2008-2009
EVANGELICAL SUNDAY SCHOOL LESSON COMMENTARY

FIFTY-SEVENTH ANNUAL VOLUME
Based on the
Evangelical Bible Lesson Series

Editorial Staff
Lance Colkmire — Editor
Tammy Hatfield — Editorial Assistant
James E. Cossey — Editor in Chief
Joseph A. Mirkovich — General Director of Publications

Lesson Exposition Writers
J. Ayodeji Adewuya   Jerald Daffee
Winfield H. Bevins   Joshua F. Rice
Lance Colkmire   Richard Keith Whitt

Published by

PATHWAY PRESS   **Cleveland, Tennessee**

* To place an order, call 1-800-553-8506.
* To contact the editor, call 423-478-7597.
or email at *Lance_Colkmire@pathwaypress.org*.

Lesson treatments in the *Evangelical Sunday School Lesson Commentary* for 2008-2009 are based upon the outlines of the Pentecostal-Charismatic Bible Lesson Series prepared by the Pentecostal-Charismatic Curriculum Commission.

Copyright 2008

PATHWAY PRESS, Cleveland, Tennessee

ISBN: 978-1-59684-353-0

ISSN: 1555-5801

Printed in the United States of America

TABLE OF CONTENTS

INTRODUCTION TO THE 2008-2009 COMMENTARY

The *Evangelical Sunday School Lesson Commentary* contains in a single volume a full study of the Sunday school lessons for the months beginning with September 2008 and running through August 2009. The 12 months of lessons draw from both the Old Testament and the New Testament in an effort to provide balance and establish relationship between these distinct but inspired writings. The lessons in this 2008-2009 volume are drawn from the third year of a seven-year series, which will be completed in August 2013. (The series is printed in full on page 15 of this volume.)

The lessons for the *Evangelical Commentary* are based on the Pentecostal-Charismatic Bible Lesson Series Outlines, prepared by the Pentecostal-Charismatic Curriculum Commission. (The Pentecostal-Charismatic Curriculum Commission is a member of the National Association of Evangelicals.) The lessons in this volume, taken together with the other annual volumes of lessons in the cycle, provide a valuable commentary on a wide range of Biblical subjects. Each quarter is divided into two or more units of study.

The 2008-2009 commentary is the work of a team of Christian scholars and writers who have developed the volume under the supervision of Pathway Press. All the major writers, introduced on the following pages, represent a team of ministers committed to a strictly Evangelical interpretation of the Scriptures. The guiding theological principles of this commentary are expressed in the following statement of faith:

1. WE BELIEVE the Bible to be the inspired, the only infallible, authoritative Word of God.

2. WE BELIEVE that there is one God, eternally existing in three persons: Father, Son, and Holy Spirit.

3. WE BELIEVE in the deity of our Lord Jesus Christ, in His virgin birth, in His sinless life, in His miracles, in His vicarious and atoning death through His shed blood, in His bodily resurrection, in His ascension to the right hand of the Father, and in His personal return in power and glory.

4. WE BELIEVE that for the salvation of lost and sinful men, personal reception of the Lord Jesus Christ and regeneration by the Holy Spirit are absolutely essential.

5. WE BELIEVE in the present ministry of the Holy Spirit by whose cleansing and indwelling the Christian is enabled to live a godly life.

6. WE BELIEVE in the personal return of the Lord Jesus Christ.

7. WE BELIEVE in the resurrection of both the saved and the lost—they that are saved, unto the resurrection of life; and they that are lost, unto the resurrection of damnation.

8. WE BELIEVE in the spiritual unity of believers in our Lord Jesus Christ.

USING THE 2008-2009 COMMENTARY

The *Evangelical Sunday School Lesson Commentary* for 2008-2009 is presented to the reader with the hope that it will become his or her weekly companion through the months ahead.

Quarterly unit themes for the 2008-2009 volume are as follows:

• Fall Quarter—Unit One: "Lessons From the Early Church (Acts, Part 1)"; Unit Two: "Wisdom From Proverbs"; Unit Three: "Learning Faithfulness From Job"

• Winter Quarter—Unit One: "1 and 2 Corinthians"; Unit Two: "Profiles of Faith in Christ"

• Spring Quarter—Unit One: "Gospel of Mark (The Servant Messiah)"; Unit Two: "Practical Christian Living (James)"

• Summer Quarter—Unit One: "Joshua and Judges"; Unit Two: "Prayers in the Psalms"

The lesson sequence used in this volume is prepared by the Pentecostal-Charismatic Curriculum Commission. The specific material used in developing each lesson is written and edited under the guidance of the editorial staff of Pathway Press.

INTRODUCTION: The opening of each week's lesson features a one-page introduction. It provides background information that sets the stage for the lesson.

CONTEXT: A time and place is given for most lessons. Where there is a wide range of ideas regarding the exact time or place, we favor the majority opinion of conservative scholars.

PRINTED TEXT: The printed text is the body of Scripture designated each week for verse-by-verse study in the classroom. Drawing on the study text the teacher delves into this printed text, exploring its content with the students.

CENTRAL TRUTH and FOCUS: The central truth states the single unifying principle that the expositors attempted to clarify in each lesson. The focus describes the overall lesson goal.

DICTIONARY: A dictionary, which attempts to bring pronunciation and clarification to difficult words or phrases, is included with many lessons. Pronunciations are based on the phonetic system used by Field Enterprises Educational Corporation of Chicago and New York in *The World Book Encyclopedia*. Definitions are generally based on *The Pictorial Bible Dictionary*, published by Zondervan Publishing Company, Grand Rapids, Michigan.

EXPOSITION and LESSON OUTLINE: The heart of this commentary—and probably the heart of the teacher's instruction each week—is the exposition of the printed text. This exposition material is organized in outline form, which indicates how the material is to be divided for study.

QUOTATIONS and ILLUSTRATIONS: Each section of every lesson contains illustrations and sayings the teacher can use in connecting the lesson to daily living.

TALK ABOUT IT: Questions are printed throughout the lesson to help students explore the Scripture text and how it speaks to believers today.

CONCLUSION: Each lesson ends with a brief conclusion that makes a summarizing statement.

GOLDEN TEXT CHALLENGE: The golden text challenge for each week is a brief reflection on that single verse. The word *challenge* is used because its purpose is to help students apply this key verse to their life.

DAILY BIBLE READINGS: The daily Bible readings are included for the teacher to use in his or her own devotions throughout the week, as well as to share with members of their class.

SCRIPTURE TEXTS USED IN LESSON EXPOSITION

Genesis
3:15	December 21

Numbers
11:24-29	May 31

Joshua
1:1-11, 16-18	June 7
2:1-5	June 21
3:14-17	June 7
4:4-7, 20-24	June 7
6:1-10, 15-27	June 14
9:1-9, 14-21	June 21
10:6-14	June 21
24:1-8, 13-15, 19-27	June 28

Judges
2:1-3	June 21
2:7, 10-23	July 5
3:7-10	July 5
6:11-17, 21, 24	July 12
7:1-22	July 12
13:1-5, 24, 25	July 19
16:4, 5, 9, 12, 14-31	July 19

Job
1:1-12, 18-22	November 9
2:4-10	November 9
13:1-22	November 16
19:1-29	November 23
42:1-17	November 30

Psalms
77:1-20	July 26
84:1-12	August 2
85:1-13	August 9
91:1-16	August 16
139:1-18, 23, 24	August 23
140:1-13	August 30
141:1-10	August 30
143:1-12	August 30

Proverbs
3:1-31	October 26
16:1-25	November 2

Isaiah
9:6, 7	December 21

Matthew
8:5-13	February 8
15:22-28	February 8
27:57-66	April 12
28:1-10, 16-20	April 12

Mark
1:1-4, 9-15, 21, 22, 29-35	March 1
2:1-12, 23-28	March 8
3:1-5	March 8
3:13-19	April 19
5:1-6, 9, 13, 15 20, 22, 23, 25-36, 41, 42	March 15
6:7-13	April 19
8:27-38	March 22
9:14-24	February 8
9:30-32	March 22
9:33-50	March 29
10:32-34	March 22
10:35-45	March 29
11:27-33	March 8
14:10, 11, 17-21 43-45, 53-65	April 5
15:15-39	April 5
16:14-20	April 19

Luke
1:32, 33	December 21
2:1-7	December 21
7:36-50	February 22

John
1:29-51	February 1
3:14-21	February 22
9:1-11, 14-21, 25-27, 35-41	February 15

Acts
1:4-8, 12-14	September 7
2:1-4, 14-18	Septmeber 7
2:1-4, 16, 17	May 31
2:37-41	September 7

Acts (con't)		2 Corinthians	
2:41-47	May 31	3:5, 6	May 31
2:42-47	September 7	4:1-18	January 18
3:1-10, 16	September 14	5:1-10	January 18
4:8-21	September 21	6:16	June 28
4:31-35	May 31	7:1	June 28
5:1-10	September 21	8:1-12	January 25
5:12-16	September 14	9:2-15	January 25
5:29, 33, 38-42	September 21		
6:8-15	September 28	**Galatians**	
7:51-60	September 28	4:4-7	December 21
8:1-8, 14-17, 26-29, 35-40	October 5	5:22-25	May 31
9:1-22, 26-31	October 12	**Ephesians**	
9:36-43	September 14	5:18-21	May 31
11:4-26	October 19		
		Hebrews	
1 Corinthians		1:1-3	December 21
1:18-31	December 7	3:12-14	July 5
2:1, 2	December 7	9:26-28	December 21
2:3-16	December 14		
3:3, 4, 16-23	December 14	**James**	
10:14-17	December 28	1:1-25	April 26
11:17-33	December 28	2:1-26	May 3
12:4-27	January 4	3:1-18	May 10
12:28-31	January 11	4:1-17	May 17
13:1-13	January 11	5:7-20	May 24
14:1-5	January 4		

SCRIPTURE TEXTS USED IN GOLDEN TEXT CHALLENGE

Numbers		Psalms (con't)	
14:18	November 30	85:7	August 9
		91:1	August 16
Joshua		139:17	August 23
4:23, 24	June 7	143:11	August 30
24:15	June 28		
		Proverbs	
Judges		3:5, 6	June 14
6:14	July 12	3:13	October 26
		16:20	November 2
Job			
1:22	November 9	**Isaiah**	
13:15	November 16	53:5	April 5
19:25	November 23		
		Matthew	
Psalms		16:24	February 1
77:12	July 26	28:6	April 12
84:10	August 2		

Mark

1:14, 15	March 1
1:27	March 8
8:34	March 22
9:23	February 8
9:35	March 29
16:15	October 19
16:15	April 19

John

3:16	February 22
9:25	February 15

Acts

1:8	September 7
5:12	September 14
4:19, 20	September 21
8:25	October 5
10:38	March 15

1 Corinthians

1:18	December 7
2:12	December 14
11:26	December 28
12:13	January 4
13:13	January 11

2 Corinthians

4:7	January 18
8:9	January 25

Galatians

4:4, 5	December 21
5:16	July 19
6:7	June 21

Ephesians

5:18, 19	May 31

Philippians

1:20	September 28

1 Timothy

1:15	October 12

Hebrews

3:12	July 5

James

1:12	April 26
2:8	May 3
3:17	May 10
4:10	May 17
5:16	May 24

ACKNOWLEDGMENTS

Many books, magazines and Web sites have been used in the research that has gone into the 2008-2009 *Evangelical Commentary*. The major books that have been used are listed below.

Bibles
King James Version, Oxford University Press, Oxford, England
Life Application Study Bible, Zondervan Publishing House, Grand Rapids
New American Standard Bible (NASB), Holman Publishers, Nashville
New International Version (NIV), Zondervan Publishing House, Grand Rapids
New King James Version (NKJV), Thomas Nelson Publishers, Nashville
The Nelson Study Bible, Thomas Nelson Publishers, Nashville
Word in Life Study Bible, Thomas Nelson Publishers, Nashville

Commentaries
Adam Clarke's Commentary, Abingdon-Cokesbury, Nashville
Barnes' Notes, BibleSoft.com
Commentaries on the Old Testament (Keil & Delitzsch), Eerdmans Publishing Co., Grand Rapids
Ellicott's Bible Commentary, Zondervan Publishing House, Grand Rapids
Expositions of Holy Scriptures, Alexander MacLaren, Eerdmans Publishing Co., Grand Rapids
Expository Thoughts on the Gospels, J.C. Ryle, Baker Books, Grand Rapids
Jamieson, Fausset and Brown Commentary, BibleSoft.com
Life Application Commentary, Tyndale House, Carol Stream, IL
Matthew Henry's Commentary, BibleSoft.com
The Bible Exposition Commentary: New Testament, Warren Wiersbe, Victor Books, Colorado Springs
The Expositor's Greek Testament, Eerdmans Publishing Co., Grand Rapids
The Interpreter's Bible, Abingdon Press, Nashville
The Pulpit Commentary, Eerdmans Publishing Co., Grand Rapids
The Wesleyan Commentary, Eerdmans Publishing Co., Grand Rapids
The Wycliffe Bible Commentary, Moody Press, Chicago
Zondervan NIV Bible Commentary, Zondervan Publishing House, Grand Rapids

Illustrations
Choice Contemporary Stories and Illustrations, Baker Books, Grand Rapids
Fresh Illustrations for Preaching and Teaching, Baker Books, Grand Rapids
Illustrations for Preaching and Teaching, Baker Books, Grand Rapids
Knight's Master Book of New Illustrations, Eerdmans Publishing Co., Grand Rapids
1,000 New Illustrations, Al Bryant, Zondervan Publishing Co., Grand Rapids
Quotable Quotations, Scripture Press Publications, Wheaton
The Encyclopedia of Religious Quotations, Fleming H. Revell Co., Old Tappan, NJ
The Heart of God, Woodrow Kroll, Elm Hill Books, Nashville
The Speaker's Sourcebook, Zondervan Publishing House, Grand Rapids
Who Said That?, George Sweeting, Moody Press, Chicago

Reference Books
Biblical Characters From the Old and New Testament, Alexander Whyte, Kregel Publications, Grand Rapids

Harper's Bible Dictionary, Harper and Brothers Publishers, New York

Pictorial Dictionary of the Bible, Zondervan Publishing House, Grand Rapids

Pronouncing Biblical Names, Broadman and Holman Publishers, Nashville

The Interpreter's Dictionary of the Bible, Abingdon Press, Nashville

Pentecostal-Charismatic Bible Lesson Series (2006-2013)**

Fall Quarter September, October, November	Winter Quarter December, January, February	Spring Quarter March, April, May	Summer Quarter June, July, August
Fall 2006 1 • Old Testament Survey 2 • New Testament Survey	**Winter 2006-07** 1 • Beginnings (Genesis 1-11) 2 • Basic Christian Doctrine	**Spring 2007** 1 • Teachings of Jesus in Matthew 2 • The Christian Family	**Summer 2007** 1 • Prayers in the Psalms 2 • God's Providence
Fall 2007 1 • Abraham (Genesis 12-25) 2 • Great Women of the Bible	**Winter 2007-08** 1 • Isaac, Jacob & Joseph 2 • Discipleship	**Spring 2008** 1 • Romans & Galatians 2 • Ecclesiastes	**Summer 2008** 1 • God Delivers His People (Exodus) 2 • Great Hymns of the Bible
Fall 2008 1 • The Early Church (Acts, part 1) 2 • Wisdom From Proverbs 3 • Job (Faithfulness)	**Winter 2008-09** 1 • 1 & 2 Corinthians 2 • Profiles of Faith in Christ	**Spring 2009** 1 • Mark* (The Servant Messiah) 2 • Practical Christian Living (James)	**Summer 2009** 1 • Joshua and Judges 2 • Prayers in the Psalms
Fall 2009 1 • The Expanding Church (Acts, Part 2) 2 • The Gospel Fulfills the Law (Leviticus-Deuteronomy)	**Winter 2009-10** 1 • Major Prophets (Isaiah, Jeremiah, & Ezekiel) 2 • Bible Answers to Crucial Questions	**Spring 2010** 1 • Ephesians 2 • Commended by Christ	**Summer 2010** 1 • Books of Samuel 2 • Sin and Holiness
Fall 2010 1 • Counsel for Christlike Living (1 & 2 Peter) 2 • The Person and Work of the Holy Spirit	**Winter 2010-11** 1 • Learning From Spiritual Leaders (1 & 2 Kings; 1 & 2 Chronicles) 2 • Christian Ethics	**Spring 2011** 1 • Life and Teachings of Jesus (Luke*) 2 • Ruth and Esther	**Summer 2011** 1 • Mature Relationships in Christ (Philippians) 2 • Whoeness in Christ (Colossians) 3 • Friendships With Jesus
Fall 2011 1 • Justice and Mercy (Minor Prophets) 2 • Priorities and Values	**Winter 2011-12** 1 • 1, 2, 3 John & Jude 2 • Growing Spiritually	**Spring 2012** 1 • Return From Exile (Ezra and Nehemiah) 2 • Gifts of the Spirit	**Summer 2012** 1 • 1 & 2 Thessalonians (The Second Coming) 2 • Redemption and Spiritual Renewal
Fall 2012 1 • Hebrews 2 • Who Is God? (The Nature of God)	**Winter 2012-13** 1 • Pastoral Epistles (1 & 2 Timothy, Titus, Philemon) 2 • Prayer	**Spring 2013** 1 • John* (The Son of God) 2 • The Church	**Summer 2013** 1 • Daniel and Revelation (Triumph of Christ's Kingdom) 2 • Help for Life's Journey

*Emphasize the uniqueness of each Gospel.
**Unit themes subject to revision

Introduction to Fall Quarter

"**L**essons From the Early Church (Acts, Part 1)" is the theme of the first seven lessons, which begin with the commissioning of the church in Acts and closes with the broadening of the church in Acts 11.

Expositions were compiled by Lance Colkmire (B.A., M.A.), editor of the *Evangelical Commentary* and *Real Life* young adult curriculum for Pathway Press. He also serves the South Cleveland (TN) Church of God as ministries coordinator.

The second and third units are "Wisdom From Proverbs" and "Learning Faithfulness From Job."

The two lessons from Proverbs address the benefits of wisdom (ch. 3) and the wisdom of a godly life (ch. 16). The four sessions from Job cover his trials, his trust in God, his faithfulness in adversity, and the mercy of God.

Expositions were written by the Reverend Joshua F. Rice (B.A., M.A., Th.M.), director of student ministries and Christian education at Mount Paran Church of God, Atlanta, Georgia. He is currently writing his doctoral dissertation toward a Ph.D. in New Testament Studies from the Lutheran School of Theology at Chicago.

The Church Commissioned and Empowered

Acts 1:1 through 2:47

INTRODUCTION

Luke's two books of Scripture are objective historical records. In his Gospel he wrote concerning "all that Jesus began both to do and teach," and in the Book of Acts he wrote of "the apostles whom he [Christ] had chosen" (Acts 1:1, 2). Luke narrates the facts like a modern news reporter.

"The former treatise" (v. 1) is the Gospel of Luke. Both books were addressed to Theophilus, whose name means "friend of God." The first book contains the life of Christ in the flesh, and the second contains the life of Christ in the Spirit and all that He continued to do and teach through the church until the time of the imprisonment of the apostle Paul in Rome.

Luke was a physician (Colossians 4:14) and, as such, was extremely interested in the perfect life of Christ in more ways than one. Christ's acts of healing of body and soul were far beyond the healing of which Luke was capable as a human doctor. Luke was convinced of Christ's divinity by His acts and by His teachings. It was said that Jesus spoke "as one having authority," and that no other man spoke as He did (Matthew 7:29; John 7:46).

The Gospel of Luke ends with a brief mention of the Ascension (24:50, 51), and the Acts begins at this same point. The reason Christ could continue to do what He "began" (Acts 1:1) was because He was yet alive (v. 3)! The grave could not contain Him. No room for doubt existed that He still lived, for He had eaten, spoken and walked with them. He had shown them His wounds. All this lasted for 40 days after the Crucifixion.

His message had not changed. Christ still spoke of His kingdom. He still was King! It would not be long before His rule over the hearts of humanity would extend around the world. He had a plan.

Unit Theme:
Lessons From the Early Church (Acts, Part 1)

Central Truth:
God calls and empowers the church to continue Christ's ministry on earth.

Focus:
Reflect on the initial empowerment of the church and determine to fulfill its purpose.

Context:
The Book of Acts is a continuation of the Gospel of Luke and was probably written around A.D. 65.

Golden Text:
"Ye shall receive power, after that the Holy Ghost is come upon you: and ye shall be witnesses unto me both in Jerusalem, and in all Judaea, and in Samaria, and unto the uttermost part of the earth" (Acts 1:8).

Study Outline:
I. Obedient to Christ's Command (Acts 1:4-8, 12-14)
II. Empowered for Ministry (Acts 2:1-4, 14-21, 37-41)
III. Devoted to Fellowship (Acts 2:42-47)

I. OBEDIENT TO CHRIST'S COMMAND (Acts 1:4-8, 12-14)

A. Wait for the Promise (vv. 4, 5)

4. And, being assembled together with them, commanded them that they should not depart from Jerusalem, but wait for the promise of the Father, which, saith he, ye have heard of me.

5. For John truly baptized with water; but ye shall be baptized with the Holy Ghost not many days hence.

Talk About It:
1. What was "the promise of the Father" (v. 4)?
2. Compare the two baptisms in verse 5.

The King issued a command. It may have disappointed some who may have been hoping for action, but the command to wait carried with it a promise. It was the same promise Jesus had made before, and it involved the integrity of the Trinity in keeping it.

The gathering of the disciples in this verse evidently took place in the city of Jerusalem (Luke 24:49, 50). After the meeting, Jesus led them out of the city to the place from which He ascended. This was their last "formal" meeting.

Their waiting was not to be a period of time spent without any activity at all. It was to be a period of preparation for being baptized in the Holy Spirit. This baptism would be preparation for an exciting spiritual ministry.

"However many blessings we expect from God, His infinite liberality will always exceed all our wishes and our thoughts."
—John Calvin

In Matthew 3:11, John had foretold and explained this new baptism. It was for sinners who had repented and prepared them for service by enduing them with superhuman power. The disciples understood that God would keep His promise within the next few days.

B. Witness Around the World (vv. 6-8)

6. When they therefore were come together, they asked of him, saying, Lord, wilt thou at this time restore again the kingdom to Israel?

7. And he said unto them, It is not for you to know the times or the seasons, which the Father hath put in his own power.

8. But ye shall receive power, after that the Holy Ghost is come upon you: and ye shall be witnesses unto me both in Jerusalem, and in all Judaea, and in Samaria, and unto the uttermost part of the earth.

Talk About It:
1. Explain the disciples' question in verse 6.
2. What is the primary purpose of the baptism in the Holy Spirit?

The disciples had been preoccupied for a long time about the age-old hope that some day the political power of Solomon's kingdom, considered the golden age of Israel, might be restored. They confused this hope with Christ's teaching concerning the spiritual kingdom of God in the hearts of men.

Jesus refused them information concerning the prophesied restoration of Israel's power. He was interested in turning their attention to the more important matter of spiritual power. Someday the other prophecy would be fulfilled also, but the Father had reserved for Himself the knowledge of the time of its fulfillment.

Christ emphasized the greater importance of spiritual power over the disciples' preoccupation with national political power. He outlined a sequence of three wonderful things that would happen to them: (1) The Holy Spirit would come upon them. (2) Divine power was to follow the Holy Spirit's coming and not come before it or without it. (3) They would be witnesses unto Christ, beginning at Jerusalem, and then, in ever-expanding influence, bring the gospel to the ends of the earth. They would certainly need all the power they could get to do this!

In the word *witnesses* is also a prophecy, for it means the same as the word *martyrs*. A great host of Christ's followers would lay down their lives for the gospel while carrying out the Lord's command.

They were to begin their witness at the most difficult place, at home. They were to saturate their own city, province and country with the gospel. Then they were to go to that region against which they were most prejudiced, Samaria. Furthermore, they were to take the gospel to the ends of the earth.

Much modern missionary theory is based on verse 8. Many mission programs begin their work in a new country by starting in the largest or capital city and then branching out. Some local churches try to follow the plan of maintaining a strong home base from which missionaries and support are sent to each of the concentric spheres represented in verse 8. Scholars emphasize the "both . . . and . . . and . . . ," insisting that all of us should give equal emphasis to local, regional, national and international missionary work; and that work on all these levels should be carried on simultaneously, without neglecting any part. It is a philosophy for a balanced missionary program. These were Christ's last words. Their importance cannot be overemphasized.

> "God shines in many ways throughout His universe. . . . He shines best of all in the lives of men and women He created and then redeemed."
> —A.W. Tozer

C. Worship in One Accord (vv. 12-14)

12. Then returned they unto Jerusalem from the mount called Olivet, which is from Jerusalem a sabbath day's journey.

13. And when they were come in, they went up into an upper room, where abode both Peter, and James, and John, and Andrew, Philip, and Thomas, Bartholomew, and Matthew, James the son of Alphaeus, and Simon Zelotes, and Judas the brother of James.

14. These all continued with one accord in prayer and supplication, with the women, and Mary the mother of Jesus, and with his brethren.

Talk About It:
1. Who was in the Upper Room (also see v. 15)?
2. Describe the attitude and actions of those in the Upper Room.

"The essence of prayer does not consist in asking God for something but in opening our hearts to God, in speaking with Him, and living with Him in perpetual communion. Prayer is continual abandonment to God."
—Sandhu Singh

cloven (v. 3)— "divided" (*NKJV*)

Christ's last instruction to His disciples was that they should wait in Jerusalem for the baptism in the Holy Spirit. They eagerly made the half-hour walk back to the city, where they were when Jesus ascended into heaven.

It is not known for certain, but the upstairs room where they gathered may have been the same room in which they had observed the Last Supper with Jesus before His crucifixion. It may have been the same room in which the disciples huddled as fugitives from the Jews and where Jesus first appeared to them in His resurrected body. The room probably was used as an assembly room as well as a dwelling by those 11 disciples mentioned in verse 13.

It was a close-knit group that met together this time. There were no status-seekers, doubters, or faultfinders among them.

Each day, between the ascension of Christ and the Day of Pentecost, the band of faithful disciples gathered in the Upper Room for worship. They were united in the love of Christ and with a common purpose and hope.

Mary, the mother of Jesus, is specifically mentioned as being present. This is the last mention made of her by name in the Scriptures. However, doubtlessly she continued to be active in the Jerusalem church for some time, but without any known official capacity or special veneration. Other women were present also, and relatives of the Lord. It is thought by some that the 70 disciples mentioned in Luke 10:1 probably were among the 120 present in these meetings (Acts 1:15).

This was one of the last times the entire group of disciples would be together. Soon they would be obedient to Christ's command and carry the gospel to the ends of the earth. Perhaps this was much in their thoughts and made their fellowship much dearer.

II. EMPOWERED FOR MINISTRY (Acts 2:1-4, 14-21, 37-41)
A. Empowered Tongues (vv. 1-4)

1. And when the day of Pentecost was fully come, they were all with one accord in one place.

2. And suddenly there came a sound from heaven as of a rushing mighty wind, and it filled all the house where they were sitting.

3. And there appeared unto them cloven tongues like as of fire, and it sat upon each of them.

4. And they were all filled with the Holy Ghost, and began to speak with other tongues, as the Spirit gave them utterance.

Pentecost was a feast of the Jews. It commemorated both the giving of the Law on Mount Sinai and the time of gathering the firstfruits of the annual harvest. The word *Pentecost* itself means "the fiftieth day" and was used to designate the fact that this feast occurred 50 days after the Passover. There were several days of preparation and observance preceding the festival day itself, much as we have a Christmas season and a Christmas Day. The outpouring of the Holy Spirit occurred on the actual day of the festival.

The phrase "with one accord" is used 11 times in the Book of Acts. Most of the time it refers to the unity and harmony among the believers in Christ. On this occasion they were in one place with a unified purpose and desire. Through prayer and supplication, the band of 120 reached a point of spiritual receptivity beyond the comprehension of merely religious people. They were vessels ready to be filled.

The infilling of the Spirit occurred with a startling suddenness. Three unusual phenomena accompanied the infilling. The first was "a sound from heaven as of a rushing mighty wind." This does not mean there was actually a blowing wind, but only a windlike sound.

The second phenomenon was the appearance of tongues or flickering flames of fire. This visible sign appeared above the head of each of the 120 believers. As the wind had been a symbol of the power of the Holy Ghost (Acts 1:8), so the flickering flames were a symbol of the fire mentioned in Matthew 3:11.

The manifestation of wind and fire was then superseded by a miracle in the tongues of the disciples themselves. They began to speak in foreign tongues, or languages. Acts 1:15 states that some 120 persons were present, and 2:4 states "they were all filled with the Holy Ghost, and began to speak with other tongues." The word *all* reveals both the number who received the Spirit and the number who spoke with other tongues. All 120 received the baptism and all 120 spoke with tongues.

The Spirit-inspired speaking was not brought about by human knowledge or effort, for "the Spirit gave them utterance." This simply means the disciples spoke the words which the Spirit put upon their lips in foreign languages that they could not understand.

B. Inspired Preaching (vv. 14-21)
(Acts 2:19-21 is not included in the printed text.)
14. But Peter, standing up with the eleven, lifted up his voice, and said unto them, Ye men of Judaea, and all ye that dwell at Jerusalem, be this known unto you, and hearken to my words:

15. For these are not drunken, as ye suppose, seeing it is but the third hour of the day.

Talk About It:
1. Describe the two uses of the word *all* in verses 1 and 4.
2. What "filled the whole house" (v. 2, *NKJV*)?
3. Explain the phrase "as the Spirit gave them utterance" (v. 4).

"There is nothing Jesus has ever done for any of His disciples that He will not do for any other of His disciples."
—A.W. Tozer

16. But this is that which was spoken by the prophet Joel;

17. And it shall come to pass in the last days, saith God, I will pour out of my Spirit upon all flesh: and your sons and your daughters shall prophesy, and your young men shall see visions, and your old men shall dream dreams:

18. And on my servants and on my handmaidens I will pour out in those days of my Spirit; and they shall prophesy.

Peter seized the opportunity to preach the gospel of Christ to the throng of Jews. He and the other apostles had preached at earlier times when Jesus sent them out (Luke 9:1, 2), but this was his first sermon since the death and resurrection of Christ. Note that the 11 remaining apostles stood with him. This signified that what he had to say was for the entire group. He was the spokesperson, but the message was that of all.

The Jewish day began about 6 a.m., or roughly at dawn. This means it was about 9 a.m., "the third hour of the day," and the Jews were ridiculous to imagine that the disciples were drunk. It was much too early in the day.

The disciples' behavior was not caused by drunkenness, but was the fulfillment of prophecy. Peter quoted Joel 2:28-32 to explain the events of the morning. As Joel had prophesied, the Holy Spirit had been poured out upon sons, daughters, young and old. The various groups are mentioned to emphasize that the Holy Spirit is for all people and all ages. Sons and daughters, under the influence of the Spirit, give Spirit-inspired utterance to the glory of Christ. By the power of the Holy Spirit, men and women, old and young, become divinely enabled to work and witness for Christ. "And . . . whosoever shall call on the name of the Lord shall be saved" (Acts 2:21).

C. Convicted Hearts (vv. 37-41)

37. Now when they heard this, they were pricked in their heart, and said unto Peter and to the rest of the apostles, Men and brethren, what shall we do?

38. Then Peter said unto them, Repent, and be baptized every one of you in the name of Jesus Christ for the remission of sins, and ye shall receive the gift of the Holy Ghost.

39. For the promise is unto you, and to your children, and to all that are afar off, even as many as the Lord our God shall call.

40. And with many other words did he testify and exhort, saying, Save yourselves from this untoward generation.

Talk About It:
1. Why did some people think the believers had been drinking?
2. Why did Peter refer to the prophet Joel?
3. Which part of Joel's prophecy (vv. 17-21) do you think is most important?

"The eternal plan to reconcile man with God and bridge the separation, to save him from judgment for that sin, to forgive him of all sins, originated in the heart of God."

—Anne Graham Lotz

remission (v. 38)— forgiveness

untoward (v. 40)— perverse or crooked

The Church Commissioned and Empowered

41. Then they that gladly received his word were baptized: and the same day there were added unto them about three thousand souls.

The truth proclaimed by Peter penetrated the minds and hearts of the people and brought deep conviction. In the light of this mighty outpouring of the Holy Spirit, in view of the transformation of this ignorant fisherman into an eloquent prophet, who referred repeatedly to their own prophets, the people were convinced. For Peter showed them clearly how these prophecies had centered on Jesus, whom they had crucified, and they suddenly saw their guilt before God.

The fact is that we are all guilty before God, "for all have sinned, and come short of the glory of God" (Romans 3:23). If no other sin has dominion over us, the sin of unbelief or rejection of Christ as Savior and Lord of our lives is enough to condemn our souls to everlasting punishment.

The tremendous feeling of guilt felt by these Jews caused them to cry out for help. They now addressed Peter and the other apostles as "Men and brethren" (Acts 2:37). What a change in attitude! They recognized that the apostles had something they needed, and they humbly asked for help.

Peter's first directive was that they must *repent*. They had to turn away from sin and unbelief, and look to Christ as Savior. In doing this they would receive forgiveness through Christ's blood shed on the cross. Only faith in His name could bring the answer.

Peter told the people to be baptized in the name of Jesus. It was important that their profession be made public. Water baptism portrayed their confession of Christ and their repentance.

Peter declared if his hearers would meet the conditions, they would "receive the gift of the Holy Ghost" (v. 38). He was speaking of the baptism in the Spirit.

Verse 39 is a promise that reaches down through the years and stands like a mighty beacon of promise to us today, to our children, and to those in the most remote parts of the earth. What a marvelous privilege is ours to have the living Holy Spirit, the third person of the Godhead, actually dwelling within us. He is our leader, our guide, our teacher, our comforter, our source of strength to overcome temptation, our source of power to witness, our source of grace to live pleasing to God. He is present to anoint, to inspire, and to give holy zeal that we might accomplish the Great Commission given to us by Christ.

We do not have all of Peter's dynamic message, for he used many other words to testify to and exhort the people. He pled with them not to be caught up in the undertow of their generation, but to come apart and take a stand for God.

Talk About It:
1. Why was the crowd "pricked in their heart" (v. 37)?
2. What "promise" is Peter referring to in verse 39?
3. What was the response to Peter's message (v. 41), and why?

Peter's Spirit-anointed message must have fallen like coals of fire on the hearts of these convicted Jews, for we are told that 3,000 gladly received his words and were baptized. The Word of God, when preached under divine anointing, will not be without effect. This timely, Spirit-filled message of Peter's made a strong foundation for the early church.

III. DEVOTED TO FELLOWSHIP (Acts 2:42-47)
A. Commencement (vv. 42, 43)

42. And they continued stedfastly in the apostles' doctrine and fellowship, and in breaking of bread, and in prayers.

43. And fear came upon every soul: and many wonders and signs were done by the apostles.

Maturity in the Christian faith does not occur the moment one accepts Christ. In fact, those who have lived longest for Christ are the first to admit their continued need for teaching from God's Word. A consuming desire to know more about God and His Son Jesus Christ accompanies true conversion.

The word *doctrine* here refers to the teaching of the apostles. They had known the Lord intimately. They had witnessed His miracles. They were present when He presented His discourses. What this early teaching was may best be judged not by the later New Testament Epistles but by the sermons recorded in the earlier chapters of Acts.

Luke described the fellowship as the intimate living of the apostles and other Christians. They "had all things common" in brotherly unselfishness (v. 44).

Alvin J. Lindgren said: "The Christian church . . . must be a loving fellowship. No man can either become or remain a Christian by himself. To be baptized into Christ is to become a part of 'the brethren' (Romans 16:14; 1 Corinthians 8:12; Galatians 6:1; Colossians 4:15). The importance of fellowship in the early church is evident throughout the New Testament. 'You are no longer strangers and foreigners, but fellow citizens with the saints and members of the household of God' (Ephesians 2:19, *NKJV*). Paul tells why this fellowship of the saints is so important: 'I long to see you so that I may impart to you some spiritual gift to make you strong—that is, that you and I may be mutually encouraged by each other's faith' (Romans 1:11, 12, *NIV*). The fellowship of Christians strengthens the faith of those involved. It is a redemptive fellowship" (*Foundations for Purposeful Church Administration*).

Some Bible scholars believe the phrase "in breaking of bread" (Acts 2:42) refers to a common meal and that every such meal in the early days of the church had a religious significance. Other New Testament scholars say this statement is the common New Testament name for the Communion service, referring of course to Jesus' breaking of the bread and giving it to the disciples at the first Lord's Supper. We know the Communion service is intended to promote fellowship, or communion, with other Christians as well as with Christ.

Prayers were a prominent feature of Christian worship in the early church. Prayers were offered at the Communion service and by groups of Christians in the Temple. And various groups met in the homes of the Christians just for prayer.

In commenting on the words "fear came upon every soul" (v. 43), J. Vernon Bartlet states: "Awe began to creep over every soul. This awe, as in the presence of the superhuman, was caused primarily by the Pentecostal outpouring and its results just recorded; but it was enhanced by other signs of divine power among the Christians" (*The New Century Bible*).

Concerning the signs and wonders done by the apostles, Richard B. Rackham observes: "These miracles served the same purpose as those of the Lord. As His works had borne witness to Him, so the works of the apostles were signs of divine approval and the credentials of the apostles" (*The Expositor's Greek Testament*).

> "Wherever we find the Word of God surely preached and heard, and the sacraments administered according to the institution of Christ, there, it is not to be doubted, is a church of God."
> —John Calvin

B. Continuation (vv. 44-47)

44. And all that believed were together, and had all things common;

45. And sold their possessions and goods, and parted them to all men, as every man had need.

46. And they, continuing daily with one accord in the temple, and breaking bread from house to house, did eat their meat with gladness and singleness of heart,

47. Praising God, and having favour with all the people. And the Lord added to the church daily such as should be saved.

Having "all things common" was an experiment that apparently never reached beyond Jerusalem. It was an idealistic sharing among the Jerusalem church and was entered into voluntarily. It was never commanded by the Lord. There is no evidence in the New Testament to indicate it is the desire of the Holy Spirit for the entire church. Small groups of Christians have tried to revive the idea from time to time in the history of the church. It has always failed, as it did in the first century. Evidence of its failure is the fact that not long after this experiment, Paul appealed to the Gentile churches to come to their assistance.

Most Bible scholars do not believe this means they divided everything and distributed it among all. It seems, rather, that they took what was their own, sold it, and gave according to the need. Note this clause: "as every man had need."

Talk About It:
1. Describe the lifestyle of the early church.
2. Explain the growth of the early church.

The early Christians were in fellowship with one another because they shared a relationship to the living Christ and His Spirit. It was a particular kind of fellowship, a fellowship of redemptive love.

The early Christians, following Pentecost, praised God for the blessings they were receiving through the gift of His Son. They had been delivered from sin. They had communion with God, and they had love one for another. Their love for God found expression in the unselfish act of sharing of their abundance with fellow believers in need. And this they did gladly—with no sense whatever of a grudging spirit. To share our earthly goods with those less fortunate out of love and generosity is to manifest true Christian character.

CONCLUSION

A certain church was filled with division and disunity. One of the concerned members was heard to say to his pastor, "If only we could have a great revival, another Pentecost! Maybe that would bring our church back together again."

Now that sounds like a sensible solution, doesn't it? But look at the Biblical pattern for a moment, and you will notice the reverse order. Pentecost did not bring the people together. They got themselves together, and that brought Pentecost. The Spirit waited until "they were all with one accord" before He descended. The old strife over who should be greatest in the Kingdom was gone. No one pointed an accusing finger at his brother as the cause for lack of revival. In one accord each one sought God for a revival beginning in himself, and the Spirit descended.

GOLDEN TEXT CHALLENGE

"YE SHALL RECEIVE POWER, AFTER THAT THE HOLY GHOST IS COME UPON YOU: AND YE SHALL BE WITNESSES UNTO ME BOTH IN JERUSALEM, AND IN ALL JUDAEA, AND IN SAMARIA, AND UNTO THE UTTERMOST PART OF THE EARTH" (Acts 1:8).

There are few statements in Scripture that are more positive, affirmative and emphatic than this one. There is no qualification here, no equivocating, no "escape clause" to provide for the possibility of something going awry.

"Ye *shall* receive power . . . and ye *shall* be witnesses unto me." This is not even a command; it is a statement of inevitable outcomes, a statement of things that are certainly to come, a bold, straightforward statement of what is going to happen. This suggests that those persons who do not receive power, and who do not become witnesses, have never been fully filled with and baptized in the Holy Spirit.

"The difference between listening to a radio sermon and going to church . . . is almost like the difference between calling your girl on the phone and spending an evening with her."
—**D.L. Moody**

Daily Devotions:
M. Fellowship With God
   Exodus 33:8-17
T. Obedience Is Better Than Sacrifice
   1 Samuel 15:16-26
W. Promise of Empowerment
   Joel 2:28-32
T. Commissioned to Minister
   Matthew 10:1-10
F. Commanded to Love
   John 15:9-17
S. Called to Fellowship
   1 Corinthians 1:1-10

The Church Commissioned and Empowered

Miraculous Ministry of the Church

Acts 3:1-16; 5:12-16; 9:36-43

INTRODUCTION

In 1 Corinthians 12:10, Paul lists the "workings of miracles" as one of the spiritual gifts the Holy Spirit gives to the church. The plural forms emphasize variety in the manifestations of this spiritual gift. In addition to healing, many different kinds of miracles occur. The term *miracles* (*dunameis*, powers) refers to extraordinary manifestations and can include healings. Usually, the "workings of miracles" is associated with God's mighty works apart from miracles of healing. Paul listed the gifts of healings as a distinct gift from the workings of miracles, which covers a wide range of supernatural manifestations, as suggested by the phrase "signs and wonders" (Hebrews 2:4; Galatians 3:5).

Miracles are associated with power. This gift to do powerful deeds far exceeds human power. It is a profound encounter with God's sovereign action and the Spirit's power to do supernatural works. The workings of miracles are an invasion against the kingdom of Satan and a sign of the breaking-in of God's kingdom into this present world. The manifestation of this gift includes the resistance and the casting out of demons (Matthew 12:28). It could just as well include events such as Paul's afflicting Elymas, a magician, with blindness (Acts 13:4-12) and bringing the physically dead back to life (9:36-42; 20:9-12). The Holy Spirit does break through in this human world and does the unusual, the extraordinary. At times, He moves through individuals and gives them the ability to work miracles.—French L. Arrington (*Encountering the Holy Spirit*)

Unit Theme:
Lessons From the Early Church (Acts, Part 1)

Central Truth:
Miracles in the church are evidences of God's presence and power.

Focus:
Acknowledge the miraculous ministry of the church and proclaim God's power today.

Context:
The Book of Acts is a continuation of the Gospel of Luke and was probably written around A.D. 65.

Golden Text:
"By the hands of the apostles were many signs and wonders wrought among the people" (Acts 5:12).

Study Outline:
I. A Lame Man Walks (Acts 3:1-10, 16)
II. The Sick Are Healed (Acts 5:12-16)
III. A Dead Woman Raised (Acts 9:36-43)

I. A LAME MAN WALKS (Acts 3:1-10, 16)
A. The Crippled Man (vv. 1-3)

ninth hour (v. 1)—
3 p.m.

1. Now Peter and John went up together into the temple at the hour of prayer, being the ninth hour.

2. And a certain man lame from his mother's womb was carried, whom they laid daily at the gate of the temple which is called Beautiful, to ask alms of them that entered into the temple;

3. Who seeing Peter and John about to go into the temple asked an alms.

The Jews observed regular times for prayer, which included 9 a.m., noon, and 3 p.m. It was at the afternoon hour that Peter and John came to the Temple on this day. Receiving the Holy Spirit had not cancelled their need for communion with God through prayer. Instead, it intensified their desire for this communion.

Talk About It:
1. How much was the lame man dependent on others?
2. Where did this man beg, and why there?

Prayer meetings and methodical praying (not mechanical praying) are sure signs of a spiritual church and spiritual people. People with needs to be prayed for, as well as people who pray for needs of others, need to meet together and do business with God.

The handicapped man was brought each day by his friends to a spot by the great brass gate where he could beg for money from the people going in and out. He had learned to appreciate the kindness of the people and the goodness of God in supplying his needs which he was so helpless to supply for himself.

"Every single one of us is handicapped—physically, mentally, socially, and spiritually—to some degree; and although we seldom think about it, the person without faith has a far greater handicap than the person without feet."
—**Frank K. Ellis**

His physical state is typical of the spiritual state of sinners who are deformed from birth by their twisted nature, which they inherit from Adam, and are powerless to deliver themselves from this plight. They have to beg for help.

As verse 3 reminds us, economic needs take precedence in our thinking over other needs so much of the time. It is so easy to put off spiritual needs, and even physical needs. As Peter and John approached him, the lame man pleaded for alms, but what he received was of immeasurably greater value.

B. The Caring Apostles (vv. 4, 5)

Talk About It:
Describe the eye contact Peter and John made with this man (v. 4). Do you suppose the lame man was used to this? Why or why not?

4. And Peter, fastening his eyes upon him with John, said, Look on us.

5. And he gave heed unto them, expecting to receive something of them.

The lame man must have been so discouraged and dejected that he did not even raise his head when he first cried out for alms. He probably only half-expected to receive something.

Peter's replying to his request for alms probably surprised him. Undoubtedly most who passed through the gate disdained

Miraculous Ministry of the Church

to look upon the afflicted man, let alone speak to him. But Peter and John, through the presence of the Holy Spirit, had become immensely sensitive to people's needs of all kinds. Meeting the total needs of people everywhere seems to be the Scriptural position of the early church, with priority given to the spiritual needs; however, not neglecting at all the physical needs and economic needs (Philippians 4:19).

The lame man's expectancy showed he had faith. He was sure that these men with such kind voices, who had called for his attention, were going to give him something. His faith is typical of the kind we need to have when we approach God in prayer. It is useless to beg for God's mercy and blessings if we are unsure that we will receive anything from Him.

C. The Believing Apostles (vv. 6-10)

6. Then Peter said, Silver and gold have I none; but such as I have give I thee: In the name of Jesus Christ of Nazareth rise up and walk.

7. And he took him by the right hand, and lifted him up: and immediately his feet and ankle bones received strength.

8. And he leaping up stood, and walked, and entered with them into the temple, walking, and leaping, and praising God.

9. And all the people saw him walking and praising God:

10. And they knew that it was he which sat for alms at the Beautiful gate of the temple: and they were filled with wonder and amazement at that which had happened unto him.

Peter had no silver or gold, but he had something better! What was it Peter had? Where did he get it? What did he do with it?

What Peter had was not material, not tangible, not something to be seen or measured. It was something that sprang from Peter's heart and mind—a power, a virtue, a force, an energy, a compulsion. It was connected with the new Peter, the revived apostle. It also was connected with God: "In the name of Jesus Christ . . ." spoke Peter. It was a cooperative, coordinative power—God working in and through Peter.

"Rise up and walk." Not long ago the only Person who had dared to say such a thing was Christ himself. Here we see that Jesus yet lives and works through His followers (see John 14:16-18). However, if the lame man had made no attempt to get up, he would not have been healed. It would have shown his lack of faith. Peter extended a helping hand, but the man had to put forth an effort. Immediately strength flowed into his muscles and bones.

Talk About It:
1. How did Peter demonstrate faith in Christ's power (vv. 6, 7)?
2. According to his actions, what did this man know about his healing (vv. 8, 9)?
3. Describe the response of the people at the Temple (v. 10).

Feeling the strength flowing for the first time in his legs, the lame man gave a great leap of exhilaration and exultation. He stood up, overcome with joy, almost delirious with praise. He walked to and fro, leaping every few steps, testing his "new" legs, bending them, feeling them. Then the men started into the Temple. But the lame man was unable to contain himself. He still had to leap once in a while out of sheer joy. No doubt he shouted and cried out in praise to God.

The miracle was done in public, in the midst of a time of great traffic in the Temple, during the afternoon hour of prayer. The man's shouts and leapings undoubtedly had attracted much attention and people had stopped to watch the spectacle, forming a large crowd. The space beneath the Beautiful Gate had become a stage for an act of God.

The healed man was as well known to the high priest. For years he was seen by all who entered the Temple. Here was a miracle that no one could deny.

D. The Healing Christ (v. 16)

16. And his name through faith in his name hath made this man strong, whom ye see and know: yea, the faith which is by him hath given him this perfect soundness in the presence of you all.

The gathering crowd afforded Peter an opportunity to preach the gospel. He discredited himself and said the miracle just done was not anything particularly marvelous, for Christ had done much more astonishing things, yet He had not been favorably received by the people (see vv. 11-26).

Although the apostles had obvious power and holiness, they made it plain to their listeners that they were dependent upon God. They were not the source, but the channels of this power.

In verse 16, Peter begins to draw the net on his simple sermon. He preaches the need for faith in Christ and points to the lame man who was healed as an example of how the living Christ responds to people's faith. Perfect soundness of mind, soul and body are possible through faith in Christ.

II. THE SICK ARE HEALED (Acts 5:12-16)

A. Signs and Wonders (vv. 12-14)

12. And by the hands of the apostles were many signs and wonders wrought among the people; (and they were all with one accord in Solomon's porch.

13. And of the rest durst no man join himself to them: but the people magnified them.

14. And believers were the more added to the Lord, multitudes both of men and women.)

"Faith sees the invisible, believes the incredible, and receives the impossible."

—*Quotable Quotes*

Talk About It:
According to Peter, how was the lame man healed?

Solomon's porch (v. 12)—a covered outer corridor of the Temple
durst (v. 13)—dared

In this passage we continue to see the vital relationship between miracles and the ongoing work of the Lord. Christ ministered through miracles, and He conveyed that ministry to the church. The apostles continued to allow the miracle-working power of God to be manifested.

Miracles are described in these verses as a very important part of the work of the church. The apostles did not cause the miracles to happen, but God performed miracles through them. The emphasis was not merely on the miraculous. The miracles served to draw people to Christ.

Signs, from the Greek *semeia*, emphasizes that the miracles pointed to some greater purpose. They were signs of the power of God—not power alone but power made possible through Christ Jesus.

Wonders, from the Greek *terata*, emphasizes the physical aspects of the miracles. They were supernatural workings, not part of the normal activity seen in nature. The word indicates that what happened drew the attention of the people.

The evangelistic connection of the miracles is recorded in verse 14: many were added to the Lord and the church as a result of the miracles. The miracles validated the gospel message in the minds of many of the people, and they received the Word of the Lord.

B. Countless Healings (vv. 15, 16)

15. Insomuch that they brought forth the sick into the streets, and laid them on beds and couches, that at the least the shadow of Peter passing by might overshadow some of them.

16. There came also a multitude out of the cities round about unto Jerusalem, bringing sick folks, and them which were vexed with unclean spirits: and they were healed every one.

Verses 15 and 16 illustrate the extent to which the miracles contributed to the ministry of the church. People began to seek out the apostles. They earnestly sought that even the shadow of Peter might fall on their sick ones. They came from other cities outside Jerusalem in order to come under their ministry.

The sick were so numerous that they could not be ministered to in their homes. Many people brought their sick ones knowing that the best they could expect was to get close enough to Peter for his shadow to fall on them. Evidently this expression of faith led to many healings, which resulted in more conversions to Christ.

No indication is given here that this was a work unique to this particular period in the history of the church. The emphasis is that people were being ministered to. In fact, the categories

Talk About It:
1. Describe the ministry of the apostles (v. 12).
2. What was the impact of the apostles' ministry (vv. 13, 14)?

Talk About It:
1. How did people of Jerusalem express their faith in God's ability to heal (v. 15)?
2. Describe the impact on surrounding towns (v. 16).
3. Why do you suppose "they were all healed" (v. 16, *NKJV*)?

of the sick—bedridden and those "vexed with unclean spirits"— are specified. The size of the crowds is stressed. Clearly, the message is that this was an effective part of the ministry of the apostles and the church. The intent of the passage is *not* to say that this was a special work to be done only by the apostles.

The physically and spiritually ill were brought from the surrounding towns. Not one person went away without receiving what he or she came for or was brought for.

Christ never turns away anyone who comes to Him for help, if that person comes in faith and is willing to accept the Lord as his or her master.

III. A DEAD WOMAN RAISED (Acts 9:36-43)
A. Dorcas' Death (vv. 36, 37)

36. Now there was at Joppa a certain disciple named Tabitha, which by interpretation is called Dorcas: this woman was full of good works and almsdeeds which she did.

37. And it came to pass in those days, that she was sick, and died: whom when they had washed, they laid her in an upper chamber.

The town of Joppa was located a few miles northwest of Lydda on the coast of the Mediterranean Sea. Here, too, we find Christian disciples, showing the results of the Jerusalem persecution and the work of Christian missionaries. Among these disciples was a beloved woman named *Tabitha*, affectionately called *Dorcas* by the Hellenist Christians. She, too, was a disciple, for under the gospel there is no distinction between male and female (Galatians 3:28). Of her it is said that she "was always doing good and helping the poor" (Acts 9:36, *NIV*).

Verse 37 is a brief statement about the grim reality of sickness and death—a reality from which even the choicest of saints have no immunity. In the midst of a life of blessed ministry and helpfulness, sickness made its entrance, and then death. Why should a life so full and useful and evidently pleasing to the Lord be cut short in the midst of the years? But the reality of death must ever be the somber evidence of the reality and presence of sin (Romans 5:12).

Although it was sometimes the custom outside of Jerusalem to delay burial a few days, a possible reason for deferring in this case was the knowledge that Peter was close at hand, and the hope that a call to him might result in a restoration by the power of Jesus through the apostle.

B. Peter's Arrival (vv. 38, 39)

38. And forasmuch as Lydda was nigh to Joppa, and the disciples had heard that Peter was there, they sent unto him two men, desiring him that he would not delay to come to them.

"Faith is believing what you do not see; the reward of faith is to see what you believe."
—St. Augustine

almsdeeds (v. 36)— charitable deeds

Talk About It:
Describe the ministry of Dorcas.

"We make a living by what we get; we make a life by what we give."
—Duane Hulse

39. Then Peter arose and went with them. When he was come, they brought him into the upper chamber: and all the widows stood by him weeping, and shewing the coats and garments which Dorcas made, while she was with them.

It is believed that Lydda was only 10 or 12 miles southeast of Joppa, hence the decision on the part of the disciples at Joppa to send for Peter at Lydda. Not only might there have been a slight hope of his performing a miracle for them, but they were greatly in need of his comfort. They sent two men to get Peter. In dangerous times and by unsafe roads, it was customary to send two messengers, both for mutual protection and that, if anything happened to one, the other might still deliver the message. Then too, it was a security against fraud, in case such were necessary.

Upon arrival at Lydda, the two messengers begged the apostle to come to Joppa without delay. Peter went with the two messengers and was brought immediately into the upper room where the body of Dorcas lay after it had been cleansed in accordance with the Jewish custom of "purifying the dead." We can be reasonably sure that the apostle was conscious of the Spirit's leading and that it would please God to help them in their distress when he set out from Lydda.

Talk About It:
How did the widows testify about Dorcas' ministry?

"What people say behind your back is your standing in the community."
—Edgar Howe

C. Dorcas' Resurrection (vv. 40-43)

40. But Peter put them all forth, and kneeled down, and prayed; and turning him to the body said, Tabitha, arise. And she opened her eyes: and when she saw Peter, she sat up.

41. And he gave her his hand, and lifted her up, and when he had called the saints and widows, presented her alive.

42. And it was known throughout all Joppa; and many believed in the Lord.

43. And it came to pass, that he tarried many days in Joppa with one Simon a tanner.

Peter's action in sending all the mourners out of the room is almost an exact reenactment of Jesus' action in the home of Jairus, whose daughter He raised from death (Mark 5:38-42). Privacy for the more earnest concentrated prayer was doubtless what Peter sought as well. Although the contents of Peter's prayer are not recorded, he probably asked God to restore the child's life.

Having been assured by the Spirit of a definite answer, Peter turned to the body and called for her to arise. What Peter said in Acts 9:40 differed only in one letter from the words of Jesus to Jairus' daughter. Whereas Jesus had said *Talitha* (little

Talk About It:
Why do you suppose God resurrected Dorcas?

girl) *cumi* (Mark 5:41), Peter now said *Tabitha cumi*—"Tabitha, arise." In response to this command, Dorcas opened her eyes and, seeing her benefactor, sat up.

It is interesting that Peter extended his helping hand after Dorcas had been restored to life, whereas in the Gospels, Jesus took the damsel's hand before she was restored (Mark 5:41; Luke 8:54). Having raised Dorcas from her deathbed, Peter presented her alive to her marveling friends and the other saints who had gathered there.

Because of Dorcas' restoration many more persons accepted the Lord, for it was in Christ's name and by His power that this miracle had been performed. The belief by the people resulting from Dorcas' restoration is like that mentioned of those who were won to the faith by the raising of Lazarus (John 11:45).

This last verse of the text indicates the connection between Peter's ministry in Lydda and Joppa and his visit to the house of Cornelius in Caesarea (ch. 10). We do not know how long Peter stayed with Simon the tanner in Joppa, but the very fact that he stayed with a man whose trade was abominable to the Jews indicates that his prejudices as a Jew were weakening. Peter's emancipation from religious and ethnic prejudice is in itself a victory for the gospel, and the evidence of this change of attitude as noted here in this verse is a step which prepares for the next chapter.

"Jesus promised those baptized in the Spirit that they would receive supernatural ability to show that Jesus is still living. This fulfillment of Jesus' promise is our inheritance as Spirit-baptized believers."
—French Arrington

CONCLUSION

Because of the restoration of Dorcas, "many believed in the Lord" (Acts 9:42). This is in accord with the purpose of the Book of Acts; that is, to show how Christianity spread from its beginning in Jerusalem to the far-flung parts of the Roman Empire and ultimately to the imperial city itself. Even as Jesus' signs recorded in the fourth Gospel had as their purpose "that ye might believe that Jesus is the Christ, the Son of God; and that believing ye might have life through his name" (John 20:31), so these signs of the apostles had as their purpose to inspire faith in the living Lord and to spread the Christian faith to many people. It should be understood that whatever miracles are permitted and performed by the Lord even today must have as their ultimate purpose the furtherance of the gospel and the glory of the Lord Jesus Christ. And the greatest of all miracles is the spiritual regeneration of believing sinners.

GOLDEN TEXT CHALLENGE

"BY THE HANDS OF THE APOSTLES WERE MANY SIGNS AND WONDERS WROUGHT AMONG THE PEOPLE" (Acts 5:12).

"Two things are given here that are remarkable. The one is that Christianity at its beginning was mightily helped and advanced by miracles done in the name of Jesus. The other remarkable thing is that the authority of the apostles as leaders of the early church was greatly strengthened by these miracles being wrought exclusively by their hands. We cannot understand either the external relationship of the early church to the world or the internal relationship of the people to the leaders unless we take these two remarkable works into account.

"Divine power always gets attention. It is as a magnet that pulls people to where God is working. Signs and wonders show that God is in immediate connection with the human family and that His presence is loving and healing. God depends on human hands and committed hearts to be instruments through whom He can work."—*Pulpit Commentary*

Daily Devotions:
M. Miraculous Provisions
1 Kings 17:8-16
T. Miracle of Resurrection
1 Kings 17:17-24
W. Miracle of Healing
2 Kings 5:8-14
T. Prayer and Fasting Required
Matthew 17:14-21
F. Signs That Follow Believers
Mark 16:15-20
S. Prayer of Faith
James 5:13-20

Bold Witness of Christ

Acts 4:1-37; 5:1-11, 17-42

Unit Theme:
Lessons From the Early Church (Acts, Part 1)

Central Truth:
A bold Christian is a powerful witness for Christ.

Focus:
Highlight the boldness the early church displayed and witness fearlessly for Christ.

Context:
Around A.D. 30, the early church boldly stands for Christ in the face of challenges.

Golden Text:
"Peter and John answered and said unto them, Whether it be right in the sight of God to hearken unto you more than unto God, judge ye. For we cannot but speak the things which we have seen and heard" (Acts 4:19, 20).

Study Outline:
I. An Inspiring Defense (Acts 4:5-21)
II. A Powerful Confrontation (Acts 5:1-10)
III. Victorious Over Opposition (Acts 5:29-42)

INTRODUCTION

There is a painting by Max Gabriel which seems to speak to the persecution of the people of God, and to the love of God that sustains them. Copies of it are in almost every gallery. The original is in the Louvre in Paris. It is called "The Last Token."

The painting depicts a scene in the days when being a Christian in the Roman Empire meant persecution, suffering or death. One of the Christians, a slender and beautiful maiden, is about to be torn apart by beasts. At her side is the great stone wall of the amphitheater, rising tier above tier and crowded with the multitude whom sin has brought to that fearful state. The iron grating into the den, or vivarium, of the beasts has been lifted, and a ferocious tiger, enraged by captivity and hunger, is stealthily creeping out of the cage toward his helpless victim.

The maiden is clad in white, except for the dark mantle around her head and shoulders. She stands only a few feet from the opening out of which the tiger is coming. But she heeds not the beast, and seems oblivious to its nearness. At her feet lies a white rose which some loved one has thrown into the arena; and her upturned and fearless eyes eagerly scan the benches above for the face of him who has cast the rose. The hate of man has condemned her to death, and the savage beast is soon to taste her virgin blood; but one single rose with one beating heart behind it has changed the whole scene. Now there are no beasts, no bloody sands, no jeering mob—only a white rose and love triumphant.

In today's lesson, the believers faced severe persecution. Behind anything they could do for themselves was a force that sustained them. That force was God's love. They never lost sight of His love, and they came forth victorious.

I. AN INSPIRING DEFENSE (Acts 4:5-21)

About 5,000 people had been converted through the Spirit-filled preaching of Peter and John and the testimony of a lame man who was healed (Acts 3:1—4:4). It was too late now to stop the floodtide of faith. While the two apostles had been thrown into jail, there was not enough room in all the jails of Jerusalem to hold all those who that night were spreading the gospel around town.

A. The Apostles' Interrogation (vv. 5-7)

(Acts 4:5-7 is not included in the printed text.)

The Jewish leaders had hurried during the evening hours to prepare for a meeting of the highest council in the land, a meeting of the Sanhedrin, to sit as a supreme court and judge the matter at hand. The power arrayed against the apostles was formidable. It included the highest religious and political leaders of the Jews. They were not a fair tribunal but a biased and prejudiced group that already knew what it would do with John and Peter if it were not for their popularity.

The same men who tried Jesus illegally and condemned Him now sat in judgment over the apostles. The same man who feared to stand by Christ during that hour and denied Him three times now was in the very place that Christ occupied and was to be judged. How would he act now?

All the influential relatives of the high priest were present. They could be counted on to vote as a block the way the high priest wanted them to vote. The Sanhedrin always sat in a circle, with those having business to do with it in the center. Thus Peter and John, surrounded and intimidated, were asked this first question: "By what power, or by what name, have ye done this?" (v. 7). An honest answer would be an admission that the miracle was not done in the name of or by the authority of the Jews. This the questioners knew very well. Peter and John really were on the spot!

B. The Apostles' Inspiration (vv. 8-12)

8. Then Peter, filled with the Holy Ghost, said unto them, Ye rulers of the people, and elders of Israel,

9. If we this day be examined of the good deed done to the impotent man, by what means he is made whole;

10. Be it known unto you all, and to all the people of Israel, that by the name of Jesus Christ of Nazareth, whom ye crucified, whom God raised from the dead, even by him doth this man stand here before you whole.

11. This is the stone which was set at nought of you builders, which is become the head of the corner.

12. Neither is there salvation in any other: for there is none other name under heaven given among men, whereby we must be saved.

Caiaphas (KY-uh-fuhs)—v. 6—the high priest under whom Jesus was crucified

Talk About It:
1. Why were the religious leaders so upset with Peter and John (see vv. 1-4)?
2. What was the central issue in this matter (v. 7)?

Nothing Real
Do they cast us out of the city? They cannot cast us out of that which is in the heavens. If they who hate us could do this, they would be doing something real against us. So long, however, as they cannot do this, they are but pelting us with drops of water or striking us with the wind.
—Gregory Nazianzen

impotent (v. 9)—helpless

Talk About It:
1. Who is the "cornerstone" (*NKJV*), who are the "builders," and what had they done (v. 11)?
2. What does Peter declare about Jesus in verse 12?

Peter's actions here are very different from his actions at the trial of Jesus. His boldness and calm confidence is inspired by the Holy Spirit, as well as his answer to the Jews' question. He addresses them formally and with respect.

Peter does not try to make his statement favor himself, nor does he commit perjury in any way. He tells the plain truth. Soon all the people in the country will have heard of the happenings in Jerusalem. Peter does not hesitate in mentioning the well-known truth that the Sanhedrin had condoned, even ordered, the slaying of Christ. The mention of Christ's resurrection must have rankled the Sadducees greatly, for they did not believe in any resurrection of the dead.

The greatest power in the world is able to break the bonds of death. That power gave Peter boldness to speak. The healed man stood near him, a living witness of Christ's healing power. The facts favored Peter, but the Sanhedrin was more interested in preserving its own authority and influence over the people.

In verse 11, Peter uses Christ's own defense of His authority (Matthew 21:42) by mentioning Isaiah 28:16. Christ was given to the Jews to become the foundation and beginning of the church, but they refused to receive Him, and thus the church began without a strictly Jewish base. The leaders of the Jews should have been wise master-builders, having all the knowledge of God's plan in the Scriptures of which they were so proud. This verse was one of Peter's favorites in all his future thinking about the church (see 1 Peter 2:1-10).

There is but one source of salvation, and that is Christ, declares Peter in Acts 4:12. We cannot save ourselves, nor can anyone else save us, nor any system.

God's name was sacred to the Jews Peter addressed. Peter knew he must gain their respect for the name of God's Son, the world's only Savior.

C. Baffled Leaders (vv. 13-18)

13. Now when they saw the boldness of Peter and John, and perceived that they were unlearned and ignorant men, they marvelled; and they took knowledge of them, that they had been with Jesus.

14. And beholding the man which was healed standing with them, they could say nothing against it.

15. But when they had commanded them to go aside out of the council, they conferred among themselves,

16. Saying, What shall we do to these men? for that indeed a notable miracle hath been done by them is manifest to all them that dwell in Jerusalem; and we cannot deny it.

17. But that it spread no further among the people, let us straitly threaten them, that they speak henceforth to no man in this name.

unlearned and ignorant (v. 13)— "uneducated and untrained" (*NKJV*)

18. And they called them, and commanded them not to speak at all nor teach in the name of Jesus.

The Holy Spirit removes fear and cowardice from Christians and empowers us for witnessing boldly. The Holy Spirit also compensates for our lack of knowledge and education in spiritual things. He causes others to take note of the outstanding lives of Christians, undeniable evidence that we have been with Christ.

Also undeniable in this case was the presence of the healed man (v. 14). This was positive proof that a superior power, a supernatural power, had worked through Peter and John. The silence following Peter's speech must have been embarrassing to the Jewish leaders present.

The Sanhedrin was unwilling to let the prisoners hear their debate that followed. With some at least, Peter's words had struck hard. The presence of the healed man too may have caused some to waver; so there could be no chance for a vote until a private conference was held. Also, they knew now their political influence would be endangered if they voted for conviction. Another solution had to be discussed.

Since the miracle was obviously genuine and acknowledged by all, it should have been obvious what they should have done. They should have received the apostles with joy and should have affirmed the miracle and the news of salvation with all their influence. But, competing with this was their pride and their fear of loss of power among people. They yielded to their selfish motives.

Their terrible decision was to try to suppress the details of the case and prevent news of it reaching beyond Jerusalem. Without giving any reasons, the council threatened the apostles, commanding them to observe strict silence concerning the miracle and Jesus. How difficult it is to understand the council's malicious reasoning—reasoning apparently aimed at the prevention of further healings. And how terrible to suppress the glad news of salvation!

D. Determined Disciples (vv. 19-21)

19. But Peter and John answered and said unto them, Whether it be right in the sight of God to hearken unto you more than unto God, judge ye.

20. For we cannot but speak the things which we have seen and heard.

21. So when they had further threatened them, they let them go, finding nothing how they might punish them, because of the people: for all men glorified God for that which was done.

Talk About It:
1. What caused the religious leaders to "marvel" (v. 13)?
2. What could the leaders not deny (v. 16)?

"God's will for us is less about our comfort than it is about our contribution. God would never choose for us safety at the cost of significance. God created you so that your life would count, not so that you could count the days of your life."
—Erwin McManus

Talk About It:
1. What did Peter and John say they *had* to do (vv. 19, 20)?
2. Why didn't the authorities punish the two apostles?

The apostles acknowledged the council's right to render a judgment, but they asked the council to consider whether one should respect more the decision of men or the command of God. The injustice of the council's decision was obvious.

Not just to be defiant, but to be faithful to the divine command to witness (Acts 1:8), the apostles declared they would have to be disobedient to the council's decision. This compulsion to tell the story of Jesus is one that every Christian should feel most strongly. And often it is this personal witness, in the face of opposition, that attracts people to Christ. Christians ought to be noted for their bravery and inspired testimony.

In spite of the further threatenings, the apostles had determined to be faithful to the Lord. They walked out of the council with the healed man beside them, knowing God was with them and approved their stand. The multitude also was with them, glorifying God for what had been done. They knew they would be victorious through Christ.

II. A POWERFUL CONFRONTATION (Acts 5:1-10)
A. Deceptive Act (vv. 1, 2)
1. But a certain man named Ananias, with Sapphira his wife, sold a possession.

2. And kept back part of the price, his wife also being privy to it, and brought a certain part, and laid it at the apostles' feet.

Talk About It:
What did Ananias and Sapphira do wrong?

Hypocrisy
The Indian tribes in Latin America have various ways to denote the hypocrite. They designate him as "a man with two faces," "a man with two hearts," "a man with two kinds of talk," "a two-headed man," "a two-sided man," and "a man with a straight mouth and a crooked heart!"

Having seen Barnabas (4:36, 37) and others blessed so much and having seen them win the affection of the apostles for having given sacrificially of their property, Ananias and Sapphira conspired to win similar acclaim. Nothing more is known of these two disciples than what is declared here.

Ananias and Sapphira plotted to deceive the apostles by selling a parcel of land as others had done, but giving only a part of the total profit to the fund being raised. Yet they would claim that they had given the total price. It was a deliberate deception, and they thought it would not be noticed. Piously Ananias brought his offering and laid it, along with other offerings, in front of the apostles who were collecting the money. Naturally he was conspicuous and thought to be a highly consecrated Christian by those who saw him make the presentation.

Hypocrisy is extremely difficult to conceal. Consecrated Christians can usually discern what is going on and who is completely loyal to God and crucified to the world.

B. Spiritual Discernment (vv. 3, 4)
3. But Peter said, Ananias, why hath Satan filled thine heart to lie to the Holy Ghost, and to keep back part of the price of the land?

4. Whiles it remained, was it not thine own? and after it was sold, was it not in thine own power? why hast thou conceived this thing in thine heart? thou hast not lied unto men, but unto God.

A person filled with the Holy Spirit generally has a perceptive insight into the personalities of others and can discern motives rather well. The hypocrisy of Ananias was obvious to Peter. He accused Ananias of lying not to him but to the Holy Spirit.

The disciples were under no obligation to sell their property and give the profit to the church, but many were doing so and were blessed thereby. The church needed funds at its beginning as much as now, especially to care for the persecuted believers who lost their source of income when they embraced the new faith.

Ananias and Sapphira could have sold their property and kept the entire price without being in the wrong, if they had not attempted the deception mentioned. They had sinned against God and the church, but principally against God who would have been glorified as the receiver of the gift. They had cheated the Lord and had been caught!

C. Divine Punishment (vv. 5-10)

5. And Ananias hearing these words fell down, and gave up the ghost: and great fear came on all them that heard these things.

6. And the young men arose, wound him up, and carried him out, and buried him.

7. And it was about the space of three hours after, when his wife, not knowing what was done, came in.

8. And Peter answered unto her, Tell me whether ye sold the land for so much? And she said, Yea, for so much.

9. Then Peter said unto her, How is it that ye have agreed together to tempt the Spirit of the Lord? behold, the feet of them which have buried thy husband are at the door, and shall carry thee out.

10. Then fell she down straightway at his feet, and yielded up the ghost: and the young men came in, and found her dead, and, carrying her forth, buried her by her husband.

It appears that Ananias died, not of a heart attack, but by execution by the Holy Spirit. God's holy wrath would not put up with such blasphemy (Matthew 12:31, 32). God had acted on other occasions with such dispatch to curb defiance of Deity (see Numbers 16; Leviticus 10:1, 2). There was a need for such an example to avert exploitation of the early church, and it seems the example was sufficient for the time being.

Talk About It:
1. How did Peter know Ananias was being dishonest?
2. Where was this sin "conceived" (v. 4)?

Talk About It:
1. What effect did Ananias' death have on all who heard about it (v. 5)?
2. Had this couple knowingly "agreed together to tempt the Spirit of the Lord" (v. 9)?
3. Why was this sin judged so suddenly and so harshly?

At first glance, it seems that they did not give Ananias a decent burial, but the fact that they took time to wrap him in burial cloths indicates that they probably observed all the usual procedures in decent burials. Bodies had to be buried soon after death since embalming was not practiced, and it was the custom of the Jews to bury their dead immediately.

It seems strange that Sapphira was not notified of the death of her husband, but it may have been that her whereabouts were not known when he died. Perhaps she was coming in to apply for her share in the common fund, hoping to qualify by having contributed a share. The fraud would now be disclosed to her face.

When Peter saw that Sapphira's story agreed with her husband's, he knew they had conspired in the fraud. As coconspirators, each was as guilty as the other in being a traitor to the cause of Christ. They must share the same fate.

Peter explained to Sapphira the extent of her guilt—she had sinned against the Holy Spirit. The same sin had brought about the death of her husband, and his buriers were just returning from doing their work. Peter pronounced the death sentence upon her, for she was condemned by her own words. The Holy Spirit took her life, and she fell down dead.

"Sin is the only thing that God abhors. It brought Christ to the cross, it damns souls, it shuts heaven, and it laid the foundations of hell."
—Thomas Brooks

III. VICTORIOUS OVER OPPOSITION (Acts 5:29-42)

The apostles were brought again before the Sanhedrin and called into account for their conduct (v. 27). They were reprimanded for having violated the previous command of the court not to teach in Christ's name. To the apostles it was inconceivable to do anything else. They were constrained to share the good news about the saving grace of the Lord Jesus Christ. John wrote of the constraint to witness: "That which was from the beginning, which we have heard, which we have seen with our eyes, which we have looked upon, and our hands have handled, of the Word of life; . . . that which we have seen and heard declare we unto you" (1 John 1:1, 3).

The high priest accused the apostles of filling Jerusalem with the Christian doctrine (Acts 5:28). Also, the apostles were accused of making the rulers of Israel responsible for the death of Christ. This was interpreted as an attempt to set the people against the rulers. Apparently the high priest forgot the tragic words recorded in Matthew 27:25. There the people, incited by the priests, had said to Pilate, "His blood be on us, and on our children."

A. Christ's Witnesses (vv. 29-32)

(Acts 5:30-32 is not included in the printed text.)

29. Then Peter and the other apostles answered and said, We ought to obey God rather than men.

The apostles were men of principle. They did not deny the charges brought against them, nor did they hesitate to reply to those charges. Always their statements strongly indicated that the rulers were fighting a losing battle against God. They responded to the leaders by telling them God's authority was greater than man's and therefore they ought to obey God.

The word translated *obey* occurs in the New Testament only four times. It refers to absolute, unquestioning submission. What other attitude can believers have if we believe that God is God, and if we have removed all other masters and authorities from our lives?

Peter reminded the Sanhedrin that the apostles were representatives of the Messiah. They were acting under His authority and, so far as they could, filling the gap caused by His absence. He asserted that their preaching and teaching had been done by divine command, which could not be set aside by any human authority, imperial or ecclesiastical. He declared the true Prince of Israel, Jesus, alone had the power and right to issue commissions to those who were committed to God.

The apostle further explained that Jesus, whom the chief priests had crucified, was still alive, reigning in glory, enthroned at the right hand of God, and that they were fulfilling His royal commands when they were teaching in the Temple. He claimed they were witness-bearers for the risen and reigning Prince and Savior and cowitnesses with "the Holy Ghost, whom God hath given to them that obey him" (v. 32).

B. Enraged Rulers (v. 33)

33. When they heard that, they were cut to the heart, and took counsel to slay them.

The members of the Sanhedrin became violently enraged over what they heard. The phrase "cut to the heart" indicates a state of extreme vexation, amounting to inward rage. This was not the "pricking" of the heart which leads to contrition and repentance (see 2:37). Rather, it was a painful indignation and envy which thought of ridding themselves of the apostles as they had done of their Master. Like maddened beasts, wounded and inescapably cornered, they now saw as their only alternative the destruction of their pursuers.

Justice was forgotten and judges' benches were forsaken as personal passion dethroned reason, bared wicked fangs, and viciously panted for blood. As Weymouth translates the verse, "They were disposed to kill the apostles."

C. The Respected Council Member (vv. 34-39)
(Acts 5:34-37 is not included in the printed text.)

Talk About It:
1. Why did God exalt Christ (v. 31)?
2. Who are the two witnesses for Jesus named in verse 32?

"Christ will be standing upright, tall and immortal, after the tumult and the shouting dies and the captains and the kings lie stretched side by side, the 'cause' that made them famous forgotten, and their whole significance reduced to a paragraph in a history book."
—A.W. Tozer

Talk About It:
How did the religious leaders react to Peter's message?

Gamaliel (guh-
MAY-li-el)—v. 34—
a well-known and
highly regarded
member of the
Sanhedrin and
teacher of the Law

forth a little space
(v. 34)—"outside for
a little while" (NIV)

Talk About It:
1. Explain Gamaliel's
references to
Theudas (v. 36)
and Judas of
Galilee (v. 37).
2. How can one "fight
against God" (v. 39)?

38. And now I say unto you, Refrain from these men, and let them alone: for if this counsel or this work be of men, it will come to nought:

39. But if it be of God, ye cannot overthrow it; lest haply ye be found even to fight against God.

There was but one calm voice in the Sanhedrin that day. It belonged to Gamaliel, who was held in great esteem by the members of that body. He warned the rulers that they should do nothing hastily. He reminded them how other men and causes had arisen before, each having embedded in them the seeds of self-destruction. They soon died out. He suggested if the apostles were not of God, the same thing would happen to them. They might flourish for a while, but their efforts would then come to nothing.

However, if the apostles really were from God, he argued, the Sanhedrin could find itself fighting against Him. Furthermore, he reminded them, if it is of God it cannot be stopped. From the standpoint of the apostles, the advice of Gamaliel to give them time was excellent.

D. The Freed Apostles (vv. 40-42)

40. And to him they agreed: and when they had called the apostles, and beaten them, they commanded that they should not speak in the name of Jesus, and let them go.

41. And they departed from the presence of the council, rejoicing that they were counted worthy to suffer shame for his name.

42. And daily in the temple, and in every house, they ceased not to teach and preach Jesus Christ.

Talk About It:
1. Why did the
apostles rejoice
(vv. 40, 41)?
2. How did their
ministry change
after this experience
(v. 42)?

Gamaliel's advice fortunately prevailed on this occasion. However, the court gave partial vent to its indignation by flogging the apostles for their disobedience to their previous command to cease teaching in the name of Jesus. They were probably administered 39 stripes each, according to Jewish law.

The rulers then renewed their futile command charging them not to speak in the name of Jesus. Surely, by this time, they realized that the apostles were not going to obey them. Nevertheless, they released them.

The attitude of the apostles toward their suffering must have baffled the rulers. Whatever they expected out of them, they witnessed a fierce loyalty to Christ. Dishonor became honor to them because they did what they did for the sake of Jesus' name. It was Mr. Valiant-for-Truth who said, "My marks and scars I carry with me" (Pilgrim's Progress).

In a real sense, the apostles identified with the Lord in this experience. Paul wrote, "That I may know him, and the power of his resurrection, and the fellowship of his sufferings, being made comformable unto his death" (Philippians 3:10). We hear very little about "the fellowship of his sufferings." Yet we must share in the cross-bearing if we hope to share in the crown-wearing.

The apostles did not heed the ban placed on speaking in the name of Jesus. They continued daily, in the Temple courts and in their own homes, to preach and teach that Jesus Christ is the Messiah. The suffering they had endured only drew attention to the message they were proclaiming.

CONCLUSION

From the very beginning, Christ's servants suffered opposition and persecution. The forces of evil were alert to protect their interests. But the same Holy Spirit who filled the disciples' hearts with love also filled their minds with conviction and determination. Their loyalty to Christ was absolute. They were more than willing to risk their lives for Christ and the gospel. God expects the same commitment level from His followers today.

GOLDEN TEXT CHALLENGE

"PETER AND JOHN ANSWERED AND SAID UNTO THEM, WHETHER IT BE RIGHT IN THE SIGHT OF GOD TO HEARKEN UNTO YOU MORE THAN UNTO GOD, JUDGE YE. FOR WE CANNOT BUT SPEAK THE THINGS WHICH WE HAVE SEEN AND HEARD" (Acts 4:19, 20).

If the Jewish leaders thought they could bully the apostles, they were mistaken. They did not reckon with the strength of spiritual conviction. Peter and John were manly and resolute in their reply. They appealed to the conscience of the priests and asked them if they thought people ought to obey God or obey man. Once again, the spiritual leaders of Israel were trapped by the logic of those whom they regarded to be ignorant and unlearned.

Not only were Peter and John unwilling to stop speaking in Jesus' name, but they also said they *could not* stop, even if they desired to. They had seen so many wonderful things and had heard such wonderful truths that they could not do otherwise than to tell others about it. They were impelled by a power stronger than themselves.

"When we are born again, we are dropped not into a maternity ward, but into a war zone. Our birthplace is less mother's womb and more battlefield earth."

—Erwin McManus

Daily Devotions:
M. False Prophets Confronted
1 Kings 18:20-29
T. The Lord Is Victorious
1 Kings 18:30-40
W. Overcoming Opposition
Nehemiah 6:10-19
T. Bold Preaching
Matthew 3:1-12
F. Finish Strong
2 Timothy 4:1-8
S. A Bold Choice
Hebrews 11:23-29

Living and Dying for Christ

Acts 6:8 through 7:60

Unit Theme:
Lessons From the Early Church (Acts, Part 1)

Central Truth:
Christians are called to be living sacrifices for Christ.

Focus:
Remember Stephen's courage and offer our lives to Christ.

Context:
Around A.D. 35, the ministry of Stephen makes an eternal impact in Jerusalem.

Golden Text:
"According to my earnest expectation and my hope, that in nothing I shall be ashamed, but that with all boldness, as always, so now also Christ shall be magnified in my body, whether it be by life, or by death" (Philippians 1:20).

Study Outline:
  I. Stephen's Arrest (Acts 6:8-15)
 II. Stephen's Defense (Acts 7:44-53)
III. Stephen's Vindication (Acts 7:54-60)

INTRODUCTION

One of the first problems to crop up in the church at Jerusalem is described in Acts 6:1: "In those days when the number of disciples was increasing, the Grecian Jews among them complained against the Hebraic Jews because their widows were being overlooked in the daily distribution of food" (*NIV*).

The 12 apostles realized they could not meet the legitimate needs of the widows in the church and still give due diligence to their primary calling of preaching God's Word. So they decided to choose seven men, "full of the Holy Ghost and wisdom" (v. 3), to take care of this ministry. One of the men chosen to be a deacon was Stephen.

Paul expounds on the qualifications for deacons in 1 Timothy 3:8-10: "Deacons must be reverent, not double-tongued, not given to much wine, not greedy for money, holding the mystery of the faith with a pure conscience. But let these also first be tested; then let them serve as deacons, being found blameless" (*NKJV*).

Stephen met these qualifications, and more. He was "a man full of faith and of the Holy Ghost" (Acts 6:5).

Beyond waiting tables, Stephen's ministry was so powerful that it was accompanied by "great wonders and miracles among the people" (v. 8), and it stirred up violent opposition. To him is attributed one of the greatest defenses of the faith in the Scriptures. In his survey of Hebrew history, Stephen emphasized the willful disobedience of the Hebrew people to the will of God and the culmination of this rebellion in the crucifixion of Jesus. Since this charge was more than his critics could stand, they seized him by mob violence and stoned him outside the city of Jerusalem. Thus, it became his honor to die as the first Christian martyr.

I. STEPHEN'S ARREST (Acts 6:8-15)

A. His Powerful Ministry (v. 8)

8. And Stephen, full of faith and power, did great wonders and miracles among the people.

This brief description of Stephen's spiritual endowment and ministry reminds us of Jesus, who was "filled with wisdom" and the grace of God (Luke 2:40), and of the people's reaction when it is said that they "wondered at the gracious words which proceeded out of his mouth" (4:22). The name *Stephen* means "crown" and, in view of Stephen's spiritual power and ministry crowned with triumph, strongly suggests a name divinely chosen.

The phrase "full of faith" is best rendered "full of grace"— that is, full of that spiritual power, charm and kindness so evident in the personality of Jesus. Stephen's fullness of divine power manifested itself in mighty works, here called "wonders and miracles."

Talk About It:
Why was Stephen able to do "great wonders and miracles"?

B. His Irresistible Wisdom (vv. 9, 10)

9. Then there arose certain of the synagogue, which is called the synagogue of the Libertines, and Cyrenians, and Alexandrians, and of them of Cilicia and of Asia, disputing with Stephen.

10. And they were not able to resist the wisdom and the spirit by which he spake.

Libertines (v. 9)— "freedmen"; liberated Jewish slaves or their descendants

The powerful ministry of Stephen aroused the opposition of a class of Jews known as *Libertines*, or "Freedmen," probably the children of Jewish captives who had been emancipated by the Romans and who had returned to Jerusalem and set up a synagogue. Among these men were certain ones from the cities of Cyrene and Alexandria as well as from Cilicia and Asia. These were all Jews of the Dispersion and probably Hellenistic in culture. The subject of their debate with Stephen is not stated, but it might have concerned the messiahship of Jesus, a most irritating subject to the Jews.

Stephen's irresistible wisdom (v. 10) is evident in his debate with his critics. The strength of his case and the force of his argument were such that his opponents in the debate found themselves hapless. Although they probably accepted his premises as based on the authority of Scriptures, they rejected his messianic conclusions as scandalous and revolutionary. The defeat of Stephen's opponents recalls the promise of Jesus that the adversary "will not be able to contradict or resist" the testimony of Jesus' disciples (Luke 21:15, *NKJV*).

Talk About It:
Why couldn't Stephen's opponents argue against him effectively?

"The Spirit gave him [Stephen] words and wisdom that none of his adversaries were able to resist or contradict. His power came as a direct result of the fullness of the Spirit."
—French Arrington

C. His Arrest and Unfair Trial (vv. 11-15)

11. Then they suborned men, which said, We have heard him speak blasphemous words against Moses, and against God.

12. And they stirred up the people, and the elders, and the scribes, and came upon him, and caught him, and brought him to the council,

13. And set up false witnesses, which said, This man ceaseth not to speak blasphemous words against this holy place, and the law:

14. For we have heard him say, that this Jesus of Nazareth shall destroy this place, and shall change the customs which Moses delivered us.

15. And all that sat in the council, looking stedfastly on him, saw his face as it had been the face of an angel.

Talk About It:
1. Compare the accusations made against Jesus (Mark 14:57, 58; John 9:28, 29) with those made against Stephen (Acts 6:13, 14).
2. How do you suppose Stephen's face resembled an angel's face (v. 15)?

Unable to resist the powerful arguments of Stephen, his determined opponents resorted to other methods. They procured informers who were willing to give false testimony and thus represent his testimony in a damaging light. The false charge of "blasphemous words against Moses and against God" was very similar to the false charges made against Christ, for there was a secret conspiracy to find Stephen guilty of a capital crime.

Verse 12 describes the widespread agitation brought about by the charges against Stephen and his resulting arrest. Any threat to the Temple, whether real or imagined, was a threat to the livelihood and religion of the Jerusalem citizens; thus both the rulers and the Jewish people were angry. The anger and malice motivated by religion can become violent. Many gruesome persecutions have been carried on in the name of religion.

Verse 13 introduces a brief explanation of the "blasphemous words" charged against Stephen by the false witnesses. Their falsity consists in the perverted turn which they give to the testimony of Stephen. We can see from the nature of his defense in the seventh chapter that he must have been heard to declare that the worship of God was no longer to be restricted, as in the past, to the Temple in Jerusalem. Just as Christ had been charged with the intention to destroy the Temple (Matthew 26:61) when He referred actually to the death and resurrection of His own body (John 2:21), even so Stephen was accused of a similar blasphemy.

There is close similarity in verse 14 to the words of Jesus recorded in Mark 14:58; and as in the case of Jesus' own words, Stephen's words were misconstrued to mean that Jesus would literally destroy the Temple. On the other hand, although it is not here recorded, it is likely that Stephen had not only repeated the words of Jesus, but also had grasped and expounded their inner meaning. Stephen probably declared that Christ's redeeming death and high-priestly ministry had superseded and made forever unnecessary the sacrificial system of the Jews. Spiritual interpretation and application cannot be understood and received by the spiritually dead, however religious they might be.

The charges having been uttered, the judges of the Sanhedrin and the other accusers now waited in the Temple for Stephen's defense. While waiting, they beheld Stephen's angelic countenance. This was not the mild, gentle look that is often seen in paintings of angels, nor the fierce look of an avenging angel, but a look that told of inspiration within, his countenance shining with the inner light of the Holy Spirit.

II. STEPHEN'S DEFENSE (Acts 7:44-53)
A. The Lord's Temple (vv. 44-50)
(Acts 7:44-50 is not included in the printed text.)

In his brief summary of Hebrew history, Stephen mentioned the Tabernacle, which was the place Israel worshiped God while wandering in the wilderness and up to the reign of David. "Since the Tabernacle was only a tent, David desired to provide a better dwelling place for the God of Jacob. But it was David's son Solomon who built the Temple. . . .

"Stephen's attack is not on the superb Temple itself or on Solomon's building it, but on the idea that God is tied to the Temple. The divine name 'the most High' (v. 48) stresses the transcendence of God. . . . God could not be limited to the Temple in Jerusalem, or Palestine. He can be truly worshiped anywhere people turn to Him with faith in Jesus Christ" (French Arrington, *The Acts of the Apostles*).

Talk About It:
1. What did Stephen declare about both the Tabernacle and the Temple that the Jews built for worshiping God (vv. 46-48)?
2. What do verses 49 and 50 reveal about the greatness of God?

B. Stiffnecked and Uncircumcised (vv. 51-53)
51. Ye stiffnecked and uncircumcised in heart and ears, ye do always resist the Holy Ghost: as your fathers did, so do ye.
52. Which of the prophets have not your fathers persecuted? and they have slain them which shewed before of the coming of the Just One; of whom ye have been now the betrayers and murderers:
53. Who have received the law by the disposition of angels, and have not kept it.

In these verses we discover the powerful attack of Stephen upon the hardness of hearts of the Jewish leaders and people. He recognized their problem for what it was: they resisted the Holy Spirit.

Stephen indicted them for being "stiffnecked and uncircumcised." Several times in the Old Testament the Lord referred to Israel as "stiffnecked" (Exodus 32:9; 33:3, 5; 34:9; Deuteronomy 9:6, 13). It was a term of rebellion and indicated pride, arrogance, and a desire to do one's own will. "Uncircumcised" is used in Leviticus 26:41; Jeremiah 6:10; 9:26; and Ezekiel 44:7, 9 in relation to God's people. It indicated a loss of covenant holiness. Stephen saw that Israel was unholy "in heart and

Talk About It:
1. Explain the phrase "uncircumcised in heart and ears" (v. 51).
2. What did Stephen accuse the authorities of doing (v. 52)?
3. What had these leaders failed to do (v. 53)?

ears." Thus, the intention of Israel was impure as well as her ability to "hear" God's voice.

The reality of "stiffnecked and uncircumcised" was related to sin against the Holy Spirit. The New Testament shows five different ways that we bring harm to ourselves by offending the Holy Spirit:

1. We may *blaspheme* against the Holy Spirit. This is the only unpardonable sin. Its description is found in Mark 3:29, 30, which indicates a position taken regarding Jesus Christ. Blasphemy accepts as truth the lie that Jesus was filled with an unclean, or demonic, spirit rather than filled with the Holy Spirit. Such a position denies that Jesus is the Son of God. If one persists in this attitude unrepentant until death, it is unpardonable.

2. We may *resist* the Holy Spirit. This is the accusation in the passage of Acts 7:51. This element of resisting the Spirit of God indicates a rebellious spirit that rejects the truth.

3. We may *quench* the Spirit (1 Thessalonians 5:19). This has to do with "extinguishing, stifling" the move of the Holy Spirit. From its usage in Isaiah 42:3 and Matthew 12:20, we can infer that it indicates a quenching spiritual life. We quench His Spirit of compassion and mercy by failing to be directed by Him.

4. We may *despise* the Holy Spirit (1 Thessalonians 4:8). In this we defiantly set aside what is clearly God's moral law and will. We, by our actions and intentions, declare invalid what God has declared to be valid.

5. We may *grieve* the Holy Spirit (Ephesians 4:30, 31). Paul made it clear that we can grieve the Spirit "with whom you are sealed for the day of redemption" (*NIV*). In other words, we fail to trust the Lord regarding His power to accomplish what He has declared. We remain insecure in our salvation. The Old Testament parallel to this is found in Numbers 20:10-13 and 27:14, where Moses grieved the Spirit when he struck the rock for water rather than obeying God's direction to speak to the rock. He broke his relationship with the Spirit and thereby grieved Him.

Stephen announced that Israel had historically resisted the Holy Spirit. The Jewish leaders of A.D. 30 were no different from their forefathers of earlier generations. They had always rejected the truth of God's Word and had persecuted those who announced God's intention to judge and thereby truly save. The "Just One" (Acts 7:52) was another way of referring to Jesus Christ as God's righteous Servant. His final indictment was that the Jewish authorities had betrayed God's purposes revealed in the Law and the Prophets. Their betrayal was against God himself and a rejection of His divine will.

Verse 53 speaks of their disobedience. It was against the Law of God, which Jewish tradition held was mediated to Moses through angels. Thus, the Law was divinely inspired and had its origins not in man (even a man as noble as Moses) but in heaven.

III. STEPHEN'S VINDICATION (Acts 7:54-60)

A. His Vision of Jesus (vv. 54-56)

54. When they heard these things, they were cut to the heart, and they gnashed on him with their teeth.

55. But he, being full of the Holy Ghost, looked up stedfastly into heaven, and saw the glory of God, and Jesus standing on the right hand of God,

56. And said, Behold, I see the heavens opened, and the Son of man standing on the right hand of God.

When suddenly it burst upon his accusers and judges that every historic reference Stephen had used indicated the divine mission of Jesus Christ and emphasized their guilt and shame in rejecting and crucifying Him, their antagonism changed to murderous wrath. When the truth regarding men's sinfulness does not convict of sin, it produces bitterness and malice against God, His message, and His messengers.

While his antagonistic audience gave vent to passion and rage, Stephen himself remained calm. Even now, on the verge of losing his life, he could remain calm, for he was "full of the Holy Ghost" (v. 55). Moreover, he was granted a vision of "the glory of God and Jesus." In some supernatural sense, Stephen was permitted to see his "one mediator between God and men, the man Christ Jesus" (1 Timothy 2:5).

Jesus standing, instead of sitting as He is elsewhere described (Matthew 26:64; Acts 2:34; Hebrews 1:3), surely indicated His readiness to strengthen and help His martyr. When Christians suffer from persecution and other trials, their divine Head in glory feels their pain and stands ready to comfort them and to receive them. By this wonderful experience, Stephen expressed a triumphant testimony. With the Lord's presence and help we can triumph in the darkest hour.

B. His Violent Execution (vv. 57, 58)

57. Then they cried out with a loud voice, and stopped their ears, and ran upon him with one accord,

58. And cast him out of the city, and stoned him: and the witnesses laid down their clothes at a young man's feet, whose name was Saul.

When Stephen echoed the claim that Jesus as the Son of Man was exalted at God's right hand, it was to his audience nothing but blasphemy, and they would hear no more. In a

Talk About It:
1. Compare Stephen's demeanor with that of his enemies.
2. What was Stephen enabled to see, and why (v. 56)?

Proper Posture
Stephen has been confessing Christ before men, and now he sees Christ confessing His servant before God. The proper posture for a witness is the standing posture. Jesus . . . stands at God's right hand as Stephen's advocate, his "paraclete."
—F.F. Bruce

Talk About It:
1. Why did Stephen's enemies cover their ears?
2. What do you suppose his enemies screamed at Stephen as they rushed at him?

"In America today, the only respectable form of bigotry is bigotry directed at religious people."
—**William Bennett**

Talk About It:
Compare Stephen's final prayer (v. 60) with Jesus' final prayer (Luke 23:34).

Ground of Hope
The fact that Jesus Christ died is more important than the fact that I shall die, and the fact that Jesus Christ rose from the dead is the sole ground of my hope that I, too, shall be raised on the last day. Our salvation is external to us. I find no salvation in my life history, but only in the history of Jesus Christ.

—**Dietrich Bonhoeffer**

---

frantic rage they hustled him out of the city and stoned him, in accord with the Jewish form of execution. It is not clear whether or not they had Roman authority for the execution, or if it was a mob action.

The witnesses who had a part in the stoning naturally divested themselves of their outer garments. Unaware of the consequences of their action, the enemies of the gospel, the Jewish officials in particular, did something that day which ultimately became their undoing. Saul of Tarsus, the young man at whose feet the witnesses laid their garments, could never shake off the testimony of Stephen's holy life and the exclamation that he had seen the risen Christ standing at the right hand of God in glory. Only a short time later, Saul was converted and became the great missionary apostle of the early church. Surely Stephen's martyrdom was a triumph for the church. Victory for the cause of Christ is often costly.

C. His Victorious Death (vv. 59, 60)

59. And they stoned Stephen, calling upon God, and saying, Lord Jesus, receive my spirit.

60. And he kneeled down, and cried with a loud voice, Lord, lay not this sin to their charge. And when he had said this, he fell asleep.

Even as the stones were flying, Stephen in a triumphant faith committed himself to the exalted Advocate whom he had just seen in a vision. Calling upon the Lord, he said, "Lord Jesus, receive my spirit." These words are reminiscent of our Lord's final utterance on the cross (Luke 23:46). There was one difference: Jesus committed His spirit to the Father, whereas Stephen committed his to Jesus. This was strong testimony to the Christian belief in Christ's essential deity.

A further evidence of the triumph of Stephen's death is the final loud cry: "Lord, lay not this sin to their charge." This was his final appeal to the heavenly court. This time it was not for his own vindication, but for mercy toward his executioners. Recall the words of Jesus on the cross: "Father, forgive them" (Luke 23:34). Another mark of triumph was the nature of Stephen's departure: "he fell asleep." These words are enough to take the sting from death. If this is death to the Christian, even in martyrdom, surely we need have no fear of life's twilight.

CONCLUSION

"He fell asleep." Did he really? The words seem incongruous. Was the martyr so blissfully unaware of the cruel treatment he was receiving? Was Luke exaggerating just a little here?

The friends of Voltaire, the famous infidel, tried to draw a veil of secrecy over the fear and terror that poor man displayed on his deathbed. Each side would like to think it has all the heroes. But God's Word is always true, and we are led to believe that the same Holy Spirit that gave Stephen such moral strength and spiritual calm overruled the cruelty of his assailants. His actual physical suffering was miraculously lightened and shortened. He really fell asleep.

His death must have been a vivid demonstration of the Christian's victory over the king of terrors, for among the witnesses that never forgot that scene was the young man, Saul of Tarsus. Long years after, when telling of the events that led him to Christ, he could say, "I saw his face as it were an angel" (see Acts 6:15; 22:20). Here is a striking example of the truth of the statement, "The blood of the martyrs is the seed of the church." Through this seed, corn fell into the stony heart of the chief persecutor; from this unlikely place it sprang forth into an infinite harvest that shall continue to be reaped as long as the church is in the earth.

Though Stephen sleeps, wherever this gospel is preached and his story retold, people shall wake to righteousness.

GOLDEN TEXT CHALLENGE

"ACCORDING TO MY EARNEST EXPECTATION AND MY HOPE, THAT IN NOTHING I SHALL BE ASHAMED, BUT THAT WITH ALL BOLDNESS, AS ALWAYS, SO NOW ALSO CHRIST SHALL BE MAGNIFIED IN MY BODY, WHETHER IT BE BY LIFE, OR BY DEATH" (Philippians 1:20).

People use their bodies for many different purposes. Some give their bodies to build things out of mortar and bricks, some give their bodies to break records of athletic or industrial nature, while others give their bodies to immoral experiences.

All of these uses of the body miss the entire point of the human existence. Our bodies are products of the love and the imagination of God. They express something about God, something about His creativeness, something about His orderliness, something about His multifaceted person.

What is the best way that a human body can be used? What is the best use to which it can be put? To magnify God!

What a shame to waste the human body—such a marvelous instrument of God's creative hand—on trivial or self-serving uses! Paul longed for Christ to be magnified in his body, even if by death, expressing the highest and noblest use to which human life may be put.

Daily Devotions:
M. Rewarded With
   Life
   2 Kings 20:1-6
T. Willing to Die
   Daniel 3:16-28
W. God's Servant
   Spared
   Daniel 6:16-23
T. Martyred for
   Truthfulness
   Matthew 14:1-12
F. Christ Lives in Me
   Galatians 2:19-21
S. To Die Is Gain
   Philippians
   1:15-24

Sharing the Gospel

Acts 8:1-40

INTRODUCTION

In Acts 1:8, Jesus told His disciples, "But ye shall receive power, after that the Holy Ghost is come upon you: and ye shall be witnesses unto me both in Jerusalem, and in all Judaea, and in Samaria, and unto the uttermost part of the earth." Today's lesson begins with Acts 8:1 in Jerusalem, where Stephen has been violently executed for preaching the gospel.

Apparently sparked by Stephen's death, persecution breaks out like wildfire against believers. Suddenly Christians flee for their lives throughout Judea, to Samaria, and to other places. Just as Jesus said would happen, His followers spread the gospel message, though probably not under the circumstances they had expected.

Philip, who along with Stephen was one of the first seven deacons ordained by the Jerusalem church, preaches in Samaria. As news of his successful evangelistic efforts spreads, the apostles Peter and John are sent to confirm his ministry. The apostles lay their hands on the new converts in prayer, and they are baptized in the Holy Spirit (vv. 15-17).

With the gospel advancing in Samaria, God calls Philip to leave Samaria to minister to one man on a lonely road south of Jerusalem. The resulting conversion becomes the means for the gospel to be taken to Ethiopia (vv. 26-39).

The chapter closes by saying, "Philip . . . appeared at Azotus and traveled about, preaching the gospel in all the towns until he reached Caesarea" (v. 40, *NIV*).

I. OPPOSITION ADVANCES THE KINGDOM (Acts 8:1-4)
A. Great Persecution (vv. 1, 2)

1. And Saul was consenting unto his death. And at that time there was a great persecution against the church which was at Jerusalem; and they were all scattered abroad throughout the regions of Judaea and Samaria, except the apostles.

2. And devout men carried Stephen to his burial, and made great lamentation over him.

The martyrdom of Stephen was the signal for a more thorough campaign of persecution of Jerusalem believers. His death was not an isolated incident. Rather it was one of the focal points of a tension that raged over a wide area. With Christianity growing, and with no way to stop it by argument, Saul and the Jews had to either accept the predicament or stamp it out by force. They chose to use legal means where possible, but they realized that alone was not enough. So they launched a full-scale persecution. What could not be done by reason and truth (as they saw it), they hoped to accomplish by force.

Consequently a large number of believers left Jerusalem and were scattered throughout Palestine and even beyond its borders. It appears, however, that the apostles were not identified in the popular mind with Stephen, since they did not leave the city. Stephen was among the Greek-speaking Christians, who conformed less to Jewish customs and beliefs than did the Aramaic-speaking Jews, which included the apostles.

Some scholars think there were devout Jews as well as Christians who took part in Stephen's burial and mourning. If so, they may have been protesting against the extreme action of the court, as happened when Nicodemus and Joseph of Arimathea buried Jesus' body (see John 19:38, 39).

B. Great Witnessing (vv. 3, 4)

3. As for Saul, he made havock of the church, entering into every house, and haling men and women committed them to prison.

4. Therefore they that were scattered abroad went every where preaching the word.

The prime mover in the repressive campaign to stamp out the faith was Saul of Tarsus. If he felt any discomfort or uncertainty over his part in the stoning of Stephen (v. 1), there is no sign of it. Armed with the authority of the Sanhedrin, he shamefully mistreated and laid waste the church, dragging both men and women from their homes to be imprisoned.

The word translated as "havoc" (v. 3) suggests the ruin and devastation caused by an army or the picture of a wild boar

Talk About It:
1. What impact did Stephen's death have on unbelievers?
2. What impact did his death have on believers?

"No pain, no palm; no thorns, no throne; no gall, no glory; no cross, no crown."
—William Penn

Talk About It:
1. Explain Saul's terrible zeal.
2. What positive effect did persecution have?

ravaging a vineyard. Saul was "exceedingly mad" against Christ's followers and hunted them "even unto strange cities" (26:11).

As terrible as the persecution was, it was overruled by divine providence for the increase of the church. The scattered believers carried the gospel with them and preached as far north as Syrian Antioch. Thus the commission of Christ was carried out by His disciples under threat of the "roaring lion" of persecution.

II. REPENTANCE BRINGS REVIVAL (Acts 8:5-8, 14-17)
A. Philip's Preaching in Samaria (vv. 5-8)

5. Then Philip went down to the city of Samaria, and preached Christ unto them.

6. And the people with one accord gave heed unto those things which Philip spake, hearing and seeing the miracles which he did.

7. For unclean spirits, crying with loud voice, came out of many that were possessed with them: and many taken with palsies, and that were lame, were healed.

8. And there was great joy in that city.

Philip the evangelist became a missionary preacher to the Samaritans. The theme of his preaching was "Christ, the Crucified and Risen Redeemer." The word *preached* in the original Greek means "to proclaim with authority as a herald." The imperfect tense implies continued action, probably meaning the evangelistic campaign lasted for weeks or even months. Philip did not waste his time discussing economic and social problems, nor political issues, nor theological controversies. He proclaimed Christ and the kingdom of God.

The response to Philip's preaching was extraordinary. Verse 6 implies that great crowds of people believed and gave their consent to Philip's message and appeal. The readiness with which his proclamation was accepted shows that in spite of racial and religious prejudices in Samaria, Philip reaped where Jesus and His disciples and the woman of Sychar had sown some years before (John 4:39-42).

Philip's preaching was attested by signs which served to convince the people that his message and mission were genuine and from the Lord. That the power of the living Lord Jesus was manifest in Philip's ministry is evident from the healing of the sick and the demon-possessed. His miracles were similar to the many cases of our Lord's healing ministry.

The cry of the unclean spirits (Acts 8:7) may have been involuntary testimony to the messiahship of Jesus and the truth of the gospel (cf. Mark 3:11; Luke 4:41). Some understand the cry here to have been an exclamation of rage or indignation

Talk About It:
1. Describe the types of miracles that took place in Philip's ministry.
2. How did the Samaritans respond to the gospel?

Sharing the Gospel

on the part of the demons because they were compelled to release their victims in the presence of divine power. The physical diseases are distinguished from demoniac possession, but Philip's ministry of spiritual power triumphed over all human maladies.

This joy among the Samaritans was inspired partly by the healing of the sick, and partly by Philip's preaching of the good news for the salvation of sinners who believed. Pessimism and unbelief lead to sadness and despair, but faith and hope in Christ inspire rejoicing and song. Recall Jesus' words: "These things have I spoken unto you, that my joy might remain in you, and that your joy might be full" (John 15:11). Recall, too, the words of the apostle John: "And these things write we unto you, that your joy may be full" (1 John 1:4).

B. The Ministry of Peter and John (vv. 14-17)

14. Now when the apostles which were at Jerusalem heard that Samaria had received the word of God, they sent unto them Peter and John:

15. Who, when they were come down, prayed for them, that they might receive the Holy Ghost:

16. (For as yet he was fallen upon none of them: only they were baptized in the name of the Lord Jesus.)

17. Then laid they their hands on them, and they received the Holy Ghost.

It is evident that Jerusalem was recognized as the mother church and that the apostles there exercised general supervision over the widespread work of evangelism. It was good news to the apostles in Jerusalem to hear that revival had come to neighboring Samaria. No better news can come from any community than this!

The communication from Philip's campaign in Samaria brought quick reaction from Jerusalem. Peter and John, the foremost leaders of the apostles, were commissioned to go to Samaria to inspect the work. It is evident that John went with a different attitude than he had before, when he wanted to call down fire from heaven on Samaria (Luke 9:54).

These believers in Samaria, although baptized by Philip "in the name of the Lord Jesus" (Acts 8:16), had not at the same time received the gift of the Holy Spirit. The apostles were at once aware of this lack and so prayed for them that they might receive this gift from God. In this early period of transition, God often used the apostles for the bestowment of the Holy Spirit.

Having believed and having been baptized in the name of the Lord Jesus indicates that these Samaritans had become Christians and truly belonged to Christ. But they were lacking the baptism in the Spirit which would enable them to witness with spiritual power.

"It is true that [people] are praying for worldwide revival. But it would be more timely, and more scriptural, for prayer to be made to the Lord of the harvest, that He would raise up and thrust forth laborers who would fearlessly and faithfully preach those truths which are calculated to bring about a revival."
—A.W. Pink

Talk About It:
1. Why did Peter and John go to Samaria?
2. Describe the two baptisms experienced by the Samaritan converts.

Beyond Salvation
The accounts in the Book of Acts . . . connect the baptizing in the Holy Spirit with charismatic power for mission and not with salvation. The gift of the Holy Spirit, says William Rodman, "goes beyond salvation; it is promised to those who repent and come to faith in Jesus Christ."
—John Lombard Jr

The laying on of hands (v. 17) was an outward sign of a special impartation of spiritual grace. The Samaritans "received the Holy Ghost."

III. WITNESSING ONE TO ONE (Acts 8:26-40)
A. Divine Guidance (vv. 26-29)

26. And the angel of the Lord spake unto Philip, saying, Arise, and go toward the south unto the way that goeth down from Jerusalem unto Gaza, which is desert.

27. And he arose and went: and, behold, a man of Ethiopia, an eunuch of great authority under Candace queen of the Ethiopians, who had the charge of all her treasure, and had come to Jerusalem for to worship,

Esaias (v. 28)—Isaiah

28. Was returning, and sitting in his chariot read Esaias the prophet.

29. Then the Spirit said unto Philip, Go near, and join thyself to this chariot.

Talk About It:
1. How specific were the Lord's directions to Philip (vv. 26, 29)?
2. Who was this man that Philip met in the desert (v. 27)?

While the apostles Peter and John were being led to preach the Word of God in various Samaritan villages on their return to Jerusalem, the evangelist Philip was about to receive divine direction from a special messenger of the Lord for a fruitful mission south of Jerusalem. From Samaria, Philip was instructed to go directly south and, leaving Jerusalem on the east, to take the road at some distance from that city. This road toward Gaza was very likely the one by way of Hebron through the desert country.

These verses describe Philip as an evangelist who was prepared to do the Lord's bidding anywhere and at any time—even to be used to witness effectively to a spiritually hungry stranger on the lonely Gaza road. Philip's obedience was prompt and complete. Although perhaps perplexed at this sudden change of plan, "he arose and went" (v. 27). Instead of preaching to crowds, as had been his privilege in Samaria, he was now to preach to one man, a task no less difficult and, to the mind of the Lord, no less important.

As soon as Philip came to the Gaza road, he found a covered wagon moving in a southerly direction. In this wagon was seated the treasurer of the Ethiopian Court. It was common in the eastern countries to employ eunuchs as government officials. Although some think he was a Jew who had made his home in Ethiopia, he was very likely a native African who had become a proselyte to Judaism. This dignitary was returning from a Jerusalem pilgrimage and was occupied in reading aloud the Greek version of the messianic prophecy of Isaiah when Philip found him.

The fact that he had traveled about 1,200 miles from his native country to worship in the capital of Judaism indicates his

Sharing the Gospel

inner hunger for a spiritual satisfaction that his position, honor and money could not buy. His reading of the Word of God had intensified this hunger, but the content of this Servant passage of Scripture had perplexed him and had created a desire for a true interpretation. The Lord had prepared an interpreter and had sent him to the side of the inquirer.

Philip was prepared for his important mission to this man by his knowledge of Scripture, his love for souls, and his responsiveness to the voice of the Holy Spirit. Hearing the eunuch read, Philip momentarily debated what to do. Then the Spirit commanded him to approach the eunuch's wagon as the Lord's witness. A.T. Pierson noted, "For the first time in the Book of Acts, we see the Holy Spirit no longer moving upon the multitude, but condescending to become the personal guide of one believer." In the Greek the words "join thyself" express strong determination to accomplish a purpose.

> "Philip being sent from a great revival in Samaria to minister to one man in the desert reminds us how much the individual is worth to God."
> —**Lance Colkmire**

B. Sincere Seeker (vv. 30-34)

(Acts 8:30-34 is not included in the printed text.)

The prompt obedience and the tactful approach of the witness indicate the true method of a Spirit-led personal evangelist. Philip used a question, "Understandest thou what thou readest?" (v. 30), to arrest the man's attention to the interpretation and application that Philip was now prepared to give. The behavior of Philip also indicates eagerness to witness and lead a hungry soul to Christ.

Talk About It:
1. What did the Ethiopian not understand?
2. What did Isaiah foretell in this scripture (Isaiah 53:7)?

The eunuch's responsive question as well as his invitation to Philip to take his place at his side in his chariot (v. 31) indicates an earnest desire for more enlightenment. The word *guide* is the one employed for the guidance given by teacher to student. Jesus used it reproachfully of the blind guidance given by the scribes and Pharisees of His day (Matthew 15:14; Luke 6:39). It is also used of the Holy Spirit as the teacher of believers (John 14:26; 16:13).

The text Philip used was Isaiah 53:7, 8. The word translated "place" (Acts 8:32) signifies the whole context of the passage, so that interpretation could be given to the text in the light of the whole Servant prophecy. The prophet was speaking of an Individual (Christ) who suffered in silence like a dumb lamb before its shearer. Moreover, in His humiliation of the violence and outrage which He endured, the human rights and justice which belonged to Him were denied Him. Who can describe the wickedness of His contemporaries, for by them the Sufferer was hurried to a violent death.

Since some of the Jews interpreted this passage as referring to the nation of Israel, some to the prophet himself, and others to the Messiah, it is no wonder that the eunuch found it difficult to understand. To him, however, the passage seemed to refer to an individual, whether it was the prophet himself or some other man. But since he needed further enlightenment and assurance, he turned to the Lord's witness for the correct interpretation.

C. Effective Witnessing (vv. 35-38)

35. Then Philip opened his mouth, and began at the same scripture, and preached unto him Jesus.

36. And as they went on their way, they came unto a certain water: and the eunuch said, See, here is water; what doth hinder me to be baptized?

37. And Philip said, If thou believest with all thine heart, thou mayest. And he answered and said, I believe that Jesus Christ is the Son of God.

38. And he commanded the chariot to stand still: and they went down both into the water, both Philip and the eunuch; and he baptized him.

Talk About It:
1. How was Isaiah 53:7 a perfect starting point for Philip's message?
2. What condition did Philip give for the Ethiopian to be baptized?

The theme for Philip's witnessing to this man was simply "Jesus." Whether or not this Ethiopian had ever heard of Jesus is not known, but that he now had heard an exposition of Christ, the fulfillment of the Suffering Servant, that enlightened his understanding and moved his heart is evident from the sequel. For it was Jesus, and no other, who suffered silently and unjustly, and offered His life in death for sin. Through His obedience unto the death of the cross, He made justification possible for all sinners by bearing their iniquities. This interpretation and application of the Servant passage alone is in accord with Jesus' own words, "Search the scriptures; for in them ye think ye have eternal life; and they are they which testify of me" (John 5:39).

Philip's witnessing evidently included instruction relative to Christian baptism. It is evident, too, that the evangelist's testimony of Christ's redeeming death and resurrection in fulfillment of the Servant prophecy had produced conviction and kindled saving faith in the heart of the Ethiopian. Hence, upon their arrival at a stream of water, the man requested baptism as a visible confession of his new faith.

Philip's words in verse 37 indicate that he was satisfied with the sincerity of the Ethiopian's testimony and that water baptism was in order. The driver of the chariot was ordered to stop, and it is probable that the whole retinue was permitted to see the beautiful and sacred ceremony. Their going "down both into the water" (v. 38) seems to be in harmony with the universality of immersion in the practice of the early church, although this is not expressly stated here. The eunuch would lay aside his outer clothing, descend chest-deep into the water, and be submerged in the name of the Lord Jesus.

"Jesus died on the cross—that's history. Jesus died for me—that's salvation."
—*Christianity Today*

D. Reason to Rejoice (vv. 39, 40)

39. And when they were come up out of the water, the Spirit of the Lord caught away Philip, that the eunuch saw him no more: and he went on his way rejoicing.

40. But Philip was found at Azotus: and passing through he preached in all the cities, till he came to Caesarea.

"The picture is not that of the eunuch left dazed upon the highway, wondering what had become of Philip. He had forgotten Philip, for he had found all for which his soul was hungry. He went on his way rejoicing with new light upon his brow, the new life thrilling through his spirit, and the new love mastering him. He was independent of Jerusalem now; he was independent even of the messenger, for he had found the Master" (G.C. Morgan).

While human feeling may have moved Philip to accompany his new convert with further instruction, a stronger and irresistible impulse from the Spirit of the Lord led Philip to an abrupt and immediate departure. The Lord had other plans for His witness and other places for him to work. Philip next appeared at Azotus, and from there he headed north along the coastal road, preaching the gospel in the cities through which he traveled until finally he reached Caesarea. There he seems to have settled down to become a family man of spiritual influence (see Acts 21:8).

CONCLUSION

Philip's witnessing to the man from Ethiopia, as well as his ministry in Samaria, are Biblical illustrations of the Holy Spirit's direction of an obedient evangelist on a specific mission. These are also examples of the Spirit's preparation of lost souls for the specific ministry of the Lord's servant. As Philip was prepared by his understanding of Scripture in the light of Christ's mission, so the eunuch was prepared by his reading of Scripture which predicted Christ's mission of salvation. As Philip was prepared to break social barriers to preach the gospel in Samaria, so the Holy Spirit prepared the Samaritans' hearts to receive the good news.

GOLDEN TEXT CHALLENGE

"THEY, WHEN THEY HAD TESTIFIED AND PREACHED THE WORD OF THE LORD, RETURNED TO JERUSALEM, AND PREACHED THE GOSPEL IN MANY VILLAGES OF THE SAMARITANS" (Acts 8:25).

When Peter and John went to Samaria, they confirmed Philip's ministry there. They witnessed how the Samaritans were responding to the gospel, and they helped evangelize them. But they did not stop there. On their way back to Jerusalem, the apostles preached the gospel in Samaritan villages.

Azotus (a-ZOH-tus) —v. 40—a primarily Gentile town that once had been the Philistine city of Ashdod

Caesarea (v. 40)— an important seaport built by King Herod between 25 and 13 B.C.

Talk About It:
1. Why do you suppose Philip made such a dramatic exit from the desert?
2. What was the significance of Philip preaching "in all the cities" from Azotus to Caesarea (v. 40)?

Who are the "Samaritans" in your community—those people who are looked down upon because of their color, their social status, or their religion? Whether they live in "villages" or in a city, the gospel of Christ is for them. Do you intentionally make efforts to be a witness to them?

The Transforming Power of Christ

Acts 9:1-31

INTRODUCTION

The study of the apostle Paul's life is one of the most interesting and rewarding studies in all of Scripture. Second only to Jesus Christ, Paul stood like a mountain peak among New Testament characters. What he did and what he said helped to establish the Christian faith in the ancient world. His activity for Christ helped to change the direction of the world. Without him the world would be a different place than it is today. The Christian faith was shaped by his Spirit-inspired life and writings.

In this lesson we see Paul at the time of his conversion as Saul of Tarsus, where he was an arrogant persecutor of the Christians. There was little in his life before his conversion to suggest what a great man for Christ he would become. Yet he had great talent and abilities that God would use in His service.

Saul was a zealous Jew, and he would become an equally zealous Christian. Frequently the same personality traits that make a man very evil will also make him very good after he is converted. Nowhere in human history is there a clearer example of that circumstance than in the life of Paul.

The first mention of Paul in the Bible is Acts 7:58: "And the witnesses laid down their clothes at a young man's feet, whose name was Saul." Acts 8:1-3 tells us that young Saul was in full agreement with the persecution of the Christians. More than that, he himself joined eagerly in the persecution. Verse 3 says that "he made havoc of the church, entering into every house, and haling men and women committed them to prison." At least seven times in his later writings Paul referred to his persecution of the Christians.

Unit Theme:
Lessons From the Early Church (Acts, Part 1)

Central Truth:
Christ can save even the worst of sinners.

Focus:
Discuss Paul's conversion and witness with confidence that no one is beyond God's grace.

Context:
Around A.D. 35, Saul (Paul) encounters Christ on the road to Damascus.

Golden Text:
"Christ Jesus came into the world to save sinners; of whom I am chief" (1 Timothy 1:15).

Study Outline:
I. Apprehended by Christ
(Acts 9:1-9)
II. Affirmed by the Spirit
(Acts 9:10-22)
III. Accepted by the Church
(Acts 9:23-31)

I. APPREHENDED BY CHRIST (Acts 9:1-9)

A. Religious Zealot (vv. 1, 2)

1. And Saul, yet breathing out threatenings and slaughter against the disciples of the Lord, went unto the high priest,

2. And desired of him letters to Damascus to the synagogues, that if he found any of this way, whether they were men or women, he might bring them bound unto Jerusalem.

Talk About It:
1. Why did Saul go to Damascus?
2. What role did the high priest play in the persecution of Christians?

Saul was angry toward the Christians because they followed Jesus Christ. The root of his rebellion lay in his zeal for the Jewish law. In his mind Jesus was a man, yet His disciples called Him God; Jesus was executed on a cross, and yet His disciples claimed that He was without sin. The hatred Saul harbored in his heart became so intense that he personally attempted to eradicate the Christian faith. In the course of his persecution, he approached the high priest with a plan of pursuit and further persecution. The fact that Saul was able to gain an audience with the high priest suggests that he stood high in the ecclesiastical world of the Jewish people.

Saul solicited from the high priest a commission whereby he could require any Christian Jew in Damascus to return to Jerusalem. It is quite clear from this verse that Saul was principally concerned with refugees who had fled to Damascus to escape the persecution in Jerusalem. No doubt there were also natives of Damascus who had become Christians, but these would not have been under the jurisdiction of the Jewish high priest. Citizens of Judea who had fled to Damascus would be.

In his blind rage Saul intended to deal harshly with both men and women. He was not content to imprison and bring to trial heads of families only, but it seems he was intent upon bringing whole families into account for their conversion to Christianity. The Pharisee Saul was so blinded by his mistaken devotion to the Jewish faith, and his hatred of the Christian faith, that it seems he had lost all gallantry or pity. Nothing blinds a man more than prejudice, and Saul was filled with an unreasonable prejudice against Jesus of Nazareth. He vented his rage upon the followers of Christ.

"One of the most expensive luxuries one can possess is to hate somebody. A deep-seated grudge in one's life eats away at his peace of mind like a deadly cancer destroying a vital organ of life."
—E.T. Wayland

The fruit of Saul's blind rebellion was that he was made much less than a man. He actually became savage and brutal in nature. If he had gotten his way, he would have stamped out the Christian way (called "this way"). Moreover, he would have removed the very memory of Jesus from the history pages. In a tragic way, Saul became a madman.

B. Stunning Revelation (vv. 3-5)

3. And as he journeyed, he came near Damascus: and suddenly there shined round about him a light from heaven:

4. And he fell to the earth, and heard a voice saying unto him, Saul, Saul, why persecutest thou me?

5. And he said, Who art thou, Lord? And the Lord said, I am Jesus whom thou persecutest: it is hard for thee to kick against the pricks.

Damascus was a six-day journey from Jerusalem. It was an ancient city, dating from before the days of Abraham, and was prominent throughout all of the Old Testament. At the time of the New Testament it was the capital of the Roman province of Syria.

Saul was accompanied on his journey to Damascus by a company of men, but it is not indicated just what sort of escorts they were. Certainly they would have been escorts with some strength of arms, for they intended to bring the Christians back to Jerusalem in bonds.

At about midday of the last day of the journey, a dazzling light shone from heaven, "above the brightness of the sun" (Acts 26:13). This was no doubt a supernatural light of the nature of the *shekinah* of the Old Testament. From 9:3 and the context, it appears that the light shone only to Paul; but comparative passages in 22:9 and 26:13 indicate that others of the company saw it too.

A supernatural voice spoke to Paul and twice stated that He was Jesus whom Paul persecuted. Jesus did not say that Saul was persecuting His followers, but that he was persecuting Him personally. This is the extent to which Jesus still identifies Himself with His followers. Any persecution of Christ's people is the same as persecution of Him. In similar fashion, any kindness to His people is the same as kindness to Him (see Matthew 25:40-45).

In his question to Jesus, Saul addressed Him as "Lord," the most intimate term that can be applied to Jesus. When the rich young ruler called Him "Master," he was referring to Jesus as a teacher. It is true that Jesus is Master, but the word *Lord* means much more. It means "ownership, absolute control." Saul was literally acknowledging himself to be the property of the One speaking to him. Later in his life this would prove to be absolutely true. Paul would frequently refer to himself as a servant of Jesus Christ (cf. Romans 1:1).

Jesus stated that Saul was "kick[ing] against the pricks." *Pricks* were sharpened points that brought great pain to beasts that kicked to get free. The rebellious animal would kick against the sharpened points and thereby inflict painful injury upon itself. Pricks were used to help control the animal. The imagery here suggested that Saul was hurting himself. He was also causing delay in the will of the Lord for his life.

Talk About It:
1. Whom had Saul been persecuting, and how?
2. What is the significance of Saul using the term "Lord"?

"The adventure of new life in Christ begins when the comfortable patterns of the old life are left behind."
—David Roher

C. Days of Blindness (vv. 6-9)

6. And he trembling and astonished said, Lord, what wilt thou have me to do? And the Lord said unto him, Arise, and go into the city, and it shall be told thee what thou must do.

7. And the men which journeyed with him stood speechless, hearing a voice, but seeing no man.

8. And Saul arose from the earth; and when his eyes were opened, he saw no man: but they led him by the hand, and brought him into Damascus.

9. And he was three days without sight, and neither did eat nor drink.

Once again Saul addressed Christ as Lord. He emphasized his submission to Christ by asking the question, "What wilt thou have me to do?" This question implied that he was ready to do the Lord's bidding, whatever that might be. Such is the meaning of commitment to Christ as Lord. His will becomes our command. When Christ is Lord of all to us, we will be submissive to His directions of life for us.

Saul's conversion was dramatic. He gave himself without reservation to the will of Christ. He did not contest the Lord's right to possess him. He gave everything to the lordship of Christ.

Instead of speaking to Saul directly to tell him what he should do, Christ directed him to proceed into the city of Damascus. There another person would tell Saul what he should do.

Acts 22:9 says that the men who traveled with Saul "saw indeed the light, and were afraid; but they heard not the voice of him that spake to me." Some imagine that there is a contradiction here, but that is not the case. Paul's company heard the sound of the voice, but they did not hear what was spoken.

Saul the great persecutor had to be led into Damascus by the hand of another. He was struck blind in order that he might see. As he lay on the ground, he was able to see the magnitude of his own sin. He also saw that the love of Christ equals the magnitude of man's sin.

The three days that Saul was blind were the most enlightened three days of his experience. Frequently in the purpose of Christ, He must slow people down. He must have time to speak to us and deal with us so He can guide us in our labors.

II. AFFIRMED BY THE SPIRIT (Acts 9:10-22)
A. Two Visions (vv. 10-12)

10. And there was a certain disciple at Damascus, named Ananias; and to him said the Lord in a vision, Ananias. And he said, Behold, I am here, Lord.

11. And the Lord said unto him, Arise, and go into the street which is called Straight, and enquire in the house

of Judas for one called Saul, of Tarsus: for, behold, he prayeth,

12. And hath seen in a vision a man named Ananias coming in, and putting his hand on him, that he might receive his sight.

At the same time Christ was dealing with Saul, He was also dealing with an older Christian concerning Saul. Ananias was apparently an elder among the Christians in Damascus. It is believed that he was the leader or pastor of the Damascus disciples. Ananias was deeply spiritual, sensitive to the will of the Lord. Christ was, therefore, able to reveal Himself to this disciple and to use him as a spiritual spokesman for the young convert Saul. Notice the similarity of the Lord's words to Ananias (v. 11) and His words to Saul (v. 6). Both were instructed to "arise, and go."

Since Ananias had great apprehension about the notorious persecutor, Saul, it was reassuring to him to learn Saul was staying with a Jew named Judas in the Jewish community along Straight Street. An important thoroughfare at that time, this street ran east and west through Damascus. Most reassuring of all was the information that Saul was praying. It was also revealed to Ananias that Saul himself had seen a vision in which Ananias would come to him. The older Christian would therefore be expected, with the way prepared for him to meet the notorious young convert.

B. Infamous Persecutor (vv. 13, 14)

13. Then Ananias answered, Lord, I have heard by many of this man, how much evil he hath done to thy saints at Jerusalem:

14. And here he hath authority from the chief priests to bind all that call on thy name.

The fame of Saul of Tarsus had spread throughout the region. His persecution of the Christians in Jerusalem had virtually stopped the Christian faith in that city. Believers in Christ had either been driven into exile, placed in prison, or made to renounce their Christian faith. This excursion into Damascus, it seems, was Saul's first attempt to press the persecution into other areas as well. Word had reached Ananias that Saul had the authorization of the Jewish leaders to bind and imprison all those of the Christian faith.

It is easy to imagine the anxiety Ananias may have felt when he was called upon to go into the presence of such a man. Saul had the nature and willingness to persecute the Christians without mercy. He, furthermore, had the authority of the Jewish leadership behind him. Would any Christian have been eager to go into the presence of such an opponent?

Talk About It:
1. What does verse 10 teach us about Ananias?
2. Why do you suppose the Lord told Ananias, "He [Saul] is praying" (v. 11, *NKJV*)?
3. Describe the vision God had given Saul.

"Men give advice; God gives guidance."
—Leonard Ravenhill

Talk About It:
What did Ananias know about Saul?

C. Chosen Vessel (vv. 15, 16)

15. But the Lord said unto him, Go thy way: for he is a chosen vessel unto me, to bear my name before the Gentiles, and kings, and the children of Israel:

16. For I will shew him how great things he must suffer for my name's sake.

Talk About It:
1. What had God "chosen" Saul to do (v. 15)?
2. What did God say He would reveal to Saul (v. 16)?

The Lord swept aside Ananias' mild objection and revealed to him there was a divine purpose for Saul. Jesus had His eye on the persecutor even while he tormented the church. Now the time had come for Jesus to exercise His claim on this one and call him into special service.

Saul was to be a messenger to the Gentiles, a people historically despised by the Jews. The Gentiles were pagan in religion and oppressive as conquerors, yet Jesus would send Saul to the Gentiles to carry the gospel. In the course of his ministry to the Gentiles, Saul would suffer greatly, just as he had caused the Jewish Christians to suffer. He who had inflicted pain and punishment upon other Christians would be subjected to pain and punishment himself.

D. Saul's Surrender (vv. 17-22)

17. And Ananias went his way, and entered into the house; and putting his hands on him said, Brother Saul, the Lord, even Jesus, that appeared unto thee in the way as thou camest, hath sent me, that thou mightest receive thy sight, and be filled with the Holy Ghost.

18. And immediately there fell from his eyes as it had been scales: and he received sight forthwith, and arose, and was baptized.

19. And when he had received meat, he was strengthened. Then was Saul certain days with the disciples which were at Damascus.

20. And straightway he preached Christ in the synagogues, that he is the Son of God.

21. But all that heard him were amazed, and said; Is not this he that destroyed them which called on this name in Jerusalem, and came hither for that intent, that he might bring them bound unto the chief priests?

22. But Saul increased the more in strength, and confounded the Jews which dwelt at Damascus, proving that this is very Christ.

Talk About It:
1. What did Ananias call Saul, and why (v. 17)?
2. How do verses 18 and 19 show Saul was a changed man?
3. What "confounded the Jews" (v. 22)?

Ananias followed the instructions of the Lord and went to Saul. As he obeyed the Lord, sight was restored to Saul and the transformation of his life was made complete. Hereafter, Saul would go in a completely opposite direction from that which he had taken earlier. He would love and promote what he had once hated; he would have fellowship with those he had caused to suffer; he would suffer himself at the hands of those who had once been his brethren and friends.

Saul surrendered himself to Christ and would thereafter travel with Him. Hereafter he would say, "I am crucified with Christ: nevertheless I live; yet not I, but Christ liveth in me: and the life which I now live in the flesh I live by the faith of the Son of God, who loved me, and gave himself for me" (Galatians 2:20).

Ananias called Saul "brother," which indicates his spiritual acceptance of the former persecutor. The disciples Saul had come to persecute also accepted him into their company, and he remained with them for a short period. In their fellowship Saul gained strength and became oriented to his new life.

Saul began to preach immediately in Damascus, asserting that Jesus Christ is the Son of God. This caused much amazement, for Saul was the one who had been so violent against the Christians because of their assertion that Jesus is the Son of God. From the beginning Saul was persuasive in his presentation of Christ, a fact that considerably confused and dismayed the unconverted Jews.

> "Salvation is moving from living death to deathless life."
> —Jack Odell

III. ACCEPTED BY THE CHURCH (Acts 9:23-31)
A. Narrow Escape (vv. 23-25)
(Acts 9:23-25 is not included in the printed text.)

Hearing of Saul's conversion, some of the Jews undertook to kill him. The marvel is not that opposition came but that it waited "many days" (v. 23). Saul had helped to set up a movement of persecution that could be expected to attack him sooner or later.

> **Talk About It:**
> Who wanted to kill Saul, and why?

Though willing to risk all to be a witness, Saul did not consider it necessary to throw all caution to the winds. He kept himself informed of the activities of the persecutors and wisely governed his affairs accordingly. When at last it seemed to be a choice between death and escape, apparently it did not appear to Saul that avoidable death would glorify God under the circumstances for the sake of a few extra converts that might be made. Perhaps his eyes were on the future ministry that God had called him to. When a way was ingeniously provided for escape, he took it. A later church father once fled under persecution, reasoning that a live Cyprian was worth more to the church than a dead one. History certainly proves Saul correct in a similar decision.

B. Bold Barnabas (vv. 26-31)
26. And when Saul was come to Jerusalem, he assayed to join himself to the disciples: but they were all afraid of him, and believed not that he was a disciple.

27. But Barnabas took him, and brought him to the apostles, and declared unto them how he had seen the Lord in the way, and that he had spoken to him, and how he had preached boldly at Damascus in the name of Jesus.

28. And he was with them coming in and going out at Jerusalem.

29. And he spake boldly in the name of the Lord Jesus, and disputed against the Grecians: but they went about to slay him.

30. Which when the brethren knew, they brought him down to Caesarea, and sent him forth to Tarsus.

31. Then had the churches rest throughout all Judaea and Galilee and Samaria, and were edified; and walking in the fear of the Lord, and in the comfort of the Holy Ghost, were multiplied.

Talk About It:
1. What did the believers fear about Saul (v. 26)?
2. How did Barnabas change the believers' thinking (v. 27)?
3. Describe the situation churches enjoyed at this time (v. 31).

The believers' memory of past horrors could not be lightly brushed aside. As every device had been used before to ferret out disciples, they kept fearing that Saul was but using subtlety to catch them.

In the dark hour God knows how to open a door. Here was Barnabas (v. 27), a brave, unselfish, generous man who dared to investigate and risk something. He learned that Saul had given evidence of genuineness and he dared to make it known. At last Saul was accepted at the mother church in Jerusalem. This was a tie that he cherished to the end, though he spent little time there and found his brief stays full of peril.

Since Saul himself was a Grecian, or a Jew from the provinces, he made a special witnessing to his former companions. But the Grecians didn't appreciate it. Bold witnessing for Christ had the same effect on them now as when Saul belonged to their number. They sought to kill him.

Saul's labors at Jerusalem were cut short in the same manner as at Damascus. Though eminently qualified to serve and though effective in convincing the Jews, there was still enough bitterness following him that it was obvious he would not long survive. Hence he went back to his hometown of Tarsus, in the province of Cilicia, from which area Barnabas later called him to Antioch for a renewed and most effective fellowship in the ministry.

After Paul forsook the cause of Judaism, persecution became less general and persistent in Palestine. The flurries that arose seemed to center on the desire to kill Paul, the deserter. When he escaped, a period of peace and growth followed for the church in Palestine.

> "*Barnabas* means 'son of prophecy,' especially as it is manifested in exhortation [encouragement] and comfort."
> —*New Unger's Bible Dictionary*

CONCLUSION

Saul was going in the direction he thought was right; however, it was not God's direction. God confronted him by asking, "Why are you fighting against Me?" Saul, being convicted of his sins, surrendered to the Lord, and said, "What will You have me to do?"

All of Christianity is summed up in what Christ said to Saul. Christ said to him, "Go into the city, and you will be told what to do." Never again would Saul take his own way. From that day forward he would take Christ's way.

The Christian is a person who has ceased to do what he wants to do, and who has begun to do what Jesus Christ wants him to do.

GOLDEN TEXT CHALLENGE

"CHRIST JESUS CAME INTO THE WORLD TO SAVE SINNERS; OF WHOM I AM CHIEF" (1 Timothy 1:15).

In our day of high-tech communications and advertising, words come easy. However, not every word we read or hear is trustworthy. We have to consider who printed the word as well as who wrote the word. There are slogans and sayings that come and go with current trends. Time has a way of burying many advertising jingles that are useful for only a particular season.

Not so with eternal truth. Paul made a statement that is just as meaningful and enriching today as when he first recorded it: "Christ Jesus came into the world to save sinners."

Does that not say it all? Let's analyze this saying together. Christ is not a product of this sinful world, yet He was sensitive to our need of being saved from the wages and results of our sins. Jesus worked out a salvation plan whereby sinners can be born again unto a holy nature and affection.

According to Paul, this statement, "Christ Jesus came into the world to save sinners," is faithful. It is 100 percent reliable and worthy of being accepted by everyone. Did you not notice that this statement has to be accepted in order for it to be valid? Oh that we who have accepted this saying and found it to be faithful and worthy would do everything within our power to get others to do the same.

Daily Devotions:
M. Encounter With God
   Genesis 32:24-30
T. Plea for Transformation
   Psalm 51:1-13
W. Transformation of the Heart
   Ezekiel 36:22-31
T. Changed by Deliverance
   Luke 8:27-35
F. Repentance and Restitution
   Luke 19:1-10
S. Transformed Through Renewal
   Romans 12:1-3

The Gospel Is for Everyone

Acts 11:1-26

Unit Theme:
Lessons From the Early Church (Acts, Part 1)

Central Truth:
The gospel demands outreach to all people.

Focus:
Explore how the church expanded across cultural barriers and obey God's call to spread the gospel.

Context:
Speaking to his Jewish brethren, Peter defends his ministry to the household of Cornelius.

Golden Text:
"Go ye into all the world, and preach the gospel to every creature" (Mark 16:15).

Study Outline:
I. Inclusiveness Commanded (Acts 11:4-10)
II. Inclusiveness Experienced (Acts 11:11-18)
III. Inclusiveness Practiced (Acts 11:19-26)

INTRODUCTION

The background for today's lesson from Acts 11 is found in chapter 10. These chapters give a graphic account of the extension of the Christian church from Jerusalem and the Jewish people to Caesarea and the Gentiles. The apostle Peter is the Lord's messenger to bring the gospel to the house of Cornelius and thus open the door of the church to Gentiles and Jews alike.

Although the Roman centurion Cornelius is praised as one who feared God, who gave liberally to the people, and who prayed constantly, he stood in need of salvation by grace and faith. In a special vision he was given directions how to secure the ministry of the apostle Peter to meet his spiritual need. In the meantime, Peter also had been prepared by a vision and a heavenly communication for his mission of salvation to the house of Cornelius. Thus he was prepared to receive the messenger from Cornelius.

Just as Peter was debating with himself as to the meaning of the strange command from heaven to kill and eat of the unclean creatures, the three men sent by Cornelius were found at the tanner's door inquiring for the apostle. Because Peter had been informed by the Holy Spirit of their coming, he introduced himself as the one they were seeking. But not knowing the exact purpose of their mission, he requested an explanation. The favorable report about Cornelius and his communication from the angel convinced Peter, and he invited the strangers in to be his guests for the night.

The next morning, Peter arose and went forth with the men who had come for him. Upon their arrival in Caesarea, Peter found Cornelius and his friends more than ready for the apostle's mission.

Acts 10:44-48 assures us that Peter's message was received by his hearers and authenticated by the Holy Spirit. Three marks of their conversion are evident. First, the Holy Spirit interrupted Peter's preaching and baptized the believers in his audience. Next, the Jewish believers present were amazed at this outpouring of the Holy Spirit. Third, they confessed their faith by water baptism.

I. INCLUSIVENESS COMMANDED (Acts 11:4-10)

The news of Peter's mission to Caesarea and his visit in the house of Cornelius had reached Jerusalem before the apostle's own return there. "The apostles and brethren" in Judea heard that the Gentiles had "received the word of God" (v. 1). This news may have been the occasion for rejoicing except for the additional information that the foremost apostle had begun to fraternize with the Gentiles.

When Peter therefore arrived in Jerusalem, he was immediately taken to task by those "that were of the circumcision" (v. 2). These were Jewish believers who were especially zealous for the Law and strong on the ban against social relationships between Jew and non-Jew. They contended with Peter because of his failure to make such discrimination.

A. The Vision (vv. 4-6)

4. But Peter rehearsed the matter from the beginning, and expounded it by order unto them, saying,

5. I was in the city of Joppa praying: and in a trance I saw a vision, A certain vessel descend, as it had been a great sheet, let down from heaven by four corners; and it came even to me:

6. Upon the which when I had fastened mine eyes, I considered, and saw fourfooted beasts of the earth, and wild beasts, and creeping things, and fowls of the air.

Peter's defense of his mission to Cornelius' house and social behavior took the form of a simple recapitulation of his experience at Caesarea. One's own experience under the direction of God is the strongest and most convincing argument.

First, Peter told them of his vision on the roof in the tanner's house at Joppa. He had gone to the housetop to pray and had become hungry. At that moment, falling into a condition of ecstasy, he saw in a vision a vessel descending in a great sheet from heaven. It was an arresting sight and a sure indication of the divine presence.

The animals contained in this vessel seemed to represent the whole animal creation, both the clean and the unclean—a mixture naturally repulsive to a Hebrew. Upon this scene the apostle gazed intently and closely, and thus received a clear mental picture of its details.

B. The Command (vv. 7-10)

7. And I heard a voice saying unto me, Arise, Peter; slay and eat.

8. But I said, Not so, Lord: for nothing common or unclean hath at any time entered into my mouth.

9. But the voice answered me again from heaven, What God hath cleansed, that call not thou common.

Talk About It:
1. How did God communicate with Peter on this occasion, and why?
2. What did Peter see?

10. And this was done three times: and all were drawn up again into heaven.

Talk About It:
1. In the vision, why did Peter tell the Lord "no"?
2. Why did God repeat the vision three times?

As Peter had been hungry before he fell into the trance, the voice of command to "slay and eat" would be a means of satisfying his hunger without distinction among the creatures before him. It was, in effect, a call to disregard the Mosaic dietary law as an object lesson for his natural Jewish prejudice.

Peter's protest against the divine injunction was emphatic and indicative of his religious prejudice against the ceremonially unclean. It recalls the prophet Ezekiel's protest to the command to prepare and eat "abominable flesh" (Ezekiel 4:14). The expression "Not so, Lord" is contradictory in a sense, but how else could an obedient servant protest his master's command?

"By one hour's intimate access to the throne of grace, where the Lord causes His glory to pass before the soul that seeks Him, you may acquire more spiritual knowledge and comfort than by a day's or a week's converse with the best of men."
—John Newton

Peter's emphatic protest was countered by a still stronger protest from the heavenly voice. It was not for him to make and regard unclean what God had cleansed. While this may be understood as an abolition of Jewish ceremonial food laws, it ought not to be interpreted as a divine disregard for such food laws as pertain to health of body. Peter himself soon grasped that the real lesson was spiritual and of a much wider application.

The threefold repetition (v. 10) probably refers to the divine command and was intended to emphasize that God had enjoined Peter with a mission of divine sanction of great significance for the Christian church.

II. INCLUSIVENESS EXPERIENCED (Acts 11:11-18)
A. Compelled by the Spirit (vv. 11, 12)

11. And, behold, immediately there were three men already come unto the house where I was, sent from Caesarea unto me.

12. And the Spirit bade me go with them, nothing doubting. Moreover these six brethren accompanied me, and we entered into the man's house.

Talk About It:
Why did Peter go with the men to Caesarea?

After the trance was over, Peter had remained on the roof in a reflective mood, when the Holy Spirit informed him of the three men from Caesarea at his door seeking his apostolic services (see 10:19). It was necessary that he now go with them on a saving mission, for the Holy Spirit had so directed. And there was to be no hesitation, misgiving, or discrimination in his mind. God had commanded, and that was final. Those Jewish brethren who had accompanied Peter from Joppa to Caesarea (see v. 23) were brought by Peter to Jerusalem to confirm his testimony, for they had been firsthand witnesses in the house of Cornelius.

B. Prepared by an Angel (vv. 13, 14)

13. And he shewed us how he had seen an angel in his house, which stood and said unto him, Send men to Joppa, and call for Simon, whose surname is Peter;

14. Who shall tell thee words, whereby thou and all thy house shall be saved.

Peter, having entered the house of Cornelius with the six Jewish brethren, now relates how that Cornelius himself had been prepared for Peter's mission by an angelic visitation. The angel's instructions to the soldier had been so specific and clear that there could be no mistake about their divine character. God had sent His angel to prepare the religiously minded Roman soldier for the apostle with his message of salvation.

The angel informed Cornelius that Peter would speak words by which the soldier and his household would receive salvation. In the previous chapter we are informed that Cornelius was accepted by God as a man who feared Him and practiced righteousness (10:35). Yet, this brief summary of the angel's instructions expressly states that he must call for the apostle to come with the gospel that he might "be saved." In other words, Cornelius was a sincere seeker who lived up to the religious knowledge he had; yet, he was hungry for the real salvation experience. He was not religiously self-righteous, for such an attitude hinders many "good" people from the salvation offered in Christ.

C. Confirmed by the Spirit (vv. 15-17)

15. And as I began to speak, the Holy Ghost fell on them, as on us at the beginning.

16. Then remembered I the word of the Lord, how that he said, John indeed baptized with water; but ye shall be baptized with the Holy Ghost.

17. Forasmuch then as God gave them the like gift as he did unto us, who believed on the Lord Jesus Christ; what was I, that I could withstand God?

Here Peter comes to the climax of his defense, telling how he had hardly begun to preach to Cornelius and his friends when he was interrupted by a manifest outpouring of the Holy Spirit. The evidence of this Spirit baptism was a glad and ecstatic utterance of praise to God (10:44-46).

The promise of the risen Christ to His disciples, "John truly baptized with water; but ye shall be baptized with the Holy Ghost not many days hence" (1:5) had been promptly fulfilled on the Day of Pentecost; but as Peter witnessed what took place in the house of Cornelius, he recalled the words of Christ and recognized a repetition of the Pentecostal outpouring for the blessing of the Gentiles. Since God had intervened and demonstrated by the gift of the Holy Spirit that He made no distinction between believing Gentiles and believing Jews, how could Peter maintain a barrier which God obviously did not recognize?

> **Talk About It:**
> What had the angel told Cornelius about Peter?

> "We pursue God because, and only because, He has first put an urge within us that spurs us to the pursuit."
> **—A.W. Tozer**

> **Talk About It:**
> 1. What does "at the beginning" (v. 15) refer to?
> 2. How did Peter explain his reasoning in verse 17?

"Who was I, that I could withstand God?" (11:17, *NKJV*). How could Peter disregard so distinct an intimation of God's will that the Gentiles should be recognized as worthy of all the privileges of the gospel, without requiring of them any other qualification than faith in Christ? Thus was the apostle's mission confirmed by divine intervention.

D. Endorsed by the Church (v. 18)

18. When they heard these things, they held their peace, and glorified God, saying, Then hath God also to the Gentiles granted repentance unto life.

Talk About It:
How did the Christian leaders respond to Peter's account?

So unanswerable were Peter's arguments, so convincing the facts, that the objectors were satisfied. Their criticism ceased, and their worship began. This was indeed a manifestation of the wisdom and graciousness of the Jerusalem brethren, not only to accede to Peter's argument, but to glorify God and to rejoice in the fact that He had granted them that change of mind by faith that results in eternal life. The principle and the commission for the evangelization for all people must ever be recognized and implemented by Christians.

III. INCLUSIVENESS PRACTICED (Acts 11:19-26)
A. The Occasion of Their Ministry (vv. 19, 20)

19. Now they which were scattered abroad upon the persecution that arose about Stephen travelled as far as Phenice, and Cyprus, and Antioch, preaching the word to none but unto the Jews only.

20. And some of them were men of Cyprus and Cyrene, which, when they were come to Antioch, spake unto the Grecians, preaching the Lord Jesus.

Talk About It:
1. As the Christians were scattered, what was the initial approach in their witnessing efforts (v. 19)?
2. How did the witnessing of Christians begin changing (v. 20)?

The same persecution that sent witnesses of Christ from Jerusalem to Judea and Samaria, including the evangelist Philip (Acts 8:4ff.), now sent some of these missionaries north and west, some going to Cyprus and others farther north to Antioch. The martyrdom of Stephen and the persecution that followed sent these witnesses to Antioch, where they spoke the word. In the original Greek the word for *preaching* in 11:19 simply means that they conversed informally about Christ and the gospel with strangers as they traveled.

"The word" (v. 19) should be a normal topic of conversation for all true Christians. They spoke to "Jews only," undoubtedly a big missionary field even in Antioch. Perhaps they feared further persecution if they should speak to the Gentiles, or perhaps they felt qualified to speak only to Jews. It was nevertheless a new day for this third-largest city of the empire when these missionaries of the Cross arrived. A center of commerce, Greek culture, pagan religion, and lax morals, Antioch now heard the message of hope, morality, righteousness and salvation.

The Christian Jews from Cyprus and Cyrene, having probably had a more cosmopolitan education and therefore having less scruples about mixing with the Gentiles than the Jews of Palestine, began to preach the gospel to the Gentiles. The word *preaching* in verse 20 is translated from another Greek word which means to "evangelize" or "preach the gospel," the good news of the Lord Jesus as Savior. The terms *Lord* and *Savior* were widely current and would be understood by the Greek population. It was a new beginning, and a great step forward in the outreach of the church.

B. The Results of Their Ministry (v. 21)

21. And the hand of the Lord was with them: and a great number believed, and turned unto the Lord.

The expression "the [good] hand of the Lord was with [or upon] them" is occasionally found in the Old Testament to indicate a direct interposition of God in the affairs of men, either for blessing or for hindrance (see Ezra 7:9; 8:18; Nehemiah 2:8). Here it is obviously indicative of great blessing from the Lord in that many "believed, and turned unto the Lord." That is, they believed the truthfulness of the Christian message and yielded their allegiance to Jesus as Lord.

Talk About It:
Is "the Lord's hand" with all evangelism efforts?

These missionaries are not named, nor were they sent out under the auspices of the church in Jerusalem; yet, their ministry was honored by the Lord in the conversion of both Jews and Gentiles.

C. The Ministry of Barnabas (vv. 22-24)

22. Then tidings of these things came unto the ears of the church which was in Jerusalem: and they sent forth Barnabas, that he should go as far as Antioch.

23. Who, when he came, and had seen the grace of God, was glad, and exhorted them all, that with purpose of heart they would cleave unto the Lord.

24. For he was a good man, and full of the Holy Ghost and of faith: and much people was added unto the Lord.

When news of the great evangelistic work in Antioch by anonymous missionaries reached the church in Jerusalem, Barnabas was immediately dispatched to Antioch on a representative mission of investigation and confirmation. The success and outcome of the work begun at Antioch depended to a great degree on the delegate sent there, and they could hardly have made a better choice.

Talk About It:
1. What kind of man was Barnabas (v. 24), and why was he sent to Antioch (v. 22)?
2. Describe Barnabas' ministry in Antioch (vv. 23, 24).

Being a Hellenist, Barnabas' sympathies were broad, and his character unimpeachable. He was a man of Cyprus as well as of Jerusalem, a friend of Jews and Gentiles. Above all, he was a man of kindly heart and genial temper and charity, fitted to soothe jealousies and allay suspicions, and thus make the alienated Gentiles feel at home in this new Christian community. There will always be a need and a place for a man like Barnabas.

Upon his arrival, instead of being scandalized at the mingling of Jews and Gentiles, Barnabas rejoiced at the astounding evidences of the grace of God among them. He saw no occasion for disapproval or need for correction. As a mature "son of exhortation" (see 4:36), he knew the dangers of temptation, and so continuously exhorted them to cleave to the Lord with steadfast purpose. *Exhortation* is an inspired encouragement to practice what we know. True to his name, Barnabas gave his encouragement to missionaries and converts alike to persevere in their service and obedience to the Lord in whom they had believed.

The praise given Barnabas in 11:24 is unusual in the Book of Acts, but certainly very refreshing to read and study. He was "a good man," a man of moral excellence and liberal enough to rise above narrow Jewish sectarianism. Like Stephen the martyr (6:5), he was also full of the Holy Spirit and faith. As C.R. Erdman puts it, "One who is full of faith is sure to be full of the Holy Spirit, and one who is filled with the Spirit will be truly good."

With the personal presence, the encouragement and help of such a dedicated servant of the Lord, the believers were edified, many new converts were added, and the church in Antioch grew rapidly.

D. Barnabas and Saul (vv. 25, 26)

25. Then departed Barnabas to Tarsus, for to seek Saul:
26. And when he had found him, he brought him unto Antioch. And it came to pass, that a whole year they assembled themselves with the church, and taught much people. And the disciples were called Christians first in Antioch.

Realizing his need of assistance in the leadership of this new and fast-growing church, Barnabas went to Tarsus to seek diligently for his friend Saul. This former persecutor of the Christians, who had been introduced by Barnabas to the brethren in Jerusalem as a new convert some 10 years earlier (9:27), was now about to be introduced to the church in Antioch as a qualified spiritual leader. For Barnabas to seek out Saul was an act of discernment, unselfishness and humility. He must have realized that to be associated with a man of such personality and ability as Saul, he himself would soon have to take a secondary role. Barnabas evidently was not concerned about his own popularity but rather the success of the cause of Christ in this great city, and he knew Saul was the right man for the job.

Saul's 10-year stay in Tarsus and Cilicia had, in all probability, been filled with evangelistic activity and had helped to prepare

Talk About It:
1. Whose help did Barnabas seek and why?
2. What is the significance of the title "Christians"?

The Gospel Is for Everyone

him for his greater work in Antioch and the great missionary expeditions to proceed from this base. Thus Barnabas was the minister used of the Lord to help both Saul and the church for the year of successful ministry that ensued in Antioch. Not only did the evangelism of these two servants result in many converts, but their faithful teaching ministry edified these believers in the Christian faith and thus increased the spiritual power of the church.

Although the name *Christians* was probably given to the disciples here in ridicule, it soon became a designation of true identity. The word is of hybrid form, a Greek word with a Latin termination, and found only in two other places in the New Testament (Acts 26:28; 1 Peter 4:16).

No longer could this new society be named by Hebraism or limited by some geographical term. Then too, the believers were evidently named for what the Antiochians saw in them. They were the people of Christ—the followers of Christ. They spoke about, sang of, and lived for Christ. To be a Christian is to be Christlike as God gives grace and power so to be.

> "A Christian is a combination of Christ and you."
> —**George Sweeting**

CONCLUSION

The testimony of Peter to the Jerusalem brethren about his wonderful experience in the house of Cornelius prepared them for cooperation with the wider movement of Gentile evangelization. This evangelization began to expand rapidly with the founding of a Christian church in Antioch of Syria. Occasioned by the persecution over Stephen, devoted disciples spoke the word of God to the Jews in Antioch; men of Cyprus and Cyrene preached the Lord Jesus to the Greeks; Barnabas exhorted the believers in Antioch; and then Barnabas and Saul taught many people there. Thus was Christianity planted and established in the third-largest city in the Roman Empire, and this new church became the base of "Operation Paul" for the Roman and Hellenistic world.

GOLDEN TEXT CHALLENGE

"GO YE INTO ALL THE WORLD, AND PREACH THE GOSPEL TO EVERY CREATURE" (Mark 16:15).

The church has certain tasks committed to it by Jesus. It has been commissioned to tell the story of God's mighty saving acts in Christ. God has been seeking to redeem people since Adam's sin in the Garden of Eden. As God is "not willing that any should perish, but that all should come to repentance" (2 Peter 3:9), the Great Commission is the natural outflow of His character. Christianity is a missionary religion in its source and total design. The early disciples became missionaries because the gospel was for all people and because of the indwelling of the Holy Spirit, the Spirit of missions.

The Great Commission was spoken by our Lord. In Mark's account of the commission, His focus is twofold:

1. *The scope.* "Go ye into all the world." Evangelism must be an all-out missionary thrust, and the church must evangelize the nations of the world. No geographical area, no culture, and no people are to be without the good news of Christ. The church must be extensive in its ministry.

2. *The method.* "Preach the gospel to every creature." Missions prospers where the gospel is genuinely heralded and experienced. Meaningful communication of the good news leads people into an experience of this grace of God made available through the death and resurrection of Christ.

The extensive and intensive proclamation of the gospel is the all-out thrust of missions, but Christians must not stop with the preaching of the good news and the offering of forgiveness of sins to all who believe on Christ. They must "make disciples" (Matthew 28:19, *NKJV*) by indoctrinating them in the teachings of their Savior and renewing their minds in the truths of God. The discharge of this task molds lifestyles and produces true Christian discipleship.

Benefits of Wisdom

Proverbs 3:1-35

INTRODUCTION

One cannot be even a novice student of the Bible without recognizing its claim to be a collection of books filled with wisdom. The concept of wisdom connects the pages of Scripture from Genesis to Revelation. To begin with, wisdom functions at the center of the fall of humanity, as Eve reaches for the fruit in the attempt to gain divine knowledge (Genesis 3:6). In the latter, John the Revelator ascribes ultimate wisdom to God alone, and calls for wisdom again and again to unlock the secrets of the visions he describes (Revelation 5:12; 7:12; 13:18; 17:9). But if the model of godly wisdom found throughout the Bible could somehow be condensed down to one book, Proverbs would be the obvious result. It has stood the test of time in order to champion the definition, nature, and proper employment of this sometimes-elusive concept of wisdom. As such, it testifies to wisdom's eternal application. It is not something that changes with the times of cultures or trends of societies. It is just as relevant today as it was on the day of its writing.

Proverbs is part of a vibrant literary tradition of the ancient Near East, and certainly not alone in its attempt to pass down morals to ancient peoples. The Bible alludes to the wisdom traditions of neighboring nations when describing the writer of its own Proverbs: "Solomon's wisdom was greater than the wisdom of all the men of the East, and greater than all the wisdom of Egypt" (1 Kings 4:30, *NIV*). Some of these traditions survive as documents today, and often take a similar form as Solomon's Proverbs—short sayings focused on practical living that appear to skip around from topic to topic. These include the Assyrian "Words of Ahikar" and Egypt's "Teaching of Ptahhotep." In fact, these sources even contain a few sayings that are uncannily similar to Solomon's. What, then, is original about the Biblical Proverbs? The answer lies in 1:7—the proverb that Old Testament scholars consider the theme or summary verse which sets the tone for the entire book. Unlike the proverbs of neighboring peoples, Solomon's wisdom stems completely from God. Without Yahweh as the source of wisdom, it fades away like the cults of Egypt and Assyria.

Unit Theme:
Wisdom From Proverbs

Central Truth:
True wisdom comes from God and results in numerous benefits.

Focus:
Survey the benefits of true wisdom and enjoy them in our daily living.

Context:
The majority of the Proverbs were written by Solomon, who completed them by 921 B.C.

Golden Text:
"Happy is the man that findeth wisdom, and the man that getteth understanding" (Proverbs 3:13).

Study Outline:
I. Prosper by Wisdom (Proverbs 3:1-10)
II. Be Blessed by Wisdom (Proverbs 3:11-20)
III. Be Secure in Wisdom (Proverbs 3:21-35)

I. PROSPER BY WISDOM (Proverbs 3:1-10)

Chapter 3 begins what might be considered the practical focus of the Book of Proverbs. Chapters 1 and 2 lay the pathway for this practical focus with powerful descriptions of the centrality of wisdom to the life of faith. These initial chapters set up the practical sayings that will touch every area of common life by loudly sounding out the theme of wisdom—claiming its origin in Yahweh and its proper place in the hearts of His faithful. In chapter 3, Solomon is ready to begin condensing the wisdom of his life and administration into the hundreds of sayings represented in chapters 3-29.

The Book of Proverbs is rooted in the grit of genuine human life and existence. This does not downplay its theological significance, because for Solomon theology and ethics cannot be disjoined. In fact, it is only in modern times that people have thought it possible to separate one's belief from his actions. It is not uncommon to hear remarks about people committing sins or even crimes such as, "They are really a good person at heart," or "They aren't living right but really do love God." Neither Solomon nor any other Biblical author could conceive of this kind of fragmentation within the human soul. Instead, Solomon's practical sayings and his burning passion for Yahweh are profoundly intertwined, and they must be read as such. Although the unbeliever could follow some of the precepts found in Proverbs and benefit, they are not meant only to serve human ingenuity or success, but to bring glory to God.

A. Wisdom Brings Profound Benefit (vv. 1, 2)

1. My son, forget not my law; but let thine heart keep my commandments:

2. For length of days, and long life, and peace, shall they add to thee.

Talk About It:
How can obedience to one's parents affect a person's life?

The *aphorisms* (concise statements of wisdom) in Proverbs are laid out in the first-person instruction of King Solomon to his son. Although the son in question is singular, Solomon was famous for his many wives and concubines (1 Kings 11:3), who in turn provided him with many children, so it is unlikely that a particular son is in view here. Rather, the sayings are meant to be wisdom for all parents to pass down to all children, especially given the fact that the mother's place as co-teacher in the home is mentioned in Proverbs 1:8. Nonetheless, they undoubtedly carried special weight for ancient Jews who knew of Solomon's particularly famous wisdom. It had been granted by God himself just as Solomon was rising to power after the death of his father, King David. Although already finding himself compromising the integrity of his father's lifestyle by intermarrying with Egypt's court and worshiping outside the prescriptions of the Torah, in 1 Kings 3 God appeared to Solomon in a dream with the promise that He would grant him one request. Instead of asking for riches or power, Solomon requested discernment to properly govern, and God declared that, in addition to being given the greatest wisdom the world had yet seen, he would also be granted wealth and power. By the time he finished writing Proverbs, Solomon's kingdom was fully established, along with the elaborate construction of God's Temple in Jerusalem.

The proverbs of Solomon are also called *sayings*, *commands*, *instructions* and *teachings* throughout the book. These are synonyms and should not be differentiated. The Hebrew word for "proverb" is *mashal*, which was used to describe a variety of shorter or pithy modes of instruction. In fact, it is also the word Jesus probably used for "parable," which in His ministry was a short story used to illustrate or to communicate a larger truth. It is not surprising that the literary setting for their delivery is not in an educational institution, nor in the Temple or synagogue, but in the family. Solomon does not call together a political assembly in order to proclaim this wisdom to the nation for the good of Israel. Instead, it is to be passed down from fathers to sons, from parents to children. This points to the centrality of the family as the key means by which children are taught godly morality. Schools certainly have their place, but ethics and values are primarily taught by the family.

The key reason for the Book of Proverbs is seen in 3:1, 2. In short, they will bring tremendous benefits when put into practice, including a long life and prosperity. It is important to note that Solomon is writing during a time of unprecedented economic growth in Israel. His policies, including a strong army and large government contracts for the building of the Temple, have brought Israel to its economic and cultural height. The arts are thriving, businesses are booming, and Jewish culture is expanding. But it is not only economic prosperity that Solomon has in mind as the result of following his teachings. The word *peace* (v. 2) is actually the Hebrew *shalom*, which is still used as a greeting in Israel today, and is one of the most important concepts in the Old Testament. Its meaning can be summarized as "wholeness and well-being through life with God." The life of *shalom* is one of peace and completion, and this is the benefit of following the Proverbs.

Claudianus Mamertus was a Roman philosopher who coined the phrase "Virtue is its own reward." Although many ascribe this concept to Biblical theology, nothing could be further from the truth. The teachings of Scripture, including the Gospels, consistently offer both temporal and eternal rewards for obedience. The Proverbs are no exception to this rule. They are not written as virtues that will only make one a better, more upright person, although they certainly will. They are not a high-minded philosophy for the person who wants to transcend the confines of earthly life. Instead, they promise benefits and rewards in the here and now.

Living the Proverbs
Several years ago, a study was performed on two groups of golfers. One group was professionals; the other was amateurs. The study tested the golfers' brain activity as they attempted putts. It found that the professionals actually had less brain activity while putting than the amateurs. This was because the professionals had learned over time to trust their swing, and they were more confident. Learning to live the wisdom of the Proverbs is similar. Results don't appear all at once, but as we practice them, they become a natural part of our consciousness.

B. Wisdom Brings Favor and Reputation (vv. 3, 4)

3. Let not mercy and truth forsake thee: bind them about thy neck; write them upon the table of thine heart:

4. So shalt thou find favour and good understanding in the sight of God and man.

Talk About It:
How valuable are "mercy [kindness] and truth" (v. 3), and why?

The benefits of *shalom* which Solomon introduces in verse 2 are systematically laid out in verses 3-10. They are straightforward and applicable to any life, whether rich or poor, male or female, ancient or modern.

Mercy and *truth* are two of the principal virtues of Old Testament faith (v. 3). The former can be translated as "loving-kindness," "favor," or "steadfast love." It refers throughout the Old Testament to the covenant love of God himself. When this degree of love is bound to the believer's external and internal self, the result is a good reputation before God and people.

It may seem a little strange that the "high" theological language of "love and faithfulness" (*NIV*) is boiled down to something as basic as social reputation, but this is the direction of the entire Book of Proverbs. They are profoundly *earthy*; unashamedly this-worldly. In them, the adherence to divine precepts always carries present rewards among one's family members, in one's business dealings, for one's health, and so on. We should not give in to the temptation to "spiritualize" them by reading in eternal rewards at every corner. Although eternal life is part of the package, the Old Testament is focused on God's dealings with us in the here and now, and this is as vital to the life of faith as the afterlife.

C. Wisdom Brings Purpose and Health (vv. 5-8)

5. Trust in the Lord with all thine heart; and lean not unto thine own understanding.

6. In all thy ways acknowledge him, and he shall direct thy paths.

7. Be not wise in thine own eyes: fear the Lord, and depart from evil.

8. It shall be health to thy navel, and marrow to thy bones.

Talk About It:
1. If we want God to direct our lives, what must we do (vv. 5, 6)?
2. What does it mean to be "wise in thine own eyes" (v. 7), and how should we live instead?

Not only does following God's wisdom benefit one with a good standing in society, there is also the blessing of individual purpose. Spoken to a young man with his life in front of him and with many choices to make, Solomon declares that trusting Yahweh will illuminate the proper path to take. There is an extraordinary focus and purpose that comes about when one realizes ultimate truth is not only external to us, but it is even outside our ability to understand as it resides in the incomprehensible being of God alone. When we acknowledge this reality, we find our path divinely directed.

Benefits of Wisdom

As if to reinforce the divine source of knowledge in verse 7, Solomon cautions us from thinking too highly of ourselves. When the benefits of following God's wisdom begin to operate in our lives, we can make the mistake of seeing ourselves as the individual centers of this wisdom. In response to this kind of internal focus, we are commanded to fear, or respect, God, which also brings physical health.

> "Woe to those who are wise in their own eyes and clever in their own sight."
> —Isaiah 5:21 (*NIV*)

D. Wisdom Brings Overflow (vv. 9, 10)

9. Honour the Lord with thy substance, and with the firstfruits of all thine increase:

10. So shall thy barns be filled with plenty, and thy presses shall burst out with new wine.

There is perhaps no better way we take our life's focus off ourselves and place it in God than by our use of the resources God has blessed us with. The reign of Solomon testifies to its robust commitment to the principles of tithing laid out in the Pentateuch, and the king considers this too a part of living in true *shalom*. These verses are just one example of the economic benefits that the Proverbs will continue to announce, a benefit that Solomon and his kingdom experienced in an unprecedented way.

II. BE BLESSED BY WISDOM (Proverbs 3:11-20)

After explaining several practical benefits of wisdom in verses 2-10, Solomon returns to interweaving this practical focus with the lyrical praise of wisdom in general. This passage poetically describes the blessings that come to the one who discovers wisdom. Note that Solomon often resorts to poetry in chapters 1-9, before adhering to strict proverbial form in chapters 10 and following. The prophets also use poetry to communicate, "Thus says the Lord," so it is not surprising to find this form in Proverbs. This is probably the reason why Proverbs is placed between Psalms and Ecclesiastes in the Old Testament order.

A. Warning Before Blessing (vv. 11, 12)

11. My son, despise not the chastening of the Lord; neither be weary of his correction:

12. For whom the Lord loveth he correcteth; even as a father the son in whom he delighteth.

Directly between two collections of the benefits of wisdom, Solomon tempers these benefits with a cautionary note. He warns us that we cannot read the Proverbs as if they are mechanistic. That is, we cannot assume that if and when we mechanically follow a precept, then life will automatically be filled with peace and prosperity. If that were the case, the Proverbs would reduce God to something like an impersonal

Talk About It:
How does the Lord discipline His children, and why should we be comforted when He does so?

vending machine, which mechanically dispenses blessings when our lives hit the right buttons. Instead, Solomon is careful to preserve the God-centered nature of the Proverbs. They are subject to God's intentions, not vice versa. Therefore, we are instructed to not despair when we go through times of trial or discipline, because God is in control of these times as much as He is the times of prosperity. He is likened to the perfect Father who cares deeply for the health and growth of His children.

B. The Value of Wisdom (vv. 13-15)

13. Happy is the man that findeth wisdom, and the man that getteth understanding.

14. For the merchandise of it is better than the merchandise of silver, and the gain thereof than fine gold.

15. She is more precious than rubies: and all the things thou canst desire are not to be compared unto her.

Talk About It:
Where can wisdom be found, and what makes it so valuable?

Following the truth that God will allow trials and discipline in the lives of the children whom He loves, the reader is encouraged to remember that the value of wisdom endures over and against any momentary trouble. A main premise of the Book of Proverbs is that wisdom is within the reach of every person. It is something that can always be "found." It is not reserved for the elites, the literate or the wealthy. In fact, the simple-minded are explicitly invited to the wisdom feast in the book's prologue (see 1:4).

In this passage we see Solomon contrasting the value of wisdom with the value of the currencies of his day. Rather than being a quick means to economic prosperity, he degrades money in comparison to the infinite value of wisdom. By doing so, Solomon cautions us against viewing the Proverbs as a simple means to an end. Although following them yields beneficial results, there is more at stake than just monetary rewards. The blessed life is concerned with more important things.

"The choices of life, not the compulsions, reveal character."
—A.W. Tozer

C. The Blessedness of the Wise (vv. 16-20)

16. Length of days is in her right hand; and in her left hand riches and honour.

17. Her ways are ways of pleasantness, and all her paths are peace.

18. She is a tree of life to them that lay hold upon her: and happy is every one that retaineth her.

19. The Lord by wisdom hath founded the earth; by understanding hath he established the heavens.

20. By his knowledge the depths are broken up, and the clouds drop down the dew.

Talk About It:
1. What does Wisdom hold in her hands?

Although still in poetic mode, Solomon returns again to the overall benefits of wisdom. In verse 2 these benefits were presented in the framework of *shalom*. Now they are subsumed under the idea of divine blessedness alongside *shalom*. Again,

Benefits of Wisdom

wisdom is something to be embraced, or found. It is always a conscious choice on the part of the God-follower. Pleasantness, peace and happiness are products of the "tree of life" (v. 18) that comes from God's wisdom. This "tree" refers to the dynamic and growing nature of wisdom. The fruit of God's wisdom is a natural result of pursuing His principles.

In finding wisdom we mysteriously tap into the mind of God himself, who used His ultimate wisdom to create the seen and unseen cosmos. Verses 19 and 20 illustrate a Creation theology that is central to the Proverbs. Just as wisdom guided the process of Creation, so divine wisdom guides us on the path of life. Men and women were created to depend on God's wisdom in the same way that the earth, seas, skies and depths depend on Him for their operation.

III. BE SECURE IN WISDOM (Proverbs 3:21-35)

Solomon's praise of wisdom continues in this series of ethical instructions. Again, we must take note of the way praise of wisdom and moral commandments are harmoniously blended, which is a key theological motif throughout the entire Book of Proverbs. We are reminded that even though wisdom points back to something as unexplainable and grand as the creation of the universe, it is also the guiding principle for normal, everyday decisions. As Old Testament scholar Derek Kidner states, "Wisdom leaves its signature on anything well made or well judged, from an apt remark to the universe itself" (*The Proverbs: An Introduction and Commentary*).

A. Poetic Focus on Discernment (vv. 21-26)

21. My son, let not them depart from thine eyes: keep sound wisdom and discretion:

22. So shall they be life unto thy soul, and grace to thy neck.

23. Then shalt thou walk in thy way safely, and thy foot shall not stumble.

24. When thou liest down, thou shalt not be afraid: yea, thou shalt lie down, and thy sleep shall be sweet.

25. Be not afraid of sudden fear, neither of the desolation of the wicked, when it cometh.

26. For the Lord shall be thy confidence, and shall keep thy foot from being taken.

Discernment ("discretion") is a key concept in the Book of Proverbs. It appears first in 1:4 as part of the prologue, specifically directed toward the benefit of young people. It appears again in 2:11 as a quality that gives security and protection, which is the theme of our present passage. In 3:21 Solomon commands that his son be the one to protect both discernment and sound judgment. If discernment is protected, it will protect

2. What did the Lord do through His wisdom and knowledge (vv. 19, 20)?

"You may know God, but not comprehend Him."
—Richard Baxter

Talk About It:
1. What is "sound wisdom and discretion," and why must it be preserved (vv. 21-23)?
2. What is the best antidote for fear (vv. 24-26)?

froward (v. 32)— perverse

its bearer with an amazing sense of security. This security is put in external and internal terms. Like an expensive necklace, a person's discernment, or the lack thereof, is easily evident to those around him or her. Internally, the man or woman of discernment experiences the peace that comes with a purposeful life and adequate sleep. The Lord himself is the wise person's confidence, providing safety and protection.

B. The Wise Man and His Neighbor (vv. 27-35)
(Proverbs 3:32-35 is not included in the printed text.)
27. Withhold not good from them to whom it is due, when it is in the power of thine hand to do it.
28. Say not unto thy neighbour, Go, and come again, and to morrow I will give; when thou hast it by thee.
29. Devise not evil against thy neighbour, seeing he dwelleth securely by thee.
30. Strive not with a man without cause, if he have done thee no harm.
31. Envy thou not the oppressor, and choose none of his ways.

Here Solomon gives specific instruction regarding the treatment of one's neighbors. These instructions increase in degree of intensity and/or conflict. They stem from the security that comes from those who preserve discernment in the preceding verses.

Interestingly, Solomon begins by illustrating not a sin of commission, but of omission. Proverbs is full of prohibitions, but they are always rooted in what we are supposed to do. In this case, we are only prohibited against doing nothing at all when it comes to treating our neighbor righteously. We must not withhold blessing when God has given it to us to use for the benefit of others. There is an urgency to Solomon's instructions. He won't allow us to wait even a single day to do good for someone else. This is where right action toward our neighbor begins, and it is rooted in the Torah. Jesus himself illustrates this urgency later when He adds the commandment to love one's neighbor to the commandment to love God (see Matthew 22:39).

In Proverbs 3:29, right action toward our neighbor picks up where it certainly does *not* begin. In the first two prohibitions, the neighbor is fully innocent. If a neighbor gives us his or her trust, we are to honor that trust by being trustworthy and refrain from seeking selfish advantage. After all, it is those who trust us that are easiest to gain selfish benefit from. Second, if someone has not harmed us, we are not to unfairly use them as a scapegoat to deflect attention away from ourselves or anyone else (v. 30). These things seem simple, and they are two of dozens of examples of proverbs that seem rather obvious. As

Kidner notes, "The samples of behavior which [Proverbs] holds up to view are all assessed by one criterion, which could be summed up in the question, 'Is this wisdom or folly?'"

The urgency and ultimate significance of this question as applied to blatantly sinful activity is brought to light by verses 32-35. We are not to mimic the ways of the wicked because God himself has turned His face against them. We can act justly in conflict because God is in control, even over evildoers. Once again, the ways of wisdom are rooted in Yahweh alone.

CONCLUSION

The Proverbs of King Solomon are a part of a larger wisdom tradition both in the Old Testament and in his own world, yet they remain distinct for their unceasing focus on Yahweh as the source of all wisdom and knowledge. Even so, their theological reality always blends with everyday life for normal people. We have the promises of prosperity, blessedness, and security for the life lived in wisdom, along with the assurance that there will be times of discipline, chastisement and trial. Through every aspect of life, God can and must be looked to as the cheerful giver of wisdom.

GOLDEN TEXT CHALLENGE

"HAPPY IS THE MAN THAT FINDETH WISDOM, AND THE MAN THAT GETTETH UNDERSTANDING" (Proverbs 3:13).

The word *happiness* is here connected with finding wisdom and understanding. Such happiness is not the fleeting feelings or experiences of joy, delight or pleasure. It is an inner contentment and a sense of blessedness that is to be found, not in the things which we possess or enjoy, but in an inner peace that possesses us in the ups and downs of life.

This happiness results from rightly determining life's values. It has a correct estimate of right and wrong, worthy or worthless, transient or permanent. As a result of this happiness having its roots in wisdom and understanding, it is lasting.

Daily Devotions:
M. Wisdom Brings Understanding
Proverbs 2:1-9
T. Wisdom Brings Honor
Proverbs 4:1-9
W. Wisdom Brings Praise
Proverbs 31:25-31
T. Christ, the Wisdom of God
1 Corinthians 1:26-31
F. Living in Christ Is Wisdom
Ephesians 1:7-12
S. Wisdom From Above
James 3:13-18

Wisdom of a Godly Life

Proverbs 16:1-25

Unit Theme:
Wisdom From Proverbs

Central Truth:
The wisdom of God's Word is necessary for right living.

Focus:
Discover the wisdom in God's Word and follow His instructions.

Context:
The majority of the Proverbs were written by Solomon, who completed them by 931 B.C.

Golden Text:
"He that handleth a matter wisely shall find good: and whoso trusteth in the Lord, happy is he" (Proverbs 16:20).

Study Outline:
 I. Wise Living (Proverbs 16:1-9)
 II. Wise Leadership (Proverbs 16:10-16)
III. Wise Counsel (Proverbs 16:17-25)

INTRODUCTION

No scripture should be read outside of its historical context. This is the foremost principle of Bible study. When it is followed, the Scriptures are allowed to speak from their own point of view. When verses are plucked out of their context and applied to our lives with no reflection, their meaning and potency can easily be distorted. This principle should always be applied to the Book of Proverbs.

Initially it might seem strange to focus on context with regard to this particular book of the Old Testament. After all, it doesn't have stories about historical people and events. It doesn't prophesy about the future or reflect on much in the past. It comes to us in a series of short statements, each of which stands on its own as a valuable piece of practical wisdom. What we are given, however, is the primary author, and elsewhere in the Old Testament we learn a lot about Solomon. Perhaps the most disturbing bit of context from his life is found in 1 Kings 11:4-6:

> As Solomon grew old, his wives turned his heart after other gods, and his heart was not fully devoted to the Lord his God, as the heart of David his father had been. He followed Ashtoreth the goddess of the Sidonians, and Molech the detestable god of the Ammonites. So Solomon did evil in the eyes of the Lord; he did not follow the Lord completely, as David his father had done (*NIV*).

To grapple with the historical context of the Proverbs means to admit that the man who wrote them spent many years of his life breaking them. It is sad but true.

Yet this reality also gives us occasion to reflect on the nature of Scripture. Does the fact that Solomon turned away from his own precepts make them somehow less effective? Of course not. If we hold onto the hope that the authors of Scripture lived perfect lives, we are not paying attention to the evidence. Even in the New Testament, Matthew, John, Peter, Paul, James and others had plenty of failures in their lives, yet this does not diminish what they wrote. So the Scriptures always transcend the life of the writer, and we must allow this truth to reinforce our belief in the Proverbs. The wisdom they espouse transcends King Solomon, whether at his best or his worst.

I. WISE LIVING (Proverbs 16:1-9)

The Book of Proverbs can be broken down into a few major sections. Chapters 1-9 represent the praise of wisdom in the setting of passing down the wisdom tradition from father to son. Chapters 10-22 contain the proverbs of Solomon, followed by other sayings from anonymous wise men in chapters 23 and 24. This shows us that Solomon himself is a part of a wisdom tradition and not the originator of wisdom in Israel. Solomon's collection picks up again in chapters 25-29, before the words of Agur and King Lemuel close out the book.

In chapter 16 we find ourselves in the middle of Solomon's sayings which, in this case, are grouped together under recognizable themes. Yet they also are tremendously diverse, offering wisdom to a variety of life settings and circumstances.

A. God's Work Alongside Us (vv. 1-4)

1. The preparations of the heart in man, and the answer of the tongue, is from the Lord.

2. All the ways of a man are clean in his own eyes; but the Lord weigheth the spirits.

3. Commit thy works unto the Lord, and thy thoughts shall be established.

4. The Lord hath made all things for himself: yea, even the wicked for the day of evil.

thoughts (v. 3)— plans

The true relationship between God and humanity is part of the foundation of the Book of Proverbs. This was a radical idea in its day. Neighboring peoples related to their pagan gods in a variety of ways, typically centered on appeasement. That is, their faith rituals were performed in order to turn away the wrath of the god, or to convince the god to bless their crops or fertility. These rituals were sometimes as extreme as child sacrifice, in the case of Molech. Baal, the other famed rival god of the Old Testament, was precisely a fertility god. Yahweh, however, works with and alongside humanity to accomplish His purposes. Old Testament faith does not imagine a large distance between God and people. Instead, God is involved in the finite details of human life. Perhaps nowhere is this better illustrated than in the opening verses of Proverbs 16.

First, the Lord is caught up in the intricacies of a person's own self. In verse 1, man is the one responsible for planning his fate, though his plans may or may not come to pass. But what is meant by the phrase "the answer of the tongue is from the Lord"? There are many ideas, including these: (1) "True, well-ordered speech is the gift of God" (Barnes). (2) "God answers as He thinks proper" (Clarke). (3) Just as God created the cosmos by speaking it into existence, so the human tongue carries the authority to chart the course of a life. (4) God alone,

Talk About It:
1. According to verse 2, how perceptive is God?
2. How do even wicked people bring glory to God (v. 4)?

in answer to the praying tongue, can make one's plans come to reality. Any way this proverb is understood, we see God intimately involved in a person's life.

In verse 2, the Lord claims His domain not just over the human tongue, but over the human heart as well. People do not have ultimate authority even over their own motives, because humanity has a huge capacity for self-deceit. Because people can always justify their flawed intentions, God steps in to weigh true motives. This sets the stage for verse 3: "Commit to the Lord whatever you do, and your plans will succeed" (*NIV*). When a person's motives and actions (which are weighed by God in the first place) are directed purely to the Lord, success is the eventual result. The truth of this rests in the fact that God is owner of all of a person's faculties. To offer them back to God means they are able to function as God intended, resulting in great achievement, with the ensuing glory and honor ascribed back to God.

Verse 4 states God is not only the originator of the human will and psyche, but the master architect over *everything*. Lest the reader think God is one who needs to be appeased by us, as if He were a faraway deity, Solomon proclaims that God is at work in history, even setting into motion the judgment of the wicked. Throughout the Proverbs, God is always the center of humanity's existence and decisions.

B. Our Moral Choices Before God (vv. 5-9)

5. Every one that is proud in heart is an abomination to the Lord: though hand join in hand, he shall not be unpunished.

6. By mercy and truth iniquity is purged: and by the fear of the Lord men depart from evil.

7. When a man's ways please the Lord, he maketh even his enemies to be at peace with him. Faux pas

8. Better is a little with righteousness than great revenues without right.

9. A man's heart deviseth his way: but the Lord directeth his steps.

After displaying the beauty of the interweaving nature of God's relationship with us, the focus now shifts to our moral behavior before God. Because God is the omniscient caregiver over our heart, mind and soul, we have a grave responsibility to follow His precepts. God alone sets the standard for what is healthy and harmful to authentic human life.

In the Hebrew, the first part of verse 5 literally reads, "An abomination to God are all the exalted things of man's heart." Pride is a chief theme of Proverbs, making it to the top of the list of the six things the Lord hates in 6:16-19. The potency of pride's sinfulness lies not so much in the claim of our own

Talk About It:
1. What can the proud person know for certain (v. 5)?
2. What causes a person to turn away from sin (v. 6)?
3. What does verse 9 say about making plans?

greatness as it does in the refusal to acknowledge our place before an almighty God. This is precisely where our morality begins—at the realization of where we stand in relation to God. Such a realization should always result in humility and leaves no room for a prideful heart.

Verse 6 of the text draws an amazing contrast to the sacrificial systems of the pagan religions of Solomon's day. Although Solomon's magnificent temple testified to the importance of animal sacrifice in the life of Israel, Scripture repeatedly reveals that the ritual of sacrifice is never enough to please God on its own (see 1 Samuel 15:22). God is not waiting on just the right bull, or the right number of bulls, in order to grant forgiveness. Solomon knew the lifestyle of "love and faithfulness" (*NIV*) brought one into right relationship to God, because such a lifestyle exemplifies the fear of the Lord (Proverbs 16:6). Note that the phrase "the fear of the Lord" reaches back to 1:7, which is the theme verse of the entire Book of Proverbs.

Those who live according to love, faithfulness, and the fear of the Lord bring pleasure to Him (16:7). These qualities express themselves in explicit action—"man's ways." When these ways line up with the internal attributes of verse 6, "peace," or *shalom*, is the result. This *shalom* is so effective that it even expands outside one's circle of relatives and friends to one's enemies.

Still centered on our responsibility to live an ethical life before God, the scope widens in verse 8 to the issue of justice, perhaps the central theme in the Old Testament overall. The proverb reminds us that this book was not written only for devotional use, but also for national use. It was written to a nation that was commanded to live obedient before God. Chief within this obedience was the concept of justice—a just society was vital to honoring Yahweh. The greatest enemy to true justice, both then and now, was of course money, which could turn one away from God's way. Therefore, the one living in love, faithfulness, and the fear of God, who reaps the benefits of *shalom*, should watch that he guards justice in his business ventures, even if this costs him greater gain.

In verse 9 Solomon comes full circle back to verse 1, illustrating the fact that our morality begins and ends with the Lord himself. We are not scrapping away trying to appease some vengeful God far off in the cosmos. Instead, we are serving the God who is intricately involved in the minutest details of our life. Throughout the Proverbs, the message of the sovereignty of God and His power rings out loud and clear.

> "The meek man cares not at all who is greater than he, for he has long ago decided that the esteem of this world is not worth the effort."
> —A.W. Tozer

II. WISE LEADERSHIP (Proverbs 16:10-16)

It is interesting that Solomon has many proverbs dealing specifically with the kingship. At first glance it might seem that since there was only one king, why should Solomon address himself? In reality, Solomon recognized the sober responsibility of holding the kingly office, and hoped to pass down wisdom to his future posterity. In addition, we know that the queen of Sheba visited Solomon on account of his famous wisdom (see 2 Chronicles 9), and there is no reason to think other nations couldn't have sent similar convoys to Jerusalem. It could be that Solomon's sayings on royalty were used to teach political morality to these same rulers.

A. The King's Moral Responsibilities (vv. 10-12)

10. A divine sentence is in the lips of the king: his mouth transgresseth not in judgment.

11. A just weight and balance are the Lord's: all the weights of the bag are his work.

12. It is an abomination to kings to commit wickedness: for the throne is established by righteousness.

Talk About It:
1. What should a leader's words *not* do (v. 10)?
2. What would our world be like if verse 11 were not true?
3. What is strong leadership built upon (v. 12)?

Although Israel was a monarchy, it was not a dictatorship. Unlike the pharaohs of Egypt and the later caesars of Rome, the king of Israel's morality was supposed to be scrutinized along with everyone else's, under the same lens of God's righteousness.

In Solomon's day, some other nations considered their king's proclamations to be automatically oracular—the words of a god. Solomon recognized the significance of any kingly pronouncement, declaring it should convey the will of God, for the king was to be His messenger. However, the king's voice was not conceived as a substitute for God's. Nevertheless, as the authoritative human voice over the nation, the king's edicts must be committed to justice; not to the gain of the few, but of the many. Verse 10 speaks alongside hundreds of Old Testament commandments that the king should always champion the causes of the poor and oppressed, rather than remain secluded among the wealthy and powerful.

Continuing the subject of justice in verse 11, Solomon reflected on the usage of honest weights. This refers to the means by which commodities were valued, normally according to weight. Currency especially, whether silver, gold or bronze, would have been measured on a small scale for transactions of many kinds. It was not terribly difficult to "fix" the scale or to dupe a buyer with false weights in order to distort the true amount to one's advantage. Proverbs consistently opposes this. One of the king's responsibilities was to enforce an economic policy that honored God.

In summing up the morality of the godly king (v. 12), Solomon uses the word *abomination*, as he did in verse 5. He declares wrongdoing is "an abomination to kings." This word carries the connotation of disgust. The king should be sickened by evil and instead be fully established in righteousness.

"True success is obeying God."
—**John Maxwell**

B. Proper Relationship to the King (vv. 13-16)

13. Righteous lips are the delight of kings; and they love him that speaketh right.

14. The wrath of a king is as messengers of death: but a wise man will pacify it.

15. In the light of the king's countenance is life; and his favour is as a cloud of the latter rain.

16. How much better is it to get wisdom than gold! and to get understanding rather to be chosen than silver!

The matter of properly relating to the king was potentially applicable to all people in Israel. Although the king's court and other government officials interacted with him on a regular basis, commoners were often granted access, especially in the event of important legal cases. We see this in Solomon's famous ruling between rival mothers in 1 Kings 3. Since the king held such a central position to the life of Israel in general and was thus held in such remarkable esteem by the people, the subject of how to relate to such a powerful ruler is found throughout Proverbs.

There was no shortage of *sycophants* when it came to those vying for a ruler's attention. In our day we might call them lobbyists, but ancient kings also had their share of savvy individuals looking to gain personal advantage from the king's benevolence. Plus, commoners might become so overwhelmed by the splendor of the king's court that they were compelled to dramatize or exaggerate the events of their case. Solomon's advice (Proverbs 16:13) is simple: The righteous king searches for the unvarnished truth alone. He should not pay attention to undue praise, but should value honesty above all.

The words in verse 14 sound harsh, but humankind had yet to conceive of democracy. The reality was that the king's decision always carried final consequences. If crimes were committed deserving capital punishment, the king was obligated to rule as such. Because of this, wisdom was necessary to navigate touchy subjects around the king. Solomon had no doubt seen this in action in his own court. He recognized the ability of those who used simple wisdom to calm his own wrath when difficult situations threatened the righteousness or stability of his kingdom. He realized that he sometimes needed help in correctly interpreting the law.

Just as the wrath of the king portends death to disturbers of his kingdom, the favor of the king dispenses life (v. 15). Under the righteous reigns of David and Solomon, Israel knew much of this life-giving favor. A sullen, mean-spirited king was not God's will for the nation, although dozens would later come who tyrannized the people. Instead, the demeanor of the king should remain bright and optimistic, so that life can be brought to all.

Talk About It:
1. What kind of person does a leader value, and why (v. 13)?
2. What is more valuable than gold and silver, and why (v. 16)?

A poetic interjection closes this segment on the kingship in verse 16: "How much better to get wisdom than gold, to choose understanding rather than silver!" (*NIV*). This, of course, is the life mantra of Solomon himself, the one who asked for wisdom above riches when God gave him the opportunity (2 Chronicles 1). After giving instruction about the righteous kingship, he praises the God-given wisdom that makes it possible in the first place.

III. WISE COUNSEL (Proverbs 16:17-25)

Decision making is a key theme throughout Proverbs. Here, the focus shifts away from the king to principles of making godly decisions. It is not surprising that since the Book of Proverbs represents a gift of wisdom from father to son, seeking and obeying wise counsel appears again and again.

A. Accepting Wise Counsel Requires Humility (vv. 17-20)

17. The highway of the upright is to depart from evil: he that keepeth his way preserveth his soul.

18. Pride goeth before destruction, and an haughty spirit before a fall.

19. Better it is to be of an humble spirit with the lowly, than to divide the spoil with the proud.

20. He that handleth a matter wisely shall find good: and whoso trusteth in the Lord, happy is he.

In Proverbs, decision making is not a matter of practicality. It does not boil down to looking at the available options and choosing the best one. Instead, it is always a matter of the heart. The ability to accept the counsel of others means choosing the right people to give counsel (v. 17). Therefore, the upright person guards his or her way closely. That person recognizes evil when he or she sees it, and can therefore avoid it.

Verse 18 shows if there is one source of evil that can prevent the acceptance of any wise counsel, it is pride. This famous proverb charts the highway of the foolish person, poetically depicting the sin of pride arriving first to bring about destruction. Why? The prideful person cannot hear, discern or accept godly counsel; he or she is too wrapped up in his or her own deceitful assurances. Sooner or later, the crash will come.

The antidote to pride is a "humble spirit" (v. 19). Such a spirit is necessary to receive sound counsel. The person with such a spirit will prefer disadvantage with humility to advantage with pride. Jesus himself expressed a similar truth in the first beatitude: "Blessed are the poor in spirit" (Matthew 5:3).

It seems a premise of the Proverbs that they won't do anyone much good who isn't open to receiving instruction in the first place. As verse 20 of the text illustrates, it takes trust that we are not the ultimate judges of our own destinies in order to accept counsel. This is, in fact, the beginning of humility—

Wisdom of a Godly Life

trusting in God instead of ourselves. When we are able to do this, wise instruction will be nourishing to our souls.

B. Accepting Wise Counsel Requires Discernment (vv. 21-25)
21. The wise in heart shall be called prudent: and the sweetness of the lips increaseth learning.
22. Understanding is a wellspring of life unto him that hath it: but the instruction of fools is folly.
23. The heart of the wise teacheth his mouth, and addeth learning to his lips.
24. Pleasant words are as an honeycomb, sweet to the soul, and health to the bones.
25. There is a way that seemeth right unto a man, but the end thereof are the ways of death.

Humility precedes all good moral attributes in Proverbs, but the moral life does not stop there. Instead, humility lays the foundation upon which to build. This group of sayings places a new layer upon this foundation—a layer characterized by discernment.

Immediately Solomon equates discernment with wisdom itself, showing its expression in one's use of words (v. 21). In the Proverbs, words are not to be taken lightly. When chosen carefully, they have the power to accomplish much. This has a lot to do with the definition of *discernment*, which is the process of choosing between multiple options. Discerning people can distill the alternatives down to the righteous choice.

Discernment goes hand in hand with understanding (v. 22). In the arid, desert climate of Israel, underwater springs or fountains held high value. To the person of discernment, understanding holds similar value. The Hebrew word for *understanding* (*shokel*) denotes prudence and insight. The discerning person gains insight into key decisions, while undiscerning persons, or fools, reap the consequences of their lack thereof.

As verse 23 illustrates, the Book of Proverbs is marked by a close connection between the heart and the mouth. The heart was considered the center of the person, including the seat of the thoughts, in ancient Jewish theology. When one's speaking is disconnected from this center, dishonesty and fragmentation result. Therefore, the discerning person's words are always preceded by the proper direction of his heart, producing instructive speech. The value of such speech is elucidated in verse 24. When speech is appropriately aligned with a righteous heart, the result is words of sweetness and healing. Discernment in Proverbs has as much to do with the words the person speaks as the ability to think rightly.

The section on discernment ends with a caution regarding the sinful proclivity of the human heart. Even the discerning person must be aware of this reality. In the end, discernment

Talk About It:
1. What is "a wellspring of life" (v. 22), and why?
2. What do verses 23 and 24 say about well-chosen words?
3. How are many people deceived (v. 25)?

Daily Devotions:
M. Rule With Wisdom
 1 Kings 3:16-28
T. Wise Behavior
 Psalm 101:1-8
W. Winning Souls Is Wise
 Proverbs 11:23-31
T. Walk in Wisdom
 Colossians 4:1-6
F. Wisdom in the Word
 2 Timothy 3:10-17
S. Ask for Wisdom
 James 1:1-12

does not come down to personal decisions, but decisions made in conjunction with God. Notice that God is conspicuously absent in verse 25. When one's decision making leaves God out, the result is always deathly.

CONCLUSION

In Proverbs 16 we see wisdom expressed in a godly lifestyle, righteous leadership, and the ready acceptance of grounded and solid counsel. None of these subjects is complete without a proper perspective on God, who is always involved at each level of wisdom. In fact, He is the source of all wisdom. We are able to find the wisdom needed for life in God alone, who freely dispenses knowledge.

GOLDEN TEXT CHALLENGE

"HE THAT HANDLETH A MATTER WISELY SHALL FIND GOOD: AND WHOSO TRUSTETH IN THE LORD, HAPPY IS HE" (Proverbs 16:20).

The *NIV* begins this verse, "Whoever gives heed to instruction prospers." Those of us who have tried to assemble a bicycle or a barbecue grill without heeding (or even reading) the instructions know all too well the value of this proverb. And its importance is multiplied when we're building our lives rather than bikes or grills.

Trusting "in the Lord" brings happiness because it means following God's instructions given to us in His Word. We will "find good"—our life will prosper—as we read and heed His "assembly" plans.

Tested and Found Faithful

Job 1:1 through 2:10

INTRODUCTION

Perhaps the most vexing question for believers in Almighty God is the problem of evil in the world. We have all heard questions like, "If God is so good, why is there so much suffering in the world?" It doesn't take long to look around at natural disasters, relatives and friends plagued by disease, and the plight of the poor and starving, and come to the same question ourselves. Indeed, Christian theologians since the apostle Paul have wrestled with this question. But Christians did not begin the dialogue. In fact, what may be the oldest book in the Bible takes on the issue directly.

The problem of how to reconcile a good and loving God with the presence of evil in the world is often called *theodicy* by theologians. Thousands of theodicies have been written in the attempt to solve the problem. Millard J. Erickson summarizes the most common approaches: "For the most part, these attempted solutions endeavor to reduce the tension by modifying one of the three elements which in combination have caused the dilemma: God's greatness, God's goodness, and the presence of evil" (*Christian Theology, Second Edition*). That is, the presence of evil is typically accounted for by either denying God's power to *do* anything about it, by denying God's goodness to *care* anything about it, or by attributing it to humanity's sinful choices alone. In the Christian worldview, none of these can be fully accepted. Instead, we are left to grapple with the reality that although God is all-powerful and could erase human suffering in an instant, He chooses another path centered in the story of the gospel. It has never been an easy truth to live with, as the Book of Job profoundly testifies.

The Book of Job stands as the Bible's great address to the problem of theodicy. It doesn't offer easy answers or quick-fix solutions, but presents the suffering, questions, and story of one man in the throes of unfairness who, nonetheless, retained his faith in the God of Israel. It also offers us an unprecedented glimpse behind the spiritual scenes of Job's calamity, assuring us that God is both all-powerful and always good.

Unit Theme:
Learning Faithfulness From Job

Central Truth:
Faith in God will help us maintain our integrity when tested.

Focus:
Observe that Job remained faithful to God and maintain our integrity when tested.

Context:
Scholars place the date of the authorship of Job anywhere from the time of Abraham to the time the Jews returned from Babylonian captivity.

Golden Text:
"In all this Job sinned not, nor charged God foolishly" (Job 1:22).

Study Outline:
I. An Exemplary Servant of God (Job 1:1-5)
II. A Tested Servant of God (Job 1:6-22)
III. A Faithful Servant of God (Job 2:1-10)

I. AN EXEMPLARY SERVANT OF GOD (Job 1:1-5)

The Book of Job comes to us as a part of the Wisdom Literature of the Bible. Specifically, the wisdom books include Job, Ecclesiastes and Proverbs, but we cannot relegate the genre of wisdom themes in the Old Testament to these books alone. As Derek Kidner states, "We may see wisdom as a thread running through the whole fabric of the Old Testament. Because God is self-consistent, what He wills can always be expressed as what wisdom dictates, and the themes of history, law, prophecy and apocalyptic can all be transposed into this key" (*The Proverbs: An Introduction and Commentary*).

Unlike the Book of Proverbs, Job and Ecclesiastes essentially are written to ask questions, not give the answers, which lead to wisdom. Even so, Job provides an exciting template for how the faithful servant of God can and should respond to suffering and grave personal loss.

A. The Greatness of Job (vv. 1-3)

perfect (v. 1)— blameless

eschewed (v. 1)— shunned

1. There was a man in the land of Uz, whose name was Job; and that man was perfect and upright, and one that feared God, and eschewed evil.

2. And there were born unto him seven sons and three daughters.

3. His substance also was seven thousand sheep, and three thousand camels, and five hundred yoke of oxen, and five hundred she asses, and a very great household; so that this man was the greatest of all the men of the east.

Talk About It:
1. How did Job's life show that he "feared God" (v. 1)?
2. How was Job "the greatest" (v. 3)?

The book begins in prose form, which stands out since the vast majority of its pages are poetry. In fact, out of its 42 chapters, only three of them are in prose—at the beginning and end. In this structural sense, the book reminds us of prophetic books such as Jeremiah and Ezekiel. Like them, we are given the narrative story surrounding the poetry so that both poetry and prose reflect meaning toward one another.

The book centers on the story of Job himself, so the opening in verse 1 is appropriate. Job's name itself is curious, especially since it shows up nowhere else in the Old Testament except Ezekiel 14:14, 20. This contributes to the problem of dating this book. It is likely that the material does predate much of the Old Testament, but came to be placed in its present form a bit later, perhaps in conjunction with the Prophetic Books after the Babylonian exile. This would explain why it is not referenced by other Old Testament writers.

Job appears to be a very ancient name, and has some parallels in a few Canaanite texts from the second millennium B.C. It might have a connection to the Hebrew root *yob*, meaning "to hate," but this is unlikely. In fact, such meanings may have

Tested and Found Faithful

been ascribed to the name after the historical Job existed. We simply know it was a current name for the historical time period.

We are also only given a few clues about the location of the land of Uz. It is not mentioned before the events of the Book of Job, and only later in Lamentations 4:21 and Jeremiah 25:20 is it possibly connected to Edom. Josephus, a first-century historian, considered it to lay north of the Sea of Galilee. The ambiguity of the location points to an important ambiguity about Job himself. That is, we are not told that he was an Israelite, and his location was probably outside the bounds of Israel. He was undoubtedly a faithful follower of Yahweh, the God of Israel, but it is exceptional that he is not specifically identified as a Jew. It is as if the writer wants his story to be applicable to all followers of God in any culture—an added benefit to our contemporary reading.

The description of Job becomes more detailed in verses 2 and 3, when his property is listed. Notably, Job has seven sons—the number of perfection and completion in Old Testament thought. These are coupled with three daughters and a tremendous amount of personal property. This list reminds us of similar lists to describe the wealth of Abraham, such as Genesis 24:35; but Job was apparently not a wandering nomad, since his homes and property appear to be stationary as the story unfolds. In the ancient world, the fundamental unit of human life and interaction was not the nuclear family, as it is in our culture today, but the larger household. Therefore, the people and assets of the entire household are listed to describe Job's greatness. There was no one in the eastern regions of the land comparable with Job.

B. The Holiness of Job (vv. 4, 5)

4. And his sons went and feasted in their houses, every one his day; and sent and called for their three sisters to eat and to drink with them.

5. And it was so, when the days of their feasting were gone about, that Job sent and sanctified them, and rose up early in the morning, and offered burnt offerings according to the number of them all: for Job said, It may be that my sons have sinned, and cursed God in their hearts. Thus did Job continually.

It is not surprising that the focus of the narrative quickly shifts from Job's wealth and popularity to his religious walk. We see throughout the Wisdom Literature that all of life, and especially one's business dealings, are intricately connected to God's work.

In verse 4, the gladness of Job's household is lavishly depicted. Job's property includes individual homes for his sons, and Job's children regularly feasted together in these homes.

A Man of Integrity
It's integrity that keeps a Promise Keeper from entering into a shady business deal. It's integrity that says he will choose to express his sexuality only within the confines of his marriage. It's integrity that makes him do the right thing instead of just the easy thing.
—*Seven Promises of a Promise Keeper*

Talk About It:
How did Job express his love for his sons and daughters?

These ancient feasts lasted for days and sometimes weeks in all of the cultures of the ancient Near East, evidenced even in the wedding Jesus attended at Cana, yet Job himself is not listed as being a part of their celebration. Instead, he is the one looking out for the things of God.

In the ancient world, feasting was always accompanied by wine, and so drunkenness is an issue in the Old Testament and in other ancient literature. This appears to be in view as Job ensures that his children do not sin by speaking something against God during the feast. First, he sends them away, presumably to a priest of Yahweh, to undergo purification rituals. These are illustrated graphically in Leviticus and were done for a variety of reasons. Second, Job sacrifices a burnt offering for each one of his children in an act of prayer and repentance on their behalf. This was a costly act of both property and time. Job proudly takes the role of spiritual, as well as natural, father over his family. He is more than a financial provider; he is ultimately responsible for their spiritual well-being, and his actions depict a marvelous love for his family. The final phrase literally reads in Hebrew, "Job did this every day," meaning on a regular, consistent basis.

> "Job understood that a father is to be the priest of his home and maintain that continuity of commitment between generations by setting a godly example."
> —Tony Evans

II. A TESTED SERVANT OF GOD (Job 1:6-22)

The rosy setting of Job's righteous life ends abruptly after the short prologue. Job has been set up as a model follower of God, who reaps the benefits of prosperity and *shalom* (peace) that accompany the godly person throughout the Wisdom Literature. The connection between righteousness and reward will soon be the primary issue treated in the Book of Job. This begins with a great test.

A. God Praises Job (vv. 6-8)

6. Now there was a day when the sons of God came to present themselves before the Lord, and Satan came also among them.

7. And the Lord said unto Satan, Whence comest thou? Then Satan answered the Lord, and said, From going to and fro in the earth, and from walking up and down in it.

8. And the Lord said unto Satan, Hast thou considered my servant Job, that there is none like him in the earth, a perfect and an upright man, one that feareth God, and escheweth evil?

In the prologue, the narrator praises Job as the greatest man in the eastern territories. He is described as a lover of his family and his God. In the story of Job's first test, we are given an unprecedented glimpse into a conversation of God himself, where He adds to the narrator's assessment by praising Job. The setting is one of the most mysterious passages in all of Scripture.

Talk About It:
1. What do verses 6 and 7 reveal about Satan?
2. How did God describe Job?

Tested and Found Faithful

Verse 6 depicts an assembly before the Lord in which Yahweh is presiding, as always. In this case, the "sons of God" arrive at the assembly along with Satan. This is only one of a handful of named references to Satan in the entire Old Testament. His name appears in 1 Chronicles 21:1, and he plays a role in one of the prophetic visions of Zechariah 3. Job contains the lengthiest treatment on Satan in the entire Bible.

Satan means "accuser," and here he is personified. He travels alongside the sons of God, but is distinct from them. The expression "sons of God" is probably an ancient term for angelic beings. Even though Satan is distinct from them, he is cast in the same light. Yahweh inquires to his whereabouts, denoting that Satan has, in fact, been separate from these other sons of God. But he has been in the same place as the sons of God in Genesis 6—on earth.

As if God did not know the answer to Satan's whereabouts in Job 1:7, He immediately betrays the knowledge of what Satan has been doing. We are not given the full revelation of this knowledge, but apparently Satan is engaged in the business of examining humanity, perhaps in the attempt to frustrate the righteous. God immediately offers His prized son, Job, as the perfect example of what Satan is apparently looking for. God praises him according to familiar Old Testament virtues. In fact, Proverbs 14:16 applauds the wisdom of the man who "fears the Lord and shuns evil" (*NIV*). The message is plain: even God is pleased with the life of Job.

> "The natural response to denials of Satan's existence is to ask, Who then runs his business?"
> —**J.I. Packer**

B. God Permits Testing (vv. 9-12)

9. Then Satan answered the Lord, and said, Doth Job fear God for nought?

10. Hast not thou made an hedge about him, and about his house, and about all that he hath on every side? thou hast blessed the work of his hands, and his substance is increased in the land.

11. But put forth thine hand now, and touch all that he hath, and he will curse thee to thy face.

12. And the Lord said unto Satan, Behold, all that he hath is in thy power; only upon himself put not forth thine hand. So Satan went forth from the presence of the Lord.

While God praises His choice servant, Satan lives up to his name by accusing Job. In fact, all of Satan's words in chapters 1 and 2 are accusatory. God has asked Satan a question in verse 8. Now Satan tersely responds, "Does Job fear God for nothing?" (v. 9, *NIV*).

This is the principal argument of the devil: Job serves God because he receives tremendous blessing in return. Satan calls God's blessing a "hedge" (v. 10)—derived from a Hebrew word that also appears in Judges 9:49 and Hosea 2:6—to

Talk About It:
1. Explain Satan's claim that God had built a "hedge" around Job (v. 10).
2. What did God give Satan permission to do (v. 12)?

describe walls built out of branches. It may be that Satan is mocking God by using the word, insinuating that the hedge God has built around Job is flimsy. Whatever the case, he proclaims the truth of God's blessing on the work of Job's hands.

Satan believes Job's wealth is the key to his trust in God, and without it he will curse God. This is an affront to Yahweh's sovereignty. In fact, it mocks Job's custom of giving burnt offerings (Job 1:5), which were for the purpose of atoning for any of his children who might curse God. It also reflects back to the third commandment prohibiting the misuse of God's name (Exodus 20:7). Satan is challenging God with the most direct and flammable language he can muster.

In an incredible acceptance of Satan's challenge, God says He will allow the accuser to test his theory that Job's faith cannot survive apart from his wealth, so God provides complete access to all of Job's goods. The only thing out of bounds is Job's very person. Without answering, Satan immediately exits the scene. He has obtained what he wants.

At first glance, the agreement God willingly makes with Satan may seem disturbing. After all, it appears God offers up His servant Job to the devil just to prove a point. However, the story goes deeper. This scene portrays the fact that God is not far from people's suffering. He is intricately involved in the process of suffering, not causing it, but redeeming it for His purposes. The Book of Job presents a sovereign God whose mind we cannot comprehend, yet who lovingly presides over the process of suffering. The character of God must be kept in mind as the story is read. This book was not constructed in a bubble, but is part of the larger Old Testament. Its original authors and readers understood it in this light, and so must we.

> "The problem isn't that there are problems. The problem is expecting otherwise and thinking that having problems is a problem."
> —Theodore Rubin

C. Job's Suffering Begins (vv. 13-19)

(Job 1:13-17 is not included in the printed text.)

18. While he was yet speaking, there came also another, and said, Thy sons and thy daughters were eating and drinking wine in their eldest brother's house:

19. And, behold, there came a great wind from the wilderness, and smote the four corners of the house, and it fell upon the young men, and they are dead; and I only am escaped alone to tell thee.

Talk About It:
1. Describe the various ways Job lost his animals.
2. Why did God allow all of Job's children to die instantly?

Although we are left to hope that Satan will destroy only Job's wealth, he takes full advantage of God's prohibition to touch anything but the man himself. Sinisterly, he strikes first during the happy occasion of the type of feast described in the prologue, in which Job's sons and daughters are enjoying God's blessings. Not only does Job lose his oxen and donkeys, and thereby his ability to plow his land for farming, he does so at the hand of the Sabeans. Job is no longer respected by neighboring peoples. His protection has been compromised. The

Tested and Found Faithful

Chaldeans also get in on the action by swiping his camels. In between these great losses, Job's sheep are burned to death by fire falling from the sky. This is most curious, as it connotes Satan's ability to manipulate nature. However, it should be remembered that Satan's ability to do anything is doled out by God himself in verse 12. The devil does not have such extraordinary powers on his own.

The final calamity eclipses the losses Job has endured thus far (vv. 18, 19). In fact, it is not until he hears the last dreaded pronouncement that he offers a response.

The same dinner parties for which Job made regular sacrifices had been the final setting for the demise of all 10 of his precious children. The catastrophes build to this point, and Job's composure finally breaks under the pressure.

D. Job Responds to Satan's Attack (vv. 20-22)

20. Then Job arose, and rent his mantle, and shaved his head, and fell down upon the ground, and worshipped,

21. And said, Naked came I out of my mother's womb, and naked shall I return thither: the Lord gave, and the Lord hath taken away; blessed be the name of the Lord.

22. In all this Job sinned not, nor charged God foolishly.

It may seem strange that Job did not collapse to the ground in response to the news of his children's death, but this also speaks of Job's character. He honors their loss by engaging in proper mourning rituals. Pulling his frantic thoughts together, he rises, tears his robes, and shaves his head. The purposes of this ritual are many, but they center on the ancient importance of publicly expressing one's mourning through changing one's clothing and appearance. Job is inviting others to mourn with him and paying homage to the memory of his children.

Job's next response, however, catches the reader by surprise. In the midst of unimaginable torment, Job bows before God in worship. Though his prayer proclaims his profound sadness, he ascribes praise to the Lord as the source of all things. Philip Yancey summarizes the potency of Job's proclamation: "[The Book of] Job is not 'about' suffering; it merely uses such ingredients in its larger story, which concerns even more important questions, cosmic questions. Seen as a whole, Job is primarily about *faith* in its starkest form" (*Disappointment With God*). In the throes of loss, Job's faith shines brilliantly, even in the absence of the answers he craves.

III. A FAITHFUL SERVANT OF GOD (Job 2:1-10)

Job has passed the first, monumental test with flying colors. Refusing to accuse God of imperfection, he continues his life as best he can, walking according to his seasoned faith. Yet the story of Job's trust in God has only just begun.

Talk About It:
1. Describe Job's act of worship (vv. 20, 21).
2. What did Job *not* do (v. 22)?

"What seem our worst prayers may really be, in God's eyes, our best. Those, I mean, which are least supported by devotional feeling. For these may come from a deeper level than feeling."
—C.S. Lewis

A. Satan's New Deal (vv. 1-6)
(Job 2:1-3 is not included in the printed text.)

4. And Satan answered the Lord, and said, Skin for skin, yea, all that a man hath will he give for his life.

5. But put forth thine hand now, and touch his bone and his flesh, and he will curse thee to thy face.

6. And the Lord said unto Satan, Behold, he is in thine hand; but save his life.

We do not know the amount of time that has elapsed between chapters 1 and 2. The scene of the council of Yahweh in verses 1-3 is set identically to chapter 1, but this time Satan is explicitly said to come on purpose. He presents himself before God as one summoned by God. The Lord repeats His praise formula for Job, adding that Satan's plan has miserably failed.

Satan complains that the trial has not been severe enough. He accuses Job of callousness and indifference to the suffering of others. Satan insists that if Job be struck in his own person, his piety will crumble. So far the calamity has affected only the lives of others. His own skin has been untouched. Let his own person be involved and he will not hold fast to his integrity.

God again allows the devil to test Job, but on His terms alone. Job's life is not to be threatened.

B. Job's Unshakable Faith (vv. 7-10)
7. So went Satan forth from the presence of the Lord, and smote Job with sore boils from the sole of his foot unto his crown.

8. And he took him a potsherd to scrape himself withal; and he sat down among the ashes.

9. Then said his wife unto him, Dost thou still retain thine integrity? curse God, and die.

10. But he said unto her, Thou speakest as one of the foolish women speaketh. What? shall we receive good at the hand of God, and shall we not receive evil? In all this did not Job sin with his lips.

Exiting God's presence, Satan immediately inflicts boils on the entire surface of Job's body. Disgustingly, they are filled with disease-ridden puss that must be scraped with pottery to gain some relief. Job takes his place among the lepers on the ash heap outside the city. There, in this place of discarded things, sits this man who had once been "the greatest of all the men of the east" (1:3).

The loss of children, wealth, and now her husband's health leaves the faith of Job's wife in ruins. She asks why should Job try to hold on to his integrity now. All is lost. He should finish the job by cursing God's name and passing from the earth. But he will have none of that.

Talk About It:
1. What had happened "without cause" (v. 3)?
2. Explain the phrase "skin for skin" (v. 4).
3. What did God allow (v. 6)?

Talk About It:
1. Describe Job's condition (vv. 7, 8).
2. Why didn't Job "curse God" (vv. 9, 10)?

Tested and Found Faithful

Though certainly shaken, Job would not let go of his faith in the goodness of God. He kept his mouth from judging God, even in the middle of physical and emotional agony. His attitude is the same as before (1:21). It is right for God to give good gifts and to retrieve them (vv. 20-22); it is also right for God to send good and evil (2:10). Job bows before the sovereign hand of God whether it bestows or takes away, whether it caresses or strikes. In all of the calamity, Job continued to remain silent in his affliction.

CONCLUSION

The Book of Job is the powerful story of one man's unbreakable faith in the midst of loss, pain, desperation and uncertainty. It is also a theological exploration of the existence of evil in our world—particularly evil that preys upon the innocent and the righteous. The first two chapters are prose narrative that set up the poetic body of the literature. In them, Satan is allowed to cause Job to suffer, but always on God's terms. Job's responses are God-centered, showing faith in God to be the focus of the Book of Job.

GOLDEN TEXT CHALLENGE

"IN ALL THIS JOB SINNED NOT, NOR CHARGED GOD FOOLISHLY" (Job 1:22).

"In all this" refers to the loss of Job's 10 children and all his possessions. Instead of "charging God with wrongdoing" (*NIV*), Job worshiped the Lord wholeheartedly. While being overwhelmed by his horrible losses and not understanding why, he recognized God as being the source of all the blessings he had known and the Sovereign over his life.

No matter what the "all this"—the sufferings and losses of our life—we must continue to believe that God is always good and always in control. As one songwriter wrote of God, "When you cannot see His hand, trust His heart."

Daily Devotions:
M. Test of Obedience
   Genesis 22:1-14
T. Test of Character
   Genesis 39:7-12
W. Prayer for Help
   Psalm 17:1-15
T. Temptation of
   Christ
   Luke 4:1-13
F. Trial of Faith
   1 Peter 1:3-9
S. Ask for Mature
   Faith
   Revelation 3:7-13

Trust in the Faithful God

Job 13:1-28

Unit Theme:
Learning Faithfulness
From Job

Central Truth:
We should trust God
because He is faithful.

Focus:
Consider Job's
steadfast faith and
trust God in every
circumstance.

Context:
Scholars place the
date of the authorship
of Job anywhere from
the time of Abraham
to the time the Jews
returned from
Babylonian captivity.

Golden Text:
"Though he [God]
slay me, yet will I trust
in him" (Job 13:15).

Study Outline:
  I. Job Pleads His
     Case
     (Job 13:1-6)
 II. Job Rebukes His
     Counselors
     (Job 13:7-14)
III. Job Asserts His
     Trust
     (Job 13:15-28)

INTRODUCTION

Unfortunately, our English word for *faith* is a poor substitute for the meaning of its ancient counterparts. In our contemporary language, *faith* is always a noun. It is static like an object. It can be considered something that a believer possesses, such as a person is said to "have" a strong faith. It can also be a word that substitutes for Christian teachings and doctrines in general, as in referring to our overall beliefs in Jesus as "the faith."

These are certainly valid meanings of the Biblical concept of faith, but they can easily miss a second key component: the action-oriented nature of real faith. Faith is something that is in motion. It pushes us to new heights. It is an action word, a verb. We see this especially in the New Testament, where the word for faith, *pistis*, is used alongside its verb form, *pisteuo*. When the noun for *faith* is transformed into a verb, we get our word meaning "to believe" or "to trust." It is exactly this type of action faith, "faithing," that the life of Job exemplifies. This is because the story is not centered on Job, but on a greater One who is always worthy of our best and most active faith.

"God is the central character in the Bible, and nowhere does this come through more clearly than in the Book of Job," Philip Yancey writes in *Disappointment With God*. The book is about faith and trust, but not because of Job's resilience in the face of suffering. Job is a champion of faith because he recognizes and acknowledges the ultimate divine reality and presence. When this reality is realized even in part, action-oriented faith takes root. This kind of faith is the proper answer to the intellectual problems that the Book of Job probes. In the end, the one thing the book can offer is faith in Yahweh.

Job Had Pride

I. JOB PLEADS HIS CASE (Job 13:1-6)

The words of Job are handed down to us in the wild, emotional pathos that can only be transmitted in poetry. Prose is, of course, the mode of writing history, of careful description, of objectively passing along the correct facts about a given historical event. Poetry is the style of writing that can best convey the desperations of one's soul, the passions of the heart, and Job does just that. In fact, Job's first words in chapter 1 are in poetic form, even though they are surrounded and framed by prose. By the time of chapter 13, Job has poured out his heart and listened to the musings of his friends. He now turns up the heat with a vehement defense of his life, his integrity, and the ways of his God.

A. Job Addresses His Friends (vv. 1, 2)

1. Lo, mine eye hath seen all this, mine ear hath heard and understood it.

2. What ye know, the same do I know also: I am not inferior unto you.

The setting of almost all of the poetic sections of Job, which comprise almost 40 complete chapters, is actually dialogue. Although spoken in poetry, Job is typically responding to the speeches of his friends, and vice versa. Chapter 13 is a prime example of one of these responses by Job, and it is a direct continuation of chapter 12. There Job lashes out at his cold-hearted friend Zophar, who demeans Job in chapter 11 for his claim to innocence, calling him to a sober repentance. Job will have none of this, mocking Zophar in chapter 12 with a long poem detailing his friend's terrible misunderstanding of the ways of God. Job's friends claim to have the ways of God nicely and cleanly mapped out, but Job knows that man can never fully comprehend the divine plan. Also, Job remains committed to his own integrity. He knows he has not brought these calamities upon himself, but has lived righteously.

After a long poem detailing the sovereignty of God who acts according to His, and not man's, own purposes, Job practically laughs at the arrogance of his friends in 13:1, 2. Job criticizes his colleagues for misrepresenting the basic right of God to act in any way He wants with regard to nature, wisdom and humanity. Job, however, acknowledges God's right to choose. He is not a deity that can be placed into a neat and tidy formula. Job's friends claim a higher insight into the divine realm, but Job rebuffs them. They attempt to talk down to him, but he will not allow it. He turns to them with the unvarnished truth that he believes, and he combats their arrogance with it. He knows they are no better off than he, and he is willing to boldly stand up for his own righteousness before God.

Talk About It:
What did Job say he had seen, heard and understood?

"Friendship is one of the sweetest joys of life. Many might have failed beneath the bitterness of their own trial had they not found a friend."
—**Charles Spurgeon**

B. Job Readies His Attack (vv. 3-6)

3. Surely I would speak to the Almighty, and I desire to reason with God.

4. But ye are forgers of lies, ye are all physicians of no value.

5. O that ye would altogether hold your peace! and it should be your wisdom.

6. Hear now my reasoning, and hearken to the pleadings of my lips.

Talk About It:
1. What was Job's desire (v. 3)?
2. How did Job describe his friends (v. 5)?

Job's "friends" include Eliphaz, Bildad and Zophar. Each has his own distinctives, but their general outlook remains unified. They are certain Job has sinned and thus brought these calamities upon himself. But Job will not be judged by them. He appeals to a higher authority.

Job knows God has not left him nor closed His ears to his cry. There is more at stake for Job than the intellectual ramblings of his friends, mere mortals. He wants to take his case directly to the top. He trusts that God will hear him fairly. This is exactly the focus that his friends have lacked. They are proficient in human categories, but ignorant of God's greatness.

In verse 4 Job calls these men "worthless physicians" (*NIV*). They arrived at his house under the premise of caring about his horrifying predicament, but they have done nothing but bring him shame and dishonor. Here is a man who has lost all of his children, his property, his physical health, his dignity, and all they can focus on are their trite explanations of how it is all Job's fault. It is the last thing he needs as he scrapes his sores with broken pottery, and they have missed the mark entirely. Although they claim to be harbingers of wisdom, their silence would provide much more wisdom than their empty and incorrect words of cold explanation. After laying down the harsh line between Job and his friends, he readies them for an elongated response to their claims, saying, "Hear now my argument; listen to the plea of my lips" (v. 6, *NIV*).

> "Job's friends spent days telling Job his suffering was his own fault. Certain of their own ideas and dogma of right, wrong, justice and God, they never took time to consider Job's feelings. They never thought they might be doing more harm than good."
> —Thomas Endicott

Like a defendant in court who has finally been given the opportunity to speak on behalf of his innocence, Job commands the ear of his audience. His response will result in a testimony about his faith in the goodness of Almighty God.

II. JOB REBUKES HIS COUNSELORS (Job 13:7-14)

Job has swept the narrative platform clean in the previous verses for what is now to follow. He has unashamedly staked his position firmly against the positions of his friends, with all of their verbose and elaborate speeches about his supposed guilt. He now addresses those friends with a litany of phrases unified by a single theme—that they should tread carefully before supposing, much less volunteering, to speak on behalf of Almighty God. Job, the champion of humility, is unafraid to take them on with full and penetrating force.

A. A Flurry of Questions (vv. 7-9)

7. Will ye speak wickedly for God? and talk deceitfully for him?

8. Will ye accept his person? will ye contend for God?

9. Is it good that he should search you out? or as one man mocketh another, do ye *so* mock him?

Job launches into his assault in the form of a quick series of rhetorical questions. Although he uses questions throughout his poems to often make points about God, such as in 12:7-9, these are presently directed toward the downfall of his friends and their arguments.

In the Bible, common wisdom is often subverted in the form of rhetorical or well-placed questions. God asks Cain, "What have you done?" after the murder of Abel in Genesis 4. Samuel asks Saul, "What is this bleating of sheep that I hear?" when the wayward king disobeys the clear command of God in 1 Samuel 15. Jesus asks poignant questions at all kinds of key turns. For example, at the end of a teaching on prayer in Luke 18, He asks, "When the Son of Man comes, will he find faith on the earth?" (v. 8, *NIV*). We can imagine the silence of the audience at such a profound question.

It is not surprising, then, that Job undermines his cruel friends with this flurry of difficult and biting questions. On the other hand, these questions show genuine concern for the spiritual state of these men. Job is aware of God's judgment on such rashness. He attempts to uncover the hilarity of their attempt to speak on behalf of God, as if the divine and righteous judge of Job's case needed help from them—mere flesh and blood—in discerning right from wrong. He attempts to bring them to their senses. As if realizing this is getting nowhere, Job then turns the table on them, asking them to take some of their own medicine. What if God truly were to lay bare the motivations and secrets of their inner hearts? Could they somehow talk God into their views with their fancy tongues and educated minds? The answer, of course, is obvious, but Job continues building his case.

B. Ashes and Clay (vv. 10-12)

10. He will surely reprove you, if ye do secretly accept persons.

11. Shall not his excellency make you afraid? and his dread fall upon you?

12. Your remembrances are like unto ashes, your bodies to bodies of clay.

The problem for Job is the inability of his friends to be objective—in fact, the inability of humanity to discern anything without being consistently partial. Job recognizes that the human

Talk About It:
1. What did Job accuse his friends of trying to do "on God's behalf" (v. 7, *NIV*)?
2. How did Job turn the tables in verse 9?

"Lots of faults we think we see in others are simply the ones we expect to find there because we have them."
—**Frank A. Clark**

remembrances (v. 12)—maxims
bodies (v. 12)—defenses

Talk About It:
1. What did Job say would happen if God judged his friends (vv. 10, 11)?
2. How did Job characterize his friends' statements (v. 12)?

heart is inevitably out for the individual's own interests, regardless of his friends' veneer of neutrality. They are biased against Job, and God knows they are trying to keep this bias a secret. If God exposed their show as a forgery, His very splendor ("excellency," v. 11) would knock them off their feet. This is the first use of the word for *splendor* (*shoet*) in Job, and it refers to the loftiness of God, literally meaning "swelling" or "uprising." If their true motives were seen in the light of God's splendor, dread would befall them. They would be defenseless as their human wisdom melted like ashes before the glory of God. The mention of "proverbs" (v. 12, *NKJV*) calls to mind the next wisdom book in the Old Testament. But in this case, his friends aren't wise enough to provide any such wisdom. Their "proverbs" are not wise, but worthless.

This is a common theme of Job's poems, as they are extraordinarily God-centered. Sometimes Job does not offer a cognitive response to his friends' arguments. In these cases, as in all cases with Job, he points to the greatness of God. He shows that all human thought, no matter how authentically focused on interpreting proper theology, is dreadfully inadequate in and of itself. It is not so much that his friends' arguments are wrong, although they certainly are, but that they are foolish to think even a correct argument somehow harnesses or transcends God. God is not a formula to Job, but a divine person with free will. Because God has invented human language and human reason, it is silly to think God is somehow locked into acting according to our own predictions or theologies. This is not to say God is not bound by His character, for that is also a vital theme to Job. In fact, his only hope is to trust fully in God's character, which he continues to do. This is the subversion of Job's questioning, as he destroys the arguments of his friends by appealing to the centrality of God's very self.

C. A Request to Speak (vv. 13, 14)
13. Hold your peace, let me alone, that I may speak, and let come on me what will.
14. Wherefore do I take my flesh in my teeth, and put my life in mine hand?

Over and over again, Job begs his friends to cease their ongoing theological debate. He has suffered irreparable loss, and their headiness is not helping at all. He also, unlike them, treads carefully with his words, even as he asks the most direct questions to God. The greatest difference between the two sides is not their theology but Job's humble heart toward Yahweh.

In verse 13 Job asks for his chance at theologizing. Yet he realizes the gravity of such a request. His friends have spewed forth their opinions about God as if there were no consequences to such speech. Job is nowhere near such ignorance. He fully recognizes the unequal playing field between himself and God. Understandably, he feels a measure of terror at the thought of directly addressing God, particularly after the catastrophes God has allowed upon his household. Nonetheless, Job is confident in his own standing before Yahweh. He has not lived a life of sin to bring these occurrences about. He has not walked in arrogance or pride. Therefore, although he realizes his life may be in jeopardy at the thought of speaking candidly with Almighty God, Job trusts in God's character to hear him out and to judge righteously.

III. JOB ASSERTS HIS TRUST (Job 13:15-28)

The prayers of Job are not clean-cut, tidy or nice. They often seem inappropriate or even unlike prayers at all. Job asks God some very difficult and impassioned questions. He is able to do this because his prayers are based on a remarkable and ongoing trust in the good, loving and gracious character of God. We see this in the second half of chapter 13, where Job asserts a bold and faithful trust in Yahweh alone.

A. Job's Ultimate Hope (vv. 15, 16)

15. Though he slay me, yet will I trust in him: but I will maintain mine own ways before him.

16. He also shall be my salvation: for an hypocrite shall not come before him.

Job has asked to speak in verse 13, though he realizes he takes his life into his own hands when addressing God himself. He does not take prayer lightly. Although Job recognizes the power of God to wipe him off the face of the earth in an instant, he has a greater hope than that. He knows he has been spared for a reason, and he wants to know what it is.

Job knows God is in control, which offers great despair, great hope, and great possibility simultaneously. The *despair* is in the fact that Job feels slain by God—"though he slay me." He fails to understand why God has unleashed such judgment upon him and his household. The *hope* is that there is no one else to help—"yet will I hope in him" (*NIV*). Job holds unswervingly to the faith he professes in Yahweh. The *possibility* is that he has the chance to defend his case before God, to vindicate his actions before the Holy One—"I will surely defend my ways to his face" (v. 15, *NIV*). This is not to insinuate God has made a mistake in allowing the calamities to occur in Job's life; rather it stands as a commitment to remain true to relationship with God.

For Job, prayer is not a one-sided act of communication. God listens and God can be swayed by human suffering. Job

Talk About It:
1. How strong was Job's faith in God?
2. How certain was Job of his own righteousness?

knows this, and also holds out hope that God will hear him because he claims God's sovereignty in his life and over the world in the first place. The godless person has no chance at all, but Job knows that is not his lot. He eagerly looks forward to the deliverance ("salvation," v. 16) he expects God to grant on his behalf. The same God who raised him up, then lowered him, will raise him up again.

B. Job's Humble Approach (vv. 17-22)

17. Hear diligently my speech, and my declaration with your ears.

18. Behold now, I have ordered my cause; I know that I shall be justified.

19. Who is he that will plead with me? for now, if I hold my tongue, I shall give up the ghost.

20. Only do not two things unto me: then will I not hide myself from thee.

21. Withdraw thine hand far from me: and let not thy dread make me afraid.

22. Then call thou, and I will answer: or let me speak, and answer thou me.

Talk About It:
1. What did Job say would silence his self-defense (v. 19)?
2. What two requests did Job make of God (vv. 20-22)?

In verses 17-19, Job continues to address his friends before directly praying to God (vv. 20ff.). He wants them to hear every word he says. They have distorted his history with God in so many ways that Job fears they may dilute the purity of his prayers. Because he trusts in God's character, Job fully expects vindication at God's hand. But if any of his friends can bring hard evidence, proof of some secret lifestyle of sin going on with Job, he will drop the matter. What is more, he will give up the fight and die without even addressing God. With no response from his friends, Job proceeds to approach the throne of God.

Job's request is measured. Although his prayer is anything but detached or diluted, he does not forget that he is in the lower position of supplicant. As such, he asks for two things in order to begin. First, he begs for mercy. Although we know from the book's opening chapters that it was the hand of Satan who specifically caused Job's various disasters, Job apparently knows little of Satan, who does not appear again after chapter 2. Even if Job did know something of Satan, we can be sure that Job also recognized God's ultimate control over and above the relatively miniscule accuser.

Job's Prayers
Job's best prayers were often untidy, questioning, and even assaulting. When we pray, we know God can handle our stuttering, our struggles, and our fears.

Job recognizes that God's hand has turned against him, and he asks for reprieve. Far from Satan's accusation that he would surely curse God, Job continues to trust that God has his best interests in mind even through this time of loss and despair. If God would grant Job some peace in the midst of this terrible trial, Job would then like to be summoned to speak and to hear God's answer. Job doesn't want to be in the dark anymore. He needs the wisdom, the counsel, and the comforting words of God. He needs to know some reason for this judgment.

C. Job's Bold Request (vv. 23-28)
(Job 13:23-28 is not included in the printed text.)
Trusting that God has granted Job a divine and tender audience, he is bold in his prayer. He asks God to count and to show him the offenses he has committed to merit this tragedy. He asks why God remains hidden and turns against him. He graphically describes the loneliness and terror in his heart that has him locked up like a prisoner. Job doesn't sugarcoat his request. He knows that God alone has the power to act, and since God is listening, He can handle Job's raw emotions. Although the answer will not come for almost 30 chapters, Job continues to pour out his heart boldly before God.

Talk About It:
1. What did Job ask God to show him (v. 23)?
2. What did Job call himself, and why (vv. 25, 26)?
3. How did Job describe himself in verse 28?

CONCLUSION
The story of Job is the story not only of God's constant sovereignty over the righteous but also of the positive effects on the life which trusts fully in that sovereignty. In the throes of sufferings that are difficult for most to even imagine, Job refuses to give up on God. He doesn't search for another religious option. He runs closer to, not further away from, the living God. As part of the Wisdom tradition of the Old Testament, Job joins a host of voices that praise the character and purposes of God, even when those purposes seem veiled to our human understanding.

GOLDEN TEXT CHALLENGE
"THOUGH HE [GOD] SLAY ME, YET WILL I TRUST IN HIM" (Job 13:15).
This is probably the greatest statement of faith in the Old Testament. Job's friends had contended he was being punished by God, and Job himself was bewildered by his suffering and could not know exactly why it had come upon him. All too often, people who suffer become bitter toward the Lord; not so with Job. He asserted that even if God should take his life, he would praise God with his dying breath. That is a supreme statement of faith, a willingness to trust God even if the outcome seems to be one of destruction rather than blessing.
Believers today should also come to the point where they can say, "Even though circumstances come into my life that are so terrible I cannot understand them, I will still keep complete confidence in God."

Daily Devotions:
M. God Keeps His Covenant
Deuteronomy 7:6-11
T. God's Enduring Faithfulness
Psalm 119:89-96
W. God's Unfailing Compassion
Lamentations 3:22-32
T. God Is Faithful to Heal
Luke 8:43-48
F. God's Promise Is Sure
Romans 4:16-22
S. Called by the Faithful God
1 Corinthians 1:4-9

Faithful in Adversity

Job 19:1-29

Unit Theme:
Learning Faithfulness From Job

Central Truth:
Through every adversity, the believer's hope is in God.

Focus:
Identify how Job remained faithful in adversity and affirm our hope in God.

Context:
Scholars place the date of the authorship of Job anywhere from the time of Abraham to the time the Jews returned from Babylonian captivity.

Golden Text:
"I know that my redeemer liveth" (Job 19:25).

Study Outline:
I. Sense of Despair (Job 19:1-12)
II. Feelings of Abandonment (Job 19:13-20)
III. Hope in the Redeemer (Job 19:21-29)

INTRODUCTION

Perhaps no one in the entire Old Testament endured so much heartbreaking loss in a single day without any recognizable cause as did Job. While the Old Testament is full of wars, revolutions, violence and intrigue, in most cases the suffering can be directed to an immediate cause. For instance, the people of Noah's day lost everything because of their increasing wickedness. King David lost his prized son by Bathsheba because of his sin against Uriah. Israel was conquered by Babylon and sent into exile because they refused to stop worshiping foreign idols. Job, however, lost his property, his wealth, his children, and his health without any clear reason. This is the crux of the argument between Job and his friends. They believed there must be sin in his life to account for these catastrophes. Job, however, discounted all other reasons outside of God alone—a cause for despair but also great hope.

It may surprise some to know that many Old Testament scriptures are full of despair. The prayers of the Psalms are not always prim and proper, much less overtly worshipful. The opening of Psalm 74 is one example of a prayer that sounds more like an assault: "Why have you rejected us forever, O God? Why does your anger smolder against the sheep of your pasture?" (v. 1, *NIV*). The Book of Lamentations is devoted fully to the despair of Jerusalem, which lies in ruins, its people exiled to a pagan land.

Yet despair is never the final word anywhere in the Bible. Biblical truth acknowledges the reality of despair, but couples it with the reality of faith in God that is constantly offered us. We must take both despair and hope seriously to be faithful to the God of the Scriptures.

I. SENSE OF DESPAIR (Job 19:1-12)

Once again, Job finds himself at a critical moment in the dialogue with and between his friends. The conversation intensifies as it lengthens on and on, with the friends taking turns pummeling Job with their theological certainties. Interestingly, Job—the hero of the narrative—is the one who claims to be the *least* certain about God's ways. He trusts in God's character alone, which brings him into despair when examined in the light of his calamities.

A. Response to Bildad (vv. 1-6)

1. Then Job answered and said,

2. How long will ye vex my soul, and break me in pieces with words?

3. These ten times have ye reproached me: ye are not ashamed that ye make yourselves strange to me.

4. And be it indeed that I have erred, mine error remaineth with myself.

5. If indeed ye will magnify yourselves against me, and plead against me my reproach:

6. Know now that God hath overthrown me, and hath compassed me with his net.

Job's speech in chapter 19 is an immediate reply to the words of Bildad in chapter 18. Bildad had mercilessly criticized Job to his face, offended by Job's dismissal of the friends' viewpoints. He offered an extended poem which represented the same argument that had been repeated from the start of the friends' speeches. He meticulously listed the consequences God brings upon the wicked person, insinuating Job's personal sin had resulted in the adversity at hand.

Job's immediate response to Bildad is not meant for him alone. In fact, the "ye" of verse 2 is plural, indicating that Job speaks to the entire group of four friends. He lashes out at them for their callousness. As if his situation isn't awful enough, they crush him with their merciless arguments. Job's reaction stems from the strong values associated with friendship and hospitality in the ancient world.

Because ancient peoples were almost constantly at risk at the hands of invading armies and militias, hospitality and friendship became the bonds that kept wider communities, especially in rural areas, protected. Friendship was the early form of political treaties and alliances. This preference for hospitality becomes the basis for many of the Ten Commandments and the Torah community laws in general. The Jews were expected to treat one another with kindness and fairness on the basis of hospitality. Later, Jesus himself commanded His disciples that when they performed ministry, they were to engage in hospitality with those who would provide a bed and food for them (Luke 10:7). It was

Talk About It:
1. How did Job describe what his friends had done to him (vv. 1-3)?
2. Rephrase Job's statement in verse 3 in your own words.
3. Whom did Job blame for his predicament?

hospitality that spread the Jesus movement. The point is that Job's supposed "friends" had broken all the rules of common hospitality. They had shown up at the peak of his pain and offered no help, only talk. In fact, Job 2:13 tells us they said no words to him for a full week after arriving at his side. Job preferred that they remain silent. Their words were of no comfort.

Job was consistently direct in combating the logic and overall message of his friends' speeches. He contended that he had not gone astray. He placed the reason for his suffering to be in God alone. God had opposed him for an unknown reason, and Job was sure God would soon return His favor to him. His friends scoffed at this notion, but Job held fast to his faith in the hope of Yahweh.

B. Alienation From God (vv. 7-12)

7. Behold, I cry out of wrong, but I am not heard: I cry aloud, but there is no judgment.

8. He hath fenced up my way that I cannot pass, and he hath set darkness in my paths.

9. He hath stripped me of my glory, and taken the crown from my head.

10. He hath destroyed me on every side, and I am gone: and mine hope hath he removed like a tree.

11. He hath also kindled his wrath against me, and he counteth me unto him as one of his enemies.

12. His troops come together, and raise up their way against me, and encamp round about my tabernacle.

Because Job rightly considers God to be at the center of his suffering, he has troubling words for Him. He doesn't explore the non-Jewish options that God is perhaps further away than he had thought or hoped. Even today, deists believe God created the universe and turned it over to us, with extremely limited personal involvement. Job won't buy such a thought. He believes God is intricately involved in his suffering, and so can also be convinced to display Himself in the middle of it.

"Justice" (v. 7, *NIV*) is a key theme of the friends' theology about God. Their point is that because God is just, the sinful are always punished and the righteous are always rewarded. To them, Job is an affront to God's justice, and he is suffering the consequences. Job also desires such a morally symmetrical universe, but he knows God is not so simple. If He were, Job would not be in this predicament. Still, he cries out for God's justice to vindicate him.

Job never blames the devil. He knows all things are subject to God and that God is fully aware of his suffering. Not only this, he presumes that God cares and is involved. For whatever reason, it is God who has hemmed Job in and kept him in the dark (v. 8). How he longs for some light to illuminate some reason, some logic for his downfall!

Talk About It:
1. In verse 7, what did Job cry out for?
2. Describe the actions Job felt God had taken against him (vv. 8-12).

Faithful in Adversity

It is so bad that God has even stripped Job's honor (v. 9). We cannot read over this without reflection, because honor is a massive concept to the ancients. In his study of the ancient Mediterranean basin, scholar Bruce Malina determined that honor was the chief value to be sought in society, especially by males. *Honor* is therefore broadly defined as "the value of a person in his or her own eyes (that is, one's claim to worth) plus that person's value in the eyes of his or her social group" (*The New Testament World*). Job's sense of personal worth, then, has been compromised by the suffering he attributes to God. God has taken away what matters most to him: his dignity and his honor, and left him with nothing to show for it.

Job does not consider God a passive spectator in his suffering (vv. 10-12). Instead, it is the intentionality of God that bothers Job the worst. God has deliberately and calculatedly gone after Job's *shalom*, leaving no hope—nothing but divine wrath. The rhetoric stops just short of a parent abusing a child, as God lays siege to Job's life like an invading army. Job gives a high place to God in the poem. He does not presume God has left him, but rather that God is just outside his tent. Job can only hope that God's presence will soon give life instead of death.

II. FEELINGS OF ABANDONMENT (Job 19:13-20)

Despair is both caused *by* and a cause *of* isolation. The two almost always go hand in hand. It is not surprising, then, that Job experiences the lowly emotions of abandonment as his speech wears on. He has already attributed his pain to the hand of God. Now we see the social consequences of Job's suffering, illustrated in graphic and painstaking detail.

A. Abandonment by His Friends (vv. 13-15)

13. He hath put my brethren far from me, and mine acquaintance are verily estranged from me.

14. My kinsfolk have failed, and my familiar friends have forgotten me.

15. They that dwell in mine house, and my maids, count me for a stranger: I am an alien in their sight.

One of the saddest aspects of Job's whole story is the fact that Eliphaz, Bildad, Zophar and Elihu are called his friends. The first three are the ones who rush to his side after Job's calamity hits. They have a history together—a cherished relationship. The friends are willing to take a week of their lives to mourn alongside Job. Yet when the exchange begins, the bonds between them are broken, and the relationship quickly turns icy. The hope that Job had for personal support is blown away like chaff in the wind, and he cries out in isolation and alienation.

Talk About It: How had Job's family members responded to his condition?

We have no external reason to believe Job is talking about literal brothers in this passage. Only his wife and children are mentioned in the narrative sections of the document. Given the fact that in these verses the brothers are listed alongside acquaintances, kinsmen, friends, guests and maidservants, it is likely that the language is figurative here for all those associates of Job. Yet there is probably also a literal component to Job's feelings of abandonment. Because of Job's loss of honor and social standing among his family, friends and community, it is probable that other people abandoned their relationship with him as well. If his own wife has turned against him, there is nothing to deny the possibility that Job does not have a single human friend left in the world. For the greatest man in the East, it is strange that only three friends show up to offer condolences at the deaths of his 10 children. Ancient peoples often abandoned those who had lost all honor to homelessness and begging, as we see in the Gospels and elsewhere. Job is apparently no different, and he feels the pain of losing friendships that once were so dear and life-giving to him.

B. Abandonment by His Household (vv. 16, 17)

16. I called my servant, and he gave me no answer; I intreated him with my mouth.

17. My breath is strange to my wife, though I intreated for the children's sake of mine own body.

Incredibly, Job's own servants no longer respond to his commands! In the ancient world, servants were always part of the larger household and often rose to prestigious positions. This is why there are several Old Testament commandments regarding the appropriate treatment of slaves. Not only has Job lost the respect of the household servants, but his very breath is repulsive to his own wife. (The odor of his breath had likely been altered by his illness.) His wife was an important part of the opening narrative, adding to Job's troubles by telling him to "curse God, and die" (2:9). The phrase "children of my own body" (see 19:17) could refer to Job's 10 children, who had left him through death, or to siblings who had turned their back on him.

Talk About It:
1. How did Job's servant treat him?
2. How was Job offensive ("strange") to his wife?

C. Abandonment by His Community (vv. 18-20)

18. Yea, young children despised me; I arose, and they spake against me.

19. All my inward friends abhorred me: and they whom I loved are turned against me.

20. My bone cleaveth to my skin and to my flesh, and I am escaped with the skin of my teeth.

Job has started the list of abandonment with a wide scope of his friends, narrowed it to his closer family, and now widens it again even further than before. His plight is known to the outside

Talk About It:
1. Who "despised" Job (v. 18), and who "abhorred" him (v. 19)?

Faithful in Adversity

world, and the nameless people out there are not at all treating him kindly. His statement "Even the little boys scorn me" (v. 18, *NIV*) is reminiscent of the story of Elisha in 2 Kings 2:23, when a group of youths began to mock the prophet because of his baldness. Job also has shaved his head, and now he is a laughingstock in his community. Little nameless boys at play make fun of him. He has lost the prestige of his former days.

It is not the abandonment of the distanced and fickle public, however, that pierces into Job's heart the most. The intimate friends sitting around him have shown him nothing but disgust (v. 19). No one he loves has stuck by him. Caught underneath the weight of his isolation, Job offers a terrible summary of his predicament in verse 20. Apparently Job has been fasting. Coupled with the diseased boils on his body, he is an emaciated frame of a man. The first phrase reads in Hebrew, "The skin of my flesh clings to the bone." Job's physical body is twisted and torn, which perfectly matches the state of his emotional trauma. He knows it is only by the will of Yahweh that he barely clings to life.

III. HOPE IN THE REDEEMER (Job 19:21-29)

Although the story of Job is unlike any other literary form in the Old Testament, it does not stand alone. In fact, it bears important resemblances to major New Testament themes. Namely, Job experiences the trials of death alongside the future hope of resurrection. In this sense he is an earlier type of Christ. Although there is no mention of the Messiah explicitly in Job, there is a great hope that the same God who allows suffering will ultimately triumph over it. Job's great hope in God lifts him and the book that bears his name above despair.

A. A Final Plea to His Friends (vv. 21, 22)

21. Have pity upon me, have pity upon me, O ye my friends; for the hand of God hath touched me.

22. Why do ye persecute me as God, and are not satisfied with my flesh?

Job has just completed his lamentation over all those who have abandoned him. These included members of his family, his household, his community, and his friends. The last group, of course, is the listeners. In a gripping display of vulnerability and raw pain, Job reaches out to them to beg for mercy.

Can his friends not see that what Job so desperately needs is pure friendship? He isn't benefited by their theological rationales; he needs their personal bonds! Instead, they provide no sympathy and no comfort. Job presents them as man-eating animals out to get him. He cannot plead with any more passion. He has lost all honor and dignity before them. He needs to break out of his isolation. Yet, when Zophar responds in chapter 20, he offers no consolation, only a defense of their speeches.

2. Explain the phrase "with the skin of my teeth" (v. 20).

"I get no respect from my dog. The other day, the dog went to the door and started to bark. I went over and opened it. The dog didn't want to go out; he wanted me to leave."
—Rodney Dangerfield

Talk About It:
What did Job plead for, and why would his friends not give it to him?

B. Job's Proclamation of Hope (vv. 23-27)

23. Oh that my words were now written! oh that they were printed in a book!

24. That they were graven with an iron pen and lead in the rock for ever!

25. For I know that my redeemer liveth, and that he shall stand at the latter day upon the earth:

26. And though after my skin worms destroy this body, yet in my flesh shall I see God:

27. Whom I shall see for myself, and mine eyes shall behold, and not another; though my reins be consumed within me.

This passage is one of the most memorable pronouncements in the book. It provides the material for numerous hymns throughout Christian history. The writer tips the reader off to the importance of what is to follow by Job's desire that the pronouncement be written down for history's sake (v. 23). The interjection "Oh" can also be taken as the interrogative "Who?" so that Job may be asking for someone to record his words. It may be that Job himself writes down what he has to say. Or this statement could be just a rhetorical device. No matter how the words get written down, Job wants to be remembered by them. This statement defines and summarizes the incredible faith of Job in the face of tremendous adversity.

Job announces that God has not ignored his faithful servant (v. 25). Although it seems all is lost, there is something and Someone greater than Job's tragedies in the mix. There is a Redeemer on his side. *Redemption* is not only a religious term, but also relates to the field of ancient economics, whereby a redeemer would purchase a plot of land often to reclaim it for his ancestral heritage. God has not abandoned Job, but will come to reclaim him on the earth.

The next line is a bit cryptic and should not be taken out of context (v. 26). By all indications it refers to Job's hope that he will see Yahweh in the afterlife with his own eyes. But this does not take Job's focus off of his present condition. The Book of Job does not present a heavenly theology which teaches that earthly wrongs will only be set right in the afterlife. Rather, it is focused on earthly justice. Note that Job first proclaims that his Redeemer will be found upon the earth. And Job then says he will see Him after death. The power of Job's announcement is in the existence of the God he claims—a God significantly distinct from the one imagined by his friends. It is this God whom Job yearns for with all of his strength.

C. Judgment on Job's Accusers (vv. 28, 29)

28. But ye should say, Why persecute we him, seeing the root of the matter is found in me?

29. Be ye afraid of the sword: for wrath bringeth the punishments of the sword, that ye may know there is a judgment.

reins (v. 27)—heart

Talk About It:
1. What did Job desire, and why (vv. 23, 24)?
2. What was Job certain about (vv. 25, 26)?
3. What did Job's heart long for (v. 27)?

Steady Faith
The life of Abraham Lincoln is a phenomenal record of leadership and faithfulness in the face of sullen adversity. President Lincoln faced the eruption of the Civil war, the lack of competent generals, the death of his son, and the mental illness of his wife. Yet he maintained a steady faith in God and saw the United States through its darkest days with character and composure. Biblical faith can always stand through difficult earthly circumstances.

Faithful in Adversity

Immediately following Job's majestic statement of faith in God's ultimate sovereignty, he turns the tables back on his friends. They are still contending that Job's sin has caused God's disfavor, yet Job's faith claims otherwise. Therefore, Job cautions his friends about their own candidacy for God's judgment. Since they feel God is unable to harm them, they put restraints on God's sovereignty. The chapter closes by exposing their hypocrisy, especially as it is cast in the light of Job's incredible faith.

Talk About It:
What did Job say his friends should be fearful of, and why (vv. 28, 29)?

CONCLUSION

The Book of Job is an assembly of the raw materials of real life. Perhaps nowhere in Scripture do the graphic descriptions of personal suffering intertwine so jaggedly with the ultimate hope in the God of the universe. In this sense, the book is a kind of microcosm, or miniature replica, of the whole of Scripture combined. The spiritual life does not come to us in a linear, packaged, step-by-step process anymore than the Bible does. Real faith is messy, just like Job discovered and his book reveals. Yet it is also the kind of faith that honors the character of God, because it is boldly authentic.

GOLDEN TEXT CHALLENGE

"I KNOW THAT MY REDEEMER LIVETH" (Job 19:25).

This verse arises from a heart that has no other course but to leap to hope and faith. Job is a modern man at the abyss of eternity and is compelled to finally trust in this God who has made him. Those opening words of the verse are recorded by Handel in the *Messiah* in the song "I Know That My Redeemer Liveth."

The word translated "Redeemer" is the Hebrew *go'el*. It has a rich usage in the Old Testament. In the *Anchor Bible*, Marvin Pope lists some ways in which it was used:

- The kinsman who redeemed his relative from slavery (Leviticus 25:48)
- The kinsman who regained family property (v. 48)
- The kinsman who would provide an heir by proxy with a widow (Ruth 4:3-6)

The emphasis falls upon the role of the kinsman as interceding for those who are powerless and oppressed (Proverbs 23:10, 11). It was used of the Lord in Exodus 6:6; 15:13, and used to indicate His role in redeeming from exile (Jeremiah 50:34). In Psalm 103:4 it was used to describe the Lord redeeming an individual from death.

Thus, it is easy to see why Job used this word. It is a powerful word of hope in the face of despair. Here was a man who knew that redemption was the final word in his life. He could trust his Creator to bring deliverance from the horrors of this life.

Daily Devotions:
M. Delivered From Adversity
   Exodus 12:29-36
T. Triumph Over Opposition
   1 Samuel 17:41-54
W. God Will Deliver
   Psalm 56:1-13
T. God's Grace Is Sufficient
   2 Corinthians 12:7-10
F. Heroes of Faith
   Hebrews 11:32-40
S. Faith Is the Victory
   1 John 5:1-5

God Is Merciful

Job 42:1-17

Unit Theme:
Learning Faithfulness
From Job

Central Truth:
God's mercy is ever-
lasting and available
to all.

Focus:
Acknowledge God's
faithfulness and thank
Him for His mercy.

Context:
Scholars place the
date of the authorship
of Job anywhere from
the time of Abraham
to the time the Jews
returned from
Babylonian captivity.

Golden Text:
"The Lord is long-
suffering, and of great
mercy, forgiving iniquity
and transgression"
(Numbers 14:18).

Study Outline:
I. Humbled Before
   God
   (Job 42:1-6)
II. Accepted by God
    (Job 42:7-9)
III. Blessed by God
     (Job 42:10-17)

INTRODUCTION

Initially it may seem strange to characterize the Book of Job as a story about God's mercy. After all, it appears to focus on the unfair suffering of a righteous man who is caught in the middle of a cosmic duel between God and the devil. Eventually Job's losses are restored back to him in the final chapter, but his 10 children are not brought back from the grave, and Job receives almost no concrete answers to the questions he and his friends have been asking for some 40 chapters. Instead, God offers His very self as the reason for Job's suffering and the reason for the existence of all things. It is not only in God's final act of restoration that we see God's mercy, but in the truth that humanity finds its home in God.

The Russian novelist Fyodor Mikhaylovich Dostoyevsky wrote, "The love of God is a harsh and dangerous love." Surely this gets to the heart of God's character in the Book of Job. Job is not looking for easy answers any more than he is looking for an easy God. His vehement disagreement with his friends centers on their effort to put God in a box—to diminish God down to a formula that can be manipulated by man. Instead, God remains the holy One of love and mercy, but it is not an easy love and mercy. God's love demands that all things return back to Him. He claims all things for Himself, even human suffering. This is a difficult lesson learned by Job, even in the end.

In Hebrew thought, God is a personal being of tremendous passions. He is a God that can be moved emotionally by the situations of people. The Greeks later conceived of a static notion of an almost mathematical form for god, who sat distant from man in perfection and glory. In contrast, the God of the Old Testament is a dynamic being who is always taking His creation by surprise. The ultimate surprise, of course, was Christ himself, whose suffering surpassed even Job's, and that many times over.

I. HUMBLED BEFORE GOD (Job 42:1-6)

Reaching the final chapter of Job is like reaching the end of a monumental piece of art, like the last panel in the Sistine Chapel or the final page of a classic novel. The book is full of so many emotions, so many twists and turns that keep us feeling the pain alongside of Job. The pain Job feels is the pain we all feel when we wonder where God is in the midst of our struggle. This final chapter is more than a "happy ending." To treat it so lightly is not to do justice to the complexity of the book's deep theology. In fact, plenty is never answered in the Book of Job. What *is* answered is Job's posture of humility before God, and God's loving concern over humanity.

A. Job Admits His Ignorance (vv. 1-3)

1. Then Job answered the Lord, and said,

2. I know that thou canst do every thing, and that no thought can be withholden from thee.

3. Who is he that hideth counsel without knowledge? therefore have I uttered that I understood not; things too wonderful for me, which I knew not.

Finally, in chapter 38, Yahweh himself appears. He has had enough of Elihu's heady ramblings. He can bear Job's grievous suffering no longer. For four chapters, He questions Job about his knowledge. Does he have any idea how to speak creation into existence, how to make mountains, how to breathe life into animals? Does he recognize the hilarity of any man attempting to instruct God in wisdom, given that wisdom originates with God alone? He asks dozens of such questions as Job remains silent. Then, Job carefully responds with the last piece of poetry in the book.

Before Job can debate about the origin of suffering in the universe, he has to acknowledge the Creator of the universe (vv. 1, 2). God is above the philosophies and theologies we use to make sense of Him. He alone is capable of doing all things. And when He does something, no man can stop it. It may seem like the obvious, but for Job it is the first step of learning to accept true humility.

In many newer translations, the introductory words "You asked" are added onto the Hebrew in verse 3 to clarify the direction of the question. The question quoted is exactly what God said to Job when He first revealed Himself in 38:2. Job has carefully listened to the word of God. He goes back to God's initial declaration, and it fills him with conviction. Job had no right to speak to God in the first place, much less to demand that He accommodate Himself to categories of human wisdom. The right to pray is, in itself, the merciful gift of God. As a result, Job claims total ignorance in the presence of Almighty God.

Talk About It:
1. According to verse 2, what had Job learned about God?
2. What did Job realize he had done wrong (v. 3)?

Job had attempted to speak of God's character, and had *not* done so incorrectly. But Job had no right to even breach the subject, apart from God's mercy to give him that right. The divine realm is unfathomable for Job to converse about. The word for "wonderful" is first found in the mouth of Job himself in 5:9 ("marvellous") to describe the miracles of God. This description has now come full circle, and not a second too late for Job.

B. Job Repents (vv. 4-6)

4. Hear, I beseech thee, and I will speak: I will demand of thee, and declare thou unto me.

5. I have heard of thee by the hearing of the ear: but now mine eye seeth thee.

6. Wherefore I abhor myself, and repent in dust and ashes.

Job's admission of unawareness and ignorance in the presence of the Lord quickly turns to full-blown repentance. Job realizes that expressing sorrow alone is not enough. He has overstepped his boundaries by portending to even speak on God's level. This process again begins with his recollection of the words of Yahweh (v. 4).

Job displays his conviction and repentant spirit by again assuring God that he has heard His every word. Once more he refers to the opening of the Lord's speech, where God commands Job to "brace yourself" for His questions (38:3, *NIV*). All along Job has been questioning God, and God shows him the futility of such words. It is not that God criticizes Job for speaking or asking difficult questions. However, God's wisdom is at a level far above what any human could understand. The Wisdom books of Job, Ecclesiastes and Proverbs were not written simply to dispense helpful theological and practical truths; they were written as impressive testimonies to the greatness of God. Here Yahweh claims to transcend the entire enterprise of wisdom altogether. At long last, Job comes to this realization.

Job's perspective has been dramatically and eternally altered. It was easier to simply hear and speak about God. At that point, Job could manipulate God as just another piece of debatable information. God was something that existed in the confines of his own ability to comprehend Him mentally. But now he has seen and experienced God, and his life is changed (42:5). He doesn't describe anything about God, for to do so would be laughably inadequate. But seeing God has put his own words and the ramblings of his friends into their proper perspective. He now believes in the sovereignty of God with his whole heart. We are reminded of a similar expression by the risen Jesus to doubting Thomas in John 20:29: "Because you have seen me, you have believed" (*NIV*). Job gets an amazing chance to experience God, and he responds appropriately.

The massive poem—the many speeches, questions, and stretches of dialogue—ends with Job 42:6. Job is completely overwhelmed by the glory and power of God. He can stand His presence no longer. He beats his breast in repentance and closes his mouth. What Job received from this entire experience of suffering is the gift of humility—a humility so deep that it eluded his friends. The one introduced in chapter 1 as the greatest man of the East is now the most humble, reminding us of Jesus' teaching that greatness is found at its best in the most humble circumstances and people.

Some scholars believe that the epilogue to the book was added later when the final form of Job was edited. Thankfully we have the information it gives about Job's restoration, but imagine if the book ended here at verse 6. It would still be a powerful expression of God's loving concern for man and man's responsibility to walk rightly before God.

II. ACCEPTED BY GOD (Job 42:7-9)

After 40-plus chapters of poetry, the book closes with a surprisingly short prose description of the aftermath of God's appearance. We might expect more information about all characters, but we do get the necessities. God remains the central character, directing the events of Job and his friends. The tone immediately shifts. At the close of the poetry, Job humbles himself down to dust and ashes. Here in the prose, however, God begins the process of raising him back up to a place even greater than his former state of life and leadership.

A. Vindicated Over His Friends (v. 7)

7. And it was so, that after the Lord had spoken these words unto Job, the Lord said to Eliphaz the Temanite, My wrath is kindled against thee, and against thy two friends: for ye have not spoken of me the thing that is right, as my servant Job hath.

God's focus immediately swings not to responding to Job's prayer, but to dealing with Job's friends. They are not going to get off with a slap on the wrist. There is too much at stake to overlook their arrogance and harsh treatment of their friend Job.

We can only imagine the peace Job must have felt at the pronouncement of these words of vindication. It is a common cliché to talk today about "the patience of Job," but there actually isn't much in the story itself to denote that he was a particularly patient man. In fact, most of his speeches are directed to the absence of God, in the attempt to get God to *hurry up* and provide an answer. When the answer comes, however, we see that Eliphaz, Bildad and Zophar spoke irrationally. Yet Elihu does not bear the brunt of God's judgment. Although he is the youngest of all the men, in chapter 32 he criticized his friends for condemning Job.

> "He upholds the whole creation, founded the earth, and still sustains it by the word of His power. What can He not do in the affairs of families and kingdoms, far beyond our conception and expectation, who hangs the earth upon nothing?"
> —**Matthew Henry**

Talk About It:
How did the Lord contrast Job with his three friends (v. 7)?

"[Elihu] is the main human solver of the problem of the book, which ultimately is resolved, by Jehovah's appearance, into a question of His absolute sovereignty that cannot err. Elihu's reasoning is not condemned, as is that of the three elder friends and previous speakers, for whom and not for Elihu Job is directed to sacrifice and intercede" (*Fausset's Bible Dictionary*).

It is notable that God does not arbitrarily throw each of the friends into the same category. He recognizes Eliphaz as the ringleader and deals with him directly. The three friends' sin lies in the incorrect things they said about God. They put God into a box, claiming that God's judgment was aroused by Job's wickedness. The fact that Job has not spoken incorrectly about God is key when it comes to understanding the previous verses in which Job repents in dust and ashes. He is not repenting for improper doctrine about God. In fact, he gets this correct. He is repenting for inadequate posture toward God, as if proper doctrine were the only thing needed to appropriately approach the heavenly throne room. Job's friends, however, have a more sobering type of repentance to endure.

> "Job's false sense of God's estrangement had been the first evil corrected. Now the defamation of Job's name among men is dealt with, and afterwards family and wealth are restored."
> —*Wycliffe Bible Commentary*

B. Job's Friends Forgiven (vv. 8, 9)

8. Therefore take unto you now seven bullocks and seven rams, and go to my servant Job, and offer up for yourselves a burnt-offering; and my servant Job shall pray for you: for him will I accept: lest I deal with you after your folly, in that ye have not spoken of me the thing which is right, like my servant Job.

9. So Eliphaz the Temanite and Bildad the Shuhite and Zophar the Naamathite went, and did according as the Lord commanded them: the Lord also accepted Job.

Incredibly, God himself takes the initiative to restore Job's ignorant friends back to a place of righteousness before Him. These are the ones who have criticized, harassed, and kicked God's servant Job when he was already down and bleeding. But God loves them and desires the best for them. His method for their reconciliation, however, had to be humiliating for these high-minded friends.

Talk About It:
1. What were the three friends commanded to do?
2. What did Job do for his friends?

When reading any Biblical document in either Testament, it should always be remembered that none of them were principally written for individual readers. Because so few common people in the ancient world were literate, Biblical documents were written to be read and performed out loud to groups of people. In light of this, scriptures such as verse 8 had to be humorous. The audience has heard many chapters of conflict as the friends criticized Job, and now he is the one God selects to pray over his friends in order to restore their purity. Of course, this is also directed toward Job's spiritual health. God will not allow a bitter root to secure itself in Job's heart and to taint his

God Is Merciful

new life. Reconciliation with God means reconciliation with one another, and God sets this in motion with Job in the spotlight. As if to rub salt in the friends' wounds, God repeats the fact that they got all their facts wrong, while His servant Job achieved success.

Eliphaz, Bildad and Zophar march off to make seven (the number of completion) costly sacrifices of two different animals and to receive Job's prayer of reconciliation (v. 9). As promised, the gracious God of heaven accepts Job's prayer, recognizing his right standing before Him. Everyone benefits from Job's righteousness, including his unrighteous friends.

III. BLESSED BY GOD (Job 42:10-17)

Job has been reconciled to God along with his friends, and God has even orchestrated their mode of forgiveness to ensure that they are adequately reconciled to one another. The slate is wiped clean, and now God can begin the rebuilding process of Job's life. He doesn't start immediately with wealth or children, but with something that Job undoubtedly craves far more—community. He has been isolated for far too long. God now blesses Job with one of His greatest gifts—meaningful human relationships.

A. Social Standing Restored (vv. 10, 11)

10. And the Lord turned the captivity of Job, when he prayed for his friends: also the Lord gave Job twice as much as he had before.

11. Then came there unto him all his brethren, and all his sisters, and all they that had been of his acquaintance before, and did eat bread with him in his house: and they bemoaned him, and comforted him over all the evil that the Lord had brought upon him: every man also gave him a piece of money, and every one an earring of gold.

This section begins with a summary statement that encompasses the rest of the epilogue. The action doesn't pick up again until Job accomplishes the final task God had given him—to pray for the restoration of his friends. We do not know whether this was difficult or joyful for Job. One can imagine his prayer either way. Whatever the case, he got the job done and so embarks on his new life. That life is epitomized by a double portion of blessing. This prosperity begins in Job's social sphere.

In chapter 19, Job had lamented the fact that everyone in his social sphere, both near and far, had turned against him. Now, however, his relatives and friends—male and female alike—arrive to restore him to the community. They had previously abandoned him, leaving him to mourn his great losses alone, perhaps expecting that his death was imminent in the face of such sufferings. But now the community gathers to celebrate

"If you hold anything against anyone, forgive him, so that your Father in heaven may forgive you your sins."
—Mark 11:25
(NIV)

Talk About It:
1. Describe the turning point for Job (v. 10).
2. How were Job's relationships affected (v. 11)?

the restoration of Job at his own house. They bring greetings and words of comfort and consolation, and also gifts of gold and silver. Notably, Job is still mourning to some degree, even if it is not ceremonial mourning. God's blessings, though immediate, do not make the pain of the loss go away, and he needs the comfort of his family and friends. The gifts of precious metals that they bring do not appear to come out of benevolence as though Job had such needs. They are just another symbol for the personal, financial and social resurrection of Job.

B. Job's Household Restored (vv. 12-15)

12. So the Lord blessed the latter end of Job more than his beginning: for he had fourteen thousand sheep, and six thousand camels, and a thousand yoke of oxen, and a thousand she asses.

13. He had also seven sons and three daughters.

14. And he called the name of the first, Jemima; and the name of the second, Kezia; and the name of the third, Keren-happuch.

15. And in all the land were no women found so fair as the daughters of Job: and their father gave them inheritance among their brethren.

After bringing the story of Job to a new height of jubilance and celebration, the writer describes the amazing restoration of Job's household. As the primary unit of communal living in the ancient world, the household consisted of an extended family's entire collection of wealth, headed by a patriarch. On these terms, Job enjoys unprecedented financial prosperity.

In the prologue, where Job is described as the greatest man in the East, he possesses nowhere near this amount of wealth. In fact, every livestock holding of Job's has been completely doubled, a 100 percent return on his former net worth. His children are restored to the same number as before, yet we cannot help but continue to hurt for Job in this area. Livestock can be replaced without pulling on the heartstrings, and Job was no doubt thankful for God's blessing on his new offspring. Yet he must have continued to miss his previous children, who were so quickly and violently taken from his household and the earth. Even so, his love for his new family is expressed by his naming of the daughters. *Jemimah* means "dove," *Keziah* means "fragrance," and *Keren-Happuch* refers to a dark setting for precious stones. The beauty of Job's daughters was unequaled.

Interestingly, in the prologue Job's greatness was said to be famous in all the land. Here his children carry on his good name. Job has plenty of wealth to leave them a large inheritance, even for his daughters, which was rare in the ancient world, denoting extensive financial security.

Jemima (jeh-MY-muh), Kezia (kih-ZYE-uh), Keren-happuch (KER-un-HAP-uk)—v. 14—Job's three daughters born after his restoration

Talk About It:
1. Why do you suppose God doubled Job's possessions?
2. Why do you suppose there is more emphasis on Job's three new daughters than his seven new sons?

Amazing Story
"Amazing Grace" was written by the most unlikely of persons. John Newton was captaining a slave ship in 1748 when he almost sank. Crying out to God, he felt God change his heart. Reflecting on that experience, he penned that great hymn, and went on to become a champion for the cessation of slavery in Britain.

God Is Merciful

C. God Restores Job's Life (vv. 16, 17)

16. After this lived Job an hundred and forty years, and saw his sons, and his sons' sons, even four generations.

17. So Job died, being old and full of days.

In a final testimony to the legacy of Job, the writer depicts the complete restoration of Job's physical health. Long gone are the days when Job must scrape disease-ridden, puss-filled sores from his flesh in order to survive the physical infliction that threatened to end his life. He now enjoys optimum health for the remainder of his days.

Talk About It:
How did God show His faithfulness to Job?

An additional 140 years is obviously a huge spread of time, reminiscent of the days of Genesis in which people lived far longer lives. We are not told how old Job was during the time of the tragedies of the book—just that he received another 140 years and saw the fourth generation of his grandchildren. That is, he was a great-grandfather three times over. It is a great compliment in the Old Testament for one to die elderly. It denotes wisdom, and it is a fitting end to this Wisdom book.

CONCLUSION

In the end, the suffering of Job is doubly compensated with blessings that overflow in his relationships, his finances, and his physical health. Seen as a whole, the story is lifted from the depths of despair to the possibilities of hope to the endurance of reward. At its close, the reader is not left to doubt the justice of God. Although His purposes for suffering are not revealed, His love for true servants is tried and true. This is the great hope that the book of Job offers. It reminds us that God is always merciful, even during the greatest of human trials.

GOLDEN TEXT CHALLENGE

"THE LORD IS LONGSUFFERING, AND OF GREAT MERCY, FORGIVING INIQUITY AND TRANSGRESSION" (Numbers 14:18).

The setting for this verse is the Wilderness of Paran. The children of Israel have rejected the faith-filled report of Joshua and Caleb, who said they should boldly advance into the promised land of Canaan, in favor of the fear-filled report of the other 10 spies. The people want to murder Joshua and Caleb and go back to Egypt. But God won't let that happen. He is ready to wipe out the rebellious Israelites until Moses intercedes for them. In his intercession, Moses prays, "The Lord is slow to anger, abounding in love and forgiving sin and rebellion" (Numbers 14:18, *NIV*).

This is unlike the portrait of God painted by Job's friends, which was a stern, harsh Deity. While God will not overlook sin, as the rest of Numbers 14:18 declares, He is ready to pardon sin and restore the rebellious when repentance takes place.

Daily Devotions:
M. God's Mercies Are Great
Nehemiah 9:24-31
T. God's Abundant Mercy
Psalm 86:1-7
W. God's Mercy Endures Forever
Psalm 136:1-9
T. God Chooses Mercy
Romans 9:14-24
F. God Is Rich in Mercy
Ephesians 2:1-10
S. God's Mercy Is Available
Hebrews 4:12-16

Introduction to Winter Quarter

The theme for the first unit is "1 and 2 Corinthians," focusing on the following needs of the local church: preaching the Cross, having Christ's mind, discerning Christ's body, having Christ's Spirit, living in Christ's love, Christ's indwelling presence, and the grace of giving.

The expositions were written by the Reverend Dr. J. Ayodeji Adewuya (Ph.D., University of Manchester), who is an associate professor of New Testament at the Church of God Theological Seminary in Cleveland, Tennessee. Prior to joining the seminary, Dr. Adewuyua served as a missionary in the Philippines for 17 years. He is an active member of the Society for Biblical Literature, Wesleyan Theological Society, and the Society for Pentecostal Studies. He is the author of *Holiness and Community in 2 Corinthians 6:14—7:1.*

The Christmas study (lesson 3) was compiled by Lance Colkmire (see biographical information on page 16).

The second unit is "Profiles of Faith in Christ," studying several New Testament personalities: John the Baptist, Nicodemus, a blind man, a desperate father, a determined mother, and a sinful woman.

The expositions were written by the Reverend Dr. Jerald Daffe (B.A., M.A., D.Min.), who earned his degrees from Northwest Bible College, Wheaton College Graduate School, and Western Conservative Baptist Seminary. An ordained minister in the Church of God, Dr. Daffe has served in the pastoral ministry for 10 years and has been a faculty member at Northwest Bible College and Lee University for 30 years. Dr. Daffe received the Excellence in Advising Award at Lee University. His books include *Speaking in Tongues, Life Challenges for Men,* and *Revival: God's Plan for His People.*

First Corinthians
by Charles W. Conn

The Pagan City

The ancient city of Corinth was one of the most unlikely cities ever to receive the gospel of the Lord Jesus Christ. It was strategically located at the narrow Isthmus of Corinth, a land bridge that connected the northern and southern sections of Greece. This meant that all land travel north and south had to pass through the city. Corinth was also a seaport so located that sea traffic east and west from Rome to the eastern Mediterranean normally passed through it. As a result, the city became a melting pot of many peoples and cultures, and religions with a "mongrel population" of many races.

It is estimated that about 700,000 inhabitants lived in the metropolis, of which 200,000 were free men and 500,000 were slaves. Numerous temples were in Corinth, dedicated to the worship of many gods and goddesses. By far the most popular were the deities of fertility, such as the Egyptian Isis, the Greek Aphrodite, and the Roman Venus. Such a temple stood on the peak of the Acrocorinthus mountain that towered above the city, and 1,000 temple prostitutes served its purposes. Numerous other fertility cults had their temple prostitutes who turned the seaport sections of the city into immoral bedlam.

The Corinthian people were aggressive in business and dissolute in their personal lives. The active commerce of Corinth had made them wealthy, and their wealth caused them to live sensual and luxurious lives. To "Corinthianize," or "to live like a Corinthian," was a byword in that ancient time. Yet, despite their love of amusements and luxuries, the Corinthians had pretensions of knowledge. Just as "to live like a Corinthian" meant to abandon all pretensions of moral decency, so the term "Corinthian words" implied proud claims of knowledge and culture.

Paul's Ministry in Corinth

Of all the cities that Paul ever visited, Corinth seemed to be the most unlikely to heed the Word of Christ. Yet it was to this city that the apostle came with a heavy heart and the message of the Cross.

Paul entered Corinth after a series of unhappy events. He had already visited four cities in Greece and had encountered extreme difficulty in each of them. In Philippi he had been beaten and unjustly imprisoned (Acts 16:19-24). In Thessalonica he had been slandered and driven from the city (17:5-10). In Berea he had been hounded by the Thessalonian Jews who followed him with their slanders and persecution (vv. 13, 14). In Athens, his ministry had been interrupted with mockery and ridicule of greater intensity than he had ever faced before (v. 32). There, for the first time in his life, Paul faced defeat and left the city without establishing a church. One can only imagine the pain with which he left Athens and traveled 40 miles south into Corinth.

In Corinth, Paul made his way to the Jewish community where he resided with a couple named Aquila and Priscilla. The apostle supported himself by tentmaking (18:1-3), and the Macedonia churches, Philippi and Thessalonica, sent him some assistance (2 Corinthians 11:9), which enabled him to preach the gospel freely. As he had done in other places, Paul preached in the synagogue and converted some of the Jews, but it seems that he was more successful in converting the Greeks to Christ. The Jewish leaders then commenced a campaign of harassment and persecution, even taking Paul to trial for his activities (Acts 18:4-17). The conflict became so sharp in Corinth that Paul finally turned his back on the Jews and began in earnest his ministry among the Gentiles. The Christian church was established next door to the Jewish synagogue, a situation that perpetuated the tension between the two groups.

The Purpose of 1 Corinthians

When Paul left Corinth after 18 months in the city, he went into Ephesus, where he remained for a short visit before returning to his home base in Antioch (Acts 18:18-22). Then he returned to Ephesus on his third missionary journey and remained there for three years. It was during those years in Ephesus that Paul received word from Corinth and sent a letter to the Corinthians (1 Corinthians 5:9), dealing with immorality that existed in the church. This epistle has not been preserved for us. The Corinthians replied to it, however, with a letter of their own, in which they sought advice about numerous church problems (7:1). A group of the Corinthian Christians, led by a person named Chloe, also contacted Paul with reports of wrangling and division in the church (1:11).

What we call 1 Corinthians is Paul's reply to the letter from the church and the report of Chloe. Still the situation in Corinth did not appreciably improve, but probably worsened. It is inferred from 2 Corinthians 2:1 that Paul returned to Corinth to try to correct the strife that reigned in the church. He then returned to Ephesus, where he wrote a very severe letter which caused the Corinthians a great deal of pain (2 Corinthians 2:4; 7:7, 8), but that letter has not been preserved for us. Following this hard letter, Paul received better news from Corinth, and it seemed that the situation had improved. It was at this juncture that he wrote a fourth letter to the Corinthians, the one which we know as 2 Corinthians.

Paul's four letters to the Corinthian church were as follows: (1) the "previous letter" (1 Corinthians 5:9); (2) 1 Corinthians; (3) the "severe letter" (2 Corinthians 7:7, 8); (4) 2 Corinthians. Only two of these letters have been preserved for us by the Holy Spirit. All of this correspondence and visiting reveals the great attention required by the Corinthian church. It has correctly been called his "problem church."

Summary of 1 Corinthians

The Spirit of Corinth the city was reflected in the Corinthian church. Paul gives us a good appraisal of the people in his letter to them (see 1:26-31; 6:9-11). The Corinthian congregation was made up of those who had been fornicators, idolaters, adulterers, homosexuals, abusers of themselves with mankind (perverts), thieves, covetous, drunkards, revilers and extortioners. The Jews, such as Sosthenes, were not of this sort. The fact that many were, however, helps to explain the troubles that persisted in the church. This should not have been, for Paul emphasizes to them that they had been washed, sanctified, justified in the name of the Lord Jesus, and by the Spirit of our God.

The entire epistle deals with errors and heresies that exist among the Corinthians. Following his salutation, Paul goes immediately into the evils that exist. Chapters 1–4 deal generally with the matter of division in the church. They are split into four factions, which Paul points out to be contrary to the nature of Christ and a sign of their carnal immaturity. Paul takes no pleasure in the fact that some of the people claim to be his adherents, but he rather emphasizes that the Corinthians belong only to Christ. Even Paul himself, and the other apostles, are nothing more than servants of the Lord.

Chapter 5 deals with a sordid case of immorality. Instead of condoning the evil of the incestuous member as they have done, Paul tells the Corinthians that the guilty person should be excommunicated from the church lest the leaven of his evil spread. It seems that the church tolerated in its company some who were fornicators, covetous, idolaters, railers, drunkards, and extortioners (1 Corinthians 5:11). If the Corinthians are to be true Christians, they must separate themselves from such evil, and put it out of the church.

In chapter 6, Paul deals with the Corinthians' improper practice of taking one another to law. They should find Christian judges and mediators to settle their disputes, for the practice of going to heathen law is a sign to the world of broken fellowship within the church. The Corinthians did not understand the sanctity of the human body (6:9-20) and regarded it as a vessel for sensual satisfaction. Instead, declares Paul, the body is the temple of the Holy Ghost.

Beginning with chapter 7, Paul answers many questions the church had sent to him. These questions concern marriage, divorce and celibacy (7:1-40), food offered to idols (8:1-13), attitudes toward support of the ministry (9:1-27), associations with idolatry (10:1-33), the role of women in the church (11:2-16), and the right way to observe the Lord's Supper (vv. 17-33).

Chapters 12–14 consider the subject of spiritual gifts. Even in the exercise of these gifts, the Corinthians had become confused and in error. Paul deals at length with these problems and states that those who have one gift should not consider themselves superior to those who have another. They are all of the same Spirit and work for the same purpose. In chapter 13 Paul writes some of the most sublime words in the entire Word of God, in his statement on the greatness of divine love. Love, he declares, is superior to all other evidences of the Christian's life. Chapter 14 reveals that Paul in no way discourages the presence and exercise of the gifts, but only endeavors to correct the misunderstandings regarding them.

Chapter 15 deals extensively with the nature of the resurrection of the dead. The question had arisen, "What sort of body will Christians have in the resurrection?" (see v. 35). Paul's answer is that it will be a spiritual body, which God will give as it pleases Him. The resurrection of the dead will be the final triumph of spirituality over carnality, and immortality over mortality. The hymn of praise on that day will be: "Death is swallowed up in victory. O death, where is thy sting? O grave, where is thy victory? . . . Thanks be to God, which giveth us the victory through our Lord Jesus Christ" (vv. 54-57).

Chapters 12–16 are very important. They show that the spiritual life is the only remedy for the carnal life. The correct use of spiritual gifts, the constant presence of divine love and the abiding hope of the resurrection will cure any church from its carnality and worldliness. Just as these things ere the answers to the Corinthian ills, so they are the answer to the ills of the church today.

The Message of the Cross

1 Corinthians 1:18 through 2:2

Unit Theme:
1 and 2 Corinthians

Central Truth:
It is wise to understand and accept Christ's redemptive work.

Focus:
Distinguish between worldly and godly wisdom and follow the way of the Cross.

Context:
Paul wrote his first letter to the Corinthian church from Ephesus around A.D. 59.

Golden Text:
"The preaching of the cross is to them that perish foolishness; but unto us which are saved it is the power of God" (1 Corinthians 1:18).

Study Outline:
I. Foolishness of Worldly Wisdom (1 Corinthians 1:18-21)
II. Christ Crucified (1 Corinthians 1:22-25)
III. Redemption Through Christ (1 Corinthians 1:26—2:2)

INTRODUCTION

In 1 Corinthians 1:10-17, Paul appeals for unity in the church. In verse 18 he moves on a different argumentative tack, launching into an extended discussion, in which, on the one hand, he teaches on the significance and meaning of the Cross and, on the other hand, shows that the prideful confidence of the Corinthians in human wisdom is contrary to the gospel. The basic theme of verses 18-31 is the opposition between human/worldly wisdom and God's wisdom, or the "word of the cross" (v. 18, *NASB*).

Although not explicitly stated, there were probably some within the Corinthian congregation that were putting inordinate emphasis on "wisdom" as understood by the world of that day. They prided themselves in their possession of human wisdom, reflecting the Greeks' fascination with wisdom and philosophy. Moreover, Paul knew that the quest for wisdom was a driving force behind the divisions taking place among the Corinthians. This section is Paul's diagnosis of the underlying causes of the problem at Corinth. Paul therefore needed to warn the Corinthians, lest the spirit of the age ruin their thinking.

In addition to his warning, Paul, at the beginning of chapter 2, refers to his own preaching practice and experience. He reminds the Corinthians that he did not come to them as a preacher of exceptional oratorical ability or intricate wisdom. He proclaimed the gospel in a simple and intelligible, yet powerful, manner, with the Corinthians themselves being the incontrovertible evidence. All that counted to Paul was the message of the crucified Christ or, in other words, a clear portrayal of the cross of Christ.

I. FOOLISHNESS OF WORLDLY WISDOM
(1 Corinthians 1:18-21)

A. Lacking God's Power (v. 18)

18. For the preaching of the cross is to them that perish foolishness; but unto us which are saved it is the power of God.

To associate power with the crucified Jesus made no sense to the unbelieving Greeks and Jews. Not so for Paul and the Corinthian believers, whose lives had been changed by the gospel message. To those who are perishing, the message of the Cross is foolishness, but to those who are being saved, it is the power of God. It is one's response to the Cross that determines one's eternal destiny. The person who rejects the Cross is on the road to eternal death, whereas the one who embraces it receives the power of God, resulting in eternal salvation.

Note that Paul spoke of only two classes of people: the perishing and the saved. All humanity falls into one of these two classes. What a sharp contrast to the way people are classified today. In today's world, people are categorized based on which part of the world they come from, the color of their skin, their level of education, and their gender. Such classifications are of no value to God. One is either a child of Satan lost in sin or a child of God saved by grace through faith in the atoning work of Christ on Calvary.

B. Made Foolish by God (vv. 19, 20)

19. For it is written, I will destroy the wisdom of the wise, and will bring to nothing the understanding of the prudent.

20. Where is the wise? where is the scribe? where is the disputer of this world? hath not God made foolish the wisdom of this world?

In verse 19, Paul quotes Isaiah 29:14 in order to show both the limitation and futility of human wisdom. In the Isaiah passage, the prophet is pronouncing judgment on Jerusalem's spiritual leaders for their hypocrisy. Their hearts were far from God, yet in their "wisdom" they had created their own rules for serving God. The Lord said their wisdom would perish and their intelligence vanish.

The four rhetorical questions in verse 20 of the text and the statements that follow in verses 21-25 further affirm Paul's claim that human wisdom as demonstrated by the Jews (who looked for signs) and the quest of the Greeks for philosophical wisdom are of no use with regards to the salvation of humankind. Instead of being instruments of salvation, the signs demanded by the Jews and the wisdom sought after by the Greeks are stumbling blocks and foolishness respectively (v. 23).

Talk About It:
1. Why is the message of the Cross foolish "to those who are perishing" (*NKJV*)?
2. What power does the Cross have?

Talk About It:
1. How does God "destroy the wisdom of the wise" (v. 19)?
2. What is the point of all the questions in verse 20?

"A word to the wise is superfluous, and a hundred words to the unwise are futile."
—Sydney Harris

C. The "Foolishness" of Preaching (v. 21)

21. For after that in the wisdom of God the world by wisdom knew not God, it pleased God by the foolishness of preaching to save them that believe.

Talk About It:
Compare the world's wisdom with God's wisdom.

Humans do not have any spiritual understanding apart from divine revelation, something Paul elaborates on in the next chapter. To the natural person, regardless of the level of education, the Cross does not make sense. Yet it is the message of the Cross that God uses to bring into existence a great spiritual family out of every tongue and nation in the world. While humanity devised complex philosophies and superstitions, none of which brought them closer to God, the Lord revealed the way of redemption is through the simple means of the Cross.

II. CHRIST CRUCIFIED (1 Corinthians 1:22-25)
A. Foolishness to the World (vv. 22, 23)

Folly and Scandal
Regardless of all the gold and silver with which it is covered, the Cross remains "a scandal for the Jews, and folly for the Gentiles" (see v. 23). In our given situation the "Jews" represent those who seek only help from religion, while the "Gentiles" are those who seek clever and easy explanations. And in this case the Cross is truly a scandal and a folly.
—**Alexander Schmemann**

22. For the Jews require a sign, and the Greeks seek after wisdom:

23. But we preach Christ crucified, unto the Jews a stumblingblock, and unto the Greeks foolishness.

Why is the message of a crucified Savior such foolishness to the Jews and Greeks? Paul provides the answer in verses 22 and 23. First, the Jews demanded a sign; that is, they expected the Messiah to perform certain signs. Second, it was not only incredible but inconceivable to them that a person who died on a cross could actually have been God's Anointed, particularly in light of their understanding of Deuteronomy 21:23.

On their part, the Greeks sought after wisdom. The concepts of sin, guilt and atonement were foreign and repugnant to Greek philosophy. Therefore, there was no need for the Cross. But for Paul, Christ's crucifixion was the crux of his message and his own understanding of God's matchless wisdom.

As Isaiah said, God's ways are not our ways and His thoughts are higher than human thoughts (55:9). Paul's fundamental theological point is that if the Cross is God's saving event, all human standards and evaluations are overturned.

B. Wisdom to the Called (vv. 24, 25)

24. But unto them which are called, both Jews and Greeks, Christ the power of God, and the wisdom of God.

25. Because the foolishness of God is wiser than men; and the weakness of God is stronger than men.

Talk About It:
Who can become wise?

God's power is displayed in the crucified Jesus. The message of the Cross has the power to speak to the human heart, to affect conscience, to make plain the nature of sin, and to give a basis for hope and life. Now those who are called can overcome the power of sin through Christ, who is the power of God and the wisdom of God. One cannot separate God's wisdom from the Cross. The Corinthians had emphasized wisdom, and the Greeks had diligently sought it. However, to them, the Cross was nothing but out-and-out folly. Yet that cross on which Christ died for humanity proved to be God's power and wisdom. In it sin was defeated. It also revealed God and gave humans the power they needed. So, on the one hand, the message of the Cross was despised by the unsaved (vv. 22, 23) while on the other hand, it was exalted by those who were being saved regardless of their nationalities (v. 24). Salvation knows no nationality barriers.

Verse 25 presents a sharp contrast. The wisdom-loving Greeks, who boasted of their intellectualism and their reasoning power and prowess, could not discern in Christ the most profound wisdom. God provided the greatest sign, yet the sign-seeking Jews could not discern it, even though it was right before their eyes. The "foolishness" of divine love is wiser than the wisdom of human pride. What the Jews regarded with contempt, God used to shake the nation.

III. REDEMPTION THROUGH CHRIST
(1 Corinthians 1:26—2:2)
A. God's Choice Revealed (vv. 26-28)

26. For ye see your calling, brethren, how that not many wise men after the flesh, not many mighty, not many noble, are called:

27. But God hath chosen the foolish things of the world to confound the wise; and God hath chosen the weak things of the world to confound the things which are mighty;

28. And base things of the world, and things which are despised, hath God chosen, yea, and things which are not, to bring to nought things that are.

To further bolster his claim that God's wisdom surpasses human folly, Paul turned the spotlight on the Corinthians themselves. The contradiction of God's method to human wisdom is illustrated by the kind of people He called. Human wisdom would concentrate on outstanding people of rank, position, wealth, philosophical knowledge and education. Although the Corinthian church must have been comprised of people from different walks of life, including some rich and knowledgeable people, Paul says that many of them were indeed poor and not highly educated (vv. 27, 28). Yet, to those people regarded as foolish and weak, God had demonstrated His power as they embraced the message of the Cross. Their Christian calling was not on the basis of their standing in society. God does not show favoritism to people based on what they have, what they know, who they are, or from where they come.

"Yes, God's grace is always sufficient, and His arms always open to give it. But, will our arms be open to receive it?"
—**Beth Moore**

Talk About It:
1. Why are "not many" of the people listed in verse 26 "called"?
2. According to verses 27 and 28, whom does God delight to "call"?

"There is no leveler like Christianity, but it levels by lifting all who receive it to the lofty tableland of a true character and of undying hope both for this world and the next."
—**Jonathan Edwards**

B. God's Wisdom Manifested (vv. 29-31)

29. That no flesh should glory in his presence.

30. But of him are ye in Christ Jesus, who of God is made unto us wisdom, and righteousness, and sanctification, and redemption:

31. That, according as it is written, He that glorieth, let him glory in the Lord.

Talk About It:
1. Why does God choose the unlikely (v. 29)?
2. According to verse 30, why should we "glory in the Lord" (v. 31)?

All people are equal before God and saved the same way. Therefore, no flesh may glory in His presence (v. 29). Paul presents the benefits of Christ to the Corinthians in particular and to all believers at large in a fourfold but not necessarily sequential manner (v. 30). First, He is the true wisdom of God as opposed to the human wisdom of which the Greeks boasted. Second, Christ is the believers' righteousness. How true are Toplady's words, "In my hand, no price I bring, simply to the Cross I cling." Third, Christ is the believers' sanctification. The holiness of believers is grounded both on the work of Christ and their relationship with Him. Fourth, Christ is the believers' redemption. The word *redemption* as used here seems to summarize all that Paul has just said. Christ paid it all. Hence, Paul concludes in verse 31 (quoting from Jeremiah 9:24), "He who glories, let him glory in the Lord" (*NKJV*).

C. God's Testimony Declared (2:1, 2)

1. And I, brethren, when I came to you, came not with excellency of speech or of wisdom, declaring unto you the testimony of God.

2. For I determined not to know any thing among you, save Jesus Christ, and him crucified.

Talk About It:
1. How did Paul *not* come to the Corinthians (v. 1)?
2. What was Paul determined to do (v. 2)?

Paul alludes to his visit to Corinth (cf. Acts 18:1-18), when the Corinthians first heard the message and believed. In 1 Corinthians 2:1, Paul contrasts himself with some other preachers by the opening word, *kago*, literally, "*I* for *my* part," which is contrastive. He then restates what he previously said in 1:17, that it was not his own clever preaching or oratorical skill which led the Corinthians to believe in Jesus Christ. Paul came to the Corinthians proclaiming to them the mystery of God.

Good preaching does not consist of words that draw attention to the preacher's personal attainments or cleverness of voice, but words that point to the presence and activity of God. Good preaching, like Paul's, is not words that express what the hearers love to hear, but words that are spoken so that the hearers may turn to God.

The mystery of God is the message not fully understood by them before, but now explained by him and illuminated by the Holy Spirit (see 2:10-14). What is the mystery that Paul preached? It relates to Christ and the Cross. As Paul earlier showed, both the Jews and Greeks had no clue concerning the significance of the Cross.

"With preaching, Christianity stands or falls because it is the declaration of a Gospel. Nay, far more—it is the Gospel prolonging and declaring itself."
—P.T. Forsyth

In verse 2, Paul stated his guiding principle. He was only concerned with what he considered as the central truths of the gospel—Christ and His crucifixion. It was the power of God through the gospel of Christ that changed the Corinthians. So, there was no reason for Paul to change his focus.

CONCLUSION

It is clear that Jessie B. Pounds understood Paul's teaching about the Cross when he wrote the great hymn "The Way of the Cross Leads Home":

I must needs go home by the way of the cross,
There's no other way but this;
I shall ne'er get sight of the gates of light,
If the way of the cross I miss.

Refrain
The way of the cross leads home,
The way of the cross leads home;
It is sweet to know as I onward go,
The way of the cross leads home.

I must needs go on in the blood-sprinkled way,
The path that the Savior trod,
If I ever climb to the heights sublime,
Where the soul is at home with God.

Then I bid farewell to the way of the world,
To walk in it never more;
For my Lord says, "Come," and I seek my home,
Where He waits at the open door.

GOLDEN TEXT CHALLENGE

"THE PREACHING OF THE CROSS IS TO THEM THAT PERISH FOOLISHNESS; BUT UNTO US WHICH ARE SAVED IT IS THE POWER OF GOD" (1 Corinthians 1:18).

The Cross to the Christian is the emblem of life. Because of the power of God demonstrated in Christ's sacrificial death on the Cross, we have passed from the sentence of death unto life.

To those who are involved in this dying world, the Cross is nonsense! For those of us who are being saved, salvation has a present and future aspect.

God ordained that the preaching of the Cross (salvation's message) should be the means and message whereby all people might be saved. The lost man, blinded by sin, cannot see how such weak and foolish attempts can ever save him. His awful mistake lies in the fact that he discounts the power of God manifested in the Cross—the power of redeeming love.

The world in its wisdom failed to know God. But God made the wisdom of the world look foolish in the simple message of the Cross!

Daily Devotions:
M. The Cross Prefigured
Numbers 21:4-8
T. Christ's Suffering Foretold
Psalm 22:1, 2, 13-19
W. Christ's Atoning Death Predicted
Isaiah 53:1-12
T. Power of the Cross
Romans 6:4-14
F. Reconciled by the Cross
Ephesians 2:13-22
S. Redemption Accomplished
Hebrews 9:12-15, 24-28

Having the Mind of Christ

1 Corinthians 2:3 through 3:23

Unit Theme:
1 and 2 Corinthians

Central Truth:
Having the mind of Christ is a result of unity with Him.

Focus:
Perceive the wisdom of yielding to the internal presence of Christ and live in unity with Him and other believers.

Context:
Paul wrote his first letter to the Corinthian church from Ephesus around A.D. 59.

Golden Text:
"We have received, not the spirit of the world, but the spirit which is of God; that we might know the things that are freely given to us of God" (1 Corinthians 2:12).

Study Outline:
I. Receiving God's Hidden Wisdom (1 Corinthians 2:3-10)
II. Being Taught by the Spirit (1 Corinthians 2:11-16)
III. Living in Unity (1 Corinthians 3:3, 4, 16-23)

INTRODUCTION

Paul must have been a great disappointment to the philosophers of Corinth when they first heard him. The Corinthians loved a display of wisdom, and Paul could have pleased them since he was a learned person. But Paul used himself as an illustration of the difference between divine and human wisdom. In general, the Corinthians were not persons of high social standing and outstanding wisdom; and when Paul appeared in Corinth, his presentation of the gospel "was not with enticing words of man's wisdom" (1 Corinthians 2:4) or with "excellency of speech or of wisdom" (v. 1).

Paul distanced himself from such sophistry and maintained that his message was simple. He refused to take any credit as orator or master of style. He had no desire to compete with his opponents who touted their rhetorical abilities and, in so doing, gain status among the worldly-wise Corinthians. To do so would empty the Cross of its power. He sought to remind the Corinthians that his own preaching to them had conformed to what he had said about the "foolishness" of gospel preaching (1:23-25).

Paul's example provides a useful lesson for preachers today. Many preachers are tempted toward oratory, possibly because it is the type of preaching people rush to hear, placing more emphasis on the delivery rather than on content. But Paul chose a simple delivery of a powerful message. He knew the message must not become subordinate to the method. Concerning wisdom, Paul could be regarded as a scholar of the highest order, but he never sought to display his scholarship when preaching.

I. RECEIVING GOD'S HIDDEN WISDOM
(1 Corinthians 2:3-10)
A. Demonstrated in Divine Power (vv. 3-5)
3. And I was with you in weakness, and in fear, and in much trembling.

4. And my speech and my preaching was not with enticing words of man's wisdom, but in demonstration of the Spirit and power:

5. That your faith should not stand in the wisdom of men, but in the power of God.

Paul describes his presence with the Corinthians as being "in weakness, and in fear, and in much trembling." He did not come to Corinth in his own strength and power. Although other passages in the New Testament alert us to weaknesses of Paul (2 Corinthians 12:7-10; Galatians 4:13-15; 6:11), it is unlikely that Paul was referring to physical weakness here. Rather, Paul was referring to his utter helplessness in convincing his hearers with ordinary human persuasive ability. Unlike some other preachers in the Corinthian congregation, Paul did not attempt to use "enticing words," nor did he attempt to speak human wisdom.

While on the one hand, Paul preached with fear and trembling, on the other hand, he preached with the power of the Holy Spirit. Here is a contrast between Paul's human weakness and the power of the gospel as it is backed up by the Holy Spirit. Paul's preaching was not validated by eloquence and sophistication, but with demonstrations of the Spirit's power. The term translated as *demonstration* carries a legal sense of irrefutable proof. The Corinthians must place their faith in the work of the Spirit rather than human wisdom.

B. Revealed Through God's Spirit (vv. 6-10)
6. Howbeit we speak wisdom among them that are perfect: yet not the wisdom of this world, nor of the princes of this world, that come to nought:

7. But we speak the wisdom of God in a mystery, even the hidden wisdom, which God ordained before the world unto our glory:

8. Which none of the princes of this world knew: for had they known it, they would not have crucified the Lord of glory.

9. But as it is written, Eye hath not seen, nor ear heard, neither have entered into the heart of man, the things which God hath prepared for them that love him.

10. But God hath revealed them unto us by his Spirit: for the Spirit searcheth all things, yea, the deep things of God.

Talk About It:
1. Explain Paul's "weakness . . . fear, and . . . much trembling" (v. 3).
2. What was the key to Paul's ministry (vv. 4, 5)?

Talk About It:
1. Who are "coming to nothing" (v. 6, *NIV*), and why?
2. What is the "mystery" Paul writes about (vv. 7-9)?

Lest some Corinthians come to the wrong conclusion that the gospel is devoid of wisdom, Paul states that he speaks wisdom, but it is only intelligible to them that are "perfect." The Greek word for "perfect" (*teleioi*) is better translated in this context as "mature." *Mature* here refers to the saved—those enlightened by the Holy Spirit—in contrast to the unsaved.

The *wisdom* (Greek, *sophia*) of which Paul speaks is not of this age nor of the rulers of this age, who are passing away. This wisdom is preached to those who are spiritually mature. It is not recognized by the secular realm nor secular rulers.

The "mystery" (v. 7) spoken of is most certainly Christ's crucifixion, which God ordained before the creation of the world. It is this mystery, Christ's crucifixion, that the church must proclaim. God chose to conceal this wisdom from the rulers of this age, and thus accomplished His divine plan. Jesus is referred to as "the Lord of glory," placing Him over the princes of the world (v. 8). If they had understood who Jesus was, Paul says, they would not have crucified Him.

If there were any in the Corinthian congregation that claimed "advanced" knowledge, Paul makes clear that one cannot obtain true wisdom except through divine revelation. Verse 9 (quoting from Isaiah 64:4) conclusively demonstrates the futility of human understanding, declaring that human hearts and minds cannot conceive what God has prepared for believers. Paul says the Holy Spirit searches the "deep things of God" (v. 10). Humans, in their intellectual and philosophical pursuits, cannot grasp the truths of God's wisdom. Only the person to whom the Spirit has been revealed can correctly comprehend God's truth.

"The Holy Spirit is a personal being. He has a mind and a will."
—French Arrington

II. BEING TAUGHT BY THE SPIRIT (1 Corinthians 2:11-16)
A. Freely Given by God (vv. 11-13)

11. For what man knoweth the things of a man, save the spirit of man which is in him? Even so the things of God knoweth no man, but the Spirit of God.

12. Now we have received, not the spirit of the world, but the spirit which is of God; that we might know the things that are freely given to us of God.

13. Which things also we speak, not in the words which man's wisdom teacheth, but which the Holy Ghost teacheth; comparing spiritual things with spiritual.

comparing spiritual things with spiritual (v. 13)—"expressing spiritual truths in spiritual words" (*NIV*)

"For" (v. 11) points to an illustration showing that the spiritual wisdom and truths of God can be understood only through the Holy Spirit, just as human wisdom needs the human spirit to understand it. Just as the soul of a person knows his or her inward thoughts, so the Spirit of God discerns the thoughts and intentions of God. In contrast to some other kind of spirit through which a person might try to know God's wisdom and truth— whether the spirit of the wisdom of this world (1:20; 2:6; 3:19) or another deceptive spirit (cf. 1 John 4:2-6)—believers have received the Spirit of God. So believers can now understand and know the things freely given to them by God (1 Corinthians 2:12).

In verse 13, Paul shows it is impossible to pass the secret to others except by the Spirit. Here Paul reverts to the nature of his own ministry (cf. vv. 4, 5). He wants it known that he speaks "not in words taught . . . by human wisdom but in words taught by the Spirit" (v. 13, *NIV*) as he and his associates express spiritual truths in words conveying the real spiritual truth. Again, the contrast is between human wisdom and wisdom from God, combining spiritual *thoughts* with spiritual *words*.

B. Having the Mind of Christ (vv. 14-16)

14. But the natural man receiveth not the things of the Spirit of God: for they are foolishness unto him: neither can he know them, because they are spiritually discerned.

15. But he that is spiritual judgeth all things, yet he himself is judged of no man.

16. For who hath known the mind of the Lord, that he may instruct him? But we have the mind of Christ.

The generic term *man*, which translates the Greek word *anthropos*, refers to the unsaved person in general, who does not accept the illumination and truths from the Spirit of God. Such a person considers those truths to be foolish and, therefore, does not accept the things of the Spirit of God, for they are foolishness to him. Such a person cannot understand the things of God, because they are spiritually discerned. He or she cannot make spiritually intelligent decisions.

In contrast to the "natural man," the one who is spiritual, being guided by the Spirit, appraises all things; that is, he or she is able to draw intelligent conclusions about all kinds of spiritual things.

At the beginning of verse 16, Paul appeals to Isaiah 40:13 to reinforce the idea that no one can fully grasp the mind of God. The quotation, in its question form, at first sight appears to speak of the possibility of knowing God's wisdom, but the latter part of verse 16 gives reassurance that the Christian does know it. This explains why the person who has God's Spirit is not subject to judgments by one who does not have the Spirit, as verse 15 says. This directly relates to Paul's situation—the Greek philosophers and the sign-seeking Jews may mock and jeer, but they are both incapable and unqualified to judge the message of Paul, who has the mind of Christ, because they do not have the Spirit of God and cannot judge spiritual truths.

Some Corinthian believers may have boasted in their ability to judge all things, while possessing immunity from judgment. Although Paul places spiritual individuals above the judgments of men, there is still accountability. One is always accountable to God, who is Spirit.

"The Holy Spirit longs to reveal to you the deeper things of God. He longs to love through you. He longs to work through you."
—T.J. Bach

Talk About It:
1. What can the unsaved person not do (v. 14)?
2. What does it mean to have "the mind of Christ" (v. 16)?

III. LIVING IN UNITY (1 Corinthians 3:3, 4, 16-23)

A. Walking as Men (vv. 3, 4)

3. For ye are yet carnal: for whereas there is among you envying, and strife, and divisions, are ye not carnal, and walk as men?

4. For while one saith, I am of Paul; and another, I am of Apollos; are ye not carnal?

Talk About It:
What marks a "carnal" church?

The Corinthians were not living in a way that identified them as "spiritual" individuals. Paul refers to envying and strife in the midst of their fellowship, attributing these actions to their fleshly living. They acted as spiritual "babes," or infants (v. 1).

"One of American Christianity's most serious evils may be the sin of 'sermon listening.' We hear, but we do not act. God is not basically interested in our listening to sermons. He wants us to be living sermons."
—Beam

They lived as those motivated by the world's thoughts and actions; thus there were divisions in the congregation. The Corinthians were acting as mere humans in being divided over human leaders. By thinking of God's work in terms of belonging to or following a particular Christian worker, they were acting on a human level and taking sides like the world does. The Corinthians were probably captivated by the outward manners of Paul and Apollos, rather than their teaching. Apollos was more eloquent than Paul. Their preferring one to another proved they were carnal—led by their senses and mere outward appearances, without being under the guidance either of reason or grace.

B. Following the Indwelling Holy Spirit (vv. 16, 17)

16. Know ye not that ye are the temple of God, and that the Spirit of God dwelleth in you?

17. If any man defile the temple of God, him shall God destroy; for the temple of God is holy, which temple ye are.

Talk About It:
1. When does a person become "the temple of God" (v. 16)?
2. How can we "defile" God's temple?

Paul has compared the Christian congregation at Corinth to a field (vv. 6-9) and then to a building (vv. 10-15). Now he compares them to a temple. When Paul said "ye are the temple of God," he was speaking corporately, rather than individually. The whole Corinthian church was the temple of God. Although made up of individuals, it is the church, corporately, that constitutes the body of Christ, a metaphor that Paul later expands on in chapter 12. The importance of these two verses is to show the danger that awaits someone that tears apart or destroys the church. God will not spare such a person.

C. Not Being Deceived (vv. 18-20)

18. Let no man deceive himself. If any man among you seemeth to be wise in this world, let him become a fool, that he may be wise.

19. For the wisdom of this world is foolishness with God. For it is written, He taketh the wise in their own craftiness.

20. And again, The Lord knoweth the thoughts of the wise, that they are vain.

Having the Mind of Christ

Paul momentarily returns to the issue of wisdom. The Corinthians' immaturity prevented them from understanding the nature of God's work and, as such, moved them away from the foundation of their faith. Quoting Job 5:13 and Psalm 94:11, Paul reinforces what he has previously said in chapters 1 through 3. These Old Testament passages are clear reminders that one must finally place their confidence in God's understanding, for the wisdom of men will surely fade away. Christians must adhere to the standards of God, rather than men, in order to obtain true wisdom. In God's eyes, human wisdom is foolishness.

D. Belonging Only to Christ (vv. 21-23)
21. Therefore let no man glory in men. For all things are your's;
22. Whether Paul, or Apollos, or Cephas, or the world, or life, or death, or things present, or things to come; all are your's.
23. And ye are Christ's; and Christ is God's.
Paul's discussion about the problem of division in the church ended with his exhortation to the Corinthians to focus on God. In our day, denominationalism is a great problem as well as often a hindrance to the proclamation of the gospel. The question is always asked: Whom do you belong to? Are you a Wesleyan or Calvinist? An Arminian or Lutheran? Pentecostal or Baptist? Paul made it clear to the Corinthians that they neither belonged to him nor to Apollos.

It is not right for a church to replace the Word of God with human wisdom and leaders. Men or women, committees, board members, or elected officials must never be allowed to usurp the leadership of the Holy Spirit. Human leaders are provided by God for His church, and they are for the edification and spiritual profit of all. However, when the congregations or individual believers become enslaved, as it were, to human leadership, they not only miss the blessing of God, but they mar the work of the churches, and this cannot be done with impunity. The Corinthians had indeed deceived themselves by placing confidence in the wisdom of particular men within the congregation.

CONCLUSION
Paul speaks of the Christian's ability to discern the mind and heart of God. This wisdom of God received by the believer is considered foolishness to the world. Believers have received the wisdom of God only through the mediating work of the Spirit. The Spirit discerns the deep things of God and can enable the Corinthians to discern God's will. However, Paul rebuked the Corinthians for considering themselves superior due to their possession of this wisdom. No person can fully know the mind of God, or enter into the wisdom of God. This wisdom of God,

Talk About It:
1. How can a person "deceive himself" (v. 18)?
2. What is "vain" (v. 20), or "futile" (NIV)?

Talk About It:
Explain the phrase, "For all things are your's" (v. 21).

"Christianity is not a system of philosophy, nor a ritual, nor a code of laws; it is the impartation of a divine vitality. Without the Way there is no going, without the Truth there is no knowing, without Life there is no living."
—**Merrill Tenney**

mediated to the believer through the Spirit, should have encouraged unity among the Corinthian congregation. Paul's broad and inclusive speech in reference to the temple of God proves that Christian unity is crucial to God. Any attempt by someone to divide a particular fellowship with superior wisdom is an act against God. Moreover, although every believer must necessarily identify with a particular Christian church or assembly, it needs to be stated unequivocally that the believer's ultimate allegiance belongs to Christ.

GOLDEN TEXT CHALLENGE

"WE HAVE RECEIVED, NOT THE SPIRIT OF THE WORLD, BUT THE SPIRIT WHICH IS OF GOD; THAT WE MIGHT KNOW THE THINGS THAT ARE FREELY GIVEN TO US OF GOD" (1 Corinthians 2:12).

We must never accept the idea that all we need to do is use sensible rules of interpretation to know the Bible. It is possible to diagram every sentence of the Bible in the original languages and yet miss some of its wonderful truths.

On the other hand, a humble Christian who doesn't have but a fifth-grade education can have a clear understanding of what the Scriptures teach. This is the result, at least in part, of reliance upon the Holy Spirit. Jesus said, "But the Comforter, which is the Holy Ghost, whom the Father will send in my name, he shall teach you all things, and bring all things to your remembrance, whatsoever I have said unto you" (John 14:26).

Every Christian should study the Bible, not only with a genuine confidence in its reliability but also with a conscious dependence upon the Holy Spirit. We must acknowledge dependence upon the Holy Spirit. He is the author of the Scriptures and the best interpreter. He will illuminate the mind. As we look to Him, our study of the Bible will be enlightening and rewarding.

Daily Devotions:
M. The Messiah's
   Triumph
   Psalm 2:1-12
T. The Lord Will
   Help Me
   Isaiah 50:4-7
W. Made New in
   Christ
   Ephesians 4:20-
   24
T. Characterized
   by Humility
   Philippians 2:1-8
F. Focus on
   Heavenly Things
   Colossians 3:1-4
S. Strength for
   Suffering
   Believers
   1 Peter 4:1, 2,
   12-16

Having the Mind of Christ

Why Christ Came (Christmas)

Genesis 3:15; Isaiah 9:6, 7; Luke 1:32, 33; 2:1-7;
Galatians 4:4-7; Hebrews 1:1-3; 9:26-28

INTRODUCTION

"No room in the inn." And it was doubtless a very ordinary inn at that. Bethlehem was not a large city. Its inns at best would be quite commonplace—but even these were not available. This is no reflection on the innkeeper. With his place filled (no advance notice from Joseph and Mary), he could hardly be blamed for offering only his second best. Rather it is a penetrating comment on the divine plan for our redemption. God willed that His Son be born in a stable.

The world would have arranged for Jesus to be born in a royal palace, suitable surroundings for the King of kings. Human planners would have placed God's only-begotten Son in the lap of luxury. Surely nothing could be quite good enough for Him.

But such an arrangement would have missed the point entirely. It would have been an attempt to use pomp and circumstance to save a fallen race. In that case an angel would have done better than a baby.

The Incarnation means infinite condescension. Not pomp but poverty is required; not heraldry but humiliation. Jesus, "being in the form of God . . . took upon him the form of a servant" that He might bring "many sons unto glory" (Philippians 2:6, 7; Hebrews 2:10). His birth made that stable glorious.

Unit Theme:
Christmas

Central Truth:
Jesus came to redeem all people from sin.

Focus:
Examine why Christ came and appropriate the benefits of His coming.

Context:
Various Old and New Testament passages regarding the coming of Christ to redeem sinners

Golden Text:
"When the fulness of the time was come, God sent forth his Son, made of a woman, made under the law, to redeem them that were under the law, that we might receive the adoption of sons" (Galatians 4:4, 5).

Study Outline:
I. Timing of Christ's Coming (Galatians 4:4; Hebrews 1:1-3; Luke 2:1-7)
II. Purpose of Christ's Coming (Galatians 4:5; Isaiah 9:6, 7; Luke 1:32, 33; Genesis 3:15)
III. Benefits of Christ's Coming (Galatians 4:6, 7; Hebrews 9:26-28)

I. TIMING OF CHRIST'S COMING
(Galatians 4:4; Hebrews 1:1-3; Luke 2:1-7)

A. The Fullness of Time (Galatians 4:4)

4. But when the fulness of the time was come, God sent forth his Son, made of a woman, made under the law.

Talk About It:
What does this scripture reveal about God's timing?

Like a capstone to all the prophecies about Christ's coming, Paul said in Galatians 4:4, "But when the time had fully come, God sent his Son, born of a woman, born under law" (*NIV*). In his view of the fullness of time, Paul sees that all things were right and proper for His coming. The world had sunk to a desperate level of sin and godlessness, and yet it had been prepared for Him in various forms of readiness.

For example, the dispersion of the Jews had established synagogues in all parts of the known world; the conquering energies of Alexander the Great had made the Greek language an international form of communication; the military genius of the Romans had made worldwide travel possible by means of its sea traffic and network of roads. Jesus came at a propitious time. God's precision in prophecy and preparation brought the world to the point that it was prepared for the Messiah.

B. In These Last Days (Hebrews 1:1-3)

sundry (v. 1)—various or different

the fathers (v. 1)—our forefathers

1. God, who at sundry times and in divers manners spake in time past unto the fathers by the prophets,

2. Hath in these last days spoken unto us by his Son, whom he hath appointed heir of all things, by whom also he made the worlds;

3. Who being the brightness of his glory, and the express image of his person, and upholding all things by the word of his power, when he had by himself purged our sins, sat down on the right hand of the Majesty on high.

Talk About It:
1. Compare God's work in the world in "time past" with "these last days" (vv. 1, 2).
2. How does verse 3 describe Christ's relationship with the Father?

The Book of Hebrews is basically a New Testament commentary on how Jesus has fulfilled Old Testament law and prophecy. It begins by affirming that the same God who spoke through Israel's prophets has now spoken through Israel's Messiah, His Son Jesus. Jesus has been "appointed heir of all things" (v. 2). The word *appointed* has the sense of "put in place" as an heir. Thus Jesus has taken His rightful place as heir to all creation.

Jesus is "the brightness of his [God's] glory" (v. 3). This means that He shines forth with the glory of the Father. Revelation 1:16 describes Christ's countenance as the noonday sun, and 22:5 reveals that Christ, as the Lamb of God, is so bright in the heavenly city that there is no need of candle or sun. Thus, the reference to His brightness is a description of the purifying, revealing, and cleansing power of holy light that is the Father and is manifested in the Son.

Why Christ Came

Finally, Hebrews 1:3 tells that Jesus is "the express image of his [God's] person." The Greek word used for "express image" is *charakter*, from whence our English word for *character* and *characteristic* are derived. It denotes an engraving and a stamped impression by which the seal makes the identical impression on the item it presses against. Vine quotes Liddon on this passage: "The phrase expresses the fact that the Son 'is both personally distinct from, and yet literally equal to, Him of whose essence He is the adequate imprint.'" Vine continues, "The Son of God is not merely His image, He is the image, or impress, of His substance, or essence."

Why is this important? Our eternal redemption had to be purchased by God and not by animals or man. Only as God made provision of Himself and gave His own holy blood as He became flesh could our redemption be secured. If Jesus is not the eternal, only begotten Son of God, then we are not saved and His death was only that of a martyr.

> "Jesus was God spelling himself out in language humanity could understand."
> —S.D. Gordon

C. In Those Days (Luke 2:1-7)

1. And it came to pass in those days, that there went out a decree from Caesar Augustus, that all the world should be taxed.

2. (And this taxing was first made when Cyrenius was governor of Syria.)

3. And all went to be taxed, every one into his own city.

4. And Joseph also went up from Galilee, out of the city of Nazareth, into Judaea, unto the city of David, which is called Bethlehem; (because he was of the house and lineage of David:)

5. To be taxed with Mary his espoused wife, being great with child.

6. And so it was, that, while they were there, the days were accomplished that she should be delivered.

7. And she brought forth her firstborn son, and wrapped him in swaddling clothes, and laid him in a manger; because there was no room for them in the inn.

Censuses were carried out in the Roman world for two reasons: to assess taxes and to discover who was eligible for military service. Since the Jews were exempt from military service, a census conducted in Palestine would be for taxation purposes.

Discoveries have been made which provide definite information about the censuses. The information has come from actual census documents written on papyrus and discovered in the dustheaps of Egyptian towns and villages, and in the sands of the desert. It is almost certain that what happened in Egypt happened in Syria, too, and Judea was part of the province of Syria.

Talk About It:
1. What does verse 4 reveal about Joseph?
2. How did Caesar's decree affect Jesus' birth?

At one time critics questioned the thought of every man going to his own city to be enrolled, but now people possess actual documents proving that this is what happened. We have here another instance of additional knowledge confirming the accuracy of the New Testament record.

Actors on the stage of the world don't always know how to evaluate their role. Caesar Augustus, the first Roman emperor, issues a decree and it is obeyed and he is in control. Joseph and Mary, peasants from Nazareth, answer his decree and make their way to Bethlehem. How insignificant they seem amid the many who are returning to their hometown. Yet this woman, marching under the orders of Caesar Augustus, is carrying in her womb the Son of God.

No longer is the little puppet in the city on seven hills, Caesar Augustus, the main character in this drama. Joseph and Mary become the most significant personalities on the stage. Caesar is only an instrument that God is using to prepare the way for the fulfillment of prophecy. The prophecy revolves around the man and the woman. Things are not always as they appear to be.

Prior to this time, Mary had been living at the wrong address for the birth of the Christ child. Caesar's decree had changed all of that. She arrived in Bethlehem in the nick of time. Soon upon her arrival, the time of her delivery came.

Jesus was born in a stable. It is probable that the stable was built out of a cave. Travelers put up in such places, that is, in the open areas, while the back parts were used as stables. When the child was born, Mary wrapped Him in "swaddling clothes" (v. 7), which consisted of a square of cloth with a long bandagelike strip coming diagonally off from one corner. The infant was first wrapped in the square of cloth and then the long strip was wound round and round Him. Jesus was then laid in a *manger*, meaning "a place where animals feed."

The fact that there was no room for Jesus in the inn anticipated the reception He would receive from humanity. John recorded, "He came unto his own, and his own received him not. But as many as received him, to them gave he power to become the sons of God, even to them that believe on his name" (John 1:11, 12). Some did come to Him reverently. God sent visitors of His own to pay homage to the newborn King. And in every generation some have come and bowed before Him.

> "Each of us is an innkeeper who decides if there is room for Jesus."
> —Neal A. Maxwell

II. PURPOSE OF CHRIST'S COMING
(Galatians 4:5; Isaiah 9:6, 7; Luke 1:32, 33; Genesis 3:15)
A. Redeem Lost People (Galatians 4:5)
5. To redeem them that were under the law, that we might receive the adoption of sons.

Why Christ Came

God's purpose is the redemption of humanity under conditions conformable to His holy nature. Past ages clearly demonstrated that men and women were unable to measure up to God's moral standard of righteousness, much less achieve a righteousness of their own. Living under law, we lived under a curse—under the law's judgment. But under grace, we receive from a gracious God the gift of sonship. Here, truly, is one of the marvels of redeeming grace: God actually adopts into His household those who formerly belonged to the family of the devil (see John 8:44), and He gives to them as a free gift the right to all the privileges and blessings of sons (1:12).

Talk About It:
Why did Christ come to earth?

B. Establish His Government (Isaiah 9:6, 7)

6. For unto us a child is born, unto us a son is given: and the government shall be upon his shoulder: and his name shall be called Wonderful, Counsellor, The mighty God, The everlasting Father, The Prince of Peace.

7. Of the increase of his government and peace there shall be no end, upon the throne of David, and upon his kingdom, to order it, and to establish it with judgment and with justice from henceforth even for ever. The zeal of the Lord of hosts will perform this.

This first proclamation of Christ's kingdom comes through the ministry of Isaiah during the latter half of the eighth century B.C. (Isaiah's ministry was from 740 to 700 B.C.). The setting is one of misery and despair. Because of the people's disobedience, in the present they can see only destruction and havoc wreaked by an invading army. However, the future provides a contrast when a remnant of this nation experiences both spiritual and material blessings.

Talk About It:
1. Why does Isaiah twice use the phrase "unto us" (v. 6)?
2. How is Jesus Christ a ruler like none other (v. 6)?
3. How is Christ's kingdom like none other (v. 7)?

The focus of this kingdom of peace is the King. It all hinges on His authority and power. The distinctiveness of this Child is seen in chapter 7 through His virgin birth (v. 14). Now the prophet proclaims His authority over the coming kingdom. The special names given to this Ruler demonstrate His distinctiveness and dominion that is different from other human rulers.

In 9:6 there are four elements to the compound name. This really isn't too unusual as can be seen in the naming of Isaiah's son (8:3, 4). However, the Child who becomes ruler over this kingdom is more than a human child. The elements of His name indicate this to be God himself through a member of the Trinity coming to earth to establish a continuous kingdom.

1. *Wonderful, Counselor.* This element is better interpreted as a single term and embodies the wisdom of future authority.

2. *Mighty God.* This is the absolute declaration of His being deity, God himself through Christ coming to bring light into the darkness.

Dangerous Peace
There comes into the world One who is announced as the world's Savior and the Prince of Peace—and this leads immediately

3. *Everlasting Father*. The term *father* provides the concept of love and protection. This future kingdom won't fade or dissolve because of the lack of authority or power. It will continue forever. Instead of temporary kingdoms, which may be fortunate to survive several centuries, this one will be without end.

4. *Prince of Peace*. The desire for the future is peace rather than war. It is important to understand that the point in time for complete peace isn't stated. We know He brings spiritual peace, but world peace would be in the distant future.

Verse 7 says this kingdom, unlike those of the world, will not cease. Also, it will be an extension of David's throne and kingdom (2 Samuel 7:13, 16). Finally, this kingdom upholds justice and righteousness, rather than personal pride and earthly greed.

C. Reign Forever (Luke 1:32, 33)

32. He shall be great, and shall be called the Son of the Highest: and the Lord God shall give unto him the throne of his father David:

33. And he shall reign over the house of Jacob for ever; and of his kingdom there shall be no end.

Having announced Mary's imminent conception and the subsequent birth of Jesus, Gabriel proceeds to define the greatness of His character and the majesty of His destiny. As to His character, He would be acknowledged as "the Son of the Most High" (*NIV*). As a divine name, "the Most High God" belongs to the early patriarchal worship of one supreme Deity. Thus Melchizedek was the priest of "the Most High God" (Genesis 14:18). So the angel declares that Mary's son is to be the unique Son of the one living and true God. It refers to Jesus' deity.

But His royalty is also clearly announced in that He is destined to inherit the dynasty of His father David, and to rule over Israel. This was a prophecy of a kingship and a perpetual kingdom which has not yet been literally fulfilled. The fact that the angelic announcement of the Savior's conception and birth was literally fulfilled in Nazareth and Bethlehem certifies a literal fulfillment of the related kingdom prophecy. This mediatorial kingdom on earth will be fully realized at Christ's second advent, and will be perpetuated and perfected in the eternal counsels of God (Acts 1:6; 15:15-18; 1 Corinthians 15:22-28).

D. Crush Satan (Genesis 3:15)

15. And I will put enmity between thee and the woman, and between thy seed and her seed; it shall bruise thy head, and thou shalt bruise his heel.

The earliest prophecy concerning the coming of Christ was in the Garden of Eden when God spoke to the Serpent following the fall of Adam and Eve. The seed of the woman would be

Jesus, who would inflict a mortal wound upon Satan. It was the plan of God that the Redeemer should be the seed of a woman, that is, becoming a man. His life on earth would be for the purpose of bruising the devil, defeating him and establishing the foundation whereby people might be restored to their rightful place with God. In the process of His bruising the head of the Serpent, His heel would also be bruised. This is a reference to the Passion and Crucifixion.

III. BENEFITS OF CHRIST'S COMING
(Galatians 4:6, 7; Hebrews 9:26-28)
A. A New Relationship (Galatians 4:6, 7)

6. And because ye are sons, God hath sent forth the Spirit of his Son into your hearts, crying, Abba, Father.

7. Wherefore thou art no more a servant, but a son; and if a son, then an heir of God through Christ.

As proof of our new status as children of God, "God sent the Spirit of his Son into our hearts" (v. 6, *NIV*). "The Spirit of his Son" suggests the intimate relation of the Spirit and the Son, just as the "Spirit of God" suggests His intimate relation to the Father. The Trinity is forever one and inseparable in essence, yet triune in its personal manifestations.

The Spirit has come in answer to the intercession of Christ the Son (John 14:16); He bears witness to the work of Christ in the heart of the newborn believer (15:26; 16:14; Romans 8:14-16). This witness is also represented here in Galatians 4:6 by the word *crying*, a verb that expresses deep, heart-moving emotion. "Abba, Father" is an Aramaic form of address which was carried over into early Christian prayer. This cry may be inarticulate, like the "groans that words cannot express" mentioned in Romans 8:26 (*NIV*), for it is the Spirit who cries within our hearts to give assurance of our adoptive position.

As grace delivers us from the power of darkness and translates us "into the kingdom of his dear Son" (Colossians 1:13), so grace lifts us out of the context and bondage of legalistic servitude (bondslaves) into the position of sons. The logical consequence of this new status is that each believer becomes "an heir of God through Christ" (Galatians 4:7). Inasmuch as the entire redemptive purpose centers in Christ the Son, it must follow that the privileges and rights of sonship and heirship come to us through Christ (Romans 8:17).

B. A New Covenant (Hebrews 9:26-28)

26. For then must he often have suffered since the foundation of the world: but now once in the end of the world hath he appeared to put away sin by the sacrifice of himself.

Talk About It:
Describe the believer's relationship with God, and how this is made possible.

"I am born for God only. Christ is nearer to me than father, or mother, or sister."
—Henry Martyn

27. And as it is appointed unto men once to die, but after this the judgment:

28. So Christ was once offered to bear the sins of many; and unto them that look for him shall he appear the second time without sin unto salvation.

Talk About It:
1. What did Christ have to do only "once" (v. 26)?
2. What is the destiny of every human being (v. 27)?
3. What is the destiny of Jesus Christ (v. 28)?

The old covenant between God and humanity was inferior. The mediator was not involved in the sacrifice itself except to offer it. In this sense the priest was removed from the sacrifice.

The new covenant was established by a new mediator (Christ) and in a new manner (in the very presence of God, v. 24). Christ gave 100 percent to the sacrifice by making Himself the sacrifice. The purity of His sacrifice was in its content and in the commitment of the One giving it. Christ was completely committed to the redemption of the lost.

The new magnitude of the covenant established by Christ is that the burden of sin's punishment is now removed for those who repent and serve the Lord. The severity of sin's penalty was certain death. Death came with the Fall and was part of the certainty of sin's guilt. However, just as certain was the all-sufficient sacrifice of Christ.

Christ's perfect sacrifice "was once offered to bear the sins of many" (v. 28). *Once* stresses the magnitude of Christ's sacrifice. So perfect, His sacrifice needed to be offered only once. *Bear* conveys the extent to which the sacrifice was efficient. All of the guilt of sin is borne by that one sacrifice.

The word *many* declares that the effect of the sacrifice reaches to everyone who believes. The sacrifice of Christ was not only perfect within itself, but it was perfect in the distance it covered—it reached thoroughly into every individual's heart who would believe.

The reconciling work of Christ's sacrifice is not only a spiritual reality within the hearts of believers, but it is also a work that will transform the very body of the Christian at the second coming of Christ. Thus transformed, the believer will be ushered into the heavenly presence of the Father. Those who "look for him" (v. 28) also "love his appearing" (2 Timothy 4:8). Loving the appearing of the Lord implies repenting of sins and renewing one's desires. There must be a heavenly desire for an eternal reunion in the heavenly presence of the Father.

"Christ was content with a stable when He was born so that we could have a mansion when we die."
—Anonymous

CONCLUSION

"Christmas—the Advent—is the first step of Calvary's journey. The coming of Christ to man was a journey no one had ever taken before—or since. But all can travel the road from man to God."—C. Neil Strait

GOLDEN TEXT CHALLENGE

"WHEN THE FULNESS OF THE TIME WAS COME, GOD SENT FORTH HIS SON, MADE OF A WOMAN, MADE UNDER THE LAW, TO REDEEM THEM THAT WERE UNDER THE LAW, THAT WE MIGHT RECEIVE THE ADOPTION OF SONS" (Galatians 4:4, 5).

The ages prior to the First Advent were *periods of preparation* for a climactic event which had been planned in the eternal counsels of the Godhead. And when God saw that the world was ready for the advent of His Son—in "the fulness of the time"—He "sent forth his Son." Previous generations had been prepared through the disciplines of conscience and external laws for the gifts of grace which God's Son came to bestow upon fallen humanity. In one sense, "God sent forth his Son"; but the Son needed no external constraint other than the will of the Father. He was "sent" in the sense that He came from a state of preexistent glory. He came voluntarily to give Himself sacrificially.

First, He identified Himself fully with humanity: He "was made of a woman," that is to say, He entered humanity by the process of birth. He was subject to the laws of human growth and development, yet this process was not initiated "by the will of man" through natural generation, but by the direct agency of the Holy Spirit (cf. Luke 1:34, 35; Matthew 1:20).

Second, Jesus was "made under the law." The Jewish people were first of all subject to the law of God, a system of moral government that set them apart from their contemporaries. Jesus was thus born "under the law"—as a growing child He was subject to its ordinances, and as Man, He honored its claims upon Himself as an expression of the will of God for the life of man.

Living under law, people lived under a curse, under the law's judgment. But under grace, people receive from a gracious God the gift of sonship.

Daily Devotions:

M. God Lights the Darkness
Isaiah 9:1-7

T. God Promises the Savior
Micah 5:1-4

W. God Redeems His People
Luke 1:67-79

T. Christ Is Found by Seekers
Matthew 2:1-11

F. Christ Makes God Known
John 1:10-18

S. Christ Is the Sin Sacrifice
John 1:25-36

Discerning the Lord's Body

Unit Theme:
1 and 2 Corinthians

Central Truth:
Observing Holy Communion is an opportunity to remember Christ's death and participate in His life.

Focus:
Study the meaning of the Lord's Supper as an ordinance and participate reverently.

Context:
Paul wrote his first letter to the Corinthian church from Ephesus around A.D. 59.

Golden Text:
"As often as ye eat this bread, and drink this cup, ye do shew the Lord's death till he come" (1 Corinthians 11:26).

Study Outline:
I. Members of Christ's Body (1 Corinthians 10:14-17)
II. Honor Christ's Body (1 Corinthians 11:17-22, 27-33)
III. Remember Christ's Sacrifice (1 Corinthians 11:23-26)

INTRODUCTION

History records that Greeks and Romans integrated the worship of their pagan gods into the entire fabric of their national and domestic life. Small altars were erected in homes, and statues were placed in gardens. The temple ceremonies, state occasions, festival events and even family gatherings involved the sacrifices of animals to the pagan gods (idols) of the day.

These things posed serious problems for the Christians in Corinth. Suppose a family gathered together in what we call a family reunion, an occasion that could take place either at home, in one of the rooms of the temple, or in the temple court. An offering would be made to the gods, and part of the offering would be prepared for the reunion. What should the Christian do? To eat or not to eat becomes a crucial question. Should the Christian eat meats that were sacrificed to idols, having been sacrificed by their priests? Virtually all of the meat available for purchase came from animals which had been offered on the altar of a pagan god. The Christian is now "between a rock and a hard place."

In the text today, Paul shows why it is inconceivable that believers could participate both in the Lord's Supper while he or she is at the same time engaged in eating food that is sacrificed to idols. Furthermore, he discusses the significance of the Lord's Supper for the understanding of the nature of the community as the body of Christ. In Corinth, a meal that was intended to unite—the Lord's Supper—had become an instrument of division. This situation was intolerable for Paul. The Corinthians in their mishandling of the Lord's Supper failed to recognize the body of Christ and the significance of Communion.

I. MEMBERS OF CHRIST'S BODY (1 Corinthians 10:14-17)

A. Flee Idolatry (vv. 14, 15)

14. Wherefore, my dearly beloved, flee from idolatry.

15. I speak as to wise men; judge ye what I say.

Paul begins by appealing to the Corinthians as dear friends. His exhortation is an urgent one—that the Corinthians flee immediately from idolatry, having just demonstrated the awful consequences of idolatry as seen in the story of Israel (vv. 1-13). Thus, Paul appeals to their common sense.

Talk About It:
What will "wise men" (v. 15) do?

Running through the whole chapter is this concern with idolatry there in Corinth (vv. 7, 14, 19, 28). The pagan sacrifices to idols in Corinth were a tough issue for the church. Does a believer eat the meat used in such sacrifices when it is resold in the market? Does one go to dinner in a person's house when they might use such meat? Could one participate in the ceremonies themselves? Idolatry was not a theoretical issue in Corinth; it was a real-life problem. And it still is today, though the idols and the sacrifices have changed.

"The worship of the false in any form is idolatry."
—**William Purcell**

B. Partake of the One Bread (vv. 16, 17)

16. The cup of blessing which we bless, is it not the communion of the blood of Christ? The bread which we break, is it not the communion of the body of Christ?

17. For we being many are one bread, and one body: for we are all partakers of that one bread.

After urging the Corinthians to flee from idolatry, Paul asks two questions, both of which pertain to observance of the Lord's Supper. The questions themselves refer to *koinonia*, or participation in the body and blood of Jesus Christ. The thanksgiving prayer is probably the likely setting for these words. When partaking of the Lord's Supper, believers enter into a communal relationship with others in their fellowship.

Talk About It:
1. Why is the Lord's Supper called "communion" (v. 16)?
2. What is the significance of partaking of "one loaf" (v. 17, *NIV*)?

Moving from this understanding of fellowship, Paul discusses unity and fellowship among individual Christians. Though there may be many members of a group, there is one congregation. Just as all believers partake in the one loaf of Communion bread, all participate in the one body of Christ. Emphasis is placed on Christian unity by the repetition of the word *one*. Christians must recognize this unity in their fellowship with Christ and with one another.

II. HONOR CHRIST'S BODY (1 Corinthians 11:17-22, 27-33)

A. One Purpose and in One Accord (vv. 17-22)

17. Now in this that I declare unto you I praise you not, that ye come together not for the better, but for the worse.

18. For first of all, when ye come together in the church, I hear that there be divisions among you; and I partly believe it.

December 28, 2008

19. For there must be also heresies among you, that they which are approved may be made manifest among you.

20. When ye come together therefore into one place, this is not to eat the Lord's supper.

21. For in eating every one taketh before other his own supper: and one is hungry, and another is drunken.

22. What? have ye not houses to eat and to drink in? or despise ye the church of God, and shame them that have not? what shall I say to you? shall I praise you in this? I praise you not.

Talk About It:
1. How was the Corinthians' coming together "for the worse" (v. 17)?
2. Why did Paul say, "I praise you not" (vv. 17, 22)?

It is likely the early church practiced the Lord's Supper in two ways. The first was a part of an *agape*, or love feast. In this setting all the members joined for a fellowship meal and made the Lord's Supper part of that meal. At other times the Lord's Supper was separate from the agape and was itself a distinctive celebration. It was this first form that created a problem in Corinth.

Paul expresses disapproval toward the Corinthians for the manner of their participation in the Lord's Supper. Paul again highlights the problem of division among the Corinthians. However, in this case, it related to their social status. In Greco-Roman society, meals were often hosted by wealthy individuals and people were usually seated according to socioeconomic status. As such, the problem seems to be the contempt of the rich for the poor, an attitude that was typically exhibited by wealthy Romans and Greeks toward the lower classes. The poor were being despised by the rich, even though they were in the same community. But it could also be a problem of selfishness, as the translation of the *New International Version* suggests; in which case, when Paul says each of them partook without waiting for anybody else, he reveals how selfish and self-centered they had become. Some were diving in without waiting, even taking all the food for themselves. Some as a result were going hungry, while others were even getting drunk. What a selfish disgrace! Understood either way, there was a real problem.

Paul does not condone such behavior. The Lord's Supper is an event that should be accessible to all social levels. By shaming those less fortunate in the community, the Corinthian church shamed herself, rather than honoring the body of Christ.

> "Going to church doesn't make you a Christian any more than going to a garage makes you an automobile."
> —Billy Sunday

B. A Worthy Manner (vv. 27-33)

27. Wherefore whosoever shall eat this bread, and drink this cup of the Lord, unworthily, shall be guilty of the body and blood of the Lord.

28. But let a man examine himself, and so let him eat of that bread, and drink of that cup.

29. For he that eateth and drinketh unworthily, eateth and drinketh damnation to himself, not discerning the Lord's body.

30. For this cause many are weak and sickly among you, and many sleep.

31. For if we would judge ourselves, we should not be judged.

32. But when we are judged, we are chastened of the Lord, that we should not be condemned with the world.

33. Wherefore, my brethren, when ye come together to eat, tarry one for another.

Paul's admonition takes a solemn tone in these verses. Their abuse of the Eucharist (a potential fellowship with the risen Christ and remembrance of the earthly Jesus) was serious and had grave consequences. Hence Paul says, "For this reason many are weak and sick among you, and many sleep. . . . But if anyone is hungry, let him eat at home, lest you come together for judgment. And the rest I will set in order when I come" (vv. 30, 34, *NKJV*). It is evident that great harm was being wrought by the Corinthians' coming together at the Lord's Table; the abuses were temporally and spiritually detrimental to them.

Participating in the Lord's Supper unworthily is equal to sinning against the body and blood of Christ. Those who drink unworthily bring judgment upon themselves. One must search his or her heart and mind before participating in the solemn act of the Lord's Supper.

Paul's advice to discern the Lord's body and blood may mean two things. First, it may mean that Christ's presence is manifest in a special way. This should create a sense of reverence instead of a party spirit when the church comes together for worship. Second, Christians must equally recognize what the Lord's Supper is intended to nurture and represent—the oneness of believers in unity (10:17). If the Corinthians would take time to judge their actions and intentions before partaking of the bread and cup, divine judgment would not fall upon them.

III. REMEMBER CHRIST'S SACRIFICE (1 Corinthians 11:23-26)
A. His Body Broken (vv. 23, 24)

23. For I have received of the Lord that which also I delivered unto you, That the Lord Jesus the same night in which he was betrayed took bread:

24. And when he had given thanks, he brake it, and said, Take, eat: this is my body, which is broken for you: this do in remembrance of me.

Paul corrects the Corinthians' degrading of the Lord's Supper by showing them its true meaning. He says it is a special meal because of its historical roots. The tradition which Paul is passing

Talk About It:
1. What does it mean to eat the Lord's Supper "unworthily" (v. 27)?
2. How can we avoid divine judgment (v. 31)?
3. Why does God discipline His people (v. 32)?

"In confession . . . we open our lives to healing, reconciling, restoring, uplifting grace of Him who loves us in spite what we are."
—**Louis Cassels**

Talk About It:
Why is the bread an appropriate symbol for Christ's body?

on came straight from the Lord. The celebration of the Lord's Supper is grounded in Jesus' final meal with His disciples before His death. As such, Paul is reminding the Corinthians that the supper they were abusing was rooted in the words and actions of Christ on the night of His betrayal, something which demands that they take time to reflect on the intense pathos of that event. Not only is the supper rooted in Christ's words and actions, it is of utmost spiritual significance and immense theological meaning. The bread and the cup symbolize the broken body and shed blood of Christ.

B. His Blood Shed (vv. 25, 26)

25. After the same manner also he took the cup, when he had supped, saying, This cup is the new testament in my blood: this do ye, as oft as ye drink it, in remembrance of me.

26. For as often as ye eat this bread, and drink this cup, ye do shew the Lord's death till he come.

Talk About It:
1. What is this "new testament" (v. 25)?
2. When should believers stop partaking of the Lord's Supper (v. 26)?

Christ's establishment of the Last Supper took place during a Passover meal, when Jesus, together with the disciples, celebrated the remembrance of Israel's deliverance from Egypt to the Promised Land. Breaking bread and drinking wine were important parts of the Passover celebration. Jesus took these important pictures and reminders of Israel's deliverance from Egypt and added to them the meanings connected with His own death on the cross for us.

Christ's death, which is remembered in the Lord's Supper, established the new covenant between God and His people— a covenant that promises forgiveness for every sinner who repents. The phrase "new testament," or "new covenant," is an echo of Jeremiah 31:31. Christ shows His solidarity and continuity of the church with the traditions of Israel and their hopeful expectations.

To be in covenant relation with God is to belong to a covenant people who are bound together by responsibilities to God as well as one another. The sharing of the meal is a visible demonstration of the character of the covenant. Because of what Jesus did on the cross, we can have a new covenant relationship with God.

Furthermore, the Lord's Supper is of crucial importance because of its confessional nature. It proclaims the Lord's death until He comes. Participation in the Lord's Supper becomes a visible proclamation of the message of the church: Christ's death and resurrection. While the Lord's Supper does look back to what Jesus did on the cross, it also looks forward to the coming of Jesus and the Marriage Supper of the Lamb (Revelation 19:9).

"The Lord's Supper has both a backward and a forward look."
—Wycliffe Bible Commentary

Discerning the Lord's Body

CONCLUSION

The Lord's Supper is the central focus of this particular passage. Paul reminded the Corinthians that when they gathered together to share in a communal meal at the Lord's holy table, it was not the table of any particular patron. Behaviors or practices that excluded members of the congregation from partaking in the Lord's Supper because of their social status were a serious hindrance to establishing authentic Christian community.

Discerning the Lord's body correctly requires right actions and practices. Also, believers must aim for unity among one another to correctly interpret and participate in the Communion meal. The church must collectively examine herself as the Lord's Supper is administered.

GOLDEN TEXT CHALLENGE

"AS OFTEN AS YE EAT THIS BREAD, AND DRINK THIS CUP, YE DO SHEW THE LORD'S DEATH TILL HE COME" (1 Corinthians 11:26).

The apostle Paul did not give any specific directions as to how often the Lord's Supper should be observed. However, it is implied that it should be done frequently so that the remembrance of our Lord is kept fresh in our minds.

Holy Communion is celebrated in remembrance of our Lord Jesus Christ. It looks back and reminds us of the night in which He was betrayed, when He kept the Passover with His disciples. It reminds us of the events of the following day when His body was broken and His blood was shed so that we may receive forgiveness for our sins and be reconciled to God.

The Lord's Supper also reminds us of His continuing presence with us. We know that He is with us always, but His nearness is rarely felt as intimately as when we reverently partake of the bread and the cup in the manner in which He himself ordained.

As we participate in Holy Communion, we *show* (proclaim continually) His death until He comes. Therefore, Holy Communion also looks to the future and reminds us of our Lord's promise to return.

When we partake of the Lord's Table, we remember that He is the crucified Christ who died for our sins. We remember that He is the continuing Christ who is ever present with us. We remember that He is the coming Christ who will soon return in glory.

Daily Devotions:
M. The Passover Instituted
   Exodus 12:11-17
T. The Passover Reestablished
   2 Kings 23:21-25
W. The Lord's Supper Established
   Mark 14:22-25
T. Passover Fulfilled in Communion
   Luke 22:7-20
F. Communion Practiced
   Acts 2:42-47
S. Identification With Christ
   Romans 6:3-11

Bible Insight

The Lord's Supper
by French Arrington

Just before His betrayal, Jesus instituted the Lord's Supper. When he gathered His disciples for their last meal together, He took a loaf of bread, broke it into pieces, and distributed it to them with these words: "This is My body which is given for you; do this in remembrance of Me" (Luke 22:19).* Later in the meal He took the cup and passed it to His disciples, saying, "This cup is the new covenant in My blood, which is shed for you" (v. 20; cf. Matthew 26:26-30; Mark 14:22-26; 1 Corinthians 11:23-26). By giving the bread and cup to the disciples, Jesus was indicating that they shared in the blessings of the new covenant. It is important to understand something about the Passover Feast and deliverance of Israel from Egypt to grasp the significance of the Lord's Supper (Luke 22:15; 1 Corinthians 5:7). The Lord's Supper means for us four things:

First, *the Supper is a remembrance of the Lord.* As we receive the bread and the cup, we recall that He died for our salvation (1 Corinthians 11:25). Thus the Supper serves to remind us frequently of our deliverance from the bondage of sin by His death. The word *remembrance* (*anamnesis*) has reference to a past event, but this word is so powerful it signifies that the death of Christ is made effective now and brings blessings into the present.

Second, *the observance of the Supper is a blessing* (1 Corinthians 10:16). The element of thanksgiving (*eucharistia*) has given rise to the Supper being called the Eucharist. We offer praises and thanksgiving to God because of His mighty act of deliverance in the cross of Christ. So in the meal we appear in the presence of God with our sacrifices of praise and thanksgiving for the Sacrifice of Calvary.

Third, *the Lord's Supper is communion* (koinonia—*fellowship, partaking, sharing*). One dimension of this fellowship is described by Paul as "communion of the blood of Christ" (1 Corinthians 10:16). There is a partaking of the blood of Christ—His saving benefits—in a spiritual way. Only by faith and through the Holy Spirit do we have fellowship with Christ and share in the blessings of His death. As Paul asked, "Is [the cup] not the communion of the blood of Christ?" (v. 16). So the Supper is a visible sign that believers are spiritually nourished by Christ (John 6:57, 58).

Another dimension of the communion of the Supper is that of believers' fellowship with one another. To use the words of Paul, "The bread which we break, is it not the communion of the body of Christ?" (1 Corinthians 10:16). "The body of Christ" refers to the church, the fellowship of believers. Our sharing in the saving benefits of Christ's death is expressed in our fellowship with one another. As the host of the Supper, Christ is present to give us the spiritual blessings signified by the bread and cup of Communion.

Through the Holy Spirit we worship and adore the one Lord Jesus Christ, and our fellowship with Him and love for one another are deepened through the appropriate celebration of His death.

Fourth, *the Supper proclaims the death of Christ until He comes again* (11:26). The celebration of this holy meal reminds us of Christ's return in glory. As believers we live between Christ's first coming and His second coming. At the Supper we look back to the Lord's triumphant death and forward to His final victory when He returns. Then we will share in the Marriage Supper of the Lamb. The Lord's Supper foreshadows the inexpressible joy we will experience at that heavenly wedding feast, and it intensifies our expectation of the glorious return of Christ. Understandably the early Christians prayed around the Lord's Table, "Maranatha," meaning "O Lord, come!" (16:22). Now the Lord is not visible; but when this prayer is answered, He will become visible again.

Like with baptism in water, the Lord's Supper requires faith for proper participation. Paul warned against eating the bread and drinking the cup "in an unworthy manner" (11:27). All are unworthy to receive the bread and the cup of Christ, but all believers can participate in the Supper in a proper manner, provided they come with a right attitude—an attitude of humility, faith, and genuine commitment to Jesus Christ as Lord, and with an attitude of love for one another and appreciation for the meaning of the Supper. As the Table of the Lord is approached, worshipers are to examine themselves to see if their attitude is appropriate to partake of the bread and cup of the Lord. In Pentecostal worship, it is customary for members to examine their own lives and have a sense of the profound presence of Christ and His blessing at the Supper. Sometimes people receive healing or the baptism in the Spirit while partaking of the bread and cup.—Excerpted from *Christian Doctrine: A Pentecostal Perspective, Vol. 3* (Pathway Press).

*Scriptures are from the *New King James Version*.

Having the Spirit of Christ

1 Corinthians 12:1-27; 14:1-25

Unit Theme:
1 and 2 Corinthians

Central Truth:
The Holy Spirit equips and unites believers in Christ.

Focus:
Review the work of the Holy Spirit in the church and cooperate with His mission.

Context:
Paul wrote his first letter to the Corinthian church from Ephesus around A.D. 59.

Golden Text:
"By one Spirit are we all baptized into one body, whether we be Jews or Gentiles, whether we be bond or free; and have been all made to drink into one Spirit" (1 Corinthians 12:13).

Study Outline:
I. The Spirit Activates the Gifts
   (1 Corinthians 12:4-11)
II. The Spirit Unifies the Body
   (1 Corinthians 12:12-27)
III. The Spirit Edifies the Church
   (1 Corinthians 14:1-5)

INTRODUCTION

Paul's long discussion about spiritual gifts (1 Corinthians 12–14) was of utmost importance both to the Corinthians to whom Paul originally wrote and to believers today. The introduction demonstrates the importance Paul attached to it as he states, "Now concerning spiritual gifts, brethren, I do not want you to be ignorant" (12:1, *NKJV*). This is one of three important truths of which Paul, in his letters, stated he did not want his readers to be ignorant. They were not to be ignorant of God's plan for Israel (Romans 11:25), of spiritual gifts (1 Corinthians 12:1), and about the second coming of Jesus (1 Thessalonians 4:13). Sadly, so many Christians are ignorant on these exact points! Although the literal translation of 1 Corinthians 12:1 suggests "spiritual things or spirituals," the addition of *gifts* is appropriate here, given the context. Because of their idolatrous background, the Corinthians were prone to a misunderstanding of the gifts.

Many times, past teaching and experiences contribute to a poor understanding of the Holy Spirit and His gifts. In a congregation such as Corinth's where supernatural manifestations were taking place, it is important to make a distinction between gifts that find their source in God and those that do not. At the start, Paul lays down a broad principle for discerning matters regarding spiritual gifts: Judge things by how they relate to Jesus Christ. "No man speaking by the Spirit of God calleth Jesus accursed" (v. 3). One must ask important questions such as, "Does a supposed spiritual gift glorify Jesus, or is it for self-promotion?" "Does it promote the true Christ, or a false one?"

I. THE SPIRIT ACTIVATES THE GIFTS (1 Corinthians 12:4-11)
A. Source of the Gifts (vv. 4-6)
4. Now there are diversities of gifts, but the same Spirit.
5. And there are differences of administrations, but the same Lord.
6. And there are diversities of operations, but it is the same God which worketh all in all.

Paul's description of the gifts begins both with their nature and source. Paul uses three important words: *gifts* (v. 4, Greek *charismata*); *administrations*, or literally "services" (v. 5, *diakonia*); and *operations*, or literally "workings" (v. 6, *energemata*). His choice of words is not merely stylistic. While the *gifts* emphasize the truth of the spiritual manifestations as an expression of God's grace, the *administrations*, or services (*diakonia*), suggest that the purpose of the gifts is not for self-enjoyment or edification. Rather the gifts are for loving ministry within the body of Christ. The *operations* suggest that in all these manifestations, God is powerfully at work through His Spirit. However, although these "diversities" go under different names, they are interchangeable labels.

Paul expresses the source of the gifts in strongly Trinitarian terms: the Spirit, the Lord, and God. It is not the Spirit alone who distributes the gifts. Paul accentuates the coherence of the gifts that God distributes as a unity-in-diversity, thus leaving no room for rivalry and competition within the body of Christ. Paul will develop this theme later in verses 12-30. One particular gift must not and cannot be viewed as superior to the others; all come from the same God. His emphasis on unity-in-diversity is rooted in the nature of the one God who is Holy Trinity.

B. For the Common Good (vv. 7-11)
7. But the manifestation of the Spirit is given to every man to profit withal.
8. For to one is given by the Spirit the word of wisdom; to another the word of knowledge by the same Spirit;
9. To another faith by the same Spirit; to another the gifts of healing by the same Spirit;
10. To another the working of miracles; to another prophecy; to another discerning of Spirits; to another divers kinds of tongues; to another the interpretation of tongues:
11. But all these worketh that one and the selfsame Spirit, dividing to every man severally as he will.

In verse 7, Paul indicates that the gifts are given to all the people of God for the benefit of all or the common good. God gives these gifts for the edification of the Body. The gifts are not to bring personal benefit, advantage or status to the individual,

administrations (v. 5)—"service" (*NIV*)
operations (v. 6)— "working" (*NIV*)

Talk About It:
What is the one clear message in these three verses?

"All the gifts are actions of the Holy Spirit, making known His presence, at times in a dramatic way. They demonstrate first and foremost the reality of His activity and presence."
—French Arrington

every man severally (v. 11)—"each one individually" (*NKJV*)

Talk About It:
1. What is the purpose of spiritual gifts (v. 7)?

2. Why is there such a variety of spiritual gifts (vv. 8-10)?
3. How are the gifts distributed (v. 11)?

but to the whole community. This advantage consists of building up the body of Christ into His image. After speaking in general terms, Paul mentions different manifestations of the Spirit in verses 8-10.

The *word of wisdom* is the ability to speak forth the wisdom of God, especially in an important situation, as shown in Solomon (1 Kings 3:16-28), Jesus (Luke 20:20-26), Stephen (Acts 7), and Paul (23:6-11). The *word of knowledge* has been the subject of different interpretations. In a classic Pentecostal fashion, Harold Horton defines it as "a divinely granted flash of revelation concerning things which were hopelessly hidden from the senses." He cites the example of God's judgment for Eli, given as a voice in the night to Samuel (1 Samuel 3:13), and God's word to Peter regarding the arrival of messengers from Cornelius (Acts 10:19).

The *gift of faith* does not refer to the initial faith that is necessary for salvation. Though faith is an essential part of every Christian's life, the gift of faith is the unique ability to trust God in all circumstances, as Peter did when he walked out of the boat onto the water (Matthew 14:22-33).

The *gifts of healing* is an indefinite plural which may suggest that the gifts are bestowed upon some believers in proportion with the illnesses present. These gifts are for the benefit of the community. The *working of miracles* encompasses supernatural activity, including healing, in which the Holy Spirit usually overrides the power of nature.

The *gift of prophecy* refers both to the foretelling of the future as well as the forthtelling of the mind of God for a particular situation. Those who believe the miraculous gifts have ceased wish to define *prophecy* as "preaching." Though this is common, it is inaccurate. The Greek words translated as "preaching" and "divinely inspired speech" are different. Paul is using the word for "divinely inspired speech," not "preaching." It is inaccurate to define *prophecy* as good preaching.

Discerning of spirits, or "distinguishing between spirits" (*NIV*), describes the God-given ability to determine whether or not a supernatural manifestation has its source in God. An example is that of Paul in Acts 16:16-18.

Divers kinds of tongues, or "speaking in different kinds of tongues" (*NIV*), refers to a supernatural utterance in a language that was not learned by the speaker; it may or may not be a language known to others. The *interpretation of tongues* refers to an intelligible presentation of the content of what was spoken in an unknown tongue.

Having listed the gifts, in verse 11 Paul reiterates the one Source of the gifts—the Spirit of God. Since they are distributed not according to human will, but as the Spirit of God wills, they should be a unifying force.

"It is a mistake to think that spiritual gifts were taken away at the end of the apostolic age. If this were true, how would the Church have survived and thrived all these many centuries?"
—**Daniel Black**

II. THE SPIRIT UNIFIES THE BODY (1 Corinthians 12:12-27)

A. One Spirit, One Body (vv. 12, 13)

12. For as the body is one, and hath many members, and all the members of that one body, being many, are one body: so also is Christ.

13. For by one Spirit are we all baptized into one body, whether we be Jews or Gentiles, whether we be bond or free; and have been all made to drink into one Spirit.

Paul begins to explain further what he summarily stated in verse 7—that the gifts are given for the advantage of all. Paul was concerned that the Corinthians' distorted view of the gifts had led to a lack of social cohesion among them. To correct the problem, Paul insisted that the Corinthians had all been immersed (baptized) in one Spirit into the body of Christ. So Paul employed the analogy of the human body to drive home the points that he had been making in verses 4-11.

B. One Body, Many Members (vv. 14-20)

14. For the body is not one member, but many.

15. If the foot shall say, Because I am not the hand, I am not of the body; is it therefore not of the body?

16. And if the ear shall say, Because I am not the eye, I am not of the body; is it therefore not of the body?

17. If the whole body were an eye, where were the hearing? If the whole were hearing, where were the smelling?

18. But now hath God set the members every one of them in the body, as it hath pleased him.

19. And if they were all one member, where were the body?

20. But now are they many members, yet but one body.

Just as it is absurd to think that the human body is made up of only the most noticeable parts, so it is foolish to think that the body could function without its less prominent parts. So there is no room for either an inferiority complex or superiority complex within the body. Each part of the body needs the other in order to function well. So is the body of Christ. We need each other to function as God intends. By application, no one of the gifts is by itself sufficient.

Paul reduced pride of individual gift, ministry, or effect to the ridiculous by stretching his imagination to picture the whole body as a monstrous eye or a monstrous ear (v. 17). The implication is that if the whole church had only one gift or one ministry or one effect, it too would be monstrous rather than the perfect creature God had planned.

In verse 20, Paul returns from the realm of imagination—from what things would be like if people's twisted concepts were true—to the realm of fact. There are *many members*, and there is *one body*. There cannot be *one body* without *many members*, and the individual members cannot survive except they be in *one body*.

Talk About It:
What makes Christians "one body"?

Talk About It:
1. How is the church like the human body?
2. Answer the question posed in verse 19.

"Salvation is baptism into a community that has so truthful a story that we forget ourselves and our anxieties long enough to become part of that story, a story God has told in Scripture and continues to tell in Israel and the church."
—*Resident Aliens*

C. Many Members, One Purpose (vv. 21-27)

21. And the eye cannot say unto the hand, I have no need of thee: nor again the head to the feet, I have no need of you.

22. Nay, much more those members of the body, which seem to be more feeble, are necessary:

23. And those members of the body, which we think to be less honourable, upon these we bestow more abundant honour; and our uncomely parts have more abundant comeliness.

24. For our comely parts have no need: but God hath tempered the body together, having given more abundant honour to that part which lacked:

25. That there should be no schism in the body; but that the members should have the same care for another.

26. And whether one member suffer, all the members suffer with it; or one member be honoured, all the members rejoice with it.

27. Now ye are the body of Christ, and members in particular.

Paul uses the body metaphor to urge that no one be seen as less important than someone else. In the body every part is important. Some parts of the body that we regard as lacking honor are absolutely essential for our survival. Those parts play an even more indispensable role in sustaining the life of the body than the eye or ear, for example. The body parts that we cover for the sake of modesty are not disgusting; we cannot survive without them.

The application to Corinth and to congregation life today is unmistakably clear. Those who may appear to have more spectacular gifts may actually turn out to be less indispensable than the quiet, faithful, prayerful, devoted, humble members whose values and contributions are often overlooked by the power-seekers. Paul's overriding concern is with the unity of the church, which he expresses in terms of a concern for the wholeness of the physical body: "There should be no division in the body, but . . . its parts should have equal concern for each other" (12:25, *NIV*). Thus, a sense of group identity supersedes a sense of individualism; bodily wholeness is thus maintained.

III. THE SPIRIT EDIFIES THE CHURCH (1 Corinthians 14:1-5)

Paul resumes his teaching concerning the gifts that began in chapter 12. He now focuses on the issue of intelligibility and order during the worship service. Evidently the somewhat chaotic situation in Corinth required that he pay more attention to two of those gifts—speaking in tongues and prophecy. Perhaps some Corinthians were misusing speaking in tongues with the result that others were against its use and wanted it stopped.

---

uncomely parts (v. 23)—"unpresentable parts" (*NKJV*)

abundant comeliness (v. 23)—"greater modesty" (*NKJV*)

Talk About It:
1. Who receives "greater honor" (v. 24, *NIV*) in Christ's body, and why (v. 25)?
2. How does God want the church to function (v. 26)?

Having the Spirit of Christ

A. Eagerly Desire Spiritual Gifts (v. 1)

1. Follow after charity, and desire spiritual gifts, but rather that ye may prophesy.

The phrase "follow after," from the Greek word *dioko*, literally means "to persecute," or in a positive sense, "to pursue." Thus, Paul is telling the Corinthians to make love the object of their pursuit. Their pursuit of love should be like a hunter's pursuit of game. It speaks of intensity, perseverance, and an attitude that always achieves its goal. The imperative form used in verse 1 is present tense, indicating a continuous and ongoing pursuit of love. Paul understood that there is much to distract a person in the Christian life. Unless one determines to constantly and intensely pursue love as the motivating and guiding principle of life, some other lesser motivation will emerge and begin to direct one's life. This thought obviously concludes chapter 13, the "love chapter."

The second command of verse 1 of the text is "desire spiritual gifts." The verb *desire* is the same word used in 12:31 ("covet earnestly"). Paul's point in verse 1 is that prophecy is a spiritual gift the Corinthians should seek.

Talk About It:
1. What does it mean to "follow after charity"?
2. Why should we "desire spiritual gifts"?

B. Seek to Edify the Church (vv. 2-5)

2. For he that speaketh in an unknown tongue speaketh not unto men, but unto God: for no man understandeth him; howbeit in the spirit he speaketh mysteries.

3. But he that prophesieth speaketh unto men to edification, and exhortation, and comfort.

4. He that speaketh in an unknown tongue edifieth himself; but he that prophesieth edifieth the church.

5. I would that ye all spake with tongues, but rather that ye prophesied: for greater is he that prophesieth than he that speaketh with tongues, except he interpret, that the church may receive edifying.

The reason Paul commands the Corinthians to pursue love and seek to prophesy is given in verses 2-4. Prophecy is superior to tongues because prophecy is understandable. A person that speaks in tongues speaks mysteries in the Spirit, but their speech is not beneficial to the congregation if it cannot be understood.

Verse 3 identifies the content of prophecy. In prophecy the person speaks to other people, and what he or she says edifies, exhorts (encourages) and comforts. Paul first used the word *edification* in its verb form in 1 Corinthians 8:1 when he wrote, "Love builds up" (*NIV*). The same verb appears in 8:10 ("emboldened"); 10:23; twice in 14:4; and in verse 17. Thus edification was one of the pivotal concepts for Paul in his dealing with the church at Corinth. Edification is a criterion Paul used to evaluate the appropriateness of behavior. If an action builds up the church,

Talk About It:
1. How does the gift of prophecy benefit the church (v. 3)?
2. How does the gift of tongues benefit the individual (v. 4)?

it is beneficial. It is clear that Paul thought of edification primarily in terms of the local Christian community. His ministry was to "build up and not to destroy" (see 2 Corinthians 10:8; 13:10).

Paul directly states the issue in verse 4 of the text. Those who speak in a tongue edify or build up themselves. Those who prophesy edify or build up the church. It is the building up of the church that matters most, not the building up of oneself.

Verse 5 attempts to soften the impact of this contrast. Paul states that he wishes that all the Corinthians spoke in tongues. However, he would rather they all prophesied. Prophesying is greater than speaking in tongues unless someone interprets the tongue. Interpretation allows the possibility for a "message from God" to be conveyed to the congregation by the utterance spoken in tongues. That offers the opportunity for the "understanding" (hearing) mentioned in verse 2. Verse 5 concludes with Paul's main point, *edification*. Interpretation allows the congregation to be built up, therefore making this gift as valuable as prophecy.

CONCLUSION

It is unfortunate that there are Christians who continue to ignore or disparage the manifestations of the Spirit. On the other hand, an overemphasis of the manifestations of the Spirit is not God's intention. So Paul's use of the body metaphor is on target. The gifts of the Spirit are needed to build up the body, but glamorizing one or more gifts is unhealthy.

Members are related to one another in the same way that the physical body knows an interconnectedness of all its parts. As an arm or leg has no life outside the body, there is no such idea as an individual's relationship to the Lord in isolation from the community of faith. Individualism simply leads to a dysfunctional body.

GOLDEN TEXT CHALLENGE

"BY ONE SPIRIT ARE WE ALL BAPTIZED INTO ONE BODY, WHETHER WE BE JEWS OR GENTILES, WHETHER WE BE BOND OR FREE; AND HAVE BEEN ALL MADE TO DRINK INTO ONE SPIRIT" (1 Corinthians 12:13).

The church had been formed out of those who were by birth *Jews* and *Gentiles*, and who were by birth, or subsequent events, *slaves* and *freemen*. But these old divisions had no validity now for those who were together in the body of Christ. That which made their present unity a reality was stronger than that which had previously made them different. Together they had experienced conversion and together they had partaken of the Spirit—this made them one body in Christ.

The same is true for believers today. Whatever our ethnicity, wherever we were born, whatever our social status, and wherever we work, as God's people we make up Christ's one body and serve Him through the one Holy Spirit.

Having the Love of Christ

1 Corinthians 12:28 through 13:13

INTRODUCTION

Throughout chapters 12-14, Paul focuses on the subject of spiritual gifts. In chapter 12, Paul sets before the Corinthians the diversity of ministries in the church, each contributing to the common good. He also teaches them that the diverse ministries function together in the one body of Christ, the church—diversity in unity. At the end of the chapter, Paul lists some of the different offices that God has given for the administration and edification of the church.

In 12:31, Paul mentions "a more excellent way." It is the way of love which he expounds in chapter 13—a passage that is commonly referred to as the "hymn of love." Strategically located before Paul's lengthy discussion on the gifts of tongues and prophecy, he argues that love must provide the context of the operation of spiritual gifts.

Paul teaches that the central issue is not the exercise of any of the gifts, but what they accomplish and how they are used. This is not to suggest an either/or approach—that is, a situation where the believer has to make a choice between love and the spiritual gifts. While it is true that the exercise of the gifts without love can become repulsive, it is just as true that the believer will be limited in his or her ability to minister to others without the gifts. Someone has said that *mis*use is not corrected by *no* use but by *right* use.

Unit Theme:
1 and 2 Corinthians

Central Truth:
Loving as Christ loves is the best way to live.

Focus:
Give thanks for the love of Christ and serve with His love.

Context:
Paul wrote his first letter to the Corinthian church from Ephesus around A.D. 59.

Golden Text:
"Now abideth faith, hope, charity, these three; but the greatest of these is charity" (1 Corinthians 13:13).

Study Outline:
I. Desire the More Excellent Way (1 Corinthians 12:28—13:3)
II. Christ's Love Described (1 Corinthians 13:4-8)
III. Christ's Love Endures (1 Corinthians 13:9-13)

I. DESIRE THE MORE EXCELLENT WAY
(1 Corinthians 12:28–13:3)
A. Gifts From God (12:28-31)

28. And God hath set some in the church, first apostles, secondarily prophets, thirdly teachers, after that miracles, then gifts of healings, helps, governments, diversities of tongues.

29. Are all apostles? are all prophets? are all teachers? are all workers of miracles?

30. Have all the gifts of healing? do all speak with tongues? do all interpret?

31. But covet earnestly the best gifts: and yet shew I unto you a more excellent way.

Talk About It:
1. What is the purpose of all the questions in verses 29 and 30?
2. What are "the best gifts" (v. 31)?
3. What is "a more excellent way" (v. 31)?

Paul ends chapter 12 with a list of some of the gifts which God bestows upon individuals. There are three important observations. First, note that the list does not exactly match the list that Paul earlier provided in verses 8-10, something that alerts us to the lack of comprehensiveness of the former. Paul discusses the ministry functions in dialogue with the existing situation at Corinth, as well as in the light of the forms of leadership that suited his own cultural context. He does not suggest that these offices are either the only or exact forms of leadership that are timeless or universally normative.

Second, these verses, in context, press home Paul's argument in the entire chapter by way of summary. If these gifts are given generously as God wills (vv. 4-11), and if they are for the common good of the whole church (v. 7), it is right to say that the gifts cannot and must not serve the purpose of comparison and competition among ministers for the sake of enhancing one's status. The members of Christ's body ought not to be in competition with one another to gain prestige, position, or power. Rather, they should work together for the well-being of the whole assembly. Moreover, Paul does not suggest that there is any individual who holds functions in all these capacities. The gifts transcend the ability of any individual to possess them. Significantly, these gifts are complementary. They function together within the community—the church. As such, the passage poses a challenge to any self-styled leader who assumes that he or she is the "answer" without reference to the gifts of others. Also, the attitude of selecting certain leaders as models of chosen spiritual attributes flies in the face of Paul's discussion here.

Third, the gifts are God-given. In the same manner that the church does not bestow the gifts of healings, tongues and interpretation of tongues, and so on, upon individuals, the church does not create apostles, prophets, teachers, and other ministry gifts. They are Spirit-given.

In verse 28 Paul lists several gifts, starting with the apostles. This has raised two questions, the first of which is whether Paul intended to grade the gifts, thereby creating a hierarchical structure, or if he is simply enumerating the gifts. While Paul did not intend to create a hierarchical structure, the list suggests some priority being given to apostles, prophets and teachers. The second question relates to whether Paul intentionally moves from "gifts" (*charismata*) to roles or offices in the church. Probably so.

The climax of Paul's argument comes in verses 29 and 30. No individual will have every kind of giftedness or fill every role in the body of Christ. The diversity of the gifts within the church is God's plan for how the body of Christ would function. Thus, Paul's argument comes in a full circle. Verse 31 is a transitional statement that not only looks back to the discussion in 12:1-30, but also anticipates the discussion that is to follow in chapter 13. Paul told the Corinthians to eagerly desire the greater gifts.

B. The Way of Love (13:1-3)

1. Though I speak with the tongues of men and of angels, and have not charity, I am become as sounding brass, or a tinkling cymbal.

2. And though I have the gift of prophecy, and understand all mysteries, and all knowledge; and though I have all faith, so that I could remove mountains, and have not charity, I am nothing.

3. And though I bestow all my goods to feed the poor, and though I give my body to be burned, and have not charity, it profiteth me nothing.

First Corinthians 13 is one of the most familiar chapters in the New Testament. It does not only provide an answer to the Corinthians' attitude to the exercise of spiritual gifts, but also offers a solution to the divisiveness that was at the root of almost all their problems. Paul was about to show them a "more excellent way"—a way that stands in sharp contrast to theirs.

The Corinthians were fascinated with spiritual gifts, particularly the gift of tongues. But Paul reminds them even the gift of tongues is meaningless without love. Without love, a person may speak with the gift of tongues, but it is as meaningless as sounding brass or a tinkling cymbal. The Greek word (*glossais*) translated "tongues" has the simple idea of "languages" in some places (Acts 2:11; Revelation 5:9). Hence, some conclude that the gift of tongues is simply the ability to communicate the gospel in other languages—it is the capability of learning languages quickly. However, its usage here shows that it not only can but usually does refer to a supernatural language by which a believer communicates with God. There is no other way the reference to "tongues of angels" can be understood here.

"As the qualities of love are to be actively pursued, so are spiritual gifts. Believers may express their desire in prayer in regard to spiritual gifts, but at the same time be receptive to whatever gifts the Spirit chooses to bestow."

—**French Arrington**

Talk About It:
1. Explain the image of "sounding brass, or a tinkling cymbal" (v. 1).
2. Why does Paul repeatedly use the word *all* in verses 2 and 3?

Paul goes on to say that prophecy, knowledge, and faith to do miracles are likewise irrelevant apart from love. Giving oneself as a sacrifice is a barren gesture unless it is inspired by love. Paul's point is unmistakably clear: the Corinthian Christians were majoring in the minor; they were missing the motive and the goal of the gifts, making the means to become their own end. So, Paul draws their attention back to the preeminence of love. Love trumps all. As said earlier, one must understand that for Paul it is not an issue of love versus the gifts. Neither must it be for us. Each of the spiritual gifts is great and, together, they constitute a formidable power. But their motivation and purpose are ineffectual unless they are guided by love.

II. CHRIST'S LOVE DESCRIBED (1 Corinthians 13:4-8)
A. An Edifying Love (vv. 4-7)

4. Charity suffereth long, and is kind; charity envieth not; charity vaunteth not itself, is not puffed up,

5. Doth not behave itself unseemly, seeketh not her own, is not easily provoked, thinketh no evil;

6. Rejoiceth not in iniquity, but rejoiceth in the truth;

7. Beareth all things, believeth all things, hopeth all things, endureth all things.

Although it has often been taken as a description of Christ's character, and rightly so, in verses 4-7 Paul shows how a Christian ought to behave and how he, as the apostle to the Corinthians, has been attempting to behave. Love is a matter of behavior, an other-directed behavior for that matter, and not feeling. Such is the character of Christian love. The word *agape*, which is likely derived from the Septuagint (Greek translation of the Old Testament), is often used of God's love, not ordinary human love. What a great privilege it is for the Christian to be a bearer, by means of God's Spirit, of God's love.

Love is not an abstract, airy concept. It is described with action words. Paul is not writing about either how he feels or how he expects the Corinthians to feel. Rather, it is about how they should act as Christians. True love is always demonstrated by action. Love suffers long, as depicted in 2 Peter 3:9: "The Lord is not slack concerning His promise, as some count slackness, but is longsuffering toward us, not willing that any should perish but that all should come to repentance" (*NKJV*). If God's love is in us, we will be long-suffering to those who annoy us and hurt us. Love is kind. Kindness is demonstrated in simple acts such as giving a cup of cold water to the thirsty (Matthew 10:42; 25:35).

In verses 4b-6 of the text (*NKJV*), Paul enumerates eight things love is not:

Talk About It:
1. Describe all the things love does *not* do (vv. 4-6).
2. What does love "rejoice in" (v. 6), and why?
3. According to verse 7, how does love act?

1. *Love does not envy.* Whereas jealousy says, "I would like to have what you have," envy says, "I wish you did not have what you have." Envy is one of the most damaging of all sins. It accomplishes nothing, except to hurt the one who harbors it. Love keeps its distance from envy, and does not resent it when someone else is promoted or blessed.

2. *Love does not parade itself.* Love in action can work anonymously. It does not have to have the limelight or the attention to do a good job, or to be satisfied with the result. Love gives because it loves to give, not out of the sense of praise it can have from showing itself off.

3. *Love is not puffed up.* Love is not arrogant and self-focused. Love doesn't get its head swelled; instead, it focuses on the needs of others.

4. *Love does not behave rudely.* Love is not ill-mannered or brash. Where there is love, there will be kindness and good manners. A person who loves does not just speak his or her mind but minds his or her speech.

5. *Love does not seek its own,* an idea that Paul expresses in a slightly different manner in Romans 12:10 and Philippians 2:4. This is being like Jesus in a basic way: being an others-centered person instead of a self-centered person.

6. *Love is not easily provoked.* This is perhaps the most difficult to understand among the characteristics of love. In plain language, love is neither touchy nor irritable.

7. *Love thinks no evil.* It does not keep an account of any wrong it has received. It puts away the hurts of the past instead of clinging to them. After all, nobody is more hurt by bitterness than the person who keeps it.

8. *Love does not rejoice in iniquity.* "I told you so" and "It serves you right" are familiar statements, but they are not the language of love. Love desires the best for others and does not derive personal satisfaction from the failure of others. Instead, love rejoices in the truth.

Paul ends the discussion of the characteristics of love on a positive note. He states things that love *does.* It "bears all things, believes all things, hopes all things, endures all things" (v. 7, *NKJV*). The word *panta,* translated "all," can also be translated as "always." Paul's point is that love never tires of support, never loses faith, never gives up hope, and never quits. Most of us can bear, believe and hope, but only for a while! The greatness of *agape* love is that it keeps on bearing, believing and hoping. It doesn't give up.

B. An Everlasting Love (v. 8)

8. Charity never faileth: but whether there be prophecies, they shall fail; whether there be tongues, they shall cease; whether there be knowledge, it shall vanish away.

Love's Actions
What does love look like? It has the hands to help others. It has the feet to hasten to the poor and needy. It has the eyes to see misery and want. It has ears to hear the sighs and sorrows of men. That is what love looks like.
—**Augustine**

Here Paul attests to the permanence of love as he continues to put the spiritual gifts and virtues in perspective. Love never fails. Paul is addressing the overemphasis the Corinthian Christians had on the gifts of the Holy Spirit. He shows they should emphasize love more than the gifts, because the gifts are temporary "containers" of God's work; love is the work itself. The spiritual gifts remain until the end, but are imperfect and will eventually come to an end. However, there is no warrant in the verse to conclude that the miraculous gifts ended with the apostles. Paul does not give the slightest hint of such interpretation. Obviously, knowledge did not pass away with Paul. Neither can it be justified to say that the church today has entered its time of perfection. The fact that one does not appreciate tongues and prophecy as legitimate gifts neither invalidates them nor justifies their being wished away.

III. CHRIST'S LOVE ENDURES (1 Corinthians 13:9-13)
A. When Perfection Comes (vv. 9-12)

9. For we know in part, and we prophesy in part.

10. But when that which is perfect is come, then that which is in part shall be done away.

11. When I was a child, I spake as a child, I understood as a child, I thought as a child: but when I became a man, I put away childish things.

12. For now we see through a glass, darkly; but then face to face: now I know in part; but then shall I know even as also I am known.

Talk About It:
1. What do we now
do "in part," and
when will that
change (vv. 9, 10,
12)?
2. What is a mark of
spiritual immaturity
(v. 11)?

Paul gives the reason why spiritual gifts, such as prophecy and knowledge, will cease. They are specifically meant to equip the believer to endure in this age. In due course, they will be brought to nothing. Paul likens the situation to that of growing up. There is a life appropriate to a child. Such is manifested in thought, speech and reasoning power. But when adulthood arrives, these characteristics are no longer viable and, as such, must be left behind.

Tongues will cease when the Lord returns and completes His plan for Christians. Partial knowledge, such as the Corinthians had and Christians now have, will be brought to nought. Therefore, all spiritual gifts can be characterized as partial, but love is eternal.

In mistaking the part for the whole and the partial for the final, the Corinthians, unlike Paul, were childish. It is wrong to suggest that verses 11 and 12 see tongues-speaking and prophecy as childishness, particularly since Paul himself claimed to do both. Paul is saying that there is an age appropriate for the gifts, and *now* is that age. When the completion of this age finally arrives, it will be time to set aside whatever is not eternal.

The word *glass* in verse 12 refers to a mirror. We look into a mirror and see the reflection of ourselves and our time. This means that the image is imperfect and still obscure. What we see in a mirror is limited in comparison to what we see in reality. It is flat and one-dimensional. At best it is limited in vision and perspective. When that which is perfect is realized, there will be unlimited vision, unlimited knowledge, and unlimited life. What we see now is a reflection of what we shall fully and truly see in the future.

B. The Greatest of These (v. 13)
13. And now abideth faith, hope, charity, these three; but the greatest of these is charity.
For Paul the three great pursuits of the Christian life are not "miracles, power and gifts." Instead, they are *faith, hope* and *love*. Though the gifts are precious, and given by the Holy Spirit today, they were never meant to be the focus or goal of our Christian lives. Instead, we must pursue faith, hope and love.

Talk About It:
1. What do faith, hope and love have in common?
2. What makes love "the greatest"?

CONCLUSION
First Corinthians 13 is not only powerful but heart-searching. It calls for a careful examination of our motivation for service. There is a reason why Paul put this chapter in the midst of his discussion of spiritual gifts. Paul wanted the Corinthian Christians to remember that giftedness is not the measure of maturity, but the display of love is. Each Christian must ask, Am I exercising God's gift out of love, in order to glorify Him and bless others, or do I have a secret motive or desire to aggrandize myself, to receive human praise, to cover up some deep personal problem, or to appear more spiritual than others?

We must allow the Holy Spirit to purify our motives. We must do all things and respond to all situations out of love. To love, we must desire to love. Love is a choice! Paul's discussion of love was not meant to persuade the Corinthians to abandon their prized spiritual gifts. Rather, it was intended to convince them to exercise their gifts with love. If otherwise exercised, they would be spiritually unfruitful.

GOLDEN TEXT CHALLENGE
"NOW ABIDETH FAITH, HOPE, CHARITY, THESE THREE; BUT THE GREATEST OF THESE IS CHARITY" (1 Corinthians 13:13).
Faith speaks of the present; *hope* speaks of the future. *Love* anchors the present to the security of the past, and it attaches our present to the expectation of the future. When we love perfectly in the present, we can have perfect assurance for the future.

Love is the greatest because it is the anchor of all other Christian qualities. It secures and holds them in our lives. Love is the greatest because it is the source and energizer of all other virtues. All that is good in us stems from the impulse of love.

Daily Devotions:
M. Love Your Neighbor
Leviticus 19:11-18
T. Love the Lord
Psalm 31:19-24
W. The Beauty of Christ's Love
Song of Solomon 2:1-4
T. Love Your Enemies
Matthew 5:43-48
F. Abide in Love
John 15:9-17
S. Love One Another
1 John 3:11-18

Second Corinthians
by Charles W. Conn

The Purpose of 2 Corinthians

If we are to understand Paul's second epistle to the Corinthians, we must understand something of his relationship to the Corinthian church. In this epistle he speaks more of himself than in any other of his writings, so that it is regarded as his most autobiographical epistle. He does not hesitate to bare his own heart, if by doing so the ills of the church can be healed. Consequently, we see in 2 Corinthians the heart of a pastor as it yearns for the welfare of his children in the Lord.

The Background

Perhaps as much as a year had passed since Paul wrote 1 Corinthians, a year in which conditions in Corinth had further deteriorated. Distressed at the continued splintering of the Corinthians into factionalism, and their grievous moral lapses, Paul made a visit to the church. The visit was not entirely satisfactory and he returned to Ephesus with a heavy heart. Paul then wrote the Corinthians an exceedingly severe letter from Ephesus and sent it by Titus to the carnal church. Hoping to visit Corinth still again as he visited the Macedonian churches, Paul crossed into Macedonia and proceeded southward. While he was passing through Macedonia, Titus joined him and brought a happy report from Corinth. The severe letter, while it hurt the Corinthians, had a telling effect on them.

Titus' good news prompted Paul to write the letter we know as 2 Corinthians in gratitude. In this he endeavored to make his reconciliation with the people. As a true pastor with genuine care for the people, he had to be willing to put his personal friendship on the line in order to help them. This is often the sternest test of real friendship.

Titus' report was not altogether favorable, for there were still some in Corinth who were bent on discrediting Paul as both man and apostle. Certain men, claiming to be true apostles, questioned Paul's apostleship and even sought to cast suspicion on his practice of working for a living, as though he had some dark, hidden motive for not calling on the Corinthians for his support (11:5-15). His critics accused Paul of being in reality a weak person, a nobody, rude and contemptible in speech and physical appearance, who enjoyed writing terrifying letters (10:8-11). Such snide criticisms should remind us that the apostles were not divine, but mortal men facing many pernicious attitudes that are common to this day. The insults modern Christians sometimes face are but ancient abuses in modern garb.

The Apostleship of Paul

Paul gave a powerful defense of his ministry; the result is an epistle that, more than any other, sets forth the glory of the Christian ministry. As has been said, 2 Corinthians is Paul's most autobiographical letter. In it we learn that he had, on five occasions, been given 39 lashes; three times he, though a Roman citizen, had been beaten by a Roman soldier; three times he had been shipwrecked; he had been starved, robbed, betrayed; he had been weary, lonely, and in pain—all for the love of Christ. Heavier than his afflictions, however, was the unrelieved burden for the churches that lay always upon his heart (11:23—12:10).

Paul's suffering for the gospel, however, was not his exclusive priority. All true ministers must endure afflictions, for God has put the treasure of the gospel in earthen vessels (4:7-10).

Summary of 2 Corinthians

Paul observes that he has suffered great danger in Asia (probably in the city of Ephesus), which amounted to a death sentence, but God delivered him (1:8-10). Having been so close to death, he certainly has no reason to be other than sincere and generous toward the Corinthians (vv. 12-14). He had hoped to visit Corinth on his way to Macedonia, but decided against it because he wished to spare them a second painful visit. His change of plans had been due to concern rather than fickleness (vv. 15-23). Paul declares several times in the epistle, however, that he will come to them from Macedonia (12:14; 13:1).

Twice Paul mentions the joy he experienced when he encountered Titus in Macedonia and heard the good news from Corinth (2:13; 7:5-16). In the last instance Paul dwells, in some detail, on Titus' good report and the great pleasure it had given him.

One additional emphasis concerned a collection that was being raised among all the churches for the needy church in Jerusalem (chs. 8, 9). He commends the Corinthians for their generosity and admonishes them not to embarrass him by being negligent toward their responsibility. He has boasted about the Corinthians too much for them to let him down!

The criticisms he has heard are unfair and untrue. Paul therefore devotes much space to a defense of his apostolic ministry (10:1–12:13). In the closing part of his defense, he observes a battle he has had with a "thorn in the flesh." Though the thorn was not removed when he sought God about it, he has received grace to bear it.

Paul finally reminds the church that he is coming to them and warns them against the evils that have so long corrupted them: debates, envyings, wraths, strifes, backbitings, whisperings, swellings, tumults, uncleanness, fornication and lasciviousness (12:14-21). He admonishes them to examine themselves and correct those things that will bring wrath upon them (ch. 13).

Treasure in Clay Pots

2 Corinthians 4:1 through 5:10

Unit Theme:
1 and 2 Corinthians

Central Truth:
The indwelling presence of Christ is the believer's source of joy and eternal hope.

Focus:
Be amazed that Christ lives in us and rejoice in His presence.

Context:
Paul's second letter to the Corinthian church was written around A.D. 56, a few months after 1 Corinthians.

Golden Text:
"We have this treasure in earthen vessels, that the excellency of the power may be of God, and not of us" (2 Corinthians 4:7).

Study Outline:
I. Christ in Us: Light (2 Corinthians 4:1-6)
II. Christ in Us: Power (2 Corinthians 4:7-18)
III. Christ in Us: Heavenly Reward (2 Corinthians 5:1-10)

INTRODUCTION

Paul begins 2 Corinthians 4 with the word *therefore*, an indication that what he is about to write is connected with what he has said in the preceding context. In this case, it connects the characteristics of the victorious Christian (ch. 3) to what God has done for Paul (ch. 4).

What are the characteristics of victorious Christians? They are "living epistles" of the gospel of Christ (see 3:1-3); they find their sufficiency in God (vv. 4, 5); they are "ministers of a new covenant [promise]—not of the letter but of the Spirit" (v. 6, *NIV*); they have freedom through the indwelling Spirit (v. 17); and they are being transformed into God's image (v. 18). God leads us in victory, makes us competent, gives us the new covenant, liberates us, gives us His Spirit, and works transformation in our lives. God does these things for all of His children in order to help us to become servants, as Paul was Christ's servant.

I. CHRIST IN US: LIGHT (2 Corinthians 4:1-6)
A. Renouncing Shameful Things (vv. 1-4)

1. Therefore seeing we have this ministry, as we have received mercy, we faint not;

2. But have renounced the hidden things of dishonesty, not walking in craftiness, nor handling the word of God deceitfully; but by manifestation of the truth commending ourselves to every man's conscience in the sight of God.

3. But if our gospel be hid, it is hid to them that are lost:

4. In whom the god of this world hath blinded the minds of them which believe not, lest the light of the glorious gospel of Christ, who is the image of God, should shine unto them.

In verse 1, Paul resumes the theme of 3:6, which is his personal as well as his colleagues' divine appointment, as well as God's provision to be ministers of the new covenant. They have not only been recipients of God's mercy but have also been called to communicate and offer it to others. They received the gospel not only as a personal way of life, but also as a ministry. As a result, they do not faint or lose heart. The glory of the commission Paul received far outweighs all the distressing experiences he might face in fulfilling or discharging it. For Paul, the commission is worth all the trials that go with it. He was filled with a great hope that eclipses everything that was capable of driving him to despair. This theme will be picked up later in 4:16.

In the meantime, in verse 2 Paul goes on to fend off the accusation of deceptive behavior that was previously addressed in 2:17, where he was maliciously accused of operating with underhanded methods. He emphatically rejects such accusations and insinuations, drawing a parallel between the nature of the gospel he preached and that of his personal character. He affirms that in the same manner that the new covenant is open and forthright, his own methods were also open. He had not manipulated the message. He is a forthright person. In this we must learn that to live the gospel is just as important as to preach it. Paul did not preach for personal gain. He did not tamper with God's message. If the character of the messenger is in question, the integrity of the message also becomes questionable.

Despite Paul's claim that he preached the gospel openly, some of Paul's critics still maintained that his message was veiled ("hid," 4:3), perhaps suggesting that he was not an effective preacher. Paul maintains that the veiling had nothing to do with his method of communicating the gospel. Instead, the fault rested in two areas: the hearers and the source of blindness. First, to those who are perishing ("lost"), the gospel neither makes sense, nor is it valuable. Second, the minds of those who are perishing have been blinded by Satan (v. 4), who is the god of this world.

Talk About It:
1. What are some qualities spiritual leaders should have (vv. 1, 2)?
2. How can the gospel "be hid" (v. 3)?
3. What keeps many people from faith in Christ (v. 4)?

"If Christians want us [atheists] to believe in a Redeemer, let them act redeemed."
—Voltaire

This does not absolve them of the responsibility for their unbelief. God enlightens everyone (John 1:9) enough to accept or reject the light (3:16; 1 Timothy 2:3, 4).

B. Preaching Christ (v. 5)

5. For we preach not ourselves, but Christ Jesus the Lord; and ourselves your servants for Jesus' sake.

Talk About It:
What was Paul's message to the Corinthians?

In our media-oriented society, the preacher is pressured to use the pulpit to display his or her eloquence and oratorical skills. The congregation, in its appetite for entertainment and desire for amusement, adds to that pressure. But Paul would not succumb to such pressure. Rather, he explained the basic thrust of his preaching: Christ as our Lord; ourselves as your slaves. As faithful heralds of the gospel, Paul and his coworkers did not draw attention to themselves. Although his ministry was more glorious than that of Moses, it was not concerned with personal glorification. He never advertised or preached himself. He had previously told the Corinthians that he did not come to them with persuasive words of human wisdom (1 Corinthians 2:1-4). Moreover, Paul defined his role as that of a servant. Although he could have commanded their obedience, he chose not to.

C. Giving Us Knowledge (v. 6)

6. For God, who commanded the light to shine out of darkness, hath shined in our hearts, to give the light of the knowledge of the glory of God in the face of Jesus Christ.

Talk About It:
What does God's light accomplish in us?

"For" indicates that the sentence introduced here explains or reaffirms the implication of what Paul has just said in verse 5; that is, why he preaches Christ. It is related to the experience of the preacher as a new creation. The key thought here is that God's light dispels darkness in every form—whether it be the physical darkness of night or the spiritual darkness of human ignorance. Unlike those who have been blinded by Satan, Paul and his fellow workers have been illuminated by God. One must note that the light that dispels darkness is to be found in the face of Jesus Christ. For Paul, to know Christ is to know God. The corollary is true: to not know Christ is to not know God.

II. CHRIST IN US: POWER (2 Corinthians 4:7-18)
A. Not From Ourselves (v. 7)

7. But we have this treasure in earthen vessels, that the excellency of the power may be of God, and not of us.

Talk About It:
Explain the phrase "treasure in earthen vessels."

In the rest of this lesson, Paul contrasts his body and its sufferings with the heavenly bodies believers will receive at the resurrection. He opens the section with a striking image. Paul carries the treasure of the gospel in an earthen vessel (jar of clay). In the Old Testament the image functioned to show the fragility of humans (Psalm 31:12, 13; Jeremiah 22:28). Specifically the image of "earthen vessels" is used in the context of suffering as punishment for Israel's sins (see Isaiah 30:14; Jeremiah 19:1, 11). Paul's suffering is that of apostolic service.

The point of the contrast in verse 7 of the text is the paradox between the inestimable value of the message and the suffering of the messenger. Behind Paul's statement is an allusion to the attack on Paul by his opponents that he is weak and fails to show he possesses divine power. However, for Paul, divine power is God's possession alone and, paradoxically, it is present in his sufferings when he preaches as an apostle. Paul is interested in showing that his bodily weakness and sufferings do not evidence a lack of apostolic commission, but rather manifest an apostleship that is derived from a suffering Lord and which has as its ultimate purpose the glory of God.

> "Though we as Christians are like Christ, having the firstfruits of the Spirit, yet we are unlike Him, having the remainders of the flesh."
> —**Thomas Watson**

B. Dying to Live (vv. 8-12)

8. We are troubled on every side, yet not distressed; we are perplexed, but not in despair;

9. Persecuted, but not forsaken; cast down, but not destroyed;

10. Always bearing about in the body the dying of the Lord Jesus, that the life also of Jesus might be made manifest in our body.

11. For we which live are always delivered unto death for Jesus' sake, that the life also of Jesus might be made manifest in our mortal flesh.

12. So then death worketh in us, but life in you.

To develop his point further, Paul turns to his "catalog of hardships." Here one finds the list of trials Paul went through. This list was not just meant to instill courage but to show that God's power was present precisely in Paul's sufferings. Paul emphasizes the weakness and insignificance of the apostles in verses 8 and 9 in a manner that is reminiscent of 1 Corinthians 4:9-13. However, Paul here draws a vivid contrast between sufferings and preservation.

In verse 10 of the text, Paul states that he bears the dying of Jesus in his body, expressing the dangers to which Paul and his coworkers were constantly exposed for Christ's sake. Those dangers constituted their sharing in sufferings. Paul's suffering, as one who was under Christ's rule, shows that God's power was present in the dying of Jesus and in his own sufferings. Similarly, Paul states that the purpose of bearing the dying of Jesus is to manifest the life of Jesus in his person.

Verse 11 elucidates the previous verse by repeating its thought in a slightly different language. That Paul was given up

Talk About It:
1. Explain the four "not's" in verses 8 and 9.
2. What did Paul and the other apostles "always" face (vv. 10, 11), and why were they willing to do so (v. 12)?

to death because of Jesus indicates his faith and willingness to conform himself to the pattern of existence found in Jesus. There is an important lesson to learn here. The Corinthians, like many Christians today, and especially Pentecostals, believed that sufferings and adversity were inconsistent with the Spirit-filled life, let alone with "victorious" or "successful" Christian living. Paul saw it in a different way. It was his hardships that validated his ministry. In Paul's day, and for many Christians around the world today, the life of the Christian is a life of suffering and for a purpose. The purpose of Paul's suffering was to benefit the Corinthians.

C. For the Glory of God (vv. 13-18)

13. We having the same spirit of faith, according as it is written, I believed, and therefore have I spoken; we also believe, and therefore speak;

14. Knowing that he which raised up the Lord Jesus shall raise up us also by Jesus, and shall present us with you.

15. For all things are for your sakes, that the abundant grace might through the thanksgiving of many redound to the glory of God.

16. For which cause we faint not; but though our outward man perish, yet the inward man is renewed day by day.

17. For our light affliction, which is but for a moment, worketh for us a far more exceeding and eternal weight of glory;

18. While we look not at the things which are seen, but at the things which are not seen: for the things which are seen are temporal; but the things which are not seen are eternal.

Paul's suffering and message are for the sake of the believing Corinthians and for the purpose of reaching out to more Corinthians. Paul speaks boldly because his faith reveals to him that beyond earthly tribulation lies the assurance of resurrection. Paul's faith is more than a subjective attitude. It has an objective content, consisting in the knowledge that God has raised Jesus from the dead, and that He will raise Paul at the end of time to be with Jesus, and implicitly that He will also raise up the Corinthian Christians.

Talk About It:
1. How did Paul act on his "spirit of faith" (v. 13)?
2. What was the source of Paul's faith (v. 14)?
3. How can believers be "renewed day by day" (v. 16)?
4. What was Paul's perspective on his suffering (vv. 17, 18)?

In verse 15, Paul concludes that his ultimate goal as Christ's apostle is to bring glory to God. The basis of all his action has been his converts and not to increase his own stature. His aim is that God's grace may spread to more people as the gospel is preached. Therefore, Paul restates what he previously said in verse 1, "we do not lose heart" (v. 16, *NIV*). Paul proceeds to draw a distinction between the outward man and inner man. The outward person is the person seen by others, or that aspect of one's humanity that is subject to various assaults and hardships such as those listed in verses 8 and 9. The inner person is the unseen personality known only to God and self. The Corinthians need to understand that, despite Paul's bodily weakness, his inner person is being transformed daily.

He then turns to the contrast between the present and the eternal future—this life and the life to come (v. 17). For Paul's opponents the present is a time of glory, but for Paul it is a time of suffering. The life to come is that of glory. Contrary to the position of his opponents, Paul can say that, according to God's surpassing gift, his present momentary suffering will be followed by eternal glory. Paul neither minimized nor glorified his sufferings. Instead, he had an eternal perspective. In other words, he took his pain in strides, looking at everything in light of eternity.

In verse 18, Paul draws a conclusion from what precedes. He fixes his gaze not upon the things that belong to this age, but upon the things that belong to the coming age. As Christians we must be careful not to base our hopes on the things we see. The unseen will endure when all else fails.

> "Hope means expectancy when things are otherwise hopeless."
> —G.K. Chesterton

III. CHRIST IN US: HEAVENLY REWARD (2 Corinthians 5:1-10)
A. An Eternal Dwelling (vv. 1-4)

1. For we know that if our earthly house of this tabernacle were dissolved, we have a building of God, an house not made with hands, eternal in the heavens.

2. For in this we groan, earnestly desiring to be clothed upon with our house which is from heaven:

3. If so be that being clothed we shall not be found naked.

4. For we that are in this tabernacle do groan, being burdened: not for that we would be unclothed, but clothed upon, that mortality might be swallowed up of life.

"For we know" suggests that the Corinthians know and believe what Paul is about to say. It is a confident assertion. It also suggests that Paul is rehearsing something he has already taught them. Paul has previously dealt with Christian hope of resurrection-transformation in his previous letter to them (1 Corinthians 15). Besides, "for" points back to 2 Corinthians 4:18 and answers why the gospel preacher must remain focused on what is not seen (permanent) rather than what is seen (temporal). In doing so, Paul switches to the imagery of a house and contrasts it with that of a tent. When Paul described our present body as an "earthly tent" (*NIV*), he was stressing the temporary nature of our body. Not only is it temporary, but it is not as stable as a building. A tent is movable and has no foundation, but a building is solid, more stable, founded and permanent. One must not lose sight of the purpose of the metaphor. The promise of resurrection provides hope for Paul.

Talk About It:
1. What is the Christian's great hope (v. 1)?
2. Why do Christians "groan" and feel "burdened" (v. 4)?

Talk About It:
What is the "guarantee" God has given believers (v. 5, *NKJV*)?

It is for this reason that he does not lose heart. What a joy to know that we have a hope beyond the grave (1 Corinthians 15:19). There is assurance of physical resurrection and transformation. Believers, particularly those who are facing physical hardships, either due to persecution or as a result of their labors in the gospel, ought to take comfort in this, knowing that a permanent house of God's own design awaits them.

Paul continues by saying that while living in this tent, we groan, longing to be clothed with a heavenly dwelling. Thus, Paul shifts his metaphor to that of clothing. Verse 4 shows that Paul's aspiration was not simply to get out of this body, which would be a glorious victory, but he had his eye on a vastly grander and more glorious enterprise, that is, "that mortality may be swallowed up by life" (*NKJV*).

B. The Spirit as a Pledge (v. 5)

5. Now he that hath wrought us for the selfsame thing is God, who also hath given unto us the earnest of the Spirit.

How could Paul and the Corinthians be so sure of what Paul has just said? The answer lies in this verse. Believers have been given the Holy Spirit. God has poured the Holy Spirit into the lives of believers as an "earnest"—surety, guarantee—for the promise of resurrection. The Holy Spirit in us begins the transformation process (3:18). We are being made new on the inside. That's what Paul meant when he said that "inwardly we are being renewed day by day" (4:16, *NIV*). The Holy Spirit equips us with the characteristics and conduct that will dominate our heavenly existence. The wonderful spiritual work already enjoyed by Paul was a foretaste of coming glorification. So the blessed work of sanctification in the heart is an advanced payment (pledge, deposit) on the illustrious glorification that awaits us. The same is true of the healing of the body, a blessed privilege in this life. With the coming of the Holy Spirit, already a taste of God's future has invaded our present existence (Hebrews 6:5).

C. Present With the Lord (vv. 6-10)

6. Therefore we are always confident, knowing that, whilst we are at home in the body, we are absent from the Lord:

7. (For we walk by faith, not by sight:)

8. We are confident, I say, and willing rather to be absent from the body, and to be present with the Lord.

9. Wherefore we labour, that, whether present or absent, we may be accepted of him.

10. For we must all appear before the judgment seat of Christ; that every one may receive the things done in his body, according to that he hath done, whether it be good or bad.

Instead of trying to escape from this body, the assurance that the Christian will live eternally and receive a new body causes him or her to take on new perspectives for living in this body. Paul's primary desire was to be "clothed upon" (v. 2) with the everlasting body which is from heaven. He longed to evacuate the temporal body and go to the glorified presence. He knew that "to be absent from the body" was "to be present with the Lord" (v. 8). There was only one other alternative: to remain in the body and be absent from the Lord. Paul kept his eyes on the bigger picture, anticipating eternity.

While we are in this body, we cannot see the Lord; so we live by faith. Of course, we are all looking forward to the time when we will be able to see Him. However, we must not make it such a focus that we fail to live here on earth in this body for our Lord. It was not Paul's environment, whether in this body or in the eternal body, that determined his life. Rather, it was his goal to please the Lord in whatever environment he found himself (v. 9). That goal was Paul's motivation for service.

Verses 9 and 10 contain an implicit warning. It is not the court of public opinion that ultimately counts. We will be held accountable by God for our actions and commitments.

CONCLUSION

In today's text, Paul explains in detail the paradox between the incredible glory and hope that was his as a minister of the new covenant and the sacrificial suffering he was undergoing. Every believer should read this passage regularly for encouragement. The hope of glory kept Paul going at all times, even in immensely difficult times. This hope is not for Paul alone, but for all believers of all ages, in all places. We must lay hold of it.

GOLDEN TEXT CHALLENGE

"WE HAVE THIS TREASURE IN EARTHEN VESSELS, THAT THE EXCELLENCY OF THE POWER MAY BE OF GOD, AND NOT OF US" (2 Corinthians 4:7).

"The treasure of gospel light and grace is put into earthen vessels. The ministers of the gospel are weak and frail creatures, and subject to like passions and infirmities as other men; they are mortal, and soon broken in pieces. And God has so ordered it that the weaker the vessels are, the stronger His power may appear to be, that the treasure itself should be valued the more.

"There is an excellence of power in the gospel of Christ, to enlighten the mind, to convince the conscience, to convert the soul, and to rejoice the heart; but all this power is from God the author, and not from men, who are but instruments, so that God in all things must be glorified" (Matthew Henry).

Talk About It:
1. How must Christians "walk," and why (v. 7)?
2. What was Paul's ministry goal (v. 9)?
3. What will Christians "receive" one day (v. 10)?

"Sometimes those of us who hold that the Lord Jesus Christ is coming again are spoken of as pessimists. I think it can be truly said that we are really the only ones who have any right to be optimistic."
—**William Culbertson**

Daily Devotions:
M. The Lord Is My Light
Psalm 27:1-10
T. Walking in the Light
Isaiah 2:1-8
W. We Are the Light
Isaiah 58:6-12
T. Heirs With Christ
Romans 8:14-17
F. Christ Dwells Within Us
Ephesians 3:14-21
S. Our Hope of Glory
Colossians 1:25-29

Grace of Giving

2 Corinthians 8:1-15; 9:1-15

Unit Theme:
1 and 2 Corinthians

Central Truth:
As followers of Jesus Christ, we should imitate His generosity.

Focus:
Recognize and emulate Christ as the ultimate example of generous giving.

Context:
Paul's second letter to the Corinthian church was written around A.D. 56, a few months after 1 Corinthians.

Golden Text:
"Ye know the grace of our Lord Jesus Christ, that, though he was rich, yet for your sakes he became poor, that ye through his poverty might be rich" (2 Corinthians 8:9).

Study Outline:
I. Give Generously (2 Corinthians 8:1-7)
II. Fulfill Your Obligations (2 Corinthians 8:8-12; 9:2-5)
III. Give Joyfully (2 Corinthians 9:6-15)

INTRODUCTION

In these two chapters Paul discussed the "collection project," something that played an important role in his apostolic ministry. Although Paul did not solicit personal financial support, he spent about 10 years soliciting funds for what is commonly referred to as the Jerusalem collection. It was a collection that Paul took up among the Gentile churches and was specifically meant for Jerusalem, where the believers were facing hard times due to the famine that ravaged the area during the mid to late 40s.

The purpose of the collection was twofold. First, it was designed to alleviate the needs of the Jerusalem church, thus constituting an expression of the interdependence of believers worldwide (2 Corinthians 8:14). Second, it was to demonstrate the nature of the church as a body that transcends national and geographical boundaries. The collection relates to the Jewish expectation that in the last days the Gentiles would come to Jerusalem with gifts. It was a tangible representation of the essence of the gospel—that all are equal in Christ; that is, in Christ "there is neither Jew nor Greek, slave nor free, male nor female" (Galatians 3:28, *NIV*).

The timing of the collection is also instructive. Paul chose not to write about the collection until he was sure that some of the outstanding issues between him and the Corinthians had been resolved, the result of which was the confidence he exuded in 2 Corinthians 7:16. It is also important to note that today's study begins and ends with what God has done through Christ (8:1; 9:15).

I. GIVE GENEROUSLY (2 Corinthians 8:1-7)
A. A Sacrificial Act (vv. 1, 2)

1. Moreover, brethren, we do you to wit of the grace of God bestowed on the churches of Macedonia;

2. How that in a great trial of affliction the abundance of their joy and their deep poverty abounded unto the riches of their liberality.

Three important things need to be noted at the start of the chapter. First, Paul uses a word of endearment, *brethren*, to show his affection for the Corinthians. Second, we see the first use of the word *grace* as it relates to Christian giving. The offering of the Macedonians was grounded in their relation to God, so Paul labeled it as "the grace of God." Third, he made an example of the Macedonians, who, though living under persecution and poverty, gave generously. This was proof of love and grace, both of which constitute sufficient motivation for giving.

There are two contrasts in verse 2: "affliction" and "joy"; "poverty" and "riches." The contrasts provide a valuable lesson: the Christian's joy has no correlation with outward circumstances. Christians can experience joy in the midst of sufferings and persecution (Matthew 5:10-12; Acts 5:41; Philippians 1:12-18; James 1:2; 1 Peter 1:6, 7). We must refuse to become creatures of circumstances. This was true of the Macedonians, hence Paul held up their sacrificial giving as a motivation for the Corinthians.

B. A Willful Act (vv. 3-5)

3. For to their power, I bear record, yea, and beyond their power they were willing of themselves;

4. Praying us with much entreaty that we would receive the gift, and take upon us the fellowship of the ministering to the saints.

5. And this they did, not as we hoped, but first gave their own selves to the Lord, and unto us by the will of God.

In spite of the extreme poverty of the Macedonians, they gave generously—not only according to their ability, but until it hurt. What mattered to Paul was not the amount or the quantity of what they gave, but the spirit in which they gave. With God, a couple of "cents" sacrificially given can outweigh billions of dollars. This was the reason Paul used the Macedonians as an example for the Corinthians to emulate. But Paul did not stop there. He described the emotional state of the Macedonians as they gave—"praying" (begging) with much entreaty to give; considering it a privilege to give. Others would have made such a situation an excuse from giving. And Paul would have gladly excused them. But not the Macedonians. They were not going to be denied the opportunity to minister grace to others through their giving in spite of their own needs.

wit (v. 1)—know

the churches of Macedonia (v. 1)—included the congregations in Philippi, Thessalonica and Berea

Talk About It:
1. What two challenges did the Macedonian churches face?
2. How did the "grace of God" minister to the Macedonian believers?

Talk About It:
1. Describe the Macedonians' attitude toward giving (vv. 3, 4).
2. What did the Macedonians do "first" (v. 5), and why was this important?

Paul put the giving of the Macedonians in the context of their commitment to God and their loyalty to him as their apostle. So intense was the desire of the Macedonians to serve the Lord that they would not allow their economic hardships to keep them from being involved in the ministry opportunity available to them. The Corinthians were left to draw the inferences.

C. A Gracious Act (vv. 6, 7)

6. Insomuch that we desired Titus, that as he had begun, so he would also finish in you the same grace also.

7. Therefore, as ye abound in every thing, in faith, and utterance, and knowledge, and in all diligence, and in your love to us, see that ye abound in this grace also.

Having looked at the example of the Macedonians, the Corinthians are now prodded by Paul to also excel in giving. The initial zeal of the Corinthians in the project had evidently sagged. Rather than scold the Corinthians for lack of completion, Paul praises them for their initial enthusiasm. He appeals to their honor by pointing to their spiritual riches—their faith, utterance (speech), knowledge, diligence (zeal), and love—and urges them to "also excel in this grace of giving" (v. 7, *NIV*). Paul announces his plan to send Titus to supervise the endeavor. Paul bragged on the Corinthians about the impression they had made on Titus (7:14). The warm reception the Corinthians had given to Titus made him an ideal candidate to carry out the task.

II. FULFILL YOUR OBLIGATIONS (2 Corinthians 8:8-12; 9:2-5)
A. Christ as Your Example (8:8, 9)

8. I speak not by commandment, but by occasion of the forwardness of others, and to prove the sincerity of your love.

9. For ye know the grace of our Lord Jesus Christ, that, though he was rich, yet for your sakes he became poor, that ye through this poverty might be rich.

Paul is not issuing a command to the Corinthians on the basis of his apostolic authority. The collection is to be a free work of love. Paul prefers that the love of the Corinthians be no less than that of the Macedonians, whose example provides a basis for testing the reality of the Corinthians' love for him and their fellow Christians. However, Paul provides a better criterion by telling the story of Jesus, who, although rich, became poor in order that they, though poor, might be rich. Christ's decision was voluntary. In His incarnation, Christ willingly surrendered His riches so humanity could share in His spiritual riches of salvation. Christ's sacrifice, rather than competition with either a local church, group, or denomination, must be the real motive for giving.

B. According to Your Ability (vv. 10-12)

10. And herein I give my advice: for this is expedient for you, who have begun before, not only to do, but also to be forward a year ago.

11. Now therefore perform the doing of it; that as there was a readiness to will, so there may be a performance also out of that which ye have.

12. For if there be first a willing mind, it is accepted according to that a man hath, and not according to that he hath not.

Paul moves to a direct application of all that he has said so far to the Corinthians, encouraging them to complete the effort they had begun a year previously. Once again, Paul does not issue a command. Instead, he reasons with them that although their original intent was good, they needed to carry it out; otherwise their good intentions amount to nothing. He exhorts them to complete the action since he presumes that the will is still present and he wants them to act according to their will. He concludes by saying that the readiness of will is more important than the amount. Paul asks them to give according to their means.

Talk About It:
1. How did the Corinthians' "readiness" need to be connected with "performance" (vv. 10, 11)?
2. What makes one's giving "acceptable" (v. 12)?

C. Fulfilling Your Promise (9:2-5)

2. For I know the forwardness of your mind, for which I boast of you to them of Macedonia, that Achaia was ready a year ago; and your zeal hath provoked very many.

3. Yet have I sent the brethren, lest our boasting of you should be in vain in this behalf; that, as I said, ye may be ready.

4. Lest haply if they of Macedonia come with me, and find you unprepared, we (that we say not, ye) should be ashamed in this same confident boasting.

5. Therefore I thought it necessary to exhort the brethren, that they would go before unto you, and make up beforehand your bounty, whereof ye had notice before, that the same might be ready, as a matter of bounty, and not as of covetousness.

Achaia (ah-KAY-yah)—v. 2—the Roman province which included Corinth

Enthusiasm is difficult to sustain over a period of time. The Corinthians were no exception. Paul had previously boasted of the enthusiasm of the Corinthians and used it to motivate the Macedonians. The Macedonians responded positively, but the Corinthians had not followed through with the collection. Paul was using reverse psychology. Although he was still affirming the Corinthians' enthusiasm, he did not want them to be ashamed due to the lack of completion. The honor of both Paul and the Corinthians was at stake. Paul had made high claims of the Corinthian generosity to the Macedonians. The Corinthians would not want to feel ashamed, nor would Paul want to "lose face."

bounty (v. 5)—"generosity" (*NKJV*)
covetousness (v. 5)—"grudging obligation" (*NKJV*)

Talk About It:
1. How had the Corinthians' initial zeal affected the Macedonian churches (v. 2)?
2. Why had Paul sent some "brethren" to Corinth (v. 5)?

III. GIVE JOYFULLY (2 Corinthians 9:6-15)
A. Pleasing to God (vv. 6, 7)

6. But this I say, He which soweth sparingly shall reap also sparingly; and he which soweth bountifully shall reap also bountifully.

7. Every man according as he purposeth in his heart, so let him give; not grudgingly, or of necessity: for God loveth a cheerful giver.

The final part of Paul's appeal presents the principles behind giving and its benefits. Paul sums up the benefit of giving by means of a proverb: "Whoever sows sparingly will also reap sparingly, and whoever sows generously will also reap generously" (v. 6, *NIV*). There is no exact Scriptural parallel, so Paul may be quoting a popular saying. The principle of the proverb is clear: we reap in proportion to our planting. God will reward according to one's generosity. Caution must be taken not to translate Paul's words here into some sort of prosperity gospel in terms of possessions and material wealth. Paul spells out the implication of the proverb in verses 8-15. But before he does so, he provides the Corinthians three important guidelines of giving.

1. *Giving is a personal matter.* The amount one gives is a question each person must answer for himself or herself.

2. *Giving requires resolve;* that is, it is to be done as one has *purposed* in his or her heart. The Greek verb translated *purpose* is found only here in the New Testament, and means "to choose deliberately" or "to make up one's mind about something."

3. *God loves a cheerful giver.* The word translated *cheerful* literally means "hilarious."

In summary, giving must be done personally without fanfare and coercion or manipulation, and it must be joyfully done. Giving must be done out of conviction rather than constraint.

B. Empowering to You (vv. 8-11)

8. And God is able to make all grace abound toward you; that ye, always having all sufficiency in all things, may abound to every good work:

(9. As it is written, He hath dispersed abroad; he hath given to the poor: his righteousness remaineth for ever.

10. Now he that ministereth seed to the sower both minister bread for your food, and multiply your seed sown, and increase the fruits of your righteousness;)

11. Being enriched in every thing to all bountifulness, which causeth through us thanksgiving to God.

Paul explains the wider theological basis of the collection, beginning with God himself. As the Source of all grace, God is both the basis and example of the Corinthians in their generosity. Paul expresses his faith that God will abundantly provide His

Talk About It:
1. Explain the law of sowing and reaping (v. 6).
2. How much should an individual give to God (v. 7)?

"A man complained to his pastor, 'It's getting to be just one continuous *give, give, give.*' Said the pastor, 'You have just given one of the best descriptions of Christianity that I've ever heard.'"

—Lucille Goodyear

Talk About It:
1. What blessings did Paul speak to the Corinthians (vv. 8, 9)?

Grace of Giving

grace for the Corinthians, so that their contentment will enable them to transcend themselves and perform "every good work" for others (v. 8). God not only rewards the gift, but also makes the action possible—the giver benefits. God makes His grace to abound to givers beyond mere replenishment of resources.

In verse 9, Paul refers to Psalm 112:9 to support his view, a passage that ascribes praise to those who give freely to the poor. The general principle is that the more we give, the more we will get from God, yet we must beware of what Paul does *not* say. He doesn't suggest that wealth or surplus income is a sign of God's approval or blessing. Nor is it giving *per se* that Paul applauds. The issue here is a lifestyle of generosity. That is what Paul applauds.

The last phrase in verse 10, "the fruits of your righteousness," introduces the final theme in the section. Paul reminds the Corinthians that they have been enriched in every way and are thus led to bountifulness (generosity) that results in thanksgiving to God.

C. Expressing Thanksgiving (vv. 12-15)

12. For the administration of this service not only supplieth the want of the saints, but is abundant also by many thanksgivings unto God;

13. Whiles by the experiment of this ministration they glorify God for your professed subjection unto the gospel of Christ, and for your liberal distribution unto them, and unto all men;

14. And by their prayer for you, which long after you for the exceeding grace of God in you.

15. Thanks be unto God for his unspeakable gift.

Paul ends his appeal by pointing out the benefits of giving beyond supporting the needs of the saints. Paul has in mind the thanksgiving by the Jerusalem church that will result from the offerings. However, there is a deeper issue. The collection is a test of commitment in faith to the gospel of Christ by the Corinthians. The completion of the collection will show they have passed the test, and the acceptance by the Jerusalem Christians will lead those Christians to glorify God for the spread of the gospel. The acceptance of the collection will indicate fellowship with all Jews who have accepted Christ. Paul adds that, in the Jerusalem Christians' prayers, "their hearts will go out" to the Corinthians (v. 14, *NIV*).

The collection is neither a tax levied by the Jerusalem church nor simply an act of generosity. More importantly for Paul, the success of the collection manifests God's redemptive act in Christ, particularly His reconciliation of Jew and Gentile by means of the gospel of Christ. In celebration of God's grace, Paul cries out, "Thanks be to God for His indescribable gift!" (v. 15, *NKJV*).

2. What is the process of giving as seen in verses 10 and 11?

"Each of us will eventually give away all of our earthly possessions. How we choose to do so, however, is a reflection of our commitment to the kingdom of God."
—Charles Stanley

Talk About It:
1. For whom was this offering being received (v. 12)?
2. What would be the result of the Corinthians' giving (vv. 13, 14)?

"No person was ever honored for what he received. Honor has been the reward for what he gave."
—Calvin Coolidge

CONCLUSION

The church's need and handling of money is as sensitive today as it was at the time Paul wrote to the Corinthian believers. It deserves to be approached with utmost sensitivity, graciousness and dignity. Fiscal responsibility and the question of how to motivate people to give is a difficult task, even when the circumstances seem ideal. Paul's lengthy discussion in chapters 8 and 9 offer important insight and direction. Generosity is not something that is innate to human beings. As such, people must be taught about how to give and receive.

GOLDEN TEXT CHALLENGE

"YE KNOW THE GRACE OF OUR LORD JESUS CHRIST, THAT, THOUGH HE WAS RICH, YET FOR YOUR SAKES HE BECAME POOR, THAT YE THROUGH HIS POVERTY MIGHT BE RICH" (2 Corinthians 8:9).

"Look at the wonderful truths here: (1) a knowledge given— 'ye know'; (2) a state relinquished—'though he was rich'; (3) a reason offered—'yet for your sakes'; (4) a state assumed—'he became poor'; (5) a resource tapped—'through his poverty'; (6) an exaltation conferred—'ye . . . might be rich'" (*The Wycliffe Bible Commentary*).

Daily Devotions:
M. Help the Poor
   Leviticus 25:35-38
T. Generous Giving
   Deuteronomy 15:7-11
W. Gifts for God's Work
   Ezra 8:24-30
T. Give Without Fanfare
   Matthew 6:1-4
F. Contrast in Giving
   Mark 12:41-44
S. Trust God and Give
   Luke 12:27-34

Faith to Follow Christ

John 1:29-51

INTRODUCTION

Faith is an ongoing part of each of our lives. Often we relegate it only to the area of the religious or spiritual, but, in reality, we daily operate in a certain realm of faith. We put our faith in mechanical devices, other people, and certain principles. Without the continuance of faith we would become recluses living in fear and never experiencing the fullness of life.

Enter the elevator on the 67th floor of a towering building. As it speedily descends, you trust it to smoothly stop at the bottom rather than destructively crash. Daily we believe the earth's gravity to continue so we are not flung out into space from this spinning planet. Driving down the highway we trust other drivers to follow the principles of safe driving for the good of us all.

Of far greater importance is our ability to place our faith in Christ. For this reason, the objective of this lesson is for each of us to be inspired by the examples studied and follow Christ wholeheartedly.

Today's lesson includes a variety of individuals at different stages of spiritual development and ministry. Yet each one faces the opportunity to be a person of faith and advance further, or reject the opportunity and make no further progression. When the latter happens, an individual will not stay at the same spiritual plateau for long. Instead, regression will eventually take place. It's much like being in a stream; if you quit paddling upstream, you float downstream.

Prior to looking at the individuals in our lesson, it's important to highlight the central truth of our study: "Following Christ without reservation leads to abundant life." Faith enables us to live joyfully in times of crises as well as in the moments of bliss. Jesus invites people of all backgrounds, interests and geographical areas to experience this life of faith.

Unit Theme:
Profiles of Faith in Christ

Central Truth:
Following Christ without reservation leads to abundant life.

Focus:
Be inspired by the faith of Christ's first disciples and follow Him wholeheartedly.

Context:
Around A.D. 27, John the Baptist identifies Jesus, who calls His first disciples.

Golden Text:
"Then said Jesus unto his disciples, If any man will come after me, let him deny himself, and take up his cross, and follow me" (Matthew 16:24).

Study Outline:
I. Recognize the Lamb of God (John 1:29-36)
II. Follow Christ Without Reservation (John 1:37-42)
III. Expect a New Vision (John 1:43-51)

I. RECOGNIZE THE LAMB OF GOD (John 1:29-36)
A. Jesus' Arrival (vv. 29-31)

29. The next day John seeth Jesus coming unto him, and saith, Behold the Lamb of God, which taketh away the sin of the world.

30. This is he of whom I said, After me cometh a man which is preferred before me: for he was before me.

31. And I knew him not: but that he should be made manifest to Israel, therefore am I come baptizing with water.

To grasp the significance of this event, it is important to remember John's background. He was a miracle baby born to an elderly couple when the hope of a child had long disappeared (Luke 1:7). As evident in similar situations recorded in the Scripture, John was destined for a particular ministry—the forerunner of Christ.

His ministry was unusual and straightforward. He was not afraid to point out people's sins while, at the same time, demanding repentance. John preached the need to demonstrate a lifestyle consistent with the claims of righteousness (Luke 3:4-8). When asked about the specifics, this minister offered guidelines spanning from caring for others to paying one's taxes (vv. 10-14).

Matthew described John as wearing a robe of camel hair with a leather girdle. His diet consisted of locusts and wild honey. Though baptizing on the other side of the Jordan River from Jerusalem, people traveled a number of miles to experience his ministry. Many listened to him, confessed their sins, and were baptized (Matthew 3:1-6).

It is in this setting where our lesson begins. John is baptizing when Jesus approaches his place of ministry. Immediately John makes a dramatic statement identifying this person. He asks everyone present to look and see "the Lamb of God" (John 1:29). This expression isn't found within the New Testament except for this location. As a result, there are many suggestions as to what is being referred to, such as the lamb of the Passover, lambs in the daily offerings in the Temple, or the triumphant Lamb in Revelation. We do know that this description refers to One who by substitution bears the sins of others.

Without hesitation John believes Jesus to be the promised Messiah. Previously, when questioned as to his own identity, John indicated he was neither Elijah nor one of the other prophets (v. 21). He described himself as a humble preparer of One to come. The next day Jesus appears at John's ministry site. Apparently those who had previously questioned John are still there, as can be seen from the wording (v. 30).

Verse 31 points to John's not knowing prior to this moment who the Messiah was. All he knows is he is to set the stage for His coming and baptize in water. While obediently fulfilling this commission, Jesus appears and His identity is revealed. John believes without hesitation and declares Christ's identity.

Talk About It:
1. What did John call Jesus, and why (v. 29)?
2. Explain the phrase "He was before me" (v. 30).
3. What was the reason for John's ministry of baptism (v. 31)?

"Either sin is with you, lying on your shoulders, or it is lying on Christ, the Lamb of God."
—Martin Luther

Faith to Follow Christ

B. Divine Confirmation (vv. 32-34)

32. And John bare record, saying, I saw the Spirit descending from heaven like a dove, and it abode upon him.

33. And I knew him not: but he that sent me to baptize with water, the same said unto me, Upon whom thou shalt see the Spirit descending, and remaining on him, the same is he which baptizeth with the Holy Ghost.

34. And I saw, and bare record that this is the Son of God.

We know John the Baptist and Jesus were related (second cousins). There isn't, however, any record as to whether or not they had met previously, even though they were only six months apart in age. Even if they did, John isn't knowledgeable of divine identity until this moment at the Jordan River.

In verse 33 we plainly see John's having some previous information as to how he could identify the One to come. When he sees "the Spirit descending, and remaining" on this person, this will be the confirmation. While John baptizes with water, this "Lamb of God" will baptize with the Holy Spirit. We know this baptism would enable believers to experience a new gift and quality of spiritual life previously unattainable for everyone.

Verse 34 is a reemphasis of John the Baptist's recognizing and believing in Jesus as the promised Messiah. There's no questioning or doubt. He accepts the divine confirmation as previously promised.

C. Continued Testimony (vv. 35, 36)

35. Again the next day after John stood, and two of his disciples;

36. And looking upon Jesus as he walked, he saith, Behold the Lamb of God!

What a week in the ministry of John the Baptist! One day he encounters a delegation of priests and Levites sent from Jerusalem to determine his identity. He plainly states he is not the Messiah. The next day Jesus comes, and John knows with assurance the identity of the promised Messiah and baptizes Him in the Jordan River. On the third day John is with two of his disciples when Jesus once again comes by.

"Disciples" need to be understood as learners who would attach themselves to a teacher. This was a common means of both formal and practical education for this time period. One of these men is identified in verse 40 as Andrew. The other may have been the apostle John, Jesus' beloved disciple, though it cannot be proven.

Upon seeing Jesus, John the Baptist repeats the identification pronounced the previous day. He directs his disciples to fix their eyes on Jesus, whom he calls "the Lamb of God." It is vital for them to recognize who is walking among them.

Talk About It:
1. What confirmation did John receive about Jesus' identity (vv. 32, 33)?
2. Why is a dove an apt symbol of the Holy Spirit?

"Taking a bodily form as a dove, the Spirit made His descent on Jesus unmistakably visible. . . . Jesus' spiritual anointing was the beginning of a new era, the age of the Spirit."
—**French Arrington**

Talk About It:
How do these verses summarize the purpose of John's ministry?

"If I was a nightingale I would sing like a nightingale; if a swan, like a swan. But since I am a rational creature, my role is to praise God."
—**Epictetus**

II. FOLLOW CHRIST WITHOUT RESERVATION
(John 1:37-42)

A. Following Immediately (vv. 37-39)

37. And the two disciples heard him speak, and they followed Jesus.

38. Then Jesus turned, and saw them following, and saith unto them, What seek ye? They said unto him, Rabbi, (which is to say, being interpreted, Master,) where dwellest thou?

39. He saith unto them, Come and see. They came and saw where he dwelt, and abode with him that day: for it was about the tenth hour.

As we begin this second section, it is important to be reminded of the lesson title "Faith to Follow Christ." We are focusing on individuals who make definite choices based on faith to accept and follow Christ. They are not ones who take an extended period of time to come to a conclusion of faith. Rather, when faced with truth and the opportunity to progress spiritually, they make a positive decision.

John the Baptist's proclamation about Jesus did not include any mention of following Him. However, knowing Jesus' identity opens the door and becomes the stimulus for John's two disciples to follow Jesus. Without hesitation they chart a new course. This following does not mean traveling along with Him for a little while. No! They are casting their lots with Jesus. It is a once-and-for-all commitment rather than a trial experience. This is not an opportunity to be missed.

Though nothing is stated concerning the details of these disciples' separating from John, this is a major step. A commitment of some considerable time and investment with John is being concluded. John doesn't restrain or discourage their moving on. Apparently he understands this is part of his diminishing role.

When the two disciples begin to follow Jesus, He turns and questions what they are wanting or looking for. While Jesus already knows their intentions, He desires for them to verbally state what is taking place.

The disciples' response isn't a real answer to Jesus' question. Varied reasons are offered for their reply. Maybe a sense of shyness or being caught off guard causes them to respond to a question with a question. Another possibility could be their question implying the need for an extended time to respond and to express their desire. If they know where He lives, then they can go there and spend the necessary time.

Notice that they address Jesus as *Rabbi*, which means "Master." This was a title given by the Jews to the teachers of the Law. Their use of it was a special designation of honor and ability.

Talk About It:
1. What did these men call Jesus, and why?
2. Why did these disciples answer Jesus' question with a question?

New Cause
Immediately after his conversion, Charles Finney, the well-known revivalist of the 19th century, became willing to leave his law practice. The next morning he refused to handle a case for which he had been retained. His explanation was, "I have a retainer from the Lord Jesus Christ to plead His causes, and I cannot plead yours."

In response to their question, Jesus invites them to come with Him to the location where He is staying. The time is specifically recorded as the "tenth hour," which would be about 4 o'clock in the afternoon. Knowing the Jewish method of calculating a day is from sunset to sunset, it appears the two disciples spend the night with Jesus.

B. Recruiting Others (vv. 40-42)

40. One of the two which heard John speak, and followed him, was Andrew, Simon Peter's brother.

41. He first findeth his own brother Simon, and saith unto him, We have found the Messias, which is, being interpreted, the Christ.

42. And he brought him to Jesus. And when Jesus beheld him, he said, Thou art Simon the son of Jona: thou shalt be called Cephas, which is by interpretation, A stone.

In verse 40 the apostle John identifies one of the two men who leave John the Baptist to follow Jesus. He is Andrew, the son of Jona, from Bethsaida on the Sea of Galilee. Andrew and his brother, Simon Peter, were fishermen by occupation and lived at Capernaum. Later Andrew would abandon fishing and follow Christ's call to discipleship. This man is often referred to as the bringer. Though not as aggressive as his brother, Andrew accomplishes ministry without being in the lead position. For example, he plays a vital role in the miracle referred to as the feeding of the 5,000, in which perhaps 15,000 men, women and children are actually fed. Andrew brings to Jesus the boy with the small individual lunch. Jesus then takes this meager amount of food and miraculously feeds the entire multitude (John 6:5-13).

Andrew's role as a bringer begins immediately after spending time with Jesus. He goes directly to his brother and recruits him for accepting Jesus as the Messiah, the Christ. This does not mean Andrew possesses a full understanding of Jesus' messiahship. But he does know on the basis of John the Baptist's declaration and the time spent with Jesus that He is the chosen One.

Simon goes with Andrew. There is no record of the questions which may have come from Simon. Apparently Andrew did not have to persuade his brother to come. Knowing the tremendous role Simon Peter would play in the development of the early church, Andrew's recruitment may be his greatest act of ministry.

Verse 42 reveals the significance of this first meeting between Jesus and Simon. Jesus looks at him in a searching manner, maybe reflecting on Simon's actions in the future. Then Jesus renames him. Reflecting on this, Leon Morris writes: "The giving of a new name when done by men is an assertion of the authority of the giver (e.g. 2 Kings 24:17). When done by God it

Talk About It:
1. What did Andrew do "first" (v. 41)?
2. What did Jesus call Simon, and why (v. 42)?

speaks of a new character in which the man henceforth appears (e.g. Genesis 32:28). There is something of both ideas here. Simon is from this time Jesus' man. But he is also a different man, and the new name points to his character as the 'rock man'" (*The New International Commentary of the New Testament*).

At this first meeting, Jesus knows Peter's potential for future ministry. Yes, he will "put his foot in his mouth" and at other times fail miserably. But with time he does become a solid minister of the gospel, expounding the borders of the early church regardless of personal cost.

III. EXPECT A NEW VISION (John 1:43-51)
A. Philip's Declaration (vv. 43-45)

43. The day following Jesus would go forth into Galilee, and findeth Philip, and saith unto him, Follow me.

44. Now Philip was of Bethsaida, the city of Andrew and Peter.

45. Philip findeth Nathanael, and saith unto him, We have found him, of whom Moses in the law, and the prophets, did write, Jesus of Nazareth, the son of Joseph.

Jesus doesn't delay in His search for those men who are to be the core group for initial discipleship. The next day after the meeting with Peter, Jesus decides to journey northward to Galilee. It is then He finds Philip, and immediately Philip is instructed to follow Him.

Verse 44 provides some insight or detail about this man. He is from Bethsaida, a fishing village on the west side of the Sea of Galilee. Apparently it is very close to the city of Capernaum, and some suggest it may have been the fishing district. Peter and Andrew are listed as being from the same area. It's very likely they are acquainted with each other prior to being Jesus' disciples. Also, it is of interest how often Philip and Andrew appear together.

Philip's name means "lover of horses." His selection points to Jesus' selecting ordinary people who at times struggle with circumstances. Reluctance, timidity and insecurity may at times be evident; however, Philip becomes an ambassador for Christ and the early church. Eusebius, the Jewish historian of the first century, describes him as a "great light of Asia."

Philip follows the same pattern as Andrew, who brought Peter to Jesus. Philip reaches out to Nathanael. Notice how Philip describes Jesus: He is the One of whom Moses and the prophets had written.

Very little is known about Nathanael. He is presumed to have been from Cana of Galilee. It is generally believed that Nathanael and Bartholomew are the same person. John uses the name *Nathanael*, while the other three Gospel writers never use it. Instead, *Bartholomew* is used in their listing of the apostles.

Before leaving this section, consider the beginning words of Philip to Nathanael: "We have found Him," or "We have found the One" (*NIV*). The Messiah they have been looking for now stands as a reality before them!

B. Nathanael's Disbelief (vv. 46-48)

46. And Nathanael said unto him, Can there any good thing come out of Nazareth? Philip saith unto him, Come and see.

47. Jesus saw Nathanael coming to him, and saith of him, Behold an Israelite indeed, in whom is no guile!

48. Nathanael saith unto him, Whence knowest thou me? Jesus answered and said unto him, Before that Philip called thee, when thou wast under the fig tree, I saw thee.

People respond in various ways when confronted with the truth. Some readily accept it with gladness. Others are hesitant, desiring further proof. Then there are those who put up resistance. A few may be doubters by nature. Others need a jarring proof to bring them to belief.

Nathanael appears to be an individual with considerable Biblical knowledge. How Philip speaks of the Messiah may imply the two of them having spent time studying those portions of Scripture which prophetically describe His coming.

Nathanael's first response is not "Take me to Him"; instead, it is a skeptical question which possibly carries overtones beyond the spiritual. Claims of knowing who the Messiah is deserves close scrutiny. False christs are a strong possibility. As a result, the true seeker needs to carefully consider the claim rather than being easily drawn into a false claim.

The questioning of Jesus' hometown of Nazareth may have been due to its being a small town of little significance. It might have stemmed from the town being known as a place of poor morals and weak religious commitments. Or, it could have stemmed from a rivalry and jealousy between Nathanael's hometown of Cana and Nazareth. Whatever the reason, Nathanael is not readily swayed to Philip's statement.

Nathanael accepts Philip's invitation to come and see for himself. Jesus' first words are a powerful indicator of who He is. Jesus describes Nathanael as an Israelite who is void of deceit or craftiness. He is a straightforward person of integrity—a true son of Israel.

Jesus says He saw Nathanael standing under a fig tree. Since Jesus offers no explanation, we cannot know for sure what is meant. One possibility is that this refers to a spiritual experience which may have occurred at Nathanael's home. Since the fig tree was symbolic of home, and people often prayed within the comfort of its shade, this may have been the case with Nathanael. Knowing Jesus is divine and is not limited in knowledge, this may be an explanation of his words to Nathanael.

Talk About It:
1. Why was Nathanael skeptical at first (v. 46)?
2. What did Jesus reveal about Nathanael (v. 48)?

"Not only do we not know God, except through Jesus Christ; we do not even know ourselves, except through Jesus Christ."
—**Blaise Pascal**

C. Nathanael's Commitment (vv. 49-51)

49. Nathanael answered and saith unto him, Rabbi, thou art the Son of God; thou art the King of Israel.

50. Jesus answered and said unto him, Because I said unto thee, I saw thee under the fig tree, believest thou? thou shalt see greater things than these.

51. And he saith unto him, Verily, verily, I say unto you, Hereafter ye shall see heaven open, and the angels of God ascending and descending upon the Son of man.

Talk About It sidebar

Talk About It:
1. What did Nathanael confess about Jesus (v. 49)?
2. What promises did Jesus make to Nathanael (vv. 50, 51)?

Jesus' answer seals the question with Nathanael. All possible doubt about identity and reaction to His hometown are gone. Nathanael's response first describes Jesus as Rabbi. This is identical to how the first two disciples responded previously (v. 38). More importantly, Nathanael states Jesus is the Son of God. It's not likely he fully understands Jesus to be the God-man with both a human and divine nature. This designation could possibly be more of a recognition of Jesus' extremely close relationship with the Father.

Nathanael's declaration of Jesus as "the King of Israel" is intriguing. At this point the Jews are under the political domination of Rome and the ruling Caesar. One could almost think this to be a treasonable statement. However, the political really isn't a consideration here. Jesus is royalty by human bloodline, a direct descendant of David and the fulfillment of God's covenant (2 Samuel 7:16). This title also reflects Jesus being the Christ, the Messiah. There could be one other aspect on which to reflect—Nathanael's personal acceptance of Jesus as his King.

Jesus responds positively to Nathanael. He seems to commend Nathanael for coming to faith. Yet, Jesus wants him to know this is just the beginning of his experiences as a believer and disciple. He will see miracles and wonders that exceed the revelation of an event in Nathanael's life.

This scene closes with Jesus making a major statement. His prefacing it with the repeated word *verily* is a pattern used prior to making a significant expression. The opening of the heavens seems to indicate a communication between heaven and earth. In Nathanael's presence is Jesus, the Son of God. He is the communicator between heaven and earth. His disciples will be able to see, to hear, and to touch the divine on a regular basis.

"God knows past, present, and future in one simple and eternal act of cognition."
—Van Harvey

CONCLUSION

Having looked at five individuals, four given by name, we see individuals who did not loiter or delay in declaring their faith. They didn't ask questions of what they may receive in return or what the cost may be. When confronted with Christ, they acknowledged and obeyed God's will for each of them. Such faith enables individuals to follow and fulfill God's plan then and today.

GOLDEN TEXT CHALLENGE

"THEN SAID JESUS UNTO HIS DISCIPLES, IF ANY MAN WILL COME AFTER ME, LET HIM DENY HIMSELF, AND TAKE UP HIS CROSS, AND FOLLOW ME" (Matthew 16:24).

Jesus made it clear that consecration begins with self-denial. Christians must realize that this means saying *no* to our own selfish will and *yes* to the will of God. Strangely enough, it is at the point where the will of God cuts across our own will that our "cross" is formed. In plain, simple language, Jesus presented the conditions by which we may follow after Him. We must deny ourselves and take up our own cross. He knew that it would be impossible for Him to give guidance to any disciple who would refuse to obey Him. There must be obedience and commitment to the will of God.

Bible Insight

Great Faith
by David C. Cooper

The greatest power a person can exercise is the power of faith. Not faith in faith, or in humanity, or in our abilities—but faith in God. Jesus said, "Have faith in God" (Mark 11:22).

Faith is a spiritual resource connecting humanity to God, the finite with the infinite, the temporal with the eternal, the powerless to the omnipotent. *Faith* is a gift God has given every person. "God has dealt to each one a measure of faith" (Romans 12:3, *NKJV*).

We have faith! The question is, what are we going to do with it? How are we to exercise faith? How can we develop faith? Faith is trust, belief and confidence in the person, power and providence of God. "Without faith it is impossible to please God, because anyone who comes to him must believe he exists and that he rewards those who earnestly seek him" (Hebrews 11:6).

Faith comes in many shapes and sizes. The Bible speaks of those who have little faith (Matthew 6:30), others with great faith (8:10), and those who have no faith (Mark 4:40). Some are faithless (John 20:27). Some have weak faith (Romans 14:1), while Abraham had a strong faith (Romans 4:20). Stephen was full of faith (Acts 6:5). Paul speaks of a growing faith (2 Thessalonians 1:3) and a sincere faith (2 Timothy 1:5). James describes those who are rich in faith (James 2:5) and who model a perfect or mature faith (v. 22). Finally, Peter speaks of a precious faith, which means unique and special (2 Peter 1:1).

The power of faith is seen throughout Scripture. Faith in God brings success, blessing and prosperity. "Believe in the Lord your God and so shall you be established; believe his prophets, and you shall prosper" (2 Chronicles 20:20, *NKJV*).

Jesus said that faith moves mountains and makes the impossible possible: "I tell you the truth, if you have faith as small as a mustard seed, you can say to this mountain, 'Move from here to there' and it will move. Nothing will be impossible for you" (Matthew 17:20).

Faith is the only requirement for salvation and receiving the gift of eternal life in Jesus Christ. "For it is by grace you have been saved, through faith—and this not from yourselves, it is the gift of God—not by works, so that no one can boast" (Ephesians 2:8, 9).

True faith in God and in Christ as Lord is the governing principle of one's entire life. "We live by faith, not by sight" (2 Corinthians 5:7). "The just shall live by faith" (Romans 1:17, *NKJV*).

Finally, faith gives us an overcoming attitude against fear, worry and doubt: "This is the victory that overcomes the world, even our faith" (1 John 5:4).

A famous French gymnast came to America a number of years ago and announced that he would walk on a tightrope across Niagara Falls, and he did. Three times. Then he said, "I am going to fill a wheelbarrow with dirt and rocks and roll it across too." And he did it twice. Then he asked the crowd present: "How many of you think I can roll a person across in the wheelbarrow?"

The crowd responded enthusiastically, "Yes. We believe you can!"

The gymnast turned to one man who was especially excited in his belief and said, "All right, sir, you're first. Get in." The man left running.

Let's meet the man Jesus said had the greatest faith He had ever seen. He models for us 10 commandments of great faith.

When Jesus had entered Capernaum, a centurion came to him, asking for help. "Lord," he said, "my servant lies at home paralyzed and in terrible suffering." Jesus said to him, "I will go and heal him." The centurion replied, "Lord, I do not deserve to have you come under my roof. But just say the word, and my servant will be healed. For I myself am a man under authority, with soldiers under me. I tell this one, 'Go,' and he goes; and that one, 'Come,' and he comes. I say to my servant, 'Do this,' and he does it." When Jesus heard this, he was astonished and said to those following him, "I tell you the truth, I have not found anyone in Israel with such great faith. I say to you that many will come from the east and the west, and will take their places at the feast with Abraham, Isaac and Jacob in the kingdom of heaven. But the subjects of the kingdom will be thrown outside, into the darkness, where there will be weeping and gnashing of teeth." Then Jesus said to the centurion, "Go! It will be done just as you believed it would." And his servant was healed at that very hour (Matthew 8:5-13).

1. Get the Right Picture of God.

This Roman centurion was a man who had the right concept of God. He had 100 men under his command. The backbone of the Roman army, he disciplined the troops and kept up their morale. Yet he believed in the one true God, which is the foundation of the great commandment: "Hear, O Israel: the Lord our God . . . is one" (Deuteronomy 6:4).

Faith begins with a deep understanding that not only does God exist, but He cares about us. Jesus asked, "Are not two sparrows sold for a penny? Yet not one of them will fall to the ground apart from the will of your Father. And even the very hairs of your head are all numbered. So don't be afraid; you are worth more than many sparrows" (Matthew 10:29-31).

After a men's meeting at our church, a young father shared an amusing story with me. He said, "For a while our 2-and-a-half-year-old son thought you were God. One Sunday you were out of town and a guest minister preached. Our son came with us to the service instead of the children's program. On the way home, our friends asked him if he went to the children's program. He said, 'No, I went to big church,' then added, 'but God wasn't there today.'"

The man said to me, "We had no idea what he was talking about when he said God wasn't there." The next Sunday they were driving to church and picked up our radio program in the car. The little boy recognized my voice and exclaimed, "That's God talking!"

Well, needless to say, I'm not God, but the story illustrates how we confuse God with someone else or something else. We may have God confused with a minister, the church, our parents, or some fictitious notion about God. Our faith level will never rise above the picture we have of God.

God is revealed to us in Scripture as Creator, Sustainer, Redeemer and Father. He is omnipotent, omnipresent and omniscient. He is just and true in all His ways. He is "glorious in holiness, fearful in praises, doing wonders" for His people (Exodus 15:11, *NKJV*). Above all, God is love! He loves us with an everlasting love and is constantly drawing us to Himself by His loving-kindness (Jeremiah 31:3). He has made us in His image and has destined us to share eternity with Him in heaven.

When you have the right picture of God, then you will "trust in the Lord with all your heart and lean not on your own understanding; in all your ways acknowledge him, and he will make your paths straight" (Proverbs 3:5, 6).

2. Believe the Evidence.

The place where the miracle of the healing of the centurion's son occurred is important. Jesus lived in Capernaum during His ministry. It was located near Nazareth in northern Israel, where Jesus had grown up as a boy, and where His family lived. Peter, Andrew, James and John lived in Capernaum where they had a fishing business.

While the people of Capernaum had heard the teachings of Jesus and had witnessed His miracles, they failed to believe the evidence. Later, Christ denounced them for their lack of faith: "And you, Capernaum, will you be lifted up to the skies? No, you will go down to the depths. If the miracles that were performed in you had been performed in Sodom, it would have remained to this day. But I tell you that it will be more bearable for Sodom on the day of judgment than for you" (Matthew 11:23, 24).

While many in Capernaum dismissed Jesus and found reasons to explain away His miracles, the centurion believed the evidence of Jesus' ministry.

Faith begins by believing the evidence of God's existence and His care for us seen in the Creation. "The heavens declare the glory of God; the skies proclaim the work of his hands" (Psalm 19:1). Paul says that people are without excuse for having no faith because of the clear revelation of God in creation: "For since the creation of the world God's invisible qualities—his eternal power and divine nature—have been clearly seen, being understood from what has been made, so that men are without excuse" (Romans 1:20).

Jesus Christ himself is the greatest evidence of God. He is "the image of the invisible God" (Colossians 1:15). There is more historical evidence that Jesus lived than there is for Julius Caesar. When we look at Jesus, we look into the face of God.

We have the evidence of the impact of Christianity that has shaped Western civilization with art, literature, music, law, justice, democracy, medicine, science and technology. The great discoveries that have produced the modern age came from nations under the influence of Christianity.

We are surrounded by evidences of God's existence through personal experience. Testimonies abound of answered prayer, the miracles of God and the power of the risen Lord. History bears out the personal testimonies of faith of those who have met the risen Lord.

Your own life is marked with the fingerprints of God as He has intervened at critical moments. God has been there for you when you needed Him, even when you were unaware of Him. But today you look back at your life and see the hand of God at work.

Kepler, the astronomer, made an intricate model of our solar system. One day a friend who was an atheist came to see him at his laboratory. He noticed the impressive model and studied carefully the intricate detail of the sun and the planets set in their rotation. Turning to Kepler he said, "This is a fantastic model with amazing detail and design. Who made it?"

Seizing the opportunity to talk to his friend about God, he replied, "Nobody made it."

"Don't be ridiculous," replied his friend. "Someone had to make it."

Kepler said, "Let me ask you a question. I cannot convince you that nobody made this model of our solar system and yet you believe that the grand design from which this model is taken formed itself by evolutionary chance. Tell me, by what kind of logic do you arrive at such an incongruous conclusion?"

3. Ask God for Help.

The first reference in Scripture to prayer is Genesis 4:26: "At that time men began to call on the name of the Lord." Ours is the secular age when men have ceased to call on God. Can science, education and technology solve all our modern problems? Unequivocally, no! We need to call on God in the time of need.

God invites us: "Call on me and I will answer you and tell you great and unsearchable things you do not know" (Jeremiah 33:3).

Listen to what Jesus tells us about how to exercise faith to see results: "Ask and it will be given to you; seek and you will find; knock and the door will be opened to you. For everyone who asks receives; he who seeks finds; and to him who knocks, the door will be opened. . . . If you, then, though you are evil, know how to give good gifts to your children, how much more will your Father in heaven give good gifts to those who ask him!" (Matthew 7:7, 11).

The apostle James hits the nail on the head: "You do not have because you do not ask God" (4:2).

I once read: "If you don't bother God, everything else will bother you." *Faith* means humbling ourselves before the Lord and seeking His power because we have come to the end of ourselves. "Humble yourselves, therefore, under God's mighty hand, that he may lift you up in due time. Cast all your anxiety on him because he cares for you" (1 Peter 5:6, 7). "Let us then approach the throne of grace with confidence, so that we may receive mercy and find grace to help us in our time of need" (Hebrews 4:16).

4. Care Deeply About Others.

The centurion came to Jesus on behalf of his servant, not himself. Great faith is always focused on others, not on one's self. "My servant lies at home suffering," was his petition to Christ.

The greatest faith is intercessory faith. Before we can be powerful in faith, we must first be powerful in love. The servant was at a lower socioeconomic level than the centurion. He was suffering greatly. Yet the centurion cared for him as though he were his son. Love is no respecter of persons. The way we treat others is deeply connected with the power of faith—"Faith working through love" (Galatians 5:6, NKJV).

When you get involved helping others, God gets involved helping you. "If a man shuts his ears to the cry of the poor, he too will cry out and not be answered" (Proverbs 21:13).

5. Focus on Jesus.

The centurion addressed Jesus as "Lord." This is amazing when you consider the fact that to call anyone Lord except Caesar was an act of treason. Yet, he recognized the One who had all authority and power, far greater than that of the Roman empire.

Jesus is the focal point of great faith. "Fix your thoughts on Jesus" (Hebrews 3:1). I have observed three great spiritual problems in our times that keep us from focusing our faith on Jesus Christ.

Distractions. We are often like Peter who walked on the water when Jesus called him out of the boat. But when he took his eyes off Jesus and looked at the winds and waves, he doubted and sank into the waters.

Discouragement. When we go through the fires of adversity, we feel alone and abandoned by God. We lose heart and feel as though the Lord has left us. But Christ is with us through the fire just as He appeared in the flames with Shadrach, Meshach and Abed-Nego. He is still the fourth man in the fire!

Deception. Our generation is trying to remake Jesus into less than He is. He is the Christ, the Son of the living God. He is the eternal, incarnate Word of God, who came in all sinlessness to offer Himself as a sacrifice of atonement for the sins of the whole world and thereby secure our eternal salvation. Yet, our age is trying to reduce Him to being merely a teacher, a miracle worker, a Buddha, an enlightened one, a moralist or a prophet. But He is "the way, the truth and the life" (John 14:6). As the centurion discerned, Jesus is *Lord*!

6. Submit to His Will.

By calling Jesus "Lord," the centurion was not demanding that Jesus do what he asked, nor was he trying to manipulate Him. He simply trusted what Jesus would do. True faith submits to God's will without question, demand or rebellion. *Trust* means to turn the situation over to God and to be content with the outcome.

Today many "faith teachers" are not teaching faith at all, but rather futile ways of manipulating God by clever prayer secrets, making a financial offering (as though God's miracles are for sale), or repeating clichés called "good confessions." Such foolishenss is not faith—it is fantasy.

Can God Almighty, Creator of heaven and earth, be manipulated by mankind? If so, He would cease to be God. The Bible is clear: "Who has known the mind of the Lord? Or who has been his counselor? Who has ever given to God, that God should repay him?" (Romans 11:34, 35). God is debtor to no man. "For from him and through him and to him are all things. To him be the glory forever! Amen" (v. 36).

Walking by faith means trusting in every circumstance of life—especially in tough times. C.S. Lewis likened God's use of adversity to walking a dog. If the dog gets its leash wrapped around a pole and tries to continue running forward, he will only tighten the leash more. Both the dog and the owner are after the same end, forward motion, but the owner must restrain the dog by pulling him opposite the direction he wants to go. The master, sharing the same intention but understanding better than the dog where he really wants to go, takes an action precisely opposite to that of the dog's will. In this way, God uses adversity.

7. Come to God Through Grace, Not Works.

The centurion expresses what many of us feel when we ask God for help: "I do not deserve for you to come to my house." We are often plagued by those four words: "I do not deserve." We find ourselves thinking and saying, "I do not deserve" the blessings of God, that job promotion, that financial blessing, the good things of life, and on and on. We suffer from a poor self-image and low self-esteem. We confuse the worthiness of God with feelings of our worthlessness. But we are made in the image of God. Our lives are endowed with divine worth and value.

Another issue in this phrase, "I do not deserve," are those who have feelings of entitlement. They believe they do deserve certain things from God—God is obligated to do what they ask, when they ask it. They need to learn the proper meaning of the phrase, "I do not deserve," and realize that all good things in life are the blessing of His grace and not our works. The centurion had a balanced perspective on knowing his worth in God's sight and his need to ask Jesus for help without thinking he deserved it on the basis of his position, power and status.

8. Trust the Word of God.

The centurion's response was so insightful that it caught Jesus off guard. In fact, Jesus was astonished by the man's spiritual insight. How astonishing that anything could astonish the Lord. But one thing that still astounds the Lord is our faith. "Speak the word and my servant will be healed." Just one word from the lips of the Son of God would bring the miracle he sought. Oh that we had the same confidence in the Word of God.

Paul said, "Faith comes by hearing the message, and the message is heard through the word of Christ" (Romans 10:17). Today we have the word of God in the Bible. God also speaks to us through dreams and visions and by the gift of prophecy. Someone has identified 7,847 promises of God in Scripture. Every promise is a personal word from God to us. The words of Jesus are powerful. When we believe and receive them, they release the power of God to us.

Jesus' words are . . .

- *Eternal:* "Heaven and earth will pass away, but my words will never pass away" (Matthew 24:35).
- *Authoritative*: "When Jesus had finished saying these things, the crowds were amazed at his teaching, because he taught as one who had authority, and not as their teachers of the law" (7:28, 29).
- *Powerful:* "The people were all so amazed that they asked each other, 'What is this? A new teaching—and with authority! He even gives orders to evil spirits and they obey him'" (Mark 1:27).
- *Gracious*: "All spoke well of him and were amazed at the gracious words that came from his lips" (Luke 4:22).
- *Spiritual*: "The Spirit gives life; the flesh counts for nothing. The words I have spoken to you are spirit and they are life" (John 6:63).
- *Life-giving:* "Simon Peter answered him, 'Lord, to whom shall we go? You have the words of eternal life'" (v. 68).
- *Incomparable*: "'No one ever spoke the way this man does,' the guards declared" (7:46).
- *Judgmental*: "There is a judge for the one who rejects me and does not accept my words; that very word which I spoke will condemn him at the last day" (12:48).
- *Divine*: "He who does not love me will not obey my teaching. These words you hear are not my own; they belong to the Father who sent me" (14:24).

Great faith rests on the unalterable truth of the word of Him who cannot lie (see Hebrews 6:18).

9. Speak the Word.

Faith is found in two places: the heart and the mouth. "If you confess with your mouth, 'Jesus is Lord,' and believe in your heart God has raised him from the dead, you will be saved" (Romans 10:9). The power of faith-filled words is unmistakable. "The tongue has the power of life and death" (Proverbs 18:21). "Out of the abundance of the heart the mouth speaks" (Matthew 12:34, *NJKV*).

We too should speak the word of God by faith. "We believe; therefore, we speak" (see 2 Corinthians 4:13). God has given us great and powerful promsises in His Word. He gives the promise, but "the 'Amen' is spoken by us to the glory of God" (1:20). The word *amen* means to agree with God. We cannot go around speaking words of doubt, complaint and negativism and expect to have great faith. Jesus told us to speak to the mountain and it would move, and to not doubt but believe that those things which we speak will come to pass: "I tell you the truth, if anyone *says* to this mountain, 'Go, throw yourself into the sea,' and does not doubt in his heart but believes that what he *says* will happen, it will be done for him" (Mark 11:23).

10. Expect Results.

The centurion came to Jesus with great expectancy, and he left with great expectancy, believing what he asked for had been accomplished. "Go!" Jesus told him, "It will be done as you have believed it would." When he arrived home, he found his servant healed. He asked his attendants when his health improved and learned that it was the very hour Jesus promised him his servant would be healed.

God wants us to raise our level of expectation in His power and provision. A close friend of mine told me a story about his grandfather who was a pioneer Pentecostal preacher in South Carolina. During the Great Depression, he and his family pastored a small, struggling congregation with limited finances.

One morning the family came for breakfast, but there was nothing to serve. They had run out of everything and had no money. So, he told his wife to set the table and they all sat down. He took out a piece of paper and told the kids and his wife to write down everything they wanted to buy at the grocery store. After finishing the list, they prayed and asked God to provide everything on the list.

Suddenly, there came a knock on the door. When he went to see who was there, he found no one, but the front porch was covered with grocery bags, filled to over-flowing. After placing the bags on the table, they took out all the items and found everything they had written on their lists, and more!

Now to him who is able to do immeasurably more
than all we ask or imagine,
according to his power that is at work within us.
Ephesians 3:20

*Unless otherwise noted, all scriptures in this article are from the *New International Version*. This Bible Insight is excerpted from the book *Ten Steps Toward a Better Life* (Pathway Press; 800-553-8506; *www.pathwaybookstore.com*).

Faith Born of Desperation

Matthew 8:5-13; 15:22-28; Mark 9:14-29

INTRODUCTION

Help! This simple four-letter word can play such a vital part in our lives, provided we are willing to announce our need. Like in most areas, there are two opposite extremes. Some people call for help needlessly. The means or solution is at hand, and all they need to do is put forth the necessary effort. Other individuals want to be so self-sufficient that they rarely ask for help, no matter how much they need it.

Crises of various types do eventually enter our lives. Illness, broken relationships, job losses, death and accidents press in. As committed Christians, will we allow despair to dominate or will we allow faith to spring into full bloom? In times of desperation, it is easy to wring our hands when we should be relying on our Lord.

The objective for this lesson is not a concept we normally emphasize. Desperation usually isn't projected as an opportunity for faith to be developed and evidenced in our lives. But stop and think. During the "good times" we tend to think differently about faith. When there are no trials or stresses, we generally have a different outlook on our life in Christ. However, the strengthening of our faith comes when we are put to the test. It begins as a matter of choice. *Will I believe in Christ through the Holy Spirit to intervene in my behalf? Will I be open to the path He chooses for me?*

Sometimes God's intervention is through dramatic deliverance. However, there are other times when He enables us to endure through divine sustenance. This latter method isn't what we prefer. It means the problem will stay for a while. We will experience discomfort and inconvenience, but God still can be glorified. The issue is whether or not we allow it to happen.

Faith developed in the crucible of desperation is no less faith than when it develops in more positive circumstances. Faith is faith. Some individuals get in a bind and think they have faith when, in reality, all they have is a desire for escape. Genuine faith believes in the power of God to accomplish what seems impossible, even when it doesn't occur.

Desperate times can enable our faith to grow. We may have to work through doubt and fear which tend to creep into our thinking, but faith enables us to overcome them.

Unit Theme:
Profiles of Faith in Christ

Central Truth:
Christ responds to those who seek Him in desperation.

Focus:
Reframe desperation as a catalyst for faith and grow in our ability to trust God.

Context:
Three accounts of individuals who sought Christ's help in desperate situations.

Golden Text:
"Jesus said unto him, If thou canst believe, all things are possible to him that believeth" (Mark 9:23).

Study Outline:
I. Acknowledge Christ's Authority (Matthew 8:5-13)
II. Be Honest About Doubt (Mark 9:14-29)
III. Persist in Seeking Him (Matthew 15:22-28)

I. ACKNOWLEDGE CHRIST'S AUTHORITY (Matthew 8:5-13)
A. The Crisis (vv. 5, 6)

5. And when Jesus was entered into Capernaum, there came unto him a centurion, beseeching him.

6. And saying, Lord, my servant lieth at home sick of the palsy, grievously tormented.

Talk About It:
What is surprising about this scene?

Matthew 8 records a number of supernatural acts, including healing from various diseases, deliverance from demon possession, and calming a furious storm on the Sea of Galilee. This portion of our lesson focuses on the healing of an unnamed individual as a result of the faith of a Roman centurion. In the process we see a demonstration of belief in the authority of Christ.

Situated on the Sea of Galilee, Capernaum not only had a lucrative fishing industry but also was on a major trade route. No wonder Jesus made this His headquarters city. By residing there, He could touch such a large number of people from various occupations and countries. Because of the trade route, a tax-collection office was located here and a ranking officer of the Roman emperor resided here.

On returning to the city, Jesus was confronted with a request from a Roman centurion—a commander of 100 soldiers. His presence in Capernaum likely implied a Roman garrison was stationed there. Luke (ch. 7) also records this event, but with greater detail and what initially appears a variance with Matthew. Matthew records a centurion coming to Jesus, while Luke says the centurion "sent some elders of the Jews" (7:3, *NIV*). Understanding this was a society where someone was often sent to represent another person erases the apparent conflict. In some areas of our world it would be like "I'll send a representative."

"Compassion is a sign of a truly great and generous heart. Compassion is understanding the trouble of others, coupled with an urgent desire to help."
—Quotable Quotes

The centurion's concern for his servant was rather unusual. Normally servants were perceived as expendable—just get another one. This intense concern for the physical suffering of a servant speaks of two possibilities. First, this individual was fortunate to have a special relationship with his master. Maybe the centurion felt indebted. Second, this could be a further reflection of this soldier's character. He was not so hardened that he could not feel sympathy for a suffering servant.

Apparently the centurion knew of Jesus' ministry and ability to heal. For that reason, he sent representatives asking for Jesus to help his dying servant (Luke 7:2, 3). The help he sought was healing—not just a moderate improvement.

B. The Response (vv. 7-9)

7. And Jesus saith unto him, I will come and heal him.

8. The centurion answered and said, Lord, I am not worthy that thou shouldest come under my roof: but speak the word only, and my servant shall be healed.

9. For I am a man under authority, having soldiers under me: and I say to this man, Go, and he goeth; and to another, Come, and he cometh; and to my servant, Do this, and he doeth it.

Once again we see the compassionate serving heart of Jesus. He shows no bias or prejudice to anyone in need. No particular group or person of position receives preferential treatment. Without hesitation or further questioning, Jesus will come to the centurion's house and heal the servant. The centurion's response indicates his belief in the authority of Jesus over disease and suffering, even from a distance.

The statement begins with a recognition of his own unworthiness. He doesn't feel his level of spirituality merits Jesus' entering his home. This seems to indicate a knowledge of his own sinfulness and the righteousness of the Lord. With this in mind, he asks for Jesus to simply speak the word of healing, and it will be so. What tremendous faith!

Continuing, the centurion speaks of authority from a military perspective. Though he is under the authority of his supervisors, he has authority over the men under his command. When he speaks and issues directives, his men understand it to not be merely a suggestion to be questioned, disregarded, or fulfilled at a later time. No! Immediately they must fulfill his orders. Because of his authority and position, they obediently comply.

In the same manner, he understands Jesus' position and authority. This man believes Jesus' authority enables Him to bring healing by speaking.

Talk About It:
Why did the centurion talk about his own authority?

"Christ heals with more ease than any other. Christ makes the devil go out with a word. Nay, He can cure with a look."
—**Thomas Watson**

C. The Faith (vv. 10-13)

10. When Jesus heard it, he marvelled, and said to them that followed, Verily I say unto you, I have not found so great faith, no, not in Israel.

11. And I say unto you, That many shall come from the east and west, and shall sit down with Abraham, and Isaac, and Jacob, in the kingdom of heaven.

12. But the children of the kingdom shall be cast out into outer darkness: there shall be weeping and gnashing of teeth.

13. And Jesus said unto the centurion, Go thy way; and as thou hast believed, so be it done unto thee. And his servant was healed in the selfsame hour.

Hearing the centurion's response, Jesus is astonished. Here is a Roman soldier whose faith and grasp of Jesus' authority far exceeds that of the ones who should have had such insight. Notice Jesus doesn't keep this knowledge to Himself. He verbalizes it to all who are present.

Talk About It:
1. What caused Jesus to "marvel" (v. 10)?
2. What point does Jesus make in verses 11 and 12?
3. How did Jesus answer the centurion's request (v. 13)?

In verses 11 and 12, Jesus makes an important observation. He refers to the harvest of souls who will accept the truth and become committed children of the King. "East and west" indicates individuals from far-flung areas of the earth coming to faith and receiving eternal life. In the future they will participate in and enjoy the kingdom of heaven. It will be as though they were the descendants of the patriarchs and recipients of the promised covenant.

Jesus then states a marked contrast with God's chosen people, the Jews. Instead of being the subjects of God's kingdom enjoying His blessings, many of them will be thrown outside into darkness. This is a contrast to the glowing lamps and light of the life and celebration within the King's residence. This will be the result of their failing to put their faith in Jesus as the Messiah and recognizing His authority as the Son of God.

Finally, after traveling a certain distance with the centurion, Jesus said, "Go! It will be done just as you believed it would" (v. 13, *NIV*). At that moment, the servant was healed.

II. BE HONEST ABOUT DOUBT (Mark 9:14-29)
A. The Questions (vv. 14-16)

14. And when he came to his disciples, he saw a great multitude about them, and the scribes questioning with them.

saluted (v. 15)—greeted

15. And straightway all the people, when they beheld him, were greatly amazed, and running to him saluted him.

16. And he asked the scribes, What question ye with them?

Asking questions of what we do not understand is one method of gaining information. However, questioning may also become the path to doubt. All of us experience doubt at some time or another. Sometimes it stems from our attempting to reason or think through everything. Also, doubt is sometimes a tool of Satan to subtly lead us into temptation and then into sin. Eve's encounter with the serpent in the Garden provides an excellent example (Genesis 3).

Talk About It:
Describe the scene when Jesus, Peter, James and John rejoined the other disciples.

In this portion of our lesson, Jesus and His inner circle of disciples—Peter, James and John—have been up on the mountain with Him. They saw Jesus transfigured before their eyes, witnessing His glory as the Son of God (Mark 9:2-9). Coming down to join the rest of the Twelve, it was evident a situation had developed. A large group of people surrounded the disciples, and the scribes were arguing with them.

How the scribes became involved here is not given. Their presence isn't unusual since a community of them lived in Galilee (Luke 5:17). Since a majority of these students and teachers of the Law were Pharisees, it was common to see them in opposition to Jesus.

Faith Born of Desperation

Immediately upon seeing Jesus, the multitude of people ran to Him. Apparently they weren't expecting Him, so this was a major surprise. After the people greeted Him, Jesus turned His attention to the scribes and directed a question to them. The *NIV* translates it, "What are you arguing with them about?" How Jesus knew about their ongoing dialogue is not mentioned. Some possibilities are divine knowledge, overall nature of the scribes, or seeing the intense speaking. Regardless of the means, Jesus now handled the issue.

B. The Crisis (vv. 17-22)

17. And one of the multitude answered and said, Master, I have brought unto thee my son, which hath a dumb spirit;

18. And wheresoever he taketh him, he teareth him: and he foameth, and gnasheth with his teeth, and pineth away: and I spake to thy disciples that they should cast him out; and they could not.

19. He answereth him, and saith, O faithless generation, how long shall I be with you? how long shall I suffer you? bring him unto me.

20. And they brought him unto him: and when he saw him, straightway the spirit tare him; and he fell on the ground, and wallowed foaming.

21. And he asked his father, How long is it ago since this came unto him? And he said, Of a child.

22. And ofttimes it hath cast him into the fire, and into the waters, to destroy him: but if thou canst do any thing, have compassion on us, and help us.

At this point it becomes beneficial to correlate Matthew's account (17:14-21), since he offers some details not given by Mark. The father of the tormented son steps forward, kneels before Jesus, and asks for mercy on his son. The boy's situation is out of control and has been for some years (Mark 9:21). Possessed of an evil spirit which robs him of speech, he suffers other results as well. The spirit "throws him to the ground. He foams at the mouth, gnashes his teeth and becomes rigid" (v. 18, *NIV*).

One can only imagine the agony the father experienced as he saw this boy tormented in so many ways! Seeking help, he brought the boy to Jesus' disciples. We know from Matthew 10:5-10 that the Twelve were sent out with the power to perform marvelous miracles. However, the father was greatly disappointed. The disciples were unable to bring deliverance and cast out the spirit.

Jesus' initial response was to berate individuals for their lack of faith. But whom did He mean? The scribes? The crowd? His disciples? The Jewish nation as a whole? No specific group is clearly indicated. Immediately following this rebuke, Jesus said to bring the boy to Him.

Talk About It:
1. Describe the son's condition (vv. 17, 18).
2. Explain the man's disappointment (v. 18).
3. Describe Jesus' lament in verse 19.
4. How did the evil spirit respond to Jesus' presence (v. 20)?

As soon as the demon-possessed boy comes into Jesus' presence, the evil spirit reacts violently in manners previously described by the father. This is not surprising. The evil spirit cannot overcome God's Son, who comes to bring deliverance. Before taking action, Jesus asks how long the child has been afflicted. Why is this of importance? Will it make any difference in what the Master does? Probably not. But it does help everyone, including us, to understand the tremendous pain this father is experiencing. No wonder he desperately desires help for this suffering son.

Can you imagine the fear of not knowing when this child could be thrown into the fire or into the water? Within him is the constant potential for severe injury, or even death. This child has no possibility of growing up and leading a good life but for the compassionate intervention of the Master.

C. The Deliverance (vv. 23-29)
(Mark 9:25-29 is not included in the printed text.)
23. Jesus said unto him, If thou canst believe, all things are possible to him that believeth.
24. And straightway the father of the child cried out, and said with tears, Lord, I believe; help thou mine unbelief.

Once again, Jesus puts faith in the forefront prior to taking an action. He asks a straightforward question of the father. In essence, if he can believe, then this deliverance is possible. Yes, Jesus can drive out the evil spirit by His own authority and will. But He chooses to involve the man who desires the miracle.

The child's father steps forward and makes a definite statement of faith. At the same time, he desires help in overcoming any dimension of doubt or disbelief which may remain. What a truthful expression with which many of us can identify! Yes, we want to believe. However, nestled within us may be those small voices of doubt fueled by reason rather than faith. They must, of necessity, be stilled for the fullness of our faith to be exercised.

People run to see what will take place. Without delay Jesus commands the spirit not only to come out but never return to torment this child again. His description of it as a "deaf and mute spirit" (v. 25, *NIV*) reflects the impact it had on the child. Though resisting as evidenced by the violent reaction, the spirit has no choice under the divine authority of Jesus. Deliverance takes place. Initially the child is perceived as a corpse by many nearby. But Jesus takes his hand and the child is able to stand, a healthy boy.

This demonstration of deliverance creates a problem for the disciples. It raises a question of their inability to minister to a needy person. When asked the reason for their failure, Jesus doesn't launch into a complicated answer. Rather, He states

Talk About It:
1. What can "belief" accomplish (v. 23)?
2. What help did the father request (v. 24)?
3. How did Jesus deliver the boy (v. 25)?
4. What did the disciples learn from this experience (vv. 28, 29)?

Modern Miracle
Severely attacked with multiple sclerosis, Margaret was carried by her husband, Truman, to an Oral Roberts' crusade for healing. After praying for her, Roberts said, "Your desire is arrested." Twenty-five years later she continues to improve to the

Faith Born of Desperation

the simple solution—intercession makes the difference. This speaks so loudly of the need for relationship with the heavenly Father in order to have authority in ministry. It further reminds us of the reality of our Enemy. The battle is not one of human ability. No, it rests in the spiritual arena.

III. PERSIST IN SEEKING HIM (Matthew 15:22-28)
A. The Crisis (vv. 22, 23)

22. And, behold a woman of Canaan came out of the same coasts, and cried unto him, saying, Have mercy on me, O Lord, thou son of David; my daughter is grievously vexed with a devil.

23. But he answered her not a word. And his disciples come and besought him, saying, Send her away; for she crieth after us.

As we continue our lesson on faith in desperation, we are introduced to a third person in great need. This woman is described only in terms of geographical location. Verse 21 indicates Jesus traveling into the area of Tyre and Sidon (east end of the Mediterranean Sea). In view of this, her identification of being from Canaan doesn't refer to the wider area known in the Old Testament. Here it refers more specifically to the coastal area known as Phoenicia. Individuals in this area often were worshipers of the Baal and Ashtoreth.

According to Mark's Gospel, the fame of Jesus' ministry precedes His coming to the area (7:24, 25). Desperately needing help, she approaches Jesus. Notice the wording of her appeal. She begins with a plea for mercy. There's no sense of her feeling worthy of His attention. Nothing she is or can offer deserves Jesus' coming to the aid of her daughter. Yet, give her credit for knowing who Jesus is and what He has done in the past.

This woman's knowledge of Jesus can be seen in her addressing Him as "Lord, thou son of David." It is the most popular of the messianic names. Having said this, the concerned mother states her need: her daughter is demon-possessed.

Jesus ignores her pleas. He does not do or say anything. She then apparently turns her attention to the disciples. Desperately needing help, she persists in her cries to the disciples. Weary of hearing her pleas, they ask Jesus to send her away. They don't ask for a miracle, just relief for themselves.

B. The Persistence (vv. 24-27)

24. But he answered and said, I am not sent but unto the lost sheep of the house of Israel.

25. Then came she and worshipped him, saying, Lord, help me.

point of leaving her wheelchair to walk in her home. She even drives the big grain truck home to the farm from a nearby town.

Talk About It:
1. How did the woman describe her daughter's condition (v. 22)?
2. What was the disciples' request (v. 23)?

"Faith in God makes a person undaunted, unafraid, undivided and unflappable."
—**William Ward**

---

26. But he answered and said, It is not meet to take the children's bread, and to cast it to dogs.

27. And she said, Truth, Lord: yet the dogs eat of the crumbs which fall from their masters' table.

Jesus' priority comes to the forefront. In terms of His life here on earth, His mission is to Israel. This is the chosen nation brought into existence through Abraham and Sarah for the redemption of humankind. He, the chosen Messiah, comes from within their bloodline. The message of the Kingdom, as well as the miracles, are to be directed for Israel's benefit primarily.

In desperation, the woman kneels before Jesus asking for His help, only to hear the words of a popular prejudice. The Jews see themselves as God's children and all other nations as "dogs"—as wild, ravenous people undeserving of special favor. In an apparent attempt to soften the concept, Jesus uses the term referring to little dogs.

Even the statement of Jewish prejudice doesn't sidetrack this woman. She knows dogs do not receive the best food from a table. If just the crumbs of Jesus' ministry can be applied to her daughter, that will suffice.

C. The Miracle (v. 28)

28. Then Jesus answered and said unto her, O woman, great is thy faith: be it unto thee even as thou wilt. And her daughter was made whole from that very hour.

This woman's faith remains strong and committed regardless of the problems she faces. Jesus commends her and grants the request for healing. Her diligence is rewarded. What's so incredible is that the faith of this woman of a Gentile nation surpasses that of the chosen people of God.

Since there is no reference to the girl, it is assumed she remained home. Here the Master simply wills the healing, and it takes place without being in her presence.

CONCLUSION

Each of the three individuals covered in this lesson found themselves in a crisis. In themselves they were helpless. But by placing their faith in Jesus, their problems were resolved.

GOLDEN TEXT CHALLENGE

"JESUS SAID UNTO HIM, IF THOU CANST BELIEVE, ALL THINGS ARE POSSIBLE TO HIM THAT BELIEVETH" (Mark 9:23).

Sounds simple, doesn't it? Everything is possible; nothing is impossible. And such a simple requirement—only believe.

What is the problem, then? Obviously, some people get hardly anything—let alone everything! There must be a clue which has eluded us.

Talk About It:
1. Explain Jesus' statement in verse 24.
2. How did the woman respond to Jesus (v. 25)?
3. How did the woman express her faith in verse 27?

"My faith has no bed to sleep upon except omnipotence."
—Samuel Rutherford

Talk About It:
What happened "that very hour"?

Faith Born of Desperation

The secret is in remembering who said it. This is not the backslapping, arm-around-the-shoulder effort of a friend to console you. This is not a whistle-in-the-dark, keep-up-your-courage sort of thing.

Remember who is speaking—Jesus, the great Friend, before whom no power of evil can stand. It is the focus of our faith that counts. Let us give our attention not to the problem, nor to our great need for an answer, but to the One who is able to turn the impossible into the possible.

Daily Devotions:
M. Desperate
   Circumstances
   1 Samuel 21:10
   through 22:2
T. Desperate for
   Help
   Psalm 142:1-7
W. Faith Takes
   Bold Action
   Daniel 3:16-18
T. Faith Overcomes
   Obstacles
   Mark 5:25-34
F. Faith Sparks
   Enthusiastic
   Praise
   Luke 17:11-19
S. Faith Gives
   Courage
   Acts 27:14-25

Faith to See

John 9:1-41

Unit Theme:
Profiles of Faith in Christ

Central Truth:
Through faith in Christ, we gain spiritual sight.

Focus:
Focus on the importance of spiritual sight and trust Jesus for clear vision of who He is.

Context:
In A.D. 28, Jesus heals a blind man in Jerusalem.

Golden Text:
"One thing I know, that, whereas I was blind, now I see" (John 9:25).

Study Outline:
I. Jesus Heals Physical Blindness (John 9:1-11)
II. Jesus' Miracle Questioned (John 9:12-34)
III. Jesus Rebukes Spiritual Blindness (John 9:35-41)

INTRODUCTION

Since today's lesson focuses on physical blindness, let's look at the situation as reported in 2006:

- 1.1 million people in the United States are legally blind.
- 42 million people are blind worldwide.
- 100 million people in the United States need corrective lenses to see properly [about 1/3 of the population] and 14 million have vision problems that cannot be fixed with corrective lenses.
- Only 3 percent of cases of blindness result from injuries. The remainder occur as a result of eye disease.

Blindness also can be categorized by various scales. *Total blindness* is described as the complete lack of form and light perception. *Legal blindness* is defined as having 20/200 vision in one's better eye, even when benefitting from the best vision correction possible. According to *Wikipedia*, "This means that a legally blind individual would have to stand 20 feet from an object to see it with the same degree of clarity as a normally sighted person could from 200 feet."

In the New Testament era, there isn't a scientific differentiation concerning the status of each of the blind individuals to be considered. The inclusion of so many in the Biblical narrative reveals the commonness of blindness. Some of this would be the result of an unsanitary myth. Many believed rubbing saliva in one's eyes would cure eye problems, when, in reality, it furthered the problem and contributed to blindness. Others experienced blindness as the result of insect bites concentrated at the eyelids.

Individuals experiencing blindness became totally dependent on the kindness of others. Without the guidance of relatives or friends, their mobility was greatly limited and even dangerous. Many blind people had to turn to begging to survive.

Jesus healed a number of blind persons during His ministry. This lesson concentrates on only one of the healing instances, which caused tremendous controversy among the religious leaders. While studying the specifics of this lesson, let's not forget the objective: Though physical sight is vitally important, it pales in contrast to the spiritual sight which enables us to clearly see Jesus for who He is.

I. JESUS HEALS PHYSICAL BLINDNESS (John 9:1-11)
A. The Reason (vv. 1-5)
   1. And as Jesus passed by, he saw a man which was blind from his birth.
   2. And his disciples asked him, saying, Master, who did sin, this man, or his parents, that he was born blind?
   3. Jesus answered, Neither hath this man sinned, nor his parents: but that the works of God should be made manifest in him.
   4. I must work the works of him that sent me, while it is day: the night cometh, when no man can work.
   5. As long as I am in the world, I am the light of the world.

To grasp the fullness of this event, we must consider the previous happening as recorded in chapter 8. An intense dialogue occurs between Jesus and the Pharisees. They have been taking refuge in their being the blood descendants of Abraham. However, Jesus points to spiritual reality. True descendants would not be slaves to sin and desiring to kill the Son of God himself. He further refutes their claims of His being demon-possessed while stating He is on earth to honor the Father.

When Jesus and His disciples slip away from the Temple grounds avoiding those who were going to stone Him, they come into contact with a blind man. By some means they have knowledge of his being born blind. This stimulates the disciples to ask an important question. They want to know whose sin is the cause of this man's handicap.

The disciples apparently want to establish a cause for this man's suffering. God's dealing with the nation of Israel demonstrates a correlation between sinful actions and divine judgment. The same can also be seen in individual cases. Mirriam's sin of speaking against Moses resulted in leprosy (Numbers 12:9, 10). David's sin of adultery resulted in suffering of varied types (2 Samuel 12:7-14).

Since the man's blindness was from birth, it was not logical for his condition to be the result of his own sin. Logically it fell back on the parents. Immediately Jesus dispelled this idea. This blindness was traced back to the counsel of God. Physical illnesses and handicaps are the result of a sinful race of people, originating with the sin of Adam and Eve. Maladies occur within the human race without respect to the actions of a person or family. However, God in His providence steps in to change the situation and bring glory to Himself. The divine plan of redemption isn't limited to the spiritual. While Jesus walked on earth in human flesh, He demonstrated the marvelous power of God in releasing many individuals from the pains and struggles of human suffering.

Talk About It:
1. What assumption did Jesus' disciples make about the blind man (v. 2)?
2. What did Jesus say was the purpose of the man's blindness (v. 3)?
3. Explain Jesus' statements about the night and light (vv. 4, 5).

> "Christ is the sun, and all the watches of our lives should be set by the dial of His motion."
> —Thomas Brooks

Talk About It:
Describe how Jesus healed the blind man.

> "Christ is the most cheap physician. He desires us to bring nothing to Him but our broken hearts; and when He has cured us He desires us to bestow nothing on Him but our love."
> —Thomas Watson

Though surrounded by a sea of darkness, Jesus stepped out as the Light of the World. He came to shine forth the light of truth. This was not limited to just preaching and teaching. It included marvelous miracles reversing the course of nature and human happenings.

B. The Process (vv. 6, 7)

6. When he had thus spoken, he spat on the ground, and made clay of the spittle, and he anointed the eyes of the blind man with clay,

7. And said unto him, Go, wash in the pool of Siloam, (which is by interpretation, Sent.) He went his way therefore, and washed, and came seeing.

Jesus did not touch the blind man's eyes or simply speak words of healing. Instead, He used mud. Roman historians record the placing of clay on blinded eyes as a prescription by some physicians. However, this was not an ordinary medical procedure used by Jesus. He began with what may have been known and then brought in the gift of divine healing.

Jesus' instructions to wash in the Pool of Siloam are without explanation. Siloam was a rock-cut reservoir located within the city walls of Jerusalem. Going there may have been a matter of expediency as the nearest water supply. Even though water from it was used in rituals of the Feast of Tabernacles, there was no perception of its having significant symbolism or medical value. The major purpose was likely a faith issue. Would this man obediently follow the instructions of the Master? Or, would he question and doubt without receiving his sight? This man followed Jesus' directions and immediately received his sight. This brings to mind the story of Naaman. Once this leprous man obediently followed the prophet's instructions to dip seven times in the Jordan River, he was totally healed (2 Kings 5:14).

C. The Discussion (vv. 8-11)

8. The neighbours therefore, and they which before had seen him that he was blind, said, Is not this he that sat and begged?

9. Some said, This is he: others said, He is like him: but he said, I am he.

10. Therefore said they unto him, How were thine eyes opened?

11. He answered and said, A man that is called Jesus made clay, and anointed mine eyes, and said unto me, Go to the pool of Siloam, and wash: and I went and washed, and I received sight.

The people are confronted with a contrast that seems unbelievable. The healed man returns home, and those who knew him as a blind man must confront his being able to see.

Many are convinced he is the one whom they have seen begging. Others insist it must be a look-alike. There's no way a blind man could now be seeing.

In their presence he boldly asserts his identity. He is one and the same. There's no mistake. So then the automatic question comes. They want to know how this miracle could occur.

With simplicity the specifics of the account are told. He begins by identifying the person responsible, the man called Jesus. Then there is the method. Some mud was placed on his eyes, followed by washing in the Pool of Siloam. The result of obediently following Jesus' directions is the ability to see. Now they know the whole story.

II. JESUS' MIRACLE QUESTIONED (John 9:12-34)
A. The Pharisees' Question (vv. 12-17)
(John 9:12, 13 is not included in the printed text.)

14. And it was the sabbath day when Jesus made the clay, and opened his eyes.

15. Then again the Pharisees also asked him how he had received his sight. He said unto them, He put clay upon mine eyes, and I washed, and do see.

16. Therefore said some of the Pharisees, This man is not of God, because he keepeth not the sabbath day. Others said, How can a man that is a sinner do such miracles? And there was a division among them.

17. They say unto the blind man again, What sayest thou of him, that he hath opened thine eyes? He said, He is a prophet.

The neighbors and other acquaintances press the issue by wanting to know where Jesus is. When this information is not available, they take this healed man to the Pharisees who are in the Temple area.

Not only are the Pharisees concerned about the miracle but also the day on which it occurs. Keep in mind the Pharisees' tremendous desire to keep the Law evolved into their having developed hundreds of extra laws. Also, there is the basic issue of working on the Sabbath. According to official decrees, no healing work was to be done on the Sabbath except in what would be perceived as emergency cases.

Immediately after learning the process of Jesus' healing this man, the Pharisees proclaim Him to be a Sabbath-breaker. If this is true, then He can't be of God. However, others wisely question, How could a sinner perform such a miracle? They cannot fathom God's choosing to miraculously work through someone who is not in right relationship with God. With this division of opinion, the Pharisees turn to the person who now can see.

Talk About It:
1. What were the differing opinions of the healed man's neighbors?
2. How did the man explain his healing?

Talk About It:
1. Why do you suppose the healed man was taken to the Pharisees?
2. Why did the Pharisees criticize the healing?
3. What was the healed man's opinion of Jesus?

The man is asked a simple but loaded question. In our time we might phrase the question, "What do you think?" Without hesitation the man labels Jesus as a prophet. This is logical since many of the Old Testament prophets were used of God to perform miracles. Elijah and Elisha are prime examples.

B. The Response (vv. 18-27)

(John 9:22-24 is not included in the printed text.)

18. But the Jews did not believe concerning him, that he had been blind, and received his sight, until they called the parents of him that had received his sight.

19. And they asked them, saying, Is this your son, who ye say was born blind? how then doth he now see?

20. His parents answered them and said, We know that this is our son, and that he was born blind:

21. But by what means he now seeth, we know not; or who hath opened his eyes, we know not: he is of age; ask him: he shall speak for himself.

25. He answered and said, Whether he be a sinner or no, I know not: one thing I know, that, whereas I was blind, now I see.

26. Then said they to him again, What did he to thee? how opened he thine eyes?

27. He answered them, I have told you already, and ye did not hear: wherefore would ye hear it again? will ye also be his disciples?

Believing is more than just seeing. Mountains of evidence may be present, but it boils down to a matter of choice. If a person doesn't believe in miracles, when confronted with one he or she will continue in unbelief. Such is the case of many in this event. Wanting more evidence, they call for this man's parents. Specific identification is requested. They affirm his being their son and his blindness from birth.

Unbelief continues seeking evidence, often hoping for a loophole to confirm its position rather than turn to belief. The doubting Pharisees want to know the means of the healing. The parents are well aware of the dilemma. Rather than face expulsion from the synagogue by acknowledging Jesus as the Healer, they sidestep. Since their son is an adult, he should answer this part of the questioning.

Notice verse 24. The Pharisees try to tilt the response so Jesus is declared a sinner. Refusing to be drawn into a debate for which he has no information, the healed man stays with the key issue. Once he was a blind man, but now he sees. When questioned about the means, he points to having already explained this. Then he offers two possibilities for being questioned again: Either they didn't listen the first time, or they want to hear it again while contemplating becoming disciples. What an explosive possibility he suggests!

C. The Evaluations (vv. 28-34)

(John 9:28-34 is not included in the printed text.)

The response of the Pharisees is what would be expected in light of their opposition to Jesus. Immediately they attack the former blind man. It begins with an accusation of discipleship. Since Jesus has been painted as a sinner, the blind man must also be a sinner. But the Pharisees call themselves followers of Moses.

Notice how they attempt to discount Jesus. God spoke to Moses face-to-face and is a known prophet. But who is Jesus? Not knowing where He comes from isn't a statement of unknown genealogy. This could easily be verified. It speaks of their pushing aside any possibilities of His having spiritual authority. To them He is a nobody.

A remarkable response of commonsense logic then confronts the Pharisees. This man finds it remarkable these religious leaders can be so ignorant concerning One who miraculously brings sight to blinded eyes. Then two statements are made. First, God listens to people who follow His will. Second, causing blinded eyes to see isn't a normal event. So, in light of this, the logical conclusion must be that Jesus is from God or this couldn't have taken place.

Unable to respond to this, the Pharisees quickly return to the issue of sin and its impact. Ignoring the miracle, they indicate sin is the reason he was born blind. The insinuation continues that he must still be a sinner and has no right to lecture these "righteous" leaders who know truth. Following these words, the man is expelled from the synagogue.

III. JESUS REBUKES SPIRITUAL BLINDNESS (John 9:35-41)

A. The Belief (vv. 35-38)

35. Jesus heard that they had cast him out; and when he had found him, he said unto him, Dost thou believe on the Son of God?

36. He answered and said, Who is he, Lord, that I might believe on him?

37. And Jesus said unto him, Thou hast both seen him, and it is he that talketh with thee.

38. And he said, Lord, I believe. And he worshipped him.

In marked contrast, we see Jesus approach the man after his expulsion from the synagogue. First, having heard about the incident, Jesus goes looking for this abused individual. Second, upon finding him, there isn't any dialogue about the series of events. Instead, He gets to the heart of the matter—belief in the Son of Man.

This is the first time the formerly blind man actually sees Jesus. Previously he only hears the voice. When questioned as to his faith, the man respectfully says he wants to believe but needs to know who the Son of Man is. That's wisdom.

reviled (v. 28)— "hurled insults" (*NIV*)

Talk About It:
1. How did the Pharisees compare Jesus with Moses (vv. 28, 29)?
2. What did the healed man say was "marvelous" (v. 30)—"remarkable" (*NIV*) or "amazing" (*NASB*)?
3. What was the healed man's conclusion about Jesus (vv. 31-33)?
4. Why did the Pharisees throw out the healed man (v. 34)?

"He who throws dirt always loses ground."
—Anonymous

Talk About It:
1. What did Jesus call Himself in verse 35, and why?
2. How did the healed man respond to Jesus' revelation (v. 38)?

Jesus' response is simple but powerful. Not only has the man seen the Son, but he is now speaking with Him. Consider the wonderful opportunity here. Physically he sees. Will he now trade spiritual blindness for spiritual sight? It's a crossroad.

The man believes on Jesus and immediately worships Him. Nothing is recorded about the words or posture. Most important is the attitude of the heart and mind. In the presence of the Son of God, he responds in worship.

B. The Guilt (vv. 39-41)

39. And Jesus said, For judgment I am come into this world, that they which see not might see; and that they which see might be made blind.

40. And some of the Pharisees which were with him heard these words, and said unto him, Are we blind also?

41. Jesus said unto them, If ye were blind, ye should have no sin: but now ye say, We see; therefore your sin remaineth.

Jesus' words present a paradox. We know He came to bring freedom from sin and condemnation to believers, but judgment for those who refuse to accept the Savior and His message. This becomes so clear in the healing of the blind man. The Pharisees, who believed in the miraculous, should be rejoicing in this miracle. Instead, they reject both Jesus and the people involved.

Some Pharisees who hear Jesus' words question whether or not He perceives them to be blind and worthy of judgment. Surely they expected this response in view of how strongly and consistently they mount their opposition. But Jesus points to another paradox. They "see" in the sense of knowing much truth about the Law and how one should live. But their choosing not to accept Jesus for who He is points to their imperfect sight which becomes a form of blindness. This, in turn, is sin, which makes them worthy of judgment.

We must ask ourselves whether or not we are like the Pharisees. In view of the Biblical and spiritual knowledge we have, do we live accordingly, or do we walk in spiritual blindness?

CONCLUSION

Our lesson centers on a man who receives both physical and spiritual sight. The physical sight comes by Jesus' mercy and the man's obediently following the instructions given by Jesus. The spiritual sight occurs when Jesus offers him the opportunity to believe and the man chooses to believe. We are reminded of faith being the means by which we gain spiritual sight.

Faith to See

GOLDEN TEXT CHALLENGE

"ONE THING I KNOW, THAT, WHEREAS I WAS BLIND, NOW I SEE" (John 9:25).

We do not need to have experienced physical blindness to know the great, gushing sense of relief and joy that promoted this statement. There can be few feelings to equal that of seeing after a period of long blindness.

That is what happens to us when we come to God for the first time as His children. He takes the carnal scales off our eyes. The things of the Spirit to which we were previously blind become apparent to us. The beauties of discipleship we formerly could not see we now see. The horrors of sin and the tragedy of a sinful life suddenly are revealed to us.

Do you remember that time, when, like the blind man of Bible times, you could only cry out in wonder, "Whereas I was blind, now I see"?

Daily Devotions:
M. Rescued From Death
   Genesis 21:14-19
T. A Donkey Sees and Speaks
   Numbers 22:21-34
W. Spiritual Sight Given
   2 Kings 6:13-17
T. Jesus Revealed
   Luke 24:13-31
F. The Veil Removed
   2 Corinthians 3:13-18
S. Faith Sees the Invisible
   Hebrews 11:24-27

Faith for Salvation

Luke 7:36-50; John 3:14-21

<table>
<tr><td valign="top">

Unit Theme:
Profiles of Faith in Christ

Central Truth:
God sent His Son into the world to save the lost.

Focus:
Recap Christ's message of salvation and be grateful for His forgiveness.

Context:
Two New Testament accounts of sinners who came to Christ

Golden Text:
"God so loved the world, that he gave his only begotten Son, that whosoever believeth in him should not perish, but have everlasting life" (John 3:16).

Study Outline:
  I. Need for Salvation (Luke 7:36-40)
 II. Gratitude for Forgiveness (Luke 7:41-50)
III. God's Provision for Salvation (John 3:14-21)

</td><td valign="top">

INTRODUCTION

Gratefulness quickly disappears when we take things for granted. The special becomes common; the common is ignored. We flick a switch or push a button and the lights come on; turn the ignition key and the engine starts; push the handle and water comes out of the faucet; pick up the phone and hear the dial tone.

But what happens when the common doesn't happen— when there is no response or it is delayed? It's amazing how our computerized world creates stress when the expected connection does not occur or seems to "take forever." Instead of being grateful for the systems which make many activities so simple or normally so fast, we react with frustration.

We can respond to our salvation in a similar manner. Though valuing our life in Christ and enjoying our relationship with our heavenly Father, we may become complacent in it. We easily forget that salvation is the basis for our relationship with every Person in the Godhead. All the blessings of life in Christ rest upon the foundation of our salvation.

This is the last of four lessons on faith. It correlates closely with the first one on having faith to follow Christ. Also, this lesson includes the golden text of the Bible, John 3:16. It reminds us why God gave us the gift of His Son, who, in turn, made the supreme sacrifice—death by crucifixion.

Besides the doctrinal importance of this lesson, we are given a glimpse of some of the cultural practices of the Eastern society during the time of Christ and the preceding centuries.

</td></tr>
</table>

I. NEED FOR SALVATION (Luke 7:36-40)

A. The Dinner (v. 36)

36. And one of the Pharisees desired him that he would eat with him. And he went unto the Pharisee's house, and sat down to meat.

When we read about an encounter between Jesus and the Pharisees in the Gospels, we usually see the Pharisees either accusing Him of false teaching or some form of law-breaking. In turn, Jesus powerfully points out their ignorance or the error of their ways. As a result, there is a tendency to lump all the Pharisees into the same category. In doing so, we miss the fact of there being some who were not antagonistic toward the Master.

This passage doesn't initially give the name of the Pharisee who invited Jesus to a meal. Jesus accepted the invitation. He appeared to let no opportunity pass when good could be accomplished. This provides a pattern for us to follow. We should be open to and ready to dialogue with anyone who wants to hear about our Savior and Lord.

Talk About It:
Is it surprising that Jesus would eat at a Pharisee's house? Why or why not?

B. The Interruption (vv. 37-40)

37. And, behold, a woman in the city, which was a sinner, when she knew that Jesus sat at meat in the Pharisee's house, brought an alabaster box of ointment.

38. And stood at his feet behind him weeping, and began to wash his feet with tears, and did wipe them with the hairs of her head, and kissed his feet, and anointed them with the ointment.

39. Now when the Pharisee which had bidden him saw it, he spake within himself, saying, This man, if he were a prophet, would have known who and what manner of woman this is that toucheth him: for she is a sinner.

40. And Jesus answering said unto him, Simon, I have somewhat to say unto thee. And he saith, Master, say on.

Into this meal setting comes an unlikely, uninvited intrusion. This woman's name isn't given. Over the centuries, names such as Mary Magdalene or Mary of Bethany are suggested; however, there are no proofs or traditions for either. The only description given is that of being a woman from the city labeled as a sinner. This reference implies her being a woman of loose morals. Hearing Jesus is at the Pharisee's house, she boldly comes into the house but exhibits a humble attitude and posture.

This woman comes with an express purpose as indicated by her bringing an alabaster box of ointment. This ointment was perfume consisting of oils from carefully cultivated flowers. Its value could be that of nearly a year's wages for a common laborer.

Talk About It:
1. Why do you suppose the woman was weeping (v. 38)?
2. Explain the thoughts of Simon the Pharisee (v. 39).

Since reclining on couches was a common posture for eating, it was possible for this woman to stand behind Jesus and still have her tears wash His feet. Wiping His feet with her hair would be greatly disturbing. No chaste woman would let down her hair in the company of men other than her husband. She went further by kissing His feet and using the expensive ointment on them. Surely those in attendance were stunned at the scene they were witnessing.

As might be expected, the host begins to privately evaluate what is taking place. Immediately he doubts Jesus' being a prophet. A person of such status would be discerning as to who this woman really is. He wouldn't allow such a woman to touch Him. This reflects the Pharisees' having a far greater concern with ceremonial cleanness than ministering to a hurting, wayward individual.

The reality of who Jesus is comes to an immediate confrontation. Looking at the host, Jesus indicates He has something distinctive to say to him. The Pharisee is open to hear what is to be said; however, notice how he refers to Jesus as "Teacher" (*NKJV*). That is a lower position than prophet and definitely not any recognition as the Son of God.

II. GRATITUDE FOR FORGIVENESS (Luke 7:41-50)
A. An Example (vv. 41-43)

41. There was a certain creditor which had two debtors: the one owed five hundred pence, and the other fifty.

42. And when they had nothing to pay, he frankly forgave them both. Tell me therefore, which of them will love him most?

43. Simon answered and said, I suppose that he, to whom he forgave most. And he said unto him, Thou hast rightly judged.

One of the distinctives of Jesus' ministry is His using common illustrations to drive home a truth or principle. Here He uses a parable of two debtors who had their debts forgiven. One owed the equivalent of 50 days' wages for a common laborer. The other debt was equal to that of 500 days. If they each worked six days per week, it is a comparison of about eight weeks of work to that of 83 weeks.

Having laid out the setting, Jesus poses a penetrating question in view of the woman's presence in the Pharisee's house. "Which of them will love him [the creditor] more?" (*NKJV*). From a logical perspective, the man names the one with the greater debt. He is right. In making this statement, he unknowingly places this "sinner woman" as the greater debtor. No wonder she is responding with tears and a special anointing. Jesus indicates the Pharisee understands the story correctly. He then

Talk About It:
Why did Jesus tell a story at this point?

follows it with a careful review of the Pharisee's actions in comparison to this woman who is being looked down on because of her lifestyle.

B. A Comparison (vv. 44-47)

44. And he turned to the woman, and said unto Simon, Seest thou this woman? I entered into thine house, thou gavest no water for my feet: but she hath washed my feet with tears, and wiped them with the hairs of her head.

45. Thou gavest me no kiss: but this woman since the time I came in hath not ceased to kiss my feet.

46. My head with oil thou didst not anoint: but this woman hath anointed my feet with ointment.

47. Wherefore I say unto thee, Her sins, which are many, are forgiven; for she loved much: but to whom little is forgiven, the same loveth little.

At this point in the narrative Luke includes the name of the Pharisee. Nothing other than his name, Simon, is given. Of special interest in these verses are the many cultural customs that are included. Some are unusual to a 21st-century person, but were common for the people of that time and place.

Jesus now speaks directly to His host. Asking if Simon sees the woman is a means of drawing attention to her actions. It also sets the stage for an important comparison. Within himself the Pharisee looks down on this woman for her previous deeds. He overlooks her actions of humility and apparent repentance, along with neglecting to recognize his own failures in the basics of hospitality when hosting a guest.

Manners and Customs of the Bible, by Fred H. Wight, includes a chapter on hospitality as a sacred duty. First, guests would remove their shoes when entering a home. This kept them from soiling the mat or cushions on which they would be sitting. Since most of them wore sandals, their feet would be dirty. As a result, guests would be offered water for washing their feet. Often a servant would pour the water over the guests' feet and wipe them. Guests also expected to be kissed, first on the right cheek and then on the left, which is similar to the handshake used in Western countries. Using the kiss as a greeting is still practiced in many countries.

Jesus also spoke of Simon's failure to anoint Him with oil. This ancient custom consisted of pouring olive oil, which could be plain or mixed with spices, on a person's head. The normalcy of this practice is seen by its being brought to Simon's attention.

Simon apparently prided himself in keeping the Law but failed to realize his inadequacy in love. In marked contrast were the seemingly extreme actions of this woman as she demonstrated humility coupled with love for the One who could make the difference in her spiritual life.

Talk About It:
1. How did Jesus contrast Simon's treatment of Jesus with the woman's (vv. 44-46)?
2. Why did the woman love Jesus so much (v. 47)?

"We may be truly said to worship God, though we lack perfection; but we cannot be said to worship Him if we lack sincerity."
—Stephen Charnock

C. A Saving Faith (vv. 48-50)

48. And he said unto her, Thy sins are forgiven.

49. And they that sat at meat with him began to say within themselves, Who is this that forgiveth sins also?

50. And he said to the woman, Thy faith hath saved thee; go in peace.

Talk About It:
1. What did the dinner guests ask themselves?
2. According to Jesus, what saved the woman (v. 50)?

After having revealed Simon's inconsistencies, Jesus turns His attention to this unnamed woman. Knowing the intent of her heart and having experienced the actions of her love, He simply says to her, "Your sins are forgiven." There's no rehashing of her previous life with all of the specific sins. What matters is they are gone! She is forgiven not because of her deeds but rather as the result of her faith. Jesus explicitly states, "Your faith has saved you" (v. 50, *NKJV*).

The number of other guests along with Jesus at Simon's house isn't indicated. However, their presence comes into the narrative at this point. They are amazed at what has been said. Immediately it fosters the question of identity: Who is this Person who boldly proclaims forgiveness of the woman's sins?

Isn't it interesting how frequently the question concerning Jesus' identity appears? It doesn't matter whether the issue is healing or forgiveness of sins, people repeatedly ask who this Jesus really is. It's no wonder there comes an occasion when Jesus questions His own disciples about their stance on this issue. First He asks, "Who do people say the Son of Man is?" (Matthew 16:13, *NIV*). After hearing the variety of responses, He asks the disciples, "But what about you? . . . Who do you say I am?" (v. 15, *NIV*).

"Karl Menninger, the famed psychiatrist, once said that if he could convince patients in psychiatric wards that their sins were forgiven, 75 percent would walk out the next day."
—*Today in the Word*

This same question needs to be addressed to us as well: Who is Jesus Christ? It is not enough to base our answer solely on what Jesus does for us. What is the identity of the One who is "the same yesterday, today, and forever" (Hebrews 13:8, *NKJV*)?

III. GOD'S PROVISION FOR SALVATION (John 3:14-21)
A. The Love (vv. 14-16)

14. And as Moses lifted up the serpent in the wilderness, even so must the Son of man be lifted up:

15. That whosoever believeth in him should not perish, but have eternal life.

16. For God so loved the world, that he gave his only begotten Son, that whosoever believeth in him should not perish, but have everlasting life.

Talk About It:
1. Why was a serpent "lifted up" (v. 14; see Numbers 21:8, 9)?

This portion of our lesson comes from Nicodemus' dialogue with Jesus. Nicodemus comes to the Master with a genuine heart believing Him to be from God. It points to there being some Pharisees who are open to the message and identity of Jesus.

When confronted with the concept of being "born again," Nicodemus struggles (vv. 3, 4). He thinks of physical birth rather than spiritual birth. As Jesus attempts to bring him to a heavenly perception, the salvation process is explained.

Jesus uses a well-known Old Testament event to illustrate His part in bringing salvation (v. 14). Numbers 21:4-9 records the event in which a bronze snake became the symbol through which healing rescued people from the poison of venomous snakebites. As a result of the Israelites' accusing Moses of bringing them to the wilderness to die, God sent a deadly punishment. Snakes invaded the camp, biting a number of the people. When many died, the people confessed their sins and asked Moses to pray for the snakes to be removed. God's response was for Moses to fashion a bronze snake and place it on a pole. Those who looked on it would be healed from the poisonous bites.

In the same manner in which those people received physical healing, so did Christ's crucifixion become the means for spiritual healing. Those who look to Him will experience the spiritual rebirth placing them in the right relationship with the heavenly Father. The poison of sin dominating human nature due to Adam and Eve's sin in the Garden of Eden, with its spiritual death, is taken away from those who will believe on Jesus. In its place they receive eternal life.

This brings us to the golden text of the Bible, John 3:16. With brevity and clarity it states why God chose to extend mercy to undeserving humanity. Salvation rests completely on God's love for His human creation. Knowing the hopelessness of the human condition, He willingly made the greatest of sacrifices. Jesus Christ took on human flesh and limited His divinity to become the sinless sacrifice needed to cover our sins.

Here we are reminded of love being far more than an emotion. Genuine love is anchored in defined actions which take effort and even sacrifice. This can be seen clearly in 1 Corinthians 13:4-7, where love is defined in terms of concrete actions.

The phenomenal aspect of God's provision for sinful humanity rests in its availability. It doesn't become our possession through a list of difficult works. Neither can it be purchased by money or the trading of other possessions. Salvation is available through believing on Jesus as God's Son and Savior. This choice enables a person to move from spiritual death to everlasting life as a forgiven child of the heavenly Father.

B. The Reason (vv. 17, 18)

17. For God sent not his Son into the world to condemn the world; but that the world through him might be saved.

18. He that believeth on him is not condemned: but he that believeth not is condemned already, because he hath not believed in the name of the only begotten Son of God.

2. How and why was Jesus "lifted up" (v. 14)?

3. Why is John 3:16 often called the Bible's "golden text"?

Cry of Faith
George Whitefield, the 18th-century English evangelist, wanted to deliver himself from "the snare of the devil." He followed an austere lifestyle, fasting two days every week. On one occasion, he spent two weeks laying quietly and eating almost nothing in an attempt to cleanse his sinfulness. Only when he cried out to God in faith, realizing his own helplessness, did he experience deliverance from his burden of sin.

Talk About It:
1. Why did Jesus come into the world (v. 17)?
2. What does it mean to "believe on" Jesus (v. 18)?

These two verses further expand the concept initiated in the previous verse. God's great love is extended to humankind for a definite purpose. He sent His Son, Jesus, for the express purpose of providing the means of salvation. However, judgment comes to those who refuse to accept God's provision.

The major emphasis of these verses is a continuation of why God willingly sent His Son. His love desired that all people would have the opportunity to escape the bondage of sin. He wants the whole world to have the blessing of salvation.

Too often God has been portrayed as a divine tyrant just waiting to pounce on anyone as soon as a sin is committed. This view does not seem to be as prominent today as in earlier decades; however, we must take care not to swing too far in the opposite direction. Instead there is a balance which needs to be presented. God's love caused Him to go to the greatest extent possible to provide for us an eternal relationship with Himself.

"Belief is a wise wager. . . . If you gain, you gain all; if you lose, you lose nothing. Wager, then, without hesitation, that He exists."
—Blaise Pascal

Also, God's holiness demands separation from sin or eventual judgment. Anyone who does not believe in Jesus lives under the condemnation of God. Sometimes God's judgment can begin to be seen during life on earth, but it will certainly be experienced in eternity.

These verses also demonstrate the role and value of faith. Without it no one can find forgiveness for sin and enter into the provision of salvation.

C. The Verdict (vv. 19-21)

19. And this is the condemnation, that light is come into the world, and men loved darkness rather than light, because their deeds were evil.

20. For every one that doeth evil hateth the light, neither cometh to the light, lest his deeds should be reproved.

21. But he that doeth truth cometh to the light, that his deeds may be made manifest, that they are wrought in God.

Here we come to the bottom line. Though God doesn't send His Son for the purpose of judging people, it will occur because of their own choice. Choosing to remain in one's own way instead of accepting God's provision produces God's judgment.

Talk About It:
1. Who loves darkness, and why (vv. 19, 20)?
2. Who "comes to the light" (v. 21, *NKJV*), and why?

These verses draw a contrast between good and evil through the description of light and darkness. This would have been a well-known analogy to Nicodemus. The emphasis here isn't so much on Christ as the Light of the World, even though it is stated at the beginning of verse 19. Rather, attention focuses on human choice.

Individuals immersed in the deeds of darkness enjoy the comfort of their sins. Shutting themselves away from the light of Christ, they continue to pursue a lifestyle that inevitably brings judgment. They do not want to hear of the error of their ways or replace short-term pleasure for eternal bliss with the heavenly Father. Instead of responding to the truth, they cling to current ideas and actions which bring destruction.

In marked contrast are those people who allow the light of Christ to impact their life. They follow truth. They put their hope in God and live in the light of His revelation.

John 3 does not record how Nicodemus responded to Jesus' teaching. However, in chapter 7 we see this Pharisee standing in defense of Christ after He called Himself the "living water," even though he makes no personal testimony of faith in Him (see vv. 37-52). In 19:39, Nicodemus boldly helps to care for the body of the crucified Lord, which appears to be a public testimony of faith in Christ.

> "It is in our hearts that evil lies, and it is from our hearts that it must be plucked out."
> —Bertrand Russell

CONCLUSION

Regardless of the darkness of sin into which we may have fallen, hope is available. The light of Jesus Christ can penetrate the darkest realms of sin and bring a complete change in thought and lifestyle. More importantly, Christ brings eternal salvation which brings us into right relationship with God. The struggle is one of choosing to put our faith in Christ while rejecting our sinfulness and self-determination. Will we humbly submit ourselves or obstinately pursue our own path?

GOLDEN TEXT CHALLENGE

"GOD SO LOVED THE WORLD, THAT HE GAVE HIS ONLY BEGOTTEN SON, THAT WHOSOEVER BELIEVETH IN HIM SHOULD NOT PERISH, BUT HAVE EVERLASTING LIFE" (John 3:16).

God's love reaches back into eternity and culminates at Calvary. Such love in the heart of God moved Him to send His Son down from heaven and to give Him to die on the cross. At an early time, humanity fell into sin and rebellion against God's plan. Being the kind of God He is, God has sought to win humanity back into His joyful fellowship. He has not remained serenely detached but has become passionately involved in our joys and heartaches—"the Word was made flesh, and dwelt among us" (1:14).

The purpose of Christ's coming has been to disclose the love of God and to redeem His people. The great outpouring of God's love has been through His Son—loving, searching, and even dying for godless sinners.

Remarkable is the self-giving love of Christ, a love that moved Him to die as a criminal on a cross. "But God commendeth his love toward us, in that, while we were yet sinners, Christ died for us" (Romans 5:8). The phrase "for us," meaning both "for our

Daily Devotions:

M. Sacrifice
Provided
Genesis 22:6-14

T. Give Thanks to
God
1 Chronicles
16:8-13

W. Song of
Forgiveness
Psalm 32:1-11

T. Salvation Only
Through Christ
Acts 4:8-12

F. Confession
Required for
Salvation
Romans 10:5-13

S. Salvation Is
God's Gift
Ephesians 2:4-10

advantage" and "in our place," is central to the message that God in Christ humbled Himself. The Holy One, the highest of all, has taken the place of sinful people and handed Himself over to death. His disgrace and pain on the cross declare the unlimited breadth and depth of divine love.

Faith for Salvation

Introduction to Spring Quarter

The theme for the first unit is the "Gospel of Mark (The Servant Messiah)." These six lessons move from the beginning of Christ's ministry to His crucifixion.

The writer of this unit is the Reverend Joshua F. Rice (see biographical information on page 16).

The second unit, "Practical Christian Living," comes from the Book of James. How Christians deal with suffering, demonstrate mercy, live in peace, overcome worldliness, and demonstrate caring are the issues.

These lessons were compiled by Lance Colkmire (see biographical information on page 16).

Lessons 7 (Easter) and 14 (Pentecost) were written by the Reverend Dr. Jerald Daffe (see biographical information on page 132).

Jesus Begins His Ministry

Mark 1:1-45

INTRODUCTION

When we approach the Gospel of Mark, we tread on sacred ground. This is because Mark is almost certainly the first Gospel written. This may seem strange given that Matthew sits in the first place of the New Testament order. However, it was Martin Luther who confirmed the order of Matthew first, based on his belief that it was the earliest Gospel, on account of its Jewish flavor.

Another factor for determining the dating of Mark as the first Gospel is the fact that it is the shortest one. It stands to reason that the teachings and narratives of Jesus were written quite simply at first, then elaborated on by later Gospel writers. This is apparently what Matthew and Luke do, given the fact that practically all of Mark's content can be found within the content of the other two books. Yet Matthew and Luke still contain material that is identical, often verbatim, that is not found in Mark. That is because Jesus' teachings and actions were being continually preached. "Constant repetition and frequent contact between the preachers tended toward fixing the content of the message" (*Zondervan Pictorial Bible Dictionary*).

John apparently writes independently of the other Gospel writers, given the fact that he does not share their structure. This is why Matthew, Mark and Luke are called the "Synoptic Gospels"—they are in sync with one another by sharing an overall structure. However, the differences in wording in each of these books was inspired by the Holy Spirit to address a particular audience: Matthew, for Christians with a Jewish background; Mark, for Gentiles; Luke, for cultured Greeks.

It is widely held that Mark was written between A.D. 50 and 70, in the very next generation after Jesus lived on earth. As such, it is the material we have about Jesus that is closest in time to the Messiah, and much comes from eyewitnesses who saw and heard the events depicted. Although the Gospel of Mark does not identify its author, a quote from Papias in A.D. 125 identifies the author as the Mark in Acts, who is a colaborer with Peter, Paul and Barnabas.

I. BEGINNING OF THE GOSPEL (Mark 1:1-13)

The beginning of Mark's Gospel is as simple and inauspicious as its ending. Mark does not spend much time setting up or wrapping up his book. There is no information about the birth of Jesus nor about appearances to His disciples after His resurrection. This book is simple, straightforward, and to the point. Whenever Mark belabors a specific story or point, we should take notice, since such passages are vital to the themes he is attempting to communicate.

A. About Jesus Christ (v. 1)

1. The beginning of the gospel of Jesus Christ, the Son of God.

Mark begins not by identifying himself, his place of origin, the date of his work, or anything about his setting. He is concerned with the history of Jesus, and that story only. The beginning of his Gospel sets a fast pace that carries throughout the book. Once the action starts, it accelerates. This fits with the major theme of the Gospels—that God's kingdom is at hand in the person of Jesus. The time for God's reign is being fulfilled right *now*, and there is a sense of urgency in all that Jesus says and does. In fact, the action moves so fast that almost half of the book is dedicated to the final week of Jesus' life! So we should not be surprised by Mark's simple introduction in verse 1.

Although Mark's introduction is incredibly brief, he tells the reader precisely what to expect. He says he is writing a "gospel." The word in the Greek denotes an announcement of good news, and its identification with a full-scale book is original in the ancient Greco-Roman world. For this reason, New Testament scholars have long worked to categorize how a "gospel" might have been understood by its original audience. Most likely, ancient readers would understand Mark's writing in terms of a Greek biography. Many ancient Greek biographies have withstood the test of time and are available today, such as Plutarch's *Lives*.

What must be recognized from the outset of Mark, however, is that ancient biographies were far different from modern biographies. This is, of course, part of our frustration with Mark—we want to know more about the life and ministry of Jesus! A modern biography on Abraham Lincoln, for example, is full of information on his childhood, his early political career, his parents and siblings, even the typical schedule of his day. The Gospels tell us almost nothing about Jesus' childhood, very little of His family, and absolutely nothing of His appearance. At times Mark gets so detailed as to tell us that Jesus was "asleep on a pillow" before He calms the storm (4:38), but such description leaves us starving for more. However, ancient biographies were never intended to provide all of the data available about a person's life, but only that information which was applicable to the goals of the writer. The reason for this is certainly cultural, but we can also point to a few practical variables.

Talk About It:
What is the significance of the word *gospel*?

First, these documents were written about 1,500 years before the invention of the printing press. Paper was quite expensive, and making copies by hand was laborious. Second, scholars of the ancient Greco-Roman world estimate that only 3 percent to 15 percent of the population of Mark's day could read at all. The Book of Mark was never intended to be read per se, but to be *heard* through a public performance of the document. Sitting through a reading of Mark's entire Gospel would take many hours, so Mark must be choosy about exactly what to include. He cues us to his overall goals via two very different titles for Jesus.

1. *Jesus the Christ. Christ* is the Greek translation of the Hebrew word for *Messiah*. Its Hebrew counterpart literally means "anointed one" and was a thoroughly Jewish term. Mark wanted the reader to know that he was writing from the historical and cultural context of Jesus' life. These events really happened, in a specifically Jewish time and place. As the Christ, Jesus was the fulfillment of the Old Testament promises about the coming Messiah, particularly found in the "suffering servant" motif in Isaiah 42 and following. This was, of course, the early church's initial proclamation to the nation of Israel; and although Mark's audience was probably not predominantly Jewish, he preserved the historical reality of the person and ministry of Jesus.

2. *The Son of God.* Before launching into the Old Testament roots for Jesus' title as Christ, Mark ascribed to Jesus a second title common to wider Greco-Roman culture—the "Son of God." By the time of Mark's writing, the Roman Empire stretched from modern-day England in Western Europe, into Russia in Asia and southward into Africa. By the end of the first century A.D. it spanned 44 nations and 4,000 cities, all ruled by one man called *Caesar*, which is another title for "emperor." However, there was a distinctly religious component to the reign of the Caesars. Beginning with Julius Caesar, who was murdered shortly before the birth of Christ, the Caesars underwent deification ceremonies and were worshiped as gods in imperial temples across the empire. Their statues, archways and coins often said verbatim, "Caesar is the Son of God." It was a term of unparalleled divinity, and Mark placed it upon Jesus, thereby saying that Jesus rivaled Caesar. No wonder Mark was careful to record how a Roman soldier echoed this title at the death of Jesus in 15:39—one of the key verses in Mark. Mark was not content to preach the salvation of Jesus to the Jews only. The evangelist knew that Jesus' message could transform the entire Roman Empire.

"The truth is that while Jesus came to preach the Gospel, His chief object in coming was that there might be a Gospel to preach."
—R.W. Dale

B. Voice in the Desert (vv. 2-8)
(Mark 1:5-8 is not included in the printed text.)

Jesus Begins His Ministry

2. As it is written in the prophets, Behold, I send my messenger before thy face, which shall prepare thy way before thee.

3. The voice of one crying in the wilderness, Prepare ye the way of the Lord, make his paths straight.

4. John did baptize in the wilderness, and preach the baptism of repentance for the remission of sins.

The quotation in verse 3 ("The voice of one crying in the wilderness . . . "), from Isaiah 40:3, is a greater factor in the Book of Mark than this initial connection to John the Baptist. In fact, Isaiah is referenced more than any other Old Testament book outside of the Psalms. This is because Isaiah contains the themes of the Suffering Servant so critical to Mark's conception of Jesus' person. As N.T. Wright says, "Isaiah was by no means the only text upon which Jesus drew for His sense of vocation . . . but it is in Isaiah, particularly the central section, that we find that combination of themes—God's coming kingdom, the renewal of creation expressed not least in remarkable healings, the power of God's 'word' to save and restore, the ultimate victory over all the 'Babylons' of the world, and the figure of the Servant itself— which we find again so strikingly in the Gospels" (*Simply Christian: Why Christianity Makes Sense*). However, Isaiah isn't the only Old Testament prophet in view here. In verse 2, Mark pairs Isaiah with a quote from Malachi (3:1)—"Behold, I send my messenger . . . "—in order to tie the prophecy directly to John the Baptist.

The introduction "and so" (Mark 1:4, *NIV*) captures the Greek sense of continuity between the prophecy and what comes next. John is the logical expression of these lines from Isaiah and Malachi. And as the final book of the Old Testament, Malachi is linked to the New Testament by the Baptist. In fact, Malachi closes the Old Testament with the promise that God will send Elijah before the "day of the Lord" (4:5).

Mark clearly identifies John the Baptist as this same "Elijah." This happens not only in the citation of these Old Testament verses, but in the description of John himself. Just like Elijah, John preaches a simple fidelity to the God of Israel in the face of pagan idolatry. Just like Elijah, John lives a simple life of wandering. And just like Elijah, John looks forward to a greater prophet to follow—in his own words, One of whom the Baptist is unworthy to even untie His sandals (Mark 1:7). This proclamation likely drew gasps from the crowds, as an ancient rabbinic saying taught, "Every service which a slave performs for his master shall a disciple do for his teacher *except* the loosing of his sandal-thong" (Leon Morris, *The Gospel According to John,* Revised Edition). John the Baptist prepares the way for Christ by lifting up the imminent coming of a powerful leader who will baptize in the Holy Spirit (v. 8). But first, John will baptize this humble ruler in water.

Talk About It:
1. Why was it important for God to send someone to "prepare the way" for the Lord's coming (vv. 2, 3)?
2. Describe John's ministry (vv. 4, 5).
3. How did John compare Himself with the coming Messiah (v. 7)?
4. Compare the two baptisms in verse 8.

"*Repent* is the translation of a Greek verb *meta-noeo*, meaning 'to have another mind, to change the mind,' and is used in the New Testament to indicate a change of mind in respect to sin, God, and self."
—*Quotable Quotations*

C. Baptism and Temptation (vv. 9-13)

9. And it came to pass in those days, that Jesus came from Nazareth of Galilee, and was baptized of John in Jordan.

10. And straightway coming up out of the water, he saw the heavens opened, and the Spirit like a dove descending upon him:

11. And there came a voice from heaven, saying, Thou art my beloved Son, in whom I am well pleased.

12. And immediately the spirit driveth him into the wilderness.

13. And he was there in the wilderness forty days, tempted of Satan; and was with the wild beasts; and the angels ministered unto him.

Talk About It:
1. How did Jesus begin His public ministry, and why (v. 9)?
2. Describe how the three Persons of the Trinity interact in verses 10 and 11.

"The doctrine of the blessed Trinity is a reminder of the supernaturalness of Biblical Christianity. The doctrine defies rationalization, yet it provides for the believer the answer to the unity and diversity of the world."
—**Robert P. Lightner**

Mark rarely gives us much time to ponder the meaning of a particular passage before racing to the next event. The One whom the prophet speaks of suddenly shows up to be baptized by John himself (vv. 9-11). Any uncertainty about the identity of Jesus is cleared up by the very voice of God. In this divine announcement, Jesus' title as the "Son of God" is given for the second time in Mark's Gospel. Important characters will repeat it at significant turns in the book.

At first glance, it is odd that Mark includes the nondescript account of Jesus' temptation in verses 12 and 13. Matthew and Luke, of course, give us a lengthy account of those 40 days, particularly the tense conversations that took place between Jesus and the devil. In Mark, however, the mention of the Temptation sets up the cosmic dimensions of the person of Jesus—Satan, creation (symbolized in the wild animals), and angels are all intricately involved. Although rarely mentioned in the Old Testament, Satan plays a significant role in the Gospels as the personality behind all oppressive forces. Yet even he is no match for Jesus Christ, the Son of God.

II. PREACHING AND CALLING DISCIPLES (Mark 1:14-20)

The first chapter of Mark continues in a virtual blur, darting into important scenes just as quickly as they disappear. After Jesus' baptism, Mark skips ahead to a later date when John is in prison, allowing an undetermined amount of time to pass between Jesus' temptation and the beginning of His public ministry. This ministry involves preaching and gathering a few close disciples.

A. Announcement of the Kingdom (vv. 14, 15)

14. Now after that John was put in prison, Jesus came into Galilee, preaching the gospel of the kingdom of God,

15. And saying, The time is fulfilled, and the kingdom of God is at hand: repent ye, and believe the gospel.

The vital connection between Jesus and John continues in Mark, since Jesus waits until John's imprisonment before beginning ministry to the masses. It seems that John must be off the scene for Jesus to take center stage.

The tiny villages of Galilee are the first recipients of Jesus' initial proclamation of the kingdom of God. This concept is the most important single term of the Gospels, used interchangeably with "kingdom of heaven." It points to the Old Testament reality that God is building a kingdom on the earth over which He exercises complete sovereignty. Only for Jesus, this kingdom is not the specific nation of Israel, but is open to all people, even sinners. The promise is for all who will repent and believe that God's kingdom stands wide open. Jesus' miracles serve as signs of the presence of God's kingdom. His teachings instruct the ways in which life must be lived in response to this kingdom.

Talk About It:
What did Jesus preach about (v. 15)?

God's Kingdom
Can you imagine a world that functions precisely according to the laws of God? It may seem like a far-off hope, but it is exactly what Jesus has in mind when He announces the availability of the kingdom of God here on earth!

B. The Founders of the Church (vv. 16-20)
(Mark 1:16-20 is not included in the printed text.)

With no further commentary on Jesus' initial proclamation of the Kingdom, Mark goes on to describe the calling of the founding leaders of the church. The pattern Mark depicts is a radical departure from the typical way Jewish rabbis gathered disciples. This took place through a rigorous process of Hebrew school, in which only top students were paired with rabbis for "official" training. Jesus, however, chooses common fishermen. Although much has been made of the disciples' selfless abandon, they were likely flabbergasted at the opportunity to follow a Rabbi, since they were unschooled laborers. From this first batch of four disciples, three go on to form Jesus' inner circle, and to become the pillars of the early church (see Galatians 2:9).

Talk About It:
1. Explain the term "fishers of men" (v. 17).
2. Describe the similarity in the responses of the four fishermen (vv. 18, 20).

III. TEACHING AND HEALING (Mark 1:21-35)

The Gospels are not handed down to us as books of philosophy or even theology. In Mark, what Jesus *does* is just as important as what He *says*. We see this as Mark shifts immediately from Jesus' proclamation of God's kingdom to His authority over demons and diseases. A tapestry of Jesus' divinity is woven to prove Mark's thesis, that He is the Christ, the Son of God.

A. The Teacher With Authority (vv. 21-28)
(Mark 1:23-28 is not included in the printed text.)

21. And they went into Capernaum; and straightway on the sabbath day he entered into the synagogue, and taught.

22. And they were astonished at his doctrine: for he taught them as one that had authority, and not as the scribes.

Jesus' ministry to the villages of Galilee is initially centered in the synagogues. It was customary for visiting rabbis to have

Talk About It:
1. What "astonished" Jesus' listeners (vv. 21, 22)?

2. Why did the evil spirit cry out, "Let us alone" (v. 24)?
3. What "amazed" the onlookers (v. 27)?

the opportunity to teach in local synagogues, somewhat like present-day evangelists in local churches. It is notable that this first major scene of His ministry takes place in Capernaum, a city mentioned only in the Gospels, but a major hub of Jesus' work. Archaeology has shown it to be an important economic hub of the area, large enough for a Roman military installation.

Jesus' teaching style immediately sets Him apart from the typical Jewish leaders, revealing the seedlings of the larger controversy that will dominate much of Mark. Time and time again, Jesus' teachings and actions go forth in direct conflict with the Pharisees and teachers of the Law. The people quickly recognize there is a difference, but not at first because of Jesus' content (that will come later), but because of His authority. What was He teaching? We have seen this in verse 15. Jesus does not expound the ins and outs of common Torah-keeping; He passionately enforces, reflects and fulfills what Torah was meant to be—the reality of living in God's kingdom. Note that the crowds do not exclaim that Jesus' teaching is anything new or original, but rather that He enforces the teaching of the Torah with a profound vigor.

The Greek word for *authority* is found 10 times in Mark—an important concept introduced here. However, it is not simply Jesus' teaching that denotes authority, but also His power over all forces seen and unseen. Already Mark and the voice of God from heaven have identified Jesus as the Christ; now the demons join them. It is the demon who first introduces Jesus' association with His small hometown of Nazareth (v. 24). It knows much about Jesus, so the Lord silences it immediately, casting it out of the man. This exorcism causes the people once again to marvel at Jesus' authority and to spread the word about Him (vv. 27, 28).

"There are two equal and opposite errors into which our race can fall about the devils. One is to disbelieve in their existence. The other is to believe, and to feel an excessive and unhealthy interest in them. They themselves are equally pleased by both errors, and hail a materialist or a magician with the same delight."
—C.S. Lewis

B. A Ministry of Power (vv. 29-35)

29. And forthwith, when they were come out of the synagogue, they entered into the house of Simon and Andrew, with James and John.

anon (v. 30)—"at once" (*NKJV*)

30. But Simon's wife's mother lay sick of a fever, and anon they tell him of her.

ministered (v. 31)— "began to wait on" (*NIV*)

31. And he came and took her by the hand, and lifted her up; and immediately the fever left her, and she ministered unto them.

32. And at even, when the sun did set, they brought unto him all that were diseased, and them that were possessed with devils.

33. And all the city was gathered together at the door.

34. And he healed many that were sick of divers diseases, and cast out many devils; and suffered not the devils to speak, because they knew him.

35. And in the morning, rising up a great while before day, he went out, and departed into a solitary place, and there prayed.

The first miracles of Jesus in each Gospel are spontaneous. That is, they seem unplanned, the product of a demon crying out or a personal friend needing help. We see Jesus' healing ministry beginning this way, as Peter's mother-in-law receives a divine cure for illness.

By this time we should expect to see Jesus cohabiting with His disciples, so there is probably nothing unusual about their visit to Peter's home. Their stay does not seem to be because of Peter's mother-in-law's illness. We are not even told that Simon asked Jesus to heal her or if the thought even crossed his mind; simply that the disciples told Jesus about her. Nonetheless, the healing takes place in the simple action of taking her by the hand. Following this healing, Jesus begins a public ministry of power in Capernaum.

The ministry of Jesus cannot remain a secret even in Mark's first chapter. The word is out, and Jesus' public ministry of miracles begins. Healing diseases and casting out demons, He will not allow His identity to be verbally proclaimed. It is unnecessary; His physical and spiritual authority over evil says it all. So we see that the public ministry of Jesus involves primarily three things, apparently in order of importance: teaching, exorcisms and healings. As the crowds grow larger, though, Jesus longs for the time with His Father that He had before, and He pursues it often (v. 35).

Mark makes it clear there was more at stake than philanthropy. Jesus was not setting out to heal every disease and to cast out every demon in the world; if that was His mission, then He failed terribly. No, these miracles were signs of something greater—the relationship Jesus maintained with His Father. For this reason, He often withdrew from the crowds to find strength and life from God.

CONCLUSION

The ministry of Jesus in the Book of Mark begins at a lightning-fast pace. Jesus is proposed to be the Messiah and the Son of God, the One proclaimed by the Old Testament and introduced by John the Baptist. He is rooted in the Jewish traditions of Galilee, and there He begins a public ministry that includes teaching the kingdom of God, calling disciples, exorcizing demons, and healing diseases. This pattern of Jesus' ministry follows throughout the Gospel of Mark, inviting us to join the adventure of Christ's life, death and resurrection.

Talk About It:
1. Describe the amazing things that took place at Simon and Andrew's house (vv. 31-34).
2. Why didn't Jesus allow the demons to speak (v. 34)?
3. What did Jesus do the next morning (v. 35)?

"Where Christ is named, idolatry is destroyed and the fraud of evil spirits is exposed; indeed, no such spirit can endure that Name, but takes to flight on sound of it. This is the work of One who lives, not of one dead; and, more than that, it is the work of God."
—Athanasius

GOLDEN TEXT CHALLENGE

"JESUS CAME INTO GALILEE, PREACHING THE GOSPEL OF THE KINGDOM OF GOD, AND SAYING, THE TIME IS FULFILLED, AND THE KINGDOM OF GOD IS AT HAND: REPENT YE, AND BELIEVE THE GOSPEL" (Mark 1:14, 15).

The apostle Mark observed from the preaching of Jesus that entrance into the Kingdom would be through repentance. Proclamation of the Kingdom must not bypass humble repentance before the Lord. The term *repent*, from the Greek term *metanoeo*, emphasizes "turning one's mind." It indicates remorse and a change in character and direction. It is an experience that reaches deep within an individual and results in lasting change.

The complement to repentance is faith. Both repentance and believing are requirements for entrance into the Kingdom. Faith is not merely a religious experience but the development of a relationship. It means trust and confidence in the Lord. It is not a formula for receiving what you want. Believing in the Lord is living in confident relationship with Him.

Mark recorded that Jesus' initial announcement of the Kingdom was "The kingdom of God is at hand." This meant the Kingdom had come into their midst. Certainly not all that the Kingdom represented was fulfilled as Jesus walked on the earth. However, Jesus was declaring that the reality of the Kingdom had come in the Incarnation. They could become part of the Kingdom by believing in Him.

Daily Devotions:
M. God Honors His Son
Psalm 2:1-12
T. God Comforts His People
Isaiah 40:1-8
W. God Sends a Forerunner
Malachi 3:1-4
T. Jesus Ministers in Galilee
Matthew 4:17-25
F. Jesus Reveals His Mission
Luke 4:16-21
S. Jesus Is God's Son
John 3:16-21

Jesus Proves His Authority

Mark 2:1 through 3:12; 11:27-33

INTRODUCTION

The authority of Jesus is a major theme in Mark. The Greek word for *authority—exousia*—appears 10 times in this Gospel. In fact, it appears throughout the other three Gospels, including 16 times in Luke. Jesus of course has authority over demons and diseases on almost every page, but He also exercises authority over nature, sins and rival religious leaders. Even in the face of execution, Jesus declares to Pilate, "You would have no power [authority] over me if it were not given to you from above" (John 19:11, *NIV*). Jesus claims a divine authority like no other man that ever lived.

Perhaps this is why the early church wrestled to properly articulate the doctrine of Christ's divinity. They had to deal with a myriad of new and difficult questions. If Jesus was equal to the Father, could He also be truly human? If He was truly human, could He also be truly divine? Is He actually equal with God or a created being? These were the vital Trinitarian issues revolving around the authority of Jesus facing the early church, yet they concluded, based on the Gospels, that Jesus' authority placed Him equal with God while not diminishing His authentic humanity. They crystallized this view of Jesus' authority at the Council of Nicea in A.D. 325: "We believe . . . in one Lord Jesus Christ, the only-begotten Son of God, begotten of the Father before all worlds, God of God, Light of Light, Very God of Very God, begotten, not made, being of one substance with the Father by whom all things were made." From the earliest annals of church history, the authority of Jesus was confirmed to be equal with the Father.

However, we must also recognize that the early church did not create Jesus' divine authority. Recently a popular television series aired titled "From Jesus to Christ." Even the title suggests that the early church formed "Jesus" into the "Christ." Yet the earliest formulations about Jesus in the New Testament maintain His divine authority as Christ. Nowhere is this more evident than in the ancient hymn Paul quotes in Philippians 2:10, 11, which probably stretches back to the first years after Jesus' ascension: "That at the name of Jesus every knee should bow, in heaven and on earth and under the earth, and every tongue confess that Jesus Christ is Lord, to the glory of God the Father" (*NIV*).

Unit Theme:
Gospel of Mark (The Servant Messiah)

Central Truth:
Jesus Christ has all authority in heaven and earth.

Focus:
Acknowledge the divine authority of Christ and submit to His lordship.

Context:
The Gospel of Mark was probably written between A.D. 50 and 70.

Golden Text:
"They were all amazed, insomuch that they questioned among themselves, saying, What thing is this? What new doctrine is this? For with authority commandeth he even the unclean spirits, and they do obey him" (Mark 1:27).

Study Outline:
I. Authority to Forgive Sins (Mark 2:1-12)
II. Lord of the Sabbath (Mark 2:23—3:5)
III. Authority From Heaven (Mark 11:27-33)

I. AUTHORITY TO FORGIVE SINS (Mark 2:1-12)

By Mark 2, Jesus' healing ministry has reached epic proportions. The curing of Simon Peter's mother-in-law led to an entire town bringing their sick to Jesus (1:31-34). In verses 40-44, He went on to cleanse a leper. This healing was as shocking as the unthinkable act of touching the leper—a taboo in Jewish culture. In verse 45 we see He was forced by practicality to stay in the wilderness to avoid being mobbed by eager crowds. This is why, upon His return to Capernaum in chapter 2, word spreads like wildfire.

A. Preaching Interrupted (vv. 1-4)

1. And again he entered into Capernaum after some days; and it was noised that he was in the house. — *PETERS HOUSE*

2. And straightway many were gathered together, insomuch that there was no room to receive them, no, not so much as about the door: and he preached the word unto them. *OLD TEST.*

3. And they come unto him, bringing one sick of the palsy, which was borne of four.

4. And when they could not come nigh unto him for the press, they uncovered the roof where he was: and when they had broken it up, they let down the bed wherein the sick of the palsy lay.

The wording of verse 1 makes it a bit unclear whether Capernaum is now being considered Jesus' new "home." He does apparently launch much of His ministry from that city, and so He may be using it as a home base of operations. After spending time in the wilderness in order to avoid crowds too large and unruly to minister to, it may be that Jesus' return to Capernaum as "home" (*NIV*) simply points to His return to civilization. However, the Greek can also be translated "house" (KJV), which would connect it directly to the story at hand. Either way, Jesus returns to the place where His authority over demons was first displayed in 1:21ff., and the people are thrilled with His arrival.

Perhaps Jesus is back at Simon and Andrew's house; we are not told. But apparently He is in a home sizeable enough to hold a group of people that spills out into the street until there is absolutely no getting in. No one will relinquish his or her place around the house; it is jam-packed. They may be there in the hopes of seeing some miracle from the Prophet-Rabbi they have heard so much about, but Jesus is there to simply speak "the word" (v. 2) to them. This is the first time the teaching of Jesus is packaged in this term *word*, which later comes to be a synonym for the entire message of the gospel in the early church. The term in Greek is *logos*, and it is used first in 1:45 when the man healed of leprosy goes about freely spreading the "news" (*NIV*) of his miraculous cure. As Jesus preaches in

one sick of the palsy (v. 3)—a paralytic

the press (v. 4)—the crowd

Talk About It:
1. How crowded did the house become, and why (vv. 1, 2)?
2. Characterize the paralytic's friends (v. 4).

the overfilled house, little does anyone know that His teaching is about to be rudely and wildly interrupted.

Verse 3 introduces us to a paralyzed man. His four friends are after more than a cure for a simple fever or a mind plagued by demonic activity. This man, unlike the leper, cannot move to get where Jesus is. Apparently he is in a physical vegetative state. If only his legs were paralyzed, there would be no need for a mat. He was likely a quadriplegic. This would make him an outcast in his community and even his family. However, he has friends who will not give up hope and are caring for him.

In an act of vandalism, the friends spring to action. People in the crowd will not make way, so the four climb to the roof and begin taking it apart. One imagines this process slowly becoming loud and distracting. The owner of the house is not consulted as his property is torn apart. Yet it is the exact kind of reckless faith that Jesus commends.

> "Inspiration without perspiration leads to frustration and stagnation."
> —Bill Bright

B. Spiritual and Physical Healing (vv. 5-12)

5. When Jesus saw their faith, he said unto the sick of the palsy, Son, thy sins be forgiven thee.

6. But there were certain of the scribes sitting there, and reasoning in their hearts,

7. Why doth this man thus speak blasphemies? who can forgive sins but God only?

8. And immediately when Jesus perceived in his spirit that they so reasoned within themselves, he said unto them, Why reason ye these things in your hearts?

9. Whether is it easier to say to the sick of the palsy, Thy sins be forgiven thee; or to say, Arise, and take up thy bed, and walk?

10. But that ye may know that the Son of man hath power on earth to forgive sins, (he saith to the sick of the palsy,)

11. I say unto thee, Arise, and take up thy bed, and go thy way into thine house.

12. And immediately he arose, took up the bed, and went forth before them all; insomuch that they were all amazed, and glorified God, saying, We never saw it on this fashion.

The scene is atrocious. The crowds must have gasped at the audacity of these men both to tear up a homeowner's roof and to interrupt the preaching of a Prophet. Jesus, however, is duly impressed.

It is not the paralyzed man who takes Jesus aback, but his friends, since the plural possessive "their" is attached to "faith" (v. 5). Although Mark uses the word *faith* less than Matthew and Luke, it is still an important term, usually used in healing narratives. It refers to something greater than what we might call "belief," which in our time is often defined as an act of the intellect alone. In the theology of Jesus, *faith* is the placement

Talk About It:
1. How could Jesus "see" the men's faith (v. 5)?
2. What were Jesus' first words to the crippled man, and why (v. 5)?
3. What did the scribes think about Jesus (vv. 6, 7)?
4. Answer Jesus' question in verse 9.

of all of one's trust and hope in God. He chides the disciples for their lack of faith in the midst of a life-threatening storm in Mark 4:40, and He commands them to have faith in prayer in 11:22. But usually *faith* is a term of commendation for those seeking healing. The four friends display a brazen and public act of trust in a new and radical Prophet to expect Him to be capable of such an unspeakable miracle. No one has hailed Jesus as the Messiah yet; His true identity is still shady. Yet these men have no one else to turn to.

Jesus' response to the man ignites a controversy. There is no reason to believe that the friends came for the paralytic's spiritual healing. Yet Jesus sees his inner torment, perhaps his fear that his own sins are the root of his condition. This was the common teaching of the day when it came to birth defects (see John 9:2). With no mention of his physical condition, Jesus heals his soul by forgiving his sins. But "some teachers of the law were sitting there, thinking to themselves, 'Why does this fellow talk like that? He's blaspheming! Who can forgive sins but God alone?'" (vv. 6, 7, *NIV*).

Blasphemy was no insignificant accusation. Strictly prohibited in the Old Testament (see Exodus 20:7; 22:28), it was expanded to include a range of meanings by Jesus' time. In fact, it is the charge of blasphemy that allows the Jewish religious leaders to bring Jesus to Pilate (Mark 14:64). In this particular instance of the term, the alleged blasphemy takes place because Jesus assumes a posture and an authority that only God can possess—the authority to forgive sins. Blasphemy was punishable by death, usually by stoning, and this appears to be what the teachers of the Law have in mind. In their interpretation of the Torah, the crowd should rise and stone Jesus to death. Yet Jesus acts quickly and boldly.

Reading their body language and knowing in His spirit their very thoughts, Jesus sets them up for proof of His divine right to forgive the man's sins. They assume that to pronounce his sins forgiven is easy—it is only empty words to them. Jesus, however, mixes the man's spiritual and physical healing in a second amazing pronouncement (2:10, 11).

Jesus' miracle seems to be spurred not by the paralyzed man's need, but by the opportunity for Jesus to prove His authority to the religious leaders. The crowds have already declared His superior authority over these teachers in 1:22, 27, but Jesus treads new ground by claiming the power to forgive sins. This is the central point of the passage, as it is the central point of Jesus' healings. They are not performed primarily to ease suffering, but to wake people up to the reality of Jesus' authority and God's kingdom. This authority is sealed by Jesus' command to the paralytic to rise, take his mat, and go home.

A Higher Authority
In a 2005 Gallup poll of a particular Christian denomination in the United States, 74 percent of the membership responded that, when it comes to difficult moral questions, they follow their own conscience rather than church teaching. Although God calls us to use our own reason and intellect, we are governed by a higher authority—Jesus Christ. Because He claims authority over all things in heaven and earth, we must look to Him as the guide for proper living, not to ourselves.

Jesus Proves His Authority

Jesus' command to the paralyzed man is extraordinarily meaningful and noticeably elongated. Simply telling him to "get up" would have met the need of miraculous recovery. However, Jesus tells him to take up his mat. If it was the Sabbath (we do not know), this would have been a violation of the instructions of the teachers of the Law about work. Yet the simple fact that the man carried out the symbol of his former helplessness is meaningful enough. What is more, he is immediately told to go home. These were perhaps the most majestic words of all for a man who probably had been separated from his household due to his infirmity. Jesus effectively heals him spiritually and physically, then restores him to his proper place in his household and community. He is now fully whole.

The crowd's response can be taken as either appropriate praise or shallow wonderment. It was likely a mix of both. The miracle astounds them, but they are fickle. Nevertheless, they had certainly heard the healing stories of Elijah and Elisha, and they counted themselves privileged to see such things in their own day.

II. LORD OF THE SABBATH (Mark 2:23—3:5)

After the healing of the paralyzed man, the conflict between Jesus and the religious leaders intensifies. These leaders are identified as primarily Pharisees (2:16) shortly after the calling of Levi (Matthew) in verse 14, then in a dispute about fasting in verse 18. We do not know if this is simply a specifying of the teachers of the Law ("scribes") mentioned previously, or if the Pharisees emerge as the Jewish sect that opposes Jesus the strongest. Their opposition often centers on the Sabbath, which is precisely the point of dispute in the passage at hand.

A. Jesus Claims the Authority of David (2:23-28)

23. And it came to pass, that he went through the corn fields on the sabbath day; and his disciples began, as they went, to pluck the ears of corn.

24. And the Pharisees said unto him, Behold, why do they on the sabbath day that which is not lawful?

25. And he said unto them, Have ye never read what David did, when he had need, and was an hungred, he, and they that were with him?

26. How he went into the house of God in the days of Abiathar the high priest, and did eat the shewbread, which is not lawful to eat but for the priests, and gave also to them which were with him?

27. And he said unto them, The sabbath was made for man, and not man for the sabbath:

28. Therefore the Son of man is Lord also of the sabbath.

Talk About It
1. What legal privilege were the disciples taking advantage of (v. 23; see Deuteronomy 23:25)?
2. Explain Jesus' statement in verse 27.
3. What did Jesus declare about Himself (v. 28)?

Mark 2 is characterized by conflict. Jesus goes head-to-head with the established religious leaders on the issues of spiritual authority (vv. 6-11), eating with sinners (vv. 16, 17), fasting (vv. 18-20), and now the Sabbath. The importance of the Sabbath issue is indicated by two consecutive scenes that bleed into chapter 3. The first centers on Jesus' interpretation of the authority of David, which He claims for Himself. The second focuses on the illogical posture of the Pharisees.

Mark 2:23 seems quite unexciting. The Old Testament made allowances for poor wanderers to pick small amounts of grain from flourishing fields, so Jesus does so with His disciples. He has already clarified the fact that it is no time for fasting—the new wine of the Kingdom has arrived! So He and His disciples enjoy some grain as they walk. The Pharisees immediately point out what they consider unlawful on the Sabbath. They may have been referring either to the walking or to the picking of grain, since they maintained stringent codes on each. They likely cited the Old Testament commandment to cease from any work on the Sabbath, and specifically the demand to stay in the home and to cook all of the bread the day before. Exodus 16:29 lays this out clearly: "Bear in mind that the Lord has given you the Sabbath; that is why on the sixth day he gives you bread for two days. Everyone is to stay where he is on the seventh day; no one is to go out" (*NIV*). The problem in Mark is not so much that the Pharisees are Biblical literalists (the Pharisees are obviously out of their homes, along with Jesus), but that they add to the teachings of the Torah with their own requirements. After all, Jesus and the disciples are not baking bread, but simply picking some pieces of grain as they walk along.

Because the Pharisees play such an important role in the Gospels, it is important to recognize some of their qualities. Israel was littered with various sects, but the four major ones were Sadducees, Pharisees, Essenes and Zealots. Theologically, Jesus was closest to the Pharisees, which is probably the reason for their clash. He had little in common with the other groups. The first-century historian Josephus, writing shortly after the time of Christ, characterizes the Pharisees in a positive light as the "populist party" in Israel: "Now, for the Pharisees, they live meanly, and despise delicacies in diet; and they follow the conduct of reason; and what that prescribes to them as good for them, they do; and they think they ought earnestly to strive to observe reason's dictates for practice . . . on account of which doctrines, they are able greatly to persuade the body of the people; and whatsoever they do about divine worship, prayers, and sacrifices, they perform them according to their direction" (*The Antiquities of the Jews*).

As Josephus describes, the Pharisees were known for their codes of "reason," including diet, doctrine, and religious practice. This posture could and should have been honoring to God. As David M. Rhoads says, their aim at its purest form was "to put the whole of life under the control of the Law" (*Israel in Revolution*). The word *Pharisee* probably means "separatist," and they considered themselves sanctified for special obedience to Yahweh. Nonetheless, that obedience had devolved into legalism. Jesus does not challenge Pharisaism as such, but the reality that they had lost the heart of their sect. This is what He looks to correct.

After their criticisms, Jesus is quick to respond with an Old Testament illustration. The Pharisees likely considered Him unlearned, but He goes on the offensive with His superior knowledge of Scripture. He is surprised by their lack of knowledge in the Old Testament, for David offered a prime example of the same behavior He and His disciples performed. In 1 Samuel 21, David replenishes the strength of his men with the only bread available—the consecrated bread blessed by the priest. But Jesus is doing more than simply backing up His actions with Scripture; He claims the authority of David to interpret the Torah in such a way that gives life. His logic reverses that of the Pharisees.

The Pharisees have missed the point of the Sabbath, and thus the point of the Torah. It was not given to oppress humanity, but to liberate people to live the way God intended (Mark 2:27, 28).

> "Christ . . . had a right to direct the manner of its [the Sabbath's] observance—undoubted proof that He is divine" (*Barnes' Notes*).

B. Jesus' Challenge Goes Public (3:1-5)

1. And he entered again into the synagogue; and there was a man there which had a withered hand.

2. And they watched him, whether he would heal him on the sabbath day; that they might accuse him.

3. And he saith unto the man which had the withered hand, Stand forth.

4. And he saith unto them, Is it lawful to do good on the sabbath days, or to do evil? to save life, or to kill? But they held their peace.

5. And when he had looked round about on them with anger, being grieved for the hardness of their hearts, he saith unto the man, Stretch forth thine hand. And he stretched it out: and his hand was restored whole as the other.

Jesus' appeal to the heart of Torah is expressed poignantly and publicly in this fifth consecutive confrontation with the Pharisees. This time, however, it is Jesus who intentionally starts the controversy. Although He had cast out a demon on the Sabbath in 1:21-26, that was a spontaneous necessity of the demon's outcry. This time, Jesus takes the initiative in setting the scene. He heals a man who has a shriveled hand.

Talk About It:
1. How did Jesus meet the Pharisees' expectation here (vv. 1-3)?
2. Why did the Pharisees "hold their peace" (v. 4)?

We are not told that Jesus even has the floor as the teacher of the service. Yet He knows He is being watched and is up to the challenge. He refuses to back down and takes His dispute with the Pharisees public. He provides no theological discourse—just a simple rationale that unveils the true nature of the Sabbath laws of Torah (vv. 1–3).

Jesus' question in verse 4—"Is it lawful to do good on the sabbath days?"—hardly needs commentary. It seems blatantly obvious to us, but the Pharisees were locked inside a strict tradition, so they had nothing to say. The Sabbath was a system of laws intended to govern all of life, and they did not question them nor reflect on their rigid interpretation of them. For the only time in Mark, Jesus is described as "angry" (see v. 5). He heals the man with a simple phrase, leading to the foreshadowing of His death for the first time in verse 6. The Pharisees have decided that Jesus is dangerous, so they seek a political alliance with the followers of Herod in order to dispose of Him.

"It is much easier
to be critical than to
be correct."
—Benjamin
Disraeli

III. AUTHORITY FROM HEAVEN (Mark 11:27-33)

Jesus' conflict with the Pharisees is peppered throughout the Gospel of Mark, and it often centers specifically on the issue of authority. After all, Jesus is a high-profile prophet doing miracles and teaching with a dynamic passion. The common response was astonishment over the origins of His abilities. Finally, in Jesus' final week before His execution, the entire religious establishment teams up in the attempt to get at the heart of the matter.

A. Intimidation Met With a Question (vv. 27-30)

27. And they come again to Jerusalem: and as he was walking in the temple, there come to him the chief priests, and the scribes, and the elders,

28. And say unto him, By what authority doest thou these things? and who gave thee this authority to do these things?

29. And Jesus answered and said unto them, I will also ask of you one question, and answer me, and I will tell you by what authority I do these things.

30. The baptism of John, was it from heaven, or of men? answer me.

The scene is set up ominously. This time the Pharisees are absent. The important and prestigious leaders of the Temple barrage Jesus with the question that would decide His true identity: "By what authority are You doing these things?" (v. 28, *NKJV*).

Jesus' enemies are constantly trying to trap Him in His own words, and this appears to be such a scene. It leads easily into chapter 12, which is dominated by conversations of conflict between Jesus and the leaders of the various religious sects. This question, however, is the gravest. These Temple leaders

Talk About It:
1. Why did the religious leaders question Jesus' source of authority (vv. 27, 28)?
2. How did Jesus answer their question? Why?

want to know who gave Jesus the presumption to be who He is and to do what He does. Seeing the trap, Jesus refuses to be defensive.

Jesus will not place Himself in a compromising position if His interrogators will not put themselves out on the line. Therefore, He asks a question with teeth, one that could put His enemies' lives in jeopardy. If they would denounce John, He would give them their answer (11:29, 30).

B. Jesus' Enemies Stand Down (vv. 31-33)
31. And they reasoned with themselves, saying, If we shall say, From heaven; he will say, Why then did ye not believe him?
32. But if we shall say, Of men; they feared the people: for all men counted John, that he was a prophet indeed.
33. And they answered and said unto Jesus, We cannot tell. And Jesus answering saith unto them, Neither do I tell you by what authority I do these things.

The religious leaders, of course, know precisely what is at stake. John the Baptist was a popular leader who died a martyr's death. The common people revered his memory. They would be foolish to trample on his grave, so they refuse to answer the question. Jesus responds in kind.

Once again, Jesus maintains the upper hand. He eludes the trap of His enemies with humility, choosing not to announce the origin of His authority, although He knows it full well. They will not believe Him even if He proclaims the truth, so He remains silent.

CONCLUSION
The Gospel of Mark presents Jesus as a prophet with authority in the tradition of Elijah. There is nothing that can defeat the power of Jesus, whether a physical debilitation or a clever question. He has authority to heal disease, cast out demons, interpret the Torah, lay down His life, and raise it up again. However, the religious leaders oppose His authority with the same tenacity as the demons themselves. For this reason, Mark focuses on the conflict narratives that lead to Jesus' execution, in order to reveal their true nature. Jesus was not put to death due to any criminal guilt, but due to the religious leaders' jealousy.

GOLDEN TEXT CHALLENGE
"THEY WERE ALL AMAZED, INSOMUCH THAT THEY QUESTIONED AMONG THEMSELVES, SAYING, WHAT THING IS THIS? WHAT NEW DOCTRINE IS THIS? FOR WITH AUTHORITY COMMANDETH HE EVEN THE UNCLEAN SPIRITS, AND THEY DO OBEY HIM" (Mark 1:27).

The authority of Christ's teaching caused astonishment, and His authority over demons caused amazement. This wonder is expressed in a question, "What is this?" Then, as though to answer their own inquiry, "A new teaching—and with authority!" (*NIV*). That the demons should so promptly obey Jesus' command was to the observers incredible. It was indeed teaching and exorcism with divine authority.

"The words and works of Jesus are never to be separated. What He taught and claimed is to be viewed in the light of what He was and did" (Erdman). Together they produce the impression of Christ's deity.

Jesus Heals and Gives Life

Mark 5:1-43

INTRODUCTION

In first-century Palestine, the hallmark of Jesus' fame was His ability to do miracles. Although known as a powerful teacher, the crowds had seen powerful teachers before. They had only heard about healing miracles in a few Old Testament instances. And even Romans, with presumably little interest in the teachings of Jesus, knew of His miracle-working power and sought Him out, including a centurion (Matthew 8:5) and even King Herod himself (Luke 23:8). At no point did Jesus' enemies deny His numerous miracles; they simply denied the miracles' source of authority. Josephus, a non-Christian Jewish historian writing in the first century shortly after the time of Christ, wrote: "Now, there was about this time Jesus, a wise man, if it be lawful to call him a man, for he was a doer of wonderful works—a teacher of such men as receive the truth with pleasure. He drew over to him both many of the Jews, and many of the Gentiles . . . and the tribe of Christians, so named from him, are not extinct at this day" (*The Antiquities of the Jews*).

The fact that we have no early evidence denying the miracles of Jesus is a powerful testimony to their historical authenticity. This begs the question about their overall impact: If people were convinced that Jesus could heal diseases and open blind eyes, why didn't they believe His message about the fulfillment of the kingdom of God? This question cuts to the heart of the reason for Jesus' miracles. They were not simply acts of philanthropy. If Jesus was trying to eradicate disease from the face of the earth, He miserably failed. No, His miracles signaled that the kingdom of God had come among the people. If they could not believe in His message of the Kingdom, the miracles would not help.

Christian author Philip Yancey explores this disconnect between miracles and true faith in the Old Testament wilderness wanderings of Israel: "The response of the Israelites to such direct [divine] intervention offers an important insight into the inherent limits of power. Power can do everything but the most important thing: it cannot control love. . . . No pyrotechnic displays of omnipotence could make them trust and follow him" (*Disappointment With God*).

Jesus' miracles are acts of power, but their ultimate aim is to point to the One worthy of our love and commitment.

Unit Theme:
The Gospel of Mark (The Servant Messiah)

Central Truth:
Jesus Christ is able to heal the mind, body and soul.

Focus:
Realize Christ has power to meet all of our needs and receive His help.

Context:
The Gospel of Mark was probably written between A.D. 50 and 70.

Golden Text:
"God anointed Jesus of Nazareth with the Holy Ghost and with power: who went about doing good, and healing all that were oppressed of the devil; for God was with him" (Acts 10:38).

Study Outline:
I. A Demoniac Made Whole (Mark 5:1-20)
II. An Incurable Illness Healed (Mark 5:25-34)
III. A Girl's Life Restored (Mark 5:21-24, 35-43)

I. A DEMONIAC MADE WHOLE (Mark 5:1-20)

In the Book of Mark, the authority of Jesus grows more pronounced as the story unfolds. Jesus has just exercised His power over nature itself by calming a storm, evoking terror in the hearts of the disciples (4:41). Although He has cast out demons already in chapter 1, the passage at hand offers a closer glimpse at a more extraordinary exorcism. As we shall see, this story actually serves as a microcosm, or little illustration, of much of Jesus' ministry in Mark.

A. A Broken Soul (vv. 1-5)

1. And they came over unto the other side of the sea, into the country of the Gadarenes.

2. And when he was come out of the ship, immediately there met him out of the tombs a man with an unclean spirit,

3. Who had his dwelling among the tombs; and no man could bind him, no, not with chains:

4. Because that he had been often bound with fetters and chains, and the chains had been plucked asunder by him, and the fetters broken in pieces: neither could any man tame him.

5. And always, night and day, he was in the mountains, and in the tombs, crying, and cutting himself with stones.

The scene takes place in conjunction with the astounding act of calming the storm. We have grown used to the accelerated pace of Mark's narrative, and this movement is no different. No sooner does Jesus get off the boat after filling His disciples with awe than another incredible opportunity presents itself. The location of the Gadarenes is an important feature of the story. Known by several different names in the textual tradition, including Gerasenes and Gadara, the region was just five miles from the Sea of Galilee, yet was known for its large population of Gentiles and pigs. Therefore, this passage represents Jesus' first journey onto what might be considered borderline Gentile soil, even though it is officially in Judean territory. In Mark, Jesus' only other foray into non-Jewish culture occurs when He heals the Syrian woman in chapter 7. However, we cannot draw many conclusions from these particular locations, since they are all under Roman occupation. The reality of Roman imperialism is the focus here, as it significantly underlies many important aspects of these verses.

Jesus steps off of the boat to find Himself immediately in conflict with an extraordinarily powerful evil spirit. There appears to be "levels" of demonic power in the Gospels. For instance, in Mark 9 the disciples are unable to exorcize a particular evil spirit due to its uncommon strength. Here we also are examining a particularly intimidating demonic possession.

Gadarenes (v. 1)— the inhabitants of Gadara, the capital of the Roman province of Perea. The city was on the east side of the Jordan River, about six miles from the Sea of Galilee.

Talk About It: Describe the unnamed man's physical, emotional and spiritual condition.

Jesus Heals and Gives Life

The Greek word translated "met" (5:2) is its only use in Mark, and sometimes denotes opposition. It is the word Jesus uses in His parable about counting the cost of discipleship in Luke 14:31, in reference to a king who amasses an army "to oppose" (*NIV*) another king. This is no ordinary meeting in Mark 5. The demoniac and the spirits that drive him appear to be challenging the authority of Jesus in a spiritual showdown.

Mark uses two terms for demonic powers with different nuances. Sometimes they are described tacitly as simply "demons." However, in this case and several others, the description is more detailed, a translation of two words that mean both "evil spirit" and "unclean spirit." Both meanings are necessary to understanding demonology in this Gospel. First, *the spirit is evil*. It opposes everything that Jesus stands for—the coming of God's reign onto the earth. Second, *the spirit is unclean*. This is of particular significance in this story due to the fact that the man resides in the tombs. First-century Jews were appalled by this idea, since Numbers 19:16 declares anyone touching a grave to be ceremonially unclean for a full seven days. The demoniac acts according to the uncleanness of the spirit who has taken over his life by living in perpetual uncleanness. Such a state drove him to utter madness and insanity. Since God's Word was given to bring order to an otherwise chaotic life, it is unsurprising that the demoniac lives in chaos.

The demoniac's action of cutting himself is in direct disobedience to the Levitical command connected to pagan rituals regarding their tombs: "Ye shall not make any cuttings in your flesh for the dead" (Leviticus 19:28). The man's soul is inexorably tied to the graves around him. Although people attempted to chain him, perhaps in the attempt to exorcize the spirits controlling his life, he was a slave to the devil. Yet even this man has a date with destiny when Jesus comes to the area.

> "There is a fundamental sense in which evil is not something that can be made sense of. The essence of evil is that it is something which is absurd, bizarre and irrational. It is the nature of evil to be inexplicable, an enigma and a stupidity."
> —**Nigel Wright**

B. Deliverance (vv. 6-13)

(Mark 5:7, 8, 10-12 is not included in the printed text.)

6. But when he saw Jesus afar off, he ran and worshipped him,

9. And he asked him, What is thy name? And he answered, saying, My name is Legion: for we are many.

13. And forthwith Jesus gave them leave. And the unclean spirits went out, and entered into the swine: and the herd ran violently down a steep place into the sea, (they were about two thousand;) and were choked in the sea.

Although the possessed man initially came from the tombs to oppose Jesus, when he approaches he must assume a humble posture. When he begins to speak, it is clear that this has nothing to do with the demon-possessed man himself. It

Talk About It
1. In what sense did this man "worship" Jesus (v. 6)?

2. Who was "Legion," and what is the name's significance (vv. 8-10)?
3. Explain the demise of the herd of pigs (vv. 11-13).

is the spirits within him that are controlling his every move. They are the ones begging for mercy before Jesus. The majestic title they give Him is found nowhere else in Mark, and it is fascinating that in the Gospel at large the demons know Jesus' identity before any people catch on.

Although hailed as the "Holy One of God" by the first demon in 1:24, these spirits unilaterally address Him as the "Son of the most high God" (5:7). This ascription to God is found in the Old Testament only throughout the Book of Daniel, which is a key to the context of the book. In Daniel, the people of God are living under the oppression of Babylon, similar to the way in which Rome dominates Israel in Jesus' day.

The demoniac identified himself as *Legion*, which was a common Roman military term for the main units of infantry that occupied colonized territories. During the time of Jesus they consisted of 5,000 to 6,000 men each, and a full legion was stationed in Jerusalem itself—an ever-present symbol of Roman oppression smack in the middle of the very city of Yahweh. Mark shows that this oppression has a spiritual side to it as well. The evil spirits are on the side of the Romans, even borrowing their terminology.

Not wanting to leave the Gentile area, the demons suggest a herd of pigs as a good place for Jesus to send them. They fear Jesus and are afraid of some kind of torture. The pig, of course, is an unclean animal in Jewish tradition as evidenced in the Torah. It is not a kosher animal for Jews to eat, yet they are being raised on Jewish soil! Jesus consents to the unclean spirits' request, and immediately the massive and expensive herd of pigs drown themselves. Their deaths indicate Jesus' authority over both demonic powers and the power of Rome.

"Jesus is the great leader in spiritual warfare, and beside Him all others are dwarfed."
—David Griffis

C. Financial Fall-Out (vv. 14-20)
(Mark 5:14, 16-19 is not included in the printed text.)
15. And they come to Jesus, and see him that was possessed with the devil, and had the legion, sitting, and clothed, and in his right mind: and they were afraid.

20. And he departed, and began to publish in Decapolis how great things Jesus had done for him: and all men did marvel.

Decapolis (v. 20)—the 10 cities

Talk About It:
1. Describe the changes in the saved man (v. 15).
2. What did the locals ask of Jesus, and why (vv. 16, 17)?
3. What did Jesus tell the man to do, and what was the result (vv. 19, 20)?

Two thousand pigs is a massive capital investment today, not to mention 2,000 years before modern livestock machinery and methods. The men in charge of the pigs are probably fearful of their lives, and they run into the town to report the tragic events (v. 14). They have lost everything for their employer. When the townspeople arrive, the scene is much more peaceful than they could have guessed. The man who had been possessed by demons is "sitting there, dressed and in his right mind; and they were afraid" (v. 15, *NIV*).

Jesus Heals and Gives Life

The demoniac was infamous in the town. He inspired fear everywhere his story was told. The townspeople heard him crying out at night and likely avoided the area entirely. Now that fear is transferred over to Jesus, who has made him well. When the people recognize the power of Jesus, and specifically what He has done to the pigs, they cannot tolerate His presence. Who knows whose property will be destroyed next? In the face of economic catastrophe, they beg Jesus to leave (v. 17).

Jesus complies without hesitation, getting back into the boat. The trip has been successful—a broken soul has been delivered. Interestingly, this is one of the rare occasions in Mark where Jesus does not instruct the healed man to be silent about the miracle. Instead, he is to be restored to his family and to give praise to God for His mercy. As a result, the man evangelizes all over the area in 10 different cities (Decapolis). His story is beyond captivating, and people are astonished. Jesus' fame grows, even in the Decapolis, which was a mostly Greek area. His message is not only for the Jews, but also for the Gentiles.

II. AN INCURABLE ILLNESS HEALED (Mark 5:25-34)
A. A Broken Body (vv. 25-29)

25. And a certain woman, which had an issue of blood twelve years,

26. And had suffered many things of many physicians, and had spent all that she had, and was nothing bettered, but rather grew worse,

27. When she had heard of Jesus, came in the press behind, and touched his garment.

28. For she said, If I may touch but his clothes, I shall be whole.

29. And straightway the fountain of her blood was dried up; and she felt in her body that she was healed of that plague.

Jesus was a magnet for those with no one else to turn to. Previously this took the form of a crazed demoniac. In stark contrast, Jairus, a high-status synagogue ruler, then seeks His help (vv. 21-24). Now it is a woman who has lived as an outcast because of her condition. Although she is one of hundreds pressing around Jesus that day, her story survives in great detail, which is often rare for this first and shortest Gospel.

Her condition was appalling in its cultural context. The Torah could not be any clearer about her uncleanness: "When a woman has a discharge of blood for many days at a time other than her monthly period or has a discharge that continues beyond her period, she will be unclean as long as she has the discharge" (Leviticus 15:25, *NIV*). What is more, anything such a woman touched was considered unclean. Therefore, she was a complete

"D.L. Moody once spoke with a woman who didn't like his method of evangelism. 'I don't really like mine all that much either. What's yours?' She replied that she didn't have one. Moody said, 'Then I like mine better than yours.'"
—**Timothy Jones**

an issue of blood (v. 25)—"subject to bleeding" (*NIV*)

Talk About It:
1. What had doctors done for this woman (v. 26)?
2. What did the woman believe (vv. 27, 28)?
3. What was the result (v. 29)?

virtue (v. 30)— power

outcast to society, barred from the synagogue and the Temple area. Whether she was married is unknown, but her condition would certainly cause childlessness. Given the fact that it had gone on for 12 years, it likely started when she was young. Most historians consider the average life expectancy of women in this time period to be around 30 years, so she had probably lived with this condition for the majority of her adult life. Medicine was primitive at this time, and trying different doctors has spiraled her into a life of poverty and despondency. Her only hope for physical, social and religious restoration lies in a new, radical Prophet.

We cannot know for certain why the woman presumed that touching the clothes of the Lord would grant her healing. However, it is likely connected with the Elijah tradition that runs throughout the Gospel of Mark, from John the Baptist onward. Recall that Elijah's cloak carried miraculous powers in 2 Kings 2. His coat parted the Jordan River as a symbol of the prophet's ministry being carried on to his attendant Elisha. The woman's faith points to the continuation of Elijah's mantle of ministry in the person of Jesus. Just like in Elisha's experience hundreds of years before, it is not without immediate effect. The woman's bleeding stops.

B. The Power of Faith (vv. 30-34)

30. And Jesus, immediately knowing in himself that virtue had gone out of him, turned him about in the press, and said, Who touched my clothes?

31. And his disciples said unto him, Thou seest the multitude thronging thee, and sayest thou, Who touched me?

32. And he looked round about to see her that had done this thing.

33. But the woman fearing and trembling, knowing what was done in her, came and fell down before him, and told him all the truth.

34. And he said unto her, Daughter, thy faith hath made thee whole; go in peace, and be whole of thy plague.

Although Jesus does not consciously heal the suffering woman, He recognizes that something extraordinary has taken place. A humorous dialogue ensues between the Lord and His disciples. Apparently a crowd is thronging Jesus on every side. One imagines a famous person today being rushed by security guards through an excited crowd that almost swallows him or her. What does Jesus mean, "Who touched Me?"

Halting His journey with Jairus, Jesus looks for the one who touched Him. Realizing she is about to be found out, she throws herself on the dirty ground in front of Him, fearful that her boldness may have crossed the line. Instead, Jesus is duly impressed by her faith.

Jesus Heals and Gives Life

She was healed by her faith in something—but what? This verse has tended to be read in the light of the woman's faith in Jesus' ability to heal, but this ability is never disputed by anyone in the Gospels. Instead, it is probably her faith in Jesus as the successor to Elijah that results in her healing. She recognizes that Jesus is no mere magician, but that He represents the continuation and fulfillment of the Old Testament promises. The word Jesus uses for "plague," or "suffering" (v. 34, *NIV*), is used for "flogging" elsewhere in the New Testament. Her horrifying daily torment is finally over, thanks to the power of Jesus over disease.

III. A GIRL'S LIFE RESTORED (Mark 5:21-24, 35-43)
Jesus' healing stories occasionally are collapsed into one another, giving the reader a sense of Jesus' popularity. In this case, the story of Jairus' daughter is sandwiched around the woman with the issue of blood, resulting in two very different scenes, one full of faith and the next of despair, before Jesus' healing authority proves victorious.
A. A Faith-Filled Request (vv. 21-24)
(Mark 5:21, 24 is not included in the printed text.)
22. And, behold, there cometh one of the rulers of the synagogue, Jairus by name; and when he saw him, he fell at his feet,
23. And besought him greatly, saying, My little daughter lieth at the point of death: I pray thee, come and lay thy hands on her, that she may be healed; and she shall live.
No sooner does Jesus exit the boat from the Gadarenes than another crowd has gathered. They watch His every move like the paparazzi, and He seldom has time to Himself. Whereas Jesus had pursued the healing of the demoniac, those with physical illnesses usually seek Him out.
In contrast to the Pharisees, this leader of a local synagogue recognizes the power of Jesus. Although his name is Greek, it is probably a Hellenistic form of a Hebrew name due to its first two letters as short for "Yahweh." His situation is dire, but not for himself. In fact, here lies the significance of this story. It is the only story in Mark in which healing is requested for someone not presently on the scene. The faith of the Syrian woman in 7:26 comprises a plea for exorcism, and is all the more remarkable given that she expects healing without Jesus' physical presence. Jairus, however, believes that Jesus must place His hands on the girl for healing to be imparted. This also casts the woman with the issue of blood in a new light. She believed Jesus' power extended to His clothing without the need for even His conscious attention. Nevertheless, Jesus agrees to accompany Jairus to his home.

Jairus (jay-EYE-ruhs)—v. 22—ruler of a synagogue near Capernaum

Talk About It:
How did Jairus' faith in Jesus differ from that of most religious leaders?

B. A Bold Prophet (vv. 35-43)

(Mark 5:37-40, 43 is not included in the printed text.)

35. While he yet spake, there came from the ruler of the synagogue's house certain which said, Thy daughter is dead: why troublest thou the Master any further?

36. As soon as Jesus heard the word that was spoken, he saith unto the ruler of the synagogue, Be not afraid, only believe.

41. And he took the damsel by the hand, and said unto her, Talitha cumi; which is, being interpreted, Damsel, I say unto thee, arise.

42. And straightway the damsel arose, and walked; for she was of the age of twelve years. And they were astonished with a great astonishment.

Talk About It:
1. What is the relationship between fear and faith (v. 36)?
2. Who ridiculed Jesus, and why (vv. 39, 40)?
3. Why did Jesus limit those who accompanied Him (vv. 37, 40)?
4. What strict command did Jesus give (v. 43)?

Mark's literary reconstruction of these events is emotionally jarring. Because Jesus stops to minister to the desperate woman, Jairus' time has run out. It seems that Jesus' authority is limited by the constraints of time—a view that Mark overturns. Here Jesus is addressed as "Teacher" (*NKJV*) in a respectful acquiescence to the reality of the girl's death (v. 35). Perhaps these men are Jairus' servants, which makes him a person of means. His plight captures the heart of Jesus.

Jesus cuts to the heart of Jairus' fear, dispelling it with the need for faith (v. 36). At this point, the story grows intense. Jesus will only let His inner circle of three—Peter, James and John—accompany Him into Jairus' house (v. 37). These were three of the four disciples He first chose in chapter 1. They arrive during a traditional Jewish mourning ceremony, known for high volume and raw emotion. It was expected that all relatives and friends of the family gather in the home for communal grieving that lasted several days. Boldly, Jesus questions the need for such pomp and circumstance. His statement to the group was probably taken as a traditional condolence. It was typical then, as it is now, to speak of the dead as "sleeping," awaiting the age to come. It was terribly rude of Jesus to invoke this empty comfort in the initial pangs of loss, and the crowd scoffs at Him. But Jesus believes that the age to come is present! He defiantly orders everyone out of the house, and He takes His disciples and the parents to the corpse.

The moment of healing was so powerful that the very Aramaic phrase Jesus spoke ("Talitha cumi") is recorded (v. 41). He spoke Aramaic the rest of the time, too, but it is almost always given in Greek translation. The miracle provides an opportunity for one of the great curiosities of Mark's Gospel, as Jesus orders those present to keep the healing a secret (v. 43). This would certainly be no easy task, given that a crowd of mourners who know the child was just dead is waiting just outside. Scholars

"Faith does not operate in the realm of the possible. There is no glory for God in that which is humanly possible. Faith begins where man's power ends."
—George Muller

Jesus Heals and Gives Life

often refer to this recurring command of Jesus as the "Markan secret." Just as Jesus speaks in parables, so His miracles are parabolic. They express the reality of the kingdom of God to the world, but are kept hidden from some.

CONCLUSION

As the fulfiller of the age to come in the Old Testament tradition, Jesus serves the world as life-giving healer. No one is out of bounds when it comes to Jesus' ministry: the unclean, the female, the demon-possessed, the Gentile. All can experience His glory. In Mark 5, Jesus' healing authority is showcased in a compressed account of a single day of Jesus' ministry, in which three very different people experience a miracle. In the final act, a dead girl is given her life back. These miracles build Jesus up as the all-powerful Messiah before more challenges to His movement come in chapter 6.

GOLDEN TEXT CHALLENGE

"GOD ANOINTED JESUS OF NAZARETH WITH THE HOLY GHOST AND WITH POWER: WHO WENT ABOUT DOING GOOD, AND HEALING ALL THAT WERE OPPRESSED OF THE DEVIL; FOR GOD WAS WITH HIM" (Acts 10:38).

The word *anointed* reports the one act of anointing which took place immediately after the baptism of Jesus (Matthew 3:16). This Jesus from Nazareth was the Anointed One, the Christ. His anointing had not only affirmed His Sonship, but it also gave Him power—power to make sons of God all who would believe in Him.

After receiving this anointing, Jesus "went about literally, went through life or through the country, or among the people doing good, not merely doing right, but doing favors, showing mercy" (Alexander). The apostle does not specify the good things He did, but he did say that He was "curing all who were overpowered by the devil" (Williams). In this one statement Peter encapsulated all that Jesus came to do—to defeat the devil.

The phrase *the devil* is found only twice in Acts, and it means "slanderer" or "false accuser." Jesus, the Anointed of God, met and defeated not only the devil himself (Luke 4:1- 14), but He also delivered many who were under the dominion of one or more of the devil's demonic spirits. He gave deliverance to the demoniac of Gadara (Mark 5:7, 15); He healed the blind and dumb demoniac "insomuch that the blind and dumb both spake and saw" (Matthew 12:22). He overpowered Satan on other occasions as well, all because "God was with him." How amazing to know that this same God is with us and in us today in the person of the Holy Spirit!

Daily Devotions:
M. God, Israel's Healer
Exodus 15:22-26
T. God's Word Brings Healing
Psalm 107:17-22
W. Messiah's Healing Ministry Foretold
Isaiah 35:3-10
T. Jesus, the Healer
Luke 4:38-40
F. Healing in Jesus' Name
Acts 3:1-10
S. Healing by Jesus' Stripes
1 Peter 2:20-25

Jesus Foretells His Death

Mark 8:27-38; 9:30-32; 10:32-34

Unit Theme:
The Gospel of Mark (The Servant Messiah)

Central Truth:
Jesus willingly chose the cross to bring us to God.

Focus:
Consider Jesus' attitude toward His death and obey His call to take up our cross and follow Him.

Context:
The Gospel of Mark was probably written between A.D. 50 and 70.

Golden Text:
"Whosoever will come after me, let him deny himself, and take up his cross, and follow me" (Mark 8:34).

Study Outline:
I. Death and Resurrection Foretold (Mark 8:27-33)
II. Discipleship Linked to the Cross (Mark 8:34-38)
III. Facing Death With Confidence (Mark 9:30-32; 10:32-34)

INTRODUCTION

It does not take long in reading through the Gospel of Mark to realize that the book is not exactly packaged in a way that crisply "sells." This does not mean it is boring, nor that his characterization of Jesus fails to show Jesus' ability to transform the lives of everyone He meets. It simply means that Mark is not as "ironed out" as we are used to in modern religious books.

Walk into any Christian bookstore and see that many of its titles mirror those of secular pop psychologists, focusing on self-help. Easy answers to every problem we face are provided at great cost to the immature believer. Christian author Donald Miller describes his frustration with the Bible after becoming a Christian when his expectations of easy self-help were not immediately met. He gives this tongue-in-cheek description of modern Christianity: "The truths of the Bible were magic, like messages from heaven, like codes, enchanting codes that offered power over life, a sort of power that turned sorrow to joy, hardship to challenge, and trial to opportunity. Nothing in my life was mundane. After I became a Christian, every aspect of human interaction had a fascinating appeal, and the intricate complexity of the natural landscape was remarkable in its perfection" (*Blue Like Jazz: Nonreligious Thoughts on Christian Spirituality*).

On the contrary, Mark pulls no punches in the message of Jesus. It is a message of self-abandonment, not self-help; of self-denial, not self-fulfillment. In short, Jesus came to die and expects the same level of self-sacrifice from His followers.

The story of Mark's Gospel is one of conflict, controversy and intrigue. From the beginning of the third chapter, he alerts the reader that the death of Jesus is on the minds of His enemies. We are left to deal with the fact that the execution of Jesus is not a historical accident. It is not something He stumbles into by opposing the wrong people. No, it is the plan of the Father from the start. We can guess that this becomes clear to Jesus during His 40 days in the wilderness before beginning ministry, but we do not know. Somehow Jesus knows that God's destiny for His life means a violent death for the sins of the world.

I. DEATH AND RESURRECTION FORETOLD (Mark 8:27-33)

In the Gospel of Mark, Jesus' death is foreshadowed from almost the very beginning. This foreshadowing always occurs in the context of His conflict with the religious leaders of Israel. At times this is overt, like when they murmur about Jesus' committing blasphemy. Other times it is hidden, like when they attempt to catch Him in a verbal trap, such as the subject of paying taxes to Caesar. Most of the time, however, the topic of Jesus' death stays under the surface of the narrative, which is strange given the fact that six chapters, more than a third of Mark's Gospel, are dedicated to the week leading up to His death.

A. The Secret Is Out (vv. 27-30)

27. And Jesus went out, and his disciples, into the towns of Caesarea Philippi: and by the way he asked his disciples, saying unto them, Whom do men say that I am?

28. And they answered, John the Baptist; but some say, Elias; and others, One of the prophets.

29. And he saith unto them, But whom say ye that I am? And Peter answereth and saith unto him, Thou art the Christ.

30. And he charged them that they should tell no man of him.

In Mark 8, Jesus is busy at work. His amazing healing ministry continues, with the addition of the miraculous feeding of a massive crowd. There seems to be nothing that Jesus cannot do, and the question of His true identity has come to a head. Surely this spiritual leader—with authority over demons, disease, nature, hunger, and the very order of reality—is a prophet. This has been recognized from the start. But it is becoming increasingly clear, especially to those closest to Him, that He is more than a prophet. He is like nothing they have seen before; could He be the One?

His ragtag band is now ministering in the far northern corner of Judea, about 40 miles from the Sea of Galilee—a long way on foot. The villages they reach are located around a major city of the area called *Caesarea Philippi*. The significance of its name should not go unnoticed. Philip, a son of King Herod, was the governor of the area. Caesar Augustus gave him rulership over the northwest area of Palestine, stretching into Syria and other regions. In gratitude he named this hub city after both himself and Caesar—"Caesar Philip." Although probably not meant as a direct insult to the Jews, the irony is thick. Here in the land given to Israel through Father Abraham sits a city named after a pagan ruler who claims to be the Son of God. In fact, it was this Caesar who first took the divine title "Augustus," a religious term denoting holiness. Caesar and Philip sought to define the nation of Israel according to new Roman rulers and standards, and this is where Jesus allows His true identity to be revealed.

Talk About It:
1. Why did Jesus ask His disciples this question (v. 27)?
2. Why do you suppose people mistakenly identified Christ as stated (v. 28)?
3. What is the meaning of the term "the Christ" (v. 29)?
4. Explain Christ's command in verse 30.

Finally, Jesus begins the conversation about His true nature. The disciples have heard the shrieks of demons testify to His divinity, but Jesus continually orders them to be silent. They have seen Him perform miracles only God can do, including raising the dead, but He rarely lets anyone talk about them afterward. He is finally ready to let the secret out—who exactly is He? The disciples rehash the familiar murmurs of the crowds. They can't imagine He is asking *them* so directly. The people mostly whisper about a powerful Prophet in the tradition of Elijah who is a lot like John the Baptist. The difference is that Jesus has the miraculous powers of Elijah while teaching with an authority like John. There are others who point to various prophets in the attempt to decipher the identity of Jesus. Jeremiah had an unpopular message for Israel's religious leaders 600 years before; perhaps this is who Jesus most resembles. Isaiah had a message of remarkable hope around the same time; could Jesus be him? At long last, Jesus silences the meandering conversation with the real question He is out for: "Those are just the crowds. They see Me for a few days at a time. They hear Me teach for an hour or two and witness some miracles here and there. But you men have been with Me every step of the way." Jesus expects them to have a greater insight than the fickle crowds.

There is no more room left for guessing. Jesus' ministry is quickly driving toward His final week, and things need to be crystal clear. Unsurprisingly, it is the impulsive Simon Peter who says it as straightforwardly as it can be said: Jesus is the Messiah, the One the entire nation has been waiting for these past centuries. He is the One that Moses predicted would come and lead Israel to a greater freedom than just freedom from Egypt. Peter's words hung in the air, and one can imagine the piercing silence. No more commentary was necessary. The phrase is so dangerous that Jesus orders them to keep it quiet. This is for their safety, and for the timing of God. If they trumpet it in the streets, they might all be killed in a hurry. The coming of God's Messiah is nothing to be handled lightly.

"Anything that one thinks of God apart from Christ is only useless thinking and vain idolatry."
—**Martin Luther**

B. A Different Kind of Messiah (vv. 31-33)

31. And he began to teach them, that the Son of man must suffer many things, and be rejected of the elders, and of the chief priests, and scribes, and be killed, and after three days rise again.

32. And he spake that saying openly. And Peter took him, and began to rebuke him.

33. But when he had turned about and looked on his disciples, he rebuked Peter, saying, Get thee behind me, Satan: for thou savourest not the things that be of God, but the things that be of men.

Jesus Foretells His Death

Christ (in Greek) and *Messiah* (in Hebrew) literally translate "Anointed One." At the close of the Jewish ordering of the Old Testament, which actually ends in 2 Chronicles, King Cyrus is celebrated as God's "anointed" for his restoration of the city of Jerusalem and the nation of Israel after the Babylonian exile (see Isaiah 44:28; 45:1). However, Isaiah also makes it clear that the story doesn't end with Cyrus. In fact, by the close of his writings, there is a need for another deliverer, and Isaiah prophesies that this leader will rule in a way never seen on earth before. He will rule as a suffering servant of God. Therefore, it is not surprising that Jesus launches into what His identity as God's Messiah will mean first for Himself, then for His followers. It is the last thing His disciples expect: suffering, rejection and death.

By all indications, the Roman occupation had heightened messianic fervor all across Israel. It had been so long since the nation had been politically free—over six centuries—with brief independence during the Maccabean revolt. When would God act to raise her up to her former greatness? False messiahs appeared from time to time, and were typically crushed by Roman might. But Jesus would not come to power by way of conventional means. In fact, He would reign by becoming utterly powerless.

His use of the term "Son of Man" furthers the irony and tension within the scene. It is Jesus' first use of this term in Mark since chapter 2, and links to an important passage in the Book of Daniel. In the visions of Daniel 7 and 8, the prophet finds himself before a powerful, divine figure—the Son of Man—who interprets the future of Israel's oppressors. Jesus gives Himself this title, yet He will not be defeating the Roman legions but instead be mocked and killed by His own people. After all of His wrestling with the Jewish religious leaders at every turn, He tells His disciples that He will let them win . . . at first. The disciples fail to understand, and Simon Peter, who had just championed Jesus' messiahship but a moment before, now pulls Jesus aside to correct Him (Mark 8:32).

Jesus' description of His death was so plain that Peter could not believe a word of it. Surely Jesus had misheard the will of the Father. Their movement was quickly spreading through the villages of Israel. Jesus was in demand everywhere that He traveled. People were being healed, saved and transformed. How on earth could it end so tragically! Peter hadn't left everything to join a mission that would ultimately fail. In his arrogance and ignorance, He tells it all to Jesus.

Jesus is indignant, returning Peter's rebuke with a scathing reprimand. Yet somehow He looks right past Peter to the true agent behind the impulsive disciple's words. It is serious for

Talk About It:
1. What did Jesus begin teaching His disciples about His destiny at this time (v. 31)?
2. Why did Peter "rebuke" Jesus (v. 32)?
3. What did Jesus call Peter in verse 33, and why?

Jesus to call someone the devil, especially someone He obviously loves so deeply. We are left to wonder if Jesus reacted so passionately because there was something in Simon's words that tempted Him. Jesus knew the temptation of the devil from His days in the wilderness. Did it come racing back in this moment when Peter offered Jesus an easy, more traditional way of coming to power? Whatever the case, Jesus is firm. What He has just told them *will* come, *must* come to pass, because it is of divine, not human, origins. Otherwise all they have been doing will come to nothing.

II. DISCIPLESHIP LINKED TO THE CROSS (Mark 8:34-38)

Peter's ignorance and arrogance not only spark anger in Jesus but also open the door for a teaching moment. If His leading disciple cannot understand His mission, then how could anyone else? Jesus brings the crowd to Him along with His disciples, and elaborates on the practical meaning behind His future. He must make sure that everyone who follows Him knows just what they are signing up for.

A. The Way of the Cross (vv. 34, 35)

34. And when he had called the people unto him with his disciples also, he said unto them, Whosoever will come after me, let him deny himself, and take up his cross, and follow me.

35. For whosoever will save his life shall lose it; but whosoever shall lose his life for my sake and the gospel's, the same shall save it.

Modern business and religious marketers would have a terrible time attempting to package Jesus for popular consumption. He has a way of speaking either very secretly or with an overwhelming boldness. Here Jesus is not interested in softening the edges of what discipleship means. His teaching has vicious teeth and conjures up the worst fears of His audience.

Verse 34 is one of the most difficult verses to see through the eyes of its original audience, both those who heard Jesus speak these words and those who heard Mark's Gospel read in the first century. There are several things working against our immersion in Jesus' context here. First, we tend to spiritualize hard sayings like this. Crosses are not everyday reality for us, so we immediately look for a spiritual meaning. Of course, there is a great spiritual significance in the verse, but it probably did not sound that way in its context. Second, crosses today are an important form of Christian art and iconography. We wear them around our necks. They adorn our church walls. They are printed on bumper stickers and T-shirts. They do not carry with them the import of terror and fear that they did in the time of Jesus and the early church. Perhaps we can compare them to

---

"High and lifted up, I see Him on the eternal Calvary, and two pierced hands are stretching east and west o'er land and sea."
—G.A. Kennedy

Talk About It:
1. What does it mean to "take up [our] cross" (v. 34)?
2. Explain the irony in verse 35.

Jesus Foretells His Death

electric chairs in our day, but only if we were forced to watch electric-chair executions as we walked along our city streets. I have never seen anyone wearing an electric-chair pendant around their necks, yet this is precisely what we do with the cross. It would have never entered the minds of Jesus' listeners to celebrate such an instrument of torture.

Crucifixion is one of the most horrific deaths ever invented by the minds of men. Its brutality is unmatched, created to maximally intensify and lengthen the suffering of the dying. However, its primary goal was to publicly warn passersby. It was official state terrorism, meant to scare the public into complying with the oppression of Rome. Principally reserved for road bandits and seditionists, Caesar Augustus' general Cassius was known for crucifying thousands of people at the same time if a rogue city fought Roman conquest. This kind of language would not draw a crowd around Jesus for long. Yet it is vital to His understanding of how life works in the kingdom of God.

The way of the cross is not a death wish. It is a way of giving up one's life so that true, authentic life can be experienced. Marcus J. Borg effectively relays this vital theological component of Jesus' teaching: "The 'way of death' did not mean physical death, even though some of the early followers of Jesus were martyred. Rather, it was a metaphor for an internal process. . . . This internal dying or death has two closely related dimensions of meaning. On the one hand, it is a dying of the self as the center of its own concern. On the other hand, it is a dying to the world as the center of security and identity. These—the self and the world—are the two great rival centers to centering in God, and the path of transformation thus involves a dying to both of them" (*Jesus: A New Vision*). In the teachings of Jesus, the path to self-fulfillment does not lie in self-help, but in giving up one's self through the way of the cross.

Come and Die
Dietrich Bonhoeffer remains one of the most celebrated Christian martyrs of the past century. Jailed in World War II for his opposition to the Nazi Party, he was eventually executed for treason. Nonetheless, he continued to write about Christian responsibility in the face of oppression. In his most famous work, *The Cost of Discipleship*, he wrote these words: "When Christ calls a man, He bids him come and die."

B. The Value of Following Jesus (vv. 36-38)

36. For what shall it profit a man, if he shall gain the whole world, and lose his own soul?

37. Or what shall a man give in exchange for his soul?

38. Whosoever therefore shall be ashamed of me and of my words in this adulterous and sinful generation; of him also shall the Son of man be ashamed, when he cometh in the glory of his Father with the holy angels.

After Jesus clearly defines the great cost of being His disciple, He turns the tables to describe the great costs of *not* following Him. Yes, the physical consequences and immediate spiritual consequences of following Jesus are severe. But the bigger picture allows the beauty of the Lord's teaching to shine through. Even if one could achieve total bliss in this world, it would be

Talk About It:
1. Answer the questions in verses 36 and 37.
2. How does one show he is "ashamed" of Christ's words (v. 38)?

worthless if the soul were left untended. It can be exchanged neither for pleasure nor riches. For this reason, Jesus expects that His followers will be able to stand unashamed of the gospel, even in the face of torture and death. None other than the Father himself will reward them.

III. FACING DEATH WITH CONFIDENCE (Mark 9:30-32; 10:32-34)

The narrative of Mark takes an ominous turn with Jesus' introduction of His impending fate. But even this serves to elevate Jesus' authority, because He never shrinks back from its conclusion. The fact that His death was not an accident was a vital component of the early church's message. After all, they were promoting a Savior who had been killed as a traitor by the Romans. The reality that this was in the plan of God all along legitimized the death of Jesus for these early Christians.

A. An Extended Meeting (9:30-32)

30. And they departed thence, and passed through Galilee; and he would not that any man should know it.

31. For he taught his disciples, and said unto them, The Son of man is delivered into the hands of men, and they shall kill him; and after that he is killed, he shall rise the third day.

32. But they understood not that saying, and were afraid to ask him.

Talk About It:
1. Why didn't Jesus want anyone to know where He was at this time (vv. 30, 31)?
2. Why didn't the disciples understand Jesus' teaching, and why were they afraid to ask (v. 32)?

Obviously, Jesus' initial announcement of His future death did not go so well. The Twelve were not ready to receive such a hard truth, as evidenced in Peter's virulent rebuke. As a result, Jesus takes an extended time away from the crowds with His disciples. He knows that they need Him now more than ever. In this setting, He explains Himself again.

By this time in Jesus' ministry, evading the crowds was more difficult than ever. Their presence had to be completely covert, which probably meant taking more arduous travel routes. The subject of discussion was grave enough to warrant such discomfort. He tells them again what He told them before in 8:31. This time, Mark gives it to us in Jesus' words. There will be a betrayal, then a murder, then a resurrection. The disciples are again shocked. How do these components fit into the reign of Messiah? How will this path restore the nation of Israel to her former greatness? Their lack of understanding is perfectly expressed in the following passage in which they argue about greatness (vv. 33, 34). They assume that Jesus as the Messiah is about to set up His earthly kingdom, and they are vying for position. Ironically, Jesus is talking in opposite terms, and "they . . . were afraid to ask him about it" (v. 32, *NIV*).

Only one other time in the Book of Mark are the disciples afraid of Jesus—when He calmed the storm back in chapter 4. What inspired their fear during this conversation? It is likely that Jesus' words were so far outside of their frame of reference, and that He spoke them with such authority and passion, that they remain silent, and the meaning of Jesus' words is again lost to them.

B. A Bold March (10:32-34)

32. And they were in the way going up to Jerusalem; and Jesus went before them: and they were amazed; and as they followed, they were afraid. And he took again the twelve, and began to tell them what things should happen unto him,

33. Saying, Behold, we go up to Jerusalem; and the Son of man shall be delivered unto the chief priests, and unto the scribes; and they shall condemn him to death, and shall deliver him to the Gentiles:

34. And they shall mock him, and shall scourge him, and shall spit upon him, and shall kill him: and the third day he shall rise again.

The time has come for Jesus to begin the journey to Jerusalem. He needs no prodding from anyone, although He knows that violence and death await Him. Luke, in his Gospel, says that he "resolutely set out" for the Holy City (9:51, *NIV*). In the Gospel of Mark, Jesus is no less determined.

The disciples can hardly believe what is happening. After all, Jerusalem is that bastion of religious oppression that Jesus has been vehemently opposing for three years. The leaders there are powerful, with plenty of Roman connections, and they hate Jesus. He has been able to survive their attacks by sticking to His own turf—the villages mostly around Galilee. He will be afforded no such protection in the big city. And with the Feast of the Passover soon approaching, neither the Jewish nor the Roman leaders will be in any mood for a new Messiah. This time it is not the disciples who are afraid, but the crowds (v. 32, *NIV*). The Twelve are astonished at the scene. Seeing their nervous eyes, Jesus takes them aside for a third explanation of His future.

Jesus' final description of what is to come is the most shockingly detailed. The Gentiles will mock His spirit and destroy His body. But given just three days, God will turn the tables on them all.

CONCLUSION

The way of the cross is central to the gospel, not only in the teachings of Jesus but also in His self-understanding. It has been said that Jesus was born to die, and this is pure truth. We

> "Love always involves responsibility, and love always involves sacrifice. And we do not really love Christ unless we are prepared to face His task and take up His Cross."
>
> **—William Barclay**

Talk About It:
1. Who was "amazed" and who was "afraid" (v. 32), and why?
2. Why do you suppose Jesus was so specific in His prophecy (v. 33)?

> "The determining factor of my existence is no longer my past. It is Christ's past."
>
> **—Sinclair Ferguson**

see it in Jesus' very words in three distinct occasions in the Gospel of Mark. We also see it foreshadowed in the growing opposition and hatred of the Pharisees, scribes, and teachers of the Law. Yet the message of Mark is not somber. It is the announcement that Jesus has conquered death and brought redemption. For this reason, His followers are also called to the way of the cross, so that the power of God's resurrection might be at work in us all.

Daily Devotions:
M. Sin Brought Death
   Genesis 3:17-24
T. Delivered From Death
   Psalm 116:1-9
W. When Death Comes
   Ecclesiastes 12:1-7
T. Jesus' Authority Over Death
   John 5:24-30
F. Jesus Laid Down His Life
   John 10:10-18
S. Why Jesus Chose Death
   Philippians 2:5-11

GOLDEN TEXT CHALLENGE

"WHOSOEVER WILL COME AFTER ME, LET HIM DENY HIMSELF, AND TAKE UP HIS CROSS, AND FOLLOW ME" (Mark 8:34).

Jesus lays down the requirement to be a faithful disciple—self-discipline. The first aspect of self-discipline is denial. *Denial* stresses a departure from self-centered interests. It is to actively move away from habits, opinions, and directions that are not consistent with a Christ-centered life.

The second aspect of self-discipline is to "take up [one's] cross." The *cross* represents an intensive commitment to the way of Christ. In the cross is represented not only a departure from self-centeredness but also a statement of commitment before the world. It implies suffering.

The final aspect of self-discipline is to *follow* Christ—to "mimic or repeat" what Christ did. This indicates that one's life is now directed by Christ. The individual's life is not his own. He has disciplined himself to follow Christ.

Jesus Foretells His Death

Jesus Teaches About True Greatness

Mark 9:33-50; 10:35-45

INTRODUCTION

The New Testament has as much to say about social standing as it does any other topic. For the Biblical writers, one's social status was just as spiritually significant as one's eternal destination. This emphasis is due to the fact that Christian theology brought a completely new way of conceiving social rank into the world. The social pyramid had never been fully inverted before Jesus. True, the Greeks did introduce democracy into the mix, but it was largely a democracy of the upper class. By the time of Jesus, the Roman emperor had disbanded any power in the representative government and ruled exactly like a king. Society was more stratified according to social rank than ever before. Virtually everyone was categorized according to title, wealth and prestige. The goal, of course, was to move up in status through securing the most powerful friends and allies possible. Jesus was the first to talk about securing status through moving *down* the social ladder by befriending the outcasts and welcoming shame. It was not often a popular message.

Henri J.M. Nouwen writes eloquently about this new view of status that God brought humanity through Jesus Christ, even in the midst of Roman abuses of power: "What was and is God's response to the diabolical power that rules the world and destroys people and their lands . . . God chose powerlessness. God chose to enter into human history in complete weakness. That divine choice forms the center of the Christian faith. In Jesus of Nazareth, the powerless God appeared among us to unmask the illusion of power, to disarm the prince of darkness who rules the world, and to bring the divided human race to a new unity. It is through total and unmitigated powerlessness that God shows us divine mercy" (*Finding My Way Home: Pathways to Life and the Spirit*).

The gospel program for power is a radical commitment to downward mobility. This is seen not only in the Gospel of Mark, but in the ministry of Paul as well. Although a high-status, educated, worldly-wise traveler who could speak multiple languages, Paul chose to work a menial job and suffer shame for Christ's sake. He lived this way as a method of expressing the gospel.

Unit Theme:
Gospel of Mark (The Servant Messiah)

Central Truth:
Jesus exemplified true greatness.

Focus:
Assess and practice what Jesus taught about the way to attain true greatness.

Context:
The Gospel of Mark was probably written between A.D. 50 and 70.

Golden Text:
"If any man desire to be first, the same shall be last of all, and servant of all" (Mark 9:35).

Study Outline:
I. Reject Vanity and Sectarian Pride (Mark 9:33-40)
II. Commit to Humility and Peace (Mark 9:41-50)
III. Achieve Greatness Through Service (Mark 10:35-45)

I. REJECT VANITY AND SECTARIAN PRIDE (Mark 9:33-40)

Jesus' teachings on power were split into two distinct scenes. In both cases they were presented in conjunction with the disciples' feuding over social position. In the performance of Mark to its original audiences, this was likely quite humorous. Obviously, the disciples did not grasp anything Jesus was trying to teach them about power. That would occur after the Resurrection, when the spirit of His words began to form a new consciousness in them.

A. Correction of the Disciples (vv. 33-35)

33. And he came to Capernaum: and being in the house he asked them, What was it that ye disputed among yourselves by the way?

34. But they held their peace: for by the way they had disputed among themselves, who should be the greatest.

35. And he sat down, and called the twelve, and saith unto them, If any man desire to be first, the same shall be last of all, and servant of all.

Talk About It:
Why do you suppose the disciples were having this argument?

After an extended time alone with Jesus, in which He explains once again His destiny to go to the cross, the motley band of brothers heads back to home base in Capernaum. It is the perfect time for the heady disciples to jostle for position. After all, they are well known in Capernaum. They have been operating out of the town from the beginnings of their ministry together. They are used to being held in high esteem by the townspeople who long to get near to Jesus. Yet their arrogance is so defiant that they cannot even keep their argument quiet in the presence of the Lord. Jesus waits for a teaching moment to present itself before asking about their discussion indoors. He wants plenty of time to address their folly.

The disciples cannot even answer the Lord's question. They are suddenly stricken by the stupidity of their childish quarreling. After Jesus tells them about His plan to give His life for the world, they are embarrassed at their behavior. Without receiving an answer, Jesus cuts to the heart of their need.

Jesus sits down as if to assume a humble posture. The disciples lean forward to hear the Master's insight. It is blistering in its simplicity. They are concerned with being the greatest, when they should be vying to become the least. In fact, they should aspire not toward greatness, but toward servanthood. The Greek word he uses is not the one for *slave*, but the one from which we get our word *deacon*. It refers literally to a waiter. The disciples are seeking to be served, rather than to serve, and Jesus offers the necessary corrective.

"The first step towards humility [is] to realize that one is proud."
—**C.S. Lewis**

B. The Humility of a Child (vv. 36, 37)

36. And he took a child, and set him in the midst of them: and when he had taken him in his arms, he said unto them,

37. Whosoever shall receive one of such children in my name, receiveth me: and whosoever shall receive me, receiveth not me, but him that sent me.

Jesus is not finished driving home His point into the minds of His wayward disciples. They need a stronger visual aid to truly grasp the significance of Jesus' words. They are renowned for missing the point entirely and then being too prideful to ask for clarification. In this instance, Jesus is teaching principles that are just too important to be overlooked.

Welcoming children was not on the disciples' priority list that day. They desired to experience the applause of the Capernaum masses, not to serve "the least of these." In Jesus' day, children were often considered expendable due to their economic drain and their lack of productivity. The Romans were especially known for the practice of ancient abortion, called *exposure*. In this practice, unwanted children, almost always female, were left to die upon rocks at a particular place outside the city. The early Christians, in response to Jesus' teachings, were known for opposing this horrid practice.

In Jesus' worldview, nothing was more sacred than serving a child. In fact, this is one of the few places in Mark where Jesus offers a direct connection with the Father. This is not to say that Mark does not consider Jesus the perfect reflection of the Father; he does. But it is not a major theme in his Gospel, as it is in John. Therefore, it is significant that Mark underscores the importance of serving the least privileged as a means of connecting with both Christ and the Father.

Talk About It:
What truth did Jesus convey by using a child?

"He chose the lowly things of this world and the despised things . . . so that no one may boast before him."
—1 Corinthians 1:28, 29, *NIV*

C. An Inclusive Community (vv. 38-40)

38. And John answered him, saying, Master, we saw one casting out devils in thy name, and he followeth not us: and we forbad him, because he followeth not us.

39. But Jesus said, Forbid him not: for there is no man which shall do a miracle in my name, that can lightly speak evil of me.

40. For he that is not against us is on our part.

The disciples still don't get it. The comic relief in the narrative continues with yet another question that reveals the ignorance of the Twelve. Here Jesus is soon to enter His final week, and they seem almost completely unchanged by the time they have spent with the Lord. This time John interrupts Jesus, not with a humble question, but with a bit of information he expects to be praised for.

Now that Jesus has stolen their opportunity for individual grandeur, John feels that they at least need to protect their exclusivity as a group. After all, everyone around the villages knows that Jesus had chosen 12 apostles, and this was likely a source of pride for them. John expects Jesus to validate his

Talk About It:
1. Why had the disciples told a man to stop casting out demons?
2. Explain the principle in verse 40.

definition of the group's boundaries, but Jesus exposes them, saying, "Whoever is not against us is for us" (v. 40, *NIV*).

Jesus is ministering and calling people all over Judea—people who will multiply His ministry by doing His works. Jesus' logic seems obvious, but His disciples are in need of straight-forward truth. If someone is doing good in the name and power of Jesus, how could he be a hindrance to their mission? In fact, the disciples shouldn't give a second thought to even the apathetic. God's kingdom is being established and it will prevail, so those straddling the fence will not hinder the disciples' ministry.

> "Most of us are umpires at heart: we like to call balls and strikes on everyone else."
> —Leo Aikman

II. COMMIT TO HUMILITY AND PEACE (Mark 9:41-50)

There is much at stake in this particular dialogue between Jesus and His disciples. He is not in a hurry as He painstakingly addresses each topic that comes up. Yet the subjects are tied together by the overarching theme of God's preferential option for those of lower status. Jesus goes on to describe the significance of God's love for those at the bottom of the social order by depicting the reality of hell. There is judgment for those who ignore God's value system—a judgment Jesus fears for at least one of His own disciples.

A. Little Rewards and Little Ones (vv. 41, 42)

41. For whosoever shall give you a cup of water to drink in my name, because ye belong to Christ, verily I say unto you, he shall not lose his reward.

42. And whosoever shall offend one of these little ones that believe in me, it is better for him that a millstone were hanged about his neck, and he were cast into the sea.

John's commitment to maintaining the hard and fast boundaries around the Twelve displays his lack of understanding of God's benevolent heart. If God is concerned with maintaining His own exclusive divine club, humanity is hopelessly lost forever. Instead, John should be seeking out allies, even weak allies, in fulfilling the mission of the kingdom of heaven.

God will not accept only those who are a part of the Twelve. Instead, even a stranger who gives them a cup of water will be lavishly rewarded. This both elevates the prestige of the 12 apostles while also encouraging them to be open to support from all quarters. Try as they may, they cannot fulfill God's mission alone. Even those who seem insignificant, like water-carriers, can greatly contribute to their efforts and to the Kingdom. This verse represents the only time Jesus explicitly calls Himself the Christ. He uses the term a few other places in teaching, but this particular use likely caught the disciples off guard. Here the Christ is *among* them right there in the room and they are bickering about greatness. What gives them status is not their own ability, but the fact that they belong to the Messiah, the One far greater than them and who humbly serves humanity.

Talk About It:
1. Who "shall not lose his reward" (v. 41)?
2. Why is it so serious to cause "little ones . . . to stumble" (v. 42, *NKJV*)?

In light of Christ's humility, the disciples should pay special attention to the weakest members of society. They should not only welcome them gladly into the community of faith, but should protect them from the evil influences of the world. In every society and culture, children are the most susceptible victims to the abuse of power. This is why Jesus highlights them in His discourse on the way power functions in the Kingdom. He displays to His disciples the end result of their power-grabbing, and it is nasty. When people lust after power, it tends to result in the weak falling into sin. We see it all around us in the way entertainment executives colonize the minds of the younger generation. Jesus saw the same thing in His day. The Romans were especially known for the sexual abuse of young boys. But whatever the specifics, Jesus doles out stiff consequences for those guilty of this abhorrent misuse of power.

"The foundation of the war for people's souls, minds and hearts is waged against our children. If they can be persuaded when they are young, it is terribly difficult to change their allegiance as they age."
—George Barna

B. The Seriousness of Misusing Power (vv. 43-50)

43. And if thy hand offend thee, cut it off: it is better for thee to enter into life maimed, than having two hands to go into hell, into the fire that never shall be quenched:

44. Where their worm dieth not, and the fire is not quenched.

45. And if thy foot offend thee, cut it off: it is better for thee to enter halt into life, than having two feet to be cast into hell, into the fire that never shall be quenched:

46. Where their worm dieth not, and the fire is not quenched.

47. And if thine eye offend thee, pluck it out: it is better for thee to enter into the kingdom of God with one eye, than having two eyes to be cast into hell fire:

48. Where their worm dieth not, and the fire is not quenched.

49. For every one shall be salted with fire, and every sacrifice shall be salted with salt.

50. Salt is good: but if the salt have lost his saltness, wherewith will ye season it? Have salt in yourselves, and have peace one with another.

To live a life of power in which those underneath are treated with contempt is completely unacceptable for the follower of Jesus. Its consequences are numerous, but Jesus hones in on the betrayal of the young and helpless. Rather than participating in that type of power system, Jesus' disciples should cut off hands and feet, even gouge out eyes. Of course, this is *hyperbole*—exaggerated speech meant to make a large point that sticks in the minds of the audience. And in the disciples' context, we can imagine that the point stuck hard. One need only consider Greco-Roman art of that period to recognize that culture's adoration of the human body. Sculptures were set up across the empire

Talk About It:
1. Why do you suppose Jesus repeats the same phrase about hell three times?
2. How can our hands, feet and eyes cause us to sin?
3. Explain the statement "Have salt in yourselves" (v. 50).

to celebrate the gift of the male and female physique, yet Jesus describes unimaginable self-mutilation. Having the hand cut off was the punishment meted out in the Torah for a woman who grabbed the genitals of a man, thus dishonoring him and his bloodline (Deuteronomy 25:11, 12). Jesus, however, takes that shameful punishment and orders it applied on the self who abuses power. Samson is the famous Old Testament figure with his eyes gouged out, yet Jesus encourages the same for the sinful person. Taken figuratively, we might consider the *hand* to represent ambition, the *foot* to stand for advancement, and the *eye* to signify the lust of the flesh for worldly possessions. These, after all, are the seeds of selfish power—*pride, vainglory,* and *covetousness.* In the theology of Jesus, there is no less at stake here than heaven and hell.

Jesus' graphic description of hell makes us uncomfortable, but He speaks of it often. Jesus believes in hell as a real place of torment. The disciples thought they were simply jostling for position, but Jesus shows them they are playing with hellfire. When power is sought after, it is bound to be misused. When it is misused, the weakest are struck first. When the weakest are abused, heaven and hell are at stake.

The disciples are filled with great energy and ambition, and it will serve them well as they continue in ministry. But if this ambition is flavored with selfishness and vainglory, they will have lost what makes them distinct. They will have become worldly. Therefore Jesus commands them to preserve their "saltiness" no matter what the cost, and to quit all the silly fighting. When they learn to be at peace with each other, they will flavor and preserve the world as God intended.

III. ACHIEVE GREATNESS THROUGH SERVICE
(Mark 10:35-45)

Even after the lengthy discourse in chapter 9, it takes but a short time and the disciples are at it again, brawling over who should get the highest positions in the Kingdom. They, of course, have grossly misunderstood the very nature of the kingdom of God. They are waiting on Jesus to take over the nation of Israel and to set up a theocratic or even militaristic government. When this happens, they expect to rule and reign over His physical kingdom. In this effort, James and John take the boldest step of any disciple yet. Jostling for position is no longer a private matter, something the disciples are ashamed of before the Lord. Instead, these two brothers engage Jesus directly in their lust for worldly prominence.

A. An Outlandish Request (vv. 35-40)

35. And James and John, the sons of Zebedee, come unto him, saying, Master, we would that thou shouldest do for us whatsoever we shall desire.

Jesus Teaches About True Greatness

36. And he said unto them, What would ye that I should do for you?

37. They said unto him, Grant unto us that we may sit, one on thy right hand, and the other on thy left hand, in thy glory.

38. But Jesus said unto them, Ye know not what ye ask: can ye drink of the cup that I drink of? and be baptized with the baptism that I am baptized with?

39. And they said unto him, We can. And Jesus said unto them, Ye shall indeed drink of the cup that I drink of; and with the baptism that I am baptized withal shall ye be baptized:

40. But to sit on my right hand and on my left hand is not mine to give; but it shall be given to them for whom it is prepared.

Once again, Jesus has just described His impending death to the disciples (vv. 32-34). He will keep nothing for Himself, but will suffer and die for the Father's glory. In the face of such self-sacrifice, His followers again up the ante in their desperate search for self-promotion.

This powerful Messiah whom they once feared has now become casual to James and John. They demand that Jesus give them an affirmative answer without even hearing the request. But these are the aptly named "sons of thunder" of 3:17, known for risk-taking and general belligerence. It is hard to believe that in a very short time they will be leading Christ's church—the fastest-growing organization in world history.

Jesus does not blast the Sons of Thunder for their arrogance. Instead, He appears quite open to their request. After all, there is something in the character of Jesus that often appreciates the unpretentious boldness of His children.

Sometimes it is much scarier getting what you ask of Jesus than it is to have Him decline. Rather than scoffing at them, Jesus tests their faith: Are they ready to take up the mantle of His cup and baptism—the destiny of His suffering? They are as confident as they can be, and we should not forget that John stands as the only disciple to comfort Jesus at His cross . . . and risks his own neck for doing so.

Nonetheless, this is simply a request that Jesus cannot grant. Although they will experience suffering and martyrdom for the cause of Christ, God alone reserves the seats for the age to come. Some decisions are in the Father's domain only. Again, their vainglory provides a teaching moment. Amazingly, Jesus never seems to tire of saying the same things over and again to His dull disciples. He shepherds them as a patient rabbi.

Talk About It:
1. Why would James and John think Jesus might give them whatever they asked (v. 35)?
2. What did they request (v. 37)?
3. What were the "cup" and "baptism" Jesus was talking about (vv. 38, 39)?

"Even I, the Son of Man, came here not to be served but to serve others, and to give my life as a ransom for many."
—Jesus (Matthew 20:28, *NLT*)

B. The Patient Teacher (vv. 41-45)

41. And when the ten heard it, they began to be much displeased with James and John.

42. But Jesus called them to him, and saith unto them, Ye know that they which are accounted to rule over the Gentiles exercise lordship over them; and their great ones exercise authority upon them.

43. But so shall it not be among you: but whosoever will be great among you, shall be your minister:

44. And whosoever of you will be the chiefest, shall be servant of all.

45. For even the Son of man came not to be ministered unto, but to minister, and to give his life a ransom for many.

Since James and John have addressed Jesus as "Teacher," He subsequently operates as such. Quite a firestorm has erupted in their little camp, thanks to the boldness of the Sons of Thunder. Jesus calms the uprising with straightforward and life-giving instruction.

The verb for "indignant" (v. 41, *NIV*) in the Greek is *aganakteo*, the root of our English word for *agony*. Jesus was indignant once before when the disciples hindered the children from reaching Him (v. 14), but this is the only recorded case where the disciples react this way. The word denotes strong feelings of resentment. Jesus describes the roots of their resentment in its context. All around them, they see power exercised in one specific way by the Gentiles. Indeed, the entire Roman political machine is ridiculously hierarchical. Caesar Augustus had stripped the senate of its power during the childhood of Jesus, leaving himself as the only ruler, so everyone reported to him. The goal in Roman society was to find an ally in Caesar's food chain in order to get a piece of the political and economic pie. The disciples are acting perfectly in line with this type of system, which has been perpetuated by the Pharisees and the Temple establishment. In the kingdom of God, though, there is another way.

Finally Jesus describes Kingdom living in the most literal terms available (vv. 43, 44). The lowest one can go in society, even lower than the status of a child, is to be a slave. The rights of slaves are not their own; they are completely decided by the master. It is this radical style of upside-down living that Jesus advocates for His disciples. They should not be setting Him up to request positions of power. They should be arguing over who gets to serve, because that is the example of Jesus himself.

The matter has now been settled, and the disciples do not revisit the subject again in Mark. This is logic that they cannot combat, try though they may. Jesus has come not just to serve, but also to pour out His life's blood (v. 45). He goes beyond the responsibilities of a slave to actually become that same example.

Talk About It:
1. What is the secular view of greatness (v. 42)?
2. What is Christ's view of greatness (vv. 43, 44)?

Number Zero
Several years ago, tennis star Serena Williams was asked during an interview what it felt like to be ranked the number one player in the world. She replied with humor: "When I was little, I always wanted to be number zero. I thought that was the best you could be. I guess I wasn't very bright" (*Homiletics Journal for Preachers*, Feb. 2003). In the math of the kingdom of God, she was right on cue.

Jesus Teaches About True Greatness

CONCLUSION

The message of the gospel does not shy away from the truly human questions about greatness. There is a drive in all of us to achieve something significant, and the teachings of Jesus do not seek to dull this ambition. Instead, Christ's instruction channels that energy into the service of both God and others. This is the radical edge to the new Christian community, a place where people look out not for themselves, but for one another. This new use of power changed the Roman Empire, and still changes our world today through the power of Jesus.

GOLDEN TEXT CHALLENGE

"IF ANY MAN DESIRE TO BE FIRST, THE SAME SHALL BE LAST OF ALL, AND SERVANT OF ALL" (Mark 9:35).

In a striking paradox, Jesus said that greatness in the Kingdom results from humility. The least is the greatest; the lowest is the highest. What is great before God is not a clamoring for prestige, but a humbling of oneself like a child. Entry comes to those who are lowly and helpless; status comes to those who have a humble spirit like children.

"A little child has no idea that he is great, and so in the kingdom of heaven the greatest is he who is least conscious of being great," said R.V. Tasker. "True humility does not hanker after greatness, does not even think of it," said R.C. Lenski (Roy Zuck, *Precious in His Sight*).

Daily Devotions:
M. Servant of the Lord
Deuteronomy 34:5-12
T. Submissive Servant of God
1 Samuel 3:1-10
W. Wholehearted Servant of God
2 Kings 23:21-25
T. The Way to Greatness
Matthew 20:20-28
F. Serving Is Ministry
Acts 6:1-7
S. Serve God and Others
Romans 12:1-13

Jesus Betrayed and Crucified

Mark 14:10 through 15:39

Unit Theme:
Gospel of Mark (The Servant Messiah)

Central Truth:
Jesus was betrayed and crucified for our sins.

Focus:
Contemplate what Jesus suffered for our salvation and trust Him as Savior and Lord.

Context:
The Gospel of Mark was probably written between A.D. 50 and 70.

Golden Text:
"He was wounded for our transgressions, he was bruised for our iniquities: the chastisement of our peace was upon him; and with his stripes we are healed" (Isaiah 53:5).

Study Outline:
I. Betrayed by a Disciple (Mark 14:10-21, 43-45)
II. Arrested and Tried (Mark 14:53-65)
III. Humiliated and Crucified (Mark 15:15-39)

INTRODUCTION

Mark spends about a third of his Gospel recounting Jesus' final week on earth. What is more, he spends two very lengthy chapters on just the final 24 hours of His life. For the historian, this emphasis is both illuminating and maddening. Mark fails to give us a sentence describing the life of Jesus before His ministry begins, yet takes pains to describe Peter's redundant denial of his Master. He rushes through Jesus' teaching ministry in a blur, but slows down to describe the most intimate dialogue at His final dinner with the Twelve. We get almost no information about Jesus' family, but an entire passage about a woman who washed His feet. The reason for all this, though, is clear: Jesus' death is the central event in the Gospel. Although His resurrection is the climactic and most important event, in that it vindicates the death, not even the Resurrection downplays the significance of the Crucifixion. Jesus' death is more important than further details about His childhood, His family, His ministry, or His post-resurrection appearances. Mark gives us what we need to know, and this includes a careful reconstruction of the events surrounding Jesus' death. But why?

We must remember that Mark is writing not directly to us, but to the Christian communities of the first century. The primary obstacle they faced in spreading the message of their fledgling faith was that their founder had been sentenced to the stiffest penalty possible under the Roman legal system. It must have been terribly difficult to convince skeptical Jews and Gentiles that such a "criminal" was the Son of God. Therefore, Mark painstakingly describes the conspiracy against Jesus and His innocence in the face of the jealousy of the religious leaders. Even the Romans are only secondarily complicit in their rage; they are not the main players. But there is more at stake than the plight of the early Christians. There is a theological emphasis as well. Mark is displaying the degree to which God is willing to go in order to present a new way of wielding power to the world. Jesus has already taught that in God's kingdom, moving to the bottom constitutes true power. At the Cross, He shows the world the extent of God's servitude. From now on, divine power will be known principally through weakness.

march 14, 445 BC.
3 o'clock in evening *april 6, A.D. 32*

+69
2 weeks
483 x 7 week
3 x 360 week
173, 360 Day
(—) 500 Day
<
Dan. 9:26

I. BETRAYED BY A DISCIPLE (Mark 14:10-21, 43-45)

The beginning of what only appears to be the end of Jesus begins with the clear intentions of the religious leaders in chapter 14. The problem is that they need to get rid of Jesus as soon as possible. In the past few days He has both acted and spoken in a way that threatens their hold over the country through the Temple system. However, Jerusalem is thronged with Jewish pilgrims celebrating the largest and most important festival on the Jewish calendar. They cannot move against Jesus in public during the Passover, as His profile is high and the people hail Him as a powerful prophet. Therefore, the conspirators need a man on the inside. *Praise of the Lord*

A. Judas Iscariot (vv. 10, 11)

10. And Judas Iscariot, one of the twelve, went unto the chief priests, to betray him unto them.

11. And when they heard it, they were glad, and promised to give him money. And he sought how he might conveniently betray him.

Perhaps no other figure in history has been as vilified as Judas Iscariot. In American history, Benedict Arnold holds the position of the most infamous turncoat, but he cannot even hold a candle to Judas' tragedy. In Mark's list of the 12 apostles chosen by Jesus, Judas Iscariot is named last. Yet his fate is unmentioned in Mark. Judas seems to appear on Jesus' final day as if to do the devil's dirty work, then disappears just as quickly. But the legacy he has left behind has spoken to generations of Christians as a warning. Even one of Jesus' own failed to truly believe.

It is clear that Jesus' acceptance of the worship of an apparently wealthy woman seals the decision of betrayal in Judas' mind (14:3-9). What is not extremely clear is why. Many have pointed to the addition of Judas' surname "Iscariot" for a clue as to his motivations. It probably refers simply to his hometown of Kerioth, and is given to separate him from the other disciple named Judas. However, *Iscariot* might also be derived from a Latin term meaning "bandit" or "assassin." This would identify Judas with a political party in Israel called the Zealots, who were known for carrying out assassinations on those complicit with Roman power. For this reason, some have suggested that Judas was only prodding Jesus to act to take power. Perhaps Judas sought to force Jesus into a situation in which He would either have to come to power or be killed. Surely the One with authority over nature and demons would rise up! Of course, if this was Judas' plan, it failed miserably. Yet Mark is clear that God was ultimately overseeing the events that led to Jesus' death.

In Mark's narrative it appears that money is Judas' chief motivation. The disciples have just rebuked Jesus for allowing an expensive vial of perfume to be "wasted" in a lavish act of worship.

Talk About It:
What "delighted" (v. 11, *NIV*) the chief priests?

Betrayed for the Bible
William Tyndale first translated the Bible from Hebrew and Greek into English, making a Bible for the common people. In 1535 he was betrayed by a friend, taken prisoner to the castle of Vilford, and continued to work on his translation. He was unable to finish his work because he was sentenced to die a heretic's death: strangulation and burning at the stake. On October 6, 1536, he cried out his last words.
—*Sermon Illustrations.com*

Jesus, however, gladly accepts the expensive offering and the one giving it. Judas goes to the chief priests to betray Jesus, and they promise him money. Mark does not say whether Judas hoped to enrich himself off of Jesus' ministry. If he was a Zealot, perhaps he resented the fact that Jesus was not storing away to finance His coming rule. But money is at the heart of Jesus' teachings about the causes for sin in the world, so it is no surprise that it becomes the cause for His very betrayal.

The key word in the narratives surrounding Jesus' arrest and death is the Greek *paradidomi*—to betray, or literally, to hand over. Judas looks for an opportunity to hand Jesus over to the chief priests, who then hand Jesus over to Pilate, who hands Jesus over to the soldiers for crucifixion. The language almost insinuates that Jesus has no control over the situation, but this is cleared up in His final meal with the Twelve. In fact, He knows exactly what will happen.

B. A Grief-Filled Passover (vv. 12-21)
(Mark 14:12-16 is not included in the printed text.)
17. And in the evening he cometh with the twelve.
18. And as they sat and did eat, Jesus said, Verily I say unto you, One of you which eateth with me shall betray me.
19. And they began to be sorrowful, and to say unto him one by one, Is it I? and another said, Is it I?
20. And he answered and said unto them, It is one of the twelve, that dippeth with me in the dish.
21. The Son of man indeed goeth, as it is written of him: but woe to that man by whom the Son of man is betrayed! good were it for that man if he had never been born.

The meal at hand is the most important celebration in Jewish tradition. At the Passover, the Jews still today remember the glorious deliverance of their ancestors out of the tyranny of Egypt. In Jesus' time period, they often left an empty seat at the table to symbolize the prophet in the line of Moses who they believed would soon deliver them from the oppression of Rome. As an observant rabbi, Jesus celebrates the Passover meal in a traditional manner. However, He has shocking news for His disciples—one of them will betray Him.

Eating in first-century Palestine was considered a sacred and intimate act. The Jews did not dine sitting in chairs as we do, but actually lay on their sides with their feet away from the table. They huddled together, and to share a meal was to welcome those around you as equal partners. This is the context for the amazement of the religious leaders that Jesus eats with sinners. Therefore the reality of Jesus' impending betrayal is intensified by the fact that the culprit shares food with Jesus right then. He takes advantage of Jesus' welcoming heart while plotting against Him. This accounts for the shock of the disciples.

goodman (v. 14)—
owner

Talk About It:
1. Describe the "minor miracle" seen in verses 13-16.
2. How did the disciples respond (v. 19) to Jesus' terrible revelation (v. 18)?
3. Compare the fate of the "Son of Man" with His betrayer (v. 21).

Jesus Betrayed and Crucified

One by one the disciples beg the Lord to identify the traitor (v. 19). They fear Jesus has mistakenly singled them out. In this most intimate occasion of eating together, they are grieved to the core that the closeness is not completely genuine. Yet in Mark, we are not told whether Jesus actually identifies His betrayer. He does insinuate that each disciple asks Him the question, and perhaps His lack of an answer denotes that Jesus is trying to give Judas one last chance to repent. Even so, the Lord knows the events that have been set in motion cannot be stopped. They are the will of His Father.

Jewish meals at this time involved sharing a loaf of bread and a single dipping bowl of broth and meat in the center of the low table. Each person at the table would dip a piece of bread into the bowl and eat the entire piece. It was an intimate, communal act, and Jesus expresses terrible judgment for the one that would share the bread and bowl with Jesus while plotting betrayal. This one receives a judgment even worse than those causing children to sin (9:42). The traitor would be better off to never have existed.

C. A Painful Kiss (vv. 43-45)

43. And immediately, while he yet spake, cometh Judas, one of the twelve, and with him a great multitude with swords and staves, from the chief priests and the scribes and the elders.

44. And he that betrayed him had given them a token, saying, Whomsoever I shall kiss, that same is he; take him, and lead him away safely.

45. And as soon as he was come, he goeth straightway to him, and saith, Master, master; and kissed him.

staves (v. 43)— clubs

In the preceding verses, important scenes transpire before Judas appears again in Mark's narrative. Not only does Jesus have a traitor, but even His outspoken disciple Peter will deny Jesus three separate times. After making this prediction, Jesus takes only His closest inner circle of three—Peter, James and John—to support Him in prayer as He agonizes in sorrow over what is about to occur. Instead, they ignore Jesus' pleas and sleep. Jesus himself wakes them a third time in the presence of the traitor.

Judas arrives with a ragtag militia unit, not the chief priests themselves but a mob sent by them. The religious leaders themselves are conspicuously absent, for they fear implication if something goes wrong. Perhaps they also fear Jesus' power. Yet even Jesus describes the hilarity of their swords and clubs, as if He is leading a violent rebellion (vv. 48, 49). However, the religious leaders want to prove just that to the Romans, and Judas is complicit. In one of the most ironic moves in history, he arranges the signal of a kiss with the mob. Sarcastically

Talk About It:
1. Describe those who came to arrest Jesus (v. 43).
2. How did Judas betray Jesus, and why (vv. 44, 45)?

greeting Jesus, he does the deed and Jesus is taken into custody after a quick skirmish. He has been handed over, and the narrative grows dreadfully dark. Jesus willfully hands Himself over to His betrayer.

II. ARRESTED AND TRIED (Mark 14:53-65)

The arrest of Jesus commences quickly, and in the blink of an eye He is left without a friend in the world. Every disciple who had claimed ultimate allegiance at the dinner just a few hours before runs away in fear of the mob sent by the chief priests. This is the first stage of Jesus' passion—the sheer loneliness of it all. It is not just Judas who betrays Jesus, it is every one of the Twelve. Jesus will face this final act in His divine drama completely alone.

A. The Problem of Valid Testimony (vv. 53-59)

53. And they led Jesus away to the high priest: and with him were assembled all the chief priests and the elders and the scribes.

54. And Peter followed him afar off, even into the palace of the high priest: and he sat with the servants, and warmed himself at the fire.

55. And the chief priests and all the council sought for witness against Jesus to put him to death; and found none.

56. For many bare false witness against him, but their witness agreed not together.

57. And there arose certain, and bare false witness against him, saying,

58. We heard him say, I will destroy this temple that is made with hands, and within three days I will build another made without hands.

59. But neither so did their witness agree together.

After Jesus' arrest, He is taken straightaway to the most powerful leader of the Jewish community—the high priest. This will be no ordinary trial; it is rigged from the start. Upon Jesus' arrival, the entire religious establishment pounces. They have been waiting for word from the high priest, and they assemble quickly when the message is dispatched. The proceedings appear to be at least somewhat open, as Peter is allowed into the high priest's courtyard. Yet there is a secretive element to the trial, since it is in the high priest's home.

Immediately the Sanhedrin runs into a major problem in gathering evidence about Jesus. They need forceful and agreeing testimony to make the charges—any charges—stick. Superficially they are following the commands throughout the Torah: "On the testimony of two or three witnesses a man shall be put to death, but no one shall be put to death on the testimony of only one witness" (Deuteronomy 17:6, *NIV*). Their formal adherence to this commandment betrays that the decision to kill Jesus has

Talk About It:
1. How did Peter follow Jesus (v. 54)?
2. What were the chief priests unable to find (v. 55)?
3. What false charge was made against Jesus (vv. 58, 59)?

already been made. They are not looking for evidence to then decide on charges. No, they have already decided on the verdict!

The problem is that they cannot seem to find the testimony they need to seal Jesus' fate. All they can gather centers on Jesus' statement, "I will destroy this temple . . . and within three days I will build another" (v. 58; see John 2:19). However, the witnesses twisted the meaning of Jesus' words, claiming that He was speaking about the literal Temple in Jerusalem. During Jesus' crucifixion, mockers used this phrase to ridicule Him: "Aha! You who destroy the temple and build it in three days . . ." (Mark 15:29, *NKJV*). However, on the third day Jesus' temple (His body) came back to life, which was His meaning all along.

B. The Crux of the Trial (vv. 60-65)

60. And the high priest stood up in the midst, and asked Jesus, saying, Answerest thou nothing? what is it which these witness against thee?

61. But he held his peace, and answered nothing. Again the high priest asked him, and said unto him, Art thou the Christ, the Son of the Blessed?

62. And Jesus said, I am: and ye shall see the Son of man sitting on the right hand of power, and coming in the clouds of heaven.

63. Then the high priest rent his clothes, and saith, What need we any further witnesses?

64. Ye have heard the blasphemy: what think ye? And they all condemned him to be guilty of death.

65. And some began to spit on him, and to cover his face, and to buffet him, and to say unto him, Prophesy: and the servants did strike him with the palms of their hands.

The high priest has quickly had enough of these technical problems with the Law, especially when Jesus refuses to engage in dialogue. Every major character in the Passion narrative is incredulous at Jesus' poise. He is perfectly resolved to His fate, and will not stoop to the level of His accusers. He has taught publicly for three years and will not debase Himself by answering their gibberish. The opportunity to answer, of course, is His legal right. But He will not exercise that right. In so doing, He appears to scoff at the entire proceeding. Therefore, if Jesus will not play by the rules, the high priest won't either.

The religious leaders want Jesus dead no matter the cost. So the high priest plays his trump card. He condemns Jesus on the basis of blasphemy. Blasphemy is prohibited specifically in Exodus 22:28, then poignantly illustrated in Leviticus 24:10-23. There, a son of mixed race curses the name of Yahweh, and becomes the basis for executing those who might similarly blaspheme God. According to the high priest, Jesus is guilty of this brand of blasphemy by claiming to be the Messiah, the Son

"Lord Jesus, You are My righteousness; I am Your sin. You have taken upon Yourself what is mine and given me what is Yours. You have become what You were not so I can become what I am not."
—**Martin Luther**

Talk About It:
1. How did Jesus respond to the charges, and why (v. 60)?
2. Who did Jesus claim to be (vv. 61, 62)?
3. Describe the initial assault on Jesus (v. 65).

Only Three Years
A surprising feature of the ministry of Jesus is its length. The Buddha taught for almost 50 years, Muhammad for about 20 years, and Moses led Israel for 40 years. Jesus, however, ended His mission after three years. According to New Testament scholar Marcus J. Borg, "Jesus' ministry was brief, a light flashing momentarily but brilliantly like a meteor in the night sky" (*Jesus: A New Vision*). Instead, the focus of Jesus' life and ministry was His death and resurrection, which accomplished what His teaching ministry could not—the salvation of the world.

of God. This claim trumps the need for witnesses or testimony. The case is closed in this kangaroo court.

Jesus' response to the high priest's question is quite shocking in Mark. He has kept His identity a secret from almost everyone, even in the face of the supernatural miracles. Here, however, Jesus is unequivocal. He is exactly what they believe Him not to be, and one day He will return at the right hand of God himself. Those who seek to categorize Jesus as a teacher of moral truths or a wise philosopher—but not the Son of God—should pay close attention to this passage. Good teachers of ethics don't go around claiming to be equal to God himself, but Jesus does. Verses like this urged C.S. Lewis to write these famous words: "A man who was merely a man and said the sort of thing Jesus said would not be a great moral teacher. He would either be a lunatic—on a level with the man who says he is a poached egg—or else he would be the Devil of hell. You must make your choice. Either this man was, and is, the Son of God: or else a madman or something worse . . . let us not come with any patronizing nonsense about His being a great human teacher. He has not left that open to us" (*Mere Christianity*).

Mark's secret about the identity of Jesus is clearly out in the open, even in front of His enemies. In response, the high priest ceremonially tears his robes to indicate the gravity of the situation. Already Jesus is condemned and the beatings begin. This is no civil proceeding. Jesus has done no wrong except to reveal His true identity. Yet He does not shrink back even in the face of torture and death.

III. HUMILIATED AND CRUCIFIED (Mark 15:15-39)

The mockery of the Sanhedrin is compounded by Peter's third denial of Jesus (14:66-72). Then in chapter 15, after a long night, He is handed over to Pilate. Condescendingly, Pilate asks Him if He is a king. Again, He confirms His identity, yet refuses to respond to the accusations of His enemies. This amazes Pilate, who quickly realizes that this is nothing but a matter of jealousy, not law. Nonetheless, his plan to release Jesus as a token to the crowds backfires, and he gives in to their whim.

A. Scourged and Mocked (vv. 15-20)

Praetorium (v. 16)—Herod's palace

15. And so Pilate, willing to content the people, released Barabbas unto them, and delivered Jesus, when he had scourged him, to be crucified.

16. And the soldiers led him away into the hall, called Praetorium; and they call together the whole band.

17. And they clothed him with purple, and platted a crown of thorns, and put it about his head,

18. And began to salute him, Hail, King of the Jews!

19. And they smote him on the head with a reed, and did spit upon him, and bowing their knees worshipped him.

20. And when they had mocked him, they took off the purple from him, and put his own clothes on him, and led him out to crucify him.

The first stage of Jesus' death is a brutal flogging. Although not described in Mark, this typically was performed by a Roman *flagellum*, a whip which sometimes served as a death sentence in itself. In fact, the Romans were careful not to kill the victim at the whipping post so the crucifixion might be carried out. Yet after this brutal flogging, the Roman soldiers gather together to mock Jesus, hailing Him as the Caesar over Israel. They dress Him in purple—the color of royalty—and have their sickening fun. Unsurprisingly, Jesus offers no response.

B. Nailed to the Cross and Insulted (vv. 21-32)

21. And they compel one Simon a Cyrenian, who passed by, coming out of the country, the father of Alexander and Rufus, to bear his cross.

22. And they bring him unto the place Golgotha, which is, being interpreted, The place of a skull.

23. And they gave him to drink wine mingled with myrrh: but he received it not.

24. And when they had crucified him, they parted his garments, casting lots upon them, what every man should take.

25. And it was the third hour, and they crucified him.

26. And the superscription of his accusation was written over, THE KING OF THE JEWS.

27. And with him they crucify two thieves; the one on his right hand, and the other on his left.

28. And the scripture was fulfilled, which saith, And he was numbered with the transgressors.

29. And they that passed by railed on him, wagging their heads, and saying, Ah, thou that destroyest the temple, and buildest it in three days,

30. Save thyself, and come down from the cross.

31. Likewise also the chief priests mocking said among themselves with the scribes, He saved others; himself he cannot save.

32. Let Christ the King of Israel descend now from the cross, that we may see and believe. And they that were crucified with him reviled him.

Although church art has depicted Jesus carrying His entire cross on the Via Dolorosa, crucifixion victims actually carried the upper beam. Tied to the sentenced, it weighed around 100 pounds. Apparently the scourging and mocking left Jesus too physically weak to meet this challenge, so an African (Simon of Cyrene) took His place. Amazingly, Jesus refused the concoction that might give His body some relief. He faced the nails with eyes wide open.

Talk About It:
1. Contrast Barabbas with Jesus (v. 15).
2. Describe the soldiers' mockery (vv. 17-19).

Talk About It:
1. Why was someone else forced to carry Jesus' cross (v. 21)?
2. What did Jesus refuse, and why (v. 23)?
3. What was posted on Jesus' cross, and why (v. 26)?
4. How was Jesus "numbered with the transgressors" (v. 28)?
5. What was Jesus repeatedly challenged to do, and why (vv. 29-32)?

At 9 a.m. the spikes were pounded into the Lord. We know from a skeleton dated to this same time period that the spikes were nailed through the wrists, with a single spike driven through the ankles. The placement was designed to hold the victim's weight to the cross, and the Romans were precise.

The insults continued all morning long. The chief priests, however, kept their mockery among themselves, for they had already poisoned the minds of the masses with their lies. They had convinced the peasants that Jesus was intending to destroy the Temple, which was never the case. Even both thieves insult Him, though one thief becomes repentant as he sees Jesus dying (see Luke 23:39-43).

C. Death and Recognition (vv. 33-39)

33. And when the sixth hour was come, there was darkness over the whole land until the ninth hour.

34. And at the ninth hour Jesus cried with a loud voice, saying, Eloi, Eloi, lama sabachthani? which is, being interpreted, My God, my God, why hast thou forsaken me?

35. And some of them that stood by, when they heard it, said, Behold, he calleth Elias.

36. And one ran and filled a spunge full of vinegar, and put it on a reed, and gave him to drink, saying, Let alone; let us see whether Elias will come to take him down.

37. And Jesus cried with a loud voice, and gave up the ghost.

38. And the veil of the temple was rent in twain from the top to the bottom.

39. And when the centurion, which stood over against him, saw that he so cried out, and gave up the ghost, he said, Truly this man was the Son of God.

In Mark, Jesus says nothing during His first three hours on the cross. It is not until noon that the people there realize this is no ordinary criminal. Jesus' outcry is so bone-wrenching that those nearby remember it in its original language. To withstand the torture, Jesus recites the Psalms, and repeats a verse from Psalm 22. Nature itself is thrown into disarray at this event. Those nearby think Elijah may come to take Jesus down. But something very different happens.

With Jesus' final breath, the curtain separating the people from the Holy of Holies is split apart. Jesus had not come to destroy the Temple, but to give it new meaning. God has been let out, unleashed onto the world with a message of salvation through Jesus' death. At the end of the scene, even a Roman centurion confirms Mark's assertion in his introduction in 1:1—"the gospel about Jesus Christ, the Son of God" (*NIV*).

Talk About It:
1. What phenomenon occurred for three hours (v. 33)?
2. How was Jesus forsaken by God the Father (v. 34)?
3. Why was the Temple's veil "rent in twain" (v. 38)?
4. What did a Roman centurion confess (v. 39)?

CONCLUSION

The trial and crucifixion of Jesus tip us off to the fact that He is, in fact, a dangerous leader. He is not just a good teacher, dispensing new and helpful spiritual truths. He is a revolutionary, and He is crucified as such. However, His revolution is not of this world, but of the human heart. His death opens up a new door for humanity's transformation, both Jew and Gentile.

GOLDEN TEXT CHALLENGE

"HE WAS WOUNDED FOR OUR TRANSGRESSIONS, HE WAS BRUISED FOR OUR INIQUITIES: THE CHASTISEMENT OF OUR PEACE WAS UPON HIM; AND WITH HIS STRIPES WE ARE HEALED" (Isaiah 53:5).

Isaiah uses an accumulation of terms to describe the awful agony of our Savior at Calvary. He piles word upon word to enable us to grasp something of the intensity and extremity of our Lord's suffering upon the cross.

With the use of the word *wounded*, the writer speaks of the piercing of Christ. The term *bruised* refers to the crushing weight of sin and woe upon the Lord, while *chastisement* tells us of the beating which left livid stripes in the flesh of Jesus. Though we read the words which describe the sufferings of our Lord, we can never fully understand all that He endured when He was beaten, bruised and bloodied at Calvary. We simply stand in amazement at such suffering.

But the great truth here is not the *revelation* of those sufferings. It is the *reason* for such sufferings. The prophet makes it clear that the Sufferer is not suffering for Himself, but for others. He was pierced, but it was for *our transgressions.* He was bruised, or crushed, but it was for *our iniquities.* He was beaten, but it was for *our healing and peace.* It is the innocent suffering for the guilty. He took our place at Calvary and suffered the punishment we so clearly deserved that we might be set free. Isaiah sums it up in verse 6: "The Lord hath laid on him the iniquity of us all." No wonder Paul declares, "The Son of God, who loved me, and gave himself for me" (Galatians 2:20).

Our Lord did not suffer and die in vain. Blessed are the results of His death. All who take His death to heart and accept Him as their sacrifice and substitute find their sins forgiven, their souls healed, and their minds resting in peace. He did it all for us that we might be made righteous in Him.

Daily Devotions:
M. Messiah's
   Coming Foretold
   Genesis 3:9-15
T. Messiah's
   Suffering Foretold
   Psalm 22:1-10
W. Messiah's
   Suffering for Us
   Isaiah 53:1-12
T. Jesus' Death
   Fulfilled Scripture
   John 19:28-37
F. Proclaim Christ
   Crucified
   1 Corinthians
   1:21-31
S. Christ's Death
   Was Reconciling
   2 Corinthians
   5:14-21

The Risen Christ (Easter)

Mark 27:57 through 28:20

Unit Theme:
Christ's Resurrection

Central Truth:
Jesus Christ rose from the dead and lives forever.

Focus:
Appreciate the significance of Christ's resurrection and exalt Him as our risen Lord.

Context:
Jesus rose from the dead in Jerusalem in A.D. 30.

Golden Text:
"He is not here: for he is risen, as he said. Come, see the place where the Lord lay" (Matthew 28:6).

Study Outline:
I. Christ's Burial (Matthew 27:57-66)
II. Christ's Resurrection (Matthew 28:1-10)
III. Christ's Mandate (Matthew 28:16-20)

INTRODUCTION

Easter—what images come to mind when you hear the word? If you take a secular approach, you think of school vacation, chocolate bunnies, fuzzy chicks, and possibly new clothes. Children can have their pictures taken with a big Easter bunny. Some people watch or participate in Easter parades. Others decorate a tree in their yard with Easter eggs.

Within the church world, Easter stands as one of the three most important celebrations—the other two being Christmas and Pentecost. Many denominations prepare for the Easter celebration with the 40 days of fasting known as Lent. During these days individuals abstain from foods or activities that are especially meaningful to them.

But let's personalize this for each one of us. *What does Easter mean to me?* Unless we grasp and value the vitality of Easter with its continuing impact throughout the centuries, the true power and hope of life in Christ is missing!

The objective of this lesson is to appreciate the significance of Christ's resurrection and exalt Him as our risen Lord. We do not view Christ as merely a miracle worker whose power ended when He took His last breath. We do not place our faith in a good teacher who offered many important life principles and then died like a common human. We serve the God-man, Jesus Christ, who came to earth, humbled Himself in human flesh, prepared the foundation for the church, and suffered the humiliation of crucifixion. How wonderful that the account doesn't end there. It continues with His marvelous resurrection.

Today's lesson takes us back to a familiar passage of Scripture as recorded by Matthew. It enables us to see the many individuals who experience the Resurrection morning. There's no uniform response. Some find it very difficult to believe even though having heard Christ's previous words. Others, like the soldiers, choose to propagate a lie rather than grasp the truth.

This lesson once again provides us with an opportunity to rejoice in a risen Savior—the true meaning of Easter.

I. CHRIST'S BURIAL (Matthew 27:57-66)
A. The Tomb (vv. 57-61)

57. When the even was come, there came a rich man of Arimathaea, named Joseph, who also himself was Jesus' disciple:

58. He went to Pilate, and begged the body of Jesus. Then Pilate commanded the body to be delivered.

59. And when Joseph had taken the body, he wrapped it in a clean linen cloth,

60. And laid it in his own new tomb, which he had hewn out in the rock: and he rolled a great stone to the door of the sepulchre, and departed.

61. And there was Mary Magdalene, and the other Mary, sitting over against the sepulchre.

Imagine what it would have been like if you were one of Jesus' disciples or followers. Within less than 24 hours your Master, Teacher and Miracle Worker is arrested, tried and crucified. Helplessly you watch the events. Surely this can't be happening. But it is true. Jesus is dead.

What will be done with the body? Time is of essence, since in just a few hours the Sabbath will begin. Jesus' body could be discarded with no care due to His being crucified as a common criminal. Or, if the body is given to His family or disciples, will they be able to arrange for a burial knowing there is only a few hours to accomplish it? Time is so short!

Into this gap steps Joseph of Arimathaea. Notice the three descriptions. First, he isn't from Jerusalem but probably a location to the northwest of the city. Second, he is a wealthy man. This explains his possession of a carved tomb. Only those of subsequent means would be able to purchase such a burial site. Third, he is described as a disciple of Jesus. However, John's Gospel records this being a secret relationship (19:38). Fear keeps him from making a public revelation. This would have been a shocking development with his being a member of the ruling Sanhedrin (Luke 23:50, 51).

Now with the death of Jesus, Joseph by his actions makes a declaration. By personally going to Pilate and requesting the body of Jesus, Joseph demonstrates loving care. Upon receiving permission, Joseph takes the body of Jesus from the cross, wraps it in a clean linen cloth, and places Jesus in his own tomb. Notice this is a new tomb. No body had even been placed there (v. 53). It's probable Joseph intended this to be his own burial place.

After placing Jesus' body in the tomb, Joseph rolls the stone in place. This large stone, which covers the tomb opening, more than likely is initially braced on a slight incline. Simply removing the brace allows one person to secure it in place. Mary Magdalene and the other Mary are at the tomb, but none of the male disciples.

Arimathaea (air-ih-muh-THEE-uh)—(v. 57)—a city in the hills northwest of Jerusalem

Talk About It:
1. What risk did Joseph take, and why (vv. 57, 58)?
2. How did Joseph express his love for Jesus (vv. 59, 60)?
3. Who witnessed Jesus' burial (v. 61)?

These women were at the cross when Jesus died and accompany His body to the tomb.

What an irony! Those men who had been Jesus' daily companions disappear after Jesus' death. Fear apparently drives them to find a safer location. But what a contrast in Joseph. The crisis of death and desire to care for the Master's body stimulates him to a public action which reflects loyalty through service.

B. The Security (vv. 62-66)

62. Now the next day, that followed the day of the preparation, the chief priests and Pharisees came together unto Pilate,

63. Saying, Sir, we remember that that deceiver said, while he was yet alive, After three days I will rise again.

64. Command therefore that the sepulchre be made sure until the third day, lest his disciples come by night, and steal him away, and say unto the people, He is risen from the dead: so the last error shall be worse than the first.

65. Pilate said unto them, Ye have a watch: go your way, make it as sure as ye can.

66. So they went, and made the sepulchre sure, sealing the stone, and setting a watch.

Having accomplished their purpose, one would think the religious leaders are feeling great satisfaction. Smugness and a sense of victory would seem to be the order of the day with a sense of celebration. Instead, they feel security measures need to be instituted to guarantee the body remains in the tomb. So the chief priests and some of the Pharisees meet with Pilate on the following day.

Their approach indicates remembering some of Jesus' teaching, specifically His rising after three days. They know He is dead and fear the disciples will perpetrate some deception to prove His words. If that occurs, they believe a greater wrong will have been accomplished than the content of His teachings while alive.

Why does Pilate continue to deal with these leaders' concerns about Jesus after being warned by his wife to have nothing to do with Jesus (v. 19)? The answer most likely is the possibility of political pressure from the leaders. Maybe this is another example of a person desiring position far more than truth.

In an attempt to keep Jesus' body in the tomb and stymie any attempt to steal it, two actions are taken. First, a seal is placed on the tomb which would indicate anyone's having moved the stone. Second, they place guards to keep a visible watch. With these two safety nets in place, they assume no hoax can be pulled. They follow Pilate's words, "Make the tomb as secure as you know how" (v. 65, NIV).

Talk About It:
1. What did the religious leaders call Jesus, and why (vv. 62, 63)?
2. Explain the statement, "So the last deception will be worse than the first" (v. 64, NKJV).
3. How was the tomb secured (v. 66)?

The Risen Christ

II. CHRIST'S RESURRECTION (Matthew 28:1-10)
A. The Divine Intervention (vv. 1-4)

1. In the end of the Sabbath, as it began to dawn toward the first day of the week, came Mary Magdalene and the other Mary to see the sepulchre.

2. And, behold, there was a great earthquake: for the angel of the Lord descended from heaven, and came and rolled back the stone from the door, and sat upon it.

3. His countenance was like lightning, and his raiment white as snow:

4. And for fear of him the keepers did shake, and became as dead men.

Human plans don't stand a chance when placed in opposition to God's sovereign will!

Since the Jewish Sabbath spans from six o'clock Friday evening to six o'clock Saturday evening, the events described here take place in the predawn hours of Sunday morning. According to the Jewish method of computing time, this is the third day of Jesus' being in the tomb. It is due to their considering just a portion of a day to be a day. In the same ways, part of a year is seen as a year. For example, we do not consider a child to be 1 year old until the exact day one year from his or her birth. In their system the child is now 2.

Christ's resurrection occurs through divine intervention. The occurrence of an earthquake is consistent with other dramatic revelations of our sovereign God. Prior to God's verbally speaking the Ten Commandments to the Israelites at Sinai, the mountain shakes (Exodus 19:18). Some translations indicate a violent movement. When Elijah flees in fear from the threats of Jezebel, God dramatically shows His presence in a variety of stages. One of them is an earthquake (1 Kings 19:11). In Acts we read about the miraculous deliverance of Paul and Silas from the Philippian jail by means of an earthquake (16:26).

Accompanying the earthquake at Christ's resurrection is an angel who rolls the stone from the tomb entrance. After completing the task this divine servant simply takes a seat on the stone and awaits the visitors (Matthew 28:2).

Verse 3 describes the angel's appearance. Can you imagine being one of the guards? All apparently is quiet in the predawn darkness when, suddenly, everything breaks loose. Besides the earthquake there is the sudden appearance of a dazzling heavenly being. The soldiers literally shake with fear and become "as dead men." This could speak of fainting due to the intense fear. Or it could simply indicate their being unable to move because their fear paralyzed them.

Now we return to verse 1. The short amount of time prior to the beginning of the Sabbath apparently hindered the normal process of preparing Christ's body for burial. However, as soon

Talk About It:
1. When did the two Marys go to the tomb?
2. Describe the appearance and the action of the angel (vv. 2, 3).
3. What impact did the angel have (v. 4)?

Sad Split
Within the first few centuries a divisive argument arose concerning the day on which to celebrate Easter. The Eastern churches wanted Easter to be celebrated on the actual date regardless what day of the week it might be. The Western churches wanted to celebrate it on the closest Sunday after the actual date when not on a Sunday.

as possible several faithful followers of Jesus take their prepared spices and perfumes to the tomb. (For further details read Luke 23:55–24:1). Mary Magdalene and the other Mary (the mother of James the Less—see Mark 15:40) had been at the tomb when Jesus' body was placed there, and now they come to complete the burial process. The embalming spices are not body preservatives; their fragrance helps to counter the odors of body decay.

The faithfulness of these women during Jesus' ministry and now at his death brings a marvelous benefit. They become the first believers to experience the empty tomb and receive the angelic announcement.

B. The Angelic Message (vv. 5-7)

5. And the angel answered and said to the women, Fear not ye: for I know that ye seek Jesus, which was crucified.

6. He is not here: for he is risen, as he said. Come, see the place where the Lord lay.

7. And go quickly, and tell his disciples that he is risen from the dead; and, behold, he goeth before you into Galilee; there shall ye see him: lo, I have told you.

As the women walk toward the tomb, their concern is moving the stone covering the entrance (Mark 16:3). Apparently recognizing their inability to move this heavy object, they are hoping someone else might be there. Then to their amazement, not only is the tomb open, but an angel is there to greet them and to give further directions.

Knowing how a certain degree of fear must have gripped their hearts, the angel begins with words of assurance, "Fear not." Repeatedly in the Scriptures there are instances where an angel or Jesus will tell an individual or a group to not be afraid. For example, it is seen when the angel announced to Mary her selection as the chosen woman to birth the Messiah (Luke 1:30). Earlier those words were spoken to Zechariah when the angel announced how, in spite of their age, he and Elizabeth would finally become parents (vv. 12, 13). When Jesus walked on the Sea of Galilee toward His disciples and they were terrified, thinking it to be a spirit, there came the encouragement to not be afraid (Matthew 14:26, 27).

In all of those instances, including the words of the angel to these women, a reason is given for not needing to be fearful. In this situation, the assurance is an empty tomb due to Christ's being raised from the dead. The angel states they are experiencing a fulfillment of Jesus' words.

So there will be no doubt, the angel wants them to see for themselves. It's not just a matter of the tomb being open; it is empty. They had been eyewitnesses of where the body was laid. Now they are eyewitnesses of a resurrected Christ evidenced by an empty tomb.

Now the angel gives the women a specific task. They are to hurry to where the disciples are and tell the news of Jesus being raised from the dead. There's a second part to the message. Jesus is going to Galilee. They are to go there, where they will be able to see their risen Master.

C. The Meeting (vv. 8-10)

8. And they departed quickly from the sepulchre with fear and great joy; and did run to bring his disciples word.

9. And as they went to tell his disciples, behold, Jesus met them saying, All hail. And they came and held him by the feet, and worshipped him.

10. Then said Jesus unto them, Be not afraid: go tell my brethren that they go into Galilee, and there shall they see me.

The women quickly leave to fulfill the angel's directive. They do not stay for further conversation filled with questions. Conflicting emotions are within them. On the one hand, they have tremendous joy in knowing Jesus is alive. But on the other hand, there is still fear. They have had a personal encounter with a heavenly messenger. These women aren't to be faulted for this. It is only right for frail humans to have a godly fear, a sense of tremendous awe, when blessed with such an encounter.

Notice the speed with which they move. They *run* to find the disciples and deliver the tremendous news. And then it happens. Jesus meets and greets them. Everything stops. They fall before Him in complete worship and hold onto His feet. Can you imagine all the thoughts which may have whirled through their minds? But most importantly, they know the priority—to fall before Him in worship. This reminds us how our thoughts and questions are always secondary to declaring adoration and worth to the Master!

Once again these women receive the message not to be afraid. Though fear would be natural for the moment, Jesus wants it dispelled in light of the total picture. He reiterates their mission of going to His disciples and telling that the risen Christ will come to them in Galilee.

III. CHRIST'S MANDATE (Matthew 28:16-20)

A. The Disciples' Response (vv. 16, 17)

16. Then the eleven disciples went away into Galilee, into a mountain where Jesus had appointed them.

17. And when they saw him, they worshipped him: but some doubted.

Matthew, the writer of this Gospel, chooses not to include many of Jesus' postresurrection appearances. This isn't a problem, since each person writes under the inspiration of the Holy Spirit to a particular audience and with a distinct theme. What a blessing to know each book of the Bible fulfills its purpose as written.

"All hail" (v. 9)—
"Greetings" (*NIV*)
or "Rejoice" (*NKJV*)

Talk About It:
1. Describe the women's mixed emotions (v. 8).
2. Why do you suppose the women "held him by the feet" (v. 9)?

"Because He lives
I can face tomorrow;
because He lives all
fear is gone."
—**William Gaither**

Talk About It:
What were the two responses to the risen Lord (v. 17)?

The Gospel of Matthew closes with a powerful mandate for all disciples of Christ. Though initially given to those who heard the words spoken, it continues to all of us who read the words of Scripture. We know it as the Great Commission. Often over-looked are the preceding verses.

The 11 disciples are privileged to hear these words due to their obedience. As noted earlier in the lesson, the women are given a message for the disciples which informs them to go to Galilee. There Jesus will meet them. They proceed as directed. Upon seeing Him, the disciples worship their risen Master.

Verse 17 says "some doubted," but who are they? We know Thomas doubted the other disciples' account of Jesus' resur-rection until he saw Jesus for himself (John 20:24-28). And the other disciples doubted the women's account of Jesus' initial appearance to them (Luke 24:9-11). Also, it could possibly refer to other individuals who experienced Christ's ministry but never made the complete commitment which would enable them to believe in Christ's bodily resurrection.

Let's pause and consider our own belief structure. Are we firm believers in the miraculous power of God through Jesus Christ, or do we fall into the class of doubters?

> "Doubts can be valuable if they force a man to search deeper and longer for answers. For to pursue the doubts is to come upon some exciting beliefs and truths."
> —C. Neil Strait

B. The Commission (vv. 18-20)

18. And Jesus came and spake unto them, saying, All power is given unto me in heaven and in earth.

19. Go ye therefore, and teach all nations, baptizing them in the name of the Father, and of the Son, and of the Holy Ghost:

20. Teaching them to observe all things whatsoever I have commanded you: and, lo, I am with you alway, even unto the end of the world. Amen.

Prior to giving the Great Commission, Jesus makes a major statement, "All authority has been given to Me" (*NKJV*). In the original language the words speak of this occurring at a particular point or event. No doubt this speaks of Jesus' resurrection from the dead. Jesus had humbled Himself by taking on the clothing of human flesh with all its frailties in order to become the sac-rificial Lamb slain for the sins of all. Now with His resurrection there is victory over death and exaltation by the heavenly Father (see Philippians 2:8-11).

Since the Great Commission is so well known, there is a tendency to gloss over the specifics or simply apply what has been said on previous occasions. Let's begin with the directive of *going*. Frequently we apply this to missions endeavors—traveling and evangelizing in other countries or cultures. This does apply, but it is only one aspect. *Going* includes witnessing to anyone who isn't a believer—in our culture, state, county, city or subdivision.

Talk About It:
1. What does "all authority" mean (v. 18, *NKJV*)?
2. What commands are in the Great Commission (vv. 19, 20)?
3. What promise is in the Great Commission (v. 20)?

The Risen Christ

Teaching "all nations" speaks of persuading individuals to come to Christ. We are to promote the specifics of the gospel through whatever means accessible to us. At that point it was through word of mouth—preaching, teaching, personal witnessing—when in their company. Now we have radio, television, DVDs, film, print, the Internet, as well as personal witnessing. It is important for us to take full advantage of what is available in the 21st century.

When individuals accept Christ, we are to provide for their following the example of our Lord in the ordinance of water baptism. This act of obedience provides an outward sign of the inner work of Christ in one's life. It also stands as a testimony to believers and unbelievers alike of one's commitment to Christ and the Christian faith. In some cultures, this is a major act since it automatically ostracizes the baptized from family and friends at great personal risk.

Discipleship must follow. Incorporating new believers into the community of believers and the specifics of the faith is vital. Without it there continues to be a high mortality rate among the young Christians within eight weeks of their first accepting Christ. Also, discipleship builds strong believers who, in turn, become part of strong churches.

As we review the Great Commission, notice its completeness. There is a progression of actions which initially bring people to Christ and then enable them to continue in the faith. Some of us are better gifted in one of the dimensions, but all of us are obligated to give our testimony. Every believer is to be an active part of the divine plan for spreading the good news of Jesus Christ.

"The simple meaning of Easter is that we are living in a world in which God has the last word."
—*Who Said That?*

CONCLUSION

The power of Christ's resurrection continues today as the power of salvation. Some may doubt the reality of Christ's rising from the grave. However, those of us who have experienced salvation know it to be true. We continue to experience joy and peace even in the middle of many life struggles. This should stimulate us to share the gospel of Jesus Christ, which frees people from sin and raises them to new life.

GOLDEN TEXT CHALLENGE

"HE IS NOT HERE: FOR HE IS RISEN, AS HE SAID. COME, SEE THE PLACE WHERE THE LORD LAY" (Matthew 28:6).

The angels offered evidence: "Come, see the place where the Lord lay." When the women calmly examined the undisturbed graveclothes, the wonderful truth dawned as clearly upon them as had the sun itself only moments before. Not only had Christ emerged, but He had obviously emerged supernaturally—so as to leave intact the linen cloth previously wound about His body. It would not take long for the truth behind this evidence to become apparent to these faithful women.

Jesus had been crucified—as the sacrificial Lamb bearing our sins in His own body on the tree. Now the efficacy of that sacrifice had been authenticated through His resurrection. Rather than a martyr, He was the living Savior with almighty power.

Moreover, "He is risen, as he said." He kept His word—precisely and on time. One can search the Scriptures from Genesis 1:1 to Revelation 22:21 and discover the marvelous truth: without exception God has always kept His word—with total accuracy and with entire fidelity in regard to time and place. Hence, whatever else Jesus Christ has said—additionally to His promise of resurrection—whether related to our salvation, our total well-being, or our ultimate destiny, we can count on Him to perform. Our Lord keeps His promises!

Jesus Commissions His Disciples

Mark 3:13-19; 6:7-13; 16:14-20

INTRODUCTION

The word *rabbi* in reference to Jesus is found throughout Mark and the other Gospels more than a dozen times. It was and remains a familiar Jewish term referring to a teacher of truth. However, the term also locates Jesus in a larger tradition of the way in which the faith of Yahweh has been passed down and disseminated in Israel. In our day, a student of the Scriptures might enter a series of classes, typically in a university setting, in order to prepare for ministry. In Jesus' day, however, rabbis were intentional about gathering students around them, not for classes, but to live life together centered on God. This is the true nature of the word *disciple*. A disciple was an apprentice who literally dwelled with the rabbi, eating together, working together, and traveling together. Rabbis looked for the best disciples they could find, and being paired with the right rabbi meant social prestige and a promising future for the top students. Each hoped someday to be a rabbi in his own right.

Jesus follows this tradition of choosing disciples, but does it "all wrong." Instead of finding the top Hebrew students, He finds ignorant, and mostly illiterate, commoners. The one disciple He chooses that has any level of sophistication is a tax collector—a despised sellout to the oppressive Roman regime. Nonetheless, He invests everything He knows and is into the hearts of the ragtag band of Twelve. As rabbinic students, they expect to one day be commissioned to carry on Jesus' ministry in their own right. Yet they could not have ever guessed just how abrupt and difficult this would be. When His time has come, Jesus departs just as suddenly as He had previously entered their lives, and they are forced to depend on the Holy Spirit to guide them in living out His mission without His physical presence.

Jesus' methodology of disciple-making leaves a legacy for the church today. When it comes to living for God, Jesus did not leave a systematic set of guidelines; He left a relational approach of living in community. The first church in Acts 2 expresses this relational quality, not primarily in some new way of doing religion (they remain worshipers in the Temple), but in their radical commitment to sharing with one another.

Unit Theme:
Gospel of Mark (The Servant Messiah)

Central Truth:
Christ commands the church to make disciples of all nations.

Focus:
Affirm that the Great Commission is given to every disciple of Christ, and be His witness.

Context:
The Gospel of Mark was probably written between A.D. 50 and 70.

Golden Text:
"Go ye into all the world, and preach the gospel to every creature" (Mark 16:15).

Study Outline:
I. Jesus Chooses the Twelve (Mark 3:13-19)
II. Jesus Sends the Twelve (Mark 6:7-13)
III. The Great Commission (Mark 16:14-20)

I. JESUS CHOOSES THE TWELVE (Mark 3:13-19)

Much has transpired in the Gospel of Mark by the time Jesus chooses His innermost circle of 12 disciples. He has already been baptized, tempted, and begun His preaching and healing ministry. Crowds are now following Him from all over Judea. In short, Jesus' ministry is in full swing. What is more, we discover throughout the first two chapters that Jesus routinely calls disciples. But by chapter 3, something has changed. Jesus' popularity has swelled to greater proportions, and He sees the need to formalize those who will be closest to Him. Nothing He will do in His grand ministry will be more important than this choice.

A. A Prayerful Selection (v. 13)

13. And he goeth up into a mountain, and calleth unto him whom he would: and they came unto him.

The previous passage centers on the logistical difficulty Jesus begins to experience because of the great multitudes coming to hear and see Him. In order to continue His teaching ministry, He has been forced into boats. In these crowds are probably hundreds of would-be disciples from across Judea and its surrounding territories. Jesus knows the time is right to identify those who will care for His needs and will receive the greatest investment of His attention. This is striking because Jesus intentionally spurns the larger crowds in favor of the smaller group. The crowds, of course, offer popularity and power. Eventually they will even try to crown Him king of Israel (John 6:15). Yet Jesus knows that although His ministry is for and to the crowds, His way of leadership is not. Only a privileged few will sit in Jesus' school of leadership.

Mark does not specifically say that Jesus journeys to the mountainside for a time of prayer and solitude, but Luke does (6:12-16). We also know from Mark 1:35 that this was His custom from the beginning. Jesus leaves the busyness of the crowds for His regular time of prayer. In this devotional, however, the Lord has something serious to wrestle with. He is not only gaining spiritual refreshment, but dealing with the Father over perhaps the most important choice of His ministry. He needs to follow the Father's will perfectly.

Note that initially Jesus appears to call a larger group up to the mountainside. Perhaps He needs the whole company of disciples around Him in order to properly select the God-ordained choices. We know from Luke 10 that Jesus has more followers who are specifically called "disciples" than just the Twelve. Here we are not told how many He calls to His place of prayer, just that they come willingly. Undoubtedly they are all hoping to be selected.

> "It is better to train 10 people than to do the work of 10 people. But it is harder."
> —D.L. Moody

B. A Powerful Appointment (vv. 14, 15)

14. And he ordained twelve, that they should be with him, and that he might send them forth to preach,

Jesus Commissions His Disciples

15. And to have power to heal sicknesses, and to cast out devils.

The number 12 is very significant, and Jesus does not arrive at it accidentally. We know this specifically from Matthew 19:28, when Jesus promises that in His future rule the disciples will sit on 12 thrones in order to judge the 12 tribes of Israel. This connection between the number of disciples and the number of tribes is vital. First, it foreshadows Jesus' plan to renew Israel. His ministry is focused on impassioning the nation to follow the Torah in the way God had intended, and thus to truly live up to their identity as the people of God.

Second, the number 12 flies in the face of the past and present disunity of Israel. For about three and a half centuries after the rule of Solomon, Israel did not exist as 12 tribes, but as a northern and southern kingdom divided against itself. In fact, Israel never truly existed as an independent unity after this, since it was at the Babylonian conquest in the sixth century B.C. that both divisions of Israel were obliterated. We have seen throughout the Book of Mark that Jesus is identified in the prophetic tradition of Elijah. Although living in the divided kingdom, Elijah was known for boldly building an altar of 12 stones to represent the unification of all 12 tribes of Israel in His standoff with the prophets of Baal (1 Kings 18:31). Jesus shows similar boldness in the context of the oppressed and fragmented nation of Israel under Roman hegemony. Everyone knows that Israel is dominated by competing religious and political sects. Yet Jesus not only announces the unity of Israel by choosing 12, but actually chooses a diverse group made up of many of these sects. With that kind of intense diversity, His 12 were bound to be a combustible group, which is exactly what we come to expect from them in Mark's Gospel.

In common Christian language today, Jesus' disciples are typically spoken of as synonymous with the Twelve. In fact, this is not true. We know that Jesus' disciples included many more than the Twelve, including 70 other preachers (Luke 10:1) and a group of faithful women (8:1-3). The Twelve carry a different title from the very beginning. They are set up to be more than just Jesus' small-time followers who do menial tasks. No, they are designated at this earliest stage as "apostles" (6:13). The word *apostle* is the noun form of the Greek verb *apostello*, which simply means "to send." In the Greco-Roman world it often referred to an emissary sent to carry an important message from one political leader to another. This meaning easily connects to Mark 3:12, where we are told that Jesus began enforcing a strict policy over the demons He exorcised of disallowing them from proclaiming His true identity. Jesus does not announce His identity to the masses just yet, but someone has to know, and this is part of the job description of an apostle. The apostles will be entrusted with the message to proclaim at the right time.

Talk About It:
What four things did Jesus appoint His disciples to do?

Plodding Process
Jesus grew up not in the elite circles of the rabbis but in the workroom of a common carpenter. Anyone who has worked with wood knows that building is a slow, painstaking process. It cannot be rushed or the quality of the item will be lessened. It is this discipline that Jesus instills into His disciples before charging them to transform the world. It will be a slow process with many setbacks and much danger. In the end, their deaths will make them appear unsuccessful. But just like woodworking, if they continue to plod ahead, God will be glorified in them.

Although the apostles will later build His church, they have only two components in their early job description: they are to preach and to drive out demons. We have seen that the content of Jesus' preaching at this point deals with the good news of the nearness of the kingdom of God, and we can assume that this is the message Jesus' new apostles pass along as well. They will demonstrate that nearness by casting out demons via the authority that Jesus confers on them.

C. The List (vv. 16-19)

16. And Simon he surnamed Peter;

17. And James the son of Zebedee, and John the brother of James; and he surnamed them Boanerges, which is, The sons of thunder:

18. And Andrew, and Philip, and Bartholomew, and Matthew, and Thomas, and James the son of Alphaeus, and Thaddaeus, and Simon the Canaanite,

19. And Judas Iscariot, which also betrayed him: and they went into an house.

The identity of the original 12 disciples was of vital importance to the early church. Even in some of the earliest letters of the New Testament, like 2 Corinthians, we see the emergence of false apostles. Perhaps these were some who had come into contact or even followed Jesus for a time, and they wanted to share equal status with the chief leaders of the early church. Paul is especially prone to attack from these intruders, since he boldly claims this status (1 Corinthians 9:1-5). However, in Galatians 1 and 2, he also protects the apostolic office as something God had instituted from the beginning and pays special homage to those chosen by Jesus. Mark gives us an early glimpse into just who those first chosen are.

The ordering of the list seems to be significant, given the fact that the first three—Peter, James and John—form Jesus' inner circle of three. The fourth addition of Andrew caps off the first four disciples that Jesus calls in Mark 1. We also know from Galatians 2:9 that Peter, James and John represent the top leadership of the early church. It is strange that Andrew plays such a prominent role in the early narratives in each Gospel, then practically disappears. In fact, any later ministry he has is unmentioned in Acts, unlike Philip, who gets no further mention anywhere else in Mark. We wish to have more information about several of these mysterious figures—Bartholomew, Thaddaeus, Simon the Canaanite (Zealot)—but can only guess at their significance in the early church. Nonetheless, we can postulate that they were known, otherwise Mark's inclusion of their names would be pointless.

Talk About It:
What specifics do you learn about the Twelve from this list?

Unlikely Trust
"We are struck by Jesus' loyalty to . . . the church, which He entrusted to an unlikely band of disciples—whom He defended, prayed for, and prepared to spread the gospel. To outsiders they (and we) must seem like incapable blunderers. But Jesus, the architect of the church, knows this structure is destined for greatness when He returns."
—John Berstecher

Jesus Commissions His Disciples

II. JESUS SENDS THE TWELVE (Mark 6:7-13)

After their designation as apostles, the Twelve essentially carried on for a while like they did before. It was Jesus' stated intention to send them out to perpetuate His ministry, but they were not ready. So, after their appointment (ch. 3) they continued to spend time with Jesus, hearing Him teach, watching Him heal. Jesus would not send them out untrained. Finally, in chapter 6, their time has come.

A. Specific Instructions (vv. 7-11)

7. And he called unto him the twelve, and began to send them forth by two and two; and gave them power over unclean spirits;

8. And commanded them that they should take nothing for their journey, save a staff only; no scrip, no bread, no money in their purse:

9. But be shod with sandals; and not put on two coats.

10. And he said unto them, In what place soever ye enter into an house, there abide till ye depart from that place.

11. And whosoever shall not receive you, nor hear you, when ye depart thence, shake off the dust under your feet for a testimony against them. Verily I say unto you, It shall be more tolerable for Sodom and Gomorrah in the day of judgment, than for that city.

Jesus pairs up the Twelve so they may provide support one for another. If left alone, the rigors of ministry might quickly extinguish their passion and hope. In order to empower them, Jesus grants them authority over demons. Note that at each step along their development, Jesus is very specific. He does not give them power to teach His entire way of life, nor to calm storms or walk on water. He knows they cannot handle such things. In fact, His instruction includes details on exactly what they should pack and how they should lodge. Jesus will allow them to take nothing on the journey with them, except a staff and good sandals for walking. They are not allowed extra food, money, or clothing. This means they will be fully dependent on God and the hospitality of strangers.

The disciples are not to bump around from house to house in any given town, although that might be a quick means of gaining a following. No, their ministry is to be characterized by modesty and by accepting the hospitality of a single family. But Jesus warns them that this hospitality will not always be given. The road of itinerant ministry will not be easy. In fact, they can expect utter rejection in some places. Again, He gives them specific instruction about what to do in these cases. They are simply to leave without a word. They should not become stressed nor should they pronounce judgment. These things are in the hands of God, who will remember their testimony as they leave. They are simple travelers with a straightforward message and specific power.

Talk About It:
1. Why do you suppose Jesus sent out the disciples in pairs?
2. What were the Twelve not to take with them (vv. 8, 9)? Why not?
3. What would "shaking the dust off their feet" symbolize (v. 11)?

"Give me one hundred preachers who fear nothing but sin and desire nothing but God, and I care not a straw whether they be clergymen or laymen: such alone will shake the gates of hell, and set up the kingdom of heaven upon earth."
—**John Wesley**

This instruction also forms the basis of ministerial compensation in the early church. Without any extra money, the disciples are forced to live off of the generosity of others. This forged an ardent dependence on God for their basic needs—a tradition that continues among many followers of Christ today. Paul especially defends this practice in 1 Corinthians 9:11: "If we have sown spiritual seed among you, is it too much if we reap a material harvest from you?" (*NIV*). So we see that Jesus' words here set an important precedent for the early church.

B. Mission Accomplished (vv. 12, 13)

12. And they went out, and preached that men should repent.

13. And they cast out many devils, and anointed with oil many that were sick, and healed them.

Talk About It:
Describe the results of the Twelve's mission.

As in many other places in Mark, the passage leaves us hungering for more information. We want to know exactly how the disciples came to enter a town, how they dealt with rejections and setbacks, and what the settings were where they preached. Alas, we simply get a basic description of their overall success in following Jesus' instructions.

The content of their preaching is summarized in the need for repentance. The good news of the Kingdom had grave implications. They were not passing along a new or trendy philosophy. Their message was urgent and required immediate action. In the wake of God's coming kingdom, it was time for the people to get serious about becoming what God intended for Israel to be. No more stagnant religiosity—God's reign had arrived in the person of Jesus! To prove this, the disciples exorcised demons and healed the sick. This second component is interesting, given the fact that it has not been mentioned before. What is more, unlike Jesus the disciples use oil in praying for the sick. This set the precedent for healing in the early church, as seen in James 5:14.

III. THE GREAT COMMISSION (Mark 16:14-20)

Jesus' postresurrection appearances are as mysterious as the Resurrection itself. He seems to exist in two worlds. He eats fish like His old, normal self, but He is also disguised in a different form on the road to Emmaus, and makes sudden appearances out of thin air. What is more, we do not know if He continues to teach the disciples much more. What we do have is a clear record of His final instruction. It represents the most intimidating, yet exhilarating, promise for the future ministry of the apostles.

A. A Ministry of Preaching (vv. 14-16)

14. Afterward he appeared unto the eleven as they sat at meat, and upbraided them with their unbelief and hardness of heart, because they believed not them which had seen him after he was risen.

15. And he said unto them, Go ye into all the world, and preach the gospel to every creature.

16. He that believeth and is baptized shall be saved; but he that believeth not shall be damned.

Interestingly, the context of the Great Commission in Mark is one of rebuke. The 11 apostles have heard about Jesus' resurrection from many sources, but they wouldn't believe a word of it. Finally, Jesus appears to them. Yet after He chides their lack of faith, He gives them the greatest challenge imaginable. His work has not been completed; it has only just begun.

Jesus first confers on them a renewed ministry of preaching. However, they are no longer bound to the villages of Israel. They are to spread throughout all creation, because the message is for creation. In fact, it is not just a message about humanity, but one about God's renewal of the entire created order. Although thrown into chaos by Adam's fall, Jesus' death and resurrection have set the world right. The disciples are charged to announce this, and to baptize those who receive the message. They have preached and healed before, but the ministry of baptism is new to them. Yet in this sacrament of the church, Mark's Gospel ends where it began. As Jesus was baptized by John to begin changing the world, so should His followers be.

B. A Ministry of Miracles (vv. 17-20)

17. And these signs shall follow them that believe; In my name shall they cast out devils; they shall speak with new tongues;

18. They shall take up serpents; and if they drink any deadly thing, it shall not hurt them; they shall lay hands on the sick, and they shall recover.

19. So then after the Lord had spoken unto them, he was received up into heaven, and sat on the right hand of God.

20. And they went forth, and preached every where, the Lord working with them, and confirming the word with signs following. Amen.

Throughout church history, some theologians have argued that the ministry of miracles should be relegated to the age of Jesus only. However, He clearly passed on this aspect of His ministry to the apostles (and to all future believers). In fact, Jesus promised that the miracles wrought through them would be "greater" (John 14:12). Yet those works would be secondary to the preached word; they would be signs to confirm their preeminent message of good news.

Talk About It:
1. Why did Jesus rebuke the apostles (v. 14)?
2. What did Jesus commission them to do (v. 15)?
3. How important is the preaching of the gospel (v. 16)?

Talk About It:
1. What is the purpose of these various signs (vv. 17, 18)?
2. What is the significance of the Lord's place in heaven (v. 19)?
3. Describe the apostles' ministry (v. 20).

The apostles had been used in exorcisms and healings, but knew nothing of speaking in tongues, not to mention snakes and poison. The gift of tongues would be given just a few weeks later (Acts 2), and we do have the record in 28:3-6 of Paul suffering no ill effect after a viper's venomous bite. The reference to drinking poison probably referred to vain attempts by some to covertly assassinate the apostles. Jesus was clear—His powerful ministry of miracles would continue in the ministry of the apostles.

Mark 16:19 may imply that Jesus' ascension took place immediately after the giving of the Great Commission. However, we do not know. Some time may have transpired between the two events. Whatever the case, Jesus' time on earth was completed and vindicated by His seat at the right hand of God, and the disciples followed the commandment to preach everywhere. Note that Mark does not say the apostles were in possession of the power to do miracles. This remained the domain of the Lord Jesus, who "worked with them" (v. 20, *NIV*).

CONCLUSION

Jesus' method of building the church does not entail simply ministering to the masses, but calling the few. He invests into an inner circle in order to build His church. Yet Jesus breaks from His tradition by allowing the ignorant, illiterate and downright sinful into that circle. Nonetheless, He builds this ragtag group into an earth-shaking force for good, sending them out to transform creation with the good news of the gospel. This effort reaches us still today, and calls the church to continue the work of Jesus and His apostles.

GOLDEN TEXT CHALLENGE

"GO YE INTO ALL THE WORLD, AND PREACH THE GOSPEL TO EVERY CREATURE" (Mark 16:15).

This call was delivered to the disciples in Galilee. It was the same as that recorded in Matthew 28:19, which was again repeated immediately before His ascension from Bethany, in Acts 1:8. "Go ye into all the world"—not into Judea only, but everywhere. This command has expanded with the discovery in later times of new portions of the inhabited earth and must ever be coextensive with geographic discovery (*Pulpit Commentary*).

In this verse, Mark gives us the method, scope and message of missions. The method is preaching, the scope is the world, and the message is the gospel. Mark emphasizes that the command of Christ obligates His church to preach the gospel in all the world for a witness to all nations. The world is the scope of our commission; the bounds of the earth are the church's only limitations. The gospel must be published among all nations, and every tribe and tongue must hear; such is the explicit will of the risen Lord.

How Christians Deal With Suffering

James 1:1-25

INTRODUCTION

The name *James* is the English form of *Jacob*, and identifies three distinct persons in the New Testament. The son of Zebedee and the son of Alphaeus, both apostles of Jesus during His earthly ministry, are not to be confused with "James the Lord's brother" (Galatians 1:19), who wrote the Epistle of James. This James is mentioned only twice by name in the Gospels as one of Jesus' "brethren" (Matthew 13:55; Mark 6:3), but is probably included among the relatives who sought to see Jesus during His Galilean tour (Matthew 12:46), who accompanied Jesus to Capernaum (John 2:12), and who sought to persuade Jesus to depart from Galilee for Judea on the eve of the Feast of Tabernacles (7:3). At the feast he was present (v. 10), but as yet not a believer in Jesus as the Christ (v. 5).

That James later became a believer in Christ is evident from the fact that the risen Christ appeared to him (1 Corinthians 15:7), that he is very likely one of "his brethren" at the Jerusalem prayer meeting (Acts 1:14), and that he appears in a prominent place of leadership in the Jerusalem church (12:17; 15:13; 21:18). It is this James who refers to himself as "a servant of God and of the Lord Jesus Christ" (James 1:1) in the epistle that bears his name.

James wrote to Jews of the 12 tribes. His readers were apparently Christians, though some dispute this. He spoke of them as brethren (1:2), he spoke of their "faith" (2:17), and he spoke of their expectation fo Christ's return (5:7). Because of severe persecution, his readers had been dispersed to places outside their home area of Palestine. The term *diaspora*, or *dispersion*, is used only two other times in the New Testament: John 7:35 and 1 Peter 1:1.

Unit Theme:
Practical Christian Living (James)

Central Truth:
Christians can stand firm and grow spiritually during trials.

Focus:
Realize that trials can lead to spiritual growth and hold on to God during times of suffering.

Context:
The Epistle of James was probably written between A.D. 47 and A.D. 51.

Golden Text:
"Blessed is the man that endureth temptation: for when he is tried, he shall receive the crown of life, which the Lord hath promised to them that love him" (James 1:12).

Study Outline:
I. By Learning From Trials
(James 1:1-11)
II. By Appreciating God's Goodness
(James 1:12-18)
III. By Obeying God's Word
(James 1:19-25)

I. BY LEARNING FROM TRIALS (James 1:1-11)

A. A Humble Servant (v. 1)

1. James, a servant of God and of the Lord Jesus Christ, to the twelve tribes which are scattered abroad, greeting.

Talk About It:
Can all Christians describe themselves as James did?

It is noteworthy that James himself does not mention his natural relationship to the Lord Jesus, but styles himself simply a bondservant of God and the Lord Jesus Christ. He was bound to Christ in devotion and love as a slave, and that alone gave him a right to speak and a claim to be herd. It is an official designation implying that neither his own will nor that of other men, but only of God and of Christ, must be done. His epistle, which is introduced by the customary "greeting," is addressed "to the twelve tribes . . . scattered abroad." That is, he was writing especially for the instruction of Christian Jews representing the whole nation and dispersed among the Gentiles outside the borders of Palestine.

B. All Joy (vv. 2-4)

divers (v. 2)—
various

2. My brethren, count it all joy when ye fall into divers temptations;

3. Knowing this, that the trying of your faith worketh patience.

4. But let patience have her perfect work, that ye may be perfect and entire, wanting nothing.

Talk About It:
1. What should produce joy in a believer's life, and why (vv. 2, 3)?
2. Describe the "perfect work" patience accomplishes through trials (v. 4).

James wrote his epistle to help people live joyfully in the midst of trials. He did not offer a way to escape trials, nor did he say they would be pleasant experiences. However, he did give helpful advice that if followed will help believers live with victory in the midst of trials.

He did not, at this juncture, indicate to the readers just what kind of trials lay in store for them. He merely spoke of various kinds. However, it may be inferred from subsequent passages that they were subjected to persecution, sickness and poverty.

One of the many excellent qualities of our Bible is its constant reference to and consideration of the stark realities of life—sin, suffering, sorrow, failure, temptation, death. Not only are all of these problems frankly faced, but the Bible reveals to believing men and women resources for every need in all the experiences of life—resources sufficient for adequate strength, for light in darkness, for victory in the hour of temptation, for peace and joy, regardless of the circumstances surrounding them.

It would have been difficult for the readers of this letter to see how any good could come out of their tribulations. The content of the epistle suggests that their own unchristian conduct brought about many of their difficulties.

Christians cannot always control their circumstances, but they can control their attitudes. Therefore, James urged, commanded, and instructed them to "count it all joy when you fall into various trials" (v. 2, *NKJV*). We are to rejoice when we fall into trials because in having victory over them, our faith will be proved genuine and we will be learning the virtue of patience.

The word *count* is interesting in that it is a financial term. Notice, we are to *count*, that is, according to W.E. Vine, "primarily to lead the way." One thing especially is to be noted from the Greek: *Count* calls for a mental evaluation that is to be adopted as a result of due deliberation. It is a conscious acceptance of a definite inner attitude. In this way, God is telling the believer to expect trials. James did not say "if" but "*when* you fall" into the various testings.

James wanted his readers to find meaning in their problems. The word he used for *know* (v. 3) suggests knowledge based on personal experience. What is it Christians know that makes it easier for them to face difficulties and to benefit from them? Is it the fact that the Word indicates our faith is to be tested? James made it plain that the "trial [genuineness] of your faith," which is "more precious than . . . gold," brings praise, honor and glory to God (1 Peter 1:7). God always tests us to bring out the best in us, while Satan tempts us to bring out the worst. Testing proves our trust in our heavenly Father. He has promised grace sufficient for our needs (2 Corinthians 12:9). The question "What does God want to produce in our lives?" arises. James indicated that it is patience. Patience is not a passive acceptance of the difficult circumstances; it is rather a courageous, aggressive steadfastness, endurance and perseverance in the face of suffering and difficulty. It leads to Christian maturity.

James also said the believer is to be "perfect and entire, wanting nothing" (v. 4). This indicates that the believer is to be complete in all parts, or spiritually sound. As we allow patience to have "her perfect work," we become increasingly complete, whole and mature in every part. Thus, this steadfastness should take full effect in us and remain effective to the very end.

C. Firm Faith (vv. 5-8)

5. If any of you lack wisdom, let him ask of God, that giveth to all men liberally, and upbraideth not; and it shall be given him.

6. But let him ask in faith, nothing wavering. For he that wavereth is like a wave of the sea driven with the wind and tossed.

7. For let not that man think that he shall receive any thing of the Lord.

8. A double minded man is unstable in all his ways.

The Power of Persistence
"Nothing in the world can take the place of persistence. Talent will not; nothing is more common than unsuccessful men with talent. Genius will not; unrewarded genius is almost a proverb. Education will not; the world is full of educated derelicts. Persistence and determination alone are omnipotent."
—Calvin Coolidge

upbraideth not (v. 5)—"without finding fault" (*NIV*)

Talk About It:
1. What is available for the asking (v. 5)?
2. What is the problem with "wavering" (vv. 6, 7)?
3. What is a "double-minded man" (v. 8)?

So many circumstances of life arise that baffle and perplex us, and we do not know what to say, what to do, which way to turn, or what to undertake. We know the decision we make is tremendously important, and yet we are not sure what decision we ought to make. For this situation, James said, the secret is to turn to God, who will give wisdom freely to all who call on Him in faith, not doubting.

James not only explained what to ask for—that is, wisdom from God—but he also described *how* to ask. However, the asking is predicated on being aware of the need for wisdom. Since the Greek verb for *ask* is in the present tense, James was advocating continual prayer. What kind of wisdom should one ask for? It appears from the context that wisdom is needed to know how to respond properly during the testing time. Wisdom is that moral discernment that enables the believer to meet life and its trials with decisions and actions consistent with God's will. The believer must recognize God's sovereignty and majesty, submitting his own will to God's will as he prays. Any failure to ask implies the believer is blind to his need. James could have said we all need wisdom, but he appealed to the individual by saying, "If any of you lack wisdom, let him ask of God." By this means he gives the reader an opportunity to examine himself, to draw his own conclusions, and to follow the advice given.

The believer is to ask of God, who gives to all. God is willing to impart wisdom to anyone who will ask humbly. Note the promise: "It shall be given him." God does not berate or scold His children for their lack of wisdom, nor does He chide them for their asking: He "upbraideth not." God gives *liberally*—that is, generously, graciously, and without constraints.

Not only must we *ask* but we must ask *in faith* (v. 6). Faith does not mean a set of theological statements, but a personal vibrant faith in the living Lord. Just as God gives without reservations, He expects believers to come to Him in prayer in the same manner.

James then painted a word picture of the one who asks with wavering faith. The representation of the sea is that of instability and restlessness—"driven" and "tossed." A wave crests, then falls. Thus, James pictures the man with his doubts. This up-and-down motion is like a man who trusts God one moment and trusts the arm of the flesh the next. Such a "double-minded" person "is unstable in all his ways" (v. 8).

The doubter here is not the person with an honest question. All of us have questions about difficult situations we cannot understand, especially in the context of trials. Our first human reaction is "Why me? Why must I go through this trial? I would surely be happier if this had not happened to me." Such feelings do not indicate doubt but are part of the tensions of trials. However, having raised these questions in our mind, we must go on and take them to the Lord. In this asking for wisdom we confess our doubts—we confess that we do not have the answer and must therefore ask God.

The person who remains in his doubts, never asking God for wisdom, is like the victim of the storm-tossed waves. He is in a turbulent state of mind because he can't decide whether or not to ask the Lord. This instability is dangerous or deadly. He will not ask for anything; therefore, he will not receive anything. He doesn't believe God can supply the answer, the strength, or the steadfastness. In this sense he is a doubter.

It should be noted that the terms *ways* and *walking* are familiar Biblical expressions for conduct; therefore, James' language here is probably more literal than figurative. The person who is divided within himself, then, will show himself as such in his doubtful prayer and also in his inability to act firmly or reliably. Thus, this person, rather than being a single-minded lover of God, is one whose character and conduct is unstable, perhaps even hypocritical. No wonder he should not expect anything from God!

"Faith is dead to doubts, dumb to discouragements, blind to impossibilities."
—Anonymous

D. Low or High? (vv. 9-11)

9. Let the brother of low degree rejoice in that he is exalted:

10. But the rich, in that he is made low: because as the flower of the grass he shall pass away.

11. For the sun is no sooner risen with a burning heat, but it withereth the grass, and the flower thereof falleth, and the grace of the fashion of it perisheth: so also shall the rich man fade away in his ways.

James turns conventional thinking upside-down in these verses. "The brother of low degree" (v. 9)—the person living in humble circumstances who is "rich in faith" (2:5)—is actually in a "high position" (1:9, *NIV*) because of his inheritance in Christ Jesus. Meanwhile, the person who is materially rich needs to realize he will be "made low" (humiliated) like a wildflower in its temporary existence (v. 10). Even while the rich person is carrying on his daily business affairs, he will "fade away" (v. 11).

Talk About It:
1. Explain the upside-down thinking in verses 9 and 10.
2. What will happen to people whose trust is in their wealth (v. 11)?

II. BY APPRECIATING GOD'S GOODNESS (James 1:12-18)
A. God Does Not Tempt Us (vv. 12-15)

12. Blessed is the man that endureth temptation: for when he is tried, he shall receive the crown of life, which the Lord hath promised to them that love him.

13. Let no man say when he is tempted, I am tempted of God: for God cannot be tempted with evil, neither tempteth he any man:

14. But every man is tempted, when he is drawn away of his own lust, and enticed.

15. Then when lust hath conceived, it bringeth forth sin: and sin, when it is finished, bringeth forth death.

Talk About It:
1. What are the perseverant promised (v. 12)?
2. What can God not do, and why not (v. 13)?
3. Describe the temptation process (vv. 14, 15).

James presents us with a beatitude: "Blessed is the man that endureth temptation" (v. 12). The expression "blessed is the man" appears frequently in the Psalms, Proverbs, the Prophets, and the Gospels. This blessedness consists not in being free from trials, or yet in being subjected to testing, but rather in enduring trials. Happy is the person who here and now, from day to day, withstands temptation. God does not want us to yield to temptation, yet neither can He spare us the experience of temptations. If we are to mature, we must face testings and temptations.

God tests our faith to show whether it is genuine. The word used here for "tried" is the same one used of testing coins and metals to establish their genuineness. There is a sense in which the believer must not only be *proved* but *approved* as having shown himself genuine. Faith that is not tried is worthless.

"When he is tried" and endures to the end, and at last wins final approval, the believer will then receive the ultimate reward—the crown of life. The reward will be given to those who love God. In verse 12 is the first mention of *love* in the Epistle of James. Man's duty of love to God is as old as any other duty in Hebrew religion. From Ezekiel onward the prophets speak often and with great emphasis on this theme. Jesus also spoke of love for God. Following His example, James and Paul did also. Love for God is the outcome of faith in Him, which produces willing endurance for Him (James 1:2-4). "He shall receive" (v. 12) indicates that the bestowal of the reward is still future.

The phrase "the crown of life" apparently was a well-known idiom in the first century. It occurs in the letter addressed to the church in Smyrna: "Be thou faithful unto death, and I will give thee a crown of life" (Revelation 2:10). Clearly James was not thinking of a fading crown, such as was given in the athletic contests, but of a crown that is imperishable. James did not say that the one who successfully endures trials earns eternal life. Man cannot *earn* eternal life; it is received as a gift through faith in Christ Jesus.

Beginning in verse 13, James turned to the nature of human temptation. James warned his readers not to blame God, but rather to understand the cause and the result of yielding to temptation. The prohibition, "Let no man say when he is tempted, I am tempted of God," is stated in the singular and demands that not a single individual—no matter how difficult or severe his testing—is to make such a claim. James did not deny that God does indeed subject people to testing, but he did deny the claim that God tests with an evil intent to lead people into sin.

God does *test* us, as He did Abraham; but He does not and cannot *tempt* us. Tempting others to evil would require that He delight in evil, which He is incapable of doing. Therefore, do not blame God for temptation. He is too holy to be tempted and too loving to tempt others.

The word *for* in verse 13 introduces a twofold reason for rejecting the claim that God is to blame when we yield to temptation: "God cannot be tempted with evil, neither tempteth he any man." These words of James are an important declaration concerning the nature of God. The gods of heathen imagination are always conceived as liable to temptations of moral evil.

In verse 14 James identifies the source of a person's temptation—"his own lust." The trouble lies with the human heart. The word *lust* is in itself a neutral term which simply means "a strong desire or craving." The context must decide the meaning of the word.

James used an illustration taken from the art of fishing; perhaps this was based on his experience as a fisherman in Galilee. A fish sees the lure and is tempted to strike. When the fish takes hold of the bait, it is suddenly dragged away and pays with its life for its ignorance.

We are *enticed* by sin. *Entice* comes from a word that means "to entrap, to allure, or to beguile." In short, it is Satan who would tempt us with evil, as he is the source of all evil. Although there are momentary pleasures of sin and the lust of the flesh, sin ultimately leads to separation from God.

"Sin, when it is finished [full-grown], bringeth forth death" (v. 15). Sin is the cause of death (both physical and spiritual). It is, in its very nature, self-destructive. James therefore gives three major elements of this destructiveness: lust, sin and death.

The primary reference seems to be spiritual death, but physical death is certainly included and, ultimately, eternal death also. The basic meaning of death is separation. When physical death occurs, there is the separation of the soul from the body. In the matter of spiritual death, it is the separation of man from God because of sin. In eternal death it is the separation of man from God forever.

Thus, we see the one who endures and overcomes the hardships, trials and temptations receives a "crown of life," while the one who yields to his lust receives death. We make the choice.

> "The temptation once yielded to gains power. The crack in the embankment which lets a drop or two ooze through is soon a hole which lets out a flood."
> **—Alexander MacLaren**

B. God Bestows Good Gifts (vv. 16-18)

16. Do not err, my beloved brethren.

17. Every good gift and every perfect gift is from above, and cometh down from the Father of lights, with whom is no variableness, neither shadow of turning.

18. Of his own will begat he us with the word of truth, that we should be a kind of firstfruits of his creatures.

Do not err (v. 16)—
"Don't be deceived."

---

1. Why is God called "the Father of lights" (v. 17)?
2. What does God do through "the word of truth" (v. 18)?

In verse 16 James gives a specific warning. He did not want his "beloved brethren" in the Lord to be deceived. Whatever you do, do not become so warped in your thinking that you accuse God, who sent His Son to die for us, of originating temptation and sin and death. This is the exact opposite of the truth.

Instead of attributing evil to God, let us realize that our heavenly Father sends only good things to us. Everything good proceeds from Him. He is called "the Father of lights" (v. 17), perhaps an allusion to God as Creator of the marvelous heavenly lights. Light speaks of purity and holiness, and these heavenly bodies, brilliant and wonderful as they are, only feebly represent the glorious light of the great Creator himself.

But these physical lights are subject to variations of light and darkness. Even the shining sun has its spots. But there are no spots—no variableness—within the perfect light of the great Creator. "Shadow of turning" could be understood as the shadow mark cast from a heavenly body in its turning or revolution, such as when the moon is eclipsed by the earth, and the sun by the moon. Even the greatest of created things may change—but God never does!

In verse 18, James points us to the greatest gift of all: this sovereign and omnipotent God, of His own free will, chose us to be heirs of eternal life through faith in His Son. He confirmed this choice by sending His Son—"the word of truth." And when we believed the Word, He regenerated us—we were born again.

Why did God deal this way with us? "That we should be a kind of firstfruits of his creatures" (v. 18). Paul said we are "created in Christ Jesus unto good works, which God hath before ordained that we should walk in them" (Ephesians 2:10).

In speaking of our being "firstfruits," James was referring to the Old Testament practice of bringing the first sheaf of the new crop of grain harvested, together with a sacrifice, for presentation in the Levitical ceremony in the Temple on the day after the Passover Sabbath. By this act, acknowledgment was made that all came from God and belonged to Him. None of the harvest was to be used for food until this ceremony of gratitude had been performed.

The firstfruits were also a representative sample of the bounteous harvest of golden grain which would follow. Firstfruits imply "afterfruits." They give assurance that the harvest is coming. In similar fashion, Paul referred to Christ as "the firstfruits of them that slept" (1 Corinthians 15:20). In His resurrection we see what God will eventually do for all believers.

III. BY OBEYING GOD'S WORD (James 1:19-25)
A. Receive the Word (vv. 19-21)
19. Wherefore, my beloved brethren, let every man be swift to hear, slow to speak, slow to wrath:

"All people that on earth do dwell
Sing to the Lord with cheerful voice. . . .
For why? The Lord our God is good:
For mercy is forever sure;
His truth at all times firmly stood,
And shall from age to age endure."
—William Kethe

How Christians Deal With Suffering

20. For the wrath of man worketh not the righteousness of God.

21. Wherefore lay apart all filthiness and superfluity of naughtiness, and receive with meekness the engrafted word, which is able to save your souls.

superfluity (v. 21)—overflow

The first statement here is more correctly rendered, "Know this, my beloved brethren," and probably refers to the truths declared in the preceding context. As the imperative mood, it might also prepare the reader for the following exhortations. The term "my beloved brethren" suggests James' humility as well as his affection for his Christian brethren. Hearing the Word of God is the emphasis of James' exhortation in verses 19 and 20. To "be swift to hear" is to improve every opportunity for learning more truth from God's Word, to listen repeatedly to the divine message and be ready to receive light from any source. To be "slow to speak" is to take the place of the learner in all humility. Apparently there were some believing Jews who thought the Christian life could be promoted by discussion and much talking rather than listening.

"Slow to wrath" is a warning against that flare of temper that often attends religious discussion. Bitterness in assailing one's opponents is not necessarily a proof of zeal and devotion. It behooves the sincere Christian to be slow to give way to anger under provocation, for such anger is never in accord with the righteousness of God which makes Him hate and punish sin. The wrath of man cannot produce the righteousness which God requires and which He looks for in the conduct of Christians.

Receiving the Word of God (v. 21) is the application of its truth to one's conduct that requires and effects sanctification. This spiritual sanctification includes the negative, the positive, and the issue of salvation for the soul. James exhorts the reader to put away every tendency to uncleanness. Both the sins of sensuality and those of malice must be cleared away for the effective growth of the Word. The Word is a seed and requires a clean soul in which to germinate and grow. "So clear away all the foul rank growth of malice, and make a soil of humble modesty for the Word which roots itself inwardly with power to save your souls" (*Moffatt*).

In the parable of the sower (Matthew 13:3ff), the seed of God's Word can only thrive and produce in the good soil which is free from all noxious weeds and conducive to a healthy growth. The Word must be accepted completely and without reservation in order that the soul might be saved in every area of its expression, for time and eternity.

Talk About It:
1. Why must we be "slow to wrath" (vv. 19, 20)?
2. What must we reject, and what must we receive (v. 21)?

"A soft answer turneth away wrath: but grievous words stir up anger."
—Proverbs 15:1

B. Do the Word (vv. 22-25)
22. But be ye doers of the word, and not hearers only, deceiving your own selves.

23. For if any be a hearer of the word, and not a doer, he is like unto a man beholding his natural face in a glass:

24. For he beholdeth himself, and goeth his way, and straightway forgetteth what manner of man he was.

25. But whoso looketh into the perfect law of liberty, and continueth therein, he being not a forgetful hearer, but a doer of the work, this man shall be blessed in his deed.

Talk About It:
1. How do some people deceive themselves (vv. 22-24)?
2. How can we lead "blessed" lives (v. 25)?

A doer of the Word is a person who acts to the full extent of his or her knowledge, whether acquired by the spoken or written Word of God. To be a "doer" implies more than to do, for it expresses a habit. A "doer of the word" is such by profession and practice. Attentive listening to lectures, or the zeal to acquire a knowledge of the contents of the Word and an insight into its meaning, was the main portion of what was required of those who attended the lectures of the philosophers and the teachers of the Law. "This is insufficient," says James. "It is the habitual practice in striving to do what is heard and understood that is of value" (A. Plummer). For unless there is obedience to the faith revealed in Scripture, it is possible by sophisticated argument to reason oneself into a state of fleshly security and thus be tragically deceived.

In verses 23 and 24 is an illustration from life, showing the folly of being led astray. As a man may behold his natural face in a mirror, so the hearer or the reader may perceive his moral complexion in God's Word. The Word of God is like a mirror of the soul, showing a man what he really is; and if he merely beholds and makes no effort to bring his life into line with the Word, the impression is soon lost. The reading or hearing of God's Word will reflect every temptation and weakness, every failing and sin, while the Holy Spirit moves the hearer to practical obedience. The ultimate responsibility, of course, lies with the hearer.

James recognizes that the Word is also a law, "the perfect law of liberty" (v. 25)—a higher standard of holiness than was generally understood by the Mosaic Law. For James, whose ethics are so similar to the ethics of Jesus as declared in the Sermon on the Mount, the Christian rule for holy conduct is a "perfect law." Moreover, it is a law of liberty and not slavery, of life and not of death. The man who looks carefully into it sees not only his actual self but the ideal and potential of a victorious Christian life. Such a sincere student of God's Word, if he persists in his study and puts into practice what he understands, will not forget but will enjoy the favor and blessing of God in his activity. "The law of Christ brings liberty and consists not so much in restraint as in guiding and guarding the new life in Christ" (A. McNabb). "For the law of the Spirit of life in Christ Jesus hath made me free from the law of sin and death" (Romans 8:2).

"It ain't those parts of the Bible I can't understand that bother me, it is the parts I do under-stand."
—**Mark Twain**

CONCLUSION

As Christians, the question is not *if* we will face suffering, temptations and trials, but rather *how* we will handle those difficulties when they come. Here is a summary of the wise truths given to us in James 1:

1. Tests come to help us mature.
2. God will give us wisdom in the midst of trials if we will ask Him in faith.
3. We should rejoice when we are humbled.
4. If we endure temptation, we will be given a crown of life.
5. Temptation comes from our own desires, not from God.
6. God gave us new birth through His Word, which He has implanted in us.
7. Hearing and obeying God's Word are keys to victory.

GOLDEN TEXT CHALLENGE

"BLESSED IS THE MAN THAT ENDURETH TEMPTATION: FOR WHEN HE IS TRIED, HE SHALL RECEIVE THE CROWN OF LIFE, WHICH THE LORD HATH PROMISED TO THEM THAT LOVE HIM" (James 1:12).

James considered trials and testings as norms for the Christian life. He had already stated that "the trying of your faith worketh patience [perseverance]" (v. 3) The word *endure* is most often used to indicate an ongoing experience rather than a onetime test. Jesus said, "He that endureth to the end shall be saved" (Matthew 10:22). The word *endureth* is the same one James used and the same one Paul used in Romans 12:12, "patient in tribulation"—*patient* and *endure* being the same word.

We as Christians tend to think of our trials in terms of episodes or incidents, and it is true that sometimes there are specific testing periods. Actually, we are in a continuous state of trial, for to live where Satan is "the prince of the power of the air" (Ephesians 2:2) is to be surrounded by the potential to do evil. To regard the Christian life in this way may seem negative, but this is one of those unique paradoxes found in the Christian experience where even testing produces joy (James 1:2; 2 Corinthians 7:4) and is of inestimable value. The promise of the eternal reward ought to help us endure the temporal trials.

Daily Devotions:
M. Dealing With Adversity
   Exodus 1:8-14
T. Disobedience Brings Distress
   Nehemiah 9:32-37
W. Protected by God
   Psalm 91:9-13
T. A Spirit of Infirmity
   Luke 13:10-17
F. Chastening of the Lord
   Hebrews 12:5-11
S. Kept by God's Power
   1 Peter 1:3-11

How Christians Demonstrate Mercy

James 2:1-26

INTRODUCTION

The Book of James is often looked at as an exposition of practical religious experience. And it is that. Its primary concern is not creed but conduct, not belief but behavior, not doctrine but deeds. However, in addition, there are important doctrinal concepts in the book. For example, the doctrine of faith is prominent in chapter 2.

The word *faith* is found frequently in James. In the New Testament only Romans, Galatians, 1 Timothy, and Hebrews have more occurrences of the noun for *faith* than James. In only six of the New Testament Epistles is the verb for *believe* found more than in James. The Book of James speaks of the testing of faith, the prayer of faith, the works of faith, the perfection of faith, being rich in faith, a dead faith, an idle faith, and more. Some scholars see the theme of James to be the tests of faith.

Many consider chapter 2 to be the heart of James' message. In it he talks about faith in relation to avoiding favoritism (vv. 1-7), faith in relation to fulfilling the law of love (vv. 8-13), and faith as being important in demonstrating good works (vv. 14-26).

I. BY NOT SHOWING FAVORITISM (James 2:1-7)

A. Principle and Illustration (vv. 1-3)

1. My brethren, have not the faith of our Lord Jesus Christ, the Lord of glory, with respect of persons.

2. For if there come unto your assembly a man with a gold ring, in goodly apparel, and there come in also a poor man in vile raiment;

3. And ye have respect to him that weareth the gay clothing, and say unto him, Sit thou here in a good place; and say to the poor, Stand thou there, or sit here under my footstool.

gay clothing (v. 3)—fine clothes

The second chapter of James opens with a command against showing favoritism. As believers in the Lord Jesus Christ, this is in keeping with His example, for He "shows no partiality" (Acts 10:34, *NKJV*). The One to whom we owe allegiance in the faith is Christ, the Anointed One of God. James was saying that Christian faith is faith in a Person who is both human and divine—a Savior who is Prophet, Priest and King, and "God with us." Faith of any less quality does not deserve the name *Christian.*

Talk About It:
What does *not* express "the faith of our Lord Jesus Christ" (vv. 1-3)?

People who have faith in Christ—who loved all and gave Himself for all—must not practice favoritism. One function of the early church was to create a sphere in which there should be neither Jew nor Gentile, Greek nor barbarian, bond nor free. The statement "All are equal within the church's gate" is true. To be like Christ, the divine Head, the church must show no favoritism. The equality of Christians, indicated by the title "brethren," is the foundation of the admonition with which chapter 2 begins.

James cited an example of the kind of favoritism that is forbidden—the respect shown to the rich in Christian assemblies. The two contrasted visitors are outsiders. One is rich, important socially, and ostentatious. The expensive ring on his finger and his costly clothing, probably a flowing robe of pure white silk or of the finest wool, attract the attention of the congregation. Then there comes in a poor man in a shabby garment. The eyes of all observe his poverty. He too has heard of these Christians and comes to see what their religion and worship are like.

The behavior of the church members shows their bias. Their favoritism is obvious. The one wearing the gold ring and expensive clothing is invited to sit in a prominent seat. Everyone is delighted that he has condescended to visit them. He is shown every consideration. No consideration whatever is shown to the poor man. He is told to stand by the wall or wherever he can be wedged in. Or he is asked by someone to sit on the floor, close to the other person's footstool, where there is just enough room for a man to stoop.

It should be remembered that most people sat cross-legged on the floor; only important people had elevated seats, chairs or benches. No one would think of asking the rich visitor to sit on the floor. Absolutely not! And this is just the point that James was making. His readers were guilty of showing favoritism. They thought like the world in relation to social status.

B. Motive (v. 4)

4. Are ye not then partial in yourselves, and are become judges of evil thoughts?

The apostle used a double question to drive his point home in verse 4. He was asking, "Aren't you being partial? Aren't you evil-thinking judges?" Their faith should have taught them to show the same consideration to all their visitors and not to make distinctions that are wrong. He said in effect, "Since when does faith in the Lord Jesus Christ justify attitudes that treat the man with a fine garment as superior and the man with a shabby garment as inferior?" Is the soul of the one worth more than the soul of the other? Are not all people, rich and poor, equal in the house of God? Something is wrong with our faith if we have not learned from Christ to treat all people with love and respect, without regard to their social or economic status in this world.

C. Explanation (vv. 5-7)

5. Hearken, my beloved brethren, Hath not God chosen the poor of this world rich in faith, and heirs of the kingdom which he hath promised to them that love him?

6. But ye have despised the poor. Do not rich men oppress you, and draw you before the judgment seats?

7. Do not they blaspheme that worthy name by the which ye are called?

Favoritism can result in snobbery, which is contrary to the purpose of God. James said that the poor are the special objects of God's concern. Discrimination against them is therefore an affront to God; it defies His will. The apostle did not mean that God's choice has been limited to the poor. Neither did he mean that all the poor will be saved. But the poor have often been more ready to hear the gospel and accept its blessings than those who are rich in this world's goods. Preaching the gospel is not left to chance but is the deliberate strategy of God. Jesus said that part of His divine mission was to preach the gospel to the poor. That mission has been delegated to the church.

James was referring to people who were poor in one respect, namely, in regard to the riches of the world. They had little money. But in another respect, they were rich. They possessed faith. James mentioned this in verse 5. Their wealth consisted of the heavenly kingdom of which they were joint heirs with Christ.

In verse 6 James dealt with the rich. He spoke primarily of the rich Jews who were, for the most part, Sadducees. At this time they were the tyrannical oppressors of poorer Jews. They also made a special effort to harass Jewish Christians. This abuse of the poor and of Jewish Christians was possible because the Roman government allowed the Jews of the Diaspora a great deal of legal control over their own people.

James said the rich oppressed the Christians and dragged them into court. According to one translation, "It is the rich who grind you down" (*Weymouth*). The Greek word used here for "oppress," meaning "to exploit, oppress, or dominate someone," is used in the Septuagint (Greek version of the Old Testament) in referring to the mistreatment of widows, orphans and the poor. In the only other place where this same Greek word occurs in the New Testament, it is used of the tyrannical rule of the devil (Acts 10:38). The class of individuals to whom favoritism was being shown was the very class that was violently mistreating the Christians.

James stated it was even more inappropriate for Christians to show favoritism to the rich because it was the rich who were blaspheming the worthy name by which Christians were called (v. 7). The rich were content to oppress the poor and spoke with contempt of the honorable name of Christ, their Lord.

II. BY FULFILLING THE ROYAL LAW (JAMES 2:8-13)
A. The Royal Law (vv. 8-11)

8. If ye fulfil the royal law according to the scripture, Thou shalt love thy neighbour as thyself, ye do well:

9. But if ye have respect to persons, ye commit sin, and are convinced of the law as transgressors.

10. For whosoever shall keep the whole law, and yet offend in one point, he is guilty of all.

11. For he that said, Do not commit adultery, said also, Do not kill. Now if thou commit no adultery, yet if thou kill, thou art become a transgressor of the law.

The *royal law* is the law of love, expressed in the command "Thou shalt love thy neighbour as thyself" (v. 8; Leviticus 19:18). Christ taught that all who need our help in any way are to be thought of as neighbors. The command to love our neighbor may then be seen as a summary of the horizontal dimension of the Law.

This command may be called "the royal law" because it is thought of as supreme, that is, "the king of all laws." It can also be considered the royal law because Christ, the true King, is its advocate. Love is the law of His kingdom. To fulfill the royal law is to put it into practice.

"Measure wealth not by the things you have, but by the things you have for which you would not take money."
—Anonymous

Talk About It:
1. What is called "the royal law," and why (v. 8)?
2. Why does one offense make us "guilty of all" (v. 10)?

James argued that the obedience his readers claimed to be giving the Law was only a partial obedience and actually contrary to the meaning of the Law. The poor man, no less than the rich, is neighbor, and to show respect to one while dishonoring the other can in no wise be called a fulfilling of the Law. James says in verse 9, "If ye have respect to persons, ye commit sin"— literally, "you work sin." The readers were not showing love but favoritism, and their actions were not acts of obedience (as they pretended) but acts of sin. "The word translated 'transgressors' (v. 9) denotes one who steps over a line. Thus it is fittingly used of those who violate a law. In the phrase 'of [by] the law,' law is personified and thought of as judge" (Curtis Vaughn, *James: A Study Guide*).

James pinpointed the showing of favoritism as a transgression of the Law by which we are to be judged, and one which, like every other, involves the guilt of breaking "the whole law" (v. 10). In verse 8, the apostle cited the words of Leviticus 19:18 as the precept which forbids showing partiality. This was the same precept Jesus used as His summary of the principle underlying the last six commandments. We are to love our neighbor—that is, anyone to whom we have it within our power to become helpful, even though he or she may be a stranger. Those who discharge this duty appropriately do well. We must not limit the precept to either our wealthy neighbor or our poor neighbor. Those who practice partiality are guilty of sin against both the Old Testament and the law of the Spirit of life in Christ Jesus.

No one should accept the idea that "respect of persons" in the church is a trivial matter to be overlooked. James distinctly tells us that partiality is sin and that he who indulges in it disobeys the whole moral law. The same God who said "Do not commit adultery" and "Do not commit murder" (v. 11, *NIV*) also said "Don't show favoritism" (v. 1, *NIV*).

B. Application (vv. 12, 13)

12. So speak ye, and so do, as they that shall be judged by the law of liberty.

13. For he shall have judgment without mercy, that hath shewed no mercy; and mercy rejoiceth against judgment.

In verse 12, James dealt with the subject of judgment. We will be held accountable for our words and our behavior. The apostle's words here echo the teaching of Jesus in Matthew 7:21-23; 12:34-37. A person's habits of speech and action are always an index of his or her moral state. If we compare human character to a tree, words correspond to its leaves, deeds to its fruit, and thoughts to its roots underground. Words and actions will be judged in connection with the counsels of the hearts of which they are the products.

"The Bible tells us to love our neighbors, and also to love our enemies; probably because generally they are the same people."

—G.K. Chesterton

rejoiceth against (v. 13)—triumphs over

Talk About It:
Who will be judge with mercy?

How Christians Demonstrate Mercy

James continued his treatment of judgment in verse 13. The doctrine of judgment to the unmerciful is emphasized in many parts of Scripture. It receives special prominence in the teaching of our Lord in the Gospel of Matthew. We can never, of course, merit eternal life by cherishing a compassionate spirit. But since mercy and love are supreme elements in the character of God, it is clear that those who do not manifest active compassion toward others have not themselves been renewed into His image. The purpose of the gospel is to restore man's likeness to God, who is love; so then, the man who exhibits no love shows that he has not permitted the gospel to exercise its sanctifying power within him, and he shall therefore be condemned for rejecting it.

There is another side. The apostle added, "Mercy triumphs over judgment" (v. 13, *NKJV*). This means that the tenderhearted and actively compassionate follower of Christ need not fear the final judgment. His mercifulness is an evidence that he is a partaker of the mercy of God in Christ.

> "Blessed are the merciful: for they shall obtain mercy."
> —**Jesus**
> **(Matthew 5:7)**

III. BY DOING GOOD WORKS (James 2:14-26)
A. Question (v. 14)

14. What doth it profit, my brethren, though a man say he hath faith, and have not works? can faith save him?

The insufficiency of barren faith is the subject of verse 14. The case James cites is not that of a hypocrite but of a self-deceiver. The man has faith, of a sort, but it is only the cold assent of the mind. It does not purify his heart, or renew his will, or change his moral nature, as saving faith always does. Its weakness is seen in the fact that it is unproductive. It does not motivate its possessor to any acts of self-denial or compassionate benevolence. This defective faith coexists with showing favoritism, or an unbridled tongue, or a passionate temper, or a disposition to decline accepting the blame for one's own sins.

Talk About It:
Answer the questions in verse 14.

B. Genuine Faith (vv. 15-20)

15. If a brother or sister be naked, and destitute of daily food,

16. And one of you say unto them, Depart in peace, be ye warmed and filled; notwithstanding ye give them not those things which are needful to the body; what doth it profit?

17. Even so faith, if it hath not works, is dead, being alone.

18. Yea, a man may say, Thou hast faith, and I have works: shew me thy faith without thy works, and I will shew thee my faith by my works.

19. Thou believest that there is one God; thou doest well: the devils also believe, and tremble.

20. But wilt thou know, O vain man, that faith without works is dead?

Talk About It:
1. What is "dead" (vv. 17, 20)?
2. What point does James make in referring to demons (v. 19)?

More Than Words
"A young boy, on an errand for his mother, had just bought a dozen eggs. Walking out of the store, he tripped and dropped the sack. All the eggs broke, and the sidewalk was a mess. The boy tried not to cry. A few people gathered to see if he was okay and to tell him how sorry they were. In the midst of the words of pity, one man handed the boy a quarter. Then he turned to the group and said, "I care 25 cents' worth. How much do the rest of you care?"
—Stanley C. Brown

wrought (v. 22)—worked together

perfect (v. 22)—complete

To illustrate what he is talking about in these verses, James said it is the bitterest mockery for a man who is himself living in ease and comfort to say to his shivering, starving brother, "Depart in peace. Do not be discouraged; God has said He will never forsake His people. He shall give His angels charge concerning you, and I myself will pray for you." Sentimental professions of concern which offer no practical help do not profit either person. They tempt the destitute man to give up, and they ruin the moral health of the false sympathizer. Mere lip compassion is not true compassion, and a professed faith that is barren of good works is dead in itself.

In verse 18 James issues a direct challenge to those who claim to be true and consistent believers. He defies professing Christians who divorce faith from practice to exhibit their faith apart from works. He says in effect, "A believer is to let his light shine. Well, I point to the new life I am now living as the appropriate example of my faith; but since you neglect good works, I challenge you to indicate how you can manifest your faith otherwise." A faith that produces no works is unable to show itself; therefore it is not true faith at all.

In verse 19, James cited an example of what he was talking about. If any professing Christian prided himself upon the correctness of his beliefs, here was a warning to him. If he was satisfied with the thought that he was holding fast to the doctrine of the unity of one God even while living in the midst of idol worshipers, this was useless unless it produced the fruit of holiness. The demons believe, and yet they remain demons—and condemned. The unclean spirits whom Jesus cast out had plenty of knowledge and belief regarding God and Christ. But their believing was a kind that made them shudder with terror when they realized the purpose of Jesus' mission and message. A mere assenting intellectual belief cannot cleanse from sin; it can only produce the fear of coming torment.

C. Examples of Genuine Faith (vv. 21-26)
21. Was not Abraham our father justified by works, when he had offered Isaac his son upon the altar?
22. Seest thou how faith wrought with his works, and by works was faith made perfect?
23. And the scripture was fulfilled which saith, Abraham believed God, and it was imputed unto him for righteousness: and he was called the Friend of God.
24. Ye see then how that by works a man is justified, and not by faith only.
25. Likewise also was not Rahab the harlot justified by works, when she had received the messengers, and had sent them out another way?
26. For as the body without the spirit is dead, so faith without works is dead also.

Paul said that Abraham was justified by faith before Isaac was born (see Romans 4). James said that he was justified by works because he offered up Isaac his son upon the altar. But, James was careful to add, in this crowning manifestation of Abraham's piety, the patriarch's faith cooperated with his works. The confidence that he had in God for so many years enabled him to be willing to obey the dreadful command to kill his only son. Only a strong faith in God's dependability could have given Abraham victorious passage through such an awful ordeal.

God surely knew Abraham well to ask him to do such a deed, knowing full well He would never allow Abraham to complete the job. On Abraham's part, he had to trust God's wisdom and purpose, as well as the final outcome, to attempt to carry out the command. After all, God had promised that Abraham's descendants would become a great nation through Isaac. So Abraham must have told God in essence, "OK, Lord, You've promised a great nation would spring from Isaac, and that can't happen if he's dead. So the only possible solution I see for this dilemma is for You to raise him back to life after I've obeyed You" (see Genesis 21:12; Hebrews 11:18, 19). Abraham had no doubts that he and Isaac would return home together (Genesis 22:5). And he put his faith into action through his obedience.

James gave Rahab as his second example. Her case seems to have been chosen because it was so unlike that of Abraham. Abraham was a Jew and the father of the chosen nation; Rahab was a pagan woman. Abraham had for many years received special training in the school of faith; Rahab had received no training at all. Abraham was a good and pure man; Rahab had lived a sinful and sensual life. Yet this degraded Canaanite obtained like precious faith with the illustrious patriarch Abraham.

These same two Old Testament examples are also cited in Hebrews 11. The contrast between Abraham and Rahab is useful to show that invariably good works flow from a living faith. Rahab's belief was expressed in her own words (Joshua 2:9-11), and her diligent attempts to guarantee the safety of the two spies at the risk of her own life brought her faith into prominence through her works.

CONCLUSION

Today's lesson is titled "How Christians Demonstrate Mercy." *Mercy* is "the outward manifestation of pity; it assumes need on the part of him who receives it, and resources adequate to meet the need on the part of him who shows it. It is used (a) of God, 'who is rich in mercy' (Ephesians 2:4) . . . and (b) of men; for since God is merciful to them, He would have them show mercy to one another (James 2:13)" (from *Vine's Expository Dictionary of Biblical Words*).

Instead of playing favorites, pouring out all our love on ourselves, and ignoring the needs of others, let's be merciful people who demonstrate our faith through our deeds.

1. What action of Abraham profoundly expressed his faith (vv. 21, 22)?
2. What was Abraham called, and why (v. 23)?
3. Why did Rahab have faith in God (see Joshua 2:8-10)?
4. How did Rahab express her faith (Joshua 2:2-4; James 2:25)?

"Faith is not belief without proof but trust without reservation."
—**D. Elton Trueblood**

GOLDEN TEXT CHALLENGE

"IF YE FULFILL THE ROYAL LAW ACCORDING TO THE SCRIPTURE, THOU SHALT LOVE THY NEIGHBOUR AS THYSELF, YE DO WELL" (James 2:8).

To avoid partiality we need to begin with the royal law of love. This deals with the two greatest commandments: "Thou shalt love the Lord thy God with all thine heart, and with all thy soul, and with all thy might" (Deuteronomy 6:5), and "Thou shalt love thy neighbour as thyself" (Leviticus 19:18).

There is no better illustration to use here than Jesus' encounter with the lawyer who was testing Him (Luke 10:25-37). After stating how to receive eternal life, Jesus was asked the question "Who is my neighbor?" He responded with the story of the Good Samaritan. After being robbed and beaten, a traveler lay helplessly on the road. Both a priest and a Levite came by. However, when they saw him, each continued on the other side of the road. Neither allowed compassion to influence his actions. Not until a Samaritan came by did help become available. Not only did he stop and bind up the man's wounds, but he also took him to the nearest inn and paid for lodging during the recuperation time.

This story illustrates not only love and compassion, but also that our loving actions are to be given to *whoever* is in need, at the time we are available and have the resources to meet the need. James 2:9 is explicit in its directive concerning avoiding partiality: it is sin. Those practicing partiality are in complete opposition to God's law. They are transgressors (sinners) just like anyone who breaks any other of God's laws.

Daily Devotions:

M. A Different Spirit
Numbers 14:20-24

T. Great in Mercy
Psalm 145:4-9

W. Show Mercy
Proverbs 3:1-4

T. Sin No More
John 8:3-11

F. God Shows Mercy to Us
Romans 5:6-11

S. God's Mercy Saved Us
Titus 3:1-6

How Christians Demonstrate Mercy

How Christians Live in Peace

James 3:1-18

INTRODUCTION

Solomon wrote, "To every thing there is a season, and a time to every purpose under the heaven: . . . a time to keep silence, and a time to speak" (Ecclesiastes 3:1, 7). That's wisdom—knowing when to speak and when to be quiet. How much more peace the Christian community would know if we as Christians practiced this advice. Perhaps more of us would do this if our tongue didn't keep getting in the way.

James said, "Consider what a great forest is set on fire by a small spark. The tongue also is a fire. . . . It corrupts the whole person . . . and is itself set on fire by hell. All kinds of animals . . . have been tamed by man, but no man can tame the tongue" (3:5-8, *NIV*).

Burning, evil, destructive, wild—such strong words to describe a four-inch, two-ounce part of our body. Yet James went even further, saying, "If anyone considers himself religious and yet does not keep a tight rein on his tongue, he deceives himself and his religion is worthless" (1:26, *NIV*).

Jesus Christ *always* ruled His tongue. He knew when to talk and when to be mum; His religion was not worthless. This frustrated and angered His chief enemies, the tongue-wagging religious leaders whose worship was hypocritical and vain (Matthew 15:7-9).

Is our attitude any better than that of the Pharisees? When we see a fellow Christian fall, do we immediately whip out our sword—the tongue—to accuse and judge, rather than seeking to redeem the person? May our tongue promote peace and hope, speaking of the second chance and the challenge to change. May we not speak about the speck in our brother's eye when there is a beam in our own eye (7:3).

Solomon wrote, "The tongue of the wise brings healing" (Proverbs 12:18, *NIV*). Does this describe your tongue?

Unit Theme:
Practical Christian Living (James)

Central Truth:
Christlike words and attitudes promote peace.

Focus:
Be warned of the destructiveness of un-Christlike words and attitudes, and abstain from these evils.

Context:
The Epistle of James was probably written between A.D. 47 and A.D. 51.

Golden Text:
"The wisdom that is from above is first pure, then peaceable, gentle, and easy to be intreated, full of mercy and good fruits, without partiality, and without hypocrisy" (James 3:17).

Study Outline:
I. By Recognizing the Tongue's Power (James 3:1-6)
II. By Taming Our Speech (James 3:7-12)
III. By Using Wisdom From God (James 3:13-18)

masters (v. 1)—
teachers

I. BY RECOGNIZING THE TONGUE'S POWER (James 3:1-6)
A. Grave Warning (vv. 1, 2)

1. My brethren, be not many masters, knowing that we shall receive the greater condemnation.

2. For in many things we offend all. If any man offend not in word, the same is a perfect man, and able also to bridle the whole body.

John Calvin may have been correct when he wrote of verse 1: "The common and almost universal interpretation of this passage is that the apostle discourages the desire for the office of teaching, and for this reason, because it is dangerous, and exposes one to a heavier judgment in case he transgresses. . . . But I take *masters* not to be those who performed a public duty in the church, but such as took upon them the right of passing judgment upon others, for such reprovers sought to be accounted as masters of morals."

The apostle's warning is against having censorious or critical tongues that are always seeking to set other people straight. To be always criticizing others is not a manifestation of godly wisdom but reveals instead our own imperfection in relation to God.

The apostle Paul declared, "Therefore thou art inexcusable, O man, whosoever thou art that judgest: for wherein thou judgest another, thou condemnest thyself; for thou that judgest doest the same things" (Romans 2:1).

James specifically addresses the problem of the unruly tongue in verse 2. The unruly tongue is a universal plague to mankind; it continually frustrates human efforts to control it. So difficult is it to control the tongue that James ascribes "perfection" to the man who does not offend with his words. We reveal the state of our inner lives by what we say. Jesus said to the Pharisees, "How can ye, being evil, speak good things? For out of the abundance of the heart the mouth speaketh" (Matthew 12:34).

B. Bits and Rudders (vv. 3-5)

3. Behold, we put bits in the horses' mouths, that they may obey us; and we turn about their whole body.

4. Behold also the ships, which though they be so great, and are driven of fierce winds, yet are they turned about with a very small helm, whithersoever the governor listeth.

5. Even so the tongue is a little member, and boasteth great things. Behold, how great a matter a little fire kindleth!

helm (v. 4)—rudder

the governor listeth (v. 4)—"the pilot desires" (*NKJV*)

Without a bit in the horse's mouth it is impossible for the rider to have control over him. Likewise, without a bridle on the tongue, no one can govern himself appropriately. David recognized this truth: "I will take heed to my ways, that I sin not with my tongue: I will keep my mouth with a bridle" (Psalm 39:1). Moses, the meekest of men, was forbidden by God to enter the Land of Promise because "he spake unadvisedly with his lips" (106:33).

How Christians Live in Peace

It has been said, "We rule irrational animals with a bit; how much more ought we to be able to govern ourselves?"

The bit is little, but the rider can control the whole body of the horse with it. The rudder (helm) is small, but it enables the steersman to guide a large boat. A tiny spark may set a huge forest on fire. Likewise, the tongue is a little member of the body, but a victory over it can save the whole person from many evils.

The evil tongue is a tormentor. It is a dagger that can stab the hearts of loved ones. It can be a scourge that tortures the lives of others. But disciplined by the grace and Spirit of God and governed by godly wisdom, the tongue ministers healing and strength and blessing to others.

C. Dangerous Fire (v. 6)

6. And the tongue is a fire, a world of iniquity: so is the tongue among our members, that it defileth the whole body, and setteth on fire the course of nature; and it is set on fire of hell.

James used the term *fire* to represent all iniquity, saying that it finds its expression in the tongue. It is almost impossible to seethe with anger or bitterness, burn with pride or selfishness, or lust for power without expressing it somehow with the tongue. James added that the tongue is "set on fire of hell." The Greek word for *hell* in this verse is not *hades* (the abode of the dead) but *gehenna*. In James' day the word *gehenna* (hell) was used to describe the torments of hell as a place of burning or punishment for the wicked. The garbage dump south of Jerusalem where the refuse of the city burned with a stench day and night was referred to as "the Valley of Gehenna." The tongue set on fire by hell evokes images of torment and filth associated with the evil tongue.

As a spark can set a forest on fire, as one lighted match can start a conflagration, so the tongue can kindle "the course of nature" (the whole life) into a flame.

II. BY TAMING OUR SPEECH (James 3:7-12)

A. Unruly Evil (vv. 7, 8)

7. For every kind of beasts, and of birds, and of serpents, and of things in the sea, is tamed, and hath been tamed of mankind:

8. But the tongue can no man tame; it is an unruly evil, full of deadly poison.

The apostle characterized the tongue as an untamed beast. We marvel at humanity's success in calming the wild nature of various animals known for their ability to hunt and kill, yet we fail to tame the muscle in our mouth. In fact, James stressed our inability to tame the tongue. Behind the teeth lies a deadly weapon; it can dispense death-dealing poisonous words.

> "You cannot be hurt by something you did not say."
> *—Marquee Messages*

nature—"his life" (*NIV*)

Talk About It:
How can the tongue defile "the whole body"?

Talk About It:
Why can no one tame the tongue (v. 8)?

> "You never see a fish on the wall with its mouth shut."
> *—Marquee Messages*

similitude (v. 9)—
likeness

9. Therewith bless we God, even the Father; and therewith curse we men, which are made after the similitude of God.

10. Out of the same mouth proceedeth blessing and cursing. My brethren, these things ought not so to be.

11. Doth a fountain send forth at the same place sweet water and bitter?

12. Can the fig tree, my brethren, bear olive berries? either a vine, figs? so can no fountain both yield salt water and fresh.

Talk About It
1. Why are "blessing God" and "cursing men" incompatible (vv. 9, 10)?
2. What is the point of the questions in verses 11 and 12?

A person may put the faculty of speech to its highest use and then almost immediately afterward wickedly abuse it. The tongue has been given us that we might bless God the Father. To utter praise of the Divine is the most ennobling exercise of human speech. The Christian calls God "Lord" and adores Him for His eternal glory; he also calls Him "Father" and blesses Him for His redeeming grace. Then with absolute inconsistency, the same mouth that raised God may be heard invoking evil upon others. How often do those who profess godliness speak spiteful words? Do not Christians who belong to the same congregation sometimes backbite one another? Do not believers of different fellowships often, out of mere sectarian rivalry, denounce one another's churches?

God is the Creator of all humanity, for we are made after the likeness of God. God and us are closely related to each other by creation and through Christ's incarnation and mission. Reverence for God requires that we respect all people as creatures of God. How inconsistent, then, for the same mouth to bless the Father but curse His children.

The inconsistency found in humans is not found in the world of nature. A spring of water cannot transgress the law of its nature. A fruit tree can only produce fruit according to its kind. How unnatural, then, that in the moral world the same fountain of speech should emit a rill of clear, sweet praise and soon afterward a torrent of bitter slander or evil utterances. In the case of a person who has experienced the renewing grace of the Holy Spirit, this unnatural inconsistency of speech ought not to be.

"The hypocrite's crime is that he bears false witness against himself."
—Hannah Arendt

III. BY USING WISDOM FROM GOD (James 3:13-18)
A. The Proof of Wisdom (v. 13)

conversation (v. 13)—conduct

13. Who is a wise man and endued with knowledge among you? let him shew out of a good conversation his works with meekness of wisdom.

Talk About It:
How does the wise and understanding person live?

James asked, "Who is really wise and understanding?" not who is just claiming to be. Is the question decided by how well one can engage in controversies with rivals, or in how he can set simple people straight? The temptation of the knowledgeable is to be arrogant and impractical. But James offered a different standard for the wise.

When James raised the question about wisdom, he did not have in mind the Greek concept of speculative or theoretical wisdom, but the idea of practical wisdom that enables one to live the life of godliness.

James' response to his own question, in effect, was that actions speak louder than words. That is, true spiritual wisdom will be seen in right conduct and in moral behavior. The wise man's *works* are not merely the facts he teaches but the deeds he does. If his wisdom does not transform his life, it is useless. A wise and understanding person demonstrates in what he says and by what he does that he possesses wisdom.

The word for *meekness* was used by James earlier to show the unresisting way God's Word is to be received (1:21). The term describes one who welcomes God's dealings even if He sends trials (cf. Romans 8:28). Such meekness puts priority on accepting God's circumstances and does not react in kind to provocations. The emphasis in James 3:13 falls on that characteristic of wisdom described as humility. It is a gentleness "that comes from wisdom" (*NIV*) or that is characteristic of wisdom. Meekness is not weakness; it is power under control. Meekness is the right use of power, and wisdom is the right use of knowledge. They go together. The phrase "meekness of wisdom" is indeed an appropriate one.

"Goodness is something so simple: Always live for others, never to seek one's own advantage."
—Dag Hammarskjold

B. False Wisdom (vv. 14-16)

14. But if ye have bitter envying and strife in your hearts, glory not, and lie not against the truth.

15. This wisdom descendeth not from above, but is earthly, sensual, devilish.

16. For where envying and strife is, there is confusion and every evil work.

The opposite of a gentle spirit controlled by wisdom is a heart filled with "bitter envy and selfish ambition" (v. 14, *NIV*). "In your hearts" is an important inclusion of this verse because in Hebrew thought the heart was the source of all moral action (Proverbs 4:23). It is evident James knew that among the members of the church were some whose spirits were characterized by bitter envy and selfish ambition. James made it clear by the adjective *bitter* that he was referring to a sinful zeal. He did not explain what caused the bitterness. However, he indicated that harboring bitter envy was a sin.

The Greek word for *bitter* is the same one used by James to describe bitter water that comes from a spring (v. 11). The word denotes a sharp, pungent characteristic. *Envy* is from the word *zelos*, which can be translated "jealousy" or "zeal." If this condition existed among his readers, he insisted, they must "not boast about it or deny the truth" (v. 14, *NIV*).

Talk About It:
1. What wisdom is "earthly, sensual" (vv. 14, 15)?
2. What does "envy and selfish ambition" (v. 16, *NIV*) cause?

When God's wisdom is at work, there is a sense of humility and submission and a desire for God to get all the glory. The word for *boast* denotes here a glorying against something. In this case, James said it is a boasting against the truth. *Lie* in Greek is the word *pseudomai*, which means "to utter an untruth or to attempt to deceive by falsehood." The prefix *pseudo* has become a part of our English vocabulary.

James used strong words in verse 15 to describe the nature of false wisdom. It could not be spiritual (that is, taught by the Spirit) because it was rooted in the earth; it is earthbound, not heaven-inspired. Further, it is unspiritual—human and sensual.

James described three sources of that kind of wisdom: earthly, sensual and devilish (demonic). *Earthly* wisdom is as simple as the word implies. Such wisdom comes from the worldly system. James emphatically stated it does not come from above. *Sensual* wisdom, rather than originating in the spiritual realm, originates in the natural, the animal, the fleshly realm. *Demonic* wisdom comes from the devil himself. James proceeded to identify the results of this kind of wisdom—envy and strife—which produce "confusion and every evil work" (v. 16).

Origin determines outcome: worldly wisdom will produce worldly results; spiritual wisdom will give spiritual results. Worldly wisdom produces trouble. The word for *confusion* means "disorder that comes from instability." It is also rendered *unstable* (1:8) and *unruly* (3:8). Confusion sets the stage for "every evil practice" (v. 16, *NIV*). *Evil* here means "worthless, of no account." This phrase refers specifically to worthless activity, to deeds that are bad because they are good-for-nothing and cannot produce any real benefit.

Instead of promoting harmony, this *wisdom* causes disruption and unruliness; instead of creating fellowship among the members, it destroys it. Such wisdom cannot come from God. James was no doubt speaking of disturbance and turmoil in the church.

C. Pure Wisdom (vv. 17, 18)

17. But the wisdom that is from above is first pure, then peaceable, gentle, and easy to be intreated, full of mercy and good fruits, without partiality, and without hypocrisy.

18. And the fruit of righteousness is sown in peace of them that make peace.

In verse 17 James gives a sevenfold description of divine wisdom.

1. *Pure.* Why is purity mentioned as the first characteristic of wisdom? Wisdom that finds its origin in God is pure because God himself is pure, that is, holy. Therefore, purity is the first requirement in the Christian's life. This quality means being chaste, clean or innocent. The word *pure* comes from the same

---

"Stop justifying selfishness because 'the world is a jungle.' It can also be a garden, depending on whether one wants to plant and water, or to plunder and uproot."
—Sydney Harris

easy to be intreated (v. 17)—"willing to yield" (*NKJV*)

Talk About It:
1. What is godly wisdom filled with, and what is it missing (v. 17)?
2. Describe the harvest in verse 18.

How Christians Live in Peace

root word as *holy, hallow* and *sanctification*, and is the opposite of the self-seeking attitude of verses 14-16. This virtue stands *first* in importance. It is logically basic to all that follows. The term *pure* is frequently mentioned in the New Testament to describe not only freedom from ceremonial defilement but sincere moral and spiritual integrity associated with Christ, as in 1 John 3:3.

2. *Peaceable.* Divine wisdom is "peace-loving" (*NIV*) in contrast to the bitter spirit of competitiveness and selfish ambition described in James 3:14. The term *peaceable* may be used to cover the narrower classical definition of "freedom from strife with others" as well as the distinctly Hebraic meaning of inward peace (*shalom*)—that is, well-being, referring especially to salvation. The Christian makes peace with God when he is justified; as he surrenders his life to God, he is further blessed with the peace of God. He then becomes a peacemaker for God. By his attitude toward others he shows that he loves peace.

The peace of God dominates the believer's thinking so that people see him or her as a tower of strength. Indeed, all of the believer's ways are pleasing and all his or her "paths are peace" (Proverbs 3:17).

3. *Gentle.* This godly wisdom is "considerate" (*NIV*). It carries the meaning of moderation without moral compromise, and is courteous and forbearing. God is gentle and kind, although He has justifiable reason to be stern and punitive toward people in their sin. This also is the very spirit of Jesus.

God's people also are marked by this Godlike quality, not insisting on their rights according to the letter of the law, but exercising love's leniency instead. Gentleness conveys the thought of respect for the feelings of others, a willingness to waive all rigor and severity in dealing with others. The gentle person quietly gathers all the facts before he gives his opinion. He refrains from placing himself first.

4. *Easy to be entreated.* This wisdom is open to reason. There should always be a certain yieldingness about us—a readiness to admit that even *we* might be wrong. This wisdom is open to new light; it is willing to learn from others. It has a conciliatory attitude and is ready to cooperate when a better way is shown.

5. *Full of mercy and good fruits.* The only double characteristic in the list, this wisdom stands in direct contrast to "every evil work" (v. 16). The word for *mercy* is used in the New Testament only in reference to God himself or to godly people. Mercy is a part of the character of God. Mercy is more than a feeling of pity; it is an attitude of compassion toward those in distress that leads to practical help. Mercy prefers to deal with the needy in terms of what is needed rather than what is deserved. It displays compassion by performing good deeds.

6. *Without partiality*. This means divine wisdom is without discrimination and without a divided mind. The Greek word emphasizes both acting with no indecision or uncertainty and making no distinction (showing no partiality) in one's dealings with others. This wisdom shows no favoritism and discriminates against no one. It also acts consistently; it does not take one position in one circumstance and another in a different one.

7. *Without hypocrisy*. Divine wisdom is sincere and genuine. It causes one's life to agree with what is in the heart. The Greek word translated *hypocrite* in the New Testament means "one who wears a mask, an actor." This wisdom does not need to work under a mask since it has nothing to hide. Wherever you find God's people pretending and hiding, you can be sure the wisdom of this world is governing their ministry.

Having noted the effects of false wisdom (vv. 14, 15), James now mentions the effect of divine wisdom using an agricultural metaphor. It produces "the fruit of righteousness" (v. 18). James returned to the use of the word *fruit* to indicate the vast difference between man-made results and God-given fruit. Fruit is the product of life and has in it the seeds of more fruit. The *NIV* renders verse 18, "Peacemakers who sow in peace raise a harvest of righteousness."

"Blessed are the peacemakers: for they shall be called the children of God."
—**Jesus**
(Matthew 5:9)

CONCLUSION

The Lord desires that peace reign in the family and in the church. For this to happen, we must gain control of our tongues and let God's wisdom guide us. If our tongues are unbridled and we lean on human wisdom, chaos and infighting will result. But if our words are held in check and we walk in divine wisdom, peace will prevail.

GOLDEN TEXT CHALLENGE

"THE WISDOM THAT IS FROM ABOVE IS FIRST PURE, THEN PEACEABLE, GENTLE, AND EASY TO BE INTREATED, FULL OF MERCY AND GOOD FRUITS, WITHOUT PARTIALITY, AND WITHOUT HYPOCRISY" (James 3:17).

God is the origin of true wisdom. It is not the product of human culture but is supernatural. And being a gift from God, it is good and perfect in all its characteristics.

James represents heavenly wisdom as distinguished by seven attributes. *Seven* was the symbolic number for perfection among the Jews. There are seven colors in the rainbow of the Christian life, which, when blended, form its pure white sunlight.

Purity, the first of these seven, is marked off from the others because it refers to what a person is within his or her own heart. The other six deal with qualities shown by true wisdom in one's behavior toward others.

How Christians Live in Peace

The heavenly wisdom is *peaceable*—it seeks peace—while earthly wisdom is characterized by rivalry and division.

Earthly wisdom is pushy and brash—selfishly seeking its own way—while divine wisdom is *gentle*, or courteous and considerate.

Heavenly wisdom is *easy to be intreated*—accessible, open to conviction—while earthly wisdom is hardheaded and close-minded.

God's wisdom is filled with *mercy and good fruits*—noted for compassionate feelings and actions—while human wisdom produces bitter fruit from a self-seeking heart.

Carnal wisdom is unpredictable and unreliable, while divine wisdom is *without partiality*—steady, persistent, and purposeful.

God's wisdom is *without hypocrisy*—always being what it appears and professes to be—while human wisdom plays power games and wears masks.

James said that this divine wisdom, which we desperately need, is ours for the asking (1:5).

Daily Devotions:
M. Peace in the Land
Leviticus 26:3-8
T. Dwelling in God's House
Psalm 84:1-4
W. Prince of Peace
Isaiah 9:3-7
T. Jesus Gives Peace
John 14:23-27
F. The Author of Peace
1 Corinthians 14:29-33
S. Christ Is Our Peace
Ephesians 2:14-18

How Christians Overcome Worldliness

James 4:1-17

Unit Theme:
Practical Christian
Living (James)

Central Truth:
Christians avoid
worldliness by living
humbly before God.

Focus:
Identify and avoid
worldliness and live
humbly before God.

Context:
The Epistle of James
was probably written
between A.D. 47 and
A.D. 51.

Golden Text:
"Humble yourselves
in the sight of the Lord,
and he shall lift you
up" (James 4:10).

Study Outline:
 I. By Controlling
    Desires
    (James 4:1-7)
 II. By Drawing Close
     to God
     (James 4:8-12)
 III. By Putting God First
     (James 4:13-17)

INTRODUCTION

Christians live between the times: between the time of our conversion and the time of our consummation, which will come at death or the second coming of Christ. We live between the time of our justification and the moment of our glorification.

During this in-between time, we find ourselves "sojourners and pilgrims" in a world where we have to wrestle with "fleshly lusts which war against the soul" (1 Peter 2:11, *NKJV*). The world continually calls us to cave in to the sinful desires of the flesh, but James warns that whoever is "a friend of the world is the enemy of God" (4:4).

Christians realize that life is full of mirages which people chase after to satisfy their cravings for earthly satisfaction. Needy, hungry, thirsty and tired souls who try to find satisfaction through power, prestige or pleasure never find lasting rest, security or peace. Proverbs 14:12 captures this distressing futility: "There is a way which seemeth right unto a man, but the end thereof are the ways of death."

The spirit of this age revolves around self and caters to the ego. So how should Christians live in this illusory world until Jesus comes again? We must realize we are facing three major foes—the world, the flesh and the devil—and place our dependence on God. It is only through faith in God and a total commitment to Him that we can overcome the spirit of worldliness.

I. BY CONTROLLING DESIRES (James 4:1-7)
A. Friendship With the World (vv. 1-4)

1. From whence come wars and fightings among you? come they not hence, even of your lusts that war in your members?

2. Ye lust, and have not: ye kill, and desire to have, and cannot obtain: ye fight and war, yet ye have not, because ye ask not.

3. Ye ask, and receive not, because ye ask amiss, that ye may consume it upon your lusts.

4. Ye adulterers and adulteresses, know ye not that the friendship of the world is enmity with God? whosoever therefore will be a friend of the world is the enemy of God.

The quality of life portrayed here by James is appallingly low. The readers are charged with wars and fightings, self-indulgence, prayerlessness, lust, adultery, envy, pride, slander, and murder. In fact, James painted such a depressing picture that many Bible scholars question whether he was addressing Christian Jews or unbelieving Jews. For example, Alfred Plummer says there are places in this letter where James "seems to go beyond the precise circle of readers addressed in the opening words, and to glance at the Jewish nation, whether outside Palestine or not, and whether Christian or not." He therefore feels that James was thinking here, in part at least, of the bitter contentions which divided Pharisees, Sadducees, Herodians, Essenes, Zealots and Samaritans from one another (*The Expositor's Bible*).

Curtis Vaughn writes: "We must not exclude the Jewish Christians entirely from these charges. The situation described must to some extent have been applicable to them. Though believers, they were still endued with the spirit of their unconverted neighbors and had some of the same evil passions at work within them.

"The whole passage, then, is an in-depth treatment of the havoc wrought when worldly wisdom rather than heavenly wisdom dominates the life. This worldly-mindedness expresses itself in choosing pleasure (the passion for self-gratification) as the chief end of life, in harsh criticism of fellow Christians, and in arrogant disregard of God" (*James: A Study Guide*).

In verse 4, James said the problem is the incompatibility of worldliness and godliness. The two simply will not mix. The Christian has been called to renounce the world and submit to God.

"The 'friend of the world' is out for pleasure," writes Russell Jones. "The end is always the opposite of pleasure—conflict and frustration. The worldly man either neglects or abuses prayer, the key to God's storehouse of satisfaction. When prayer is neglected, when God as the source of all is ignored, we fail

Talk About It:
1. Where do "fights and quarrels" (v. 1, *NIV*) originate?
2. Name two reasons a person might not receive from God (vv. 2, 3).
3. Why is friendship with the world hatred toward God (v. 4)?

"We are safe at sea, safer in the storm God sends us, than when we are befriended by the world."
—Jeremy Taylor

to get what the deeper self desires. Frustration is the result of not going to God for our needs. If we attempt to use prayer selfishly, we fail again. God cannot give us the things that will build up our sinful self. To do so would be contrary to His deity" (*Preacher's Homiletic Library*).

B. More Grace (vv. 5, 6)

5. Do ye think that the scripture saith in vain, The spirit that dwelleth in us lusteth to envy?

6. But he giveth more grace. Wherefore he saith, God resisteth the proud, but giveth grace unto the humble.

lusteth to envy (v. 5)—"envies intensely" (*NIV*)

Talk About It:
Contrast God's response to the proud with His response to the humble.

Verse 5 is a confirmation of the fact that friendship with the world and friendship with God are incompatible. "The Spirit who dwells in us yearns jealously" (*NKJV*). God has put His Holy Spirit within the Christian and regards with intense concern the Christian's harboring of any rival spirit in his heart. God claims us entirely for Himself. No alien relationship, such as friendship with the world, will be tolerated by Him. He wants the undivided devotion of every human heart.

Verse 6 emphasizes that although God makes great demands on His people, He also makes great provision for them: "He giveth more grace." The word *grace* is used here to describe God's generous and effective help. "More grace" means that He gives abundant grace, all the help that people need. The difficulties of living a separated life for God in a wicked world are many and formidable, but God's grace is more than adequate for all our needs. God is indeed a jealous God and makes exacting demands of us, but He provides what is necessary to enable us to resist those influences and forces that would draw us away to the world. The greater our needs, the greater is God's supply of grace.

"The proud man is possessed by things; the humble man possesses things and uses them for the good of others and the glory of God."
—Warren Wiersbe

C. Submission and Resistance (v. 7)

7. Submit yourselves therefore to God. Resist the devil, and he will flee from you.

Talk About It:
What makes the devil flee?

A literal rendering of "Submit yourselves . . . to God" is "Set yourselves under God." To set ourselves under God is to subordinate ourselves to Him to bring our will under His control, to yield sincere obedience to His commands.

The call for submission is followed by a command to resist the devil. Actually this is involved in our submission to God. To be a loyal subject of God's, one must, of necessity, resist God's archfoe. The Greek word used here for *resist* means "take your stand against." It is used by Paul in Ephesians 6:13, where we are charged to "withstand" the assaulting forces of evil. The word is also used by Peter in 1 Peter 5:9 in another command to "resist" the devil. We resist him when we refuse to yield to him, when we fearlessly defy him.

How Christians Overcome Worldliness

II. BY DRAWING CLOSE TO GOD (James 4:8-12)

A. Come Near (v. 8)

8. Draw nigh to God, and he will draw nigh to you. Cleanse your hands, ye sinners; and purify your hearts, ye double minded.

We are to earnestly seek for God, and the assurance is given that if we do so, He will unfailingly respond. No one has ever really sought Him in vain. Since God is omnipresent, He is always near. This reference has to do with fellowship and communion.

How are we to draw near to God? We cannot walk in harmony with God and with the world; we cannot live in sin and have fellowship with God. So we have to "cleanse" our hands if we want to hold the hand of God. The double-minded person— the one whose heart is divided between God and the world— is called upon to purify his heart, to set it completely on God.

Note that in Old Testament times the washing of the hands was a ritual required especially of the priests as a part of the process that qualified them to perform their ceremonial duties (Exodus 30:20). By adding "purify your hearts," James further accentuated the symbolism of cleansing he had already used in this verse.

Talk About It:
How do we "draw nigh to God"?

"God doesn't seek for golden vessels, and does not ask for silver ones, but He must have clean ones."
—**David Livingstone**

B. Humble Yourselves (vv. 9, 10)

9. Be afflicted, and mourn, and weep: let your laughter be turned to mourning, and your joy to heaviness.

10. Humble yourselves in the sight of the Lord, and he shall lift you up.

There is nothing wrong with joy and laughter in themselves. The Lord wants our mouths to be filled with laughter and our hearts with joy. But if we are not right with Him, if sin has come between us and God, if we are out of fellowship with Him, if our hands are soiled with sin and our hearts are divided—we ought to "be afflicted [grieve], mourn, and weep." Only through sorrow for our sins, through repentance in true humility, will God lift us up to sit with Him in "heavenly places." Then we can experience joy everlasting in His presence.

Talk About It:
1. When must we "grieve, mourn and wail" (v. 9, *NIV*)?
2. What does it mean to be lifted up by God?

C. Don't Judge (vv. 11, 12)

11. Speak not evil one of another, brethren. He that speaketh evil of his brother, and judgeth his brother, speaketh evil of the law, and judgeth the law: but if thou judge the law, thou art not a doer of the law, but a judge.

12. There is one lawgiver, who is able to save and to destroy: who art thou that judgest another?

Verse 11 warns us not to slander another person. This is an evil act which contradicts the law of God. For instance, Leviticus 19:16 commands, "You shall not go about as a slanderer among your people" (*NASB*). Proverbs 10:18 declares, "Whoever spreads slander is a fool" (*NIV*).

Talk About It:
1. If we condemn other people, what are we really doing (v. 11)?

"Wanted: people who overlook the faults of others as easily as they do their own."
—*Marquee Messages*

By breaking the law of God through speaking evil of others, we are putting ourselves above the law of God. Rather than being a "doer" of God's command, James says, we make ourselves a "judge" of His command. However, verse 12 emphasizes, "There is only one Lawgiver and Judge" (*NIV*). The Lord God, the only One who is able both to save and destroy life, is also the One who establishes the laws we must live by.

So James raises the question, "Who are you to judge your neighbor?" (*NIV*). The answer is, we have no right or authority to sit in judgment on others.

III. BY PUTTING GOD FIRST (James 4:13-17)
A. Don't Be Presumptuous (vv. 13-16)

13. Go to now, ye that say, To day or to morrow we will go into such a city, and continue there a year, and buy and sell, and get gain:

14. Whereas ye know not what shall be on the morrow. For what is your life? It is even a vapour, that appeareth for a little time, and then vanisheth away.

15. For that ye ought to say, If the Lord will, we shall live, and do this, or that.

16. But now ye rejoice in your boastings: all such rejoicing is evil.

Talk About It:
1. What is our life like (v. 14)?
2. How should we approach tomorrow (v. 15)?
3. What is "evil," and why (v. 16)?

In this section James points out contrasting attitudes toward plans for the future and the will of God. Of course, considering God's will in all our actions is the attitude every Christian should cultivate. Some believers were confidently asserting that they could make plans for a year. Of course, their plans included making a profit. They were giving exclusive attention to the affairs of this life with little or no thought for God. They acted as if they had complete control of the future.

No allowance was made for unforeseen circumstances. These businessmen were confident they would be able to carry their plans all the way to completion. James pointed out the fallacy of their thinking. They were ignorant concerning the future: "Whereas ye know not what shall be on the morrow" (v. 14). They were disregarding the scriptural warning "Boast not thyself of to morrow; for thou knowest not what a day may bring forth" (Proverbs 27:1). Their planning in absolute disregard of God and this admonition was the essence of worldliness.

No Christian can safely assume that he can live independent of God. To leave God out of one's plans is an arrogant assumption of self-sufficiency. Whether people recognize it or not, they will "live and do this or that" only *if* it is the Lord's will (James 4:15). Obviously, the early Christians did not regard the words "if the Lord will" as a ritual of piety that would validate the plans they had made.

This recognition of our dependence on God for the future is not an excuse for inactivity, nor should it discourage us from planning for the future. Having committed our all to Him, we may continue our planned activities under the encouraging sense of God's sustaining grace.

Human boasting (v. 16) is worthless, for it gives man and not God the glory. Boasting of what they could or could not do, without subjecting themselves to God's will, was sinful. Ignoring Divine Providence, the Jewish businesspeople were holding themselves up before others, claiming success. They claimed to control their destiny. James viewed such talk as *evil*, using a Greek word meaning "wicked."

B. Do Good (v. 17)

17. Therefore to him that knoweth to do good, and doeth it not, to him it is sin.

James concluded the section with a proverbial saying that perhaps circulated in the Jewish world of his day: "Anyone, then, who knows the good he ought to do and doesn't do it, sins" (v. 17, *NIV*). Although this statement may apply to any number of situations, James intended it to refer to the immediately preceding text.

Talk About It:
Explain the meaning of verse 17.

Sin should not be taken lightly. This is especially true of the sin of omission. Neglecting the needs of our neighbor is the equivalent of ignoring God and is therefore a sin against the law of God.

CONCLUSION

Here are the aspects of worldliness found in James: fights, quarrels, covetousness, greed, double-mindedness, slander, rebellion, boasting, selfishness, and hard-heartedness. The tragedy is that not only do we find these things in the secular world we live in but also in the church. It is up to us as individual believers to humble ourselves before the Lord, grieve over our worldly attitudes and actions, purify our hearts and minds, and draw near to God.

If we will submit to God, the devil will flee from us, and God will draw near to us and lift us up. We can lead holy lives in an unholy world.

GOLDEN TEXT CHALLENGE

"HUMBLE YOURSELVES IN THE SIGHT OF THE LORD, AND HE SHALL LIFT YOU UP" (James 4:10).

Philippians 2:10 declares that "every knee should bow" and "every tongue should confess that Jesus Christ is Lord." Not only *should* this happen, but one day even unbelievers *will* humble themselves before God (see Revelation 20:11-15).

In our Golden Text, James tells his readers it is time to humble themselves before God. Self-abasement is a decisive act, and James urges his readers to do so at once. This is not to be a forced humiliation but a voluntary submission unto God. The submissive believer will be lifted up by God in both this life and the life to come.

How Christians Demonstrate Caring

James 5:7-20

INTRODUCTION

In the first six verses of chapter 5, James wrote to people who believed they were self-sufficient because of their wealth. They were hoarding their riches, which they gained by abusing the weak. James said they should "weep and howl" because of the miseries that awaited them (v. 1).

Verse 4 describes one way the wealthy had been taking advantage of others—by cheating common laborers. These workers were like slaves who had no legal action open to them. They had been cheated by their bosses, and no court would hear their case. So they turned to the Lord, and He heard their cry.

The Lord had seen every selfish act of the rich. They had been *wanton* (v. 5), meaning "self-indulgent," and lived in luxury. Just as cattle are unaware that their feasting will end in their slaughter, so the rich were ignorant that their sensual indulgences would bring them down.

In their complete self-absorption, the wealthy "oppressed and acted very unjustly, to get estates; when they had them, they gave way to luxury and sensuality, till they had lost all sense and feeling of the wants or afflictions of others; and they [would] persecute and kill without remorse" (Matthew Henry).

The remainder of chapter 5—the subject of today's lesson—portrays how Christians must not live like the self-absorbed rich. Instead of greedily grabbing everything they can, believers should stand firm and patiently await the Lord's coming, trusting in His compassion and mercy. Rather than seeking satisfaction through gold and silver, Christians should find lasting strength and joy through prayer and praise.

Instead of cheating people who are weak, Christians should pray for them. Rather than condemning people, believers must reach out to forgive and restore. Instead of living in coldhearted pride, Christians should confess their faults to each other and pray together.

Unit Theme:
Practical Christian Living (James)

Central Truth:
Compassionate prayer can bring spiritual and physical healing.

Focus:
Perceive the importance of caring for others and show Christ's love to them.

Context:
The Epistle of James was probably written between A.D. 47 and A.D. 51.

Golden Text:
"Confess your faults one to another, and pray one for another, that ye may be healed. The effectual fervent prayer of a righteous man availeth much" (James 5:16).

Study Outline:
I. By Exhibiting Patience (James 5:7-12)
II. By Praying for One Another (James 5:13-18)
III. By Rescuing the Erring (James 5:19, 20)

I. BY EXHIBITING PATIENCE (James 5:7-12)

A. With Hope (vv. 7, 8)

7. Be patient therefore, brethren, unto the coming of the Lord. Behold, the husbandman waiteth for the precious fruit of the earth, and hath long patience for it, until he receive the early and latter rain.

8. Be ye also patient; stablish your hearts: for the coming of the Lord draweth nigh.

We will never outgrow the need for patience. This virtue is useful regardless of our station in life. James' present discussion grew logically out of the account of the oppression by the rich (vv. 1-6), as indicated by the word *therefore* (v. 7). After James vented his indignation toward the rich, he turned his attention to the "brethren." He expressed his concern for them, urging them to exercise the virtue of patience. He resorted to repetition; four times he employed the term *patience* (vv. 7-10).

The first part of chapter 5 describes the terrible oppression of the righteous. Their suffering was both economic and physical. James did not give a complete listing of how the righteous suffer, but his command to be patient must be seen against the Christian's life in a hostile environment. "Be patient therefore" looks back to sieges of suffering. But to be patient, as James used the word, is much more than passively waiting for the time to pass.

The Greek verb for "be patient" means "to be long-tempered and long-suffering, to use self-restraint so as not to retaliate." The opposite conduct would be to display wrath and to take revenge. James knew that the readers of this epistle were unable to defend themselves against the oppressors; therefore, he urged them to exercise patience and leave matters in the hands of God, who would come to deliver them. The word for *coming* refers to the bodily presence of the Lord. So James was calling for an experience in patience that would last "until the Lord's coming" (*NIV*). That event was held before them as a motive for patience because it would terminate their subjection to oppression and injustice. James took it for granted that the Lord's return was a living hope in the early church.

In counseling for patience, James used the example of the farmer who waits for the "precious fruit of the earth" (v. 7) until it is ready for harvest. He waits for the early rains and the latter rains. The crops are precious because they provide food to sustain physical life. The farmer works long and hard to receive the harvest. The ground has to be prepared. During Bible times this often meant clearing away the stones and thorns so that a crop could be planted. In the parable of the sower, Jesus said some of the seed sowed fell on stony ground, some among thorns, and some on good ground. The seed in the good ground

Talk About It:
1. What can agriculture teach us about the coming of the Lord?
2. What does it mean to "establish" (v. 8, *NKJV*) your heart?

How Christians Demonstrate Caring

produced a thirty-, sixty-, or hundredfold harvest. From the perspective of a hardworking farmer, each crop is precious.

The early rains, generally arriving in a series of thunderstorms, come in the latter part of October or in early November. The farmer anxiously awaits these rains, since they are necessary to soften the hard-baked soil for plowing and sowing. The bulk of the rains come during December through February. The latter rains fall during late April or May. These late rains, accompanied by warmer temperatures than in winter, are important for the maturing of the crops. That is a long time to wait for the harvest, yet the farmer patiently waits, realizing he cannot hurry the process.

In the same way, James assured the early believers, God is always on time, and we cannot hurry the process. Instead, they were instructed to "establish" (v. 8, *NKJV*) their hearts. Thus, they were urged to strengthen and make firm their inner life as a decisive act. The verb conveys the thought of strengthening and supporting something so that it will stand firm and unmovable. The reason given for standing firm is that "the Lord's coming is near" (*NIV*).

> "Prayer of the modern American: 'Dear God, I pray for patience. And I want it right now!'"
> —Oden Arnold

B. Without Complaining (v. 9)

9. Grudge not one against another, brethren, lest ye be condemned: behold, the judge standeth before the door.

The biblical concept of patience is not simply to endure something but to do so without complaint. In today's language the Greek word translated "grudge" (v. 9) might be better translated "complain." Some authorities tell us the verb literally signifies a groan. The readers of this epistle were experiencing pressures from within and from without the assembly because of the oppressive situations in which they found themselves. James' readers lost their patience. In time they gave vent to their repressed feelings and lashed out at those who were close to them.

Talk About It:
Explain the warning in this verse.

Groaning and grumbling is the opposite of being joyful, contented, and thankful. At times the believer may find himself in difficult circumstances, begin to grumble, and fall into sin. To continue this kind of practice results in judgment. To make the picture more graphic, James wrote that "the Judge is standing at the door!" (v. 9, *NKJV*).

C. With Perspective (vv. 10, 11)

10. Take, my brethren, the prophets, who have spoken in the name of the Lord, for an example of suffering affliction, and of patience.

11. Behold, we count them happy which endure. Ye have heard of the patience of Job, and have seen the end of the Lord; that the Lord is very pitiful, and of tender mercy.

James was writing to a suffering church. To encourage them, he bade his readers to turn their attention back to the religious history of their own people. By this means they would see great examples of "suffering affliction, and of patience" (v. 10). The Book of Hebrews describes some of the things these people suffered. Although they were honored by God, who used them as His representatives, they did not escape harsh treatment. James seems to be saying that if these honored believers did not escape persecution, those of lesser positions in His service should not expect to escape.

In the statement "We count them happy which endure" (v. 11), we hear the echo of one of Jesus' beatitudes in Matthew 5:11, 12: "Blessed are ye, when men shall revile you, and persecute you, and shall say all manner of evil against you falsely, for my sake. Rejoice, and be exceeding glad: for great is your reward in heaven." No doubt the readers were familiar with these words of Jesus.

James also expected his readers to be familiar with Job's story: "Ye have heard of the patience of Job." *Heard* seems to indicate that the readers had gained their knowledge of Job in public readings and instructions in synagogues and churches. This is the only place in the New Testament where Job is specifically mentioned.

The "patience of Job" does not seem to fit the picture of him as it appears in the book bearing his name. There we see the impassioned outburst at his so-called comforters and his distressed protest to God himself. He was, however, an outstanding example of perseverance in the most trying situations. Because "in all this Job did not sin with his lips" (Job 2:10, *NKJV*). God eventually blessed him with twice as many possessions as he had before (42:10, 12, 13).

Job had his ups and downs, but in the total picture he trusted the Lord. Job saw "the end of the Lord" (James 5:11). The Greek word translated "end" (*telos*) may also be used to indicate the goal toward which a movement is directed. Thus, it may also mean "design" or "purpose."

Our Lord offers us a quality of happiness we can experience even in the midst of difficulties; therefore, it is understandable that "we count them blessed who endure" (*NKJV*). Be patient and endure because the Lord is compassionate and merciful.

D. Without Swearing (v. 12)

12. But above all things, my brethren, swear not, neither by heaven, neither by the earth, neither by any other oath: but let your yea be yea; and your nay, nay; lest ye fall into condemnation.

The use of the tongue is a recurrent theme in this epistle. Depending on the person, the tongue can be either very useful or very abusive. The expression "above all things" (v. 12) makes good sense when interpreted in the context of losing one's patience. James called to mind the teachings of Jesus in Matthew 5:34-37, which forbid swearing altogether. It should be obvious that what is referred to in both Matthew and here is the casual use of oaths in informal conversation and not the taking of formal oaths in such places as courts of law. The people knew the commandment about the use of God's name in oaths; therefore, to avoid that problem they made a distinction between binding and nonbinding oaths. Instead of using God's name, which would be binding, they swore by heaven or by earth or anything else. By doing this they thought they would avoid incurring the wrath of God. Both Jesus and James denounced this practice.

Rather than having to make such oaths, the Christian is to speak clearly and mean what he says. If he says "Yes," he is to mean it; likewise, if he says "No." Thus no oath would be necessary, and there would be no further need to support his sincerity.

Talk About It:
What does it mean to "let your 'Yes' be yes, and your 'No,' no" (*NIV*)?

II. BY PRAYING FOR ONE ANOTHER (James 5:13-18)
A. Is Anyone Suffering? (v. 13)

13. Is any among you afflicted? let him pray. Is any merry? let him sing psalms.

Prayer and patience go hand in hand; therefore, the praying person will be a patient person. Prayer provides the inner strength to be patient. In this section James commanded prayer for a variety of needs and circumstances both physical and spiritual. In this passage James turns from suffering to joy and then back to suffering.

The Christian does not always live on the mountaintop of faith. Because of this, James makes another practical suggestion concerning how the believer should relate to suffering. His counsel is simple: "Is any among you afflicted? Let him pray" (v. 13). The word *afflicted* in the King James Version would be better translated *suffering*. The primary meaning is "to endure hardship; to experience some misfortune or calamity." Therefore, it need not be limited to physical suffering; it is a general term that may include trouble and distress as well as sickness.

Every verse in this section (vv. 13-18) contains an explicit reference to prayer. It is through prayer that the believer can habitually lay hold on God's power for victory through all these different experiences. We should continually pray about our own needs and the needs of others.

Therefore, when James said, "Let him pray," he was not being unsympathetic toward the individual with a problem. The believer should make it a practice to turn to God whenever he is distressed. His prayer may not change the situation, but it can give him strength to bear it bravely as he submits himself to Divine Providence. We should also pray for fellow believers who are suffering.

"Is any merry? Let him sing psalms." This sentence shows the radical swing the emotions can make. It indicates there will be periods of sadness as well as periods of joy. The word *merry* in Greek is a blend of two words meaning "well" and "soul." Thus, it means being in good spirits or in a happy mood. Praise comes as a song—many times a song is a praise. Often when things go well with us, we forget to pray. However, when the pressures let up, we should respond to God in worshipful adoration.

B. Is Anyone Sick? (vv. 14, 15)

14. Is any sick among you? let him call for the elders of the church; and let them pray over him, anointing him with oil in the name of the Lord:

15. And the prayer of faith shall save the sick, and the Lord shall raise him up; and if he have committed sins, they shall be forgiven him.

We come now to the matter of physical ailment. The Greek word for *sick* (v. 14) refers to being weak or without strength. James asked, "Is any sick among you?" He answered that important question by sharing a three-part solution to the problem of sickness in the life of the believer.

First, "Let him call for the elders of the church" indicates that the person who is sick is to take the initiative. This is the only passage in the New Testament that gives direct advice concerning the ministry of healing within the church. However, there are a number of other passages which do address this vital subject.

Second, at the summons the elders are to go to the home of the sick rather than the sick person's being brought to a healer at a public service. James was not introducing a new procedure but was reminding his readers of the importance of prayer in time of a brother's need.

Finally, the elders are to anoint the sick man with oil in the name of the Lord. The Scriptures mention two important uses of oil: for medicinal purposes, as in the parable of the Good Samaritan (Luke 10:34), and symbolically or sacramentally as in the Old Testament. The use of oil for the anointing of the sick was a common practice among the Jews. The disciples did this when Jesus sent them out in pairs to preach and heal (Mark 6:13). The oil was thought to have healing properties, but here it seems to be symbolic of healing. The emphasis is not on the oil but on "the prayer of faith" (v. 15).

"I have been driven many times to my knees by the overwhelming conviction that I had absolutely no other place to go."
—Abraham Lincoln

Talk About It:
1. Who are the church elders?
2. What is the purpose of anointing the sick with oil?
3. What is "the prayer of faith"?

How Christians Demonstrate Caring

Since the root cause of sickness and suffering is sin, it is essential that the forgiveness of sin be vitally involved in the divine healing of the body. Here it is even suggested that the illness is part of the divine chastening for sins committed. Recall the paralyzed man brought to Jesus for healing (Matthew 9:2-8) and Jesus' word of absolution: "Son . . . thy sins be forgiven thee." This is not to say all sickness is the result of personal sin, as Jesus made clear in John 9:2, 3. But all sickness does result from living in a sin-cursed world.

C. Confess Your Faults (v. 16)

16. Confess your faults one to another, and pray one for another, that ye may be healed. The effectual fervent prayer of a righteous man availeth much.

Believers are to confess their faults to one another and pray for each other. It is not just the elders who are to pray but all Christians. If a person has sinned against a brother, he should confess the sin to him. This should result in mutual confession—"one to another." Then the two believers are to pray for each other. The scene must not be restricted to the sick room, nor does it seem James was thinking of a public service. It seems, rather, to be a private gathering where confidences are shared for the purpose of mutual help and intercession. James added the assurance that "the prayer of a righteous man is powerful and effective" (*NIV*). The "righteous man" referred to here is the person whose sins have been confessed and forgiven.

D. Consider Elijah (vv. 17, 18)

17. Elias was a man subject to like passions as we are, and he prayed earnestly that it might not rain: and it rained not on the earth by the space of three years and six months.

18. And he prayed again, and the heaven gave rain, and the earth brought forth her fruit.

As an encouragement to believing, enduring, and persisting in prayer, he recalled the example of Elijah. The principle is that prayer has great power. How do we know? "Elijah," said James, "was a man just like us" (v. 17, *NIV*). He was not a superman; he, too, needed to pray. James thus disarmed the natural reaction of his readers that common mortals like themselves could never expect to achieve the prayer results of a grand person like Elijah. The phrase "[of] like passions" does not mean that he was excitable or irritable nor subject to corrupt passion, but rather that he was subject to the same weaknesses other men have. The explanation of his power in prayer is twofold: He was a righteous man, and "he prayed earnestly." So James assured his readers that such answers to prayer are within the reach of any believer.

III. BY RESCUING THE ERRING (James 5:19, 20)

19. Brethren, if any of you do err from the truth, and one convert him;

20. Let him know, that he which converteth the sinner from the error of his way shall save a soul from death, and shall hide a multitude of sins.

Talk About It:
1. What does it mean to "err from the truth" (v. 19).
2. How should we reach out to backsliders?

What do you do with a brother who strays from the truth—do you give up on him, or do you patiently love him back? After having discussed the ministry of physical healing, James closes his letter with some practical teachings on the important subject of spiritual healing. It may well be called "the ministry of restoration." James' purpose in these closing verses is to encourage Christians to make an effort to bring back those who have wandered.

James, addressing his readers as "brethren," concluded his message with a weighty word of good cheer for those whose hearts are set on a greater task than that of praying for the sick—for those who are seeking to bring lost men and women back to the paths of righteousness. The people who are to be sought after and brought back to these paths are evidently Christians who have become backsliders and have strayed from the truth. The Greek word used for "err" suggests the familiar metaphor of a sheep wandering astray. Although gregarious by nature, a sheep nibbling the grass among the rocks and crags could easily become lost. One thing is sure—his wandering from the path places him in grave danger.

This is decidedly true for one who errs from the truth. To wander from the truth inevitably involves the loss of a vital relationship with God. The gospel involves not only principles to be understood but also a life to be lived. Therefore, the person must be turned from the wrong way to the right one—from falsehood to truth. The promise James made is to those in the community who observe a person in error and, in proper meekness and humility, attempt to turn him back to the true way and to the religious community.

This is an extremely important ministry of love. Too often those who err are discarded; no effort is made to bring them back into the fellowship of the church. Sometimes such efforts are rebuffed, but persistence is the key. People find it hard to refuse persistent love.

What happens when the wandering believer is reclaimed? James approved and encouraged the work of restoration by showing its important results. "Let him know" (v. 20) is a personal word of assurance for the individual instrumental in restoring the erring one. In view of the far-reaching results, it is a work to be appreciated and warmly encouraged. The phrase "whoever turns a sinner from the error of his way" (*NIV*) stresses this crucial point.

James called the one who has erred "a sinner." This person has missed the mark of God's will by wandering from the truth. "His way," as contrasted to the way of truth, is the way of *error* or delusion. "Shall save a soul from death" refers to the soul of the restored sinner. That he is saved "from death" stresses the seriousness of the condition from which he is rescued. James did not say that the wandering one is spiritually dead or is dying, but that he is saved from death, which unmistakably is at the end of the path he was following. The concept of saving a soul from death is clear enough, for death is plainly the final result of sin, usually thought of as eternal death.

James' reference to covering "a multitude of sins" seems to be an allusion to Proverbs 10:12—"Love covereth all sins"— which is also quoted in 1 Peter 4:8. It is God, not people, who does the covering. When a sinner turns from his wandering from the truth and returns to God, all the resources of God's love are unleashed. The psalmist declared that as far as the east is from the west, so far does our Lord remove our sins from us when they are confessed to Him (Psalm 103:12). He forgives and forgets. James intended to show that forgiven Christians ought to work together for the mutual well-being of the church.

CONCLUSION

Christians demonstrate caring by exhibiting patience, praying for one another, and rescuing the erring. These are acts of caring we cannot accomplish in our power. We bear godly patience as a fruit of the Spirit in our lives; we pray effectively through the Spirit's enablement; and we help to restore the errant believer through the Spirit's convicting power.

GOLDEN TEXT CHALLENGE

"CONFESS YOUR FAULTS ONE TO ANOTHER, AND PRAY ONE FOR ANOTHER, THAT YE MAY BE HEALED. THE EFFECTUAL FERVENT PRAYER OF A RIGHTEOUS MAN AVAILETH MUCH" (James 5:16).

Normal exposition of this verse boils down to this: Prayer changes things.

From preceding verses we know that James addressed himself to practical matters. He did not speak subjectively. He was not philosophizing. He spoke of the sick and of their healing through prayer. He spoke of the sinful and of their forgiveness through prayer. He spoke of our confessing faults one to another, of our need to pray for each other, and of organized methods by which such spiritual help is requested and administered.

James used two qualifying phrases to set forth his concept of effective prayer. First, *prayer must be fervent*: not cold or apathetic or halfhearted, but hot with passion and concern. This conforms with the promise of Christ: "What things soever ye desire, when ye pray, believe that ye receive them, and ye shall have them" (Mark 11:24). It is also in keeping with human experience. Burning desire and fervent prayer are Siamese twins.

Second, *effective prayer must be sincere*: it must be backed by decision and action. James' "righteous man" is more than talk. He is not necessarily saintly or beyond human frailty, but he is one who sincerely believes and who backs faith with a life of commitment.

Elijah was James' example (v. 17). Live as Elijah, then pray as Elijah, and God will answer.

Be Filled With the Spirit (Pentecost)

Numbers 11:10-29; Acts 2:1-17, 41-47; 4:31-35;
2 Corinthians 3:1-8; Galatians 5:22-26; Ephesians 5:18-21

INTRODUCTION

Frequently, when speaking of God's will, we tend to think of specific actions such as vocations, marriage, even purchases. Rarely do individuals think about God's will in terms of spiritual growth and experiences. Today's lesson directs our attention to God's will for us in terms of the Holy Spirit's active work in our lives. The specific objective is to acknowledge it is God's will for every Christian to be filled with the Holy Spirit and live a Spirit-filled life.

The breadth of this lesson takes us to both sides of the outpouring of the Holy Spirit. We will begin with the work of the Spirit in the Old Testament and end with ministry in a New Testament congregation. This reminds us of the ongoing ministry of the Holy Spirit, which precedes the Day of Pentecost in Jerusalem and continues to this present day.

Since this is Pentecost Sunday, it would be good for us to understand the background of Pentecost with its origin in Judaism. Pentecost is a feast observed 50 days after the Passover. Devout Jews believe this day marks the anniversary of God's giving the Law. They carefully review the Torah (Pentateuch) and may stay up all night in order to do so.

In the New Testament era of the early church, Pentecost stands as that important day when the promised Comforter descends on the gathered disciples. Obediently they have been waiting for 10 days. During this time, prayer and unity prevails. Then they experience the baptism of the Holy Spirit with the initial evidence of speaking in tongues. Immediately the church grows as 3,000 come to faith in Christ.

This entire lesson points to the Spirit-filled life in both the Old Testament and the New Testament. However, it doesn't stop there. The Spirit-filled life isn't to be just a historical item of the past. God's will is for each of us to daily live the Spirit-filled life. This enables us to live with confidence as we face some of the difficulties that are common to life. It also empowers us to be witnesses of the saving and keeping power of the Lord Jesus Christ.

While studying this lesson, be sure to pay special attention to the diverse areas in which the Spirit-filled life can make a difference. It ranges from skills to community to worship. No dimension of our lives is to be separated from the impact of the Holy Spirit's ministry.

Unit Theme:
Gift of the Holy Spirit

Central Truth:
Scripture commands Christians to be filled with the Holy Spirit.

Focus:
Acknowledge that it is God's will for every Christian to be filled with the Holy Spirit, and live a Spirit-filled life.

Context:
Various passages on being filled with God's Spirit

Golden Text:
"Be filled with the Spirit; speaking to yourselves in psalms and hymns and spiritual songs, singing and making melody in your heart to the Lord" (Ephesians 5:18, 19).

Study Outline:
I. Filled With the Spirit (Numbers 11:24-29; Acts 2:1-4, 16, 17)
II. Spirit-Filled Living (Acts 2:41-47; Ephesians 5:18-21; Galatians 5:22-25)
III. Spirit-Filled Unity and Service (Acts 4:31-35; 2 Corinthians 3:5, 6)

I. FILLED WITH THE SPIRIT (Numbers 11:24-29;
Acts 2:1-4, 16, 17)

A. The Elders (Numbers 11:24-29)

24. And Moses went out, and told the people the words of the Lord, and gathered the seventy men of the elders of the people, and set them round about the tabernacle.

25. And the Lord came down in a cloud, and spake unto him, and took of the spirit that was upon him, and gave it unto the seventy elders: and it came to pass, that, when the spirit rested upon them, they prophesied, and did not cease.

26. But there remained two of the men in the camp, the name of the one was Eldad, and the name of the other Medad: and the spirit rested upon them; and they were of them that were written, but went not out unto the tabernacle: and they prophesied in the camp.

27. And there ran a young man, and told Moses, and said, Eldad and Medad do prophesy in the camp.

28. And Joshua the son of Nun, the servant of Moses, one of his young men, answered and said, My lord Moses, forbid them.

29. And Moses said unto him, Enviest thou for my sake? would God that all the Lord's people were prophets, and that the Lord would put his spirit upon them!

It is difficult to realize the heavy load of leadership which Moses bears as Israel progresses toward the Promised Land. Regardless of God's miraculous provisions, the people repeatedly lapse into complaining. Often they direct it as a personal attack against Moses. The people's griping over their continuous diet of manna finally becomes too much for him, and Moses pours out his frustration to God (vv. 4-10).

Moses feels God has placed too great a burden on him. He didn't choose this position for himself. The people's attitudes and actions make it similar to a father needing to carry a nursing child. There isn't meat available to satisfy their appetites. Moses says he is unable to carry this burden alone. In fact, death appears to be more desirable than to continue in this path (vv. 11-15).

God doesn't deal specifically with Moses in terms of what he feels or states. Instead, He gives Moses the plan of action to alleviate the distress. First, he is to gather the leaders of Israel and have them stand at the Tabernacle. Second, the Lord will take some of the spiritual anointing which covers Moses and put it on the elders. Third, the Spirit upon the elders will enable them to share in the burden of leadership. Fourth, the people are to sanctify themselves in preparation for divine provision. Fifth, God will provide meat which will last a whole month (vv. 16-20).

of them that were written (v. 26)—
"listed among the elders" (*NIV*)
ONE MIND
ONE ACCORD

Talk About It:
1. Why do you suppose "the Lord came down in a cloud" (v. 25)?
2. What did God do for the elders, and why (vv. 25, 26)?
3. Explain Moses' desire expressed in verse 29.

In his frustrated mind-set, Moses questions the provision of so much meat. Even killing all their livestock wouldn't provide enough. God gently reminds him of His ability (vv. 21-23). Isn't it interesting how this man who experienced the power of God in the 10 plagues on Egypt and the crossing of the Red Sea must now deal with doubt? This reminds us of the need to keep our faith strong, even in the time of crisis.

When the elders of Israel gather with Moses at the Tabernacle, they are given the Holy Spirit just as was upon their leader. Notice there is a verbal sign of this covering—they prophesy. It is an initial evidence which does not continue. The latter portion of verse 25 is most accurately translated "but they did not do so again" (*NIV*).

Two of the men listed as elders, Eldad and Medad, do not join the others at the Tabernacle. For some reason not stated, they are still in the camp when the Holy Spirit is given. However, that doesn't matter. They receive Him where they are and begin to prophesy. A messenger runs to Moses with this information. Joshua, the right-hand man of Moses, misunderstands or mis-interprets what is taking place. He sees it as being "out of order" or possibly insubordination to Moses' leadership. In any case, he asks Moses to stop them.

Moses' reply indicates his mature grasp of what is taking place. He isn't threatened by these elders prophesying, even if it is in the camp away from the main group. This is a mighty blessing for individuals and for the whole nation. Moses desires for everyone to have this experience and empowerment.

How blessed we are to know that the fullness of the Holy Spirit is now available to all! We just need to be open to receiving and seek this blessing for service.

> "We do not use the Holy Spirit; He uses us."
> —**Warren Wiersbe**

B. The Obedient (Acts 2:1-4)

1. And when the day of Pentecost was fully come, they were all with one accord in one place.

2. And suddenly there came a sound from heaven as of a rushing mighty wind, and it filled all the house where they were sitting.

3. And there appeared unto them cloven tongues like as of fire, and it sat upon each of them.

4. And they were all filled with the Holy Ghost, and began to speak with other tongues, as the Spirit gave them utterance.

cloven (v. 3)—
"divided" (*NKJV*)

When studying this passage, there is a tendency to emphasize the phenomena described in verses 2 and 3. It is hard to imagine what it would have been like to be in that room, more than likely rather crowded, and seen and heard what took place.

Talk About It:
1. What were the two sounds heard that testified to the Holy Spirit's coming (vv. 2, 4)?

2. What happened to "each of them" (v. 3), and why?

For today's lesson, let's focus on the people. Just prior to His ascension, Jesus directs His followers to go to Jerusalem and wait for the promised gift of the Holy Spirit (Luke 24:49; Acts 1:4, 5). There is a definite place for this to take place, but no specific timetable other than "in a few days" (Acts 1:5, *NIV*). Obedient to His word, 120 of them gather in Jerusalem. Instead of scattering throughout the city, they wait as a unified body.

Acts 1:12-26 describes some of their activities. Foremost is their continued emphasis and commitment to prayer (v. 14). They also did some business by filling Judas' vacant position in the Twelve. There's no hint of their spending time in aimless waiting or casual visiting. They aren't complaining about how much longer will it take.

In 2:1-4 the Holy Spirit comes upon this gathered group with audible and visual phenomena. More important is the evidence of their being filled with the Holy Spirit. The Holy Spirit enables them to speak languages they had never learned but could be understood by the various nationalities gathered in Jerusalem for the Feast of Pentecost.

C. The Fulfillment (vv. 16, 17)

16. But this is that which was spoken by the prophet Joel.

17. And it shall come to pass in the last days, saith God, I will pour out of my Spirit upon all flesh: and your sons and your daughters shall prophesy, and your young men shall see visions, and your old men shall dream dreams.

Talk About It:
What is the significance of the term "all flesh" (v. 17)?

The events within the location where the believers were waiting for the promise apparently spills out into the streets. Knowing how narrow the streets are and how closely houses are packed together, it quickly becomes evident to people in the area that a phenomenon is occurring. They respond with amazement, since they know these Galileans could not possibly be fluent in all the languages of their native areas (vv. 7-10). Notice there isn't the thought of each one simply speaking a few words or phrases which may be easily learned. Instead, there is the sense of speaking fluently.

Besides the amazement of the multitude witnessing this mighty outpouring, they also are perplexed. What is the significance or meaning? In response to the people's questioning, the Twelve address the group. Beginning at verse 14, Peter stands out as the primary spokesperson. Notice how he addresses them. He recognizes some as visiting during the feast time and others as residents of Jerusalem.

It's interesting how Peter orders his presentation. First, he addresses those who have discarded these actions as the result of drunkenness. It's only 9:00 in the morning. No group would begin partying so early, enabling them to be intoxicated at this hour. Though Peter didn't, he could have pointed to wine causing slurred speech. Its influence never enables anyone to speak precisely and in a language never learned.

Having eliminated the scoffers' suggestion, Peter points to the Scriptures. He announces with clarity their seeing the fulfillment of the prophecy of Joel 2:28, 29. Though given centuries earlier, they now are privileged to witness its taking place. Through the outpouring of the Holy Spirit, all can experience His ministry through them in what was previously limited to a select few. Neither gender nor age are qualifications for this blessing.

II. SPIRIT-FILLED LIVING (Acts 2:41-47; Ephesians 5:18-21; Galatians 5:22-25)

A. A Fellowship Community (Acts 2:41-47)

41. Then they that gladly received his word were baptized: and the same day there were added unto them about three thousand souls.

42. And they continued stedfastly in the apostles' doctrine and fellowship, and in breaking of bread, and in prayers.

43. And fear came upon every soul: and many wonders and signs were done by the apostles.

44. And all that believed were together, and had all things common;

45. And sold their possessions and goods, and parted them to all men, as every man had need.

46. And they, continuing daily with one accord in the temple, and breaking bread from house to house, did eat their meat with gladness and singleness of heart,

47. Praising God, and having favour with all the people. And the Lord added to the church daily such as should be saved.

After the Day of Pentecost the fledgling church numbers over 3,000. There is no structured government other than the informal leadership of the Twelve. They have no church buildings, but they do have a bond of community. Verse 42 shows they follow a set of doctrinal beliefs. This centers on the life and teachings of Jesus as well as the Old Testament Scriptures. From this we see the importance of doctrine rather than personal experience being the foundation of the church. First Timothy 4:16 speaks clearly of this: "Watch your life and doctrine closely. Persevere in them, because if you do, you will save both yourself and your hearers" (*NIV*).

The early church's fellowship is seen in their praying and eating together. Sharing food around a table provides an intimate approach which enables conversation to flow. It quickly becomes an opportunity to know others on a deeper level beyond the

Talk About It:
1. Who "gladly received" Peter's message, and what was the evidence (v. 41)?
2. What were the believers devoted to (v. 42)?
3. Describe the relationships of the early Christians (vv. 44-46).
4. How was the world influenced by the church (v. 47)?

When asked how she knew she was a Christian, one lady who worked as a maid responded, "Now I sweep the dirt into a dust pan instead of under the carpet." This raises a further consideration. Having received the baptism of the Holy Spirit, what impact has it made in my lifestyle?

to yourselves (v. 19)—"to one another"

Talk About It:
1. What does it mean to be "filled with the Spirit" (v. 18)?
2. What does verse 19 teach about worship?
3. What should "the fear of God" cause us to do (v. 21)?

usual topics of the weather and various current events. Verse 46 indicates this to be a regular, daily practice. Being in the same city and sharing the special relationship in Christ causes them to seek out each other. This verse also points to the attitude. These were joyous actions arising from sincere hearts.

This fellowship community then experiences marvelous spiritual results. The miraculous occurs within their community and those who are interested in what is being said and done. Also, more individuals are accepting Christ and becoming a part of the church. Note the response of those observing this body of believers. They are positive toward them. Positive behavior, coupled with the joy of the Lord, impacts those with whom we come in contact.

B. A Worshiping Community (Ephesians 5:18-21)

18. And be not drunk with wine, wherein is excess; but be filled with the Spirit;

19. Speaking to yourselves in psalms and hymns and spiritual songs, singing and making melody in your heart to the Lord;

20. Giving thanks always for all things unto God and the Father in the name of our Lord Jesus Christ;

21. Submitting yourselves one to another in the fear of God.

Spirit-filled living must include the dimension of worship. To adore and offer our thanksgiving to the Sovereign Lord is to be an ongoing response of believers who are filled with the Holy Spirit and continuing to walk in His influence.

Verse 18 begins with a concept contrast. The apostle Paul points to those individuals who submit to the gratification of wine. They recklessly pursue the taste and short-lived excitement of heavy indulgence with significant negative results. In marked contrast to such a behavior, believers are encouraged to allow the continuance of the Holy Spirit's guiding and fulfilling of their lives. We are to open ourselves daily to the divine impact of the Spirit.

"Speaking to one another" (v. 19, *NKJV*) through godly songs should be an ongoing part of the Spirit-filled life whenever and wherever believers are in the company of each other. Music is a universal language of cultures to express joy and sorrow. It is only logical for the melodies of the heart to be released into audible song.

The apostle Paul points to a variety of musical literature which is to fulfill our need and desire for expression. This should be a reminder to the worship leader in local congregations to use different types of music. The *psalms* mentioned here most likely refer to the Old Testament psalms, which were a part of Jewish worship. *Hymns* very likely were the new songs written by believers in the early church to express doctrinal concepts. *Spiritual songs* refer to those that are testimonial, expressing an experience with God.

A worshiping community is also to be a thankful group of believers (v. 20). Thankfulness should include the "small things" of life as well as the larger, seemingly more important aspects. Listening to a small child's simple prayer of thanks can expand our horizon of thankfulness.

Verse 21 teaches that submission to one another plays a part in a Spirit-filled community as we worship together. No one is exempt from being in submission to others. Being filled with the Spirit and operating in the gifts doesn't release anyone from ecclesiastical authority or even parental authority when it applies. Divine order includes both leadership and submission "out of reverence for Christ" (*NIV*).

C. A Fruitful Community (Galatians 5:22-25)

22. But the fruit of the Spirit is love, joy, peace, longsuffering, gentleness, goodness, faith,

23. Meekness, temperance: against such there is no law.

24. And they that are Christ's have crucified the flesh with the affections and lusts.

25. If we live in the Spirit, let us also walk in the Spirit.

Here we reach the final evidence or test of Spirit-filled living. The claim is to be backed by genuine, visible evidence. The expression "The proof is in the pudding" also applies to Spirit-filled living. We must demonstrate our testimony.

Before considering the initial two verses, it is vital to understand our position in Christ. Verse 24 reminds us that Christ's children have experienced a crucifixion of their sinful nature with its passions and desires. Since the Spirit has quickened us who were dead in our sins, it becomes our responsibility to practice the new life empowered by the Divine working in our being. We can't mature in Christ and fulfill His purpose if we sit by passively.

Galatians 5:22, 23 is a familiar passage. However, familiarity doesn't guarantee either a good understanding or fulfillment of it. First, consider the unity indicated here. The "fruit" is singular, not plural. All the nine virtues listed here are part of a single whole. The implication is that no one can claim to be evidencing the fruit of the Spirit without working to cultivate each of the individual virtues.

Following is a brief statement of what each of these virtues demonstrates:

> "A Christian man is the most free lord of all, and subject to none; a Christian man is the most dutiful servant of all, and subject to everyone."
> —**Martin Luther**

Talk About It:
How do these verses describe the Spirit-filled life?

Love—the distinctive mark of the Christian, which is an act of the will God accomplishes through us

Joy—a cheerful gladness that flows from our salvation, regardless of our circumstances

Peace—the reconciliation with God that enables us to be free from tension, even when in conflict situations

Longsuffering (*patience*)—being forbearing and non-retaliatory, even when individuals deliberately attempt to provoke us

Gentleness—kindness and politeness that treats others with utmost respect

Goodness—inner character development expressed by moral and ethical values

Faith—faithfulness seen in loyalty and trustworthiness

Meekness (*gentleness*)—submissiveness and humility before God and others

Temperance (*self-control*)—self-mastery enabling one to control his or her thoughts and actions

Here we see how the Holy Spirit longs to work in our lives as individuals and as a corporate body of believers. Our claim of the Spirit's fullness in our lives must be reflected in words and actions.

> "There never will exist anything permanently noble and excellent in the character which is a stranger to resolute self-denial."
> —Sir Walter Scott

DENY
BLAST
Lie against
grieve
quinch

III. SPIRIT-FILLED UNITY AND SERVICE (Acts 4:31-35; 2 Corinthians 3:5, 6)

A. Unity and Generosity (Acts 4:31-35)

31. And when they had prayed, the place was shaken where they were assembled together; and they were all filled with the Holy Ghost, and they spake the word of God with boldness.

32. And the multitude of them that believed were of one heart and of one soul: neither said any of them that ought of the things which he possessed was his own; but they had all things common.

33. And with great power gave the apostles witness of the resurrection of the Lord Jesus: and great grace was upon them all.

34. Neither was there any among them that lacked: for as many as were possessors of lands or houses sold them, and brought the prices of the things that were sold,

35. And laid them down at the apostles' feet: and distribution was made unto every man according as he had need.

After the disciples had praised and glorified God (see vv. 24-28), they presented to Him a single and a simple petition. They did not ask for deliverance from the threatenings of the Sanhedrin, or for protection from violence. They knew He would do this if it were His will for them. Their one petition was that He grant them boldness to preach His Word (vv. 29, 30).

Talk About It:
1. How and why was "the place . . . shaken" (v. 31)?
2. Explain the significance of "great grace" (v. 33).

Be Filled With the Spirit

Unexpectedly the prayer was followed by a tremendous spiritual outpouring upon them. The place where they were gathered was shaken, and the disciples were filled anew with the Holy Ghost. This does not indicate that there had been any diminution of the Spirit in their lives since the Day of Pentecost; there was nothing lacking in spiritual fullness. But this powerful repetition of the infilling further emboldened the disciples to speak His Word in the face of danger.

The common sharing of goods which the Christians had begun earlier (2:44, 45) was greatly increased in the face of danger. The Christians sold their houses and lands, pooled their resources, and lived together in unity. Because they were fully united in faith, purpose and service, the common sharing of material goods was both desirable and spontaneous. No brother of the church desired to have more than any other.

Despite the danger they faced, the disciples of Christ enjoyed a glorious period of power and growth (4:33). The unity of the church was not a pretense, for the people worshiped, worked, believed and shared together. Growth and grace were the consequence of this unity and fellowship. The emphasis of their ministry was the resurrection of Jesus. This was the great hope and confidence of the church then, and it still is today.

In verses 34 and 35, we read about the common sharing of goods that was practiced at this point in the early church history. God did not command the people to sell their houses and pool their money; it was an ideal of the people themselves. Love made them desire to share, and share alike. Moreover, the disciples were fully expecting the Lord to return momentarily, at which time they would have no need of houses and lands. The practice of community sharing began as a generous gesture of brotherly love; there was no duress or pressure about it. Each person acted voluntarily. It is good when Christians can be thus concerned and feel such responsibility for one another. While there was no commandment from God regarding this practice, He does call upon His people to give and to assist when a fellow Christian is in need (1 John 3:17).

B. Able Ministers (2 Corinthians 3:5, 6)

5. Not that we are sufficient of ourselves to think any thing as of ourselves; but our sufficiency is of God;

6. Who also hath made us able ministers of the new testament; not of the letter, but of the spirit: for the letter killeth, but the spirit giveth life.

In verses 1-3, the apostle Paul said he did not need "letters of recommendation" to prove the legitimacy of his ministry. Instead, he said the Corinthian converts themselves were "our letter, written on our hearts, known and read by everybody" (NIV).

3. Why were there "no needy persons among them" (v. 34, NIV)?

"The church exists to train its members through the practice of the presence of God to be servants of others, to the end that Christlikeness may become common property."
—William Adams Brown

Talk About It:
Explain the sufficiency, or competence, of believers.

In verse 5 he makes it clear that he could not boast of his success in ministry, for his "sufficiency"—competence, capability, qualification—"is of God." He had no competence in himself to claim anything for himself. When we as Christians realize that our ability to minister to others comes from Christ and we are willing to glorify Christ for what He accomplishes through us, we will find success in our service.

Paul said that God "has made us competent as ministers of a new covenant" (v. 6, *NIV*). This "new covenant" is the gospel of Jesus Christ—the message that "giveth life" by the Holy Spirit.

We as members of the church of Christ have been entrusted with the gospel of Christ. It is written on our hearts, transforming us into messengers of the good news who can eternally influence other people through the competence Christ gives us.

CONCLUSION

When considering the work of the Holy Spirit, it is important to see His work evidenced in both Testaments. Since the Day of Pentecost and up to the present, we are blessed to experience the fullness of both Spirit baptism and daily empowerment. Those of us who have been so privileged to be part of a Spirit-filled community understand the blessings of His ministry in our lives.

GOLDEN TEXT CHALLENGE

"BE FILLED WITH THE SPIRIT; SPEAKING TO YOURSELVES IN PSALMS AND HYMNS AND SPIRITUAL SONGS, SINGING AND MAKING MELODY IN YOUR HEART TO THE LORD" (Ephesians 5:18, 19).

Daily Devotions:
M. God's Spirit in a Ruler
   Genesis 41:37-43
T. Artisans Enabled by the Spirit
   Exodus 31:1-6
W. Spirit-Anointed King
   2 Samuel 23:1-5
T. Filled Again With the Spirit
   Acts 4:23-33
F. Gentiles Receive the Spirit
   Acts 10:44-48
S. Living in the Spirit
   Galatians 5:16-25

The service of song is a part of worship in which the Holy Ghost must be vitally involved. How often would barren and cold services be transformed into warm, lively, victorious events if the Holy Spirit were allowed to direct and anoint for the occasion. However much a song is perfect in practice and however fine in technique and performance, unless it is anointed by the Spirit, it will fail to accomplish the purpose of glorifying Christ.

Paul said singing and praise proceed from the heart and is unto the Lord. If singing is only from the lips, it will not bless the singer and surely will not touch others. All songs should be spiritual. Spirit-anointed singing will glorify Jesus, touch hardened hearts, and bless others.

Introduction to Summer Quarter

" Joshua and Judges" is the theme of the first unit. The lessons from Joshua explore Israel's entering the Promised Land, defeating Jericho, making a treaty with Gibeon, and hearing Joshua's final commission. The lessons from Judges study three deliverers: Othniel, Gideon and Samson.

The expositions were written by the Reverend Winfield H. Bevins (B.A., M.Div.). Winfield is founding pastor of Church of the Outer Banks (*www.churchobx.com*), a growing and innovative church in Nags Head, North Carolina. He is the author of seven Pathway Press publications including *Developing a Powerful Prayer Life*, *Discovering the Holy Spirit*, *Heroes of the Faith*, *Introducing the Spiritual Disciplines*, *Rediscovering John Wesley*, and *Truth for Living*.

The second unit, "Prayers in the Psalms," are studies of Psalms 77, 84, 85, 91, 139, 140, 141 and 143.

The expositions were written by the Reverend Dr. Jerald Daffe (see biographical information on page 132).

MOSES: Taken out of water (saved from the water —

Entering the Promised Land

Joshua 1:1 through 4:24

Unit Theme:
Joshua and Judges

Central Truth:
Christians receive God's promises by faith.

Focus:
Observe how Israel received God's promised blessing through obedience and testify to God's faithfulness by our obedience.

Context:
Around 1406 B.C., Joshua leads Israel through the Jordan River into Canaan.

Golden Text:
"The Lord your God dried up the waters of Jordan from before you, . . . that all the people of the earth might know the hand of the Lord, that it is mighty: that ye might fear the Lord your God for ever" (Joshua 4:23, 24).

Study Outline:
I. Preparing to Enter (Joshua 1:1-18)
II. Stepping Out in Faith (Joshua 3:9-17)
III. Testifying to God's Power (Joshua 4:1-9, 15-24)

INTRODUCTION

The Book of Joshua is the sixth book of the Old Testament and it covers nearly a 25-year period of Israel's history under the leadership of Joshua, who was Moses' successor. In this book we see God lead a new generation of believers to enter the Promised Land by faith.

Joshua was born in Egyptian slavery. His father was Nun, of the tribe of Ephraim (see 1 Chronicles 7:20-27). *Joshua* means "Jehovah saves" or "Jehovah is salvation." Joshua had been Moses' assistant since the giving of the Commandments at Mount Sinai and continued to serve Moses through the wilderness wandering. Because of Joshua's courage and strong leadership, God selected him to lead the nation of Israel after Moses' death.

Under the leadership of Moses, the previous generation of Hebrews was told to leave Egypt and travel to Canaan. The possession of Canaan was originally promised to Abraham in Genesis 12:1-3. In this passage God initiated a covenant with Abraham while he was living in Ur of the Chaldeans, promising him land, descendants and blessings. This promise was passed to Abraham's offspring, who later became known as the nation of Israel.

Moses successfully led the people of Israel out of Egypt and to the edge of the Promised Land nearly 1,000 years after God promised the land to Abraham. Joshua and Caleb were in favor of conquering the land, but the Israelites didn't have enough faith to enter it. Therefore, Israel wandered in the wilderness for 40 years, and eventually stopped on the edge of Canaan. God was unhappy with their disobedience and allowed that generation to die out without ever receiving the promise.

When Moses died on Mount Nebo (Deuteronomy 34), Joshua was probably already in his 80s or 90s. He was a very qualified leader who was full of faith and wisdom, and was obedient to God. As a result, Joshua was able to do in a few short months what his generation was not able to do in 40 years!

The Lord is truly the God of second chances. No matter if we fall, God is always there to pick us up. This lesson will focus on how Israel received God's promised blessing through obedience and testify to God's faithfulness and power.

I. PREPARING TO ENTER (Joshua 1:1-18)

A. Forget the Past (vv. 1, 2)

1. Now after the death of Moses the servant of the Lord it came to pass, that the Lord spake unto Joshua the son of Nun, Moses' minister, saying,

2. Moses my servant is dead; now therefore arise, go over this Jordan, thou, and all this people, unto the land which I do give to them, even to the children of Israel.

Before Israel could receive the Promised Land, they had to let go of the past. Israel had followed Moses' leadership since their final days in Egypt and during 40 years in the wilderness, and they had become comfortable with his leadership. The Lord reminded them that Moses was dead, along with his way of doing things. God was going to use Joshua to do a new thing that Moses and his generation did not do.

The Lord then told Joshua to focus on the task at hand. The Jordan River was the only thing separating the Israelites from the Promised Land. All Israel needed to do was to let go of the past and cross over into Canaan through the intervention of God.

In our generation many Christians and churches are living in the past, even though their blessing is right in front of them. Their mantra is, "We've never done it that way before." If we are not careful we will only perpetuate and repeat the traditions of the past without engaging the future. Many churches think that if they could just return to the "good old days" everything would be all right. This is the reason many churches are empty. Much of what worked back then will not work now. Times change, people change, but God is always the same.

One of Joshua's greatest legacies is that he led the people out of the past and into the future. God does not want us to rely on stale manna of the past. The Lord wants to give us fresh manna every day. Manna is a reminder of our need for God in the present. The first step for Israel to get out of the wilderness and into the Promised Land was to let go of the past.

B. Look to the Future (vv. 3, 4)

3. Every place that the sole of your foot shall tread upon, that have I given unto you, as I said unto Moses.

4. From the wilderness and this Lebanon even unto the great river, the river Euphrates, all the land of the Hittites, and unto the great sea toward the going down of the sun, shall be your coast.

The Lord began to remind Israel of the promises that He gave to them by saying, "I will give you every place where you set your foot, as I promised Moses" (v. 3, *NIV*). Their future was not to die in the wilderness, but to inherit the Promised Land through faith and obedience. Faith moves us to obedience.

Talk About It:
Describe the challenge God gave to Joshua.

"There has never yet been a person in our history who led a life of ease whose name is worth remembering."
—**Theodore Roosevelt**

Talk About It:
How was Joshua to complete Moses' mission (see Deuteronomy 11:24)?

God wanted them to see and understand the full extent of the Promised Land. They could literally stare over into the Promised Land and behold their future. All they had to do was open their eyes and believe.

The reason so many people are stuck in the past is that they have no faith to look to the future. That's why men and women of faith are visionaries. They can see what no one else can see. It takes eyes of faith to see what is not already there. It could be said that vision is the ability to see what can and will be. We must become visionaries who can see the future if we are going to stand on God's promises and receive His blessings.

C. God Will Be With You (vv. 5-9)

5. There shall not any man be able to stand before thee all the days of thy life: as I was with Moses, so I will be with thee: I will not fail thee, nor forsake thee.

6. Be strong and of a good courage: for unto this people shalt thou divide for an inheritance the land, which I sware unto their fathers to give them.

7. Only be thou strong and very courageous, that thou mayest observe to do according to all the law, which Moses my servant commanded thee: turn not from it to the right hand or to the left, that thou mayest prosper whithersoever thou goest.

8. This book of the law shall not depart out of thy mouth; but thou shalt meditate therein day and night, that thou mayest observe to do according to all that is written therein: for then thou shalt make thy way prosperous, and then thou shalt have good success.

9. Have not I commanded thee? Be strong and of a good courage; be not afraid, neither be thou dismayed: for the Lord thy God is with thee whithersoever thou goest.

Here God promises Joshua and the nation of Israel that He will be with them wherever they go. He is *Immanuel*, "God with us." Israel was broken and discouraged from wandering in the wilderness for 40 years, but God was speaking a new word of hope and healing through His leader, Joshua. It was a message full of promise and fulfillment. The Lord exhorted them to "be strong and courageous" three times in these few verses.

Joshua 1:5-9 shows us that there is no greater promise than having God's presence in our lives. John Wesley cried on his deathbed, "Best of all God is with us." We can find meaning for the present and hope for the future when we know that God is going to be with us. Faith began to rise up in Israel once they realized that God would be with them. God's presence will be with us as we step out in faith and begin to stand on His promises.

Talk About It:
1. What promise did God give to Joshua (v. 5)?
2. Why did Joshua need courage (vv. 6, 7)?
3. What would bring Joshua success (vv. 7, 8)?

"We teach what we know, but we reproduce what we are."
—John Maxwell

Entering the Promised Land

D. We Will Obey (vv. 10-18)
(Joshua 1:12-15 is not included in the printed text.)

10. Then Joshua commanded the officers of the people, saying,

11. Pass through the host, and command the people, saying, Prepare you victuals; for within three days ye shall pass over this Jordan, to go in to possess the land, which the Lord your God giveth you to possess it.

16. And they answered Joshua, saying, All that thou commandest us we will do, and whithersoever thou sendest us, we will go.

17. According as we hearkened unto Moses in all things, so will we hearken unto thee: only the Lord thy God be with thee, as he was with Moses.

18. Whosoever he be that doth rebel against thy commandment, and will not hearken unto thy words in all that thou commandest him, he shall be put to death: only be strong and of a good courage.

victuals (v. 11)—provisions

The word "then" (v. 10) indicates the decisiveness of Joshua. The context conveys the immediate and obedient response by Joshua to God's command. There is no hesitation at the promises and responsibilities given by God. The Christian should strive for spontaneous obedience to God.

The Bible is careful to note Joshua's use of administrative structure by mentioning the word *officers*. Joshua could have dealt directly with the people. The Scripture could have bypassed this notation. However, administrative structure can be an essential tool in accomplishing God's plan, and it is noted here.

The heart of Joshua's command to the officers was to prepare. Joshua was confident of the promise of God, and he made preparation for that promise. The basis of his preparation and confidence about crossing the river was the provision of God. He proclaimed that God would give the land for their possession. Joshua's leadership began here with preparation based on the provision of God.

The people responded to Joshua with complete obedience indicated by the words "all" and "wherever" (v. 16, *NIV*). They committed themselves completely to the content of Joshua's commands and the places those commands would take them.

The people indicated the example and standard by which their obedience could be measured. That standard was their obedience to Moses. This generation of people represented a new generation of obedience for the nation. This was not the initial generation which left Egypt. That generation had continually disobeyed God and Moses. They were sentenced to wander in the wilderness for 40 years and to die there. This new generation that arose during the wandering period was obedient.

Talk About It:
1. What command did Joshua give to the officers (v. 11)?
2. What promises were made to Joshua in verses 16-18?

True Leadership
In order to be a leader, a man must have followers. And to have followers, a man must have their confidence. Hence the supreme quality of a leader is unquestionably integrity. Without it, no real success is possible,

Talk About It:
What did Joshua confidently say?

This generation's obedience made it possible for them to conquer the lands they had crossed on the way from the wilderness to the shores east of Jordan. Their obedience would make it possible for them to cross the Jordan and conquer Jericho in a resounding manner. They were now pledging their obedience to Joshua.

The phrase "only the Lord thy God be with thee" (v. 17) indicated the basis of the nation's obedience to Joshua. Their obedience was service to God before service to man. They needed the assurance that Joshua was directed by God before they would follow him. They did not blindly obey a man. They obeyed God by their obedience to God's leader.

This places a serious responsibility on the people of God and God's chosen leaders. The people of God must follow divinely appointed leadership as an act of service to God. Leaders commissioned by God are responsible to God for the manner in which they lead.

II. STEPPING OUT IN FAITH (Joshua 3:9-17)
A. Listening to the Word of God (vv. 9, 10)
   (Joshua 3:9, 10 is not included in the printed text.)
   Stepping out in faith begins and ends with listening to the Word of God. In verse 9, Joshua tells the people, "Come here and listen to the words of the Lord your God" (*NIV*). One of the reasons why Israel wandered in the wilderness for 40 years was because they listened to a false report by men who didn't have faith in God. They chose to listen to these faithless men rather than listen to God. This happens today. God will give us a promise, but then someone will tell us that it cannot come to pass, so we lose faith in the promise.

Under Joshua's leadership, Israel chose to listen to the word of the Lord. Before when they did not listen to God's Word, they had suffered. After they listened to His Word, they were able to have enough faith to enter the Promised Land.

Studying the Bible is very important for you to be able to grow in your faith. Keep in mind that the Bible is for you. Let it speak to you just as if it were written specifically to you. God speaks through His Word.

B. Following the Ark (vv. 11-17)
   (Joshua 3:11-13 is not included in the printed text.)
   14. And it came to pass, when the people removed from their tents, to pass over Jordan, and the priests bearing the ark of the covenant before the people;

   15. And as they that bare the ark were come unto Jordan, and the feet of the priests that bare the ark were dipped in the brim of the water, (for Jordan overfloweth all his banks all the time of harvest,)

16. That the waters which came down from above stood and rose up upon an heap very far from the city Adam, that is beside Zaretan: and those that came down toward the sea of the plain, even the salt sea, failed, and were cut off: and the people passed over right against Jericho.

17. And the priests that bare the ark of the covenant of the Lord stood firm on dry ground in the midst of Jordan, and all the Israelites passed over on dry ground, until all the people were passed clean over Jordan.

The first part of verse 15 describes the approach of the priests with the ark. The text is so specific it notes the feet of the priests touching the river. This reflects the precision of this miracle. God had said in verse 13 that when the soles of the feet of the priests touch the river, He would cut off the waters. This is precisely what happened. The miracle began at the moment specifically chosen by God.

There is a parenthetical notation recognizing that it was spring ("harvest"). This was the time of harvest when the snows on the high mountains at the headwaters of the Jordan were melting. The most prominent of these mountains was Mount Hermon (elevation, 9,200 feet). The waters of the river were flooding at their fullest. This removes all speculation that the crossing coincided with some natural drying of the river.

Joshua commanded the people to follow the ark of the covenant. The ark was made of acacia wood overlaid with gold. It contained manna, Aaron's rod, and the Ten Commandments. The ark was symbolic of God's gracious presence among His people and was Israel's most sacred possession.

Today, God's presence is manifest in and among His people through the Holy Spirit. We get into trouble when we do not follow God's Spirit. Jesus said, "When He, the Spirit of truth, has come, He will guide you into all truth" (John 16:13, *NKJV*). The Holy Spirit wants to give us wisdom and direction in everything we do. We should never make a major decision in our life without asking God's Spirit to lead us.

Verse 17 of the text says the priests "stood firm on dry ground" in the middle of the river. The phrase "dry ground" indicates the thoroughness of the miracle. Not only did the waters stop flowing, but the riverbed became dry. The priests were able to stand "firm" on the dry riverbed.

III. TESTIFYING TO GOD'S POWER (Joshua 4:1-9, 15-24)
A. God's Power Demonstrated (vv. 1-9)
    (Joshua 4:1-3, 8, 9 is not included in the printed text.)
4. Then Joshua called the twelve men, whom he had prepared of the children of Israel, out of every tribe a man:

rose up upon an heap (v. 16)—the waters were miraculously dammed up

right against Jericho (v. 16)—near Jericho

Talk About It:
1. What would lead Israel's way (v. 11), and why?
2. When was a path made through the Jordan (v. 13)?
3. Contrast this miracle with the Red Sea crossing (see Exodus 14:28-30).

"Do not follow where the path may lead, go instead where there is no path and leave a trail."
—*Sermon Illustrations.com*

5. And Joshua said unto them, Pass over before the ark of the Lord your God into the midst of Jordan, and take you up every man of you a stone upon his shoulder, according unto the number of the tribes of the children of Israel:

6. That this may be a sign among you, that when your children ask their fathers in time to come, saying, What mean ye by these stones?

7. Then ye shall answer them, That the waters of Jordan were cut off before the ark of the covenant of the Lord; when it passed over Jordan, the waters of Jordan were cut off: and these stones shall be for a memorial unto the children of Israel for ever.

Talk About It:
1. What was the significance of the number of stones (vv. 4, 5, 8)?
2. What was the purpose of the stones (vv. 6, 7)?

In verses 1-3 God instructs Joshua regarding the 12-stone memorial to be made. After the people had crossed the Jordan, God instructed Joshua to select 12 men. These men were to be representatives from each of the 12 tribes. Each man was to take a stone from the middle of the river where the priests were standing. They were to take them to that night's lodging place.

There were 12 stones and 12 representatives chosen to signify the thoroughness of God's blessing upon the entire nation. The stones were taken from the precise place where the ark had stood in the riverbed. This was to signify the work done there by the presence of God.

Verses 6 and 7 give the reason for setting the stones up— they were to be a "sign." The Hebrew word for *sign* is *ot* and is pronounced like the English word *oath*. The word meant "a token to induce consideration of something." In the context of this passage it meant "a memorial to induce memory and belief."

Those seeing the stones would remember what occurred at the river Jordan that day. Two things were to be remembered— the stopping of the waters and the role of the ark. The role of the ark was of particular importance. The description of its role is repeated in verse 7 for emphasis. This clearly indicates that the agency of God was of greater importance than the wonder of the miracle.

The power of God occurs not just for the benefit of believers in one generation. God's ability to miraculously work among His people must be communicated from one generation to the next. Parents hold a special responsibility to "raise up signs" (see v. 6) unto their children. These signs should highlight God's ability. If one generation fails to further this remembrance and memory, the children of that generation would be greatly threatened by what they were not told about the way God works in behalf of His people.

The most specific thing the memorial stones were to signify was the fact that the waters were stopped only when the ark came to the middle of the river. The emphasis upon the centrality of the ark was so critical that human participation is not mentioned. The priests carried the ark to the middle of the river. Joshua was the leader who received and gave the commands from God for the crossing. However, none of these individuals are mentioned. The ark signifying God's presence was to receive full attention and credit for the stopping of the waters.

The place of encampment where the stones were laid was Gilgal (vv. 19, 20). It would become a prominent city in the history of Israel. The monument of 12 stones was later erected there. The rite of circumcision was performed there by the nation (5:8). The Passover was first observed there by the nation in the Promised Land (v. 10). Most significantly, the city became the battle headquarters for Joshua as he conquered the Promised Land. Later, Saul would be anointed king there.

The presence of the memorial of stones would become an important source of inspiration. With all of the many events and victories surrounding the city, the ark would be a reminder of God's miraculous intervention. The remembrance of God's miraculous intervention can be a source of victory for the life of the believer.

B. God's Might Remembered (vv. 15-24)
(Joshua 4:15-19 is not included in the printed text.)
20. And those twelve stones, which they took out of Jordan, did Joshua pitch in Gilgal.

21. And he spake unto the children of Israel, saying, When your children shall ask their fathers in time to come, saying, What mean these stones?

22. Then ye shall let your children know, saying, Israel came over this Jordan on dry land.

23. For the Lord your God dried up the waters of Jordan from before you, until ye were passed over, as the Lord your God did to the Red sea, which he dried up from before us, until we were gone over:

24. That all the people of the earth might know the hand of the Lord, that it is mighty: that ye might fear the Lord your God for ever.

The miracle of crossing the Jordan was completed. The ark had led the way. God had commanded that 12 stones be taken from the river and a memorial be erected on the other side. Joshua also erected a memorial in the middle of the river. God's work was powerful and a mighty witness to the faithfulness of the Lord.

Passing It On
Our faith is never meant to keep to ourselves, but to pass on to the next generation. We need to pass our faith on to our children so they will keep it and do the same when they have children. There is no greater calling than this. Our children are paying careful attention to all that we do. They can sense whether we are genuine or not. We must live an authentic faith before them every day.

Talk About It:
1. When did the water return to its normal position (v. 18)?

2. Why did Joshua refer to the Red Sea miracle (v. 23)?
3. What was the ultimate purpose of the Red Sea and the Jordan crossings (v. 24; Exodus 14:31)?

The memorial represented yet another act of obedience of the children of Israel. They took the stones and built the memorial because they were commanded to do so.

The memorial was to be a remembrance to successive generations—that they might know the hand of God had brought them to this land against overwhelming odds. The event must never be forgotten. It was an act of God as significant as the crossing of the Red Sea. They were to know that the Lord himself had dried up the waters. Just as the Lord had delivered the children of Israel out of Egyptian bondage, He had brought the children of the wanderings into victory. God had not forgotten His covenant with His people. He was still working to fulfill His will for them.

The final emphasis of the memorial was the fear of the Lord. A contemporary translation of the Hebrew term used for *fear* in this passage is the word *reverence*. The fear of the Lord is the idea of being overwhelmed by the majesty of God, to be awestruck. The forces of nature and the efforts of men are so much smaller than His ability and might. In the light of His presence and power, individuals are overwhelmed by Him. The sense of overwhelming awe was to permeate all those who recognized the hand of God as a result of the memorial. The fear of the Lord was to be the final and climactic witness of the memorial on the outer side of the Jordan.

"The Christian faith is a faith in the miraculous; if we do not believe in miracles, we do not believe in Him."
—**Will Oursler**

CONCLUSION

As Joshua and the nation of Israel were called to inherit the Promised Land, so we are to receive the promises of God in our life by faith. A lack of faith was the reason why Israel wandered in the wilderness for 40 years. Lack of faith is the reason why many churches and Christians live defeated and broken lives. Hebrews 11:6 says, "Without faith it is impossible to please Him, for he who comes to God must believe that He is, and that He is a rewarder of those who diligently seek Him" (*NKJV*).

Let us follow the example of Joshua and receive the promises of God by faith. Let faith rise in your life, your family, and your church. Start believing God for the things that you know He has promised to you and your family. Like Joshua and the nation of Israel, step out in faith and begin to inherit the blessings of God.

GOLDEN TEXT CHALLENGE

"THE LORD YOUR GOD DRIED UP THE WATERS OF JORDAN FROM BEFORE YOU, . . . THAT ALL THE PEOPLE OF THE EARTH MIGHT KNOW THE HAND OF THE LORD, THAT IT IS MIGHTY: THAT YE MIGHT FEAR THE LORD YOUR GOD FOR EVER" (Joshua 4:23, 24).

One reason the Lord led the Israelites into Canaan through such a dramatic fashion—by parting the Jordan River—was so "all the people of the earth" would hear about it and realize the Almighty was on the side of Israel. The Israelites would face strong enemies in Canaan, but now those peoples would realize that the same God who had parted the Red Sea some 40 years earlier had also dried up the Jordan for His people. They were moving into Canaan under His authority.

This miraculous crossing also struck fear of the Lord into this new generation of Israelites, most of whom had only heard about the Red Sea crossing. Their obedience to God under Joshua's leadership had brought them into the Promised Land and could make anything possible if they continued to obey.

Daily Devotions:
M. Crossing the Red Sea
   Exodus 14:13-22
T. Consecrate Yourself
   Exodus 19:10-14
W. Blessed by God
   Isaiah 54:1-3
T. Doubt Not the Lord
   Matthew 14:25-33
F. Call to Obedience Through Faith
   Romans 1:8-17
S. Be Strong in Faith
   Romans 4:16-25

Bible Insight

The Art of Supernatural Living
(Joshua 3)
by Allan Lockerman

What have you experienced in your life that can only be explained by the super-naturalness of God? (I am not sure that *supernaturalness* is really a word, but I like the way it sounds, so I am going to say it again.) I repeat, What have you experienced in your life that can only be explained by the supernaturalness of God?

You may be one of those people who can honestly say your life is filled with the supernatural. As Adrian Rogers says, you might be "naturally supernatural." Your motto may be, "A miracle a day keeps the devil away." But if you are like many people, you are not sure you have ever truly experienced supernaturalness. What a pity . . . what a shame. I have already stated that the promised life is not a 24/7 life of super-naturalness, but I do believe that it is a life that knows the touch of the supernatural. Or stated more succinctly, there is a supernatural dimension to the promised life.

Joshua 3 begins the epic conquest of the Promised Land. From the outset, it was supernatural. Let me set the scene. The children of Israel were poised to cross into Canaan. Ahead of them was a formidable barrier—the mighty Jordan River. If you have been to that part of the world, you may snicker when I talk about the Jordan River as mighty and formidable. Ordinarily, it is anything *but* a raging torrent. Those who have never seen it often have the mistaken idea that the Jordan is a major trib-utary like the Mississippi. It is not. In fact, in my neck of the woods, we wouldn't call it a river. We would probably call it a creek and name a Baptist church after it. It isn't much of a river, as rivers go. In fact, at points you can wade across it.

But at this particular time, the Jordan River was at flood stage. "For the Jordan overflows all its banks during the whole time of harvest" (Joshua 3:15). The rains had come and the snows had melted on Mount Hermon, so the water was raging. I find it interesting that the Lord told them to move across at the worst possible time. God was testing them. They had a choice to make: Would they step out in faith, or play it safe? They stepped out in faith. The priests moved into the water carrying the ark of the covenant, and as they did, the water dried up for 60 miles—all the way to the city of Adam.

This is an incredible account—déjà vu of the Red Sea crossing. It is a story of God's people experiencing the dimension of the supernatural. To be sure, this is *not* the kind of thing that happens every day. But it did happen, and from it we can learn some powerful truths about the supernaturalness of the promised life.

Before we go further, I want to issue a disclaimer. This is going to be simple stuff, so simple it may offend your sophistication. But though it is simple, most people are not going to understand it. I doubt that one in 10 will "get it," because it deals with things supernatural. Writing to the Corinthians, the apostle Paul made it clear that some people simply are not equipped to perceive the supernatural. There are some Paul refers to as "natural" (see 1 Corinthians 2:14)—people who do not possess the Spirit of God in their lives and cannot discern spiritual (supernatural) things. But you can possess the Spirit of God and still not grasp the supernatural. If you are a Christian whose focus is always on the natural, you will have difficulty believing, accepting and experiencing something that is beyond the natural. Why bother with a passage that 90 percent of the people reading it will not fully understand? Because, if only 10 percent get it, it will revolutionize the church.

Believe in the Possibility

If you are to experience the supernatural dimension, you must believe in the possibility of supernatural living. Joshua clearly did.

"Sanctify yourselves, for tomorrow the Lord will do wonders among you" (Joshua 3:5). I like Joshua. He believed in the possibility of supernatural living. He believed in a God who "can." There are many, both outside the faith and within the faith, who do not believe that God can. The apostle Paul warned that this day would come. Speaking to Timothy, he made the following statement: "In the last days . . . [men will have] a form of godliness but denying its power. And from such people turn away" (2 Timothy 3:1, 5).

Please note that last phrase, "From such people turn away." The language means "run away." If you're around people who call themselves Christians, yet who do not believe in the supernaturalness of God, leave them alone. They are bad news. There are people who want us to believe that the miraculous, if it *ever* happened, is only a thing of the past. They would have us to believe that now, having the completed canon of Scripture, supernatural things don't happen—at least not as they happened in the past. Now we can read His Word and live under natural law.

Allow me to say a word about "natural" laws. There are none. There is no such thing as a "natural" law. In fact, there is no Mother Nature; there is only Father God. Therefore, there are no "laws of nature"—only laws of God. And if God made them, He can suspend them.

My family and I were on a vacation trip. The five of us were crowded into one small car. Every 30 minutes or so, somebody would need to stop. It didn't take long for that to get old and my patience to run thin. Finally, after one stop too many, I announced that I was making a new law: "No stopping until we are at least halfway there."

Thirty minutes later, we stopped again, only this time, nature was calling me. My kids were brutal. "What about the law? You laid down the law!" To which I replied, "I make the laws, I break the laws." I know what you are thinking—*That is very bad parenting.* You are right. But it is good theology. If God makes the laws, God can suspend the laws of nature. God is a supernatural God.

Just so you understand where I'm coming from and who I am, let me make it abundantly clear. I am a thoroughgoing supernaturalist. I don't just believe in a God who can—I believe in a God who will! I don't just believe in a God who once did—I believe in a God who still does!

I don't mean that I walk on water or call down fire from heaven. I don't anoint handkerchiefs and send them out at $49.99, VISA and MasterCard accepted. But I do believe in a God who will enable you and me to live beyond the natural capacity of our lives.

Some time ago, I was listening to a broadcast of a high school football game. Playing on the defensive line was a young man who was too small for the position. He stood 5 feet 8 inches tall and weighed 150 pounds and was playing against two huge, offensive linemen, each weighing over 200 pounds. Evidently he was doing quite well. One of the commentators said, "You know, the little guy just plays bigger than himself." That young man was not playing by supernatural power; he was simply maximizing his natural capacity. But when I heard that statement, I remember thinking, *That is exactly the way we are supposed to live—bigger than ourselves. Life is supposed to be lived beyond natural capacity.*

If the truth were known, when it comes to the spiritual life, most of us don't even live up to the natural capacities that we possess. If we did, there is so much more we could do. But God designed us not to live beneath, or even within, but *beyond* our capacities. God designed us to be people of faith who live boldly and trust God for the results. A.W. Tozer said, "God is looking for people through whom He can do the impossible. What a pity that we plan only the things we can do by ourselves."

The apostle Paul wrote, "I can do all things through Christ who strengthens me" (Philippians 4:13). It is not a can-do attitude we're talking about. It is a God-can-do attitude. If you want to experience the supernatural dimension, you must believe in the possibility of supernatural living.

Go With God

Believing in the possibility is not enough. If you want to experience the supernatural dimension, you must place yourself in the flow of what God is doing. Joshua told the people to watch the ark and follow after it. What was the ark of the covenant? What did it mean to the people?

The ark was actually a furnishing from the Holy of Holies in the Tabernacle. It was a wooden chest overlaid with gold. It measured approximately 2 feet by 4 feet. Inside the ark was the Book of the Law, the tablets with the Commandments upon them, Aaron's rod that budded in the wilderness, and a gold pot containing some of the manna that had fallen from heaven.

Incidentally, we do not know what happened to the ark of the covenant. There are many legends and myths concerning it, and scholars are divided. Some believe it was stolen in 950 B.C. by foreign invaders. Others believe Nebuchadnezzar destroyed it in 586 B.C., along with some of the utensils in the Temple. One theory holds that the ark of the covenant is buried deep within the western wall of the Temple mount in a secret chamber that no one knows about anymore. Many people in Israel believe the day will come when the Temple will be rebuilt and in the process, the ark will be recovered.

The ark of the covenant represented the presence of God in their midst. It served as the visible reminder of the invisible God with them. It was there that the Shekinah (or presence of God) dwelled. Now you can understand Joshua's instruction, "Watch the ark, and wherever the ark goes, you go." Wherever God is going, we must go with Him.

There is a principle here that most of us miss. Good people will sometimes say, "I've been a Christian for years, and I have never experienced the supernatural." The problem is they are not looking for the hand of God, so they never see it.

Let me dispel a myth. There is the idea that when we become Christians, God joins Himself to our life, and we can exercise His power as we see fit. We seem to think God wants to join in our plan. People will say, "God is on our side." I have heard people pray before a volleyball game and ask God to "be on their side." Let's get it straight. God doesn't join us. God allows us to join *Him*. We don't do our thing in His power. That is backward. Here is a revelation: *God is not on your side.* He is not on anybody's side. God *is* the side! Be very careful when you pray. Do not ask God to be on your side. Instead pray, "Dear God, help me to be on Your side." Joshua was saying, "Go after God." How does this work? Let me put this in practical terms.

1. *Pay attention to what God is doing in your community.* Henry Blackaby says it well: "If you see God doing something, drop everything and get in on it." Go with God. I am not encouraging church hopping to find the best show in town. But I am saying when God is doing something in your community, don't let your loyalty to a dead church keep you from a living work of God.

2. *Pay attention to what God is doing in your church.* What is God anointing and blessing? What kind of worship does God seem to be blessing? Move in that direction. What ministries does God seem to be anointing these days? Move in that direction.

3. *Pay attention to what God may be doing in your home.* Do you want a touch of the supernatural in your marriage? I have a suggestion for you: Pay attention to what God is doing in your spouse's life, and go in that direction. There are marriages on the rocks for this very reason. God is doing something in the husband or the wife, and the other is not paying attention. I have known wives whose husbands are struggling as God does a new work in them, but they fail to see God's hand in it. Many a man in the throes of a mid-life crisis is like Jacob wrestling with God. Some wives are not in tune with God, or their husband, enough to sense what is happening. The same goes for husbands who never sense what God is doing in their wives. What is God doing in your mate? Don't fight it. Join it, and see what God will do in your home.

What is God doing in the lives of your children? What are the gifts God is developing in them? What is the natural inclination God has given them? Watch for it, and then get in on it. Rather than trying to shape that child in your image, let that child grow up in God's image—the image that God has put in his or her life.

4. *Pay attention to what God is doing in your sphere of influence.* What is God doing at your office among your coworkers and friends? Do you want to be an effective witness? Pay attention to what God is doing, and get in on it. Go in that direction. The idea is this: God is *always* doing something. There is never a time when He is not. Pay attention, and put yourself in the flow of what God's doing.

5. *Pay attention to what God is doing in your life.* What things are changing around you and in you? I find that most people are aware that things are constantly changing in them and around them, but they never seem to pick up on the idea that God is doing a new work in their life. In my own life, there are areas of ministry I no longer feel God blessing as He once did. But there are new areas of ministry that He seems to be opening to me. Could God be changing me? Do I just keep doing what I have always done, or do I move in the new direction God seems to be blessing? Go with the flow of God, not against it, if you want to see the supernatural dimension of the promised life.

One last word: Stay in the flow. It is important that you not lose sight of where God is going next. There is a strange caveat to Joshua's instruction. In Joshua 3:4, the people are told to follow the ark, but not too closely: "Yet there shall be a space between you and it, about two thousand cubits by measure."

Two thousand cubits is roughly half a mile. They are to follow after the ark, but they are to maintain a half-mile radius around it. Why? Verse 4 continues and gives us the rationale. "Do not come near it, that you may know the way by which you must go, for you have not passed this way before."

The idea is simple. Don't get so close to it that you obscure the view. Make sure it is kept out front, so the people can keep their focus on it at all times. If you ever lose focus on where God's going, you are in trouble.

How does that apply? Follow God, and don't lose track of what God is doing now. Don't lose focus. There are whole generations that have done just that. They have lost the focus of what God is doing now. In a previous generation, we discerned where God was going and followed, but if we are not careful, we will lose our focus on what God is doing now. Following God is not a onetime affair; it is a day-by-day thing. Where is God going now? The constant prayer of every believer must be, "What next, Lord? What next, Lord?" That is the only way we will continue in the supernatural dimension of the promised life.

*Unless otherwise indicated, Scripture quotations are taken from the *New King James Version*. This Bible Insight is excerpted from *When Good Enough Is Not Enough*. It is available from Pathway Press online at *www.pathwaybookstore.com* or by calling 1-800-553-8506.

Victory by Submission to God

INTRODUCTION

If Joshua 1–5 is about preparing to inherit the Promised Land, then chapter 6 is about possessing the Promised Land. Israel had to learn some valuable lessons as they stood on the edge of the land of Canaan: Submission brings victory, and sin brings defeat. When Israel obeyed and submitted to God's plan, they had victory (ch. 6); but when they let sin in, they were defeated in battle (ch. 7). To submit to God means that we must bring ourselves under the rule and the mission of God. As we shall see, we can overcome life's greatest challenges by submitting to God's plan and obeying His instructions for our life.

The first great battle that Israel won was against the city of Jericho. One of the most ancient cities in the world, Jericho is first mentioned in Numbers 22:1. The walls of the city enclosed about seven acres. A large portion of Jericho's people lived outside the walls and retreated inside whenever there was an attack. The Lord had an unusual battle plan for Israel to bring down the walls and gain victory over the ancient city.

There is a simple way to explain the conquest of Jericho: Israel obeyed God. If any are not satisfied with that explanation, they don't appreciate the value of obedience. Any of God's miraculous works involve obedience in some manner. We must do what we are told first, and then if necessary, all nature will allow her normal course to be interrupted and superseded, and give priority to God's higher law. Wind and waves will obey Him, the solid earth will give way to His commands, and towering walls will fall in obeisance as we dare first to act upon God's Word.

We can be more than conquerors, for it is more than we who are doing the fighting. If God does not have to fight *with* us, He will fight *for* us, and His incalculable resources will be tuned to a powerful response to our obedience.

Unit Theme:
Joshua and Judges

Central Truth:
Victorious Christian living results from obedience to God's Word.

Focus:
Realize we can overcome life's greatest challenges by submitting to God's plan and obey His instructions.

Context:
Around 1400 B.C. the Israelites conquer Jericho.

Golden Text:
"Trust in the Lord with all thine heart; and lean not unto thine own understanding. In all thy ways acknowledge him, and he shall direct thy paths" (Proverbs 3:5, 6).

Study Outline:
I. An Unusual Battle Plan (Joshua 6:1-7)
II. An Obedient People (Joshua 6:8-19)
III. A Victorious Outcome (Joshua 6:20-27)

I. AN UNUSUAL BATTLE PLAN (Joshua 6:1-7)

A. A Battle Already Won (vv. 1-5)

1. Now Jericho was straitly shut up because of the children of Israel: none went out, and none came in.

2. And the Lord said unto Joshua, See, I have given into thine hand Jericho, and the king thereof, and the mighty men of valour.

3. And ye shall compass the city, all ye men of war, and go round about the city once. Thus shalt thou do six days.

4. And seven priests shall bear before the ark seven trumpets of rams' horns: and the seventh day ye shall compass the city seven times, and the priests shall blow with the trumpets.

5. And it shall come to pass, that when they make a long blast with the ram's horn, and when ye hear the sound of the trumpet, all the people shall shout with a great shout; and the wall of the city shall fall down flat, and the people shall ascend up every man straight before him.

The phrase "straitly shut up" (v. 1) is a special construction in Hebrew and indicates that the people of Jericho did not only shut the gate, but kept it strongly closed continually. God had not only been working *for* the children of Israel, but He had been working *with* the people of Jericho; for "because of the children of Israel" the city was shut up. God had instilled fear into their hearts through the report of the miracles that He had been doing (2:9-11).

God had an unusual battle strategy for Israel that included waiting, walking, and not talking. This unconventional strategy was a test of Israel's faith and obedience. Israel could have been overwhelmed by their enemy and their circumstances. The wall of Jericho must have seemed large and intimidating to the nomadic people of God who had never had their own fortified land. There was probably no way they could have won this battle on their own. They had no military experience, weaponry, or training. Therefore God told them, "I have given Jericho into your hands" (v. 2, *NASB*). He had already won the battle for them. They just needed to have faith, submit, and obey His word.

The Lord commanded them to circle the city of Jericho (v. 3). Circling a fortified city was an ancient ritual of siege designed to intimidate its inhabitants. Circling the city built the faith of the Israelites and put fear in the hearts of the people of Jericho. The Lord also commanded them to blow trumpets that were made from the horns of rams (v. 4). These horns produced a loud tone and were used to make a signal rather than music. They were used to summon people to an assembly or gathering. Each of these commands was given to teach Israel that God's promises are fulfilled whenever His commands are obeyed.

Talk About It:
1. Why was Jericho "shut up" (v. 1)?
2. How is the number 7 significant in this story (v. 4)?
3. What amazing outcome did God reveal (v. 5)?

"Faith is deliberate confidence in the character of God, whose ways you may not understand at the time."

—Oswald Chambers

Victory by Submission to God

B. Spoken Promise (vv. 6, 7)

6. And Joshua the son of Nun called the priests, and said unto them, Take up the ark of the covenant, and let seven priests bear seven trumpets of rams' horns before the ark of the Lord.

7. And he said unto the people, Pass on, and compass the city, and let him that is armed pass on before the ark of the Lord.

Once Joshua received the word of encouragement from God (vv. 1-5), he then spoke the word to the people. When the Lord gives us a message of promise, we must speak it to others. We also should constantly remind ourselves of God's Word by meditating on it. In Hebrew thought, to meditate on Scriptures is to quietly repeat them, giving oneself entirely to God and abandoning outside distractions. Paul tells us, "Whatever is true, whatever is noble, whatever is just, whatever is pure, whatever is lovely, whatever things are of good report . . . *meditate* on these things" (see Philippians 4:8).

In a world full of distractions, we need to allow God to speak to us. It takes time to drown out the cares of the world, sit and prayerfully meditate on God's Word, and then allow Him to speak to us. It is the Word that builds our faith and trust in the Lord. When Joshua began to speak the word to Israel, God's promises began to take root in their hearts and they were spiritually prepared to receive the Promised Land. If we are going to stand on God's promises, we should speak them. The more of the Word we have in our hearts and lives, the more we will be able to live victorious Christian lives.

> **Talk About It:**
> How did Joshua respond to God's directives?

II. AN OBEDIENT PEOPLE (Joshua 6:8-19)

A. Victory Plan (vv. 8, 9)

8. And it came to pass, when Joshua had spoken unto the people, that the seven priests bearing the seven trumpets of rams' horns passed on before the Lord, and blew with the trumpets: and the ark of the covenant of the Lord followed them.

9. And the armed men went before the priests that blew with the trumpets, and the rereward came after the ark, the priests going on, and blowing with the trumpets.

Here we are given the order of march: the armed men first, the priests with their ark and the trumpets, and then the "rear guard" (v. 9, *NIV*). The army of Israel consisted of all the able-bodied and willing men age 20 and older.

The people of Jericho must have been awestruck by the sight of perhaps 400,000 soldiers marching around their city day after day. It obviously was not a military maneuver, for this procession only invited attack. The small Jericho army must

> **Talk About It:**
> Describe the procession.

have sensed divine sanction in Israel's actions. Though they did not know exactly what would happen, they were helpless before the God of Israel.

Israel was commanded to follow exactly what God had ordered them to do in order to receive the victory. Seven priests were to blow seven trumpets and they were to march around Jericho for six days. On the seventh day they were to march around the walls seven times (vv. 13-15). *Seven* is God's perfect number and symbolized completeness and perfection. Paralleling Creation, the seventh day of the siege was God's appointed time for the destruction of Jericho.

Rather than using weapons to show military power, the army was commanded to shout to the Lord for victory. Although this seems like a foolish military strategy, the significance of this battle is found in Israel's obedience to what God asked them to do. What they were commanded to do didn't matter as much as their obedience to what He had commanded. The Bible says obedience is "better than sacrifice" (1 Samuel 15:22). They were commanded to march, and that's what they did. Whenever we obey God, no matter how silly it may seem, He promises to bless us. God always honors obedience. Victory comes through obedience!

One of the most important lessons we can ever learn is that the battle belongs to God. It is so easy to get tunnel vision when we are in the midst of trials and difficulties. As a result, our problems and circumstances seem bigger than God. The lesson to be learned is that Almighty God will give us victory when we submit to His plan and His Word.

B. Silent Belief (vv. 10-15)
(Joshua 6:11-14 is not included in the printed text.)

10. And Joshua had commanded the people, saying, Ye shall not shout, nor make any noise with your voice, neither shall any word proceed out of your mouth, until the day I bid you shout; then shall ye shout.

15. And it came to pass on the seventh day, that they rose early about the dawning of the day, and compassed the city after the same manner seven times: only on that day they compassed the city seven times.

Joshua commands the people not to speak as they walk around the city of Jericho. Why? One reason would be to keep the people from speaking unbelief. Joshua knew one of the main reasons Israel wandered in the wilderness for 40 years was that they murmured among themselves in unbelief. Joshua wasn't going to take that chance again.

When facing overwhelming circumstances, it is better to say nothing at all than to speak unbelief. Many Christians are quick

"It is difficult to steer a parked car, so get moving."
—Henrietta Mears

Talk About It:
1. When was there to be silence, and when was there to be shouting (v. 10)?
2. What was different about the seventh day (v. 15)?

Victory by Submission to God

to speak words of unbelief. It is amazing how many times we get ourselves into trouble by saying the wrong thing. The lesson we should learn is to watch every word that comes out of our mouth. Words can bind us or they can set us free.

A second reason for the soldiers to march in silence was to foster a growing sense of awe as the people of Jericho watched the march. There were no threats nor words of boasting coming from Israel's soldiers. Instead, they march in calm, quiet obedience to their all-powerful God. Their trust was in Him alone.

C. Time to Shout (v. 16)

16. And it came to pass at the seventh time, when the priests blew with the trumpets, Joshua said unto the people, Shout; for the Lord hath given you the city.

Joshua commands Israel to shout for the victory after they silently march around Jericho seven times on the seventh day. In the middle of a battle, if you say anything, let it be a shout unto the Lord for victory. Rather than speaking words of unbelief, shout words of faith, hope and love. Remind yourself of the promises of God. Preach to yourself. Remember, "Faith comes by hearing, and hearing by the word of God" (Romans 10:17, *NKJV*).

D. Devotion to God (vv. 17-19)

17. And the city shall be accursed, even it, and all that are therein, to the Lord: only Rahab the harlot shall live, she and all that are with her in the house, because she hid the messengers that we sent.

18. And ye, in any wise keep yourselves from the accursed thing, lest ye make yourselves accursed, when ye take of the accursed thing, and make the camp of Israel a curse, and trouble it.

19. But all the silver, and gold, and vessels of brass and iron, are consecrated unto the Lord: they shall come into the treasury of the Lord.

Joshua commanded the Israelites before they went into Jericho not to defile themselves with unclean things. He said, "Keep away from the devoted things, so that you will not bring about your own destruction by taking any of them" (v. 18, *NIV*). He warned them not to allow themselves to become contaminated with the things of the world. Many times, our greatest temptations come after our greatest victory.

The silver and gold in verse 19 are symbolic of the things that tempt us daily. If we are not careful, the very things we once conquered can influence us. As we go into battle, we must be sure not to covet the very thing we are trying to conquer. We have to guard our thoughts, hearts and lives from "the accursed thing" (v. 18) that pulls us away from holiness.

"We must not be still and look for miracles; up and be doing, and the Lord will be with thee."
—John Eliot

Talk About It:
Why should we shout to the Lord (see Psalm 47:1)?

accursed (v. 18)— devoted

Talk About It:
1. Who was to be spared, and why (v. 17)?
2. What was the warning about "the accursed thing" (v. 18)?
3. What was to be brought to the Lord (v. 19)?

"If the guilt of sin is so great that nothing can satisfy it but the blood of Jesus; and the filth of sin is so great that nothing can fetch out the stain thereof but the blood of Jesus, how great, how heinous, how sinful must the evil of sin be."
—William Bridge

III. A VICTORIOUS OUTCOME (Joshua 6:20-27)

A. Walls Will Fall (vv. 20, 21)

20. So the people shouted when the priests blew with the trumpets: and it came to pass, when the people heard the sound of the trumpet, and the people shouted with a great shout, that the wall fell down flat, so that the people went up into the city, every man straight before him, and they took the city.

21. And they utterly destroyed all that was in the city, both man and woman, young and old, and ox, and sheep, and ass, with the edge of the sword.

Talk About It:
Why was Jericho "utterly destroyed" (v. 21)?

After Israel did everything God had commanded them to do, the walls of Jericho fell (v. 20). Archaeological excavations of Jericho have revealed that the account as we have it describes exactly what happened on that eventful day. It has been determined that the outer wall fell outward, and down the hillside. The houses setting on the top between the outer and inner walls dragged the inner walls with them. Numerous traces were also found of an earthquake. Some believe an earthquake caused the collapse of the walls. If it did or didn't, the important thing is that God ordained that the walls should fall when the sound of the trumpet was heard, and when the people shouted with a great shout.

The walls of Jericho fell as Israel submitted themselves to God. In the same way, we can overcome life's greatest obstacles by submitting to God's plan and obeying His instructions. Whatever walls are in our life have no chance when we submit to God. James tells us, "Submit . . . to God. Resist the devil, and he will flee from you" (James 4:7).

Israel was commanded to destroy all that was in the city because the Canaanite culture was extremely corrupt. If Israel didn't utterly destroy the inhabitants, they would become a serious threat to the spiritual welfare of the nation of Israel. At the same time, Israel became God's instrument of divine judgment against the Canaanites. Therefore, Israel "destroyed with the sword every living thing" in Jericho (Joshua 6:21, *NIV*).

"Sin fascinates you; then it assassinates you."
—Christians Quoting.org

This is a spiritual metaphor for contemporary believers to examine ourselves and see if there is any wicked way in us. If we are not careful to walk in holiness unto the Lord, the things of the world can creep into our lives and destroy us spiritually. Through television, movies, the Internet, and other subtle influences, the world can work its way back into our lives. Therefore, we should take every precaution to make sure we guard ourselves from the Enemy.

B. God Honors His Promises (vv. 22-25)

22. But Joshua had said unto the two men that had spied out the country, Go into the harlot's house, and bring

out thence the woman, and all that she hath, as ye sware unto her.

23. And the young men that were spies went in, and brought out Rahab, and her father, and her mother, and her brethren, and all that she had; and they brought out all her kindred, and left them without the camp of Israel.

24. And they burnt the city with fire, and all that was therein: only the silver, and the gold, and the vessels of brass and of iron, they put into the treasury of the house of the Lord.

25. And Joshua saved Rahab the harlot alive, and her father's household, and all that she had; and she dwelleth in Israel even unto this day; because she hid the messengers, which Joshua sent to spy out Jericho.

Earlier (ch. 2), Rahab the harlot had opened her home to protect the Hebrew spies from the Jericho authorities. As a result, the Lord promised to spare Rahab when judgment came to Jericho. True to His word, God had the Israelites destroy all of the inhabitants of Jericho with the exception of Rahab and her family. Amazingly, Rahab became the great-great-grandmother of King David (see Matthew 1:5, 6).

Even though Rahab was a harlot living among an idol-worshiping people, God offered her redemption from judgment. God is a God of grace. Throughout the Bible, we can see that God is seeking to restore a people to Himself. He offers this free gift to us by His grace and mercy. We are "saved by grace through faith . . . not of works, lest anyone should boast" (see Ephesians 2:8, 9). We can never be good enough to earn God's love. In fact, there is nothing we can do to make God love us more than He already does. When asked by a multitude what God wanted from them, Jesus replied, "Believe on him whom he hath sent" (John 6:29). It is the work of grace through faith, not of anything we can do.

C. God Will Bless You (vv. 26, 27)

26. And Joshua adjured them at that time, saying, Cursed be the man before the Lord, that riseth up and buildeth this city Jericho: he shall lay the foundation thereof in his firstborn, and in his youngest son shall he set up the gates of it.

27. So the Lord was with Joshua; and his fame was noised throughout all the country.

We can see an amazing contrast in the last two verses of chapter 6: "Cursed before the Lord is the man who rises up and builds this city Jericho. . . . So the Lord was with Joshua, and his fame was in all the land" (*NASB*). God's curse remained on the land of Jericho for over 500 years, and was later mentioned in 1 Kings 16:34. The curse was to make the pagan city

Talk About It:
What does the treatment of Rahab reveal about God (also see Hebrews 11:31)?

"Faith is the gaze of a soul upon a saving God."
—A.W. Tozer

Talk About It:
1. Describe the curse on Jericho (v. 26).
2. What happened to Joshua (v. 27)?

of Jericho a permanent reminder of God's judgment against evil.

In contrast, we see that Joshua will always be remembered as the man who led Israel into the Promised Land. He has a godly legacy alongside other patriarchs such as Moses, Abraham and Isaac. What sets these men apart is their total submission and obedience to God and His word. When we honor and obey God, He not only blesses us but our ancestors after us. As the psalmist said, "I have been young, and now am old; yet I have not seen the righteous forsaken, nor his descendants begging bread. He is ever merciful, and lends; his descendants are blessed" (Psalm 37:25, 26, *NKJV*).

CONCLUSION

We will never inherit the promised land of heaven without some battles. We must do whatever God asks of us, no matter how unusual or insignificant it might seem. Throughout the Bible we see where the Lord asked people to do things that didn't make sense according to the world's wisdom. We need to submit and obey God's Word and plan for our lives. When we become obedient to God in every area of our lives, we will experience victorious Christian living.

GOLDEN TEXT CHALLENGE

"TRUST IN THE LORD WITH ALL THINE HEART; AND LEAN NOT UNTO THINE OWN UNDERSTANDING. IN ALL THY WAYS ACKNOWLEDGE HIM, AND HE SHALL DIRECT THY PATHS" (Proverbs 3:5, 6).

We are urged to trust in the Lord totally, abandoning ourselves to Him and His grace. There is a natural inclination to hold back a part of ourselves for ourselves or to trust in our human ability to chart the course of our life. Human understanding is not adequate for this responsibility, however, and our only safe alternative is to trust the Lord and depend on His understanding. At least four other times the Bible admonishes us to trust or love the Lord with all our heart (see Matthew 22:37; Joshua 22:5; 1 Samuel 12:20; Deuteronomy 11:13).

Our Golden Text tells us to acknowledge God in *all* our ways, which means in all our activities, thoughts, aspirations and plans. In everything that concerns our life, we should acknowledge God as Lord and Master. In so doing, we can be sure He will direct our paths. We are thus called upon for total commitment to the Lord, total trust in Him, and total acknowledgment of His lordship.

"Nothing can more raise a man's reputation, nor make him appear more truly great, than to have the evidences of God's presence with him."
—**Matthew Henry**

Daily Devotions:
M. Victory Through Obedience
   2 Samuel 5:22-25
T. Walk Away From Sin
   Ezra 10:1-4
W. God Is With His People
   Zechariah 8:20-23
T. Overcome Evil With Good
   Romans 12:14-21
F. Victorious in Christ
   2 Corinthians 2:14-17
S. God Remembers Your Obedience
   Hebrews 6:9-12

Victory by Submission to God

Sin's Consequences and God's Faithfulness

Joshua 9:1 through 10:14; Judges 2:1-5

INTRODUCTION

Joshua 9 teaches us about the consequences of sin and the faithfulness of God. Joshua and the nation of Israel were deceived into making a covenant with the Gibeonites, which resulted in sin and failure. Gibeon was one of the four Hivite cities, about six miles west of Jerusalem. The Gibeonites desired to make a covenant with Israel because they knew that God commanded Israel to destroy all of the inhabitants of the land. As Christians, we need to learn that the world will deceive us and that sin has dire consequences.

The Bible tells us repeatedly that we will reap what we sow, whether good or bad (Galatians 6:7). Therefore, we must be careful not to sow to sin or the flesh. In contrast we should sow to the Spirit, which will result in everlasting life. This means there are serious consequences for our thoughts, words and deeds. We have a responsibility to live for God. To be responsible means we have the ability to respond. We are not victims of sin, but free agents who must take responsibility for the consequences of our actions.

Not seeking God's counsel and not praying will bring failure. If we don't seek the Lord, we will end up making decisions on our own which result in sin and suffering. However, God is always faithful to restore and revive when we call upon His name and repent.

Unit Theme:
Joshua and Judges

Central Truth:
God is faithful to help believers who seek Him.

Focus:
Reflect on God's faithfulness to His people despite their failure, and trust Him to work on our behalf.

Context:
Around 1400 B.C., Joshua continues leading Israel in the Promised Land.

Golden Text:
"Be not deceived; God is not mocked: for whatsoever a man soweth, that shall he also reap" (Galatians 6:7).

Study Outline:
I. Failure to Seek God's Counsel (Joshua 9:1-15)
II. Consequences of Prayerlessness (Joshua 9:16-27; Judges 2:1-5)
III. God Remains Faithful (Joshua 10:6-14)

I. FAILURE TO SEEK GOD'S COUNSEL (Joshua 9:1-15)

A. United Against God's People (vv. 1, 2)

1. And it came to pass, when all the kings which were on this side Jordan, in the hills, and in the valleys, and in all the coasts of the great sea over against Lebanon, the Hittite, and the Amorite, the Canaanite, the Perizzite, the Hivite, and the Jebusite, heard thereof;

2. That they gathered themselves together, to fight with Joshua and with Israel, with one accord.

When news of the conquest of Ai (ch. 8) reached the kings on the west side of Jordan, they banded themselves together to wage war on the Israelites. They imagined they were strong enough to defeat the Lord God of Israel himself. In their madness they were blind to the fact that He who had brought His people out of Egypt, sustained them in the wilderness for 40 years, and fought their battles for them, could be overwhelmed by man's devices.

People who bind themselves together to oppose God's plans and work will certainly fail in their wicked designs. So long as any people walk in the way of the Lord, they will be victorious. Opposition to those engaged in God's work is rebellion against God himself. As once the Canaanites banded together to fight Israel, so the foes of Christ combine to wage war upon Him and His church.

B. Deceiving God's People (vv. 3-13)

(Joshua 9:10-13 is not included in the printed text.)

3. And when the inhabitants of Gibeon heard what Joshua had done unto Jericho and to Ai,

4. They did work wilily, and went and made as if they had been ambassadors, and took old sacks upon their asses, and wine bottles, old, and rent, and bound up;

5. And old shoes and clouted upon their feet, and old garments upon them; and all the bread of their provision was dry and mouldy.

6. And they went to Joshua unto the camp at Gilgal, and said unto him, and to the men of Israel, We be come from a far country: now therefore make ye a league with us.

7. And the men of Israel said unto the Hivites, Peradventure ye dwell among us; and how shall we make a league with you?

8. And they said unto Joshua, We are thy servants. And Joshua said unto them, Who are ye? and from whence come ye?

9. And they said unto him, From a very far country thy servants are come because of the name of the Lord thy God: for we have heard the fame of him, and all that he did in Egypt.

Talk About It:
1. What had "all the kings . . . heard about" (v. 1, *NIV*)?
2. What happened "with one accord" (v. 2)?

wilily (v. 4)—"craftily" (*NKJV*)

clouted (v. 5)— "patched" (*NKJV*)

Being alarmed at what had happened at Jericho and Ai, and knowing all the Canaanites were to be cut off, the Gibeonites resorted to a strategy different from that employed by the kings. Instead of relying upon power, they would resort to guile and deception and make peace with Israel. Disguising themselves so that they appeared as men who had traveled from a far country, they rode to the camp of Israel and sought out Joshua. Being cunning men, and desperate to save their own lives as well as those of their people, they pretended to have undergone the fatigues and hardships of a very long journey. The condition of their clothing and other possessions seemed to confirm what they said.

When Joshua asked them who they were, they said they were ambassadors from a country a long way off. Although the Israelites had been solemnly forbidden to make a covenant with any of the Canaanites, and the slaughter of them had already begun, God spared the Gibeonites in spite of their hypocrisy because they believed in His power to protect them. He saw their faith, poor as it was, and refrained from exposing them to Joshua. Even limited, imperfect faith is honored by God, and it is better than none at all, in that it may develop into greater faith.

The Gibeonites came to Joshua and the nation of Israel in order to deceive them into making a covenant with them so that they might live. *Deception* means being tricked into believing something that is a lie. It has its origins with the devil, who is "the father of lies" (John 8:44, *NIV*). He has been deceiving people since he came in the form of a serpent to Adam and Eve in the Garden of Eden (Genesis 3:1-15). The fruit Satan used to deceive Adam and Eve seemed harmless and even good for them. Often temptation seems harmless and even good for us. If we are not careful the devil will deceive us with his lies in order to make us fall into sin. The secular media is filled with deception, as are many businesses and organizations. We must be careful not to buy into the lies and deceptions that are in the world, which ultimately are the lies of the Enemy.

C. Making a Covenant With the World (vv. 14, 15)

14. And the men took of their victuals, and asked not counsel at the mouth of the Lord.

15. And Joshua made peace with them, and made a league with them, to let them live: and the princes of the congregation sware unto them.

The Gibeonites deceived Israel into making a covenant with them, which resulted from Israel's not seeking the counsel of the Lord (v. 14). Once Joshua made a covenant with the Gibeonites, he could not go back on his word. Had he broken his covenant with the Gibeonites, he would have sinned against God, which would have brought the wrath of God upon Israel.

Talk About It:
1. Who did these Gibeonites pretend to be (v. 4)?
2. In verses 9 and 10, what did the Gibeonites say that was true? What was false?

"One of the striking differences between a cat and a lie is that the cat has only nine lives."
—**Mark Twain**

victuals (v. 14)— provisions

Talk About It:
1. What mistake did the Israelites make (v. 14)?
2. Describe the treaty that was agreed upon (v. 15).

The blame in this transaction is not that a "league," or treaty, was made, but that it was done hastily and rashly without consulting God. Joshua and the princes relied so completely upon their own wisdom that they thought it unnecessary to consult Him. He who trusts his own wisdom need not be surprised to find he does foolish things. Within three days Joshua and the princes discovered the deception, but having made the treaty with the Gibeonites, they observed it to the letter.

If the devil can get us to make a covenant with the world, he has us and he gets the glory. That's the battle—who is going to get the glory? Instead of making a covenant with the world, we should rely on God for strength and wisdom. That will bring God glory. If we live for the devil, whether we realize it or not, we glorify him. The best way to keep from being deceived by the Enemy and making a covenant with the world is to continually seek the Lord in prayer. Prayer is the key to the victory.

II. CONSEQUENCES OF PRAYERLESSNESS
   (Joshua 9:16-27; Judges 2:1-5)
A. Lack of Discernment (Joshua 9:16-27)
   (Joshua 9:22-27 is not included in the printed text.)
   16. And it came to pass at the end of three days after they had made a league with them, that they heard that they were their neighbours, and that they dwelt among them.
   17. And the children of Israel journeyed, and came unto their cities on the third day. Now their cities were Gibeon, and Chephirah, and Beeroth, and Kirjath-jearim.
   18. And the children of Israel smote them not, because the princes of the congregation had sworn unto them by the Lord God of Israel. And all the congregation murmured against the princes.
   19. But all the princes said unto all the congregation, We have sworn unto them by the Lord God of Israel: now therefore we may not touch them.
   20. This we will do to them; we will even let them live, lest wrath be upon us, because of the oath which we sware unto them.
   21. And the princes said unto them, Let them live; but let them be hewers of wood and drawers of water unto all the congregation; as the princes had promised them.

When the Israelites realized their leaders had been deceived by the neighboring Gibeonites, they grumbled against their leaders. Their complaining may have resulted from their being unable to gain the spoils of Gibeon and/or because they saw this as a breach of God's command.

This trouble stemmed from the root of prayerlessness. The Gibeonites deceived Joshua and the nation of Israel into making

Talk About It:
1. What happened after three days (v. 16)?
2. What caused murmuring (v. 18)?
3. How did the Gibeonites feel about their fate (vv. 23-25)?

a covenant because they had not inquired of God. What would cause the people of God to overlook prayer after winning so many battles? Pride. Believers are in danger of spiritual pride whenever they start to think they can do it themselves.

One of the main consequences of prayerlessness is a lack of discernment. Joshua and the nation of Israel weren't able to discern the true intention of the Gibeonites because they did not rely on God. When we live a life of prayer, God gives us discernment to know people's true motivations and intentions. There are several examples of discernment in the New Testament, such as Jesus and the woman at the well (John 4:16-18) and Peter and Ananias and Sapphira (Acts 5:1-4). There are times when God reveals to us certain knowledge and discernment that can only be known through supernatural means.

The Gibeonites willingly became servants in the nation of Israel—a far better alternative than being wiped out. Specifically they became wood-choppers and water carriers for the ministry of the Tabernacle.

> "No treaty is ever an impediment to a cheat."
> —**Sophocles**

B. A Thorn in Your Side (Judges 2:1-5)

1. And an angel of the Lord came up from Gilgal to Bochim, and said, I made you to go up out of Egypt, and have brought you unto the land which I sware unto your fathers; and I said, I will never break my covenant with you.

2. And ye shall make no league with the inhabitants of this land; ye shall throw down their altars: but ye have not obeyed my voice: why have ye done this?

3. Wherefore I also said, I will not drive them out from before you; but they shall be as thorns in your sides, and their gods shall be a snare unto you.

4. And it came to pass, when the angel of the Lord spake these words unto all the children of Israel, that the people lifted up their voice, and wept.

5. And they called the name of that place Bochim: and they sacrificed there unto the Lord.

Talk About It:
Why and how would Israel's treaty with Gibeon cause problems (vv. 2, 3)?

One of the main reasons the Lord commanded Israel to destroy all of the inhabitants of the land was because any survivors would become a thorn in their side. The Canaanites were a corrupt people, and coexisting with them would have been a threat to the spiritual well-being of the nation of Israel. Among their sins were idol worship, sacrifice of infant children, and sexual perversion. Every level of their society was corrupt, therefore God commanded Israel to destroy them.

Israel's first failure in this regard was their treaty with Gibeon. But that was just the beginning. In Judges 1 we read how, after Joshua's death, the Israelites failed to completely drive out various peoples of Canaan (vv. 21, 27-35). So the angel of the Lord

Sin Thorn
When we become Christians, God starts the process of sanctification, which literally means to be made holy. The goal of sanctification is to enable us to put to death the deeds of the flesh (Romans 8:13). If we don't allow God to sanctify us of our sin, it will

continue to have a stronghold in our lives and become a thorn in our side.

declares, "You have disobeyed me. Why have you done this?" (2:2, *NIV*). The people responded by crying aloud, offering sacrifices to the Lord and naming that place *Bochim*, which means "weepers."

III. GOD REMAINS FAITHFUL (Joshua 10:6-14)

A. Power Over Enemies (vv. 6-8)

6. And the men of Gibeon sent unto Joshua to the camp to Gilgal, saying, Slack not thy hand from thy servants; come up to us quickly, and save us, and help us: for all the kings of the Amorites that dwell in the mountains are gathered together against us.

7. So Joshua ascended from Gilgal, he, and all the people of war with him, and all the mighty men of valour.

8. And the Lord said unto Joshua, Fear them not: for I have delivered them into thine hand; there shall not a man of them stand before thee.

Israel, through the destruction of Jericho and Ai, and the treaty between Joshua and the Gibeonites, had gained a firm bridgehead in Canaan. Should they continue their victorious advance, they would soon conquer all the inhabitants of the land. Therefore the five kings became allies, combined their armies, and marched upon Gibeon (vv. 1-5).

The Gibeonites had deceived Joshua, but since he afterward ratified the covenant with them, they concluded he was obliged to defend them. They were right, for in making them "hewers of wood and drawers of water" to the Israelites (9:21, 27), they became servants, and entitled to the protection of their master.

Upon receiving the appeal of the Gibeonites, Joshua immediately proceeded to make plans to relieve them. The situation demanded swift action, for the army of the five kings was already before the walls of the city.

As they were preparing to go into battle, the Lord said to Joshua not to be afraid, for God had already given Israel the victory. The Lord was reminding Joshua that He was in control. Many times when we are in a battle we try to fight in the power of our own strength. However, we should give our battle to the Lord because He will give us the power to defeat our enemies.

The Bible tells us that we are in the midst of a spiritual battle, and our adversary, the devil, is like a roaring lion seeking to destroy our lives (1 Peter 5:8). Paul says, "We do not wrestle against flesh and blood, but against . . . the rulers of the darkness of this age, against spiritual hosts of wickedness in the heavenly places" (Ephesians 6:12, *NKJV*). Satan and his forces are trying to destroy our life, and it is imperative that we pray against these powers of darkness in order to gain victory.

Talk About It:
1. What request did the Gibeonites make (v. 6)?
2. Why should Joshua not be afraid (v. 8)?

"God incarnate is the end of fear; and the heart that realizes that He is in the midst . . . will be quiet in the middle of alarm."
—F.B. Meyer

Sin's Consequences and God's Faithfulness

B. Power Over Nature (vv. 9-14)

9. Joshua therefore came unto them suddenly, and went up from Gilgal all night.

10. And the Lord discomfited them before Israel, and slew them with a great slaughter at Gibeon, and chased them along the way that goeth up to Beth-horon, and smote them to Azekah, and unto Makkedah.

11. And it came to pass, as they fled from before Israel, and were in the going down to Beth-horon, that the Lord cast down great stones from heaven upon them unto Azekah, and they died: they were more which died with hailstones than they whom the children of Israel slew with the sword.

12. Then spake Joshua to the Lord in the day when the Lord delivered up the Amorites before the children of Israel, and he said in the sight of Israel, Sun, stand thou still upon Gibeon; and thou, Moon, in the valley of Ajalon.

13. And the sun stood still, and the moon stayed, until the people had avenged themselves upon their enemies. Is not this written in the book of Jasher? So the sun stood still in the midst of heaven, and hasted not to go down about a whole day.

14. And there was no day like that before it or after it, that the Lord hearkened unto the voice of a man: for the Lord fought for Israel.

discomfited (v. 10)— "confounded" (*NASB*)

Beth-horon (v. 10)— the name of two towns, an "upper" and a "lower, on the road from Gibeon to Azekah" (*Unger's Bible Dictionary*)

Azekah (v. 10)—a fortified city of Judah

Joshua made a rapid night march of 15 to 18 miles, and threw his army against the enemy the following morning in a surprise attack. The result was all he could have hoped for. The five kings were decisively defeated with great slaughter, and put to flight. The Israelites bravely did their duty, but it was God who gave them the victory. He showed His great power in completely defeating the enemy Joshua had hurried to attack. So in the Christian's warfare against the world, the flesh, and the devil, we may be assured of victory with the help of Christ (1 Corinthians 15:57).

The Canaanite army might flee from the battlefield, but they could not rid themselves of the triumphant Israelites or their God who had given them the victory. Both relentlessly pursued them. God opened the windows of heaven and poured giant hailstones upon them. Those who make an enemy of God shall perish miserably, for "it is a fearful thing to fall into [His] hands" (Hebrews 10:31). He is never at a loss for a weapon or a method with which to suspend the laws of nature or use them to achieve His purposes. The Scriptures are filled with revelations of this sublime fact. If He is willing to move heaven and earth to help His people, He will not be slow to use less spectacular means. "My help," said David, "cometh from the Lord, which made heaven and earth" (Psalm 121:2).

Talk About It:
1. How did Joshua surprise the enemy (v. 9)?
2. How was this day unlike any "before it or after it" (v. 14)?

The prayer Joshua prayed was so powerful that the sun stood still. Though he had marched all night and fought all day, he wished for nothing so much as the prolonging of the day. He believed in the sovereignty of God over nature, and that His favor to Israel would lead Him to grant the request. Never was there a day like it before or since, in which God so honored faith and prayer. Never did He comply with such a request from a man, nor so miraculously fight for His people. By it He magnified Joshua, and made clear to all the world what He was doing for Israel in Canaan. Today, if we honor God by praying to Him, He will honor us by answering us.

CONCLUSION

Joshua and Israel made the mistake of not seeking God, and they ended up letting the inhabitants of the land live among them. Therefore, they experienced constant turmoil and confusion. Earlier, when Achan kept forbidden treasure, Israel lost the battle (ch. 7).

Sin still defeats people and keeps them from God's will. Let us examine ourselves to make sure that sin and worldliness are not controlling our hearts.

The Lord is always faithful to His people despite their failure. If we turn to God in faith, He will work on our behalf. We need the Lord in our lives if we are going to win life's many battles. Prayer is the key to overcoming the Enemy and receiving God's blessings. What battles are you facing today? Seek the Lord and He will give you the strength you need to overcome.

GOLDEN TEXT CHALLENGE

"BE NOT DECEIVED; GOD IS NOT MOCKED: FOR WHATSOEVER A MAN SOWETH THAT SHALL HE ALSO REAP" (Galatians 6:7).

In a world dominated by physical and material values, Paul shouts the great message that an unchanging God has created a universe in which mental, physical and spiritual laws also operate in an unchanging manner. Paul uses the commonly known metaphor of sowing and reaping to illustrate this regularity in the realm of things spiritual.

It is a common fallacy to think that we are exceptions to this regularity; God's great universe does not provide for exceptions. He is able to forgive our sins, but the consequences must still be borne individually.

Paul further tells us that we cannot expect to sow one thing and reap another. The person whose field is full of thorns cannot anticipate a rich yield of wheat. The final product must be chosen before seed time. The great joy in the rule of regularity is that efforts expended upon things spiritual and eternal will produce life everlasting as certainly as living for the flesh will produce corruption. An unchanging and loving God has thus decreed it.

Daily Devotions:
M. The Curse of Sin
   Genesis 3:8-11, 14-19
T. Obey God's Commands
   2 Chronicles 16:7-14
W. God's Great Faithfulness
   Lamentations 3:21-26
T. Be Careful What You Plant
   Galatians 6:7-10
F. God's Keeping Power
   2 Timothy 2:11-13
S. Heed God's Word
   Hebrews 2:1-4

We Will Serve the Lord

Joshua 24:1-27; 2 Corinthians 6:16 through 7:1

INTRODUCTION

This lesson carries us to the end of Joshua's long, useful career, and closes our four studies of his life and work. Much has happened since the events recorded in last Sunday's lesson (chs. 9, 10). Though the conquest was not fully completed, and would not be for many generations, Canaan was allotted to the several tribes, the wars ended, and the people settled down to build homes for themselves.

Having become old, and knowing his days were numbered, Joshua called the people together at Shechem to address them for the last time. The setting for this important meeting was altogether appropriate. Here Abraham received the promise of the Holy Land, nearby the bones of Joseph had been deposited, and here the blessings and curses of the Law had been solemnly pronounced.

Shechem was a large natural amphitheater where a gathering of all the tribes could assemble to hear Joshua's farewell message to call the Israelites to renew their covenant with the Lord. The covenant between Israel and God was that they would worship and serve the Lord alone. Joshua also commanded the Israelites to throw out all of their foreign gods and idols. The purpose of the covenant was so Israel would become a holy nation that would be God's light to the nations. Shortly after making his final speech, Joshua died and was buried in his hometown of Timnath-serah.

Joshua 24 reminds us that the decision to serve God must not be made lightly, but with serious commitment and followed through in every area of our life. Serving God begins by acknowledging that God has a rightful claim on us. First Corinthians 6:19, 20 says, "You are not your own; you were bought at a price. Therefore honor God with your body" (*NIV*). God has created us by His Spirit and redeemed us through the sacrificial gift of His Son. This lesson will focus on the importance of making a decision to serve the Lord with all of our being.

Unit Theme:
Joshua and Judges

Central Truth:
The decision to serve God must not be made lightly, but with serious commitment.

Focus:
Acknowledge that God has a rightful claim on our lives and serve Him wholeheartedly.

Context:
In Shechem around 1350 B.C.

Golden Text:
"Choose you this day whom ye will serve; . . . but as for me and my house, we will serve the Lord" (Joshua 24:15).

Study Outline:
 I. Recount God's Faithfulness (Joshua 24:1-13)
 II. Serve No Other Gods (Joshua 24:14-21)
III. Live as God's People (Joshua 24:22-27; 2 Corinthians 6:16 through 7:1)

I. RECOUNT GOD'S FAITHFULNESS (Joshua 24:1-13)

A. Faithful to the Patriarchs (vv. 1-4)

1. And Joshua gathered all the tribes of Israel to Shechem, and called for the elders of Israel, and for their heads, and for their judges, and for their officers; and they presented themselves before God.

2. And Joshua said unto all the people, Thus saith the Lord God of Israel, Your fathers dwelt on the other side of the flood in old time, even Terah, the father of Abraham, and the father of Nachor: and they served other gods.

3. And I took your father Abraham from the other side of the flood, and led him throughout all the land of Canaan, and multiplied his seed, and gave him Isaac.

4. And I gave unto Isaac Jacob and Esau: and I gave unto Esau mount Seir, to possess it; but Jacob and his children went down into Egypt.

Joshua begins his speech by reminding the nation of Israel not to forget where the Lord had brought them from. He spoke to them prophetically by saying, "Thus saith the Lord" (v. 2). These were not his words, but the very words of God. The Lord wanted to remind them of how He had redeemed them as a people for Himself. Israel's history is His story. Their story tells the story of God throughout the ages. In history we can see the unfolding of the Lord's plans and purposes.

Jewish tradition has it that Terah (v. 2) actually manufactured idols, and that Abraham broke some of them; he was finally driven out of his country for refusing to worship idols. Though it is not mentioned in the Bible, we know from archaeology that the moon god Sin was the main deity, but there were many others worshiped also. Abraham learned to abhor this idolatrous and cruel worship of his countrymen. With his family he set out for Haran, but that godless city with its star-worship was no resting place for him who "looked for a city which hath foundations, whose builder and maker is God" (Hebrews 11:10).

In verse 4 of the text the people are being shown that Abraham's son, Isaac, was given two sons by God, Jacob and Esau, who became the ancestors of two great nations. To the latter He gave the mountains of Seir for a possession (Genesis 36:6-9); these were the Edomites. To the descendants of the former He gave Canaan as a sole possession; these were the Israelites.

Joshua does not mention the inheritance of Jacob, since his hearers are well acquainted with the history of the patriarchs; he satisfies himself with mentioning the migration of Jacob and his sons to Egypt, that he might pass to the second great proof of the guidance of God, the miraculous deliverance of Israel out of bondage in Egypt.

B. Faithful in the Exodus (vv. 5-7)

5. I sent Moses also and Aaron, and I plagued Egypt, according to that which I did among them: and afterward I brought you out.

6. And I brought your fathers out of Egypt: and ye came unto the sea; and the Egyptians pursued after your fathers with chariots and horsemen unto the Red sea.

7. And when they cried unto the Lord, he put darkness between you and the Egyptians, and brought the sea upon them, and covered them; and your eyes have seen what I have done in Egypt: and ye dwelt in the wilderness a long season.

The very brief outline of God's activities is continued. Only the leading points are mentioned: the sending of Moses and Aaron, and then the plagues inflicted upon Egypt. The Hebrew word for *plagued* is literally "smote," indicating that both land and people suffered.

The second half of verse 5 refers to Exodus 3:20 and shows how God was faithful to the promise given to Moses at his call. God always keeps His promises; any lack of dependability is always on people's part.

C. Faithful Across the Jordan (vv. 8-10)

(Joshua 24:9, 10 is not included in the printed text.)

8. And I brought you into the land of the Amorites, which dwelt on the other side Jordan; and they fought with you: and I gave them into your hand, that ye might possess their land; and I destroyed them from before you.

The giving up of the Amorites into the hands of the Israelites was the third great act of God for Israel. This enabled them to conquer their land. Verses 9 and 10 mention the frustration of the attack made by Balak, king of the Moabites, through the instrumentality of Balaam, when the Lord did not permit him to curse Israel, but instead induced him to bless them (Numbers 22–24).

D. Faithful in Canaan (vv. 11-13)

(Joshua 24:11, 12 is not included in the printed text.)

13. And I have given you a land for which ye did not labour, and cities which ye built not, and ye dwell in them; of the vineyards and oliveyards which ye planted not do ye eat.

The Lord reminds the Israelites that He gave them the Promised Land. The Bible tells us nothing is too hard for God because He is in control. The Lord gave Israel the victory to show them that He is all-powerful. He is intimately aware of everything that happens to every person and living thing. Paul

Talk About It:
Explain the three uses of the word *brought* in these three verses.

Talk About It:
How did God show His favor upon Israel?

Talk About It:
1. Explain the phrase "sent the hornet" (v. 12).
2. What possessions did the Israelites inherit (v. 13)?

tells us God is able to do far more abundantly than all that we ask or think (Ephesians 3:20). C.S. Lewis describes God's omnipotence as the power to do all that is intrinsically possible, not to do the intrinsically impossible. This means God will not do anything that is contrary to His law and decrees. Israel would fall into sin whenever they forgot that God was in control.

Joshua wanted to remind them that God is in control. The Creator upholds, directs and governs all creation by His sovereign will and holy providence. In His foreknowledge He governs and directs the affairs of the nations. His plans and purposes cannot be thwarted or overturned. He works all things together for good to those who love Him according to His will. Understanding the greatness of God helps us better understand ourselves as well as others. It gives us glimpse into the eternal realities of the kingdom of God. It inspires us to pray, "Your kingdom come, your will be done on earth as it is in heaven" (Matthew 6:10, *NIV*).

II. SERVE NO OTHER GODS (Joshua 24:14-21)
A. Choose Today (vv. 14, 15)

14. Now therefore fear the Lord, and serve him in sincerity and in truth: and put away the gods which your fathers served on the other side of the flood, and in Egypt; and serve ye the Lord.

15. And if it seem evil unto you to serve the Lord, choose you this day whom ye will serve; whether the gods which your fathers served that were on the other side of the flood, or the gods of the Amorites, in whose land ye dwell: but as for me and my house, we will serve the Lord.

Joshua begins his charge to the nation of Israel with the challenge to "fear the Lord." This is an odd statement for our contemporary culture. The fear of the Lord is missing in many of our churches, our prayers, and our personal life. So what does it mean to fear Him? It refers to the reverence and awe we should have in the presence of our awesome and almighty God.

Joshua told the Israelites to fear the Lord in order to give them a proper perspective of their relationship to God. The fear of the Lord means that we have an accurate understanding of the reality of God's greatness and our weakness. The Bible declares, "The fear of the Lord is the beginning of wisdom" (Psalm 111:10). Holy fear gives us a solid foundation and unlocks the keys to wisdom and knowledge.

The word *serve* is used seven times in verses 14 and 15. Joshua declares that they should serve the Lord with sincerity and truth. This refers to the motivation for serving the Lord. Being sincere means we have the right motivation and purity

Talk About It:
1. What would it take for the Israelites to serve the Lord "in sincerity and in truth" (v. 14)?
2. Describe the two false gods they could choose to serve (v. 15).

of heart. There are a lot of people who think that serving God is just about what God can do for us. This causes us to miss out on the real blessings of loving God for who He is and not for what He can do for us. People fall into the trap of seeking His hand and not His face. But when we seek His face we get His hand. God blesses those who seek Him from a pure heart and motive.

There is only one true God. The Bible opens with the words "In the beginning, God." God has no beginning and no end. There was never a time when God was not. Many of the world's religions believe in many gods, as did the ancient Amorites. However, Jews and Christians believe there is only one God who is sovereign over all things, including the devil, time and humanity. Like Israel, we need a correct understanding of the supremacy of God.

Serving the Lord is a choice each of us must make. Many gods are out there, but we are called to serve the one true God. Joshua wanted to make sure the nation of Israel would continue to serve the Lord alone after his death. He set the example by declaring, "As for me and my household, we will serve the Lord" (*NIV*).

We should worship and serve God out of a deep desire rather than duty. We should check our motivation to see whether we are serving the Lord from our hearts or from a sense of obligation. God wants people to worship and serve Him in sincerity and truth. Jesus tells us, "But the hour is coming, and now is, when the true worshipers will worship the Father in spirit and truth; for the Father is seeking such to worship Him. God is Spirit, and those who worship Him must worship in spirit and truth" (John 4:23, 24, *NKJV*). Our prayer and our worship should be offered to God with all our hearts and all of our souls.

B. We Will Serve the Lord (vv. 16-21)
(Joshua 24:16-18 is not included in the printed text.)

19. And Joshua said unto the people, Ye cannot serve the Lord: for he is an holy God; he is a jealous God; he will not forgive your transgressions nor your sins.

20. If ye forsake the Lord, and serve strange gods, then he will turn and do you hurt, and consume you, after that he hath done you good.

21. And the people said unto Joshua, Nay; but we will serve the Lord.

To revert to idolatry was too repulsive to consider, and the people cried out their horror at even the thought of forsaking the Lord. Of course, it is easy to make a commitment when everyone else is doing so, but it is much harder when one has to stand alone. This commitment that the Israelites made as a group would be tested individually in the days ahead.

Choices
One's philosophy is not best expressed in words. It is expressed in the choices one makes. In the long run, we shape our lives and we shape ourselves. The process never ends until we die. And the choices we make are ultimately our responsibility.
—**Eleanor Roosevelt**

Talk About It:
1. What did the people credit God for doing (vv. 17, 18)?
2. Explain the statement "He is a jealous God" (v. 19).

It was unthinkable that, after experiencing such great deliverances and providences at the hands of God, they would turn their backs on Him now (v. 17). The Israelites were willing to face the facts of history and to recognize the hand of God in their present success and prosperity and safety. The idols of the Amorites had been proven powerless before the God of all the earth (v. 18).

In verse 19, Joshua reminded the people that God does not play games with us. If we make a commitment to Him, He will expect us to keep it, and His wrath will fall hard upon us if we turn our back on Him or trifle with the seriousness of this commitment. "He is a jealous God" and will not share His glory with idols. His judgment of evil and idolatry is proclaimed in dozens of passages of Scripture, so that we are without excuse if we turn aside from serving Him (v. 20).

In verse 21 the people repeated their allegiance to God. They insisted that they had made up their minds once and for all. This is what all of us should do.

> "Though we do not face a pantheon of false gods like the Israelites did, we face pressures from a pantheon of false values—materialism, love of leisure, sensuality, worship of self, security, and many others."
> —*Today in the Word*

III. LIVE AS GOD'S PEOPLE (Joshua 24:22-27;
2 Corinthians 6:16-18; 7:1)

A. Serving God Together (Joshua 24:22-27)

22. And Joshua said unto the people, Ye are witnesses against yourselves that ye have chosen you the Lord, to serve him. And they said, We are witnesses.

23. Now therefore put away, said he, the strange gods which are among you, and incline your heart unto the Lord God of Israel.

incline your heart (v. 23)—"yield your hearts" (*NIV*)

24. And the people said unto Joshua, The Lord our God will we serve, and his voice will we obey.

25. So Joshua made a covenant with the people that day, and set them a statute and an ordinance in Shechem.

26. And Joshua wrote these words in the book of the law of God, and took a great stone, and set it up there under an oak, that was by the sanctuary of the Lord.

27. And Joshua said unto all the people, Behold, this stone shall be a witness unto us; for it hath heard all the words of the Lord which he spake unto us: it shall be therefore a witness unto you, lest ye deny your God.

The people insisted that they understood the solemn responsibility of the commitment that they were making. They believed they were ready to go forth to serve God. Joshua knew his people well, and he realized that their history was full of high points of solemn commitment, followed by backsliding and failure, but he would have to take them at their word.

Joshua must have known that some of his people had secreted idols in their tents, and he knew full well how serious

Talk About It:
1. How were the people witnesses against themselves (v. 22)?
2. What did the people vow to God (v. 24)?

We Will Serve the Lord

this was. If the people meant business, they would return home and destroy every vestige of idol worship immediately (v. 23). If they did not begin immediately to act to carry out their commitment they had just made, they would tend to forget it and to compromise more with the world.

Three times Joshua had the people to affirm their faith in the Lord and their commitment to Him. The check and double-check was designed to impress upon them the deadly seriousness of what they were doing.

Joshua recorded the solemn covenant that his people had made with the Lord and set up a large stone monument there at Shechem as a memorial to this event. Thus, the people had one another as witnesses to their vow, plus the written record in the Law, and the great stone monument. Joshua had done all he could do to forge a strong relationship between Israel and God—they would need such a relationship through the years ahead. He dismissed the people, and they returned home. Joshua died soon after this at the age of 110 (v. 29).

The people of Israel needed to make a clean break with idolatry. Not only did the unity of their new nation depend on it, but the very moral foundations of their personal, family and national life were at stake. Joshua made them face the issue and make a decision, hopefully once and for all. It would be well if every person living today would do the same thing.

B. Being a Holy People (2 Corinthians 6:16-18; 7:1)

16. And what agreement hath the temple of God with idols? for ye are the temple of the living God; as God hath said, I will dwell in them, and walk in them; and I will be their God, and they shall be my people.

17. Wherefore come out from among them, and be ye separate, saith the Lord, and touch not the unclean thing; and I will receive you,

18. And will be a Father unto you, and ye shall be my sons and daughters, saith the Lord Almighty.

7:1. Having therefore these promises, dearly beloved, let us cleanse ourselves from all filthiness of the flesh and spirit, perfecting holiness in the fear of God.

We are the temple of the living God. We are called to be a holy people. Today there is a tremendous need to rediscover the call to holy living. Holiness is something for us as Christians to aspire to attain in our daily life. It is not based on works of righteousness but on our daily relationship with Jesus Christ. It is not a perfection of our actions but a perfection of love. Too often there is a misunderstanding of the discipline of holiness, and no one has misunderstood it more than the church. It has been the cause of countless splits within Christianity.

---

3. What did Joshua record (vv. 25, 26)?

Community of Faith
First, the church is a place for believers to live together in community. The Christian faith is a social religion, not a solitary one. Second, it is a place for believers to pray for one another. Third, the church is a place to hear and learn from the Word of God. Fourth, God has instituted the church as a place where we can find, grow, and use our gifts and talents for Him.

Talk About It:
1. Who is "the temple of the living God" (6:16)?
2. To whom is God a Father (v. 18)?
3. Explain the phrase "perfecting holiness" (7:1).

The basic biblical meaning for the word *holiness* is "separation and consecration." To be *holy* is to be *wholly* God's. The Lord separates us for His unique purposes and plans. Second Corinthians 7:1 tells us we are to bring "holiness to completion" (paraphrase). This means there is a goal or purpose to holiness. Holiness draws us closer to God. The Bible tells us that only the pure in heart will see the Lord. As we draw closer to God through the discipline of holy living, our hearts are cleansed from sin and worldly desires. As a result, we are able to see His face more and more. Holiness also makes us more like God. As we give ourselves completely to the Lord through the discipline of holy living, we become holy as He is holy.

There is another purpose for holiness. In 2 Timothy 2:21, Paul says, "If a man therefore purge himself from these, he shall be a vessel unto honour, sanctified, and meet for the master's use, and prepared unto every good work." The term *vessel* parallels the Old Testament idea of vessels being sanctified so they may be holy for temple use. The idea that Paul gives here is that a believer must be set apart or sanctified before he or she can be used. Therefore holiness is not just separation, but is the process of being set apart in order to know God and to be used by the Lord.

> "How little people know who think that holiness is dull. When one meets the real thing, it is irresistible."
> —C.S. Lewis

CONCLUSION

Joshua's farewell message to Israel is a call to serve the Lord and not other gods. The decision to serve the Lord should not be taken lightly, but demands a wholehearted commitment to Him. Serving the Lord is not just an individual responsibility, but involves being a part of a community of faith or local church. Let us stand with Joshua and say, "We will serve the Lord" (24:15). Let us live as "sons and daughters . . . [to] the Lord Almighty" (2 Corinthians 6:18).

GOLDEN TEXT CHALLENGE

"CHOOSE YOU THIS DAY WHOM YE WILL SERVE; . . . BUT AS FOR ME AND MY HOUSE, WE WILL SERVE THE LORD" (Joshua 24:15).

The power of choice is tremendous—indeed, sometimes frightening—in its implications. By it destinies are settled. God respects that power as a sacred room in the home of human personality. He will not invade it. He never compels anyone to serve Him. Will it be God or the devil? Heaven or hell? It is up to us.

Whether we like it or not, we *must* choose. The neutralists of Joshua's day, intent on evading their responsibility, were actually deciding against the Lord. Their procrastination was fatal. "Choose you *this* day . . . " was the wise admonition of their aged leader. Their habit of halting between two opinions was ruining them.

Joshua and his family, thank God, had decided long since. He had chosen his Lord while still a youth. And how signally God had honored him!

Have you decided to serve Him? If not, "choose you this day"! Decide now, once and for all, to serve the Lord Jesus Christ.

Daily Devotions:
M. Be Faithful to God
Genesis 39:2-10
T. Love God Wholeheartedly
Deuteronomy 6:4-9
W. Testimony in Song
Psalm 111:1-10
T. Serve One Master
Matthew 6:24-33
F. Count on God's Faithfulness
Romans 3:1-4
S. Love One Another
Romans 13:8-10

Bible Insight

THE BOOK OF JUDGES
by Charles W. Conn

The Message of Judges

The Book of Judges is the record of Israel's early years in their national homeland. In that primitive period all of those who had participated in the exodus from Egypt and the conquest of Canaan disappeared from the scene and leadership of the nation passed into other hands. Those were confused and uncertain days in Jewish history, and Judges presents a graphic account of the young nation's troubles and failures. The period was punctuated by a dreary succession of apostasies by Israel, each followed by invasion and oppression by a neighboring enemy. In those years Israel had no king or permanent leader, and national crises were met by individuals divinely endowed to lead the nation. These men and one woman were known as "judges," from which the book gets its name. There are 13 judges mentioned in the book, but none continued to lead the nation on a permanent basis; each returned to private life as soon as their crisis was over.

Their names are carefully listed, but only a few of them are familiar to us today. Even in the Scriptural record there are detailed accounts of some and a mere mention of others. Yet each in his time did a tremendous service for his land and people. The judges were as follows:

1. Othniel
2. Ehud
3. Shamgar
4. Deborah
5. Barak
6. Gideon
7. Tola
8. Jair
9. Jephthah
10. Ibzan
11. Elon
12. Abdon
13. Samson

Two final judges are recorded in 1 Samuel, making a total of 15 judges. These were Eli and Samuel. Their service was not the same as the 13 in Judges, but was more permanent in nature.

Outline of Judges

I. Israel Corrupted by the Canaanites (1:1–2:15)
   A. Israel's Incomplete Victories (1:1-36)
   B. Israel's Spiritual Defeat (2:1-15)
II. History of the Thirteen Judges (2:16–16:31)
   A. Condition of the Times (2:16–3:7)
   B. Othniel, the First Judge (3:8-11)
   C. Ehud Against the Moabites (vv. 12-30)
   D. Shamgar and the Philistines (v. 31)
   E. Deborah and Barak, Co-Judges (4:1–5:31)
   F. Gideon and the Midianites (6:1–8:35)
   G. Usurpation of Gideon's Son, Abimelech (9:1-57)

H. Tola, the Seventh Judge (10:1, 2)
I. Jair, the Eighth Judge (vv. 3-5)
J. Jephthah and the Ammonites (10:6–11:40)
K. Civil War in Israel (12:1-7)
L. Ibzan, the Tenth Judge (vv. 8-10)
M. Elon, the Eleventh Judge (vv. 11, 12)
N. Abdon, the Twelfth Judge (vv. 13-15)
O. Samson's Miraculous Birth (13:1-25)
P. Samson and the Philistines (14:1–16:31)
III. A Time of Anarchy and Violence (17:1–21:25)
A. Micah and the Levites (17:1-13)
B. The Danite Migration (18:1-31)
C. The Atrocity of Gibeah (19:1–21:25)

Synopsis of Judges
I. Israel Corrupted by the Canaanites

Following the initial conquest of Canaan, many pockets of resistance remained among or alongside the Israelites. The Book of Judges opens with an account of efforts by individual tribes to defeat the remaining Canaanite strongholds. There is no indication that the Hebrews sought to destroy the enemies. This was a mistake, for the Canaanites would live like thorns in their sides, and the thorns would one day fester and contaminate the nation of Israel. Six times in chapter 1 we are told of Israel's incomplete victories (1:19, 21, 27, 30, 32, 33). The defeated people were subjugated but not destroyed, and in time they came to be acceptable neighbors who influenced Israel more than they were influenced by them.

This military compromise sowed the seed of spiritual failure. While Joshua lived, the people maintained a measure of obedience to the laws of God. When he died, and his generation with him, there remained little remembrance of God and His wonderful works. The Hebrews intermarried with the heathenish people of Canaan, and gradually adopted their idolatrous practices. "And they forsook the Lord, and served Baal and Ashtaroth" (2:13). Baal worship was cruel, frequently savage, and involved great indignity and reprobation. Ashtaroth was a goddess of lust and impurity, worshiped by overt acts of indecency and licentiousness.

II. The Thirteen Judges

Until the death of Joshua, the Hebrews had a leader whom God specifically called and ordained for leadership; first Moses, then Joshua. But no one was appointed to take Joshua's place. There was no single person or place to give the people a sense of unity. Each tribe was its own entity, and the 12 were yet to be welded into a united nation. Just as each tribe operated alone, so "every man did that which was right in his own eyes" (17:6).

Disorder was inevitable. The people adopted the evil practices of their neighbors, for which they suffered greatly. The pattern we see throughout Judges is this: (1) First, the people forsook God; (2) then God punished them by allowing an enemy to oppress them; (3) which resulted in repentance and prayer for deliverance; (4) which God answered by raising up a leader to deliver them.

There were seven periods of apostasy, with seven times of oppression, followed with seven occasions of deliverance. Thirteen judges were raised up to meet the need, but few of them were permanent, and none ever set up a dynasty or was succeeded by an heir to his judgeship. The word *judge* was not used in the sense that we think of today. Rather than national judiciary officials or administrators, the judges were local chieftains who rallied the people of their particular tribe to repel their oppressor. All 12 of the tribes never united under a leader, but only the one tribe affected, or those few other tribes who chose to cooperate. Some of the judges were contemporaries; two or more may well have worked at the same time in different sections of the nation. If the years the judges ruled were consecutive, the period would be about 400 years. That is not likely. The period of the judges, allowing for the difficulties of chronological computation, was probably nearer 300 years.

Othniel (Judges 3:9-11)

Othniel, the nephew of Caleb, was the first judge. His service came as a result of Israel's first widespread apostasy, for which they were punished with eight years of bondage to the king of Mesopotamia. The specific sin of Israel was an abandonment of worship of God, and the practice of idolatry, wherein they worshiped Baal, god of the Canaanites (v. 7). When the children of Israel repented of their idolatry, God raised up Othniel to deliver them. "The Spirit of the Lord came upon him, and he judged Israel, and went out to war" (v. 10). Othniel's campaign was successful, and Israel enjoyed 40 years of peace.

Ehud (3:15-30)

After Othniel's death, the pattern of apostasy, punishment, repentance and deliverance began anew. Because of Israel's sins, Eglon, the king of Moab, with the assistance of the Ammonites, was enabled to conquer and enslave the Hebrews around the region of Ephraim. This servitude lasted for 18 years before Ehud, of the tribe of Benjamin, rose up and delivered the people. Ehud conveyed Israel's tribute, or tax, to Eglon in Moab. When the two men were alone, Ehud, who was left-handed, assassinated Eglon, who was a very fat man, by thrusting a dagger into his belly (vv. 15-29). Ehud escaped and rallied the tribe of Ephraim, who invaded Moab and killed 10,000 soldiers of the Moabite army. Israel then had 80 years of rest.

Shamgar (3:31)

The Philistines were the next enemies to oppress Israel. During their occupation it became dangerous to use the regular roads, so the Hebrews had to travel through fields and byways instead (5:6). Nothing is told of Shamgar, except that in the course of delivering Israel he slew 600 Philistines with an ox goad, a long metal-tipped pole for prodding oxen. This indicates that Shamgar was a man of tremendous physical strength.

Deborah and Barak (4:4–5:31)

Once again the Israelites resorted to evil. God punished them by allowing them to be enslaved by Jabin, the king of Canaan. For 20 years they were cruelly treated, especially by Sisera, captain of the Canaanite army, who had 900 chariots under his command. Deborah, a prophetess and judge at the time, appointed Barak to help her deliver Israel from Jabin and Sisera. Deborah was a remarkable woman, who inspired Barak to gather an army of 10,000 men from the tribes of Naphtali and Zebulun. This army gathered at Mount Tabor in the mountains of Samaria, where it defeated Sisera with his chariot horde. Sisera did not die in battle, but was killed by a woman named Jael as he slept in her tent trying to escape from the Israelites. She drove a tent peg through the head of the sleeping captain (4:21). Following this deliverance from the Canaanites, Israel had 40 years of peace.

Gideon (6:11–8:32)

The greatest of the judges was Gideon, who came to leadership when Israel had been in severe bondage to the Midianites for seven years. Gideon was from Ophrah, a city of Manasseh located 16 miles north of Jericho. Gideon was threshing wheat when an angel appeared to him and called him to deliver Israel. Being a humble man, Gideon questioned his ability to accomplish such a task, whereupon God assured him, "Surely I will be with thee, and thou shalt smite the Midianites as one man" (6:16).

Gideon began his work by building an altar to the Lord and destroying an altar of Baal that stood on his father's property. The spiritual climate was so wretched that Gideon, fearing reprisals by the townspeople, or even his father's household, tore the altar down at night. The people indeed were angry that Baal's altar was destroyed and they contended with Gideon's father, Joash, about the matter. They wanted to kill Gideon.

Sensing that Gideon was intent upon driving them out of Israel, the Midianites, along with the Amalekites, prepared for battle and camped in the valley of Jezreel. Gideon sent messengers to the tribes of Asher, Zebulun and Naphtali, calling them together to save Israel. Thousands of men responded to his call; in fact, so many responded that all of them could not be used.

Gideon thinned his army down to a mere 300 so they and all Israel would have to know that it was God and not their own power that delivered them from Midian. The final method of elimination concerned the manner in which the people drank water. Three hundred were so eager for the battle that they scooped water into their hands and lapped it as they prepared to attack.

The 300 were divided into three companies, who used trumpets, torches and empty pitchers to confuse the Midianites and win one of the most famous victories in Hebrew history. The land was "in quietness forty years in the days of Gideon" (8:28).

When Gideon died "in a good old age," one of his 70 sons, Abimelech, attempted to set himself up as king. Abimelech killed his brothers (or half-brothers, since Gideon had—according to 8:30—70 sons by many wives) and reigned as king for three years. The ambitious son of Gideon was killed as he tried to secure himself as king. The time for dynasties in Israel had not yet come (9:1-57).

Tola (10:1, 2)

Tola was the next judge, but nothing is told about him except that he was of the tribe of Issachar, lived in Ephraim, and judged Israel 23 years.

Jair (10:3-5)

Jair, a man of Gilead, next judged Israel for 22 years. He had 30 sons, who rode on 30 donkeys and were the leaders of 30 villages of Gilead, a land east of the Jordan River. Riding donkeys was a sign of authority and affluence.

Jephthah (11:1–12:7)

One of the most pathetic incidents of Hebrew history concerned Jephthah, the ninth judge. A Gileadite, he was called to deliver Israel from servitude to the Ammonites and the Philistines, an oppression that lasted 18 years. Jephthah had an unhappy background. The illegitimate son of a harlot, he was cast out of his father's house by his brethren. He thereupon went to the land of Tob, where he associated with a band of desperadoes. This was his circumstance when the men of Gilead called on him to fight the Ammonites.

During the battle against the Ammonites, Jephthah rashly vowed to sacrifice as a burnt offering the first thing that greeted him when he returned home. Tragically, it was his only child, a daughter—not a ram or goat or bullock—that met him. Jephthah kept his vow, but there is some uncertainty about how it was done. The earliest interpretation was that the daughter was literally offered as a "burnt offering," according to the terms of Jephthah's vow (11:31). Later interpretation is that the daughter was dedicated to the service of God, and lived her lifetime unmarried and isolated from the world. If the former were correct, there would be much difficulty in understanding how a champion of Israel could resort to human sacrifice, one of the most terrible evils of the people whom he defeated. It was human sacrifice in the "high places" of heathen worship that made them so abominable to the Lord. The Hebrews were to stamp it out, not practice it. It is a much more humane and reasonable interpretation that Jephthah's daughter remained a virgin, dedicated to God's service in some way apart from the world. Each year the women of Gilead spent four days lamenting the unhappy situation created by Jephthah's rash vow (vv. 37-40).

Jephthah judged Israel only six years, and this brief time was further saddened by a war between Gilead and the tribe of Ephraim. The war was over Ephraim's complaint that they were not involved in the war against the Ammonites (21:1). It was a bitter inter-tribal conflict that emphasizes the disunity of the times.

Ibzan (12:8-10)

Ibzan, of Bethlehem, was the 10th judge, but nothing is known of him except that he had 30 sons and 30 daughters. He gave his daughters in marriage to men outside Bethlehem, and arranged for his sons to marry girls from outside Bethlehem.

Elon (12:11, 12)

Elon, of Zebulun, was judge for 10 years, but the record tells only that he was "buried in Aijalon in the country of Zebulun."

Abdon (12:13-15)

Abdon, of Ephraim, judged Israel for eight years. We only know that he had 40 sons and 30 nephews who rode on donkeys, which was an indication of his wealth.

Samson (13:2–16:31)

Samson, the 13th judge, and last of those listed in the Book of Judges, was by all means the most colorful and extraordinary of all. He was the only one born to be a judge. The Philistines had ruled Israel for 40 years when an angel of the Lord appeared to the wife of Manoah in Zorah, about 14 miles west of Jerusalem (13:3). The angel announced that a son would be born to the woman, and he should be a "Nazarite" (v. 5), one dedicated for special service to God. As a Nazarite, the son should abstain from wine or any unclean food and should allow his hair to grow long.

As Samson matured, the Spirit of the Lord moved upon him and he showed extraordinary strength. Almost immediately, however, he revealed a tragic fondness for Philistines. He married a Philistine woman (14:2), became involved with a Philistine harlot (16:1-3), and had a fatal affair with a Philistine named Delilah (vv. 4-21). Most of his opposition to the Philistines was prankish or mischievous rather than purposeful assault. He killed 30 men in Ashkelon (14:19), but this was the consequence of a riddle told at a party with the Philistines. As an act of personal spite, he tied fire-brands to the tails of foxes and burned the Philistine fields (15:4, 5). He slew a thousand Philistines with the jawbone of a donkey only after his own people arranged his capture by them (vv. 11-15). He carried away the gates of the walls around Gaza, but only after his alliance with a woman there (16:1-3).

One writer has observed that "not all of the persons mentioned in the Book of Judges were tribal or national leaders. This is especially true of Samson. He led no rising, gathered no army. He did not attack the foe as the champion and deliverer, and even in his prayer for renewal of strength he thinks only of being avenged on the Philistines for his two eyes."

Samson betrayed his Nazarite vows to the scheming Delilah, and was then betrayed by her. Captured by the Philistines, he was blinded and put to work as a beast. Then the Philistines made him into a clown for their entertainment. Samson is included in the register of the faithful (Hebrews 11:32) because in his death he caused the collapse of an idol's temple, which killed "more than they which he slew in his life" (Judges 16:30).

In his dramatic death, Samson exhibited a redeeming faith, but he still fell short of what God raised him up to do. His brethren carried his body back to the place of his birth, "and buried him between Zorah and Eshtaol in the burying place of Manoah his father" (16:31).

In reality, Samson left Israel in great trouble, for it was a time of great evil in the land. The final five chapters of Judges tell of a sorry time in the nation's history.

III. A Time of Anarchy and Violence (17:1–21:25)

It was a time when "there was no king in Israel, but every man did that which was right in his own eyes" (17:6). This anarchy is summed up in three stories of evil. A young Ephraimite named *Micah* used money stolen from his mother to make a shrine of household gods (v. 5). Micah employed a Levite to be priest of his pagan shrine.

A band of Danites on their way north saw Micah's shrine, stole it and lured the hireling priest away with them (vv. 16-20). They took the idols and the priest into the country of the Zidonians and set up a shrine there. In the process, they attacked the city of Laish and destroyed all the people. The behavior of the Danites violated every higher moral code we recognize today.

The third story tells how a certain Levite's wife was abused and murdered in the town of Gibeah (19:1-30). It is an abhorrent account of such perversion, lust and vio-lence that it created disbelief even in that day. In grief and anger, the husband cut his wife's body into 12 pieces and sent one part to each of the 12 tribes to demonstrate what "lewdness and folly" had been committed in Israel. The result was civil war in which the innocent suffered more than the guilty, and the tribe of Benjamin was almost exterminated (20:21). It was, indeed, a day of anarchy, when "every man did that which was right in his own eyes."

*All scriptures in this Bible Insight are from the King James Version. This Bible Insight is reprinted from *The Living Book*.

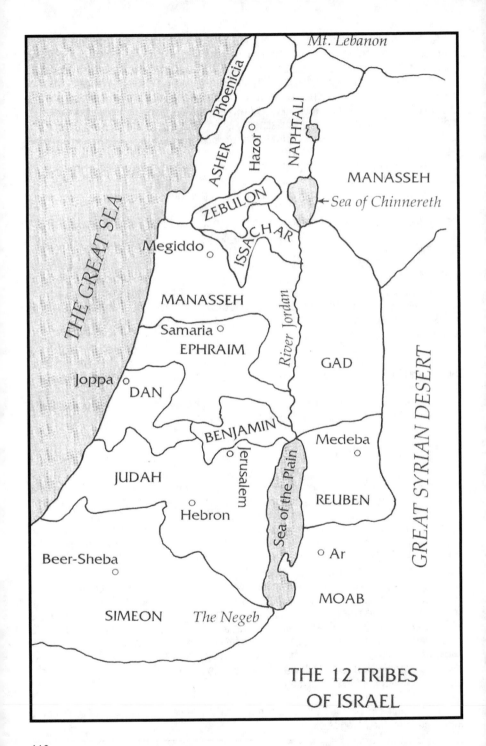

THE 12 TRIBES
OF ISRAEL

Sin and Deliverance

Judges 2:6-23; 3:7-10; Hebrews 3:12-14

INTRODUCTION

Have you ever observed or experienced the damaging effects that the cycle of sin can have in a person's life? From the Book of Judges we learn from Israel's tragic cycle of sin. Judges illustrates the tragic consequences of breaking fellowship with God. The book covers a chaotic time period in Israel's history where they repeatedly broke their fellowship with the Lord to serve foreign gods. As a result, the Lord would deliver them into the hands of other nations.

The Book of Judges begins with the death of Joshua and concludes with the rise of the monarchy in Israel. It covers a period in Israel's history from about 1380 to 1050 B.C. It has four main themes: (1) Israel would fall away from the Lord, (2) God would deliver them into the hands of their enemies, (3) Israel would repent, and (4) God would raise up a deliverer.

When the people cried out in repentance to God, He would anoint men and women to bring deliverance to His people. God empowered them by the Spirit to deliver Israel from their enemies. There were six major judges—Othniel, Ehud, Deborah, Gideon, Jephthah and Samson. These judges were anointed by the Spirit to be civil and military leaders.

The Book of Judges reminds us of our personal need for a Deliverer. We all have sinned and fallen short of God's glory; therefore we need the blood of Jesus to receive forgiveness from our sins. We also need the power of the Holy Spirit in our everyday life. The Spirit gives us power to live victorious Christian lives.

Unit Theme:
Joshua and Judges

Central Truth:
Christians avoid the tragic cycle of sin by holding firmly to faith in Christ.

Focus:
Learn from Israel's tragic cycle of sin and hold firmly to our faith in Christ.

Context:
The events began taking place in 1394 B.C.

Golden Text:
"Take heed, brethren, lest there be in any of you an evil heart of unbelief, in departing from the living God" (Hebrews 3:12).

Study Outline:
I. Disobedience Leads to Judgment (Judges 2:6-15; 3:7, 8)
II. Repentance Brings God's Deliverance (Judges 3:9, 10; 2:16)
III. Heed God's Warning (Judges 2:17-23; Hebrews 3:12-14)

I. DISOBEDIENCE LEADS TO JUDGMENT
   (Judges 2:6-15; 3:7, 8)
A. Joshua's Generation (2:6-9)
   (Judges 2:6, 8, 9 is not included in the printed text.)
   7. And the people served the Lord all the days of Joshua, and all the days of the elders that outlived Joshua, who had seen all the great works of the Lord, that he did for Israel.

Talk About It:
Describe Joshua's influence on the nation of Israel.

Joshua's generation is noted as the one that had seen the great miracles wrought by the Lord in Exodus and the conquest of the Promised Land. The generation had been mightily used by God. During the time of Joshua's leadership and for the rest of the lives of those who were contemporaries of Joshua, the nation remained faithful to God.

Verses 8 and 9 note the passing of Joshua. They identify four things about the great leader. Each item noted is a testimony to the power and providence of God.

First is Joshua's place in the nation—*he was the son of Nun*. He was part of the nation and people that God had blessed. Second, *he was a servant of the Lord*. Even though Joshua was of the holy nation, his ultimate allegiance was not to his family or country. He was first of all God's servant.

"Leadership is the discipline of deliberately exerting special influence within a group to move it toward goals of beneficial permanence that fulfills the group's real needs."
—**John Haggai**

Third, *he was 110 years old*. God had blessed him with longevity. This stood as a testimony to the enduring care of God through so many years. Fourth, *he was buried in the place of his inheritance*. He was not buried a stranger in a strange land. God had been faithful in His promise to give him a land for his own inheritance, and God had faithfully delivered Joshua to this place.

B. Another Generation (vv. 10-15)
   10. And also all that generation were gathered unto their fathers: and there arose another generation after them, which knew not the Lord, nor yet the works which he had done for Israel.

Baalim (v. 11)—the plural form of *Baal*, the chief male deity of the Canaanites

11. And the children of Israel did evil in the sight of the Lord, and served Baalim:

12. And they forsook the Lord God of their fathers, which brought them out of the land of Egypt, and followed other gods, of the gods of the people that were round about them, and bowed themselves unto them, and provoked the Lord to anger.

Ashtaroth (v. 13)—the plural form of a pagan goddess, Ashtoreth

13. And they forsook the Lord, and served Baal and Ashtaroth.

14. And the anger of the Lord was hot against Israel, and he delivered them into the hands of spoilers that spoiled them, and he sold them into the hands of their enemies round about, so that they could not any longer stand before their enemies.

15. Whithersoever they went out, the hand of the Lord was against them for evil, as the Lord had said, and as the Lord had sworn unto them: and they were greatly distressed.

The generation that followed Joshua's generation is described in basically two ways. First, *they did not know the Lord.* This is amplified in the specific notation that they did not know the *works* of the Lord. The faithfulness of one generation does not guarantee the faithfulness of the next generation. The demonstration of God's power in one generation does not guarantee the faithfulness of the next generation. This is why a generation must not merely retell the events of God's power recorded in a previous generation. Each generation must fervently pray that God will reveal Himself and His power anew.

The second description of this wicked generation is that *they worshiped other gods.* If a generation does not worship the Lord, it will worship something or someone else. This generation worshiped the idols of the nations around them, Baal and Ashtaroth (v. 13). This is a fulfillment of the prediction that was made in verse 3. The altars and gods that were not destroyed during the conquest became the very gods that were worshiped by the next generation after the conquest.

God judged the backslidden generation by delivering them over to the nations which surrounded them. They experienced military defeat and severe hardship. This was a time of chastisement for the people as well as necessary judgment.

In our day there are a lot of people who have been raised in a Christian home with a godly legacy but have never come to know God for themselves. It does not matter how well your mom or dad knew the Lord if you don't know Him for yourself. You must have a personal relationship with the Lord.

C. Divine Judgment (3:7, 8)

7. And the children of Israel did evil in the sight of the Lord, and forgat the Lord their God, and served Baalim and the groves.

8. Therefore the anger of the Lord was hot against Israel, and he sold them into the hand of Chushan-rishathaim king of Mesopotamia: and the children of Israel served Chushan-rishathaim eight years.

There is a real consequence to sin. Judges 2:11, 12 tells us Israel committed three sins, which marks the beginning of the cycle of sin and judgment. First, they "did evil in the sight of the Lord." Sin is frightening when we understand the judgment of God. Second, Israel "forsook the Lord God." Once Israel moved into the Promised Land, they forgot the Lord and began to do

Talk About It:
1. What did the new generation *not* know (v. 10)?
2. Describe the Israelites' relationship with the Lord (vv. 11-13).
3. What promise to Israel did the Lord keep (vv. 14, 15)?

"Collapse in the Christian life is seldom a blowout; it is usually a small leak."
—**Paul Little**

groves (v. 7)—Ashtoreth idols

Chushan-rishathaim (KU-shan-RISH-a-THA-im)—v. 8—an obscure Hittite conqueror who dominated Israel for eight years

Talk About It:
Describe Israel's punishment.

what was evil in His sight. People have a tendency to forget the Lord when everything is all right. This is one of the reasons Joshua (ch. 24) challenged them to not forget the Lord. Third, Israel "followed other gods."

As a result of Israel's sins, "the anger of the Lord burned against Israel" (3:8, *NIV*). He allowed them to be oppressed by a ruler known as "doubly-wicked Chushan" (Wycliffe). He ruled a district known as Mesopotamia, or "Syria of the two rivers," situated between the Euphrates and the Tigris rivers. This tyrant's forces overran Israel and forced them to pay tribute for eight years.

II. REPENTANCE BRINGS GOD'S DELIVERANCE
(Judges 3:9, 10; 2:16)
A. Cry to the Lord (3:9, 10)

9. And when the children of Israel cried unto the Lord, the Lord raised up a deliverer to the children of Israel, who delivered them, even Othniel the son of Kenaz, Caleb's younger brother.

10. And the Spirit of the Lord came upon him, and he judged Israel, and went out to war: and the Lord delivered Chushan-rishathaim king of Mesopotamia into his hand; and his hand prevailed against Chushan-rishathaim.

"The children of Israel cried unto the Lord" is a recurring expression throughout Judges (3:9, 15; 4:3; 6:7; 10:10, 12). To *cry out* here means to call on the Lord in repentance. The Lord is great in His mercy to hear us when we call on His name and repent of our sins. God is our Father in heaven and we are His children. He loves us and wants to take care of us. James tells us, "Every good and perfect gift comes from above, . . . from the Father of lights" (see 1:17). Prayer begins by understanding that God is our loving Father and we are His children.

In Judges 3 the Lord raises up a deliverer named *Othniel*, which means "lion of God," or "powerful one of God." He is the brother of Caleb. When Caleb promised to give his daughter Achsah in marriage to any hero who took the town of Debir, Othniel responded, effected its capture and received Achsah (see Joshua 15:15-17; Judges 1:11-13).

When the people sought the face of God, He raised up Othniel to deliver them. He became Israel's judge, took them to war against Cushan-Rishathaim and overpowered him. The result was that Israel lived in peace for 40 years (3:11). Where did Othniel get the ability to judge the nation, plan military strategy, and maintain peace for 40 years? The Scripture says, "The Spirit of the Lord came upon him" (v. 10). The secret of his success rests in the fact that the Holy Spirit led him in his service.

"The ladder of life is full of splinters that we don't feel until we backslide."
—Quotable Quotations

Othniel (OATH-ni-el)—v. 9—His name means "lion of God."

Talk About It:
1. How was Othniel able to deliver Israel?
2. Why is Caleb, Othniel's uncle, mentioned (see Joshua 15:17)?

Deliverance Today
No one is perfect, except for Jesus. We all need forgiveness and deliverance. In prayer, we must confess our faults and sins before God. In repentance we can come to God broken and sinful and leave cleansed and whole.

B. Deliverance From Above (2:16)

16. Nevertheless the Lord raised up judges, which delivered them out of the hand of those that spoiled them.

Othniel was one of many judges God raised up to save Israel. The *judges* were "military heroes or deliverers who led the nation of Israel against the period between the death of Joshua and the reestablishment of the kingship" (*Nelson's Bible Dictionary*).

The Lord repeatedly "saved them out of the hands of these raiders" (*NIV*). We need to be reminded that there are spiritual forces of darkness in this world and we need God's help to protect us.

Just as the Lord raised up deliverers to rescue the Israelites from their enemies, so He is there to deliver us from our trials and temptations whenever we call on His name. The judges are types and shadows of Christ. They show us the need for a Deliverer and Savior.

Rather than sending a different deliverer each time we fall, God has already sent His Son Jesus to deliver and set us free. Through His death in our place, Jesus Christ revealed the divine love and upheld divine justice, removing our guilt and reconciling us to God. Jesus Christ is the fulfillment of the Old Testament prophecies about the Messiah. Hundreds of years before Jesus' birth, prophets predicted the coming of a Jewish Messiah. The Hebrew words for *Messiah* mean "chosen one," "anointed one," and "deliverer." Jesus was specifically chosen by God to bring redemption to the world. Jesus Christ is our Savior, Deliverer, King and Lord.

> "Nothing splendid was ever achieved except by those who dared believe that something inside them was superior to circumstances."
> —**Bruce Barton**

III. HEED GOD'S WARNING (Judges 2:17-23; Hebrews 3:12-14)
A. God's Word (Judges 2:17-19)

17. And yet they would not hearken unto their judges, but they went a whoring after other gods, and bowed themselves unto them: they turned quickly out of the way which their fathers walked in, obeying the commandments of the Lord; but they did not so.

18. And when the Lord raised them up judges, then the Lord was with the judge, and delivered them out of the hand of their enemies all the days of the judge: for it repented the Lord because of their groanings by reason of them that oppressed them and vexed them.

19. And it came to pass, when the judge was dead, that they returned, and corrupted themselves more than their fathers, in following other gods to serve them, and to bow down unto them; they ceased not from their own doings, nor from their stubborn way.

The Book of Judges is a call to listen to the Word of God and obey His commandments. Tragically, the Israelites "did not listen to their judges. . . . They turned aside quickly from the way in which their fathers had walked in obeying the commandments of the Lord" (v. 17, *NASB*). Israel would have never fallen into sin if they had listened to the word of the Lord.

God's Word will guide us and keep us from falling back into sin. It is given to us so we may grow as we walk the path of God. The Bible will strengthen our faith, speak to our heart, and guide us in all of life's decisions.

Sadly, the Israelites became like Egypt's Pharaoh. Just as God sent message after message to Pharaoh through Moses, so God kept speaking to the Israelites through the various judges. But just as Pharaoh continually hardened his heart, so Israel repeatedly hardened her heart. And just as the plagues on Egypt steadily worsened, so the oppression from Israel's enemies grew worse and longer as they failed to heed judge after judge. The Israelites "refused to give up their evil practices and stubborn ways" (v. 19, *NIV*).

B. God's Anger (vv. 20-23)

20. And the anger of the Lord was hot against Israel; and he said, Because that this people hath transgressed my covenant which I commanded their fathers, and have not hearkened unto my voice;

21. I also will not henceforth drive out any from before them of the nations which Joshua left when he died:

22. That through them I may prove Israel, whether they will keep the way of the Lord to walk therein, as their fathers did keep it, or not.

23. Therefore the Lord left those nations, without driving them out hastily; neither delivered he them into the hand of Joshua.

In these verses God gave the reason why He did not drive out all the people of Canaan who were persecuting the Israelites. They were to become the instrument of God's chastening. This is God's clear response to the people's unfaithfulness.

God's response in verse 20 to the people's sinfulness was strong. His anger was "hot" against Israel. God is not passive toward sin. God hates sin and sinfulness; He will not tolerate it. However, His anger, even hot anger, is not destructive. God's purposes of deliverance and mercy are not changed, even in the midst of His anger.

The purpose of allowing the kingdoms surrounding Israel to trouble them was to *prove* the nation, whether it would walk in the ways of God or not (v. 22). The Hebrew word for *prove* in this verse literally means "to smell." In this context the word

"There are many [Old Testament] examples of God's judgment on backsliders

means "to test or try" as someone would test something by smelling it. God's purpose for chastisement was to test and see if Israel was truly faithful.

God's desire, even in the midst of chastisement, was to search for the faithfulness of the nation. His ultimate purpose was their deliverance and redemption. However, this could not be done while they were backslidden and faithless.

C. Self-Examination (Hebrews 3:12)

12. Take heed, brethren, lest there be in any of you an evil heart of unbelief, in departing from the living God.

We are encouraged to examine ourselves to make sure there is not any evil in our hearts from unbelief. We must "take heed," or "beware" (*NKJV*), which is a warning of impending danger. It is a call to check what is in our heart and in our life before something bad happens. The writer of Hebrews is giving us a warning before it is too late. As Christians, we should daily evaluate where we are spiritually.

Most of us go to the doctor for an annual checkup to make sure we are in good physical health. How much more important should it be for us to check our heart? Unbelief comes from a hardening of the heart, which is the result of sin. We need to make sure that we are living in the faith daily because sin creeps its way in a little at a time. We need the Holy Spirit to examine us so we don't have a heart that "falls away from the living God" (*NASB*).

We should pray like the psalmist: "Search me, O God, and know my heart: try me, and know my thoughts: And see if there be any wicked way in me, and lead me in the way everlasting" (139:23, 24).

D. Accountability to Others (vv. 13, 14)

13. But exhort one another daily, while it is called To day; lest any of you be hardened through the deceitfulness of sin.

14. For we are made partakers of Christ, if we hold the beginning of our confidence stedfast unto the end.

It is not enough to examine ourselves, but we should also be accountable to other Christians. We need real fellowship that we can only get from other believers. At the heart of the word for *fellowship* is the idea of participation together. No single word in the English language captures the beautiful meaning of this Greek word. The Christian life is living together in community with one another and Christ.

The writer of Hebrews realized that constant encouragement from a close fellowship was the cure from falling away from the Lord. God has given us the blessing of fellowship to provide a

and the ungodly, but God promised to heal their backslidings and restore them to fellowship with Himself if they repented."
—French Arrington

Talk About It:
What causes people to depart from God?

"[The Hebrews] had experienced the delivering power of the Cross, but now they were in danger of hardening their hearts in unbelief, turning their backs on Christ, and falling into apostasy."
—French Arrington

Talk About It:
Explain the importance of the word "if" in verse 14.

place for spiritual growth, intimacy, accountability and protection. To prevent an evil, unbelieving heart, we must stay in fellowship with other believers and encourage each other with love and care. Then we can "hold firmly till the end" (v. 14, *NIV*).

CONCLUSION

No one plans to fall from the Lord; rather it usually begins with something small, like a sinful thought that grows into a sinful action. The important truth is that God always remains faithful, even when we don't. Whenever Israel would cry out in repentance to the Lord for help, He would deliver them. In the same way, whenever we call on the name of the Lord in repentance, He is there to deliver us.

GOLDEN TEXT CHALLENGE

"TAKE HEED, BRETHREN, LEST THERE BE IN ANY OF YOU AN EVIL HEART OF UNBELIEF, IN DEPARTING FROM THE LIVING GOD" (Hebrews 3:12).

It is dangerous to develop an unbelieving heart. Faith is at the center of all Christian endeavor. In fact, the writer of Hebrews later said, "But without faith it is impossible to please him: for he that cometh to God must believe that he is, and that he is a rewarder of them that diligently seek him" (11:6).

The result of a sinful and unbelieving heart is apostasy. It leads to an attitude that refuses to cleave to, trust in, or rely upon the Lord. The ultimate outcome is a denial of the faith and a forfeiture of the blessings and benefits of knowing God.

Daily Devotions:
M. Consequences of Sin
Daniel 9:1-11
T. Fasting and Deliverance
Isaiah 58:6-12
W. Repent and Live
Ezekiel 18:30-32
T. Receive Forgiveness in Christ
Acts 2:37-41
F. Times of Refreshing
Acts 3:17-26
S. Earthly or Heavenly Minded?
Philippians 3:17-21

Sin and Deliverance

A Mighty Man of Valor

Judges 6:1 through 7:25

INTRODUCTION

The Book of Judges tells us about the story of several great men and women of faith who changed the course of Israel's history and influenced the ancient Near Eastern world for God. These great leaders have left a distinct mark on the pages of history, and their life, ministry, and contributions must not be forgotten. Their lives are a testimony of what God can do through a single person who has the faith to believe. One of the great people of faith in the Book of Judges is Gideon.

In Judges 6:1–8:35 we find the story of Gideon, an ordinary farmer whom God used to do extraordinary things. Gideon's story is one of the great stories of faith in the Bible because we see that the Lord can use anybody. Gideon became Israel's fifth judge. Though he was sometimes slow to action, God used him to defeat the Midianite army. Gideon's legacy is also remembered in the great faith chapter, Hebrews 11.

God is looking for people with a humble heart and willingness to be used. If we submit ourselves to God, He will do great things in and through our lives. Simple faith in God has the power to move mountains.

Gideon's story is filled with the promise and hope of God's empowering presence. Gideon was filled with the Holy Spirit to lead God's people into battle. When we are filled with the Holy Spirit, we are empowered to do amazing things for the Lord. Like Gideon, we need to be full of the Spirit and faith. God's power and presence comes to those who have a pure and humble heart.

Unit Theme:
Joshua and Judges

Central Truth:
Through faithfulness to God, we are empowered by Him to do His will.

Focus:
Examine how God empowered Gideon and serve in God's strength.

Context:
Around 1150 B.C. in the Valley of Jezreel, God raises up Gideon.

Golden Text:
"The Lord looked upon him, and said, Go in this thy might, and thou shalt save Israel from the hand of the Midianites: have not I sent thee?" (Judges 6:14).

Study Outline:
  I. Answer God's Call (Judges 6:11-24)
  II. Use What God Provides (Judges 7:1-8)
  III. Triumph in God's Strength (Judges 7:9-25)

I. ANSWER GOD'S CALL (Judges 6:11-24)

A. Unexpected Visitor (vv. 11, 12)

Ophrah (AHF-rah)—
v. 11—the place
where Gideon was
born, lived, and died

11. And there came an angel of the Lord, and sat under an oak which was in Ophrah, that pertained unto Joash the Abi-ezrite: and his son Gideon threshed wheat by the winepress, to hide it from the Midianites.

12. And the angel of the Lord appeared unto him, and said unto him, The Lord is with thee, thou mighty man of valour.

Talk About It:
1. Where did Gideon thresh wheat, and why (v. 11)?
2. What is ironic about what the angel calls Gideon (v. 12)?

The Israelites had lapsed into one of their periodic backslidings, neglecting their attention to God's laws, delving into idolatry, and with everybody doing his or her own thing. As a result, God allowed the surrounding desert nomadic tribes to grow strong, and for seven years Israel was harassed and plundered by these barbaric people, who would swoop in suddenly from the desert on their camels, laying waste to the crops, carrying off the cattle and wealth, and forcing the people to flee to caves and strongholds in the mountains.

One day the angel of the Lord appeared to Gideon, the youngest son of Joash, under a well-known oak tree in the town of Ophrah and declared to him, "The Lord is with you, you mighty man of valor!" (v. 12, *NKJV*). This was a promise that God's presence would be with Gideon to do all that He commanded him to do. Was this an angel or God? The writer uses both "the angel of the Lord" (vv. 11, 12) and "the Lord" (v. 14) interchangeably. The appearance of the Lord in angelic form occurs several times throughout the Old Testament.

The Lord calling Gideon a "mighty warrior" (*NIV*) was not based on anything Gideon had accomplished so far in his life. In fact, at this point Gideon was "distressed; he was threshing his wheat, not in the threshing floor, the proper place, but by the winepress, in some private unsuspected corner, for fear of the Midianites. He himself shared in the common calamity, and now the angel came to animate him against Midian when he himself could speak so feelingly of the heaviness of their yoke. The day of the greatest distress is God's time to appear for his people's relief" (Matthew Henry).

"We, too, are called to a path filled with uncertainty, mystery, and risk."

—Erwin McManus

B. Specific Call (vv. 13-15)

13. And Gideon said unto him, Oh my Lord, if the Lord be with us, why then is all this befallen us? and where be all his miracles which our fathers told us of, saying, Did not the Lord bring us up from Egypt? but now the Lord hath forsaken us, and delivered us into the hands of the Midianites.

14. And the Lord looked upon him, and said, Go in this thy might, and thou shalt save Israel from the hand of the Midianites: have not I sent thee?

A Mighty Man of Valor

15. And he said unto him, Oh my Lord, wherewith shall I save Israel? behold, my family is poor in Manasseh, and I am the least in my father's house.

Gideon raised questions. If God really was with Israel, why were they suffering such oppression? Why had He delivered them from Egypt only to allow Midianites to terrorize them? The angel answered by saying Gideon himself was the answer—God was calling *him* to deliver Israel.

Now Gideon began to make excuses. How could he save Israel? He saw no qualifications in himself or in his family that would enable him to be a rescuer. This is exactly how we may feel in our life. We may feel small and insignificant, but God calls ordinary people to do extraordinary things. The truth is we *are* small and insignificant, and the battles and challenges we face are often greater than we are. The answer is that our God is bigger than our problems.

As in the case of Gideon, the only requirement that God is looking for is a willing vessel. The Bible is full of common people whom the Lord used: Jacob, Moses, Gideon, David, Esther, Jeremiah, Peter, Barnabas, and so on. Paul says in 2 Timothy 2:21, "If a man therefore purge himself . . . he shall be a vessel unto honour, sanctified, and meet for the master's use, and prepared unto every good work." The term *vessel* parallels the Old Testament idea of items being sanctified so they may be used in the Temple. As believers, we must be set apart for God before we can be used by Him.

C. Divine Sign (vv. 16-24)

(Judges 6:18-20, 22, 23 is not included in the printed text.)

16. And the Lord said unto him, Surely I will be with thee, and thou shalt smite the Midianites as one man.

17. And he said unto him, If now I have found grace in thy sight, then shew me a sign that thou talkest with me.

21. Then the angel of the Lord put forth the end of the staff that was in his hand, and touched the flesh and the unleavened cakes; and there rose up fire out of the rock, and consumed the flesh and the unleavened cakes. Then the angel of the Lord departed out of his sight.

24. Then Gideon built an altar there unto the Lord, and called it Jehovah-shalom: unto this day it is yet in Ophrah of the Abi-ezrites.

When the angel told Gideon that he would "quickly destroy the Midianite hordes" (v. 16, *TLB*), Gideon asked for a sign to show him it was really God talking to him. Then Gideon made one more request, asking the angel to wait while Gideon prepared an offering. While the angel waited, Gideon cooked a young goat and unleavened bread. When Gideon returned, the angel directed him to lay the meat and the bread on a large

Talk About It:
1. What questions did Gideon ask (vv. 13, 15)?
2. Explain the statement "Go in this might of yours" (v. 14, *NKJV*).

Talk About It:
1. What did the Lord promise Gideon (v. 16)?
2. Why did Gideon want a sign (v. 17)?
3. What did Gideon name the altar, and why (v. 24)?

rock. When the angel touched the offering with the tip of his staff, fire supernaturally came up from the rock and consumed the sacrifice. Then the angel disappeared, and Gideon was convinced he had seen an angel face-to-face.

Gideon was afraid. Israel was in turmoil and Gideon was overwhelmed by the presence of God. Therefore, the angel of the Lord proclaimed to Gideon, "Peace be with you; do not fear" (v. 23, *NKJV*). Gideon must have received the peace of the Lord in his heart, because he built an altar to the Lord and called it "The Lord is Peace," or "Jehovan-Shalom" (v. 24). The Hebrew word *Shalom* means "wholeness, peace, security and well-being." Gideon experienced firsthand the shalom of God in his heart.

Philippians 4:7 says, "The peace of God, which passeth all understanding, shall keep your hearts and minds through Christ Jesus." Jesus is the Prince of Peace. God gives peace whenever Jesus Christ comes into our heart. We live in a world full of war and turmoil and, more than ever, we need the peace of God.

God's peace gives us rest that each of us so desperately need. Our souls need to have Scriptural rest in the same way our bodies need physical rest. Throughout the Bible, God promises rest to His people. The Biblical word for *rest* literally means "a quiet place, peace, trust and reliance." Rest is the reason God commanded us to keep the Sabbath. Jesus said, "The sabbath was made for man, and not man for the sabbath" (Mark 2:27).

II. USE WHAT GOD PROVIDES (Judges 7:1-8)

1. Then Jerubbaal, who is Gideon, and all the people that were with him, rose up early, and pitched beside the well of Harod: so that the host of the Midianites were on the north side of them, by the hill of Moreh, in the valley.

2. And the Lord said unto Gideon, The people that are with thee are too many for me to give the Midianites into their hands, lest Israel vaunt themselves against me, saying, Mine own hand hath saved me.

3. Now therefore go to, proclaim in the ears of the people, saying, Whosoever is fearful and afraid, let him return and depart early from mount Gilead. And there returned of the people twenty and two thousand; and there remained ten thousand.

4. And the Lord said unto Gideon, The people are yet too many; bring them down unto the water, and I will try them for thee there: and it shall be, that of whom I say unto thee, This shall go with thee, the same shall go with thee; and of whomsoever I say unto thee, This shall not go with thee, the same shall not go.

Limiting God

How often people say, "Show me a miracle, and I will believe, but until then, I won't believe anything I don't see. I won't accept anything I can't touch."

There is a main reason that we limit an unlimited God: . . . because we do not see Him as who He really is.

—Morris Cerullo

Jerubbaal (jer-uh-BAY-ul)—v. 1— Meaning "let Baal contend," it was the name given to Gideon by his father when Gideon tore down an altar to Baal (6:32).

A Mighty Man of Valor

5. So he brought down the people unto the water: and the Lord said unto Gideon, Every one that lappeth of the water with his tongue, as a dog lappeth, him shalt thou set by himself; likewise every one that boweth down upon his knees to drink.

6. And the number of them that lapped, putting their hand to their mouth, were three hundred men: but all the rest of the people bowed down upon their knees to drink water.

7. And the Lord said unto Gideon, By the three hundred men that lapped will I save you, and deliver the Midianites into thine hand: and let all the other people go every man unto his place.

8. So the people took victuals in their hand, and their trumpets: and he sent all the rest of Israel every man unto his tent, and retained those three hundred men: and the host of Midian was beneath him in the valley.

In Judges 6:33-40 we see Gideon requesting one more test of God. He needed further assurance that divine power would assist him in the fight against the Midianites. Gideon set out a fleece at night and said, "Let there be dew on the fleece in the morning, but no dew on the ground around it" (see v. 37). The Lord complied. Then Gideon asked, "This time let there be dew on the ground but none on the fleece" (see v. 39). The next morning it was as he had asked. Gideon was ready to do exploits for God, as we see in chapter 7.

Thirty-two thousand Israelites gathered together under Gideon to fight the Midianites, but the Lord told Gideon that there were too many. Gideon told them that any who were afraid to fight could go home, and two-thirds of them did so. But 10,000 were still too many, God said, so Gideon screened out all but 300 through an unusual process. Gideon camped on a hill with his 300 men and looked down upon the Midianite camp.

God reduced their number from 32,000 to 300 men to prevent the Israelites from being self-sufficient. With an army this small, there could be no doubt that the victory was from God, for there were 135,000 soldiers in the enemy army. Gideon only needed a few good men to go into battle according to God's plan.

The significance of this part of our lesson is that God will provide exactly what we need when we need it. Our God is *Jehovah-Jireh*, "the Lord our provider." He will make a way where there seems to be no way. When all the world seems like it is against you and you don't know what to do, simply put your trust in the Lord and He will make a way.

Talk About It:
1. Why did God say Gideon had too many men (v. 2)?
2. Whom did God allow to not take up the fight (v. 3)?
3. What did God promise Gideon (v. 7)?

The Lord told Gideon to only select the men who drank from the water by putting their cupped hands to their mouth. What is the significance of only selecting the men who drank in this fashion? Albert Barnes says, "They who threw themselves on the ground and drank freely were the more self-indulgent; while they who, remembering the near presence of the enemy, slaked their thirst with moderation, and without being off their guard for an instant, were the true soldiers of the army of God" (*Barnes' Notes*). These 300 men would have the Spirit of the Lord on them when they went into battle. Like those men who drank of the water before the battle, we must drink of the living water of the Holy Spirit. Jesus said, "'He who believes in Me, as the Scripture has said, out of his heart will flow rivers of living water.' But this He spoke concerning the Spirit, whom those believing in Him would receive" (John 7:38, 39, *NKJV*).

III. TRIUMPH IN GOD'S STRENGTH (Judges 7:9-25)
A. A Dream From God (vv. 9-15)

9. And it came to pass the same night, that the Lord said unto him, Arise, get thee down unto the host; for I have delivered it into thine hand.

10. But if thou fear to go down, go thou with Phurah thy servant down to the host:

11. And thou shalt hear what they say; and afterward shall thine hands be strengthened to go down unto the host. Then went he down with Phurah his servant unto the outside of the armed men that were in the host.

12. And the Midianites and the Amalekites and all the children of the east lay along in the valley like grasshoppers for multitude; and their camels were without number, as the sand by the sea side for multitude.

13. And when Gideon was come, behold, there was a man that told a dream unto his fellow, and said, Behold, I dreamed a dream, and, lo, a cake of barley bread tumbled into the host of Midian, and came unto a tent, and smote it that it fell, and overturned it, that the tent lay along.

14. And his fellow answered and said, This is nothing else save the sword of Gideon the son of Joash, a man of Israel: for into his hand hath God delivered Midian, and all the host.

15. And it was so, when Gideon heard the telling of the dream, and the interpretation thereof, that he worshipped, and returned into the host of Israel, and said, Arise; for the Lord hath delivered into your hand the host of Midian.

The Lord told Gideon that he would either go down immediately and defeat the Midianites or, if he was still afraid, he and his servant Phurah could sneak down and spy them out. The cautious Gideon decided on the latter course.

"The real question to be asked about any miracle is not how it happened but why: what was God saying to us in this significant act?"
—Louis Cassels

Phurah (FU-rah)—
v. 10—Gideon's servant and armor bearer

Talk About It:
1. How does verse 12 describe the opposition?

It must have been an impressive and terrifying sight when Gideon and his servant drew near the enemy camp. The cutthroat, marauding horde in the valley outnumbered Gideon's band many times. Sneaking up to the edge of the Midianite camp in the shadows, Gideon eavesdropped on this conversation between two men, one of whom was telling of a dream he recently had. At that time dreams were highly regarded as having a relationship to future events. This dream seemed almost comic in its telling, but the persons who heard it considered it very seriously.

It must have startled Gideon to hear his own name mentioned by this enemy soldier. And the dream fit him perfectly. He was like a poor little barley cake, with no power in himself, but the Lord would cause him to flip-flop into the camp of the Midianites and smash them decisively. It helped Gideon also to know how much his enemies feared him.

Gideon hastened back to his camp, praising God all the way. He wasted no time in getting his men together and mobilizing them for the attack.

B. An Imaginative Plan (vv. 16-18)

16. And he divided the three hundred men into three companies, and he put a trumpet in every man's hand, with empty pitchers, and lamps within the pitchers.

17. And he said unto them, Look on me, and do likewise: and, behold, when I come to the outside of the camp, it shall be that, as I do, so shall ye do.

18. When I blow with a trumpet, I and all that are with me, then blow ye the trumpets also on every side of all the camp, and say, The sword of the Lord, and of Gideon.

Gideon's strategy must have been guided by the Lord. It was highly imaginative. The *lamps* were torches placed inside the pitchers; the *trumpets* were rams' horns. Probably only one man in most military companies would have a trumpet. The many trumpets and lights would deceive the enemy into thinking that Gideon's men were several thousand in number, and that they had them surrounded. The three groups of 100 each were to sneak upon the Midianites from different directions and spread out to make a circle around them.

The men were all to go to their places around the Midianite camp and wait for the signal from Gideon. When they saw his light and heard his trumpet, then they would show their lights, blow their trumpets, and shout. The operation depended on strict obedience and the help of God.

Gideon put the Lord before himself. He knew that the victory depended more on what the Lord would do than on what he would do, but he understood that God was depending on him to be the instrument by which victory would be gained.

2. Explain the confidence Gideon shows in verse 15.

"Faith is to believe what you do not yet see; the reward for this faith is to see what you believe."
—Augustine

Talk About It:
How does Gideon demonstrate leadership?

C. Total Victory (vv. 19-25)

(Judges 7:23-25 is not included in the printed text.)

19. So Gideon, and the hundred men that were with him, came unto the outside of the camp in the beginning of the middle watch; and they had but newly set the watch: and they blew the trumpets, and brake the pitchers that were in their hands.

20. And the three companies blew the trumpets, and brake the pitchers, and held the lamps in their left hands, and the trumpets in their right hands to blow withal: and they cried, The sword of the Lord, and of Gideon.

21. And they stood every man in his place round about the camp: and all the host ran, and cried, and fled.

22. And the three hundred blew the trumpets, and the Lord set every man's sword against his fellow, even throughout all the host: and the host fled to Beth-shittah in Zererath, and to the border of Abel-meholah, unto Tabbath.

Talk About It:
1. How did Gideon's sudden charge affect the enemy (v. 21)?
2. How did Gideon's army of 300 suddenly grow (vv. 23, 24)?

It was about 10 p.m. when Gideon and his men reached the far side of the camp. The other two bands of Gideon's men would already be in their places by now and waiting for the signal. It was the ideal time for a night attack. The new guards would not have had time to become familiar with their surroundings and their beats. The other soldiers would be most deeply slumbering at this time.

The still of the night erupted into sounds—first the sound of the trumpets and the breaking of the pitchers, then the shouts of the Israelites, then the alarms of the guards, followed by the startled cries of the Midianites and the sounds of movements of men and camels in utter confusion.

The forces of evil are not always as well-organized and invulnerable as we Christians think. A few well-directed, God-blessed actions can give His people great victories.

All this motion in the darkness in the Midianite camp, punctuated by the trumpet blasts and shouts of the Israelites, wrought complete chaos. No one could be sure who was a Midianite and who was an Israelite, for the Midianites thought the Israelites were right among them. It was every man for himself, they thought. No time to organize a group defense.

The Midianites began to slash out at anyone near them in the dark, and many of their hosts were killed by their own men. The Midianites scattered, many on foot, leaving their camels, which probably had stampeded anyway by this time.

Gideon's men pursued them, calling on his countrymen to help pursue the enemy wherever they went. Eventually several thousand more Israelites joined the fray. The two princes of the Midianites were found and slain, and the victory was complete (vv. 23-25). Israel would have rest again from their enemies—until the next time they lapsed into indifference, grew cold in their spiritual lives, and began to dabble around in strange religions and immorality.

A Mighty Man of Valor

Gideon and his men were empowered by the Spirit of the Lord to fight the battle. Earlier in Judges 6:34, we were told that "the Spirit of the Lord came upon Gideon." In Hebrew this literally means "The Spirit of the Lord clothed Gideon." Like Gideon, the Holy Spirit will give us power to do what God is calling us to do if we will ask.

To be *empowered* by the Spirit is synonymous with being *filled* with the Spirit, which is an experience in God where our spirit is totally immersed with and in the Holy Spirit. This should be an ongoing experience throughout our life of faith. To be full of the Spirit is not that we have more of God; rather that God has more of us.

> "Rest in this—it is His business to lead, command, impel, send, call, or whatever you want to call it. It is your business to obey, follow, move, respond, or what have you."
> —Jim Elliot

CONCLUSION

The story of Gideon reminds us that the Lord uses ordinary people to accomplish His purposes in the world. Ordinary men and women of the Bible changed their world for God. They stepped out of their comfort zone and dared to do great and mighty things. Likewise, their stories should also inspire us to do great things for God.

GOLDEN TEXT CHALLENGE

"THE LORD LOOKED UPON HIM, AND SAID, GO IN THIS THY MIGHT, AND THOU SHALT SAVE ISRAEL FROM THE HAND OF THE MIDIANITES: HAVE NOT I SENT THEE?" (Judges 6:14).

In this verse the angel of the Lord is identified as the Lord himself ("Jehovah" in the Hebrew text). This coincides with the firm declaration given at this time to Gideon. It was so forceful that Gideon addressed the speaker in verse 15 as the Lord God.

In this second declaration to Gideon, the Lord commissioned Gideon to *go*. The basis of the commission is revealed in the words "this thy might." This refers to the promise of the Lord's presence given in verse 12. The might of Gideon would be the presence of the Lord with him.

God sent Gideon specifically to deliver the nation, even though he had just given a number of excuses. The Hebrew word used here for *save* emphasized "deliverance from dangers and distresses." God did not ignore the excuses of Gideon. Rather, the assurance of His sovereignty and presence would still enable Gideon to lead the deliverance of the people.

In the last phrase of verse 14, "Have not I sent thee?" the Lord calls on Gideon to recognize it is the Lord himself that has commissioned him. Recognition that God's plan originates with God himself is a primary source of faith and motivation for the believer. Along with recognition of the plan must come recognition that the plan is from God.

Daily Devotions:
M. Equipping for Service
   Exodus 4:1-7
T. God Turns the Table
   Esther 9:1-10
W. Call to Service
   Jeremiah 1:1-10
T. Set Apart for Service
   Galatians 1:11-17
F. Walk in the Spirit
   Galatians 5:16-25
S. Use the Gift You Have
   1 Peter 4:7-11

A Weak Strong Man

Judges 13:1-25; 16:1-31

Unit Theme:
Joshua and Judges

Central Truth:
Christians are to live by the Spirit, not gratifying the desires of the sinful nature.

Focus:
Analyze the cause of Samson's downfall and avoid the pitfalls that bring ruin to a Christian's life.

Context:
Between 1085 and 1065 B.C. near Zorah and in the Valley of Sorek

Golden Text:
"Walk in the Spirit, and ye shall not fulfill the lust of the flesh" (Galatians 5:16).

Study Outline:
 I. Consecrated for Service
(Judges 13:1-5, 24, 25)
 II. Weakened by Compromise
(Judges 16:1-21)
III. Restored to God's Purpose
(Judges 16:22-31)

INTRODUCTION

The title of this lesson is "A Weak Strong Man." This is an *oxymoron*, or a contradiction of terms. How can a weak man be strong? The story of Samson makes it plain. Samson is one of the most well-known characters of the Old Testament. He was anointed a judge over Israel and had superhuman strength, but compromised by giving the secret of his power to Delilah, who, in turn, cut off his hair and turned him over to the Philistines. Even though Samson was a strong man physically, he was weak because he lacked moral character.

Samson was dedicated to the Lord from his birth as a Nazarite. A *Nazarite* was a person who took a special vow of consecration to the Lord. The Nazarite vow included abstinence from wine and alcohol, refraining from cutting hair, and refusing to go near a dead body for a specific period of time. Sadly, Samson did not live up to this commitment to the Lord. In this lesson we will analyze the cause of Samson's downfall.

Samson's story reminds us that Christians are to live by the Spirit and not gratify the lusts of the flesh, as the Golden Text declares. Samson fell because he allowed sin to gradually creep into his life. Sin finally cost him strength and anointing. We need to be careful that we don't open the door for sin and worldliness to creep into our lives. Even though Samson fell into sin, which ultimately led to his demise, in the bittersweet end he called on the name of the Lord and regained his strength. This is a powerful lesson of God's forgiveness and love. No one is perfect, and we all need the grace and love of God.

I. CONSECRATED FOR SERVICE (Judges 13:1-5, 24, 25)

A. The Call of God (vv. 1-5)

1. And the children of Israel did evil again in the sight of the Lord; and the Lord delivered them into the hand of the Philistines forty years.

2. And there was a certain man of Zorah, of the family of the Danites, whose name was Manoah; and his wife was barren, and bare not.

Jesus **3. And the angel of the Lord appeared unto the woman, and said unto her, Behold now, thou art barren, and bearest not: but thou shalt conceive, and bear a son.**

4. Now therefore beware, I pray thee, and drink not wine nor strong drink, and eat not any unclean thing:

5. For, lo, thou shalt conceive, and bear a son; and no razor shall come on his head: for the child shall be a Nazarite unto God from the womb: and he shall begin to deliver Israel out of the hand of the Philistines.

Human proneness to sin is well attested by the repetitious relapses of the Israelites during the days of the judges. Here for the seventh time they turned away from Jehovah to serve the agricultural and fertility gods led by Baal. This was worldliness in its most flagrant form. Whereas the Lord God wanted Israelite life to be governed by heavenly criteria, Baalism sought to tie life to the earth. God's punishment was bondage to the Philistines of the costal plain for 40 years. What meager living the Israelites eked out in the hill country was quickly consumed by these marauders.

In the midst of unfaithful Israel, Manoah and his wife had set up a godly home. This is indicated by his unhesitating obedience to God's commands. Yet, sorrow marred the family circle, for they had no children.

Just as the angel of the Lord had unexpectedly appeared to Gideon (6:11), so it happened to Manoah's wife. "The angel of the Lord" is God's presence in a form perceptible to human sight. In this act God shows Himself immanent as well as transcendent; He is not far off but nigh, near enough to care for and be concerned about human problems. In giving a promise to the wife of Manoah, God was meeting the personal need of the woman for a child as well as the social need of the nation for a deliverer.

The first restriction was for the mother. Her life was to be set aside for holy purposes. Not only were there restrictions for the mother, but there were restrictions for the son. It would be challenging for the wife of Manoah to convince the young child that he was to be different from the other children. Yet, she tackled the task with courage and heroism, convinced that only as she

Talk About It:
1. What was Manoah's wife warned not to do (v. 4)?
2. What instructions were given regarding Manoah's son, and why (v. 5)?

Samson (v. 24)—means "distinguished" or "little sun"

Talk About It:
What do these verses say about the relationship between the Lord and Samson?

obeyed God could deliverance be wrought. Samson's real strength lay not in his hair but in his obedience to the will of God.

The words of the angel were prophetic: "He shall begin to deliver Israel." The full deliverance did not lie in Samson but in those who followed him and truly walked with God.

B. The Stirring of the Spirit (vv. 24, 25)

24. And the woman bare a son, and called his name Samson: and the child grew, and the Lord blessed him.

25. And the Spirit of the Lord began to move him at times in the camp of Dan between Zorah and Eshtaol.

The Spirit of the Lord anointed Samson to perform extraordinary tasks. While still living with his parents, the Holy Spirit began to stir Samson about his calling to be a deliverer. Once when a young lion came upon him, the Spirit empowered Samson to tear the lion apart with his bare hands (14:6). In verse 19 we read how he struck down 30 Philistines. Later on he killed a thousand Philistines with the jawbone of a donkey (15:14, 15).

The key to understanding Samson's power is the Holy Spirit. Some people don't believe the miraculous gifts of the Spirit are for today. Does the Lord still anoint people who seek Him? The answer is yes! In the Old Testament era, the Holy Spirit came upon only a few select individuals (such as Samson, Gideon, Samuel and David) to perform particular tasks. In the Christian era, however, the Holy Spirit's infilling is for all believers who will receive it. You and I can experience His fullness in our everyday life by surrendering ourselves to Him and His purposes.

II. WEAKENED BY COMPROMISE (Judges 16:1-21)

A. Samson's Love (vv. 1-14)

(Judges 16:1-3, 6-8, 10, 11, 13 are not included in the printed text.)

Gaza (GAY-zuh)— v. 1—One of the five main Philistine cities, its name means "strong" or "fortified."

withs (v. 7)—"bowstrings" (*NKJV*)

tow (v. 9)—string or yarn

4. And it came to pass afterward, that he loved a woman in the valley of Sorek, whose name was Delilah.

5. And the lords of the Philistines came up unto her, and said unto her, Entice him, and see wherein his great strength lieth, and by what means we may prevail against him, that we may bind him to afflict him; and we will give thee every one of us eleven hundred pieces of silver.

9. Now there were men lying in wait, abiding with her in the chamber. And she said unto him, The Philistines be upon thee, Samson. And he brake the withs, as a thread of tow is broken when it toucheth the fire. So his strength was not known.

12. Delilah therefore took new ropes, and bound him therewith, and said unto him, The Philistines be upon thee, Samson. And there were liers in wait abiding in the chamber. And he brake them from off his arms like a thread.

14. And she fastened it with the pin, and said unto him, The Philistines be upon thee, Samson. And he awaked out of his sleep, and went away with the pin of the beam, and with the web.

The strength of Samson was demonstrated at Gaza and in the house of Delilah. At Gaza, the men waited at the gate of the city to kill Samson. However, at midnight he "took the doors of the gate of the city, and the two posts, and went away with them, bar and all, and put them upon his shoulders, and carried them up to the top of an hill that is before Hebron" (v. 3). The city of Gaza was probably not less than three-quarters of an hour from the mount where Samson took the gates. To have climbed to the top of this hill with the ponderous doors and their bolts on his shoulders, through a road of thick sand, was a feat that none but Samson could have accomplished.

While the Philistines could not stop Samson, he stopped himself. His licentious conduct at last involved him in a situation where his strength could be forfeited and his effectiveness destroyed.

The Philistines were willing to pay a high price for the head of Samson. When they learned of the romance between Delilah and Samson, they offered her a fabulous bribe (1,100 shekels of silver) if she could discover the secret of his strength. Since the value of a silver shekel was somewhere between 60 and 65 cents, the price for Samson's betrayal was for that time enormous. To Delilah the lure of the bribe was stronger than her love for Samson, and she urged him to tell her the secret of his strength.

Samson told her that if they would bind him with seven green "withs" (bowstrings), he would lose his strength. However, when she bound him with the bowstrings, he easily broke them. Then, he told her that he would become weak if he was bound with new ropes. Again, the ropes were futile against his strength. Next, he told her that if she would weave the seven braids of his hair "into the fabric on the loom and tighten it with the pin" (v. 13, *NIV*), his might would be gone. She did so, but when he awoke, he walked away with "the pin and the loom, with the fabric" (v. 14, *NIV*).

B. Samson's Foolishness (vv. 15-20)

15. And she said unto him, How canst thou say, I love thee, when thine heart is not with me? thou hast mocked me these three times, and hast not told me wherein thy great strength lieth.

Talk About It:
1. What was Samson's weakness (vv. 1, 4)?
2. Why did Samson keep playing this cat-and-mouse game with Delilah (vv. 5-14)?

"The flesh is a worse enemy than the devil himself."
—Isaac Ambrose

wist (v. 20)—knew

Talk About It:
1. What did Delilah keep doing, and how did it affect Samson (vv. 15, 16)?
2. What did Samson wrongly assume (v. 20)?

Sin's Insanity
After the news of rock musician Jonathan Melvoin's death of a drug overdose hit the media in 1996, the demand for the drug that killed him, Red Rum (a

16. And it came to pass, when she pressed him daily with her words, and urged him, so that his soul was vexed unto death;

17. That he told her all his heart, and said unto her, There hath not come a razor upon mine head; for I have been a Nazarite unto God from my mother's womb: if I be shaven, then my strength will go from me, and I shall become weak, and be like any other man.

18. And when Delilah saw that he had told her all his heart, she sent and called for the lords of the Philistines, saying, Come up this once, for he hath shewed me all his heart. Then the lords of the Philistines came up unto her, and brought money in their hand.

19. And she made him sleep upon her knees; and she called for a man, and she caused him to shave off the seven locks of his head; and she began to afflict him, and his strength went from him.

20. And she said, The Philistines be upon thee, Samson. And he awoke out of his sleep, and said, I will go out as at other times before, and shake myself. And he wist not that the Lord was departed from him. *DID NOT KNOW*

Samson received several warnings throughout his life to not commit sin, but he refused to listen. God was trying to warn him by allowing the enemy to almost catch him, but Samson refused to repent and change his ways. It was at this time that Delilah came into his life and led him down the path of destruction just like the adulterous woman in Proverbs 7.

Little by little, Samson allowed sin to creep into his heart and eventually his life. Eventually Samson's heart grew far from God. Over time he was in the lap of a wicked woman who was conspiring to destroy him. This is what happens when people choose to constantly reject the counsel of the Lord.

At last Samson told Delilah the secret of his strength: He was a Nazarite—a man set apart—and the sign of his consecration was his long hair. If that was cut off, his consecration would be gone. And if his consecration was gone, the heavenly support would be gone, and Samson would be as other men. In disclosing this secret, Samson was tampering with that which was sacred. He was selling away a power God had especially given him for accomplishing a work that was to be for the honor of His great name in the world.

Jewish expositors say that Delilah knew Samson had given her the secret because "words of truth are readily recognizable," and because she felt sure he would not "take the name of God in vain."

Once Delilah had gained the information she sought, she then prepared everything for Samson's destruction. A person would think that after such a disclosure, Samson would have taken care not to put himself in her power. Yet behold, he soon afterward fell asleep with his head in her lap, and afforded her an opportunity of employing a man to cut off his hair. What foolishness!

Having had the seven locks of Samson's head shaved off, Delilah woke him, as on former occasions; and he, unconscious that the Lord had departed from him, went forth to shake himself as at other times. But his strength was gone.

C. Sin's Slavery (v. 21)

21. But the Philistines took him, and put out his eyes, and brought him down to Gaza, and bound him with fetters of brass; and he did grind in the prison house.

Samson the mighty warrior became a slave. He lost his freedom because he became a spiritual slave to sin, which made him a literal slave to the Philistines. After Delilah cut his hair, Samson had no power to fight against the Philistines. They came in and blinded him and then bound him with fetters of brass. Then they tied him to a mill to grind.

Samson loses his hair, which is a symbol of his Nazarite vow. He loses his eyes, which is a symbol of his spiritual state. He could no longer see the truth of God. He loses his strength, which is a symbol of the presence of God working in his life to do extraordinary things. He loses his testimony of faith. He was supposed to be a man of God, but instead he became a sinful man of compromise.

Samson thought his strength was in his hair. His strength, of course, was in the Lord. It was a God-given endowment. His long hair, untouched through his life by a razor, was but the sign and seal of his consecration as a Nazarite. God had given him his strength that he might deliver Israel. His long hair was a sign that he was a committed man. But, like Esau who had lived centuries before, Samson despised his birthright. He was a weakling, not because he had lost his hair but because the Spirit of the Lord had departed from him.

If we are not careful we can also fall into sin. Samson's spiral into destruction shows us the following about the progression of the slavery of sin: (1) We are blinded to the truth. (2) We are bound by the sin. (3) We live for the sin. (4) We die by the sin.

III. RESTORED TO GOD'S PURPOSE (Judges 16:22-31)
A. Samson's Humiliation (vv. 22-25)

22. Howbeit the hair of his head began to grow again after he was shaven.

23. Then the lords of the Philistines gathered them together for to offer a great sacrifice unto Dagon their god,

form of heroin), exploded. *Red Rum* is "murder" spelled backward. This is one example of sin's insanity.
—Choice Contemporary Stories and Illustrations

Talk About It:
Use three adjectives to describe Samson's condition.

"All human sin seems so much worse in its consequences than in its intentions."
—Reinhold Niebuhr

and to rejoice: for they said, Our god hath delivered Samson our enemy into our hand.

24. And when the people saw him, they praised their god: for they said, Our god hath delivered into our hands our enemy, and the destroyer of our country, which slew many of us.

25. And it came to pass, when their hearts were merry, that they said, Call for Samson, that he may make us sport. And they called for Samson out of the prison house; and he made them sport: and they set him between the pillars.

Talk About It:
1. What mistaken idea did the Philistines have (vv. 23, 24)?
2. Why did they call for Samson (v. 25)?

The growth of Samson's hair was not here mentioned as a mere natural fact, nor with the superstitious notion that his hair made him strong. God made him strong on the condition that he keep his vow of consecration. The loss of his hair was the consequence of his voluntary breach of the vow. So its growth was the visible token that the fault was being repaired.

It was a common practice in heathen nations, during their solemn religious festivals, to bring forth the war prisoners from their places of confinement or slavery. In heaping on them every species of indignity, they offered tribute to the gods by whose aid they had triumphed over their enemies. In Philistia a vast temple was erected to Dagon, a sea idol. He was usually represented as having the head and upper parts of a man, and the lower body of a fish.

Verse 23 describes the reaction of the lords of the Philistines to the capture of Samson. Verse 24 describes the reaction of the people and shows how universally Samson's capture was ascribed to Dagon. Rulers and people alike praised Dagon.

"After the pastor's seething sermon on the congregation's myriad sins, one member said, 'At least I haven't made any graven images.'"
—*Christians Quoting*

The feasts of heathenism were wild orgies, unlike the pure joy of the sacrificial means in Jehovah's worship. Dagon's temple was filled with a drunken crowd who called for Samson. He had to dance and laugh while 3,000 gaping Philistines fed their hatred by the sight.

B. Samson's Repentance (vv. 26-28)

26. And Samson said unto the lad that held him by the hand, Suffer me that I may feel the pillars whereupon the house standeth, that I may lean upon them.

27. Now the house was full of men and women; and all the lords of the Philistines were there; and there were upon the roof about three thousand men and women, that beheld while Samson made sport.

28. And Samson called unto the Lord, and said, O Lord God, remember me, I pray thee, and strengthen me, I pray thee, only this once, O God, that I may be at once avenged of the Philistines for my two eyes.

Wearied with his humiliating exertions, Samson begged the boy who guided him to let him lean, till he could breathe again, on the pillars that held up the building. The people were clustered together waiting to see what the blind captive would do next after he had caught his breath.

Samson humbled himself before the Lord and asked the Lord to remember him. He willingly devoted himself to death that he might be an instrument of God's vengeance on the Philistines. He leaned against the two middle pillars. It is quite easy to understand how, if there was a row of them, knocking out the two strongest central ones would bring the whole building down.

Talk About It:
1. Describe the crowd (v. 27).
2. What did Samson request from God (v. 28)?

C. Samson's Death (vv. 29-31)

29. And Samson took hold of the two middle pillars upon which the house stood, and on which it was borne up, of the one with his right hand, and of the other with his left.

30. And Samson said, Let me die with the Philistines. And he bowed himself with all his might; and the house fell upon the lords, and upon all the people that were therein. So the dead which he slew at his death were more than they which he slew in his life.

31. Then his brethren and all the house of his father came down, and took him, and brought him up, and buried him between Zorah and Eshtaol in the buryingplace of Manoah his father. And he judged Israel twenty years.

God used Samson one final time to defeat the Philistines. The temple of Dagon was at the center of the city where the Philistine townspeople gathered. The temple was completely filled with people when Samson pushed down its central pillars. The Lord empowered Samson to slay more Philistines in his death than he had slain in his life.

Talk About It:
How was Samson a deliverer in death (vv. 29, 30)?

Repentance brings restoration, and restoration bears fruit. The fruit of the Spirit is the opposite of the works of the flesh. Samson's earlier life was marked with works of the flesh, such as lust, deceit and drunkenness. But at the end of his life—in a state of humiliation, blindness and weakness—Samson allowed God's Spirit to move upon him one last time to accomplish God's purpose.

CONCLUSION

Samson's downward spiral happened because he began to trust in himself rather than God. He relied on the flesh instead of the Spirit. The Bible tells us that if we live by the Spirit, we will not gratify the desires of the flesh and sinful nature (Galatians 5:16). Therefore, we need to be full of the Holy Spirit and walk in His power and strength.

GOLDEN TEXT CHALLENGE

"WALK IN THE SPIRIT, AND YE SHALL NOT FULFILL THE LUST OF THE FLESH" (Galatians 5:16).

"Walking in the Spirit" conveys the idea of continuous activity, motivated by, energized by, enabled by, and for the benefit of the Holy Spirit. It is living unceasingly for the glory of God. The walk indicates a calm and steady progress that is pleasing to God and productive in His service.

Many people's lives are so up and down, so fluctuating in victories and defeats, that there is little consistency to them. The walk in the Spirit is both consistent and victorious.

The alternative to this life is to walk in the flesh, which is a self-centered, pleasure-seeking lifestyle that disregards the will of God and yields to temptations easily. It is neither victorious nor productive, and its only consistency is in the constant trouble that characterizes such a life.

Bible Insight

PSALMS & HYMNS

The Book of Psalms was Israel's "hymnbook." There were psalms for every situation the Israelites might face.

In conjunction with this six-lesson series "Prayers in the Psalms," we have selected six hymns that have been composed and widely sung by Christians. These hymns connect with the themes of these lessons as shown:

- Lesson 8, Pray Through Your Troubles ("What a Friend We Have in Jesus")
- Lesson 9, Abiding With God ("Sweet Hour of Prayer")
- Lesson 10, A Prayer for Mercy ("At the Cross")
- Lesson 11, Secure in God ("O God, Our Help in Ages Past")
- Lesson 12, Amazing Care of Our Creator ("This Is My Father's World")
- Lesson 13, God Delivers Us From Evil ("Leaning on the Everlasting Arms")

Each week you may choose to reflect on the chosen hymn by reading its lyrics or leading the class in singing it together.

Pray Through Your Troubles

Psalm 77:1-20

Unit Theme:
Prayers in the Psalms

Central Truth:
Christians can deal with their doubts by praying and reminding themselves of God's goodness.

Focus:
Explore how to deal with doubt when troubled and focus on God and His works in prayer.

Context:
Psalm 77 was written by Asaph, appointed over the service of praise in the reigns of David and Solomon.

Golden Text:
"I will meditate also of all thy work, and talk of thy doings" (Psalm 77:12).

Study Outline:
I. Call on God When Troubled (Psalm 77:1-3)
II. Confess Your Doubts When Perplexed (Psalm 77:4-9)
III. Meditate on God's Redemptive Works (Psalm 77:10-20)

INTRODUCTION

When studying one of the Psalms, we first need to correctly identify who wrote it. This enables us to have a better understanding of both the content and the context. Second, even though many joyous expressions are found in the Psalms, we should recognize that expressions of sorrow in the process of seeking God's deliverance are common. Third, since we experience some of the same situations which bring hurt and harm, we should find it easy to identify with prayers for deliverance. Yes, the authors lived millenniums before us. But that doesn't change their feelings and desire for God's intervention.

Troubles of different types come into our lives. Sometimes our physical bodies are attacked by germs or viruses which bring great discomfort and may even have long-term side effects. Our body may suffer injury. Then we are faced with pain, restrictions or the possibility of death.

Some troubles come to us from the actions of others. It may be the result of our being at the wrong place at the wrong time or being touched by the ripple effect of their deeds. An example would be many individuals losing their investments and/or pension plans due to the corruption and scandalous actions of company officers.

Other troubles are the result of our own actions. Impetuousness drives some to attempt what wisdom would always disapprove. Others find themselves being driven by temptations to fill their desire for wealth, position or pleasure. But when the bottom line becomes visible, they experience a new reality.

When troubles barge into our lives, regardless of the reason, there is one action that should be constant—*prayer*. Prayer should be a regular part of our spiritual relationship. However, if it is not, the time of trouble provides a strong impetus to begin. And, though we may not deserve it, God in His mercy hears and decides what is best for us.

I. CALL ON GOD WHEN TROUBLED (Psalm 77:1-3)
1. I cried unto God with my voice, even unto God with my voice; and he gave ear unto me.

2. In the day of my trouble I sought the Lord: my sore ran in the night, and ceased not: my soul refused to be comforted.

3. I remembered God, and was troubled: I complained, and my spirit was overwhelmed. Selah.

As we consider the opening words of Psalm 77, let's review the authorship. This psalm, along with 11 others, are attributed to Asaph (Psalm 50; 73–83). He is a Levite from the Gershonite family who serves in the reigns of David and Solomon. His responsibility is the services of praise where he leads in singing and sounding the cymbals before the ark of the covenant (see 1 Chronicles 16:5; 2 Chronicles 5:12).

The particular situation that leads Asaph to write such a prayer of trouble is unknown. We cannot determine whether it was personal, family-related or an event in the kingdom. Regardless of the situation, we see this man sorrowing and crying out to God. He needs help and knows to whom he should turn.

This psalm begins with two statements of the author's call for help. This parallelism is common to Hebrew poetry, but it also serves to emphasize the urgency of the action. One translation reads, "I cried out to God for help; I cried out to God to hear me" (*NIV*). The wording speaks of the intensity of this man's cry for help. It isn't a casual, off-hand request. Asaph presents a crisis call for help. He is in the middle of trouble and needs divine intervention.

Verse 2 is better interpreted, "When I was in distress, I sought the Lord; at night I stretched out untiring hands and my soul refused to be comforted" (*NIV*). Asaph describes a situation which is so distressing he continues crying out to the Lord for an extended time. There is no thought of a simple prayer for help and then turning away with a sense of peace. The reference to untiring hands speaks of persistence. Satisfaction or comfort in his spirit will come only when receiving an answer.

The inner grief of this man is so great he groans within. He takes the situation to God. But his dwelling on the situation causes a sigh to rise within. The more he thinks of the circumstances, the greater the physical impact. It drains him emotionally; he is "overwhelmed" (v. 3).

II. CONFESS YOUR DOUBTS WHEN PERPLEXED (Psalm 77:4-9)
A. Past Remembered (vv. 4-6)
4. Thou holdest mine eyes waking: I am so troubled that I cannot speak.

"my sore ran" (v. 2)—"my hand was stretched out" (*NKJV*)

Talk About It:
1. What can we learn from verse 1?
2. How does the psalmist describe his condition (vv. 2, 3)?

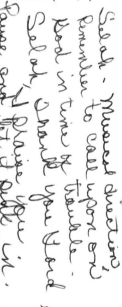

"Trouble and perplexity drive us to prayer, and prayer driveth away trouble and perplexity."
—**Philipp Melancthon**

5. I have considered the days of old, the years of ancient times.

6. I call to remembrance my song in the night: I commune with mine own heart: and my spirit made diligent search.

Talk About It:
1. What two things could the psalmist not do (v. 4)?
2. What was "considered" by the psalmist (vv. 5, 6)?

Asaph's concern over the undescribed situation causes him to be sleepless and speechless. His saying that God is holding his eyes open isn't the thought of being awakened or forced to stay awake. It is better understood in light of God's not responding to the cry for help, and thus being responsible for his being awake in the night. The distress which Asaph experiences restricts or prohibits speaking about it to anyone.

When confronted with such a situation, each of us is forced to decide how the sleeplessness will be handled. One can toss and turn or make this a productive time of reflection or meditation. It appears Asaph attempts to make this a positive experience. He begins by remembering past days. The length of this backward search is not indicated. However, "days of old" and "ancient times" speaks of long ago. Charles H. Spurgeon wrote of this passage: "If no good was in the present, memory ransacked the past to find consolation. She fain would borrow a light from the altars of yesterday to light the gloom of today. It is our duty to search for comfort, and not in sullen indolence yield to despair" (*Psalms*).

When considering some of the major addresses of Israel's leaders, we see them reviewing events of the past—both positive and negative (see Deuteronomy 9; Joshua 24). The same can be found among the prophets (see Isaiah 48; Jeremiah 2). It seems logical for Asaph to consider some specific events when God came to the rescue of His people. Maybe it is the deliverance from Egypt, the provision of food and water, or the many enemies to which God brought defeat. Reviewing the past can build faith. Reminding ourselves of how God intervenes enables us to keep a glimmer of hope alive, even when encased in frustration and near hopelessness.

Asaph also turns to his personal past. He begins to think of songs which he may have personally composed and/or possibly sang on a regular basis. There may have been a special song he favored, much in the same way we have a song or chorus that continues to be a strength and comfort. The words may be sung audibly or quietly within. Either way, they can minister. Sometimes a succession of them provides a ministering presence of the Holy Spirit, which enables us to eventually sleep.

"God has been consistently affectionate and true to us. He has shared His great wealth with us. How can we doubt the all-powerful, all-sufficient Lord?"
—C.H. Spurgeon

Asaph notes another step of remembering. He does a careful job of introspection. Maybe there is something within his own heart and spirit that contributes to the current situation. Genuine introspection necessitates an honest review of one's motives and emotions. It can be painful if the results show a less than positive picture.

Pray Through Your Troubles

When seemingly swimming in despair, an individual can make one of two choices. Either he or she resolutely confronts the situation seeking answers, or hopelessly waits for whatever fate may come. Asaph chooses the first option.

B. Current Questions (vv. 7-9)

7. Will the Lord cast off for ever? and will he be favourable no more?
8. Is his mercy clean gone for ever? doth his promise fail for evermore?
9. Hath God forgotten to be gracious? hath he in anger shut up his tender mercies? Selah.

When oppressed by situations beyond one's control with no relief in sight, it's common to ask questions. They may be about God or pointed toward God's actions. This is a normal human response. Too often people believe questioning God is a sin. But remember how God made us. We are rational beings enabled to think and to respond to our surroundings.

However, there are times when questioning is a sin. It's a sin to continue questioning too long and not moving to the next question, which is "How can we handle this, Lord?" It's a sin to continue questioning once the answer has already been given. Neither of these are the case in our study.

A further study of an individual's asking some tough questions of God can be seen in the Book of Habakkuk. The prophet asks questions such as "How long do I have to cry and You do not hear?" Or "How long do I have to look at the violence around me?" (see 1:1-3). Bold, yes! But God never rebukes him for exposing the questions of his heart. Instead, God answers Habakkuk (vv. 5-11).

Jeremiah also questions God (12:1-4). These too are strong inquiries. It is encouraging to see God responding with answers to his questions (vv. 5-17).

As Asaph reviews what is taking place (Psalm 77:7-9), he asks if God's people have been rejected by Him. Since no answer has been coming, there is the thought of God's permanent rejection of these in need. If true, this signals a horrible change in God's attitude toward His people. This has not been experienced by them or seen in the recorded past! If true, it signals the end of His mercy and favor. This would not only be distressing but a major disaster.

Apparently God's silence and noninvolvement causes questions which indicate a certain sense of uncertainty about their God. Could it be His compassion will no longer be extended? Will there be the withdrawal of His promises and provisions? Verse 9 suggests sins had been committed which could cause God's anger to be unleashed as punishment for their sins. If

Talk About It:
What is similar about all six of the psalmist's questions?

All people that on earth do dwell
Sing to the Lord with cheerful voice....
For why? The Lord our God is good:
For His mercy is forever sure;
His truth at all times firmly stood,
And shall from age to age endure.
—**William Kethe**

this is taking place, will God never again be merciful and compassionate?

Without knowing the specifics of this situation, we still find a principle. It's all right to openly confess one's doubts and fears to God through questions motivated by right intentions.

III. MEDITATE ON GOD'S REDEMPTIVE WORKS (Psalm 77:10-20)
A. God's Greatness (vv. 10-14)

10. And I said, This is my infirmity: but I will remember the years of the right hand of the most High.

11. I will remember the works of the Lord: surely I will remember thy wonders of old.

12. I will meditate also of all thy work, and talk of thy doings.

13. Thy way, O God, is in the sanctuary: who is so great a God as our God?

14. Thou art the God that doest wonders: thou hast declared thy strength among the people.

Talk About It:
1. What did the psalmist decide to "remember" and "meditate" on (vv. 10-12)? Why was this important?
2. How did he describe God in verses 13 and 14?

There comes a point in any situation where continued questioning simply furthers a sense of distress or anxiety. Rehashing the events, searching for reasons for them, and the seeming silence of God serve no benefit. Instead of this negative approach, the believer needs to begin a positive practice of meditating on God's saving works in the past. It's amazing how this changes a person's outlook. Asaph chooses this approach. We can compare it to switching from petition to praise.

A person can't simply disregard the negative situation, but the focus can change. In verse 10 the author chooses a new direction. He is going to dwell on the Lord God and on His deeds. "Remembering" here goes beyond Asaph's own life. It includes the knowledge of God's wondrous works in the generations of previous centuries. This provides a balanced perspective between the personal and corporate care of God for His people.

Verse 12 shows a dual approach to this remembering. It includes personally thinking or meditating on God's works. But it does not stop there. We reap a tremendous benefit of faith and assurance when verbally sharing it with others. For this reason, testimony of what God has done in the past and is still doing produces a positive blessing within the community of believers.

Another benefit of remembering and meditating on God's greatness is the realization again of some marvelous truths. One of these is the greatness of God. There is nothing to compare. Isaiah 40 provides a glimpse of His greatness by stating He holds the waters of the earth in His hand and measures the heavens with the span of His hand. This picture demonstrates

"When you have nothing left but God, then you become aware that God is enough."
—Maude Royden

Pray Through Your Troubles

the unbelievable dimensions of the God we serve. No wonder the miracles of the past and present are the normal works of our great God.

B. God's Redemption (vv. 15-20)

15. Thou hast with thine arm redeemed thy people, the sons of Jacob and Joseph. Selah.

16. The waters saw thee, O God, the waters saw thee; they were afraid: the depths also were troubled.

17. The clouds poured out water: the skies sent out a sound: thine arrows also went abroad.

18. The voice of thy thunder was in the heaven: the lightnings lightened the world: the earth trembled and shook.

19. Thy way is in the sea, and thy path in the great waters, and thy footsteps are not known.

20. Thou leddest thy people like a flock by the hand of Moses and Aaron.

As Asaph meditates on the past, he begins to concentrate specifically on God's redemption of His people Israel. The focus is the redemption from Egyptian bondage with the highlight being the crossing of the Red Sea. It would seem as though the plagues on Egypt could be some of what he was thinking about in verses 12 and 14. But, the crossing of the Red Sea finalizes the people's freedom from the Egyptians. The record is found in Exodus 14.

Believing the Hebrews (Israelites) were trapped by natural boundaries, Pharaoh changed his mind about their release. He sent the Egyptian army for the intent of returning them to the position of slaves. God miraculously interceded to the point of destroying Pharaoh's military force.

In verse 15 of the text, Asaph refers to the Hebrews as the sons of Jacob and Joseph instead of the more frequent statement of being the sons of Abraham. Possibly this is a reflection of its being Jacob's family who entered Egypt to escape the famine. And Joseph became the key person in enabling them to receive provisions and settle in a good part of the land.

The writer of this psalm uses a number of descriptives to emphasize what a troubling situation the people were experiencing. Lightning, thunder and deep water all speak of elements beyond the people's control. In themselves there was no hope. Into this crisis came God. He held the solution in His hand and provided leaders to guide the people. Their path through the seas was one of God's choosing. Through difficulty He carefully protected and led them safely to the other side (v. 19).

What comfort and assurance must have come to Asaph with this realization. God not only knows our difficult situation, but on some occasions it is part of His planned way for us.

Talk About It:
1. What "trembled" (vv. 16, 18), and why?
2. Where was God's presence seen but unseen (vv. 19, 20)?

"God's grace and power seem to reach their peak when we are at our weakest point."
—Anne Graham Lotz

Time to Pray
Got a cold, headache or an upset stomach? Take a quick stroll down the aisle of your local drug store. The number of choices are overwhelming. Do you want a cold remedy which specifically works on sore throats or aching muscles or congestion? Do you want extra strength or just regular strength?

The remedy God provides for our troubles is much simpler. Just pray.

CONCLUSION

Praying through our trouble usually includes much more than crying, "Help, deliver me!" There is room for us to question why certain circumstances come into our lives. Then we must move on to meditating on God's goodness and previous provision. This provides strength for endurance. It speaks of assurance of God's entering the events of our lives. This in turn allows us to rest in Him until the answer comes.

GOLDEN TEXT CHALLENGE

"I WILL MEDITATE ALSO OF ALL THY WORK, AND TALK OF THY DOINGS" (Psalm 77:12).

When we need to reflect on God's great interventions to help us through a current crisis, we can recall our personal experiences and our local church's experiences. In addition, and most importantly, we have the amazing accounts in Scripture, from Genesis to Revelation, to remind us of how God intervened in times past.

The Word of God is a faith-building force as we meditate on its accounts of God's mighty deeds. God's Word is a life-giving, dynamic channel through which God can pour out life, health, hope, and specific directions for our current crisis.

Between the covers of the Bible—somewhere, in a place God will reveal—is light in darkness, bread for nourishment, and peace for a troubled heart. Meditating on God's greatness and goodness can lay a foundation for praying through our troubles.

48   What A Friend We Have In Jesus

Joseph Scriven   Charles C. Converse

1. What a friend we have in Je - sus,   All our sins and griefs to bear!
2. Have we tri - als and temp-ta-tions? Is there trou - ble an - y - where?
3. Are we weak and heav-y lad - en, Cum-bered with a load of care?

What a priv - i - lege to car - ry   Ev - 'ry-thing to God in prayer!
We should nev-er be dis-cour-aged, Take it to the Lord in prayer:
Pre-cious Sav-iour still our ref - uge; Take it to the Lord in prayer.

Oh, what peace we of - ten for - feit, Oh, what need-less pain we bear,
Can we find a friend so faith - ful Who will all our sor-rows share?
Do thy friends de-spise, for-sake thee? Take it to the Lord in prayer;

All be-cause we do not car - ry Ev - 'ry-thing to God in prayer!
Je - sus knows our ev-'ry weak - ness, Take it to the Lord in prayer.
In His arms He'll take and shield thee; Thou wilt find a sol - ace there .

Abiding With God

Psalm 84:1-12

Unit Theme:
Prayers in the Psalms

Central Truth:
Abiding with God brings the joy of intimate communion with Him.

Focus:
Conclude that abiding in God's presence brings strength and joy, and consecrate our lives to Him.

Context:
A psalm written for the sons of Korah to be sung in Temple worship

Golden Text:
"A day in thy courts is better than a thousand. I had rather be a door-keeper in the house of my God, than to dwell in the tents of wickedness" (Psalm 84:10).

Study Outline:
I. Dwell in God's House
(Psalm 84:1-4)
II. Grow Strong in God
(Psalm 84:5-9)
III. Abide in God's Presence
(Psalm 84:10-12)

INTRODUCTION

It's much easier to talk about relationships than it is to maintain healthy ones. It is sad to see close friends who would, at one time, do anything for each other drift apart. Sometimes this results from a difference or disagreement that cannot be resolved. Other times it simply develops from a casual acceptance of this friendship and a false assumption it will always remain strong.

Of far greater consequences is when relationships within families disintegrate. It may be parents and children, siblings with other siblings, or husband and wife. The environment or stimulus may vary greatly. Regardless, usually there hasn't been that special tending and nurturing which needs to be taking place. As a result, a gradual distancing can eventually or, in some cases, quickly result in a great gap. Misunderstandings arise. Happiness and fulfillment degenerate. If allowed to continue, separations occur.

The same is true in our spiritual lives. Accepting Jesus as our Savior is only the beginning step of the relationship God desires for us to have with Him. Even after having received the baptism in the Holy Spirit with the initial evidence of speaking in tongues, there continues to be more, if we are going to experience the fullness of abiding in our Lord.

We may, on occasion, experience special blessings as waves of the Holy Spirit's presence bathe our hearts and souls until we are overflowing with joy and praise. These are marvelous times of adoration and communion. But what happens between these times? How closely do we walk with God in those common days as we go through the normal actions working, caring for families and interacting with our neighbors? This becomes the test of whether or not we are abiding with Him.

Sometimes a crisis becomes the stimulus for abiding with God. After having prayed our "Help me, God" petitions, it's amazing how it can result in our staying closer to the Master. When an Eastern shepherd is forced to inflict the harshest discipline on an often straying sheep, he breaks one of its forelegs. He then splints it and, when necessary, carries the sheep. As a result, this sheep becomes so accustomed to being by the shepherd's side that even when healthy again it stays close.

Hopefully our love for God will cause us to remain close to Him. This enables us to offer an abundance of adoration, thanksgiving and praise to God. Then, in such a pleasant relationship, we can offer our petitions and intercessions.

Today's lesson provides a broad framework in which we not only can draw close to the Master but also maintain this relationship on a regular basis.

I. DWELL IN GOD'S HOUSE (Psalm 84:1-4)

A. The Desire (vv. 1-3)

1. How amiable are thy tabernacles, O Lord of hosts!

2. My soul longeth, yea, even fainteth for the courts of the Lord: my heart and my flesh crieth out for the living God.

3. Yea, the sparrow hath found an house, and the swallow a nest for herself, where she may lay her young, even thine altars, O Lord of hosts, my King, and my God.

amiable (v. 1)—
lovely

Before reviewing the opening verses of this psalm, it would seem beneficial to ask ourselves several questions: (1) Do I look forward to going to church and being in the presence of God with fellow believers? (2) When forced to miss service due to circumstances beyond my control, do I eagerly look forward for the next opportunity to worship in the house of God? (3) When not within the security of the four walls of a church, do I still worship God and rest in His presence?

The identity of the author of this psalm is not given. We also have no knowledge of a distinctive event which triggers this marvelous expression of desire to be in the house of God and experience His presence. Some commentators believe this stems from within a caravan of Israelites as they return to Jerusalem from Babylonian exile. Regardless of the setting, the words can easily become an expression of believers today.

Verse 1 begins with a marvelous expression of love for the Lord's dwelling place. In this case, it surely refers to the Temple which had been built after the first restoration led by Zerubbabel. Individuals born during the Captivity have never experienced either seeing the Temple of the Lord or being able to worship in it. Maybe this individual isn't an exile. He may have not been able or allowed to come to the Temple for some reason. Either way, the result is an intense desire developing within.

The longing to be in the house of the Lord permeates his whole being. Nothing is withheld. His crying out for the Lord is like a cry or shout of soldiers going into battle. Every aspect of this person strains forward to be involved in worshiping God in the environment of His Temple.

H.C. Leupold, in his *Exposition of Psalms*, explains the mention of swallows in verse 3 as follows: "These birds were continually to be seen in the Temple area; they felt at home there." The application is that humans need to find security and comfort in the house of the Lord from a spiritual perspective like the birds did physically.

B. The Blessing (v. 4)

4. Blessed are they that dwell in thy house: they will be still praising thee. Selah.

Talk About It:
1. How did the psalmist describe his desperation for God's presence (vv. 1, 2)?
2. Why did the psalmist envy certain sparrows (v. 3)?

Wilted Flowers
The impatiens in our flower box at the backside of the yard were blooming so beautiful. What a delight to drive up to the garage and see the flourishing flowers. Then it seemed there were less flower stems and fewer blossoms. Gently pulling on the stalks, they came out of the ground. Some insects chewed them off above the roots and below the soil. They wilted and died. That's what we can expect when failing to abide in our God.

Verse 4 contains a vital principle that can be stated as follows: Dwelling in the presence of God causes the believer to magnify the name of the Lord. Dwelling in the house of the Lord includes two dimensions. The first dimension is attending and participating in the worship of God in the specific place designated as His house. For a period of time in Israel's history was the Temple. In our era it is the church building.

The second dimension is opening our hearts and minds to the continued presence of God, regardless of where we are. He is omnipresent, enabling us to worship Him at any time. It's this dimension which more believers need to cultivate in their lives. We do not need to wait until a particular time or place to dwell in the presence of God. We can offer our adoration, praise and thanksgiving regardless of the setting.

> "The activity which is of primary importance in the life of every believer is true spiritual worship."
> —Robert Rayburn

Any time we open ourselves to the presence of God, there are bountiful blessings to experience. Feeling His nearness as He speaks to our hearts and minds strengthens us and helps us to mature spiritually.

II. GROW STRONG IN GOD (Psalm 84:5-9)
A. The Journey (vv. 5, 6)

5. Blessed is the man whose strength is in thee; in whose heart are the ways of them.

6. Who passing through the valley of Baca make it a well; the rain also filleth the pools.

Weeping
sorrow into joy

Talk About It:
What does it mean for a person's strength to be in God (v. 5)?

In these verses we see how the Hebrews would often blend a literal event with a spiritual dimension. Verse 5 has been translated, "Blessed are those whose strength is in you, who have set their hearts on pilgrimage" (*NIV*). On the one hand, there is the physical journey which they are experiencing. On the other hand, there is the spiritual journey which occurs simultaneously.

Verse 5 points to the issue of personal strength. It can be physical, spiritual and emotional. Many equate this to be the true test of whether or not one is a true man or woman. The danger is to become self-sufficient. Dependency is seen as weakness. The truth is that we all are dependent on God, whether we realize it or not. We should find our strength in Him.

When we place our trust in the Lord, it changes the condition of our heart, our inner being. Left to itself without the influence of the Holy Spirit, the heart may lead us on a rocky road. We will go through peaks and valleys depending on our environment, our emotions, and our feeble attempts to find truth. In marked contrast is the heart of a person who trusts in the Lord. He or she follows a smooth road, even when surrounded by the most difficult of circumstances.

In verse 6 the reference to "the valley of Baca" is translated by some as "the Valley of Weeping" or "the valley of the balsam trees" (*Zondervan's Pictorial Bible Dictionary*). "The tree is called a weeper probably because it exudes tears of gum. There is no trace of a real tree with this name. The phrase refers figuratively to an experience of sorrow turned into joy."

Here we are reminded of our life journeys. Sometimes there are extremely difficult events which cause tears of sorrow to flow freely. However, we also are privileged to enjoy heights of joy which produce laughter. During these times we put the dark days behind us. As believers, the constant reality continues to be one of living in the strength of the Lord regardless of the current circumstances of our physical and spiritual journeys.

B. The Strength (vv. 7-9)

7. They go from strength to strength, every one of them in Zion appeareth before God.

8. O Lord God of hosts, hear my prayer: give ear, O God of Jacob. Selah.

9. Behold, O God our shield, and look upon the face of thine anointed.

These verses continue the dual concept of pilgrims traveling to Jerusalem and the spiritual journey. Some translate verse 7 as "They go from battlement to battlement" or "from walled city to walled city." This indicates the peril of the journey necessitating their taking shelter at night whenever possible. The risk is well worth the effort in order to reach Jerusalem and worship at the Temple. Their willing sacrifice enables them to have a spiritual encounter.

This raises some practical spiritual considerations as well. Life in Christ necessitates our taking refuge in His Word and the directives of the Holy Spirit. Our adversary, the devil, will pursue and attempt to destroy us at worst or sidetrack us at best. However, he is a defeated foe!

In verse 8 we hear an urgent prayer petition. The phrase "give ear" was used in public worship when presenting petitions. It appears the author desired the same strength referred to in verse 7.

Notice the two separate references to God in verse 8. The first, "Lord God of hosts," indicates His tremendous power, authority and sovereignty. The second is more personal. He is the "God of Jacob" who guides as well as disciplines. He seeks His people's well-being and hears their prayers.

In verse 9 God is referred to as a *shield*. There is strength in His protection. The shield thwarts the thrusts of the enemy's sword as well as the arrows in flight. We are reminded of our

"God is to be honored on every level of life so His children don't become hypocrites—given to a practice of consecration only on Sundays at 10 a.m., while behaving like those who have no knowledge of Him the rest of the week."
—**David Morris**

Talk About It:
1. Spiritually, how can we go "from strength to strength" (v. 7)?
2. What does the psalmist call God in verse 9, and why?

spiritual armor as listed in Ephesians 6. Here the shield represents faith by which the believer is protected from "flaming arrows of the evil one" (v. 16, *NIV*).

The second part of Psalm 84:9 says, "Look upon the face of Your anointed" (*NKJV*). This prayer could be directed to God for the benefit of the current king, or for the people of Israel, asking for God's favor on the leader or the people He has chosen. Or it might be directed to the Messiah, through whom our prayers reach the Father, who looks upon His face.

Though the specific references in these verses may be clouded, a principle definitely stands out: We can find no strength beyond what our God possesses. For physical protection we may wear body armor and reside in superstrong structures. But our God continues to be the true Strength. He supersedes all other earthly and heavenly powers.

III. ABIDE IN GOD'S PRESENCE (Psalm 84:10-12)
A. The Dwelling (vv. 10, 11)

10. For a day in thy courts is better than a thousand. I had rather be a doorkeeper in the house of my God, than to dwell in the tents of wickedness.

11. For the Lord God is a sun and shield: the Lord will give grace and glory: no good thing will he withhold from them that walk uprightly.

This portion of our lesson includes both the Golden Text and the concept of the central truth. They emphasize the distinctive of abiding in God's presence. Here we are strongly reminded of our life in Christ not being an occasional encounter on special days or crisis events. It is to be a constant relationship which includes communication through prayer, reading the Word, hearing the voice of the Holy Spirit, and being confident in God's strength.

In verse 10 the psalmist emphatically demonstrates his devotion to the Lord. At first glance it appears to be an exaggeration. However, this is a normal process of description when attempting to share the intensity of one's commitment. He would rather be positioned at the lowest level in God's house than to be in a higher realm of comfort among the wicked.

This description does open the door to some practical application in our lives. For example, from an economic viewpoint, what choice may we have to make? If stretching the truth or compromising our lifestyle is required to make more money, will the materialism be more important than our spiritual relationship? If associating with unbelievers while disassociating with believers provides a greater status, whom will I choose?

All of these decisions become much simpler when we consider the God we serve. He is the Almighty who rules over

"O God, our help in ages past,
Our hope for years to come,
Our shelter from the stormy blast,
And our eternal home!"
—Isaac Watts

Talk About It:
1. What does the psalmist say is "better" (v. 10)?
2. What would the writer "rather be," and why (v. 10)?
3. What can the "upright" expect from God (v. 11)?

everything. When we are in true relationship He becomes all we could need or ever hope for. Referring to God as the *sun* (v. 11) shows He provides light and warmth, enabling life to flourish. As a *shield*, He is our protector and refuge. There is safety which calms our fears, replacing them with peace.

This verse furthers the concept of blessings and rewards to those who faithfully serve God. These must always be secondary considerations in our Christian walk; however, they should not be overlooked. Our primary reason for service is to love. It stands as the binding principle. God, our heavenly Father, loves us as sons and daughters. He desires our love on the basis of who He is rather than what He does. We earthly parents understand this in light of expectations of our children.

When we continue to enter God's presence with faithfulness, there are blessings which He places upon us. His favor and honor may include material possessions, positions of influence, good health, and physical protection. Not having these is by no means a sign of God's disfavor! These simply are examples of what might occur.

It is important to recognize the gracious giving which is part of God's relationship with those who abide in Him. He is not a stingy God who grudgingly offers a few spare blessings. No, He is a generous God caring for His children in a host of different ways.

The key to all of this is our lifestyle. Do we obediently follow the Biblical guidelines which provide a wholesome life—both physical and spiritual?

B. The Trusting (v. 12)

12. O Lord of hosts, blessed is the man that trusteth in thee.

What a conclusion! It drives us to carefully evaluate our lives. Are we completely surrendered to the will and ways of God? Or, are we keeping some areas of our lives reserved for our own selfish desires? This is called *compartmentalization*.

Trusting in the Lord includes the total path of life events on a daily basis. When we abide in God, it involves trusting Him to help us in our decision making. We seek His guidance in the process rather than hoping He will agree to our decision once it has been made. Trusting involves depending on God through the Holy Spirit to offer comfort and peace in the middle of oppressive circumstances.

One of the greatest realities of trusting in God is our not needing to go to a particular location to experience His presence. Our God isn't limited to a certain building or holy site. His omnipresence enables us to be in constant communication wherever we are. We never need to be out of touch with our heavenly Father.

Who's Flying?
Have you seen the bumper sticker, "God is my co-pilot"? It sounds good, but it means God is second. One writer suggests, "The best thing we can possibly do is change seats." In the airline industry the goal of pilots is to be the senior pilot on board. For believers, our goal should be to always remain as the subordinate to our heavenly Father.

Talk About It:
Restate this verse in your own words.

"The issue of faith is not so much whether we believe in God, but whether we believe the God we believe in."
—R.C. Sproul

CONCLUSION

Abiding with God is a blessing believers can enjoy all the time. When we consecrate our lives to Him, there is a constant source of strength and joy. However, it requires ongoing prayer, meditation, and reading the Scriptures. It is easy to assume our relationship with Him is fine because of our not being involved in obvious sins. But a relationship is built and continued with constant contact—abiding in God.

GOLDEN TEXT CHALLENGE

"A DAY IN THY COURTS IS BETTER THAN A THOUSAND. I HAD RATHER BE A DOORKEEPER IN THE HOUSE OF MY GOD, THAN TO DWELL IN THE TENTS OF WICKEDNESS" (Psalm 84:10).

The *day* mentioned here is doubtless a feast day. This day so spent is far more profitable in lasting value than a thousand days spent elsewhere.

"I had rather be a doorkeeper" is literally "be at the threshold." The psalmist is saying, "I had rather be on the threshold of God's house than dwell inside the tents of wickedness." It could also refer to the "keeper of the threshold" (cf. 2 Kings 22:4; 25:18), meaning that he would rather have the humblest service at the Temple where God is than be a guest where wickedness lives.

Daily Devotions:
M. Meeting With God
  Exodus 33:7-11
T. Confident in
  God's Strength
  1 Samuel 17:32-
  37, 50, 51
W. The Promise of
  God's Presence
  Isaiah 43:1-7
T. Lifelong Worship
  Luke 2:36-38
F. Abide in the Vine
  John 15:1-8
S. Be Strong on the
  Inside
  Ephesians 3:14-
  21

Abiding With God

Sweet Hour Of Prayer

William W. Walford

William B. Bradbury

1. Sweet hour of prayer, sweet hour of prayer, That calls me from a world of care,
2. Sweet hour of prayer, sweet hour of prayer, The joys I feel, the bliss I share
3. Sweet hour of prayer, sweet hour of prayer, Thy wings shall my pe - ti - tion bear

And bids me at my Fa - ther's throne, Make all my wants and wish - es known!
Of those whose anx-ious spir-its burn With strong de-sires for thy re - turn!
To Him, whose truth and faith-ful-ness En - gage the wait-ing soul to bless:

In sea - sons of dis-tress and grief, My soul has of - ten found re - lief,
With such I has-ten to the place Where God my Sav - iour shows His face,
And since He bids me seek His face, Be - lieve His word, and trust His grace,

And oft es-caped the temp-ter's snare By thy re - turn, sweet hour of prayer.
And glad-ly take my sta - tion there, And wait for thee, sweet hour of prayer.
I'll cast on Him my ev - 'ry care, And wait for thee, sweet hour of prayer.

A Prayer for Mercy

Psalm 85:1-13

Unit Theme:
Prayers in the Psalms

Central Truth:
Because of His great mercy, God forgives the sins of those who call on Him.

Focus:
Recognize forgiveness is characteristic of God's merciful nature and accept His forgiveness.

Context:
Psalm 85 is a national lament that was probably written after the Babylonian Captivity.

Golden Text:
"Shew us thy mercy, O Lord, and grant us thy salvation" (Psalm 85:7).

Study Outline:
I. Remember God's Forgiveness (Psalm 85:1-3)
II. Call to God for Mercy (Psalm 85:4-7)
III. Receive the Blessings of Renewal (Psalm 85:8-13)

INTRODUCTION

Consider this question: Are we more likely to desire mercy in our time of difficulty than to offer it to others when they desperately desire it?

Hopefully, as believers who are following the example of Christ and living within the realm of the Spirit, we offer mercy when it doesn't stand in opposition to another Biblical principle. However, there can be obstacles to our being individuals of mercy. Consider our forgetfulness. We may, for some unviable reason, not remember God's great mercy to us or even the mercy offered by another person. Then there is the issue of retribution. In our wanting someone to get what he or she deserves, we overlook how glad we may be not having to suffer the consequences of our negative actions.

Another possible obstacle is our lack of foresight or even purposeful blindness. Either we can't see what a certain person may become, or choose not to consider the possibility of the impact of mercy. Also, we may not know how to be a person of mercy. For some, life is hard. Perhaps no one ever gave us a break, so there is difficulty in attempting to offer actions of mercy.

Psalm 85 brings God's merciful nature to our attention. It's one of His divine characteristics. Otherwise, there would be no hope for us in view of our inherent sinfulness and tendency to follow paths of least resistance. Those paths generally lead us away from the truth and the narrow way which leads to eternal life.

The specific circumstances for the writing of this psalm and the specific author cannot be determined with certainty. It seems logical for it to have been written after the Babylonian Captivity of the sixth century B.C. Israel's persistent sinning in spite of repeated warnings had necessitated extreme punishment. Yet God offered Israel hope. Here is a good place to note the Evangelism Emphasis: Because of His great mercy, God forgives the sins of those who call on Him.

I. REMEMBER GOD'S FORGIVENESS (Psalm 85:1-3)

A. His Favor (v. 1)

1. Lord, thou hast been favourable unto thy land: thou hast brought back the captivity of Jacob.

There are many ways in which God demonstrates His favor. None is greater than to experience undeserved forgiveness. This is especially true when His children have knowingly sinned and refused to answer His calls to return.

Talk About It:
How did God show favor to His people?

The southern kingdom of Judah is a prime example. They knew of God's destructive judgment on their kinsmen to the north. He allowed the Assyrians to invade and destroy the northern kingdom, never to be restored again. Some of the people were carried off into captivity and relocated as part of the Assyrian transplant policy. Those who remained behind were then influenced as other peoples were relocated in their areas. The intermarriage with those individuals eventually resulted in a people group known as the Samaritans.

Repeatedly God warned His people in Judah to turn from their wicked ways of idolatry, oppression of the poor, and false religious practices. The word of the Lord through Jeremiah stated plainly, "Reform your ways and your actions, and I will let you live in this place" (7:3, *NIV*). Failure to do so would result in death, destruction, and captivity. This did occur as God raised up Nebuchadnezzar and the Babylonians as His instrument of judgment.

The Babylonian oppression lasted for 70 years. Then provision was made for their return (see Jeremiah 25:11, 12). The specific fulfillment is recorded in the Book of Ezra. Citing the Lord God of heaven as being the director of his actions, King Cyrus opens the door for the transplanted Jews to return to Jerusalem and build the Temple. Those choosing not to return are to donate silver, gold and other goods. Under the civil leadership of Zerubbabel, nearly 50,000 Jews undertake the journey back to their homeland.

> "We are wound with mercy round and round as if with air."
> **—Gerard Hopkins**

B. His Forgiveness (vv. 2, 3)

2. Thou hast forgiven the iniquity of thy people, thou hast covered all their sin. Selah.

3. Thou hast taken away all thy wrath: thou hast turned thyself from the fierceness of thine anger.

God in His omniscience knew prior to the establishment of Israel as the chosen nation through Abraham how they would at times be unfaithful. He was fully aware how sin would at times entice them into idolatry. He attempted through various means such as prophets and circumstances to warn and to draw them back to Himself. However, when they persisted in following their selfish desires, there was no choice but to bring punishment on His own people.

Talk About It:
1. What does God desire to do with our sins (v. 2)?
2. What should we want God to turn from, and why (v. 3)?

In Isaiah 1 we see a picture of a rebellious nation. They are a sin-sick, guilt-ridden group of evildoers who persist in their corruption. Difficult times are upon them, but still there is no change in behavior. In spite of this, the Lord God offers forgiveness: "Though your sins are like scarlet, they shall be as white as snow" (v. 18, *NIV*). Failure to change this path of resistance and rebellion will result in their being devoured by the sword.

The fierceness of God's wrath on these sinning people is seen in the destruction of the northern kingdom (Israel) by the Assyrians and the destruction as well as captivity of the southern kingdom (Judah). However, God blessed Judah because of His promise to David that his lineage would sit forever on the throne. This would have its ultimate fulfillment in the coming of Jesus, the promised Messiah. Another fulfilled promise was the Babylonian Captivity being limited to 70 years. God chose to rescind His wrath. Sovereign grace and mercy replaced judgment.

While we may not have been involved in some of the same rebellious sins as the Israelites, each of us was born in sin and a state of rebellion. Through the sacrificial death of Jesus and the conviction of the Holy Spirit, we come to Christ and experience God's love rather than His anger.

II. CALL TO GOD FOR MERCY (Psalm 85:4-7)

A. Restoration (vv. 4, 5)

4. Turn us, O God of our salvation, and cause thine anger toward us to cease.

5. Wilt thou be angry with us for ever? Wilt thou draw out thine anger to all generations?

We have a responsibility in returning to a right relationship with our heavenly Father. Though His anger is turned aside, we must demonstrate a personal and corporate responsibility.

Let us review sin as evidenced within the corporate life of the Israelites. They were guilty of intentional sin, choosing to indulge in apostasy and idolatry. Continual disregard for God's prophets and the appeals to turn away from their sinful ways set the stage for justice rather than mercy. However, when the people repented and threw themselves on God's mercy, He was ready to restore.

In the Book of Judges we see the cycle of the people's backsliding into sin, receiving God's punishment, and then turning back to their God. He raised up deliverers through whom restorations took place. We see the same thing here in verses 4 and 5 of our text. The people know salvation and spiritual restoration come only through the work of their God.

It appears these individuals do have an understanding of God's anger. They know that its limitation or extension is a

> "God forgives universally, on the grounds of an Atonement and on the condition of repentance and faith."
> —Richard Storrs

Talk About It
1. What does it mean for God to "turn us" (v. 4)?
2. What concern did the psalmist express in verse 5?

A Prayer for Mercy

matter of His choice. It can be limited to a single generation or extended to generation after generation. Unless God chooses to turn from His anger, there is no salvation.

This call for mercy and restoration is reminiscent of Jonah's prayer from within the belly of the great fish. Disobedience placed this prophet in a circumstance never thought possible. In the throes of death he called to the Lord and vowed to fulfill his task. One statement stands out: "Salvation comes from the Lord" (Jonah 2:9, *NIV*).

Only by the Lord's mercy can any person find restoration to relationship with the heavenly Father.

B. Revival (v. 6)

6. Wilt thou not revive us again: that thy people may rejoice in thee?

The need for revival indicates the loss of a previous condition or relationship. Individuals and entire groups or nations, through simple neglect or outright rebellion, distance themselves from their God. When there's a desire to return, God in His mercy brings them back to Himself. Revival is more than a simple refreshing that can quickly fade or be overshadowed by difficulty. Genuine reviving enables the person or group to once again burst out in bloom, demonstrating their true identity.

In the case of the Israelites, God graciously made it possible for them to return to their homeland. However, as one reads the books of Ezra and Nehemiah, it becomes evident how spiritual reviving isn't guaranteed to last over the generations. When Ezra led the second group back to Jerusalem in 457 B.C., he was appalled at the conditions. The Jewish men had intermarried with women from other nations, which God had expressly forbidden. Initially Ezra tore his garments and pulled out the hair of his head and beard in the anguish of mourning (9:3). Later he threw himself down on the ground in weeping and confessing the sins of Israel (10:1).

When Nehemiah returned to Jerusalem from a trip to Babylon, he found a multitude of spiritual abuses. Instead of keeping the Sabbath, the people were working as well as buying and selling. The priests were not being supported with the people's tithes. Once again there was intermarriage with heathen women (Nehemiah 13).

True rejoicing in God, our heavenly Father, cannot take place until a spiritual renewal occurs. This is far more than an emotional experience which may fade. A revival brings a renewal of heart, mind and action. Only then can there be rejoicing which continues both in the gathering of the saints and in the confines of one's home and work.

"Repentance does not mean *remorse*. Repentance means giving up sin."
—**W.E. Biederwolf**

Talk About It:
What was the psalmist's desire?

Justice Given
In 1951, Ethel and Julius Rosenberg were placed on trial for passing nuclear weapons secrets to the Soviet Union. In the summation their lawyer said, "Your Honor, what my clients ask for is justice." Presiding Judge Kaufman replied, "The court has given what you ask for—justice. What you really want is mercy. But that is something this court has no right to give."
On April 5 they were sentenced to death, which took place two months later.

True revival comes as a matter of God's choice. We can't conjure it up; however, we can prepare for it. Revival changes people. It restores those who are separated from God and spiritually dying.

C. Love (v. 7)

7. Shew us thy mercy, O Lord, and grant us thy salvation.

The *NIV* renders this verse, "Show us your unfailing love, O Lord, and grant us your salvation."

This verse takes us back to God's covenant with Israel. Repeatedly in the Old Testament there are appeals to His love and mercy. This is the basis for the provision of salvation. However, obedience needs to be exhibited by God's people. Consider Deuteronomy 7:9, 12: "Know therefore that the Lord your God is God; he is the faithful God keeping his covenant of love to a thousand generations of those who love him and keep his commands. . . . If you pay attention to these laws and are careful to follow them, then the Lord your God will keep his covenant of love with you, as he swore to your forefathers" (*NIV*).

Psalm 85:7 can be seen as a request for God's covenant to be reestablished with His people. Without it there is no salvation. They are a hopeless people.

As believers today, without God's love being extended to us through the new covenant, we are helplessly mired in sin. It is only through His love extended by the substitutionary death of Jesus and His resurrection from the grave that we have life. It is the means of our present and eternal salvation.

> "The mercy of God (may be found) between the bridge and the stream."
> —Augustine, *said of a man falling into a river*

III. RECEIVE THE BLESSINGS OF RENEWAL (Psalm 85:8-13)

A. His Peace (vv. 8, 9)

8. I will hear what God the Lord will speak: for he will speak peace unto his people, and to his saints: but let them not turn again to folly.

9. Surely his salvation is nigh them that fear him; that glory may dwell in our land.

It's wonderful to be the recipient of God's blessings as He offers a renewed relationship. However, it isn't a one-sided action. The people need to be open to what the Lord is saying and will say in the future. A review of Israel's history demonstrates how quickly they would move from acclaiming their willingness to obediently follow the Lord to complaining and wanting to determine their future.

There is little value in stating one's willingness to hear what God is saying through His word and messengers unless there is follow-up. This adherence needs to be on a continued basis rather than an occasional occurrence attempting to be in His good graces.

Talk About It:
1. What "folly" must be avoided (v. 8)?
2. What is the reward for fearing God (v. 9)?

A Prayer for Mercy

One of the tremendous blessings of spiritual renewal continues to be the peace which can dominate our inner being. It's the same peace Jesus offers in the New Testament as He prepares the disciples for His leaving (John 14:27). This is not the absence of conflict and difficulties. Our heavenly Father offers a calmness of spirit based on sins forgiven and living in harmony with Him. Though we do not merit such mercy, His love opens the door to salvation. Our responsibility then becomes to "not turn again to folly" (Psalm 85:8).

Verse 9 reminds us of the nearness of salvation. God does not attempt to hide it from us and force a torturous game of hide-and-seek. Anyone who stands in awe of the Father, confesses his or her sins, and seeks daily to be close to Him will experience His marvelous glory. God's intention for Israel as a nation includes their entire group of people experiencing His power and presence.

> "Our sins, like our shadows when day is in its glory, scarce appear; toward evening, how great and monstrous they are!"
> —**John Suckling**

B. His Love (vv. 10, 11)

10. Mercy and truth are met together; righteousness and peace have kissed each other.

11. Truth shall spring out of the earth; and righteousness shall look down from heaven.

These two verses provide us with a picture of unity between God and His people. God chooses to flood them with His lovingkindness, or mercy. The people are responding with truth, ("faithfulness," *NIV*). God's loyalty and love for Israel can once again be revealed as they have turned back to Him. Forsaken are the rebellion and rejection which initiated the separation and inevitable punishment.

God's love enables Him to patiently wait for the reconciliation. The picture of two individuals embracing and kissing each other in the Oriental manner of greeting reminds us of Jacob and Esau. Though previously bitterly estranged even to the point of Esau's planning Jacob's death (Genesis 27:41), later there is reconciliation. "Esau ran to meet Jacob and embraced him; he threw his arms around his neck and kissed him. And they wept" (33:4, *NIV*).

Talk About It:
1. What is the relationship between mercy and truth (v. 10)?
2. What is the connection between righteousness and peace (v. 10)?
3. How can truth "spring out of the earth" (v. 11)?

C. His Provision (vv. 12, 13)

12. Yea, the Lord shall give that which is good; and our land shall yield her increase.

13. Righteousness shall go before him; and shall set us in the way of his steps.

When righteousness marks the course for God's people, they can expect His provision in a tangible manner. Prior to the Israelites' ever entering the land of Canaan, God provides this principle: If they are obedient, there will be prosperity. Rain will fall for the c ops and the grasslands. However, if they turn away,

Talk About It:
1. How practical are the blessings of God (v. 12)?
2. How can we find the right path in life (v. 13)?

they can expect God's anger in a tangible manner of drought (Deuteronomy 11:13-17).

This concept is clearly seen in Haggai's words to the people as he encourages them to resume building the Temple (Haggai 2:15-19). Their disobedience impacts all areas of productivity. The prophet repeatedly admonishes them to "give careful thought" to how they had suffered because of their disobedience (1:5, 7; 2:15, 18, *NIV*).

One caution does need to be inserted here. There is no promise to believers of material riches because of their righteousness. If that were the case, the apostle Paul would be a dismal failure due to his being dependent on other believers for the continuance of ministry. However, let's not forget how many believers do see an increase in their economic level due to giving up sinful, expensive habits. And God still does bless His people in a material manner so they can bless others.

> "It is a great deal easier to do that which God gives us to do, no matter how hard it is, than to face the responsibilities of not doing it."
> —J.R. Miller

CONCLUSION

When we pray for God's mercy and forgiveness, He comes to us and brings renewal. Our relationship with Him is restored as He mercifully transforms us. Never are we deserving of our Father's mercy, but in love He willingly offers it to the repentant heart.

GOLDEN TEXT CHALLENGE

"SHEW US THY MERCY, O LORD, AND GRANT US THY SALVATION" (Psalm 85:7).

It is told that one winter's night in 1935, New York Mayor Fiorello LaGuardia showed up at a night court in the city's poorest section. He dismissed the judge for that night and took over the bench. A poor woman was brought before him, charged with stealing a loaf of bread for her hungry grandchildren. The shopkeeper pressed charges to teach a lesson to other people in their rough neighborhood.

LaGuardia told the old woman, "I've got to punish you; the law says 10 dollars or 10 days in jail." As he spoke, he pulled a 10-dollar bill out of his pocket and said, "Here's the 10-dollar fine, which I now remit, and furthermore, I'm going to fine everyone in the courtroom 50 cents for living in a town where a person has to steal bread so her grandchildren can eat."

Forty-seven dollars was reportedly collected from a red-faced storekeeper, 70 petty criminals, and a few New York police officers.

Just as the bewildered grandmother was shown mercy and grace in the face of judgment, so the people of Israel received mercy and salvation when they cried out to the Lord. They didn't deserve God's mercy, nor do we; yet He offers it to us so we might be saved and not condemned.

Daily Devotions:
M. God's Compassion and Grace Exodus 34:1-7
T. Good News to Tell 2 Kings 7:3-11
W. God Will Hear the Repentant 2 Chronicles 6:24-31
T. Mercy Sought Luke 18:9-14
F. Witness of Forgiveness Acts 26:9-18
S. God's Love Demonstrated Romans 5:6-11

A Prayer for Mercy

58   At The Cross

Issac Watts   Ralph E. Hudson

1. A - las! and did my Sav - ior bleed? And did my Sov'reign die?
2. Was it for crimes that I had done, He groaned up - on the tree?
3. Well might the sun in dark - ness hide, And shut his glo - ries in,
4. But drops of grief can ne'er re - pay The debt of love I owe,

Would He de - vote that sa - cred head For sin - ners such as I?
A - maz - ing pit - y! grace unknown! And love be - yond de - gree!
When Christ, the mighty Mak - er, died For man the crea - ture's sin.
Here, Lord, I give my - self a - way, 'Tis all that I can do.

REFRAIN

At the cross, at the cross where I first saw the light, And the

bur - den of my heart rolled a - way,   It was there by
rolled a - way,

faith I re - ceived my sight, and now I am hap - py all the day.

Secure in God

Psalm 91:1-16

Unit Theme:
Prayers in the Psalms

Central Truth:
Christians can trust God's love, regardless of the perils of life.

Focus:
Affirm that God is our refuge and depend on Him for security in times of trouble.

Context:
Date and writer unknown

Golden Text:
"He that dwelleth in the secret place of the most High shall abide under the shadow of the Almighty" (Psalm 91:1).

Study Outline:
I. God Is Our Refuge (Psalm 91:1-8)
II. God Is Our Protector (Psalm 91:9-13)
III. God Is Our Deliverer (Psalm 91:14-16)

INTRODUCTION

Some of us were raised in communities where no one bothered to lock their doors. If your house had those old common locks, anyone could go to the hardware store and buy a "skeleton key" which would work. So, why bother to lock the doors?

In most places today there's a totally different attitude. Instead of being secure in the honesty of other people, we are pressed to find security in a wide variety of programs, passwords and locks. There are virus protection programs and passwords for our computers. We have alarm systems for our homes and cars. Some install iron security doors and window guards. Others use bank vaults, safe-deposit boxes, and home/business safes.

Security can be looked for by other means as well. Some seek for it in insurance policies, stocks, mutual funds and savings accounts. The amassing of property, businesses and influence also fit into the quest for security. As valuable and beneficial all of these may be, not one of them can provide security for our soul, the innermost part of our being.

Neither the author nor the date of Psalm 91 can be determined. It is, however, a glowing testimony of the security which the believer can have in God. Only someone who has a relationship with God could write with such assurance.

This psalm provides comfort for those who are undergoing times of trouble that are associated with life in general. It also can be a comfort for those whose trials are the direct result of their living for Christ and being an active witness to family, friends and associates. When an individual is secure in God, he or she can look into the face of the darkest clouds with faith and confidence.

Shadrach, Meshach and Abednego reflected this security in the face of Nebuchadnezzar's rage. Hear their reply to his threat: "O Nebuchadnezzar . . . If we are thrown into the blazing furnace, the God we serve is able to save us from it, and he will rescue us from your hand, O king. But even if he does not, we want you to know, O king, that we will not serve your gods or worship the image of gold you have set up" (Daniel 3:16-18, *NIV*).

I. GOD IS OUR REFUGE (Psalm 91:1-8)

A. A Fortress (vv. 1, 2)

1. He that dwelleth in the secret place of the most High shall abide under the shadow of the Almighty.

2. I will say of the Lord, He is my refuge and my fortress: my God; in him will I trust.

The psalm begins by identifying God as the invincible Almighty One, the concealing One, the protecting One. Each of these reflects the security which becomes ours when we choose God as our refuge. Nothing or no one can penetrate this security. This allows us to rest. There is respite from the turmoil and tormentors that attempt to disrupt and destroy.

"Secret place" (v. 1) can be translated as "shelter." This in turn may refer to the Temple and the presence of God. In several other psalms the house of God, the Temple, is presented as a place of safety (27:4, 5; 31:20). This is not to be seen as a physical place to hide, but rather, a spiritual environment where the presence of God "wraps us up" and we are held close to Him.

Verse 2 of the text indicates our will in God's becoming our security. We must choose to allow the heavenly Father to become our refuge and fortress. He does not force us to come and take shelter. Instead He calls and invites us, but the decision is ours. This coming will occur as we put our trust in Him. Many individuals say "Trust me" but provide no guarantee of their trustworthiness. That isn't the case with the Almighty, who has no equal and never fails to fulfill His word.

It is not sufficient to see the Lord as a refuge and believe in Him; we must place ourselves under His care and protection without qualification or reservation. He must become "my God . . . my shelter." Placing ourselves in the secure presence of God is similar to the trust pilots place in their instruments. Unable to see the ground because of cloud cover or fog, they trust the instruments to keep them on course and at the proper elevation.

B. His Faithfulness (vv. 3, 4)

3. Surely he shall deliver thee from the snare of the fowler, and from the noisome pestilence.

4. He shall cover thee with his feathers, and under his wings shalt thou trust; his truth shall be thy shield and buckler.

Life can be treacherous. Hidden dangers in the forms of accidents, illnesses, and human predators may spring at us. Even day-to-day living can be difficult. While we are in the middle of these encounters, as Christians we possess the ability to be secure in God. The "snare of the fowler" in verse 3 is a figurative expression for the difficulties of life which we may encounter.

Talk About It:
1. What does "dwelleth in the secret place" mean (v. 1)?
2. What did the psalmist "say of the Lord" (v. 2)?

"I would rather walk with God in the dark than go alone in the light."
—Mary Brainard

noisome (v. 3)— "deadly" (*NIV*) or "perilous" (*NKJV*)

Talk About It:
How do these verses compare God's people with birds?

"Deadly pestilence" (*NIV*) speaks of a variety of problems which may sweep across the land such as drought, insect infestations or disease.

Verse 4 gives a beautiful description of God's protection which has parallels in both Testaments. In Psalm 17:8, 9, David writes, "Hide me in the shadow of your wings from the wicked who assail me" (*NIV*). In Deuteronomy 32:11, Moses describes the Lord's care "like an eagle that stirs up its nest and hovers over its young, that spreads its wings to catch them and carries them on its pinions" (*NIV*).

In the New Testament, Jesus speaks of His desiring to provide shelter as that of a hen gathering her chicks under her wings (Matthew 23:37; Luke 13:34). The hen calls strongly to the little chicks and spreads her wings. Under the shadow of her wings each one is safe from the circling hawks. When she closes her wings, and settles down, her chicks are warm and safe. Occasionally one may poke its head out from under the wing for a quick look around, but then quickly retreats to the security.

Verse 4 of the text also says God's truth (or faithfulness) can be our "shield and bulwark" (*NASB*). All which He offers can be ours. He will not tantalize us with promises and then withdraw them. The contrary is true. The security of His presence will always be there for us.

C. Our Security (vv. 5-8)

5. Thou shalt not be afraid for the terror by night; nor for the arrow that flieth by day;

6. Nor for the pestilence that walketh in darkness; nor for the destruction that wasteth at noonday.

7. A thousand shall fall at thy side, and ten thousand at thy right hand; but it shall not come nigh thee.

8. Only with thine eyes shalt thou behold and see the reward of the wicked.

God protects His own. The refuge He provides cannot be overcome by the forces of evil. It is an impenetrable defense. In these verses we see references to wartime tactics such as a surprise attack at night or the intense battles during daylight hours.

The *pestilence* mentioned in verse 6 seems to be a direct reference to the plagues God sent on Egypt as part of delivering His people. Locusts, boils, darkness, hail, and other plagues overcame the Egyptians, but God's people were untouched. The death of the firstborn as the destroying angel passed through the country can be seen in verse 7. Though thousands of Egyptians fell all around them, the Israelites were safe! They saw the death but were preserved from it.

Talk About It:
1. How do verses 5-7 describe the protective power of God?
2. What is "the reward of the wicked" (v. 8)?

These verses remind us of physical security; however, let's not forget emotional and spiritual security. The Lord God is our fortress in these areas as well. Even when it appears there is no relief or escape in sight, we can stand strong knowing the Master of all is in control of our lives. That's security!

II. GOD IS OUR PROTECTOR (Psalm 91:9-13)
A. Our Commitment (vv. 9, 10)

9. Because thou hast made the Lord, which is my refuge, even the most High, thy habitation;

10. There shall no evil befall thee, neither shall any plague come nigh thy dwelling.

It is wonderful to lounge in the knowledge of God's protection. When the enemy comes against us strongly, it is reassuring to know we can "hunker in God's bunker" and be safe. What a blessing! However, we have a role to play. We must commit our whole self at all times to God's Word and will. The plan is not for us to do what we want and simply run to Him when storm clouds begin to threaten. If we follow this pattern we become like the teenager who wants complete freedom to come and go as he or she pleases, yet expects Mom and Dad to pay the bills and provide a home.

Verse 9 says we are to make the Lord our habitation, or dwelling place. During the eras when the Jews had a Temple, they could refer to the Holy of Holies as the place God inhabits or dwells. However, God is not limited to a single location. He is omnipresent. Yes, that flies beyond our comprehension. It is one of those mysterious truths which our finite limitations make it difficult to understand. It also is the reason why each one of us can make the Lord our dwelling place.

Each of us can make the Lord our habitation when we choose to practice the presence of God. It is not necessary to go to the church sanctuary or to be part of a special worship event to experience God's presence, though these are important. All it takes is for us to open our hearts and minds and be flooded with His presence. As we read and meditate on Scripture, sing songs of the church, and listen to the testimonies of other believers, we make Him our dwelling place—our refuge.

Verse 10 opens the door to some special promises. Special favor is given to those who commit themselves to the presence of the Lord, specifically personal protection. God cares for His children. Yes, we live in a sin-dominated world where often bad things happen to good people. Can you imagine what it would be like if we were not the benefactors of His protective presence?

B. Angelic Protection (vv. 11-13)

11. For he shall give his angels charge over thee, to keep thee in all thy ways.

Saved From Harm

"Sir, I can't get any gas into the tank," the mechanic tells me.

Several minutes later he pulls a paper towel and an extinguished cigarette from the neck of the gas tank. He says, "Someone tried to blow up your car, but they shoved the towel in too tight."

If the culprits would have been successful, our car would have exploded in the street of a Chicago suburb with my wife, our baby and myself in it. Thank You, Lord, for Your protection!

—Jerald Daffe

12. They shall bear thee up in their hands, lest thou dash thy foot against a stone.

13. Thou shalt tread upon the lion and adder: the young lion and the dragon shalt thou trample under feet.

Talk About It:
1. How can the Lord's angels help us?
2. What is the message in verse 13?

Here we see one of the marvelous benefits of making the Lord our refuge; namely, angelic protection. Careful attention needs to be given to the specifics of these verses. First, there is no indication of everyone who serves the Lord having a personal guardian angel. Nor is there any idea of an angel being given a certain number of individuals to oversee. Second, we do have the assurance of God's sending angels to assist and protect in time of need. Angels have probably kept us from various mishaps and accidents.

Satan quoted verses 11 and 12 to Jesus during the threefold temptation in the desert. At the highest point of the Temple, Satan told Jesus to throw Himself over, because if He really were the Son of God, no harm would come to Him (Matthew 4:5-7; Luke 4:9-12). Of course Jesus rejected this twisting of the Scripture, telling Satan, "You shall not tempt the Lord your God" (*NKJV*).

Psalm 91:13 needs to be understood in the proper context. This is not a statement of recklessly attacking lions and cobras or putting ourselves in harm's way. It does underscore how the angels of the Lord can rescue us from the common danger that each offers. In Daniel 6 we see that Daniel was thrown into a den of lions due to his praying in opposition to King Darius' decree. The next morning, in response to the king's inquiry, Daniel replied: "My God hath sent his angel, and hath shut the lions' mouths, that they have not hurt me" (v. 22).

In Acts 28, the apostle Paul is shipwrecked on the island of Malta. As he was gathering brushwood and putting it on a fire, a poisonous snake attached itself to his hand. The islanders expected a severe physical reaction, or even death. When nothing happened to him, this miracle caused them to think Paul was a god (vv. 1-6)!

"Angels . . . regard our safety, undertake our defense, direct our ways."
—John Calvin

Needlessly putting ourselves in danger and expecting God to intervene is one means of tempting God. On the other hand, we have the assurance of God's ability to protect us through the ministry of His angels when dangers confront us.

III. GOD IS OUR DELIVERER (Psalm 91:14-16)
A. Our Love (v. 14)

14. Because he hath set his love upon me, therefore will I deliver him: I will set him on high, because he hath known my name.

Talk About It:
Who can expect help from the Lord?

This passage reminds us how God's deliverance is built upon a foundation or relationship of love. It's amazing how human love for another will, without thought, drive someone into danger for the purpose of rescue. A mother attacks a wild animal barehanded to save her little boy. Another mother descends into a deep well on a rope to rescue her small daughter who has fallen into it. If human love will stimulate such self-sacrificing action, how much more our heavenly Father will involve Himself in the lives of us, His children.

We cannot force God into any obligation. Even at our best, we are still finite beings who are shortsighted and often fail. But when we commit ourselves to God and love Him with all our heart, soul and mind, He is moved to work in our behalf. Our love for Him becomes the stimulus for our deliverance. God sets us "on high"—in a position where our enemies cannot reach us—because we acknowledge Him.

No wonder the greatest commandment is to love the Lord our God. It indicates a relationship commitment upon which our entire life rotates. The challenge for us is to keep our love focused on God who, through Jesus Christ, is our salvation. Only then can we realistically expect His deliverance in our time of trouble.

> "Love is the greatest thing that God can give to us, for Himself is love; and it is the greatest thing we can give to God, for it will also give ourselves, and carry with it all that is ours."
> —**Jeremy Taylor**

B. Our Call (v. 15)

15. He shall call upon me, and I will answer him: I will be with him in trouble; I will deliver him, and honour him.

When we are in difficulty and in need of help, there's no stigma in calling for the Lord's assistance. Just as a parent expects his or her child to ask for help, so does our heavenly Father. There's definitely a problem if our relationship is halfhearted, or on-again and off-again. Then calling for the Lord's help appears as an escape mechanism.

Notice the definite response. We call, and God responds to our appeal. This reminds us of God's active participation in our lives. He hears and then makes a response. There's no distance here. We have the assurance of His being right there in the time of our trouble. Our God is a constant presence for those who choose to follow His will and trust in Him.

With assurance the writer of this psalm speaks of God's triumphing and delivering from whatever the problem may be. The size or type of difficulty cannot hinder the end result. When our omnipotent God responds to the call of distress, He overcomes.

Psalm 18 is David's testimony of how he cried to the Lord and experienced deliverance from enemies who desired to take his life. This psalm begins with David declaring his love for God and calling Him "my rock, and my fortress, and my deliverer" (vv. 1, 2). Only then does the psalm move to the circumstances of David's distress.

Could it be we believers often underestimate the desire of our heavenly Father to help us in our dilemmas?

Talk About It:
When we face trouble, what should we do?

> "Every evening I turn my troubles over to God; He's going to be up all night anyway."
> —**Donald Morgan**

C. His Salvation (v. 16)

16. With long life will I satisfy him, and shew him my salvation.

The final result of God's intervention here is to provide a long life. No specific years are stated; however, it really isn't important. The issue here is the inability of the pestilence or problem to limit one's lifespan. In general, Christians live longer, healthier, and more satisfying lives than do unbelievers.

In this verse we see salvation in a different perspective. Usually we speak of salvation in terms of sins forgiven and our being placed in a right relationship with the Father. This is the spiritual realm—salvation bringing deliverance from the bondage of sin and its eternal judgment. Here the psalmist writes of salvation in the physical sense. Hopefully this expands our concept of salvation. Through our relationship with the heavenly Father, the full dimension of salvation becomes ours to experience.

CONCLUSION

Living in an era when the dangers of terrorism and spreading viral diseases are becoming common threats to a growing percentage of the world's population, Psalm 91 becomes a special word of assurance. We can be secure in God and experience His deliverance. Our heavenly Father will answer our call for help.

GOLDEN TEXT CHALLENGE

"HE THAT DWELLETH IN THE SECRET PLACE OF THE MOST HIGH SHALL ABIDE UNDER THE SHADOW OF THE ALMIGHTY" (Psalm 91:1).

This is one of the most beautiful examples of spiritual truth expressed with poetic imagery to be found in Scripture. He who puts his trust in God is seen dwelling under the shadow, under the protection, of the Almighty.

In the ancient world, and in Europe during medieval times, the inhabitants of a land lived near the armed castles and took refuge in them in time of war. These fortresses were generally built on high places overlooking the plains; thus, constant lookout for enemies could be made. The people of the land, seeing the fortress in the distance, felt safe because of its presence. They were regarded as living in the shadow of the fortress. Most of the inhabitants lived in villages and valleys and sheltered places of the countryside.

The psalmist made a spiritual application: He who lives in the secret chambers of prayer lives under the protection of Almighty God.

Talk About It:
What blessing is specified here?

"He liveth long who liveth well!
All other life is short and vain;
He liveth longest who can tell
Of living most for heavenly gain."
—**Horatius Bonar**

Daily Devotions:
M. Saved From the Flood
   Genesis 6:17—7:1
T. Saved From the Lions
   Daniel 6:14-23
W. God Blesses His People
   Joel 3:16-21
T. Saved From Shipwreck
   Acts 27:27-34, 43, 44
F. Protection for Spiritual Battle
   Ephesians 6:13-18
S. Kept From God's Wrath
   1 Thessalonians 5:1-11

32

O God, Our Help In Ages Past

Isaac Watts

Probably by William Croft

1. O God, our help in a - ges past, Our hope for years to come,
2. Un - der the shad - ow of Thy throne Thy saints have dwelt se - cure;
3. Be - fore the hills in or - der stood, Or earth re - ceived her frame,
4. A thou - sand a - ges in Thy sight Are like an eve - ning gone;
5. O God, our help in a - ges past, Our hope for years to come,

Our shel - ter from the storm - y blast, And our e - ter - nal home!
Suf - fi - cient is Thine arm. a - lone, And our de - fense is sure.
From ev - er - last - ing Thou art God, To end - less years the same.
Short as the watch that ends the night Be - fore the ris - ing sun.
Be Thou our guard while life shall last, And our e - ter - nal home.

Amazing Care of Our Creator

Psalm 139:1-24

Unit Theme:
Prayers in the Psalms

Central Truth:
God is intimately involved in caring for His people.

Focus:
Reflect on how God cares for us and praise Him for His care.

Context:
Written by David around 1000 B.C., perhaps in Jerusalem

Golden Text:
"How precious also are thy thoughts unto me, O God! How great is the sum of them!" (Psalm 139:17).

Study Outline:
I. God Knows Us Intimately (Psalm 139:1-6)
II. God Is Always Near Us (Psalm 139:7-12)
III. God Cares for Us (Psalm 139:13-24)

INTRODUCTION

Most of us have no idea what it would be like to worship a god made of wood or stone, who never speaks directly to us, and who can't comfort, care or rescue. We who have been reared in Christian homes are so blessed! We have always known that God is the Creator and Jesus is Savior and Lord. However, it is possible for us to have a token knowledge of God and not pursue a deeper understanding of our heavenly Father.

We must begin with the reality that God is Creator. Life is not the result of millions of years of evolutionary process. Spontaneous generation did not occur once, never to happen again, beginning the slow spiral process which eventually brought humans into a high life form. Chance could not produce our bodies with such distinct systems (digestive, skeletal, nervous, etc.) which work so closely together to form a superior life that supersedes all other life forms.

This lesson causes us to be reminded of the marvelous attributes of our God. His omnipotence, omnipresence and omniscience are not easily comprehended by our limited, rational minds. We are faced with accepting who God is by faith in the Scriptures while, at the same time, accepting the mystery of the divine.

While studying this lesson, take time to reflect on how God continually cares for us in all the areas of our lives. In class, allow several individuals to give a short testimony of God's intervening through protection or provision.

Keep in mind King David is the author of this psalm. Experienced throughout his life and repeatedly expressed in his writings is the greatness of God's care.

I. GOD KNOWS US INTIMATELY (Psalm 139:1-6)

A. The Lord Examines (vv. 1-4)

1. O Lord, thou hast searched me, and known me.

2. Thou knowest my downsitting and mine uprising, thou understandest my thought afar off.

3. Thou compassest my path and my lying down, and art acquainted with all my ways.

4. For there is not a word in my tongue, but, lo, O Lord, thou knowest it altogether.

compassest (v. 3)— comprehend or discern

This passage of Scripture emphasizes the omniscience of God. There is nothing which has happened in the past, which is currently occurring, or which will take place in the future that He doesn't know. Contrast this with our knowledge. In spite of our best efforts to analyze a broad variety of circumstances and factors, we can only guess at the future. And so much is happening so fast in the world around us, our knowledge of the present is limited. And we are dependent on historical records to know what we can about the past. But God knows everything—past, present and future—in one eternal act of knowing!

David applies God's omniscience to us personally. What no one could possibly know about us, He does. What a sobering, somber thought! His omniscience enables Him to not only see our specific actions but also discern our thoughts. He knows the "real us" and is not sidetracked by our outward facade.

Frequently we are prone to think God needs our permission to search our hearts and know our thoughts. What a fallacy! He already knows us and all our actions. Regardless of our posture, attitudes and desires, God knows them all. Our geographical location doesn't impact Him at all. We may be limited by our distances, but God isn't.

Verse 4 says God knows our words before we speak them. Even more intimately, God knows what we want to say but refrain from saying. The unspoken words on the "tip of our tongues" are known to Him. Thinking them though maintaining silence doesn't change God's true evaluation. He knows!

This concept of God's searching us and knowing the reality of each of us can be found in a number of other passages. Jeremiah 17:10 states, "I the Lord search the heart and examine the mind, to reward a man according to his conduct, according to what his deeds deserve" (*NIV*). In Psalm 7:9 David writes, "O righteous God, who searches minds and hearts . . . " (*NIV*).

The account of David's sin with Bathsheba demonstrates God's knowing what one may consider carefully hidden. David's adulterous meeting with Bathsheba and his subsequent arranging for her husband's death appeared to hide the truth regarding her pregnancy. David married Bathsheba after the days of mourning. The child was born and everything seemed to be proper. Then God sent the prophet Nathan with the revelation of David's sin (2 Samuel 11; 12).

Talk About It:
1. Explain the phrase "You understand my thought afar off" (v. 2, *NKJV*).
2. What does God know about our words (v. 4)?

"The heart of God is all-knowing. Even when nobody else is watching, God is watching."
—Woodrow Kroll

5. Thou hast beset me behind and before, and laid thine hand upon me.

6. Such knowledge is too wonderful for me; it is high, I cannot attain unto it.

beset (v. 5)—
"hedged" (*NKJV*)

Not only does God know everything, but He is everywhere. God's being everywhere does not mean He is *in* everything, as taught by *pantheism*; that is an unbiblical view.

In verse 5 the writer shows how God surrounds him. *Beset* can be translated as "hemmed in." It speaks of being not able to move or to escape because of God's presence. Furthering this idea is the description of God's placing His hand on David, restricting his freedom.

Talk About It:
What was "too wonderful" (v. 6) for the psalmist?

The intent of verse 5 is not to project God as a tyrant who dominants or controls our every movement. Not only would this take away from our freedom of choice, but it destroys the emphasis of a God who can be everywhere. This verse should be seen as a source of security. We are never alone. His presence is around us. The challenge for each of us is to recognize and be sensitive to His nearness.

"God is both free from men and yet bound to them; far above, yet with them; distant, yet near; powerful and yet loving, loving and yet powerful at the same time."
—Shirley Guthrie

Occasionally in a worship service one of the leaders may say, "Lord, we invite You into this place." They mean well, but are theologically incorrect. He is already present. What should be said is, "Lord, help us to recognize Your presence."

Verse 6 indicates the wonder of this truth. Though the concept supersedes our reasoning ability, it continues to be true. God's works and attributes exceed our capacities but provide blessings and protection beyond measure.

II. GOD IS ALWAYS NEAR US (Psalm 139:7-12)
A. No Distance by Place (vv. 7-10)

7. Whither shall I go from thy spirit? or whither shall I flee from thy presence?

8. If I ascend up into heaven, thou art there: if I make my bed in hell, behold, thou art there.

9. If I take the wings of the morning, and dwell in the uttermost parts of the sea;

10. Even there shall thy hand lead me, and thy right hand shall hold me.

Talk About It:
1. Why can't we flee from God?
2. What did David say about the hand of God (v. 10)?

By using various images David helps us to understand the expanse of God's presence. At the same time, he encourages us to believe in the care of our God for each person regardless of where we may be.

Is there any place we may journey and God not be there? Adam and Eve hid and made a feeble attempt to cover themselves after eating of the forbidden fruit (Genesis 3). God knew where they were, but wanted them to identify their location and condition. In Genesis 4, Cain feigned ignorance of where his brother was. He attempted to hide his role in the homicide. When the walls of Jericho crumbled and the Israelites destroyed the city, Achan assumed no one saw his forbidden actions. But God saw his taking the precious metals and special garment as well as hiding them in his tent (Joshua 7). When the prophet Jonah ran from his assignment, he could not get away from God (Jonah 1). In each of these situations God made His presence known.

His omnipresence is due to not being limited to a physical body or location. He is a spiritual being. "Where can I go from Your Spirit?" (Psalm 139:7, *NKJV*) should remind us of the dialog Jesus had with a woman of Samaria. When she asked about the proper place to worship, Jesus responded by explaining *how*—"in spirit and in truth" (John 4:24).

In verse 8 of the lesson text, the author says God is in the heights of heaven as well as the depths of Sheol ("hell"). God's presence in heaven is obvious. Yet this psalm points to even the underworld not being exempt from His vigilance and visitation. Such a description presses the concept of God's omnipresence beyond the normal borders of thought.

Rising on "the wings of the morning" (v. 9) speaks of the swiftness of which the dawn breaks across the earth. If we as humans travel at that speed or even the greater speeds of modern propulsion, we cannot outrun God's presence. As for distance, no matter how far we can travel from our current location—even to "the remotest part of the sea" (*NASB*)—we can never be out of God's presence.

The bottom line is the impossibility of escaping from the presence of God. He is always there to offer guidance. He is there to hold us to Himself and keep us secure, even when facing the most difficult situations.

> "There is no place—not even hell itself—where He is not present, this God who is sovereign in His love and loving in His sovereignty."
> —**Shirley Guthrie**

B. No Covering Will Hide (vv. 11, 12)

11. If I say, Surely the darkness shall cover me; even the night shall be light about me.

12. Yea, the darkness hideth not from thee; but the night shineth as the day: the darkness and the light are both alike to thee.

David uses a common element which separates and hides. Under the cover of darkness, one can slip away unnoticed or stay separated from others. It is a natural barrier for humans. In some ways darkness is a security blanket so no one knows our true being—attitudes and actions. But God is not limited by darkness.

Talk About It:
How are daytime and darkness alike?

These verses remind us how unlimited our God is. To Him darkness is like light. He sees and is with us equally in the light and in the darkness. What we may think covers or hides us is only wishful, deceiving thinking.

God is far beyond our human concepts. No matter where we may go or what we may use for a covering, God knows and is there.

III. GOD CARES FOR US (Psalm 139:13-24)
A. His Creation (vv. 13-16)

13. For thou hast possessed my reins: thou hast covered me in my mother's womb.

14. I will praise thee; for I am fearfully and wonderfully made: marvellous are thy works; and that my soul knoweth right well.

15. My substance was not hid from thee, when I was made in secret, and curiously wrought in the lowest parts of the earth.

16. Thine eyes did see my substance, yet being unperfect; and in thy book all my members were written, which in continuance were fashioned, when as yet there was none of them.

These verses provide us with more insight about the greatness of God and why He is to be praised. The focus is on God's work as the Creator, specifically in terms of us humans. He created us and, as a result, deeply cares for each one of us.

The phrase "possessed my reins" (v. 13) means "created my inmost being" (*NIV*). The word *reins* refers to the "seat of the tenderest, most secret emotions" (Kiel & Delitzsch). From the moment of conception and the beginning of development in our mother's womb, God was there.

Even in today's age of technology enabling parents to see the child and discover the gender, and enabling physicians to operate on the child prior to birth, there's still a sense of mystery in the development of a baby. How much more of a mystery would individuals of David's era see in the conception and growth of the baby in the mother's womb until delivery! Yet it is no mystery to God, who sees everything. In the intimacy and secrecy of a mother's womb, God cares for this developing unborn child. The awesomeness of God's creation becomes evident each time a child is conceived and develops until birth.

Knowing how complex yet unified our bodies are ("fearfully and wonderfully made," v. 14) continues to be a reason for praising our Creator. Each time a new medical procedure becomes a reality in saving or improving life, it should remind us how special a creation we are. Yes, God grants men and women the ability to develop these methods. However, if our bodies did not have the "standard systems," there could never be widespread availability.

Talk About It:
1. What does it mean to be "fearfully and wonderfully made" (v. 14)?
2. In verses 13 and 15, what does David say about a mother's womb?
3. What does God know about our future (v. 16)?

Amazing Care of Our Creator

The reference to the "lowest parts of the earth" (v. 15) as being where the child is formed provides an interesting reminder of the creation of man. God took the dust of the earth to form Adam. Then, with a rib from Adam and dust of the earth, He formed Eve. Every human being is tied to the earth through the means by which the founding parents of the human race were created. This statement also reminds us of the temporary nature of our bodies.

God's care for us prior to our birth is possible because He sees and knows us even in our undeveloped form. Not only does our God know the process unfolding in our mother's womb, He also knows the length of our lives prior to our having lived even one day (v. 16).

B. His Thoughts (vv. 17, 18)

17. How precious also are thy thoughts unto me, O God! how great is the sum of them!

18. If I should count them, they are more in number than the sand: when I awake, I am still with thee.

Once again the author of this psalm confronts us with the greatness of God. His knowledge is so vast we as humans cannot even come close to counting all of the individual items it contains. Here we consider what God knows—the beginning, the present, and the future. Not only does this include the major events of history, but also all the details of the billions of people who have ever lived, are currently living, and will be born in the future.

No wonder the writer considers God's thoughts to be so vast as to outnumber the grains of sand. Continued contemplation of this brings fatigue and resulting sleep. Yet, when he awakes and is refreshed, no end is in sight. Consider this simple experiment to gain a sense of the magnitude. Take a child's sand pail and fill it with even a coarse grade of sand. Then painstakingly attempt to count each grain. How long will it take to count just one pail? Then consider the vastness of sand around the world.

Notice how the psalmist indicates that after awakening from sleep, he seems to have a greater sense of the presence and greatness of God. No wonder he earlier states how precious the thoughts of God are to him. They enable God to care and to control according to His will. Due to God's unlimitedness, not one of us is ever beyond His care.

C. His Enemies (vv. 19-22)

(Psalm 139:19-22 is not included in the printed text.)

We the readers are jolted with David's abrupt change beginning in verse 19 and continuing through verse 22. He cries out

"A woman who intentionally destroys a fetus is guilty of murder. And we do not even talk about the fine distinction as to its being completely formed or unformed."
—**Basil the Great (A.D. 329-379)**

Talk About It:
What is uncountable?

Who fathoms the Eternal Thought?
Who talks of scheme and plan?
The Lord is God! He needeth not
The poor device of man.
—**John Whittier**

for God's enemies to be destroyed. This does not appear as a discussion of the presence of evil, which is a constant in the world. Rather, it appears to be a response to some specific act or persons presently in opposition to God and His truths. This is consistent with the Hebrew mind-set of not speculating about the problem of sin but dealing with a concrete happening.

D. His Examination (vv. 23, 24)

23. Search me, O God, and know my heart: try me, and know my thoughts:

24. And see if there be any wicked way in me, and lead me in the way everlasting.

After having spoken against evil in strong tones, David turns to introspection. It is important for him not to be guilty of wrong while exposing it in others. His petition for God to search him is very personal and immediate. In verse 1 of the psalm he stated the reality of God's having searched him and known about him. Here he appeals to have his opened heart searched, not only in light of his deeds, but the intent and content of his thought life. This is total exposure—nothing held back.

Too often, even we as Christians tend to compartmentalize our lives. We try to reserve certain aspects of our lives to be governed by our desires and guidelines. To do so indicates a lack of total commitment to God.

Asking God to search our heart exposes our motives. Why am I doing or not doing a particular action? For example, why do I give my tithes to the church? Is it a habit? Is it a bribe hoping God will bless me? Is it an act of love for God?

David prays to God, "Try me," or "Test me" (v. 23, *NIV*). He wants to be sure no offensive thoughts or actions have crept into his life. It's amazing how our lives may tilt toward sin and we not be acutely aware of the danger we are in from a spiritual perspective. Without realizing it we may slowly but steadily slide further from God and into the clutches of sin.

The last line of Psalm 139—"Lead me in the way everlasting"—should be the constant desire of every believer. When we faithfully offer this prayer and place God in the driver's seat, we will stay on the path of righteousness which leads to life everlasting with our God. Being led by God necessitates our surrendering control. We no longer determine the rules. We submit to the Scriptures in our lifestyle. We make plans for our lives such as marriage, vocation and location, but they are always subject to what God desires and knows to be best.

Desiring to be led by God is the way to wisdom. Since He knows everything, why would we attempt to design our life path while hindered by our own ignorance and lack of foresight? It makes no sense.

CONCLUSION

It's no wonder the Psalms are so special to us. We identify with the many cries for help and the statements of frustration. We also are comforted by the declarations of the greatness of God and His special care for the saints.

Psalm 139 reminds us of God's omniscience, omnipotence and omnipresence. His greatness is so far beyond our finite ability to comprehend. Yet we can know His loving care for each one of us.

GOLDEN TEXT CHALLENGE

"HOW PRECIOUS ALSO ARE THY THOUGHTS UNTO ME, O GOD! HOW GREAT IS THE SUM OF THEM!" (Psalm 139:17).

David called the thoughts of God toward us *precious*, which means "of great value or high price, highly esteemed or cherished." The psalmist could not even guess at how right he was, for he lived during the Old Testament era, when God's plan of salvation had not been fully revealed.

The thoughts of God about each of us began in eternity past in a marvelous plan for our salvation, which was accomplished through Jesus and results in eternal life. John 1:1, 14 says Jesus Christ came to earth as "the Word [*Logos*]," meaning "that which is spoken or thought." Now we know, in a way David never could, that all life on earth as well as eternal life for believers was brought about through the work of Jesus, God's *thought* for you and me.

Not only are God's thoughts of us precious, but their sum is "vast" (*NIV*). It is awesome to know that in our darkest hour, when troubles overwhelm us, there is never a time when we are not on God's mind.

Daily Devotions:
M. God Answers Prayer for Guidance Genesis 24:12-19
T. Plea for God's Presence Exodus 33:14-17
W. Renewal of Strength Isaiah 40:25-31
T. Jesus Is With Us Always Matthew 28:16-20
F. Mercy and Grace in Jesus Hebrews 4:12-16
S. Pray for All Our Needs James 5:13-16

This Is My Father's World

Maltbie D. Babcock

Franklin L. Sheppard

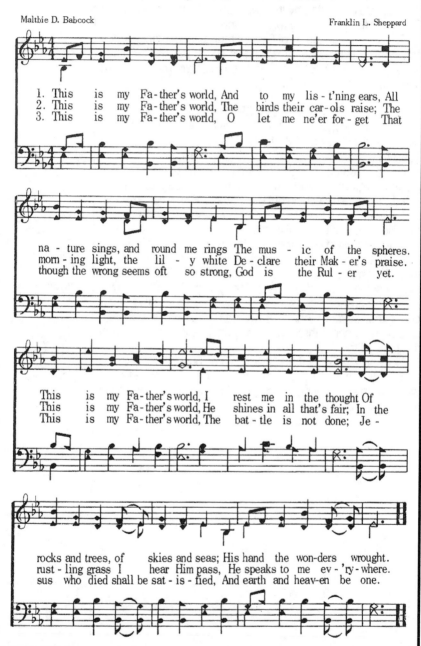

1. This is my Fa-ther's world, And to my lis-t'ning ears, All
2. This is my Fa-ther's world, The birds their car-ols raise; The
3. This is my Fa-ther's world, O let me ne'er for-get That

na - ture sings, and round me rings The mus - ic of the spheres.
morn-ing light, the lil - y white De - clare their Mak - er's praise.
though the wrong seems oft so strong, God is the Rul - er yet.

This is my Fa-ther's world, I rest me in the thought Of
This is my Fa-ther's world, He shines in all that's fair; In the
This is my Fa-ther's world, The bat - tle is not done; Je -

rocks and trees, of skies and seas; His hand the won-ders wrought.
rust - ling grass I hear Him pass, He speaks to me ev - 'ry-where.
sus who died shall be sat - is - fied, And earth and heav-en be one.

God Delivers Us From Evil

Psalms 140:1-13; 141:1-10; 143:1-12

INTRODUCTION

This last lesson on prayers in the Psalms emphasizes the concepts of protection and deliverance as we rely on our God. Each one of the three psalms which comprise this lesson reflects the troubles that are inflicted on the righteous by those who are committed to evil. They intend violence and would be successful but for God's intervention.

The concept of protection surrounds all of us whether or not we are desiring it. Multiple government regulations assure that our vehicles be equipped with seat belts and air bags. "Click it or ticket" campaigns enforce the use of seat belts or pay a fine. Then there's all the various locks and security systems to protect homes, vehicles and businesses from theft. The Food and Drug Administration attempts to regulate which chemicals, food additives and medicines are safe for human consumption. Whenever you buy a piece of equipment, the accompanying manual includes safety tips for the operator's protection. For instance, buy a ladder and attached to it are directions of where not to stand. But those directions have no value unless followed. In the same way, there's no value in God's divine ability to protect us unless we are willing to reside under His protective shield.

All three of these psalms may have been written by David. Regardless of their authorship, each psalm reflects the presence of sin and wicked people from whom the righteous need protection. There is an ongoing assault from which only God can bring deliverance.

Today's lesson can provide an ideal opportunity for individuals to share brief testimonies of God's deliverance in their lives. His protective care and rescue from enemies who would do believers harm isn't just an item of history. It continues to be a present potential for each one of us.

Unit Theme:
Prayers in the Psalms

Central Truth:
Christians trust God to deliver them from evil.

Focus:
Acknowledge that God is our protector and rely on Him for deliverance from evil.

Context:
Three psalms in which the writer cries out for deliverance

Golden Text:
"Quicken me, O Lord, for thy name's sake: for thy righteousness' sake bring my soul out of trouble" (Psalm 143:11).

Study Outline:
I. Protection From Evil People (Psalm 140:1-13)
II. Protection From Evil Ways (Psalm 141:1-10)
III. Protection From Evil Consequences (Psalm 143:1-12)

I. PROTECTION FROM EVIL PEOPLE (Psalm 140:1-13)

A. The Threat (vv. 1-5)

1. Deliver me, O Lord, from the evil man: preserve me from the violent man;

2. Which imagine mischiefs in their heart; continually are they gathered together for war.

3. They have sharpened their tongues like a serpent; adders' poison is under their lips. Selah.

4. Keep me, O Lord, from the hands of the wicked; preserve me from the violent man; who have purposed to overthrow my goings.

5. The proud have hid a snare for me, and cords; they have spread a net by the wayside; they have set gins for me. Selah.

Talk About It:
1. Describe the hearts of David's enemies (v. 2).
2. Describe his enemies' tongues (v. 3).
3. What were the hands of David's enemies trying to do (vv. 4, 5)?

The wording of these verses does not suggest some minor difficulty. Instead, individuals are plotting to bring harm. If David writes this psalm, it possibly refers to Saul and his supporters as they repeatedly attempt to trap him. Or, if written at a later period, it may be an indication of neighboring nations who want to dominate Israel. Whichever the case, the Lord's help is needed desperately.

Notice several specifics. First, the oppressors are evil with violent intent. Second, the harm is premeditated. Third, the intent of the violence is death. Having listed these three concepts, let's consider each one.

First, this threat resides in the evil, sinful heart of the oppressors. It is not an isolated problem, but one which is at the forefront of their minds. Verse 2 points of this being an ongoing attempt to harm and to destroy. It is deeply ingrained within the heart and mind of these individuals. No wonder the writer understands the need for God's intervention. This problem isn't going to fade away, and it can't be handled outside of divine intervention.

Second, we see the planning which goes into their attack. Their verbal statements are likened to the sharp sting of a poisonous snake (v. 3). Striking without warning, they can bring death to their victims. This imagery of the wicked can also be seen in other passages in the Psalms (58:3-5; 64:2-4).

The third specific is the intended outcome. By setting traps, these violent individuals of evil purposely hunt their intended victims. They try to cause the downfall of the righteous person and/or community. Because our God is powerful and overcomes evil, it is only logical for His children to cry out for deliverance from their enemy's plots of destruction.

B. The Deliverer (vv. 6, 7)

6. I said unto the Lord, Thou art my God: hear the voice of my supplications, O Lord.

"You shall judge a man by his foes as well as by his friends."
—**Joseph Conrad**

7. O God the Lord, the strength of my salvation, thou hast covered my head in the day of battle.

The author of this psalm identifies with his Lord while seeking deliverance. His "my" (v. 6) speaks of a relationship—personal ownership and commitment. This isn't a plea for help from an unknown or passing relationship.

"Salvation," as referred to in verse 7, isn't the same as we experience through Jesus Christ. The Cross is still very much in the future. However, this salvation is similar in that it stems from God's choosing to offer a means for the people of that age to be in relationship with Him. For without God's merciful actions, there is no salvation for people of any era.

As the writer speaks of salvation, he refers to his head being covered or shielded in battle. A helmet is always a vital part of a warrior's protective equipment as it shields a major area of the body, which controls all of the other functions. Ephesians 6:17 names this protective armament as "the helmet of salvation," which is part of our redemption and continuance, in spite of difficulties that may arise.

C. The Protection (vv. 8-13)

8. Grant not, O Lord, the desires of the wicked: further not his wicked devise; lest they exalt themselves. Selah.

9. As for the head of those that compass me about, let the mischief of their own lips cover them.

10. Let burning coals fall upon them: let them be cast into the fire; into deep pits, that they rise not up again.

11. Let not an evil speaker be established in the earth: evil shall hunt the violent man to overthrow him.

12. I know that the Lord will maintain the cause of the afflicted, and the right of the poor.

13. Surely the righteous shall give thanks unto thy name: the upright shall dwell in thy presence.

While in the process of affirming the Lord's protection, the writer takes considerable liberty in offering to God his wishes for the oppressors. He begins by asking God to withhold success from those who are plotting the evil deeds. Besides not wanting to experience the suffering of their intent, there is also the issue of these individuals not becoming proud in their sinfulness.

In verse 9 the author prays for the oppressors to be overwhelmed by their evil intent. It's much more than asking for what they planned to happen to themselves. Verse 10 indicates their receiving the fire of God's judgment. The deep pits (or miry pits) would seem to indicate punishment within the realm of the dead. So, not only is there the request for these men not to flourish here on earth but also experience eternal punishment.

Talk About It:
How does David describe God in these verses?

Talk About It:
1. What did David pray concerning his enemies' lips (v. 9)?
2. How does the hunter become the hunted (v. 11)?
3. What did David "know" (v. 12)?

Talk About It:
1. Explain what David wanted his prayers to be like (v. 2).
2. What did David pray regarding his mouth (v. 3)?
3. What did he pray concerning his heart (v. 4)?

The final two verses are a marked contrast to the previous three. Instead of doom and punishment for evil we see God's protective care for the righteous. Though self-seeking men and women bring harm and oppression to the poor, widowed and disadvantaged, God seeks justice and provision for them. An important key to this occurrence is to live righteously before the Lord and give thanks.

This part of our lesson seems to indicate the acceptability to pray for oppressors to be stopped and experience God's correction and punishment. At the same time, we must be living righteously in accord with God's Word.

II. PROTECTION FROM EVIL WAYS (Psalm 141:1-10)
A. The Request (vv. 1-4)

1. Lord, I cry unto thee: make haste unto me; give ear unto my voice, when I cry unto thee.

2. Let my prayer be set forth before thee as incense; and the lifting up of my hands as the evening sacrifice.

3. Set a watch, O Lord, before my mouth; keep the door of my lips.

4. Incline not my heart to any evil thing, to practice wicked works with men that work iniquity: and let me not eat of their dainties.

This second section of the lesson takes a definite shift. Instead of looking at the actions of others, we now focus on ourselves. It is much easier to look at the faults and sins of others. Introspection is more difficult. However, evil can infiltrate our thinking and lifestyle if we do not take a careful inventory.

The opening verses of this psalm are intense. There is a desire for a quick response on God's part. Yet, this isn't an off-the-cuff prayer. The author points to this prayer as having been prepared in the same careful manner as the evening sacrifice in the Temple.

This request deals with two aspects—mouth and heart. It's only logical since they are closely related. Psalm 19:14 says, "Let the words of my mouth, and the meditation of my heart, be acceptable in thy sight, O Lord, my strength, and my redeemer." In Matthew 12:34, Jesus said, "Out of the abundance of the heart the mouth speaketh."

Maybe you have heard someone say, "It just slipped out!" It wasn't his or her intention to speak in a certain manner or say certain words, but it occurred. These are the moments when one realizes the necessity of God's helping us to know when to speak and what to speak when we do. There are two opposites addressed here: (1) speaking when or what we shouldn't; (2) being silent when we should be speaking truth, direction, or comfort.

Closely tied to the actions of our mouth is the condition of our heart. Remember, the people of this culture perceived the heart as the seat of emotions and intent. We see this as referring to the mind.

Here we see the need to protect our thought processes. What we dwell on and decide is acceptable will at some point become evident in our words and our actions. While evil may remain hidden in our heart for years, unless it is eradicated through the ministry of the Holy Spirit and our choices, we may find ourselves in situations not even imagined. We join the ranks of "men who are evildoers" (Psalm 141:4, *NIV*).

B. The Desire (vv. 5-7)

5. Let the righteous smite me; it shall be a kindness: and let him reprove me; it shall be an excellent oil, which shall not break my head: for yet my prayer also shall be in their calamities.

6. When their judges are overthrown in stony places, they shall hear my words; for they are sweet.

7. Our bones are scattered at the grave's mouth, as when one cutteth and cleaveth wood upon the earth.

In verse 5 we see a desire to be disciplined, if one's words or actions are of an evil nature. Even slanting toward wrong is to be an opportunity for the righteous to take disciplinary actions. It is perceived as an action of kindness, a healing of woundedness. Discipline here is welcomed. Too often discipline is perceived as a negative because it restrains or may even hurt. Yet, there can be no true discipleship without discipline. If we begin to stray from truth toward sin, we need mature believers to help bring correction.

If Psalm 141 was written by David, it is possible that "the judges" (v. 6) is a reference to King Saul and his officers, who sought to kill David "in stony places"—in the rocky region of Engedi, where David and his men hid in caves (see 1 Samuel 24:1-7). "My words" (Psalm 141:6)—the words of David—would be heard by the officials because God would deliver him from Saul and one day place him on the throne of Israel.

While running from Saul, it appeared David's future was as hopeless as scattered bones or as broken up as plowed ground (v. 7, *NKJV*). But his eyes were on God (v. 8).

C. The Commitment (vv. 8-10)

8. But mine eyes are unto thee, O God the Lord: in thee is my trust; leave not my soul destitute.

9. Keep me from the snares which they have laid for me, and the gins of the workers of iniquity.

10. Let the wicked fall into their own nets, whilst that I withal escape.

"We have all been guilty, not of 15 idle words, but of 15 million idle words. And we must beg God's forgiveness."
—**George Sweeting**

overthrown in stony places (v. 6)—"thrown down from the cliffs" (*NIV*)

cutteth and cleveath wood (v. 7)—"plows and breaks up the earth" (*NKJV*)

Talk About It:
1. What did David call "excellent" and "a kindness" (v. 5)?
2. When would the evildoers finally listen to David (vv. 6, 7)?

"He is a fine friend. He stabs you in the front."
—**Leonard Louis Levinson**

Talk About It:
1. What did David pray for himself?
2. What did he pray regarding his enemies?

A modern translation of verse 8 helps us to see the commitment which the writer made: "But my eyes are fixed on you, O Sovereign Lord; in you I take refuge—do not give me over to death" (*NIV*). Only disaster was on the horizon except for God's help. The psalmist's ability would not suffice. Nor could others intervene.

This writer puts his complete trust in the Lord. There's no looking to the left or right. He knows there is only one refuge, one place of safety, one place of deliverance. Notice the dual results he expects. First, there will be safety from the enemy regardless of all the plotting and carefully laid traps. Second, the enemy will fall into their own traps. This reminds us of the end of Haman. He was hanged on the gallows he had prepared for Mordecai (Esther 7:10). And Haman's 10 sons were also hanged on the gallows several days later (9:13, 14).

III. PROTECTION FROM EVIL CONSEQUENCES
(Psalm 143:1-12)
A. The Appeal (vv. 1-7)

1. Hear my prayer, O Lord, give ear to my supplications: in thy faithfulness answer me, and in thy righteousness.

2. And enter not into judgment with thy servant: for in thy sight shall no man living be justified.

3. For the enemy hath persecuted my soul; he hath smitten my life down to the ground; he hath made me to dwell in darkness, as those that have been long dead.

4. Therefore is my spirit overwhelmed within me; my heart within me is desolate.

5. I remember the days of old; I meditate on all thy works; I muse on the work of thy hands.

6. I stretch forth my hands unto thee: my soul thirsteth after thee, as a thirsty land. Selah.

7. Hear me speedily, O Lord: my spirit faileth: hide not thy face from me, lest I be like unto them that go down into the pit.

Talk About It:
1. What did David ask God *not* to do (v. 2)?
2. What had David's enemies done to him (v. 3)?
3. How did David describe his condition (vv. 4, 7)?
4. Explain David's thirst (v. 6).

Have you ever felt so spiritually desolate and depleted you were sure your prayers were not getting past the ceiling? Of course, that's assuming you were still praying. In this psalm David finds himself in a spiritual desert, but is sufficiently wise to prayerfully appeal for God's protection.

His appeal for God's intervention is based on His characteristics of faithfulness and righteousness. David desires mercy evidenced by relief from the circumstances and nonjudgment for his sins. This isn't to be seen as asking God to compromise His holiness. Instead, it is a reminder of humankind's original sin and the ongoing struggle with sinful temptation and weaknesses.

Into this normal problem comes the additional burden of oppressing enemies. Many of us can identify with this. Our spiritual condition can be pressed down by evildoers and difficult situations. When negative job situations, medical conditions, accidents and financial crises squeeze our lives, we must work harder than ever to "stay close to the Lord."

In this darkness of pressing circumstances the psalmist turns his thoughts to a more positive time. He meditates on the Lord's work in previous days (v. 5). It would seem he is remembering God's deliverance and protection of Israel in the centuries prior to his life.

David's appeal to the Lord is with outstretched hands. Not only is this a gesture of prayer, but it also reflects the intense desire for God's help. The imagery of a dry desert (v. 6) is used to reflect his spiritual thirst and need for God to come and deliver. Without speedy assistance, he will soon go to the place of the dead.

David is asking for God's help in two forms. First and foremost is the need for spiritual renewal in his life. Second is the appeal for deliverance from the enemy.

> "Once a man is united to God, how could he not live forever? Once a man is separated from God, what can he do but wither and die?"
> —**C.S. Lewis**

B. The Rescue (vv. 8-12)

8. Cause me to hear thy lovingkindness in the morning; for in thee do I trust: cause me to know the way wherein I should walk; for I lift up my soul unto thee.

9. Deliver me, O Lord, from mine enemies: I flee unto thee to hide me.

10. Teach me to do thy will; for thou art my God: thy spirit is good; lead me into the land of uprightness.

11. Quicken me, O Lord, for thy name's sake: for thy righteousness' sake bring my soul out of trouble.

12. And of thy mercy cut off mine enemies, and destroy all them that afflict my soul: for I am thy servant.

Having expressed his spiritual desolation, the psalmist now turns his attention to the need for God's grace to assist in living a life that pleases the Lord. Each one of us is limited in our ability to live righteously. Even the strongest personality and person of great commitment need the undergirding and direction of God through the working of the Holy Spirit.

In verse 8 there is the sense of waking up in the morning and having a knowledge and assurance of what to do. This comes by having put complete trust in the ways and words of the Lord. Nothing is held back. Everything we have and are is offered to Him. We relinquish control. When we place ourselves in God's hand, there can be a legitimate request for His rescuing us from our enemies.

Talk About It:
1. Describe the path David wanted to follow (vv. 8, 10).
2. How would God be lifted up (vv. 11, 12)?

Placing ourselves in such a relationship with God is a process which comes through discipleship. Being taught includes several aspects. Usually we think of learning the facts—head knowledge. There is also experiential learning—trial and error in some cases. And there is relational learning—spiritual times of God's speaking to our heart.

All of us, regardless of our spiritual and/or church background, need to allow ourselves to be taught. This is a means of growth throughout our lives as believers. We also need to be followers going in the right direction. As Paul said to the Corinthians, "Follow my example, as I follow the example of Christ" (1 Corinthians 11:1, *NIV*). Jesus called various individuals to be His disciples by saying, "Follow Me." In John 12:26 He said, "Whoever serves me must follow me; and where I am, my servant also will be" (*NIV*).

In Psalm 143:11 the psalmist asks to be preserved (*NIV*). Though he will benefit personally, the request is to bring glory to God. All honor will be given to Him for the divine intervention. This is a reminder that we cannot expect God to come to our rescue without our taking refuge in Him. Why should God intervene in behalf of someone who is unwilling to follow and to rest in Him? And even then we're not worthy of His efforts on our behalf. It's always an outreach of grace.

This psalm ends by the writer returning to the issue of his enemies. In very strong language he asks for them to be silenced or destroyed. Some commentators suggest this to be an overflow of the bitterness of heart which seethes even when David is wanting his own soul to be revived. This may be true. Sometimes the hurt and oppression is so deep and severe it comes out when least expected.

There is another possibility for consideration. Since David is God's servant and the recipient of God's love, it may be a reasonable way to conclude. If this person or people are not stopped in some manner, David may not be able to fulfill God's will. If someone is speaking words of harm against us, would it not be reasonable to ask for his or her mouth to be stopped? Done in love and desiring for that person to come to a right relationship with God would be a double benefit.

The final sentence of this psalm is a firm declaration of David's relationship with God. To be His servant speaks of commitment and intent. It should be the declarative statement of every believer.

> "Don't trust in your ability to follow God—trust in His ability to lead you."
> —*Christians Quoting.org*

CONCLUSION

When we look around us and see all the injustices, immorality and crime, it is so easy to have a negative outlook on life. But we as believers can have a positive view of life when we

God Delivers Us From Evil

remember our strength and refuge is in the Lord. He protects from harm and delivers from evil. Yes, sometimes bad things do happen to God's people. We live in a sin-dominated world, but our God is still in control. He is the Shepherd who feeds, disciplines and delivers.

GOLDEN TEXT CHALLENGE

"QUICKEN ME, O LORD, FOR THY NAME'S SAKE: FOR THY RIGHTEOUSNESS' SAKE BRING MY SOUL OUT OF TROUBLE" (Psalm 143:11).

If we are the children of God, being in an "impossible" situation is not a bad place to be. As one songwriter said, "God specializes in things thought impossible."

If we are bound by a sinful habit or overwhelmed by emotional stress, we can cry out, "For the glory of your name, O Lord, save me" (*NLT*). If we are dominated by a disease or trapped in a financial vise, we can pray, "In your righteousness, bring me out of this distress" (*NLT*).

When the Lord saves us, bringing us out of despair into delight, His name will be lifted up and His righteousness proclaimed.

Daily Devotions:
M. Blessing, Not Cursing
   Numbers 23:1-12
T. Punishment Ended
   2 Samuel 24:10-16
W. Going God's Way
   Proverbs 3:1-6
T. Paul Escapes His Enemies
   Acts 9:19-25
F. Forgive Others
   2 Corinthians 2:5-11
S. Be Spiritually Transformed
   Ephesians 4:17-24

Leaning On The Everlasting Arms

Elisha A. Hoffman

Anthony J. Showalter

1. What a fel - low - ship, what a joy di - vine, Lean-ing on the ev - er -
2. Oh, how sweet to walk in this pil - grim way, Lean-ing on the ev - er -
3. What have I to dread, what have I to fear, Lean-ing on the ev - er -

last - ing arms; What a bless - ed - ness, what a peace is mine,
last - ing arms; Oh, how bright the path grows from day to day,
last - ing arms? I have bless - ed peace with my Lord so near,

REFRAIN

Lean - ing on the ev - er - last - ing arms. Lean - ing,
Lean-ing on Je - sus,

lean - ing, Safe and se - cure from all a - larms; Lean -
lean-ing on Je - sus, Lean-ing on

ing, lean - ing, Lean-ing on the ev - er - last - ing arms.
Je - sus, lean-ing on Je - sus,